Canadian Labour
and Employment Relations

Canadian Labour
and Employment Relations

MORLEY GUNDERSON
UNIVERSITY OF TORONTO

DAPHNE TARAS
UNIVERSITY OF CALGARY

SIXTH EDITION

PEARSON

Addison
Wesley

Toronto

Library and Archives Canada Cataloguing in Publication

Canadian labour and employment relations/ [edited by] Morley Gunderson, Daphne Taras.—6th ed.

Includes index.
Previous eds. published under title: Union-management relations in Canada.
ISBN 978-0-321-50413-5

1. Industrial relations—Canada—Textbooks.   I. Gunderson, Morley, 1945–   II. Taras, Daphne Gottlieb, 1956–
HD8106.5.C3385 2009   331.0971   C2008-902155-X

ISBN-13: 978-0-321-50413-5
ISBN-10: 0-321-50413-5

Vice President, Editorial Director: Gary Bennett
Acquisitions Editor: Karen Elliott
Executive Marketing Manager: Cas Shields
Developmental Editor: Mary Wong/Christina Lee
Production Editor: Imee Salumbides
Copy Editor: Lenore Latta
Proofreader: Martin Tooke
Production Coordinator: Deborah Starks
Composition: Christine Velakis
Photo Researcher: Amanda McCormick
Permissions Researchers: Beth McAuley and Dayle Furlong
Art Director: Julia Hall
Cover Designer: Jennifer Stimson
Interior Designer: Michelle Bellemare
Cover Image: Jim Frazier/Getty Images

1 2 3 4 5   12 11 10 09 08

Printed and bound in the United States of America.

PEARSON
Addison
Wesley

Brief Contents

Contents

Preface

THE NEW EDITION

This sixth edition of *Canadian Labour and Employment Relations* incorporates a number of changes that reflect new developments in the field. This begins at the top, with the title change from "Union–Management" to "Canadian Labour" Relations. That change reflects the reality that the field is broader than simply union–management issues. Political, social, and economic changes in this country continue to exert their influence as do global competitive pressures, free trade issues, deregulation, privatization, mergers and acquisitions, labour market adjustment, and industrial restructuring toward services and the information economy. New issues are also entering the radar screen, including "green" and environmental issues, the resource boom in the West (especially in Alberta), an unstable relationship between the United States and Canadian dollars that makes long-term employment planning more difficult, and macroeconomic instability associated with financial shocks. The legal environment also is changing quickly, beginning with the Supreme Court's unexpected declaration in 2007 that collective bargaining has become a fundamental right, protected by freedom of association guarantees in the *Canadian Charter of Rights and Freedoms*.

Significant content changes in this edition reflect these issues. The introduction adds material on the diversity of forms of employee representation and on the pressures of modern work. Many of the distinctive features of Canadian industrial relations are highlighted, and this chapter anchors the efforts of subsequent chapters to explain noteworthy features of Canadian theory and practice. Part 1, Chapter 2, discusses the impetus for unions and collective action in this new edition, using more examples that appeal to student readers. Chapter 3 examines labour history and adds evocative images. Chapter 4 provides a portrait of unions, updating the statistics on which we base our discussions. Chapter 5 discusses the management of industrial relations, and adds new research findings. Chapter 6 assesses employee involvement, updating findings and sorting facts from myths. Chapters 5 and 6 together bolster the presence of management as an important actor in the industrial relations setting.

In Part 2, Chapter 7 examines the social, political, and economic environments and includes new information on a number of topics: new evidence on the impact of minimum wages; the growing importance of the offshore outsourcing of business services; the trend toward banning mandatory retirement; environmental issues; and productivity changes emanating from information technology. Chapter 8 is completely rewritten and reorganized, introducing a new author, Sara Slinn, to the book. She provides a comprehensive examination of labour law, with attention to such important issues as card-versus vote-based certification, duty of fair representation, a review of the Supreme Court's 2007 *B.C. Health Services* decision, and a discussion of the difficulties that are presented by the intersection of privacy rights, human rights, and labour law. Chapter 9 focuses on employment law in nonunion settings, allowing readers to appreciate the dramatic differences in legal regimes between unionized and nonunion workplaces. It includes new research from the report by the Arthurs Commission.

In Part 3, Chapter 10 includes new discussions on effective bargaining tactics. Chapter 11 contains new examples of clauses in collective agreements. Chapter 12 updates the materials on strikes, lockouts, and dispute resolution and adds new information on the potentially historic recent CAW–Magna agreement as well as on the use of the internet during a strike. Chapter 13, on grievance arbitration, contains more material on the grievance procedure and on the court-directed expansion of the role of arbitration in labour relations. Chapter 14 (Part 4), on the impact of unions, provides the latest research findings, especially important given the constraints on unions imposed by globalization and union decline in many countries. It also provides new information on the changing trend of the union impact in the public and private sectors, as well as the union threat effect on nonunion workplace and human resource practices.

In Part 5, Chapter 15 includes new material on the continuing skirmishes between governments and their unions. Chapter 16, on union–management relations in Quebec, updates the information in that chapter in light of the political changes occurring in that province. Of particular importance is new information on controversial legislative initiatives in a number of areas: the public sector and especially the health sector; work–family balance; and the implementation of pay and employment equity. Chapter 17, on the comparative perspective, expands on issues pertaining to globalization and its impact, with particular attention to areas such as outsourcing, non-standard employment, union decline, the feminization of employment and—of particular current concern—the implications of global warming and environmental change. Every chapter of this edition has been thoroughly updated and revised to reflect recent developments.

Features that contributed to the popularity of the first five editions remain intact. The book continues to benefit from the participation of many of the country's leading scholars and teachers of industrial relations. In a country as diverse as Canada, this ensures that the experiences in all regions are reflected in analyses, examples, and conclusions. This approach exposes readers to the lively mix of views and perspectives found within a very vibrant industrial relations community. Many chapters present material that is on the leading edge of research in industrial relations and, in some cases, contain analyses that are appearing in teaching materials for the first time. Chapters provide extensive reference lists to direct the interested reader to more specific information and applications of the theory, research, and statistical evidence. Since industrial relations events appear daily on the evening news and in the press, this book pays special attention to how the academic analysis relates to real-world problems and issues.

We are particularly excited by four features of this edition, which we believe make it more accessible, relevant, and valuable as a reference:

- **The pedagogy has been retained** Each chapter begins with an opening vignette to ground the subsequent discussions. Practical examples are used throughout each chapter. Fewer websites are given than in the previous edition, as web addresses quickly change and most readers are quite adept at finding appropriate information. This sixth edition reflects the realities of individual workers and worksites, and helps future industrial relations practitioners acquire concrete knowledge and applications.

- **There is more emphasis on the role of management in the first half of the book** Reviewers of previous editions asked us to provide more material on management to counterbalance the many chapters on unions. As a result, Chapter 5 and Chapter 6 can be read as companion pieces to give a broader understanding of management functions.

- **The differences between unionized and nonunion workers are highlighted** Readers are able to move from chapter to chapter, acquiring specific insights from a variety of perspectives. Students will grasp more clearly the point that unionized and nonunion workers are covered under different legal frameworks and dispute resolution mechanisms, and form part of distinctive sets of practices designed to suit the unionized or nonunion setting. Material has been retained about the possibilities for representation by nonunion workers, including professional and staff associations, committees, and forums.

- **Canadian industrial relations contains features that are distinctive, and in some cases, unique** As competitive and global pressures bring greater awareness of international issues, Canadian students need to understand the features that make Canada different. We must know ourselves in order to appreciate our place on the world stage. As declining union density in the United States and elsewhere draws considerable attention, it is vitally important that we monitor developments in our own country carefully. Most chapters now explicitly discuss Canada in comparative perspective.

These four themes—greater applications, greater understanding of management to balance the emphasis on unions, union–nonunion differences, and sensitivity to international comparisons—are incorporated throughout the book, and add value without sacrificing any of the rigour of the previous editions.

FEATURES

- **Opening vignette:** Each chapter begins with a vignette, taken from a news article or other text, that draws the reader into the material anecdotally and provides a firm practical context for the following material.

"For the sake of the auto industry, we've put aside our differences."

Frank Stronach, Buzz Hargrove

Canada's auto industry and the entire manufacturing base face a moment of truth. New challenges in global competition mean the industry must change, or else it will continue to wither away. Magna International and the Canadian Auto Workers (CAW) Union signed a "Framework of Fairness" that will govern how they work to~~~~~~~~~~~~~~~~~years to come. Like a normal union contract, this ~~~~~~~~~~~~~~

- **Supporting film:** In four of the chapters—5, 6, 13, and 15—the opening vignettes are based on an award-winning video by Allen Ponak and Bert Painter entitled *Beyond Collision: High Integrity Labour Relations.* It is now possible for instructors to show 10-minute video segments that explicitly document the opening vignettes.

- **Exhibits:** Most chapters contain several exhibits that provide examples, expand on topics, and provide additional information related to the text.

Exhibit 6.4
Operation of the Production District Joint Industrial Council, Imperial Oil

1. MANAGEMENT VALUES, PRINCIPLES, LEADERSHIP STYLE

The values and principles of senior management are critical. Delegates and employees are sensitive to such questions as:

- Does the management team believe that employees have a role to play in ~~~~~~~~~

- **Tables and figures:** Throughout the text, tables and figures are used to present current data, to draw comparisons, and to clarify information by offering it in a clear graphical form.

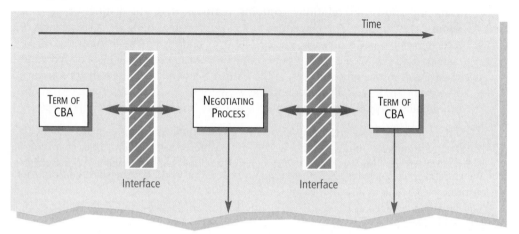

- **Weblinks:** Website information is included at the end of each chapter. Some of these sites provide further information on specific topics discussed in the text, while other links point to industrial relations journals, sources of labour data, union sites, and labour legislation.

Weblinks

Human Resources and Social Development Canada Labour Information:
www.hrsdc.gc.ca/en/lp/wid/info.shtml

Canadian Labour Congress:
www.clc-ctc.ca

AFL–CIO:

- **Questions:** Each chapter ends with a series of questions that review the material covered in the chapter and point to possibilities for further discussion or research.
- **References:** The references list not only provides sources for the information within the text but also acts as a suggested list for further reading and research.

INSTRUCTOR'S SUPPLEMENTS

- **Instructor's Manual with Testing Materials:** Each chapter in this comprehensive Instructor's Manual includes a Chapter Overview, Lecture Outline, Test Items (Within-the-Text Questions and Beyond-the-Text Questions), and Class Activities. Collective Bargaining Simulations and Arbitration Cases are also provided.
- **PowerPoint®Presentations:** The PowerPoint presentations include the key concepts featured in the text.

These supplements can be downloaded from Pearson Education Canada's online catalogue at **http://vig.pearsoned.ca**.

- Through a special arrangement between Allen Ponak and Bert Painter and Pearson, the film *Beyond Collision* is available at no charge to instructors who adopt this book.

ACKNOWLEDGMENTS

We would like to express our appreciation to numerous colleagues who provided excellent suggestions for material to include in this edition. We are indebted to the following reviewers: Claude Dupuis (Athabasca University); Tony Ransom (Laurentian University); and Robert Swidinsky (University of Guelph).

The Instructor's Manual that supported the fifth edition was authored by Claude Dupuis, a faculty member in the School of Business, Athabasca University. Claude has a Master's degree in industrial relations from Queen's University, and has taught courses in industrial relations at several universities and colleges using previous editions of the textbook. We gratefully acknowledge his contribution and excellent work. For the sixth edition, the Instructor's Manual has been updated by Cameron Bean.

Thanks to Cameron Bean, A. Tarik Timur, Frederick Jacques, and Kelly Williams for their comments on portions of the book, with particular acknowledgment to Cameron for his help in updating statistics and reviewing the appeal of various chapters to students, and to Tarik for his help with obtaining permissions to reproduce copyright materials that appear in the fifth and sixth editions. We gratefully thank Mary Wong, Karen Elliott, and Pamela Voves for overseeing the revision, editing, and production of this edition, and for having faith in the product.

GENERAL EDITORS

Morley Gunderson (BA, Queen's University; PhD, University of Wisconsin–Madison) holds the Canadian Imperial Bank of Commerce Chair in Youth Employment at the University of Toronto, where he is a professor at the Centre for Industrial Relations and Human Resources (Director from 1985 to 1997). He has been a visiting scholar at the International Institute for Labour Research in Geneva, Switzerland, and the National Bureau of Economic Research, the Institute for International Studies, and the Hoover Institution at Stanford.

His publications include the books *Women in the Canadian Labour Market*; *Forging Business–Labour Partnerships: The Emergence of Sector Councils in Canada*; *Labour Market Economics: Theory, Evidence and Policy in Canada*, Sixth Edition; *Comparable Worth and Gender Discrimination: An International Perspective*; *Pay Equity*; *Women and Labour Market Poverty*; and *Economics of Poverty and Income Distribution*. He has published numerous journal articles on various topics: gender discrimination and pay and employment equity; the aging workforce, pensions, and mandatory retirement; youth employment; public-sector wage determination; the determinants and impact of immigration; the causes and consequences of strikes; child care; workers' compensation and reasonable accommodation; volunteering; non-standard employment; labour market adjustment and training; and the impact of trade liberalization and globalization on labour markets, labour policy, labour standards, industrial relations, human resource management, and workplace practices. He is on numerous editorial boards and has been on the Executive Board of the Industrial Relations Research Association and an advisor/consultant to various organizations: Labour Canada; Ontario Ministry of Labour; Statistics Canada; Macdonald Commission; Abella Commission on Employment Equity; Canadian Human Rights Commission; Ontario Task Force on Hours of Work and Overtime; Ontario Task Force on

Mandatory Retirement; Centre for Policy Studies on Youth and Family; Ontario Pay Equity Commission; B.C. Task Force on Employment and Training; Ontario Workers' Compensation Board; Canadian Policy Research Network; Federal Task Force on Working Time; Federal Task Force on Employment Standards; Ontario Royal Commission on Workers' Compensation; Human Resources Development Canada; British Columbia Royal Commission on Workers' Compensation; North America Forum at Stanford; International Labour Organization; and the Harvard Institute for International Development.

In 2002 Gunderson received the Industrial Relations Research Association Award for Excellence in Teaching in Labour Economics, and in 2003 he received the Gérard Dion Award for Outstanding Contribution to the Field of Industrial Relations.

Daphne G. Taras (BA, York University; MA, Duke University; MBA and PhD, University of Calgary; LLM, Osgoode Hall) is a professor of Industrial Relations in the Haskayne School of Business, University of Calgary. She is a fellow at the Institute for Advanced Policy Research at the University of Calgary. Her teaching interests focus on the employment relationship, employee representation, worksite issues, and public policy.

Her publications include the books *Nonunion Employee Representation* (2000, M. E. Sharpe) and *Information Technology and the World of Employment* (2004, Rutgers University Transaction Publishers). Within industrial relations, her principal research interest is formal nonunion forms of employee representation. She has examined industrial relations and human resources issues in a number of major petroleum firms, including Petro-Canada and Imperial Oil. Dr. Taras has published articles in *Industrial and Labor Relations Review*, *Industrial Relations*, *British Journal of Industrial Relations*, *Relations industrielles/Industrial Relations*, *Canadian Public Policy*, and numerous other scholarly journals. She edited seven symposia for the *Journal of Labor Research*. In 1997, she organized a major international conference on nonunion employee representation held in Banff.

Professor Taras has mediated labour relations disputes and has facilitated union–management committees. For the University of Calgary, she acted as mediator in sexual harassment cases. She was co-author of a submission on nonunion representation to the U.S. Task Force on Reconstructing America's Labor Market Institutions at MIT (1999) and co-author of a submission on right-to-work to the Alberta Economic Development Authority (1995). She was her School's Outstanding New Scholar in 1997 and the recipient of the Dean's Award for Outstanding Research Achievement in 2000. She served as Associate Dean (Research) for her faculty, and oversaw both the PhD and MBA-Thesis programs. She was elected to the executive board of the Industrial Relations Research Association, and has been a member of the editorial boards of the *British Journal of Industrial Relations*, *Journal of Labor Research*, *Relations industrielles*, and other journals. In 2005, she was appointed by the Minister of Labour to be an Expert Advisor to the *Federal Review of Employment Standards, Canada Labour Code (Part III)*, chaired by Harry Arthurs, which resulted in *Fairness at Work*, known widely as the *Arthurs Report*. In 2007 she was recipient of the Labor and Employment Research Association's Excellence in Education Award.

CHAPTER CONTRIBUTORS

Marie-Pierre Beaumont (MA, Université Laval) is a research professional at the Département des relations industrielles, Université Laval, Québec. Her research interests include public policies, work organization, and work–family balance, and she currently coordinates a research project on pay equity. She is also a lecturer at the Département de management and the Département des relations industrielles, Université Laval. Finally, she is active in organizing the annual conference of the Département des relations industrielles and is a contributor to the journal *Relations industrielles/Industrial Relations*.

Richard Chaykowski (PhD, Cornell University) is a faculty member in the School of Policy Studies and in the Faculty of Law (cross-appointed) at Queen's University. He has been a Visiting Scholar at the MIT and a visitor at the University of Toronto and at McGill University. Dr. Chaykowski recently completed an appointment as Visiting Chair at Human Resources and Social Development Canada where he worked in Strategic Policy.

Professor Chaykowski's teaching and research interests include labour policy and its role in the new economy, the intersection of labour policy and law, labour market institutions, labour relations and collective bargaining, North American labour markets, workplace training and innovation, and the impacts of technological change in the workplace. Among his published books are *Contract and Commitment: Employment Relations in the New Economy* (co-edited with Anil Verma) and *Women and Work* (co-edited with Lisa Powell).

Esther Déom (PhD, Université de Montréal) is a professor of Industrial Relations at the Département des relations industrielles, Université Laval, Québec. She is the editor of *Relations industrielles/Industrial Relations*, the world's first academic journal in industrial relations and the only journal in the field in Canada. Her current research interests include pay equity and job evaluation, employment equity, collective bargaining, and work organization. She has also acted as spokesperson for the faculty union during collective bargaining since 2006 and as a neutral third party in many employment equity committees throughout her career. She was the representative for the Quebec Coalition for Pay Equity and part of the governmental consultation commission for Pay Equity Legislation. Esther Déom was also president of the Canadian Industrial Relations Association (CIRA) from 1993 to 1994.

Geoffrey England (LLB, London School of Economics; LLM, Dalhousie University; MA, Industrial Relations, University of Warwick) is a professor at the College of Commerce and associate member of the College of Law at the University of Saskatchewan. His main area of research is individual employment law, and he co-authored, along with Professor Rod Wood of the Law Faculty, University of Alberta, *Employment Law in Canada*, Fourth Edition, published by Lexis Nexis/Butterworths. He is also an employment standards and collective agreement adjudicator.

Ann C. Frost (PhD, Massachusetts Institute of Technology) is an associate professor at the Richard Ivey School of Business, University of Western Ontario. She teaches undergraduate and graduate courses in organizational behaviour and negotiations. Professor Frost's main research focus is workplace restructuring, and she has examined the ability of local unions to deal effectively with changing shop-floor conditions in the steel industry. Professor Frost's articles have appeared in *Advances in Industrial and Labor Relations*, the *Journal of Labor Research*, the *British Journal of Industrial Relations*, and the *Industrial and Labor Relations Review*. Her current research interests include models of labour–management co-operation, restructuring in the health care sector, employment practices in Canadian call centres, and the impact of recent changes in work organization on the careers of low-wage workers. Professor Frost's research has been funded by the Social Sciences and Humanities Research Council, MIT's Industrial Performance Center, and the Russell-Sage and Rockefeller Foundations.

Anthony Giles (PhD, University of Warwick) taught industrial relations at the University of New Brunswick from 1983 to 1992 and then at Université Laval from 1992 to 2001. In 2004, Dr. Giles was appointed Director of Research at the Commission for Labor Cooperation in Washington, D.C., where he was responsible for managing research in the fields of labour law, labour economics, and employment relations in Canada, Mexico, and the United States. Since 2004, he has worked for Human Resources and Social Development Canada, first as Director General, International and Intergovernmental Labour Affairs and, since 2007, as Director General, Strategic Labour Policy, Analysis and Workplace Information. Dr. Giles has conducted research and has published articles and books on a wide range of industrial relations topics, including collective agreements, workplace change, comparative and international industrial relations, and industrial relations theory.

Rafael Gomez (PhD, University of Toronto) has been a Lecturer in the Department of Management at the London School of Economics; Professor of Economics at Glendon College; and Visiting Professor of Management at Moscow State University's Graduate School of Business Administration. He has been a Visiting Research Fellow at the Central Bank of Spain and a Research Fellow at the University of Toronto's Centre for Industrial Relations. He has published in numerous journals including the *British Journal of Industrial Relations*, *Journal of Population Economics*, *Canadian Public Policy*, and the *Canadian Journal of Economics*. In January 2006, he was awarded the Labor and Employment Relations Association's 2005 John T. Dunlop Outstanding Scholar Award for exceptional contributions to international and comparative labour and employment research.

Jean-Noël Grenier (PhD, Université Laval) is professor of Industrial Relations at the Département des relations industrielles, Université Laval, Québec. He also acts as the secretary-treasurer of the Canadian Industrial Relations Association (CIRA). From 1996 to 2004, he was an active member and an officer of the FNEEQ-CSN, an important college teachers' federation in Québec. His domain of expertise is labour relations in the public services and the broader public sectors. He is currently conducting research to examine how work conditions of public-service employees and the users of these services are affected by the recent restructurings of the public-service sector in Québec.

Bob Hebdon (PhD, University of Toronto) is associate professor of Industrial Relations at McGill University. Dr. Hebdon was the 2006 Gunderson prize winner (offered to alumnae of the Centre for Industrial Relations and Human Resources at the University of Toronto) for his outstanding scholarship and contribution to the Centre. He is chair of the undergraduate program in industrial relations in the Faculty of Arts at McGill and coordinator of the labour–management concentration in the Faculty of Management. He teaches collective bargaining, public-sector labour relations, international labour relations, and industrial relations policy. His research interests include industrial conflict, public-sector restructuring, and dispute resolution. He has published in the *Industrial and Labor Relations Review*, *Industrial Relations*, *Local Government Studies*, the *Journal of Policy Analysis and Management*, the *American Economic Review*, and *Relations industrielles/ Industrial Relations*.

Doug Hyatt (PhD, University of Toronto) is a professor of Business Economics at the Rotman School of Management, University of Toronto. His articles have appeared in the *Industrial and Labor Relations Review*, *Industrial Relations*, the *American Economic Review*, and the *Canadian Journal of Economics*. His current areas of research include valuation of the intellectual property of copyright collectives, the labour market for child care workers, occupational health and safety, and workers' compensation.

Patrice Jalette (PhD, Université de Montréal) is associate professor of Industrial Relations at Université de Montréal. He has taught there since 2001, after working for four years at the *Institut de recherche et d'information sur la rémunération*, at the *Institut de la statistique du Québec*, and at the *Conseil consultatif du travail et de la main-d'oeuvre*, which advises Québec's Minister of Labour on policy matters. He is a co-researcher at the Inter-University Research Centre on Globalization and Work, where he conducts research to answer questions relating to outsourcing, global value chain restructuring, multinational corporations, unions' response to globalization, and restructuring within the municipal sector. He co-authored *La convention collective au Québec*, published by Gaëtan Morin Éditeur in 2003.

Carla Lipsig-Mummé (MA, Boston University; PhD, Université de Montréal) is Professor and Coordinator of Labour Studies, York University, and Professor (Honorary) of Political and Social Inquiry, Monash University in Australia.

The Founding Director of the Centre for Research on Work and Society, York University (1990–2001), Dr. Lipsig-Mummé writes on work, labour, and global political economy. Most recently her work focuses on the impact of climate change on work and employment, and the renewed marginalization of the working young. Her work has been published in French and English, in Canada, Australia, Russia, South Africa, New Zealand, and France, and has been widely translated. Formerly a union organizer with the United Farm Workers and International Ladies' Garment Workers' Union, she is also a consultant to unions in Canada and Australia.

Richard Marsden (PhD, University of Warwick) is associate professor in the graduate Centre for Integrated Studies, at Athabasca University, Canada's open university specializing in distance education. He has published in the *Cambridge Journal of Economics*, *Sociology*, *Critical Perspectives on Accounting*, *Organization Studies*, the *Journal of Historical Sociology*, and the *Handbook of Organization Studies*. His book, *The Nature of Capital: Marx After Foucault*, was published by Routledge in 1999.

Noah M. Meltz (BComm, University of Toronto; PhD, Princeton University) was professor of Economics and Industrial Relations in the Department of Economics and the Centre for Industrial Relations, University of Toronto, and professor, School of Business, Netanya Academic College, Israel. He was director of the Centre for Industrial Relations from 1975 to 1985, and principal of Woodsworth College, University of Toronto, 1991 to 1998. His recent books include *Human Resource Management in Canada* (co-author of the fourth edition), *Theorizing in Industrial Relations: Approaches and Applications* (co-editor), and *Industrial Relations Theory, Its Nature, Scope and Pedagogy* (co-editor). Recent papers include "Canadian and American Attitudes Toward Work and Institutions" (co-author) and "Developments in Industrial Relations and Human Resource Practices in Canada" (co-author). He is a past president of the Canadian Industrial Relations Association and was their 1998 recipient of the Gérard Dion Award for contributions to industrial relations. He was the chair of the Advisory Committee on Labour Statistics, to Statistics Canada. On January 29, 2002, Noah Meltz died in Jerusalem. As a mentor and friend to the industrial relations community, he will be missed and never forgotten.

Gregor Murray (PhD, Warwick University) is director of the Inter-University Research Centre on Globalization and Work (CRIMT—www.CRIMT.org), Canada Research Chair in Globalization and Work, and professor in the School of Industrial Relations at the University of Montreal. His research focuses on unionism, work organization, globalization, multinational firms, and industrial relations theory. His publications include *The Social Regulation of the Global Firm* (2008), *Travail et citoyenneté* (2008), *L'organisation de la production et du travail: vers un nouveau modèle* (2004), *Work and Employment Relations in the High-Performance Workplace* (2002), *La representation syndicale* (1999), and *L'état des relations professionnelles* (1996). He has worked extensively with union organizations in Canada and internationally on the paths for union renewal in a changing economy. Principal investigator in Social Sciences and Humanities Research Council's Major Collaborative Research Initiatives program, Gregor leads a project involving 70 researchers who are looking at institutions and capabilities for employment in a global era.

Frank Reid (MSc, London School of Economics; PhD, Queen's University) holds a cross-appointment at the University of Toronto as a professor in the Department of Economics and as a professor of Employment Relations. For the past 10 years he has served as the Director of the Centre for Industrial Relations and Human Resources at the University of Toronto and he is also a former president of the Canadian Industrial Relations Association. He has published in various academic journals in both economics and industrial relations as well as in numerous books and chapters in books. His current research continues his established interests in the labour market and organizational impacts of mandatory retirement policies, as well as the impacts of worksharing, jobsharing, and other alternative work arrangements.

Sara Slinn (LLB, University of British Columbia; MIR, Queen's University; PhD, University of Toronto). Sara Slinn joined the Osgoode Hall Law School faculty in 2007, after five years at Queen's Faculty of Law. Her research interests are in the areas of labour and employment law, focusing on different approaches and impediments to collective employee representation, and the intersection of *Charter* rights and labour law. Reflecting her interdisciplinary graduate work, including a PhD in Industrial Relations from the University of Toronto, Professor Slinn's research is interdisciplinary and uses empirical methods of analysis. She has also practised labour and employment law with both the British Columbia Labour Relations Board and a private law firm in Vancouver.

Akivah Starkman (PhD, University of Kent at Canterbury, England) is Director General of the Federal Mediation and Conciliation Service (FMCS). FMCS is responsible for providing collective bargaining mediation to federal jurisdiction employers and unions. Previously, he was Executive Director and Registrar of the Canada Industrial Relations Board (CIRB). Prior to joining the CIRB, Dr. Starkman was the Director of Operations and Acting Director General of FMCS, Executive Director of Labour Canada's Bureau of Labour Information, and Executive Co-ordinator of the federal Advisory Group on Working Time and the Distribution of Work. In 1995, he was a member of the Governor General's Study Tour to examine the employee–employer relationship in Canada. Formerly, he was a representative for a Canadian union. He is also an Executive Board member of the Association of Labor Relations Agencies, and a founding board member and past co-chair of the Canadian Workplace Research Network.

Mark Thompson (PhD, Cornell University) is professor emeritus of Industrial Relations in the Sauder School of Business, University of British Columbia. From 1985 to 2002, he was the William M. Hamilton Professor of Industrial Relations at the Faculty of Commerce, University of British Columbia. His research has appeared in major journals in Canada, the United States, and Britain. He has co-edited volumes on comparative industrial relations (published by the Industrial Relations Research Association), public-sector industrial relations in Canada, and regional differences in Canadian industrial relations. He has arbitrated grievances for over 20 years. He is a member of the National Academy of Arbitrators and a past president of the Canadian Industrial Relations Association. He was a governor of the Workers' Compensation Board of B.C. from 1991 to 1995. He chaired a commission to review the *Employment Standards Act* of British Columbia in 1993 to 1994 and was a member of the Advisory Committee on Labour Management Relations in the Federal Public Service in 1999 to 2000.

Kenneth Wm. Thornicroft (LLB, University of British Columbia; PhD, Case Western Reserve University) is Professor of Law & Labour Relations with the University of Victoria's Faculty of Business and also is an adjunct professor with the University of British Columbia Sauder School of Business and the Royal Roads University Faculty of Tourism and Hotel Management. He has received numerous teaching awards, including six separate "Professor of the Year" awards, and several other research and scholarship awards. Dr. Thornicoft is a former member of the B.C. Arbitration Review Panel, the B.C. Parole Board, the B.C. Employment Standards Tribunal, and the Delta Police Board. He is a current member of the B.C. Property Assessment Appeal Board and an adjudicator with the Ministry of Education's Student Appeals Branch. Dr. Thornicroft has served as a third-party neutral in over 1500 disputes. He is the author of over 70 journal articles, conference papers, book reviews, and book chapters.

Anil Verma (PhD, Massachusetts Institute of Technology) is professor of Industrial Relations and Human Resource Management at the University of Toronto, where he holds a joint appointment at the Rotman School of Management and the Centre for Industrial Relations. His primary research interests are in the areas of management responses to unionization, participative forms of work organization, and the contribution of human resource management policies—such as employment stabilization practices and other innovations in industrial relations—to organizational effectiveness and performance. Professor Verma is the author of numerous articles and has co-edited eight books including *Unions in the 21st Century* (Palgrave, U.K., 2004). He has taught previously at the University of Saskatchewan, the University of California (Los Angeles), and the University of British Columbia. He also worked in the steel industry as an engineer for five years.

Chapter 1
Canadian Labour and Employment Relations

Daphne G. Taras and Morley Gunderson

Conditions endured by the women who worked in the restaurants of the cities were as poor as can be imagined, as members of the 1919 Mathers Commission discovered. The federal government's fair wage officer admitted "that it was impossible to his mind that any girl could live and remain decent on $9 a week, which is the minimum allowed by the *Alberta Factory Act.*"

Restaurant workers laboured nine or ten hours a day, often in split shifts, seven days a week, all year, for as small a pay packet as the proprietor could get away with. In some cases, café owners doled out wages a dollar or two at a time. Rent for a cot in the basement could cost as much as $5 a week. Some café owners, afraid of getting caught in one of the far-too-infrequent visits by a *Factory Act* inspector, would pay their help with a cheque for the minimum wage and then demand that it be cashed at the till so they could take some back.

Restaurant workers were [among] the forgotten underclass of western Canada. The predominantly middle-class suffragists were fighting for things that meant little to women sleeping in café basements. The right to vote, the right to access to the professions, the right to smoke cigarettes in public—what could these things mean to women who were working every day of the year for less than the minimum wage?

Between 1916 and 1922, Edmonton waitresses had succeeded in cutting their work week to 48 hours over six days and bringing wages to about $25 a week, but their gains had not come easily. The first significant restaurant strike in Alberta took place in 1916. In 1922, the Edmonton local of the Hotel and Restaurant Employees Union called a strike against four city cafés that were demanding a wage cut of 27.5 percent. The union was offering to accept a cut of 10 percent and the waitresses stayed out 39 days to win their point. Three of the café proprietors then compromised and cut wages only 12.5 percent. Individually, workers were powerless; when they acted together they could sometimes make things happen.[1]

The image on page 2 is of Edmonton Club waitresses on strike in 1961. Conditions for service workers in many Canadian establishments are problematic, but these workers are very difficult to unionize because they often work for small employers, are part-time workers, tend to have high turnover, and fear employer reprisal. Even in the large operations, such as McDonald's or Wal-Mart, the rate of unionization is negligible for the same reasons. In addition, these large employers have access to sophisticated ways of opposing unions.

This discussion and the photo were chosen to illustrate the types of labour problems that brought the field of industrial relations into being and that continue to give the field its relevance and vitality. We could have illustrated a century of employment relationships by discussing the mining industry. The standard caricature of underground mining that involves a miner with a pick, a shovel, and a (hopefully) live canary at his side has transformed into a high technology enterprise. We could have opened with the public sector, in which most employees were not given the right to unionize until the 1960s, but which now has the highest level of unionism in the economy. Labour relations at Canada Post also could have provided fodder for lively discussion. Even nonunion companies, usually not thought of as having labour relations practices, often operate with employee voice mechanisms that range from simple suggestion systems to complex joint employee–manager councils.

In short, no matter where you live in Canada or what industries surround you, the impact of labour and employment relations will be felt.

The last 20 to 25 years have been a time of dramatic change. Workers compete across national boundaries, and indeed internet-enabled communication erodes the whole concept of boundaries. At the same time, though, national choices of foreign policies and domestic investments lead to currency fluctuations, and these trickle down to affect almost every employment setting in Canada. (For example, the United States' policy decision to fight a war in Iraq affects U.S. currency, which in turn creates challenges and opportunities for Canadian businesses.) Canadian companies are seeking greater planning flexibility, and workers are expected to cope with change by training themselves for versatility. The Canadian workforce is diverse in more ways than simply racial, ethnic, and any other grounds enumerated in human rights legislation. Immigration has long been a mainstay of Canadian development, but now serious labour market concerns are caused by internal migrations among the provinces. As one Newfoundlander aptly put it, "Alberta's recruitment problem is Eastern Canada's retention problem." There is a growing recognition that a one-size-fits-all approach to accommodating differences cannot be effective when each worker is under pressure to balance different family care-giving duties, religious and cultural obligations, and expectations about education and training. Workers now must also consider whether they prefer standard forms of work design, or new forms such as home-based work and telework. How does a country develop policies that cope with the latest developments and then anticipate the challenges of this century?

Laws often lag behind grass-roots developments. Unions existed long before they were legally recognized entities. Once treated as conspiracies, workers' efforts to strengthen their power through collective action came to be benignly tolerated by the courts as long as no real damage was done to employers' interests. Then, with the passage of labour laws and a collective bargaining regime, labour boards and courts interpreted the statutory provisions. But even in law the change has been unexpectedly dramatic.

Here was the lay of the land in 1987. The Supreme Court of Canada was asked to take collective bargaining under the protective embrace of the guarantee by the *Canadian Charter of Rights and Freedoms* of the fundamental right for freedom of association, Section 2(d). No, said the Court. Eminent legal scholars, though disappointed with the Court's approach, were not at all surprised (Fudge, 1988; Arthurs, 1988). For 20 years, the dust settled and unions learned to keep their aspirations to a very low level when approaching the legal system.

Then in 2007, the Supreme Court of Canada astonished the labour relations community—both union and management—by issuing a proclamation that explicitly overturned its own earlier decisions:

> Freedom of association guaranteed by s.2(d) of the Charter includes a procedural right to collective bargaining. The grounds advanced in the earlier decisions of this Court for the exclusion of collective bargaining from the s.2(d)'s protection do not withstand principled scrutiny and should be rejected. . . . Further, the right to collective bargaining is neither of recent origin nor merely a creature of statute. . . . Association for purposes of collective bargaining has long been recognized as a fundamental Canadian right which predated the Charter. The protection enshrined in s.2(d) of the Charter may properly be seen as the culmination of a historical movement towards the recognition of a procedural right to collective bargaining. Canada's adherence to international documents recognizing a right to collective bargaining also supports recognition of that right in s.2(d). The Charter should be presumed to provide at least as great a level of protection as is found in the international human rights documents that Canada has ratified. Lastly, the protection of collective bargaining under s.2(d) is consistent with and supportive of the values underlying the Charter and the purposes of the Charter as a whole. Recognizing that workers have the right to bargain collectively as part of their freedom to associate reaffirms the values of dignity, personal autonomy, equality and democracy. . . . (*Health Services and Support—Facilities Subsector Bargaining Assn. v. British Columbia*, [2007] S.C.C. 27)

Note that the Court referred favourably to the International Labour Organization's Declaration, reproduced in Exhibit 1.1.[2]

It remains to be seen what impact the Supreme Court's proclamation may have on the landscape of Canadian labour and employment. Certainly, the proclamation diminishes the likelihood that anti-union activities from managers or companies will receive kind treatment from legal adjudicators as this century matures.

SETTING THE BASIC TERMINOLOGY

Canadian Labour and Employment Relations is an industrial relations text with a distinctive content and outlook born of its home discipline. At one time, it was widely accepted that industrial relations focused on union–management relations, and most people writing in the field examined unions, collective bargaining, labour laws, strikes, grievance resolution, and other topics derived from the interplay between unions and management. Industrial relations was presumed to regulate the relationship between management and *organized* labour. This definition has become outdated.

The term "industrial relations" was first used in North America in 1912 when American President William Howard Taft and Congress created the Commission of Industrial Relations (Kaufman, 1993) in response to a 1910 labour dispute that culminated in the bombing deaths of 20 persons in the *Los Angeles Times* building caused by two union leaders. The Commission's mandate was to determine the conditions responsible for conflict and to suggest remedies. Prior to the Commission, the term used to describe its field of study was simply "the relations between labour and capital in industry."

Early Canadian terminology embraced such terms as the "Labour Problem" and "Industrial Troubles."[3] One of the first government investigations was the 1903 Royal Commission on Industrial Disputes in British Columbia. One of Canada's earliest labour relations statutes was the *Industrial Disputes Investigation Act* of 1907. Canadians adopted the term "industrial relations" soon thereafter. The Canadian government launched the Royal Commission to Enquire into Industrial Relations in Canada, and its *Report* was issued in 1919. William Lyon Mackenzie King (the first deputy minister of labour and long-serving prime minister of Canada, and arguably the single most influential individual in Canadian industrial relations [Ferns and Ostry, 1955: 293]) wrote a book in 1918 entitled *Industry and Humanity* and the term "industrial relations" was adopted throughout his book.

To this day, "labour relations" means the study of organized labour (unions) and management. In contrast, "employment relations" focuses on the relationship between individual employees—including those who are not organized into unions—and their employers. Similarly, labour law deals with collective bargaining matters, while employment law deals mostly with nonunion employees.

Industrial relations became an academic field because of the magnitude of labour–management warfare and the instability caused by that warfare throughout the industrializing world. In Canada, disputes in the coal mines and railways catapulted "the labour problem" to the forefront of social and public policy matters for many generations. The 1919 Winnipeg General Strike terrified politicians and industrialists alike. Workers were discovering that through collective action they could redress the worst abuses of private enterprise and raise their power substantially even in the face of management hostility. Society needed a cadre of experts who could be relied upon both to analyze and to solve the increasingly intractable dilemmas in the relations between employers and workers. Hence, the industrial relations academic field "came to the labor problem to *do* something about labor's inequities in the employment relationship" (Barbash, 1997: 17).

As a result, the industrial relations field has a strong practical orientation. One definition suggested by a leading scholar is that industrial relations is "problem solving [on] behalf of equity in the employment relationship" (Barbash, 1997: 17). Industrial relations scholars have often been social activists and reformers as well as academics, and this tradition of activism has invigorated the field.

The emerging consensus today is that industrial relations is "a broad, interdisciplinary field of study and practice that encompasses all aspects of the employment relationship."[4] Rather than examining only workers organized by unions, industrial relations has begun laying claim to all workers—union and nonunion—in all work settings. Most recently, distinguished scholars have been urging us to make the transition from the last century's use of "industrial relations" to a new label of "work and employment relations." The latter is perhaps more sensitive to the transition from an industrial society to one that also includes a significant amount of service and specialized knowledge-based work (Whalen, 2008; Kochan, 2008). Thus, industrial relations consists of both labour and employment relations, and it has broadened its scope to much more than factory and traditional production settings. We retain the elements "study and practice" to capture the debt we owe to academics, practitioners, and social activists. This is the pluralistic approach we accept for this book.

Ordinarily, endless debates about a definition would be of little interest to most readers. But, as we will describe throughout this chapter, the field is in considerable turmoil, and this grappling over the definition is symptomatic of some of the workplace pressures currently confronting employees, managers, and policy-makers.

CORE PREMISES OF THE FIELD

For a number of years, industrial relations scholarship had been splitting into two camps, one espousing systems theory and the other embracing political economy. (In the legal community, the debate was framed as being between "realists" and "idealists.") The two industrial relations camps will be described very briefly, and then we shall move on to more recent initiatives to unify the field.

The Systems Model This model situates the actors (unions, employers, and governments) within their social, political, economic, technological, and legal environment. The actors interact with each other according to a "web of rules," and the results of the system are such matters as wage rates, conditions of employment, strikes and lockouts, productivity rates, and so on (Dunlop, 1958/1993). A simple systems model begins with external inputs into labour relations such as the labour market, political system, and natural resource endowments. Then, arrows are drawn to the labour-management actors such as unions, companies, and the various agencies (mostly government) that specialize in labour. Each has goals that are affected by relations with the other actors' goals. Through a variety of simple mechanisms such as day-to-day interactions as well as laws and procedures, the actors interact with each other to produce the outputs of the system, which include wages, union security provisions, job rights, benefits, and even such outcomes as strikes and lockouts. From these outcomes is a feedback loop that allows learning and adjustment. Notice the emphasis on identifying the variables that can be quantified, coded, and entered into large data sets. Scholars became less preoccupied with solving the labour problem, and more involved in simply studying it. This was the heyday of "objective" social science.

Political Economists Political economists tend to focus on macro-level explanations and the identification of forces that shape social and economic relations. They argue that industrial relations is born of the larger organization of relations of production in society. Only with an understanding of power, the distribution of privilege, and social relations of production can industrial relations be appreciated. The economic and social aspects of the employment relationship generate tension. Political economists broadened their field so that they could move outside the systems model confines. They study all workers—be they union or nonunion—and their families, as well as business interests and the corporate elite, and the relationship between the accrual of influence and the development of public policy.

Differences between the systems approach and political economy are enormous. Crudely put, while systems theorists enumerate and scrutinize the *variables* in their models, political economists explore the *arrows and paths* in the model. Critics of systems theory argue that it has a dangerous bias toward consensus and stability, while critics of political economy argue that it exaggerates conflict and exploitation. Both approaches have contributed to our understanding of Canadian industrial relations. Systems work has carefully amassed data and evidence about matters of importance to Canadians such as the terms and conditions of employment, the incidence of industrial unrest, and the relationship between the strength of the economy and changes in the labour market. Political economy has drawn our attention to major public policy concerns such as poverty, fragility of employment for a social underclass, the ability of workers to influence public policy, and the relationship between unions and political movements.

However, the debate became increasingly irrelevant and sterile. After the field has existed for about 100 years, scholars want to celebrate commonalities. Many assumptions are taken for granted by almost all industrial relations scholars. These seven form the bedrock and are fairly easily discernible in this book:

- Labour is not just a commodity, or an input into production. Crudely put, steel does not cry when laid off; wheat does not have to feed its children; and a computer does not pay for rent, food, or tuition.

- While efficiency is important, it is not the only key objective.

- Themes such as equity, equality, and fairness also are important considerations (Budd, 2004; Arthurs, 2006).

- The field tries to obtain a solution that maximizes efficiency, equity, fairness, and dignity, so that each achieves its optimal point without sacrificing the others (Kochan, 2008).

- There is much emphasis on finding the appropriate balance. Pragmatism is needed to find the balance. Bargaining and power are preoccupations because they help resolve the balance issue.

- Workers are entitled to express themselves in their employment setting and outside it. The legitimacy of "voice" is key.

- Collective action enhances worker voice, and is a socially legitimate activity, especially so with the 2007 Supreme Court decision.

Scholars have dozens of vehicles within which to publish their studies. Exhibit 1.2 offers a few examples of our journals.

Exhibit 1.2
Selected Leading Journals in Industrial Relations

Canadian

- *Relations industrielles/Industrial Relations* (Laval University): Diversity of perspectives, including systems theory and political economy, and diversity of methodologies including quantitative analysis and case studies. Bilingual.
  Web address: www.riir.ulaval.ca

- *Labour/Le Travail* (Memorial University of Newfoundland): Labour history, case studies, and political economy. English.

    Web address: www.mun.ca/cclh/llt

AMERICAN

- *Industrial and Labor Relations Review* (Cornell University): Mostly systems theory–based econometric studies.

    Web address: www.ilr.cornell.edu/ilrreview

- *Industrial Relations* (University of California at Berkeley): Deliberately moving away from econometric studies toward a multi-disciplinary, international focus, with symposia on public policy matters.

    Web address: www.irle.berkeley.edu/indrel/

- *Journal of Labor Research* (Springer): Often opens with a symposium. Tries to position itself as more reader-friendly but still academic.

    Web address: www.springer.com (and follow links under Social Sciences to JLR)

- *Advances in Industrial and Labor Relations* (Elsevier): Published less often; longer, more chapter-like contributions.

    Web address: www.sciencedirect.com/science/bookseries/07426186

BRITISH

- *British Journal of Industrial Relations* (London School of Economics): Diversity of perspectives; most influential of the overseas journals.

    Web address: www.blackwellpublishing.com/journals/BJIR

INDUSTRIAL RELATIONS AND HUMAN RESOURCE MANAGEMENT: WHAT'S THE DIFFERENCE?

Human resource management (HRM) emerged as a subfield of management studies from its initial beginnings as personnel management (Marciano, 1995). The term "human resource" was first used by management guru Peter F. Drucker in his 1954 book, *The Practice of Management*. Drucker argues that, unlike other firm resources (equipment, land, money, etc.), the *human* resource has unique qualities: "the ability to coordinate, to integrate, to judge, and to imagine."

HRM has become a dominant focus of management research, often at the expense of industrial relations (Lewin, 1991; Kaufman, 2004). The HRM section of the influential (U.S.) Academy of Management has grown exponentially over the past decades. The HRM division of the Administrative Sciences Association of Canada is well established, although it is overshadowed by the Academy of Management. Both the Canadian Industrial Relations Association and the (American) Labor and Employment Relations Association have battled membership declines.

The lines between industrial relations (IR) and HRM are blurred.[5] Both fields appreciate that labour is not just a commodity, and that people are complex, deserving of dignity, and dependent upon employment. HR managers are familiar with issues raised by unionization, and IR managers are trained to appreciate many personnel planning and compensation issues. In smaller companies, and in nonunion companies, the distinctions between IR and HRM are relatively unimportant. But in some large organizations that are partially or fully unionized, HR departments are physically separate from IR departments.

Each field developed its own expertise and vocabulary, and, based on our interviews with practitioners, certain stereotypes have emerged. IR managers see themselves occupying a tougher, more conflictual world consisting of negotiating and then administering collective agreements and resolving disputes as they arise at the worksite. As a group, IR managers have a fairly cynical outlook. They see HR managers as living in a kinder, gentler world, or, alternatively, as manipulative but naive. By contrast, HR managers feel more connected to firm strategy and believe they have a better understanding of the firm as a whole. They see their counterparts in IR as marginalized, having specific technical expertise that, while vital within the unionized portion of the firm, tends to wax and wane in importance depending on the state of labour relations in the company and industry. They see IR as more reactive, and view themselves as having cutting-edge skills and techniques that can transform the workplace into a more productive and flexible place. Union officers often understand their management counterparts in IR quite well: although on opposite sides of the bargaining table, union and IR managers share a similar view of the employment setting. But unions sometimes view HRM with deep suspicion. Obviously, subtle differences exist between IR and HRM, but what are they?

Academic treatment of these subjects within universities and colleges does not help clarify the matter. Except for a few free-standing research and degree-granting industrial relations institutes within Canada—at Université Laval, Université de Montréal, University of Toronto, and Queen's University (where the IR Centre is now part of the Public Policy School)—most industrial relations courses are taught within other faculties, particularly business schools (Chaykowski and Weber, 1993; Taras, 2008). Business schools offer an array of courses focusing on the *people* aspects of organizations, including organizational behaviour, organizational theory, basic human resource management, and specialty courses in subjects such as compensation and benefits, and recruitment and training. In addition, students often are offered introductions to industrial relations and some smattering of collective bargaining, labour economics, employment law, and employment dispute resolution methods. Many subtopics within all these courses tend to overlap. Understandably, there is considerable confusion about the place of IR.

Most students believe IR is about unions and do not understand that the field can encompass the full employment relationship in both unionized and nonunion workplaces. As well, there is little appreciation for the four important differences that divide IR from HRM. At times, these differences are profound. Although the topics studied within IR and HRM can be identical—for example, the study of wages, the development of employee involvement and participation plans, and so on—each field has its own unique set of assumptions about human behaviour and about the place of collective action within the employment relationship (see Table 1.1).

Table 1.1 Similarities and Differences Between IR and HRM

General Stereotypes

	Industrial Relations	Human Resource Management
View of People	Not a commodity	Not a commodity
General Outlook	Tougher, conflictual world	Problem-solving
Place in the Firm	Marginalized to vital, depending on state of labour relations	Connected to firm strategy

Differences in Approach (Exaggerated for Clarity)

	Industrial Relations	Human Resource Management
Focus	Inherent conflict Zero-sum	Common interests Win–win
Assumption	Pluralist Worker agenda vs. company agenda Intersection of two organizations	Unitarist Unions are external
Policy Implications	Regulation, rules, dispute resolution Voice in the workplace	Attachment, motivation, loyalty Alignment and harmony
Orientation and Level of Analysis	Collectivist	Individual and small group

1. *The basic paradigm is different.* HRM focuses on the shared interests of workers and managers in the success of their enterprise. Conflict is de-emphasized in favour of "win–win" scenarios in which problems are solved or put aside to fulfill organizational objectives. Human resource management focuses mainly on the individual within the organization: how to enhance the fit among talents, tasks, and behaviours for the purpose of meeting organizational objectives (Horwitz, 1991: 11). According to leading HRM textbooks, the goal is "to influence the effectiveness of an organization's employees" (Heneman et al., 1989: 6).

   A premise shared by most IR scholars is that inherent conflicts of interest between employees and managers may exist. These can be brought into alignment for periods of relative stability, but conflict also is a normal state of affairs. Conflict is not viewed as pathological; however, efforts should be made to reduce the scope and frequency of discord since the parties share the same work setting and have a mutual interest in ensuring its continued viability.[6] IR approaches often feature conflictual situations, power struggles, and fixed-sum games involving resource distribution that must be solved rather than sidelined.

2. *HRM tends to be unitarist while IR is pluralist.* HRM holds that workers are meant to be absorbed into the corporation fairly seamlessly, minimizing any friction and maximizing the common agenda. Unions are treated as external to the organization, akin to

uninvited dinner guests. Managers who hold this view often speak of unions as "third parties," and say "we don't believe it is necessary to have any third parties come between us and our employees." HRM textbooks often imply that unions are an "external threat," and the inference is clear that unions cause conflict.

IR recognizes that employee interests and management interests are not necessarily the same. Workers may seek to advance their interests through collective action by, for example, joining a union to increase their power. Unions are the result of, not the cause of, conflict. As Barbash (1984: 49) has put it, "It is the labor problem which creates unions, not unions which create the labor problem." IR accepts that employees might have dual loyalties—to the firm and to a union—or even a single loyalty to the union against the firm.

3. *Approaches to organizational policy are different.* The expertise of both HRM and IR departments has been called upon in the development of employment policies and practices such as drug testing, accommodations for injured workers, and even the regulation of computer use (primarily to remove pornography from the worksite). The regulation of individual rights and behaviours at the workplace is a fast-growing area for both fields.

HRM guides the development of these and other policies to encourage employee attachment to the organization, for example, by providing extrinsic or intrinsic rewards to individuals who contribute to corporate performance. The idea is to *align* worker goals with those of the organization, for example, by offering profit-sharing schemes. HRM strategies help organizations recruit, select, and motivate employees; compensate them appropriately; and improve the fit between the employee and the organization.

IR focuses on the policies that *regulate* employment relations, particularly the development and administration of collective agreements. The emphasis is on developing rules and procedures through which conflict can be channelled. IR managers are knowledgeable about unionization processes, collective agreement negotiations, prerequisites for lawful work stoppages, and grievance procedures.

4. *The unit of analysis—the thing we study—is different.* HRM tends to examine the individual, while IR is collectivist. HRM usually is concerned with the harnessing of individual talents. Though HRM often examines the workings of small groups or teams and employee input and participation plans, usually it does so with the aim of achieving corporate goals or adding value to individual efforts. For example, small, self-managed work teams are applauded when they help increase productivity or solve work-scheduling blockages. IR is almost exclusively collectivist in orientation, and assumes that individual power in an employment situation is enhanced through coordinated collective mobilization. Since IR accepts that employees often have different interests than their employers, IR then is concerned with how employees band together to advance their interests. And IR is not just about the study of unions: there has been an upsurge of interest in using IR concepts to study how nonunion workers represent their interests within their organizations (Kaufman and Taras, 2000). IR studies are concerned with power, employee voice, and the manner in which the terms and conditions of employment are set. What is the bargain—implicit or otherwise—that is struck between workers who provide their services and companies that employ them?

What can be drawn from this examination of the differences between human resource management and industrial relations? Some employee outcomes—wages, benefits, employee participation schemes, to name but a few—can be the result of IR policies, HRM policies, or both. At the worksite level, they are virtually indistinguishable, particularly in nonunion settings. Where variability exists in personnel practices within and among firms, the question is whether differences originate from IR strategies, HRM strategies, both, or some other organizational imperative. This becomes an important area of investigation when HRM policies are used to forestall unionization. Modern managers are urged to listen to employees, to model expected behaviours, to "walk the talk," and to promote greater employee involvement and participation. These practices could form a cluster demonstrating the use of an excellent progressive HRM philosophy. These same practices could be adopted for the sole purpose of preventing workers from joining unions. We urge students to develop sensitivity to the underlying goals of common worksite practices.

Canadian Industrial Relations: The Critical Ingredients

The editors and the majority of our contributors are IR scholars and, in many cases, influential practitioners and policy-makers. At international conferences and meetings, we are frequently asked to articulate the main features of Canada's labour and employment setting. In this section, we alert our readers to five important pillars of the Canadian approach.

Decentralization, Experimentation, and Diffusion Canada's federal system of government is one of the most decentralized in the world. Broadly speaking, industrial relations belong to the provinces. Only about 8.4 percent of the Canadian workforce is covered by federal labour and employment laws, including employees of the federal government, banks, interprovincial transport, maritime trade, and telecommunications. Employees of national companies such as Tim Hortons or Roots are covered by laws in each of the provinces in which their stores or franchises are located. International companies such as Starbucks which have outlets across Canada must abide by the laws of each province in which outlets are situated. (What does this mean for labour relations in that great Canadian preoccupation, hockey?[7]) As a result, from province to province there are differences in minimum wage rates, working conditions, and procedures to follow in the event that employees become interested in unionizing. To illustrate some of the differences, the Province of Saskatchewan has posted a table online comparing its employment standards with those of the federal government at www.readyforwork.sk.ca/fast-facts/Factsheet-LSRFWComparison.pdf.

This decentralization was not by design. In fact, early policy-makers wrote standard laws for all Canadians, assuming that, for efficient development and for "peace, order, and good government," employment matters should be centrally regulated. It came as a considerable shock when the British Privy Council declared (in the 1925 *Snider* case)[8] that federal government labour laws were infringing on provincial powers. For over 20 years, the federal government withdrew from any activism in labour matters, and wrote only a temporary national labour law in 1944 (known as PC 1003) when World War II gave the federal government extraordinary power for the war's duration. Before and after the war, provinces adopted their own laws.

As a result of this complexity, an unwary practitioner easily can make serious mistakes. Although all provinces and the federal government have adopted similar overall approaches, there is a multitude of small differences (Thompson, Rose, and Smith, 2004). For example, a company such as Petro-Canada can use replacement workers during a strike in Alberta, but cannot do so in Quebec or British Columbia. In some provinces, workers who want to be represented by the United Steelworkers (USW) need only sign cards, while in others they must in addition hold a secret ballot vote. On the negative side, there is "too much law and too much inconsequential diversity" in Canada (Sims, 1994: 6). On the positive side, this decentralization has led to a rich tradition of experimentation and the cross-fertilization of ideas, as well as enough flexibility to meet diverse preferences and needs.

Serious unresolved issues remain. The conundrum of being Canadian is illustrated in Exhibit 1.3.

Exhibit 1.3
Canadian Brainteasers

1. If Canada puts the federal signature to an international treaty or ILO convention, can it bind the provinces? Can provinces argue, instead, that their exclusive jurisdiction over labour and employment invalidates the ability of Ottawa to enforce any of its international labour-related obligations?

2. If a Manitoba bus company has one bus in its fleet of 10 that crosses into Saskatchewan, while the remainder of the fleet covers only provincial routes, is the company a federal or provincial undertaking?

3. If a bank contracts a New Brunswick employment agency to provide call centre services, are the call centre employees who do 100 percent bank work governed by employment laws of New Brunswick or by the federal statutes?

4. If the federal government issues immigration permits for foreign workers to undertake seasonal work on Ontario farms, which jurisdiction has responsibility for the welfare of these workers?

Note: These types of questions were put before the Arthurs Commission in its work from 2004 to 2006. There are no easy answers. Some questions are not answerable.

Canadian Values Is there a distinctive Canadian culture and approach that affects the practice of industrial relations? Some have made the argument that Canadians are not merely "decaffeinated Americans" (Taras, 1997). At various points in Canadian evolution, influential groups of citizens and policy-makers within Canada tried to preserve a remnant of their British deference to hierarchy, to authority, together with an overlay of respect for "red Toryism." This important red Tory element combines economic conservatism with simultaneously held principles of collective rights and state intervention for the provision of comprehensive social welfare policies. There was no revolutionary overthrow of British influences.

Into this mix was added the unique history and traditions of French Canada, offering alternative social and economic visions embedded in intellectual, linguistic, and cultural influences quite different from those elsewhere in North America. The fierce nationalism of many in Quebec, reflected in successive elections, reinforced the already powerful decentralizing forces within Canada. At the same time, Quebec leaders have dominated federal politics since World War II, with Louis St. Laurent, Pierre Trudeau, Brian Mulroney, and Jean Chrétien enjoying long stints as prime minister.

Canadians were encouraged to consider themselves part of a "mosaic" of diverse ethnic or identity-based groupings, and the notion of a "hyphenated Canadian" was accepted—Italian-Canadian, Jewish-Canadian, Korean-Canadian, and so on. Canada is now one of the few countries in the world that recognizes the legality of gay marriages. Historically, the settlement of the Canadian hinterland proceeded in a more orderly fashion than was the case in the American West, with major institutions like railways, banks, and the national police (RCMP, formerly NWMP) directing Canadian settlement. It is commonly believed that most Canadians are more deferential to authority than Americans are, more accepting of collective rights, and more willing to forgo individual freedoms that clash with social norms (e.g., Canadian acceptance of gun control, enforced seat belt laws, higher taxation rates than in the United States, and universal access to medical care). Seymour Martin Lipset (1995) labels Canada as "leftist collectivist," which is likely an overstatement today, but it does capture the historical Canadian tendency toward brokering competing interests.

Canadians are strongly aware that government is a powerful player that can both apply legitimate coercion on other groups and set the public-policy framework within which the other actors must operate.

A contemporary example of how this Canadian impulse to balance individualism with collectivism has had an impact on industrial relations involves the crafting of the 1982 *Canadian Charter of Rights and Freedoms*. The Charter guarantees certain fundamental freedoms including freedom of association, thought, belief, opinion, and expression. But these individual rights are not paramount and absolute (as they are in the United States under the *Bill of Rights*). In Canada, Section 1 of the Charter holds that fundamental rights are subject to "such reasonable limits as can be demonstrably justified in a free and democratic society." There is a presumption that a fettering of individual rights is necessary for democracy, and there must be an obligation to subordinate some rights for the good of the majority. This balancing act is extremely important in the labour relations arena, where the ability of unions to represent members, collect union dues, and exercise the right to strike depends on a legal regime that allows for collective action even over the protests of individuals who believe their own rights are being diminished.

We believe that it is no coincidence that three of the longest-serving prime ministers in the 20th century—William Lyon Mackenzie King, Pierre Trudeau, and Brian Mulroney—had substantial training and expertise in industrial relations (though they did not necessarily share the same views on the subject). In the labour relations setting, pragmatism and the ability to find a compromise position for combatants is highly valued, as it is in the political arena. *Seeking a Balance* is the apt title of the 1995 federal task force to investigate reform to Canada's federal labour laws (Sims, 1995). The title captures the Canadian desire to find that elusive middle ground on which alliances can be fashioned and discord can be minimized.[9]

Multiparty Democracy Canadian unions historically formed a close alliance with the New Democratic Party.[10] In Quebec, where the NDP did not make inroads, unions aligned themselves with other parties, most recently the Parti Québécois. The movement of unions onto the political stage had significant ramifications for the regulation of employment relations. Federally, the major labour law (PC 1003) was passed in 1944 because of the Liberal Party's fear that its failure to offer basic protections for labour organizing and bargaining to appease unions would drive voters into the arms of the rival Co-operative Commonwealth Federation (CCF, as the NDP was then known). The provincial adoption of strong legislative measures to promote collective rights in employment settings was directly attributable to the influence of the NDP, either as the provincial governing party spearheading labour law reform in a number of provinces (including British Columbia, Saskatchewan, Manitoba, and Ontario) or as a strong and vociferous opposition and a serious electoral threat.

Although many unions aligned their interests with the NDP, they have found it increasingly difficult to "deliver" the votes of their members. For example, in the 1990s— while union leaders decried the policies of provincial Conservative governments in Alberta and Ontario—Premiers Klein and Harris both enjoyed tremendous popular support even among unionized workers. The powerful Canadian Auto Workers union (CAW) broke its labour–NDP alliance in the late 1990s, and once-cordial relations became strained. Today, the link between labour and the NDP, while still evident, is weaker and more fragile than during the previous century.

Mackenzie King Nowhere in the world is there a tighter linkage between a single individual and the development of a long-term statutory regime for workers than in Canada. William Lyon Mackenzie King's official approval or "imprimatur" can be found in virtually all labour policy initiatives from the turn of the century to the mid-1940s, and many distinctive features of Canada's approach reflect his thinking to this day.

A brief biography is in order. Mackenzie King was formally educated at the Universities of Toronto, Chicago, and then Harvard for a PhD in labour relations. As a graduate student, he wrote a series of newspaper exposés based on his eyewitness investigations of the appalling conditions in the needle trade sweatshops. These articles, along with his educational qualifications, launched his brilliant parliamentary career.

Mackenzie King entered the newly formed Ministry of Labour as its resident expert in 1900 and was called upon to investigate and mediate some of Canada's most difficult labour disputes. He was the principal architect of every piece of early labour legislation. Later, as prime minister during World War II, he oversaw the introduction of comprehensive labour statutes that guaranteed all workers the right to organize and unions the right to represent the interests of their members.

Mackenzie King's watchword was "conciliation," whether voluntary or by government decree. Through the magic of the conciliation process, he believed that the veils of self-interest would fall and that the disputant parties would come to appreciate the "public interest." He sought to impose order on chaos and fervently yearned for a humane society in which "Reason" and "Truth" would prevail. To create greater discipline, he drafted laws that emphasized third-party expertise and prohibited work stoppage. The failure of employers to ameliorate abusive treatment of their workers would be a victory for "Evil," just as self-serving and narrow union demands would divert humanity toward disorder. His interventions consistently compelled state involvement to restore industrial peace. He

favoured government intervention because he saw it was feasible and felt it to be morally correct. He believed, first, that the state realistically could find and employ appropriate third-party expertise (and here he viewed his own early career as the exemplar) and take on the role he described as "impartial umpire," and second, that the state was duty-bound to protect the interests of citizens from the discord created by irrationality between labour and management (Craven, 1980).

Due to his influence, a persistent theme in the development of Canadian labour law has been the preference for reason over passion, and humanism rather than simply macro-economic planning. There was a strong moral tone in King's energies. In his own words,

> For Industry and Nationality alike, the last word lies in the supremacy of Humanity. . . . The national or industrial economy based on a lesser vision, in the final analysis, is anti-social, and lacks the essentials of indefinite expansion and durability. The failure to look beyond the State, and beyond Industry as a revenue-producing process, has brought chaos instead of order. (King, 1918/1973: 28)

More than 60 years later, the same sentiments were expressed by Paul Weiler (1980: 29) in his important book on Canadian labour policy, *Reconcilable Differences: New Directions in Canadian Labour Law*: "The economic function is the beginning, not the end, of the case for collective bargaining. . . . The true function of economic bargaining consists in its civilizing impact upon the working life and environment of employees."

Following are some of the many elements in Canadian industrial relations that have their origins in Mackenzie King's approach:

■ A ban on strikes and lockouts during the life of the collective agreement. In Canada, a strike is lawful only after the expiry of the collective agreement, when the parties are in a position to bargain. During the collective agreement (which normally is in force for about two years, on average), all disputes must be referred to third-party arbitration for binding resolution.

■ Before any strike can occur, there must be a cooling-off period and an attempt at conciliation.

- Various measures are written into labour codes that give ministers of labour the power to order investigations into labour disputes that threaten the public interest.

- Government employees were not given the right to unionize until almost two decades after Mackenzie King left office. He felt that unionization of the public service would lead to chaos, as government services were essential for the welfare of the state and its citizens.

Influence of American Developments   Like many aspects of Canadian life, industrial relations has long been affected by American developments. Given the historical interdependence between the two economies, strengthened by recent free trade agreements and the pervasive influence of American culture, it would be surprising if this were not the case.

More than a century ago, U.S. labour leaders began organizing Canadian workers and integrating them into North American "international" unions. By the early 1900s, international unions dominated the Canadian labour movement, exporting to Canada a union philosophy that came to be known as "business unionism." Business unions were economically and socially conservative, unaffiliated with political parties, and focused on the needs of skilled craft workers. There is no doubt that the U.S. linkages gave Canadian workers access to greater resources and expertise than might otherwise have been the case and likely accelerated union growth in this country. However, American dominance hindered the development of alternative approaches to unionism that might have better addressed Canadian needs, such as a labour political party. Even today, about one-third of Canadian union members belong to unions such as the Teamsters, United Steelworkers, and the United Food and Commercial Workers (UFCW), all headquartered in the United States. The sole international union located in Canada is the NHL Players' Association, with its Toronto head office.

Canadian and American union linkages have fostered tight linkages in labour law. Mackenzie King's conciliation legislation probably influenced the U.S. *National Railway Act* of 1928, which in turn was an important stepping stone to the (American) *National Labor Relations Act* of 1935 (also known as the *Wagner Act*). The *Wagner Act* constituted a watershed in the evolution of North American labour law. It outlawed a variety of union-busting tactics, required employers to recognize and bargain with a union chosen by a majority of employees, and established a labour relations board to interpret and apply the new legislation. The result was a surge in union membership. In Canada, international unions lobbied hard for similar legislation, and in 1944 the *Wagner Act* principles were adopted into Canadian law alongside the traditional conciliation approach. The 1944 legislation (PC 1003) remains the basis for Canadian labour law to this day.

American influence is felt in another way. Union membership in the United States has experienced a precipitous decline in the past 25 years. In an integrated North American economy, where Canada often seems to follow U.S. trends with a time lag, the question remains whether Canadian unions will undergo the same decline (Lipset et al., 2004). Management strategies aimed at combatting union growth have been transplanted to Canada, and the workforce structural changes that have contributed to union decline in the United States, such as outsourcing and contract work, are prevalent in both countries. The Canadian public sector, the source of most union growth in the last quarter-century, has been declining. Union density in Canada, close to 40 percent in the 1980s, is at 30 percent today. See Figure 1.1.[11]

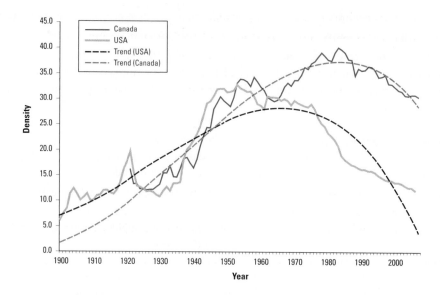

Figure 1.1 Canadian vs. U.S. Union Density

Nevertheless, it is important to recognize that union density in Canada remains more than double that of the United States, and the fate of U.S. unions should not cause us to believe that unions are less relevant in Canada. At the same time, we need to be aware that American industrial relations developments have influenced Canadian trends in the past and will do so in the future.

Why Are Canadian–American Unionization Differences Important to Educators?

Historically, Canadian and American rates of union density (the proportion of non-agricultural workers represented by organized labour unions) were virtually identical. The fortunes of the union movements in the two countries began sharply diverging in the 1970s, and today the trend lines in Figure 1.1 show significant differences (see Chapter 4 for details). With the sharp decline of American union density, industrial relations began disappearing from courses and teaching textbooks. American industrial relations scholars were encouraged to examine HRM topics, and many left the field. Employment prospects dwindled for new IR managers.

Despite some union decline during the 1990s, the Canadian labour movement remains a significant force in Canadian society. Almost all government services are unionized, including those services—such as policing, air traffic control, education, and health care—that are widely seen as essential. Most telecommunications, transportation, and hydro employees are unionized. Our automobile industry, resource-extraction industries such as logging and mining, and commercial construction all have high rates of union penetration. While some parts of the economy, such as banking, insurance, and retail sales (especially "mall" stores like Gap or Eddie Bauer) are almost union-free, those parts of our economy that are unionized continue to have a substantial impact on our daily lives. In 2007, after decades of running union-free, the giant auto-parts maker Magna voluntarily recognized the right of the Canadian Auto Workers union to hold elections in exchange for a no-strike guarantee, a move that must cause business strategy professors to scratch their heads in confusion.

Yet standard Canadian textbooks in such fields as organizational behaviour, organizational theory, strategy, and accounting and finance are virtually silent on the strong presence of unions in the Canadian landscape. This is no coincidence. The field of management education has deep roots in the United States, and Canadians tend to adopt American approaches. Until recently, most Canadian business schools hired U.S.-educated professors, and even if they were Canadian citizens, many were strongly influenced by their years of training in the United States. Standard textbooks are created for the much larger U.S. market and are adopted by Canadian classes, either directly or in a "Canadianized" version of the original. Even when books are wholly Canadian, the table of contents and rough proportion of topics are drawn from popular American texts.[12] Labour relations texts, including this book, are an exception.

We believe that Canadian students are being done a disservice by not receiving the exposure to industrial relations that would be warranted by our substantial degree of union density. For example, Canadians should know more about the impact of unions on benefits plans, union pension-based investments, wage setting, and corporate strategic planning.

The Changing Workplace

Other features of the workplace should also be added to our discussion. In addition to unions, the following types of arrangements exist in many Canadian workplaces (Taras, 2002):

- professional organizations such as those that represent doctors, lawyers, pharmacists, accountants, and engineers;
- nonunion staff associations that provide some representation rights to workers who are not unionized, including administrators; and
- complex company-initiated representation plans such as joint industrial councils, employee–management advisory committees, and forums that allow employees to discuss their terms and conditions of employment with managers.

Nineteen percent of Canadians belong to professional associations, and 10 percent belong to staff associations (Lowe and Schellenberg, 2001: 26–29). Roughly 14 percent of Canadians are represented by nonunion representation systems described in the third bullet above (Lipset and Meltz, 2000). Combining these types of figures and eliminating some double-counting problems, we estimate that approximately 48 percent of Canadian employees enjoy some access to formal collective representation.

Advances also have been made that have enhanced employment rights for all workers:

- the statutory rights arena has expanded greatly and allows for investigation and sometimes advocacy work by government officials when employees' human rights, employment standards, and universal access to certain benefits are threatened;
- most large employers are required to have health and safety committees;
- nonunion employees in several provinces and the federal sector have access to a statutory low-cost arbitration process in the event of dismissal; and
- individual employees use the internet to locate employment information that once was difficult to find without unions.

rise of precarious work

The labour market has been fundamentally transformed. In the past, public policy associated with employment relations was governed by the assumption that most or all jobs were permanent with defined working hours and a central physical location within which work was accomplished. Currently, only 54 percent of Canadians work under these conditions; the remaining 46 percent are self-employed or work in part-time, sub-contracted, or multiple employment situations (HRDC, 2001). According to a federal government report (Duxbury, Higgins, and Coghill, 2003), only about 33 percent of the workforce keeps standard business hours (Monday to Friday, 9:00 a.m. to 5:00 p.m., in a full-time job at the employer's workplace). Roughly 25 percent of workers now put in 50 hours per week or more (counting overtime, travel, and office work brought home). Most working parents report that they feel guilty about not spending time with their families and not keeping up as employees. They are caught between the two responsibilities and are dissatisfied with their lack of work–life balance. Exhibit 1.4 features other significant changes.

Exhibit 1.4
The Rapidly Changing Canadian Workforce

- Fifty-eight percent of women 15 and over are in the paid workforce, accounting for 47 percent of the total workforce. The 1976 figures were 42 percent and 37 percent respectively.
- The percentage of double income families increased from 19 percent to 62 percent during the period from 1961 to 2001.
- In 2001, 20 percent of families were headed by a single female parent, up from 10 percent in 1971.
- Seventy percent of new jobs require post-secondary education, including 25 percent that require a university degree. Only 6 percent of new jobs are suitable for those who have not completed high school.
- Immigration accounts for 70 percent of current population growth, up from 20 percent in 1976.
- Between 1991 and 2001, the median age within the core working group (20 to 64 years) rose 3.2 years to 41.3, the biggest increase since 1921. By 2011, median age will reach 43.7. This causes far-reaching effects, including job shortages, and a "hot" market for younger workers.
- Seventy-five percent of temporary employees prefer permanent employment, as do 25 percent of own-account self-employed workers. Twenty-five percent of part-time workers would prefer full-time work.
- Temporary full-time workers are much more likely to have low incomes and no access to benefits; own-account self-employed workers are much more likely to have low incomes and no access to benefits; and low-income workers generally are far less likely to have insurance or pension benefits or to be unionized.
- Precarious work is persistent, not transitory. Fifty percent of workers earning less than $10 per hour find themselves in the same situation five years later.
- In 2002, over 1.7 million adults aged 45 to 64 provided informal care to almost 2.3 million seniors with long-term disabilities or physical limitations. Seventy percent of caregivers aged 45 to 64 are employed.

Source: Arthurs (2006: 18–20, 26); final bullet point from "Balancing Career and Care" by Wendy Pyper from *Perspectives on Labour*, Vol. 7, No. 11 http://www.statcan.ca/English/freepub/75-001-XIE/11106/art-1.htm. Copyright © 2006 Statistics Canada.

Employers have been transformed too. Across the Canadian economy and almost all of its traditional industry sectors, large companies have been shrinking in employment size (Verma and Chaykowski, 1999). At Canadian Pacific Railway (CPR), for example, the number of employees was halved between 1980 and 2000, while technological advances allowed an expansion in traffic volumes by 35 percent (Timur and Ponak, 2002). At Canada Post, the total number of hours worked between 1984 and 1997 declined by over 24 percent, but the number of part-time hours as a percentage of total hours increased by over 87 percent (Fudge, 1999).

The problem for unions has been deciding how to adapt to these changes. Workplaces based on stable, long-term employment practices, on which most union–management relations were built, are rapidly disappearing. Policy-makers, managers, and employees have all struggled to adjust. As sociologist Graham Lowe puts it,

> The crucial point is that we can no longer assume that most people follow a standard life course and experience common transitions at similar times. Policy-makers now must take into account how an individual's unique life-course trajectory may influence his or her work needs, expectations, and behaviour at different stages along the way. Consider the situation of older (50+) workers who started their paid work careers later in life, or who have young dependent children in a second marriage, or experienced transitions in and out of the labour market, or are not full-time "standard" employees. We cannot assume that a traditional, linear model of retirement will be suited to the needs of these individuals. (Lowe, 2002: 98)

It is alarming that a recent study finds that the economic prosperity of the new century has not resulted in an overall improvement in job quality (Lowe, 2007). Though the unemployment rate fell by 45 percent between 1993 and 2006 (a substantial change), the resulting job shortage did not lead to widespread employer attention to the development of high-quality jobs. There is a growing rhetoric about workforce renewal and the need to retain and motivate employees, but measurable positive changes are slow to appear.

Challenges to Canadian Industrial Relations

We end by recapping some of the current strains in the study and practice of industrial relations:

1. The challenge is for industrial relations to remain a coherent field, with its own intellectual foundation and outlook on the employment relationship, despite the allure of the larger and rapidly growing field of human resource management. The key is to absorb the knowledge and scope of HRM into industrial relations, without weakening IR's emphasis on collective action, social justice, worksite equity, and the use of power to achieve a different allocation and distribution of resources.

2. Though unions and collective action are a relatively stable and enduring feature of the Canadian workplace, students are given the erroneous impression that unions are irrelevant today, or are incidental players. The challenge is to ensure adequate coverage of industrial relations topics and concerns in Canadian academic and policy institutions. The fact that 88 percent of American workers are not unionized has greatly threatened the field of industrial relations in the United States. In Canada, with almost one worker in three covered by unionized work arrangements, and a much higher percentage than

that in key industries, there is every reason to incorporate important industrial relations topics into teaching materials. When we include professional organizations, staff associations, and formal nonunion representation vehicles, almost half of Canadian workers have some form of collective representation. Rarely a week goes by in which industrial relations topics are not front-page news. Canadian citizens should be able to understand developments at the worksite.

3. The transition away from stable employment models to a more fragile employment setting poses challenges. If we concentrate only on mature labour–management relationships involving long-term employees in permanent jobs, we will miss analyzing the emergence of new forms of employment, including part-time, sub-contracting, and self-employment. We also might miss key demographic shifts.

Questions

1. Why has the definition of "industrial relations" changed over time?
2. Locate an issue of *Relations industrielles/Industrial Relations* and describe the types of topics covered and the approaches used.
3. Why has HRM posed such a strong challenge to the field of IR?
4. How can you determine whether a manager has adopted an IR or an HRM paradigm? What questions would you ask a manager to determine his/her underlying assumptions?
5. Locate the front pages of newspapers over a one-month period. What types of industrial relations and employment issues capture media attention?
6. Why is pragmatism and the ability to find a compromise position so highly valued in the development of Canadian public policy?
7. What ingredients make Canadian industrial relations unique?
8. How have developments in the United States affected industrial relations in Canada?
9. What is life like among the Canadians who are not employed in traditional settings, and what types of public policies are necessary for them? How could unions or other types of representation be more appealing to them?

Weblinks

A comprehensive web source from the University of Toronto's Centre for Industrial Relations and Human Resources:
www.chass.utoronto.ca/cir/library/hrirwebsites.html

Canadian Industrial Relations Association:
www.cira-acri.ca

U.S. Labor and Employment Relations Association:
www.lera.uiuc.edu

Canadian Policy Research Networks:
www.cprn.com

Human Resources and Social Development Canada (a source of detailed information on labour market trends):
www.hrsdc.gc.ca/en/corporate/topics/index.shtml

Chapter 2
Understanding the Unionization Decision

Ann C. Frost and Daphne G. Taras

"For the sake of the auto industry, we've put aside our differences."

Frank Stronach, Buzz Hargrove

Canada's auto industry and the entire manufacturing base face a moment of truth. New challenges in global competition mean the industry must change, or else it will continue to wither away. Magna International and the Canadian Auto Workers (CAW) Union signed a "Framework of Fairness" that will govern how they work together for many years to come. Like a normal union contract, this new national agreement will continue to offer excellent provisions governing wages and benefits, hours and work rules, vacations and holidays, seniority and safety.

Here is a joint statement made by Frank Stronach, chairman of the board of Aurora, Ontario-based Magna International, and Buzz Hargrove, president of the Toronto-based CAW Union.

We come from opposite sides of the labour relations street: A manufacturing executive and a union leader. And we've had our share of battles and controversies over the years. Union drives. Legal appeals. Tough negotiations. Even a strike or two. But in recent years, we've noticed there are a surprising number of issues on which we now see eye to eye.

We're both passionate about Canada. We both love autos. Not just to drive, but because of the immense economic and social benefits a healthy auto industry can generate. Yet we both recognize that Canada's auto industry and our entire manufacturing base face a moment of truth. New challenges in global competition mean our industry must change, or else it will continue to wither away.

And we both agree the best ace in Canada's automotive hand is our people. As we find ways to evolve and survive, our most valuable asset is the skill, the productivity and the work ethic of Canadian auto workers—matched with the knowledge and creativity of Canadian scientists, engineers and managers.

If we are going to preserve this crucial industry in the face of globalization, a dollar at parity and climate change, then we need to leverage our "human advantage" to the greatest possible degree.

Which brings us to our announcement that we are turning a new page in our relationship. Magna and the Canadian Auto Workers (CAW) Union signed a "Framework of Fairness" that will govern how we work together for many years to come.

Through this agreement, Magna accepts the CAW as a genuine partner, with a crucial role to safeguard the interests of Magna's workers as the company grows and changes. And the CAW accepts Magna's culture of "fair enterprise" and the unique structures we've

Photo 2.1

Frank Stronach and Buzz
Hargrove celebrating their
historic agreement.

Source: The Canadian Press/Frank Gunn

put in place over the years to make decisions and resolve concerns with maximum worker participation.

We think we are combining the best of both worlds: The best traditions of union protection and security and the best features of Magna's fair enterprise corporate culture. Indeed, economic studies have suggested that companies that pair union representation with extensive mechanisms for worker involvement and participation attain the best possible combination of high productivity and high morale.

Here's how it will work. Production workers at Magna's Canadian facilities will have the opportunity, in supervised secret ballot votes, to consider a new labour contract and join the CAW. In facilities where a majority of the workforce supports the union, the CAW will become the recognized bargaining agent, and the employees will be covered by a new Magna–CAW national collective agreement.

Like a normal union contract, this new national agreement will continue to offer excellent provisions governing wages and benefits, hours and work rules, vacations and holidays, seniority and safety. But it will have several unprecedented features, too. Instead of union stewards, "employee advocates" will work with "fairness committees" in each plant to make local decisions and resolve concerns. Instead of traditional grievances, a "concern–resolution process" will give workers several avenues to pursue and resolve a concern. Instead of strikes and lockouts, unresolved contract matters will be referred for final-offer arbitration.

This is an experimental approach to labour relations. We believe it will enhance our shared effort to build a successful competitive industry, but in a manner that respects and invests in working people, their families and their communities.

Magna is Canada's largest automotive employer. The CAW is Canada's largest private-sector union. Both our organizations have demonstrated incredible innovation over the years, as we've evolved to perform our respective functions to the fullest. In our own ways, we've put a unique Canadian stamp on our auto industry: What we make, how we make it and how we share the fruits of what we've produced.

Our new system of labour relations, we believe, will also be uniquely Canadian—melding North American and European aspects with a homegrown emphasis on fairness, mutual respect and hard work. We enter this new phase in our relationship optimistic that it will make a significant contribution to the future success of Canada's most important industry.[1]

Workers join unions for a variety of reasons and to accomplish a range of objectives. This chapter seeks to understand the decision to unionize from an individual's perspective. Why would Magna workers vote for a union now that they are being given this unique chance? The functions of unions and their attractiveness are inextricably linked. It is necessary to understand pre-existing conditions in the workplace and what unions offer to best appreciate why people join them. The Magna–CAW "Framework of Fairness" is very unusual in private sector Canadian labour relations (although voluntary recognition is quite common in the public sector). It means that Magna is willing to radically alter its previously union-free approach to employment relations and the CAW has offered, in return, a no-strike pledge.

There are many triggers that cause workers to contemplate joining a union. Some workers are motivated by the economic factors that often come to mind first when considering the decision to unionize. They are seeking to win higher wages through unionization. These workers also see unionization as a way to increase equity in the workplace. They believe that it is only fair that their profitable employer share a larger proportion of the pie created in part by its employees. Unionization may also be a way to gain voice at the workplace. Through their union, workers gain a say over the terms and conditions of employment, have access to a system of due process to ensure protection from unreasonable management actions, and have input into decisions that affect their lives at the workplace. Other workers at their worksite may not want to be in a union at all, but if a majority of their co-workers support the union in a certification election, the law determines that the union will be their bargaining agent.

In this chapter we review each of these aspects of unions (economics, voice, and condition-of-employment unionism) and describe the conditions that persuade workers to unionize. We discuss what the survey evidence from both Canada and the United States tells us about what workers want from collective representation. We also provide some insight into an individual's propensity to unionize—not only the determinants of his or her desire to join a union, but also the factors that influence the opportunity to do so. Finally, we address the changes that the new competitive environment is creating in the workplace and assess what these changes mean for unions. What role are unions to play in the future? How can they attract members to ensure their continued relevance and vitality?

THE ECONOMIC RATIONALE

Most people, when they think of what unions are all about, focus on unions' ability to win increased wages and benefits. Such traditional bread-and-butter concerns have brought many members into unions. In 1983, Samuel Gompers, the first president of the American Federation of Labor, stated labour's singular goal when he responded to the question "What does labour want?" essentially by saying "more."[2] This traditional function of winning more remains a critical part of what unions do. Unions do things that are instrumentally useful to people who are searching for a better deal at work.

Fairness, Equity, and the Wage–Effort Bargain

However, despite Gompers' credo, many people are drawn to unions not just for "more," but rather for reasons of fairness and equity. When firms are highly profitable, workers perceive it is only fair that some of the prosperity born of their efforts be shared with them. Similarly, workers doing a job in one firm believe it is only fair that they be paid the same as other workers doing identical work in similar firms in their industry, regardless of differences in firm profitability. Logically, unions believe that workers in the higher-cost firm should not be forced to bear the brunt of management's inefficiencies.

Unions also serve to increase workers' perceptions of equity within the firm itself. Equity theory, a psychologically based theory of work motivation, posits that people will engage in activities to the extent that they perceive the situation to be fair and equitable (Adams, 1965). Workers compare what they receive in return for their efforts with what others in similar situations receive for theirs. If this comparison of input to output ratios is equal, then equity is perceived and people will continue with the activity. In assessing inputs, people consider factors such as effort, performance level, education, and time. In assessing outputs they consider factors such as pay, recognition, and other rewards.

Inequity results from people's feelings that they are being over- or under-rewarded. Perceptions of over-reward are rare, but when they occur, people tend to feel guilty and may feel they should work harder or produce higher quality work. When people perceive that they are under-rewarded, however, they are even more inclined to take actions to restore their sense of fairness. They try to bring the situation into balance by either working less or lowering the quality of their work. In more extreme instances, they simply quit.

It is natural that workers will look to comparison groups to determine whether their own employer is fair. It is quite rankling to discover that another person is paid more, or treated better, for exactly the same type of work.

In periods of relative stability, workers also have a tendency to feel comfort in having achieved some sort of equilibrium between their input of effort and their receipt of compensation for that amount of effort. This is known as the "wage–effort bargain."[3] If management tries to lower the compensation or the quality of working conditions, workers attempt to maintain equilibrium by reducing their amount of effort or finding other means to restore lost wages. For example, if wages are cut by 5 percent, to achieve a balance workers might decrease their work pace, declare more sick days, develop cynicism about the employer, or even pilfer office supplies. If management desires a higher level of effort, according to this model of behaviour, workers will expect some enhanced compensation. When jobs are enlarged or enriched, workers naturally expect some gain in the form of higher wages, more job security, or better treatment.

If workers feel their equilibrium state is threatened—either by a demand for greater effort or by a reduction in compensation or security—they might turn to a union to redress the balance. Unions can negotiate pay systems that employees perceive to be fair. Union contracts often contain job-evaluation systems to rate jobs on the basis of difficulty, unpleasantness, and responsibility, and then pay job incumbents accordingly. Union contracts also often specify the criteria which allow job incumbents to move from one job to another. And collective agreements "lock in" wage–effort positions so that workers can achieve the stability necessary to develop a psychologically satisfying equilibrium state.

Unions also seek to improve equity of pay scales between the bargaining unit and management. In most unionized firms, the management wage premium tends to be smaller than in nonunion companies. Unions are also concerned with wage inequality within the economy as a whole. In the words of Buzz Hargrove, the president of the Canadian Auto Workers union,

These are certainly good times if you're wealthy. But what if you're not? Since 1989, the average income of the bottom fifth of all Canadians has fallen 32 percent, the number of poor children has grown by 46 percent, and the number of Canadians living on social assistance has grown by 68 percent. Yet federal spending on social programs, as a percentage of Gross Domestic Product, is at its lowest level since 1949. Good times if you've been invited to the party, not so good if your nose is pressed against the glass. [At the same time] executive salaries, bonuses, pensions, and other perks reached unprecedented heights. The typical chief executive officer's take-home pay went up 112 percent. The average Canadian worker's after-tax income, meanwhile, dropped 9 percent between 1990 and 1997. In real terms, most Canadian workers now earn less than they would have in 1975.[4]

In addition to equity and fairness, workers also turn to unions because they want to increase their bargaining power. One of the major union goals is to raise wages and benefits. Unions are expected to deliver tangible gains. Figure 2.1 shows the 1969 tongue-in-cheek effort of the oil industry's union to use the Imperial Oil mascot (the "Esso Tiger") and advertising slogan "Put a tiger in your tank" against the company in a union organizing campaign promising to deliver improvements in wages and working conditions.

Figure 2.1

Source: "Two Faces of the Tiger," Archives of the Energy and Chemical Workers Union, Provincial Archives of Alberta in Edmonton, 91-378/162. Reprinted with permission.

In negotiating successfully with employers, unions are able to transfer some profits from the employer's pocket to the employees'. For example, unions have been highly successful in organizing the automobile, steel, rubber, and telecommunications industries, which are all examples of industries in which employers enjoyed periods of high profitability due to barriers to entry, oligopolistic pricing behaviour, and/or regulated monopoly status. One example of this process of organizing a highly profitable and oligopolistic industry involves the National Hockey League Players' Association (NHLPA), formed in June 1967. The CBC-produced film *Net Worth* documents the struggles of the players in the then six NHL teams to organize and become certified by the Canada Labour Relations Board. For years, team owners had earned large profits from the proceeds of games that could not have been played without the talents of players. They accomplished this by holding pay down. Gordie Howe of the Detroit Red Wings—unquestionably one of the finest hockey players of the 1950s, and indeed of all time—was paid (and accepted) compensation considerably below his value, much to the delight and relief of the club owners. The NHL club owners also did nothing to provide for hockey players at the conclusion of their often short-lived careers. Eventually, players banded together to form the NHLPA and greatly increased their bargaining power, winning higher salaries and valuable pension benefits.[5]

In highly competitive industries, where profit margins are thin, less profit may be available to be transferred to union members through collective bargaining. Unions extract such concessions at the risk of driving such firms out of business. In these settings, unions must appeal to workers on a basis other than higher wages, such as providing a means to check managerial authority or gaining a greater say at work. But even in these circumstances unions have made great inroads. In the low-wage Canadian child care industry, unionized workers were found to have 15 percent higher wages and better fringe benefits than their nonunion counterparts (Cleveland, Gunderson, and Hyatt, 2003).

In general, the Canadian union–nonunion wage differential is estimated to be in the 10 to 25 percent range. The differential is largest for unskilled occupations, is larger across small enterprises, is higher for blue-collar than for white-collar workers, and apparently is shrinking over time (Fang and Verma, 2002). When statistical adjustments are made for the effects of industries, workplaces, regions, and other characteristics, the wage differential is 7.7 percent. Unions also deliver improved benefits packages. Comprehensive benefits plans are available to 69 percent of the unionized workforce, compared to 37 percent of nonunion workers. Eighty percent of unionized workers have pension plan coverage versus 27 percent of nonunion workers (Akyeampong, 2002). Some of this difference is due to the very high levels of unionization among public-sector workers and large employers, but it is clear that unions have fought for the expansion of benefits to those outside of management.

Not all employees want, or need, a union for its economic benefits. People who have high individual bargaining power because they are star performers, or because they have valued skills or attributes, often feel that they can achieve a better deal individually than they could as part of a collective. They also may move around from employer to employer, or engage in activities with little expectation of a permanent job. A novel Canadian approach to help these types of workers that exists in the film industry could be a model for the future. See the Canadian Artists and Producers Professional Relations Tribunal (www.capprt-tcrpap.gc.ca) for details.

High-tech workers are an example of those who have long believed unions to be irrelevant to their daily work experience. However, as their skills increasingly are in greater supply and as employers find cheaper, offshore sources of talent, even high-tech workers are beginning to pay attention to union overtures. In the United States, the Communications Workers of America is trying hard to appeal to these workers. At the same time, unions understand that workers expect "more" from them, and are struggling to identify those elements of the employment setting that dissatisfy such workers. In some cases, wages remain an appropriate focus, but in other settings, benefits and job security are more important to workers. New organizing campaigns, such as the one described in Exhibit 2.1, are being launched on issues such as these.

Exhibit 2.1
Union Organizing Strategies in Silicon Valley

With a Prada bag and the air of an entrepreneur, Amy Dean is an unlikely labour trailblazer. But as head of the AFL-CIO's Silicon Valley office, Ms. Dean, at just 37 years of age, has become the labour movement's chief navigator in the roiling and uncharted seas of the new economy.

To help the valley's horde of temporary workers who have no health insurance, she has taken the unorthodox step of creating a non-profit temp agency that, unlike most for-profit agencies, offers health coverage that temporary workers can afford.

And she has proposed using a hiring-hall concept to provide uninterrupted health and pension benefits to high-tech workers, who often jump from job to job. So far, all her strategizing has failed to strike a chord with the valley's "haves," like software designers, who, happy with their stock options, often think unions are as useful as manual typewriters. Her biggest challenge is figuring out a way for unions to connect to these high-tech workers.

Ms. Dean acknowledges that labour's traditional contracts-are-everything model is largely irrelevant to high-tech workers because it is based on a 1930s notion of people working at industrial behemoths, not agile start-ups, and of workers spending decades at one corporation, not jumping like grasshoppers between companies.

Recognizing this, Ms. Dean has become the foremost exponent of a provocative theory: Labour should return to its craft guild and hiring-hall roots as a way to keep up with the fast-changing high-tech world.

For high-tech workers, who often hold 10 jobs over a career, constantly losing and regaining health and pension coverage, Ms. Dean says unions should be a source of stability and protection. No other institution, she says, is as well-equipped to provide such workers with the two things they say they need most: portable benefits and continual upgrading of their skills.

Her most innovative work has come in seeking to help the thousands of temporary workers who flood in and out of high-tech companies—secretaries, clerks, bookkeepers, software testers. Aided by foundation grants, she has set up a non-profit agency that is placing temporary workers, for the most part secretaries, who start at $10 an hour, compared with the $8.50 paid by many agencies. Unlike most for-profit agencies, her agency offers low-cost health coverage, paid sick leave, and paid holidays, and works with a community college to furnish subsidized courses to upgrade the workers' skills.

Ms. Dean has also set up an association, in essence a fledgling union, where temporary workers can compare notes, air grievances, and map strategies to win better working conditions. The latest idea is to pressure agencies to adhere to a code of conduct requiring health insurance and a respectable wage.

"Is the current model that unions are offering relevant to the knowledge workers of today? No," Ms. Dean said. "Are the principles and benefits that unions offer relevant? Yes."

Source: Steven Greenhouse, "The Most Innovative Figure in Silicon Valley?" *The New York Times* (Sunday, November 14, 1999), p. 26.

Take Wages Out of Competition

Workers also turn to unions to protect themselves from competitive impulses among firms, which cause top management to try to lower overall firm costs by reducing the rate paid to labour.[6] By bargaining a rate of pay and fixing it for the life of the contract, unions take away management's ability to reduce pay unilaterally. At the same time, unions seek to "organize to the extent of the market" to ensure that all employers in an industry are similarly constrained. Thus, employers are forced to find some dimension other than the livelihood of their workers on which to compete. For a shorthand description, we call this union function "taking wages out of competition," but it isn't confined just to wages. It includes benefits, conditions of work, and all the components that go into the total compensation package paid for labour.

This interaction between employer strategies and union organizing is illustrated by one of the classic studies in North American industrial relations. John R. Commons (1909) documented the process of workers' banding together into unions in reaction to the expansion of the product market.[7] Commons used a case history of American shoemakers from 1648 to 1895. Shoemakers originally organized into city-based guild-like organizations to protect the wages and working conditions of members working in a delimited geographic area (the city of Philadelphia in this case). Employers, confronted with organized shoemakers in one city, simply moved production to a location lacking such organization. In response, the shoemakers' trade union began to organize shoemakers in all centres and got them to agree upon the terms and conditions under which they would work. This process of organizing workers wherever employers moved the work took wages out of competition and forced employers to compete on a basis other than cheap labour: for example, on quality of the goods, diversity of styles, or speed of delivery.

Another example of this process is the strategy followed by the International Brotherhood of Teamsters under the presidency of Jimmy Hoffa in organizing the American trucking industry. Although trucking is a highly competitive industry, by organizing a great proportion of the industry under a Master Freight Agreement, the Teamsters effectively took wages out of competition and delivered significant wage and benefit increases to union members.

A similar process occurred during the organization of the mass-production industries in the 1930s and 1940s in North America. With the advent of mass-production technologies, skilled workers (who traditionally had been organized into craft unions) could be replaced by semi-skilled and unskilled workers, many of whom were new immigrants. Such employment practices posed serious threats to the craft unions and their members. The labour movement's response was, once again, to organize to the extent of the market (this time the labour market) and bring the semi-skilled and unskilled into the labour movement.

Indeed, this process of taking wages out of competition largely explains the initial organizing impetus behind the unionization of Canadian workers by American-based international unions.[8] American unions became active in Canada, particularly between World War I and World War II, to prevent Canadian subsidiaries of American-owned firms from using cheaper Canadian labour to undercut American workers. This process was repeated within Canada as unions sought to develop national wage programs to prevent firms from using wage disparities among the provinces as a basis upon which to compete. For example, the Energy and Chemical Workers Union[9] engaged in a formal program of pattern bargaining to keep wages uniform within the petroleum industry. Likewise, highly centralized bargaining structures in British Columbia, in which employer associations bargained with a union (or council of trade unions), kept wages and working conditions in the forest products industry and the pulp and paper industry virtually identical across the vast majority of employers.

This process of organizing to the extent of the market in order to take wages out of competition remains a fundamental goal of the labour movement. The Canadian Auto Workers Union, which represents workers in the Big Three automotive manufacturers (General Motors, Ford, and DaimlerChrysler), has watched the industry's employers outsource to smaller, often nonunion, parts suppliers. As a result, the CAW has redoubled efforts to organize these suppliers. The Magna–CAW deal (described at the beginning of this chapter) is an extraordinarily unusual conclusion to the CAW's decades of efforts—no one would have predicted that the staunchly nonunion company founded by Frank Stronach would voluntarily recognize the union. Many articles had been written about Magna's commitment to remain union-free. The threat posed by nonunion grocery stores, including Wal-Mart, greatly weakens the United Food and Commercial Workers' (UFCW) bargaining power. Similarly, in Canada's film industry, unions try to organize nonunion film extras. Exhibit 2.2 describes how nonunion extras are substantially less expensive to hire than their unionized counterparts. No doubt the ACTRA (Alliance of Canadian Cinema, Television and Radio Artists) union would like to take wages out of competition to prevent film industry employers from hiring nonunion workers to the detriment of union members.

Exhibit 2.2
Nonunion Extras Plan Union Rally

Background performers in Toronto's film and TV industry are so angry that they're taking to the streets in protest.

A mass rally and union-organizing campaign planned for this weekend is expected to attract between 500 and 1000 people.

The background performers, also known as extras, are upset that they only earn $7 an hour, compared to the $19.50 earned by extras who are unionized members of ACTRA.

"We would like to be paid $10 or $12 an hour," said Ray Miller, the president of the newly formed Professional Alliance of Canadian Talent. "At $7 an hour, we're grossly underpaid." ACTRA has agreed to support the group's efforts.

Source: "Non-union extras plan union rally," *Calgary Herald* (September 1, 1999), p. D2.

Defending workers against market instability remains a relevant union goal, as Canadian and American unions react with alarm to the relocation of firms hoping to capitalize on low wage costs in Mexico and the Far East. Canadian unions have made efforts to mobilize unionization in Mexico. The International Labour Organization (ILO) has been attempting to publicize the evils of child labour, sweatshop conditions, and the abuse of workers in countries with weak unions and little protection from exploitation. While the amelioration of the worst conditions for workers is a moral stance, it also is consistent with the goal of organizing to the extent of the market to standardize employment conditions and take wages out of competition on a worldwide basis.

THE VOICE RATIONALE

Unions are attractive to members not only because of economic rationales, but also because they are vehicles for expressing employee voice (Freeman and Medoff, 1984). Voice means many things, and we provide a number of examples of voice in this section, ranging from workers' desire for more influence and sense of belonging at work, to their activity in the national and international political arenas.

Societies have two basic mechanisms for dealing with social or economic problems: exit and voice (Hirschman, 1971). The first is the market mechanism of exit in which an individual expresses his or her displeasure with current conditions by simply going elsewhere. If a store's service is found to be lacking, the shopper walks away. If a restaurant's meal is disappointing, the diner leaves, never to return. If a school fails to deliver expected academic results, parents transfer their children to another school. In the labour market, exit translates into quitting—if a worker is dissatisfied with his or her employment conditions (the pay is too low, the supervision too demanding, or the conditions too unpleasant), he or she quits and seeks employment elsewhere. This action, in theory, rewards good employers and punishes bad ones.

The second mechanism for dealing with dissatisfaction is voice. Rather than leave the store or restaurant, never to return, the disgruntled shopper or diner informs the clerk, manager, waiter, or chef of his or her displeasure and seeks to correct the problem. Through the subsequent exchange of a faulty product or the replacement of a too-salty meal, the individual is satisfied and the store or restaurant's performance improves. Likewise, rather than removing their children from a problematic school, parents using the voice option would join with other parents to lobby through the Parent Teacher Association for an improvement in teaching staff, facilities, or resources. In the employment context, voice translates into discussing with the employer conditions that need to be remedied, rather than quitting the job. Exercising the voice option creates a social good: one or more employees taking their grievances to management and having the problems corrected improves the conditions for all. Further, by exercising voice at work, employees are merely engaging in the same rights to speak out that they have in a civil society. Unions help workers gain a form of "industrial citizenship."

Clearly, the benefit to workers of the voice mechanism is a potential improvement in job conditions without the costs associated with having to quit, search for a new job, and relocate. The voice mechanism is also of benefit to the employer by increasing firm productivity via a number of different mechanisms: the "union shock effect," lowering quit rates, and harnessing worker knowledge and insight about the production process.

The simple act of becoming unionized often leads to significant improvements in firm performance through what has been termed the "union shock effect."[10] The entry of a union often prompts the employer to professionalize its management, and to replace vague, paternalistic, authoritarian personnel practices with explicit rules. Figure 2.2 depicts the UFCW's effort to allow its members to wear nose studs at Superstore—certainly many young workers simply did not understand why managers would find this body piercing to be so objectionable.[11]

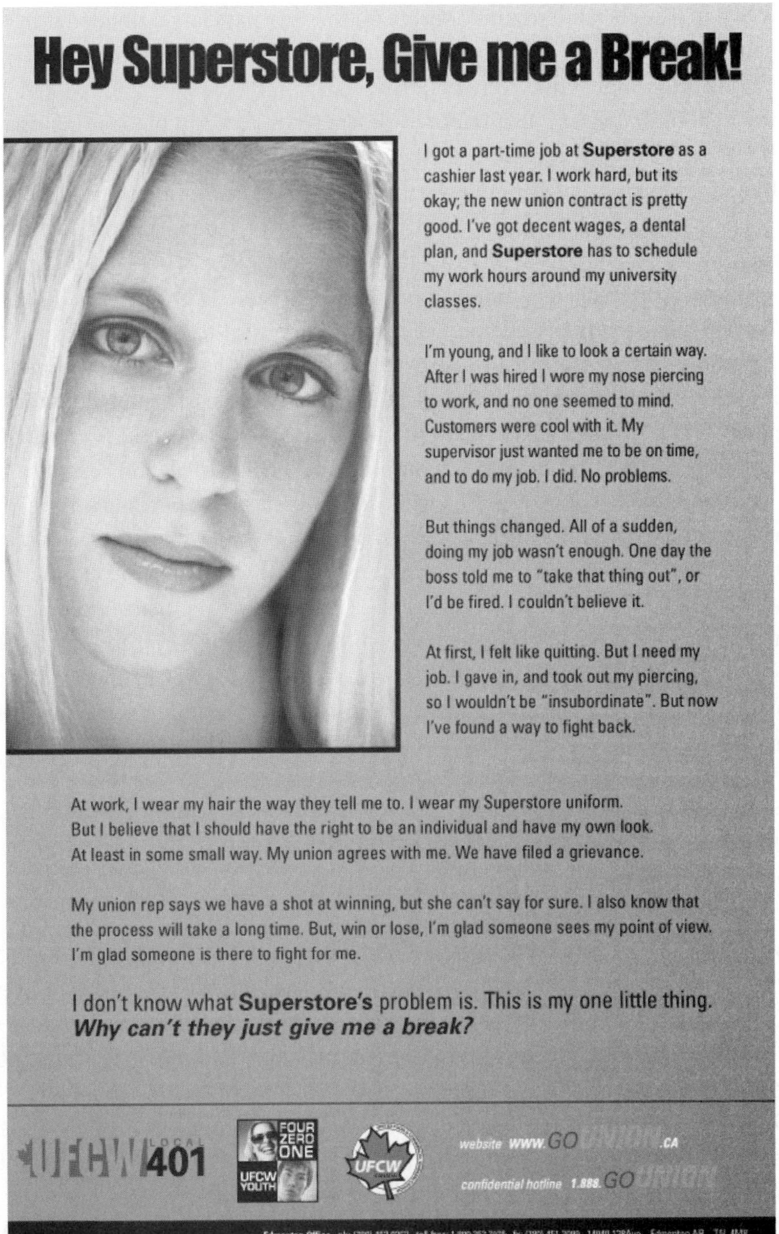

Figure 2.2 Union Poster

Poster Design: GRAPHOS. Copyright © United Food & Commercial Workers Canada. Reprinted by permission of UFCW.

The voice mechanism enables workers to solve irritating workplace problems and lowers quit rates by 20 to 30 percent (Freeman, 1980, 1984). Having some influence over the terms and conditions of employment through the collective bargaining process, as well as the presence of a grievance and arbitration system, helps to reduce quits. By decreasing turnover, management is encouraged to invest in training. Employers are more likely to invest in upgrading employee skills when the employee is more likely to remain with the firm, thus giving the firm that paid for the training the ongoing benefit of the enhanced skill and increased worker productivity. At the same time, lower quit rates imply that work groups remain intact longer. As production techniques come to rely increasingly on interdependent functions, team stability pays larger dividends by enabling team members to become more familiar with one another, to develop positive work norms, and to work more effectively together.

The voice function can also improve productivity directly by opening channels of communication between front-line workers and management that yield insights into more efficient production techniques. To the degree that worker insights can be tapped to improve operations, product quality and productivity can improve, often dramatically. The benefits of such improvements can then be apportioned to both management and workers through collective bargaining.

While enhanced voice is one reason that workers turn to unions, it is important to note that unionized workers are not likely to report greater levels of job satisfaction than their nonunion counterparts. Even though "satisfaction" is clearly a nebulous term, industrial relations studies have consistently found that unionized workers report equal, or lower, satisfaction than comparable nonunion workers.[12] While the exercise of voice results in measurable benefits, reported work satisfaction is not necessarily one of them.

Sometimes, to protest injustice, workers who cannot exit will band together, as collective action limits the chance of reprisal against individual workers. If management makes a tremendous error, or a series of niggling provocations, then workers will contemplate unions. To prove the point, we examine the reactions of the most right-wing, anti-union people in Canada—arguably Calgary business students—in Exhibit 2.3. How many minutes might it take to get four classes of business students to collectively organize? Some would say "not possible." Actually, with clever provocation, it took between six and eleven minutes.

Exhibit 2.3
How to Get B-Students to Organize

In November 2004, Professors Taras and Steel decided that it was important to their teaching to have students experience arbitrary and unsympathetic decisions. They conspired to produce a deception that would give students a mild taste of what it might feel like to be an Enron employee, losing pensions, jobs, and dignity through no fault of their own.

Steel was the regular professor in a one-semester introductory HRM course. Late in the term, Taras appeared in his class, announcing that Steel had been "suspended pending an investigation." She proceeded to tell the students that she was being forced to take over his classes, and that she had to alter the course outline because he

---

had been too generous to these classes, and had unfairly advantaged them relative to other sections of the course and relative to other years. She cancelled their 4 percent bonus assignments and made the final exam cumulative of the term work.

With the help of an accomplice—the president of an undergraduate student club—who gave an ersatz union-organizing speech, it took only six minutes for the first class of business students to commence joining the student club and signing a petition.

The teaching deception was then revealed and students were debriefed.

The deception was repeated in three additional classes. The longest it took to "unionize" the students was 11 minutes.

Source: Daphne G. Taras and Piers D. G. Steel (2007), "We Provoked our Students to Unionize: Deception Creates a Lasting IR Message," *British Journal of Industrial Relations*, 45, Vol. 1: 179–198. Copyright © Blackwell Publishing. Reprinted with permission of Blackwell Publishing UK.

Voice: Increasing Justice in the Workplace

In supporting our democratic system of government, we prize citizenship behaviours, including voting and the open expression of political beliefs. People are expected, through a democratic process, to have a say in how they are governed. By contrast, such practices typically stop at the factory gates. Workers are expected to follow all reasonable orders, adhere to company rules and policies, and work faithfully at executing their job duties. Unions are attractive to many workers because they provide workers with some say and a means to check the unfettered exercise of managerial authority. At the workplace, unions enable workers to have some access to due process, to counter unilateral management action, and to have some input into the codification of the rules that govern their daily work lives. In many cases, workers unionize primarily to gain the latter benefits—mismanagement and unpredictable behaviour on the part of first-line supervisors often will do more than low wages will to drive employees to unionize.

By law, each collective agreement must contain a grievance procedure to resolve contractual disputes. The collective bargaining agreement is the document that contains the clauses governing the employment relationship for the life of the contract (generally two or three years). It sets out the myriad details of the employment relationship (see Chapter 11). In doing so, it gives the parties, both union and management, a degree of certainty over the nature of their relationship for a fixed period of time.

Often, collective agreements are copied and bound in small sizes, intended to fit into the pockets of workers and their union shop stewards, to be referred to at work in the event of a dispute. In the famous Canadian documentary *Final Offer*, auto workers are shown in a tense shop-floor standoff with General Motors in the mid-1980s as their union negotiates an agreement at the Royal York Hotel in Toronto. The workers can quote chapter and verse from their collective agreement. Workers both use it as a shield against management decisions they believe violate their contractual rights and wield it as a sword to get at management.

The grievance procedure provides workers with due process on the job. The union grievance procedure is an alternative system to the courts and one that is accessible by unionized employees. Few wronged employees would take their cases to court—the costs and the length of time a hearing would take prohibit such action in all but the most extreme cases. However, many employees in unionized workplaces take advantage of the grievance procedure to seek redress to wrongs they believe have been committed against them; for example, how promotions were handled, what the pay for a particular job is, or how discipline was applied. The UFCW filed a grievance on Superstore's facial jewellery prohibition (see Figure 2.2), and in 2006 an arbitrator ruled in favour of the UFCW. The company ban was struck down.

Having access to this process provides obvious benefits to employees. Those whose grievances are upheld feel vindicated. Those whose grievances are denied by the independent and neutral arbitrator still, for the most part, believe that through the process they were treated fairly. Without such a process, an aggrieved employee might quit or find other ways of getting back at the employer (through loafing or even sabotage).

It is noteworthy that very few nonunion Canadian companies provide their workers with access to an impartial third party to arbitrate work-related disputes. Even among the companies that do pay a great deal of attention to the provision of justice in the workplace, the overwhelming majority settle disagreements by making a senior human resources executive or vice president the final arbiter in a multi-step system of dispute resolution. Disputes are kept "in-house." Although nonunion workers may take employers to court, this strategy is not taken when an employee wants to preserve a working relationship with the employer. The union serves a watchdog function for employee interests. Exhibit 2.4 shows two examples of unions challenging managerial decisions through the arbitration process.

In the first case, the union unsuccessfully challenged management's application of time-and-motion studies. In the second case, an arbitrator found that the union was correct in arguing that management was unreasonable in refusing to allow workers to take a third washroom break per day without losing pay. In nonunion worksites, there is no mechanism to challenge management's decisions in such matters. Many managers deeply resent having to give up the power to make decisions about employment relationships or work processes, and the flip side of the coin is that many workers are grateful for union protection.

Exhibit 2.4
Two Examples of Unions Challenging Managerial Decisions

CASE 1

The Issue: Whether the employer had a basis to conduct new "time-and-motion" studies. The union filed a policy grievance alleging that the company acted in breach of article 17 of the collective agreement in 1996. Specifically, it was alleged that the company did not provide an adequate reason for doing the new studies because there was no triggering event.

The Arbitrator's Decision: The collective agreement does not restrict the Company's right to initiate time-and-motion studies on jobs with established rates to only those circumstances where there have been triggering events, such as a change in the number of elements in the job, a change in the method of production, or a change in technology. The fact that the nine challenged time-and-motion studies were done on jobs that allegedly had established rates does not create a breach of the collective agreement because it is expressly provided for in article 17.02(a). The Board finds that as a reason, "verification" of the "integrity of the piece rate structure" falls within the Company's entitlement under the agreement. Article 17.02(b) speaks to maintaining a balance of fairness between the Company's interests and the employees' interests by means of correcting both rates that are "too tight" (and therefore unfavourable to the operator) and rates that are "too loose" (and therefore unfavourable to the Company).

Source: Ranpro Inc. and UNITE, Local 2426. Pamela Cooper Picher, arbitrator (August 6, 1999).

CASE 2

The Issue: The company would not permit employees to take paid washroom breaks. The workforce employed by a meat-processing plant was in the habit of taking washroom breaks subject to personal necessity. The company then notified the workforce that washroom breaks were adding to operating expenses and the company would no longer "foot the bill" for these breaks. A new schedule was posted, amounting to an extra 30 unpaid minutes a day. The company allotted two 15-minute breaks, unpaid, when the employees could use the washrooms. If an employee's bladder did not co-operate with the new schedule and the employee needed another break to use the washroom, 15 minutes' pay would be deducted from his or her pay. The union grieved the new policy and asked for damages to be paid to the employees for all their unpaid work.

The Arbitrator's Decision: I do not find that the intent of the parties and the agreement that sprang from that intent allowed the company to act as it did upon this occasion. Even if I am wrong in that conclusion, and the company did have the discretion to so act, I would not find the exercise of that discretion in this instance to be reasonable. I am of the belief that some damages should be paid [to the employees for the amount of unpaid time taken for washroom breaks until the time of the arbitrator's award].

Source: Burns Meats, A Division of Burns Foods (1985) Limited, and the United Food and Commercial Workers Union. Paul S. Teskey, arbitrator (March 31, 1993).

By law, management cannot fire or otherwise punish workers for speaking out through their union. Workers channel their grievances through their union representatives. Any unreasonable management interference with the ability of workers to select and be represented by a union is unlawful. Thus, all things being equal, workers should have a higher sense of security and less fear of reprisal for speaking out within a unionized worksite than in a comparable nonunion setting. Although Canadians generally are satisfied with their work lives, 51 percent of Canadian workers, both union and nonunion, believe that the possibility of management reprisal still exists (Lipset and Meltz, 1997).

As a result of union vigilance, managers feel that unions create rigid and adversarial worksites at a time when managers value flexibility and co-operation. For example, managers frequently complain that firing problem employees is exceedingly difficult. There is a great deal of truth to this view. According to a variety of studies, arbitrators reinstate dismissed employees about 50 percent of the time (Williams and Taras, 2000). Discharging an employee in a unionized workplace is much more difficult than in a nonunion workplace (which is one reason why workers join unions). One solution for management in unionized settings is to pay special attention to recruitment and selection of employees, and if problems emerge, to use reasonable discipline and proper documentation. The probationary period is especially important in easily weeding out employees with poor prognosis for successful future performance. In unionized settings, competent personnel management is essential: sophisticated managers know that in a unionized environment, their decisions have to be fair, consistent, and honour the collective agreement in order to be upheld in arbitration. When managers have not been trained in labour relations, they will make mistakes.

Voice: To Lobby Government and Take Political Action

Unions also seek to intervene on their members' behalf in society at large. By joining a union, workers hope to gain additional control over their experience at work. At the societal level, unions are a lobbying force of which politicians are well aware.

One of the measures of the vitality of any democracy in the world is the freedom workers enjoy to exercise their collective rights, both at the worksite and in the larger political sphere. As Lynn Williams (1997: 47), Canadian former president of the United Steelworkers of America, says, "The heart of the matter is that, in a democratic society, one of the most fundamental rights is that workers have open and non-threatening access to unionization and collective bargaining, if they so choose." The participation of organized labour in the larger political scene of a nation is an important measure of a society's level of democracy.

Because of the progressive and democratic role that organized labour can play within a civil society, one of the repressive measures often taken by dictatorships is the weakening or banning of unions. Conversely, one of the first groups to oppose totalitarian regimes and to work toward their demise is organized labour. One of the best examples of the role of unions in political action is the Dutch dockworkers and their manifesto distributed throughout the Netherlands on the eve of the Nazi invasion. The dockworkers listed a number of means of resistance and ended their list with a plea to hide a Jewish child. Similarly, the democratization of Poland was spearheaded by the Solidarity Trade Union, a union that broke away from Communist control and eventually formed the first democratically elected government of Poland. Social transformation in South Africa included giving blacks the right to vote and unionize.

Unions are the only national lobby group available for worker interests. Nonunion workers have few ways of gaining entry into the political arena on workplace issues of concern to them because they have no well-established organizations to lobby on their behalf. By contrast, unions have an institutional structure that can be activated to mobilize workers from firm to firm, across industries, and throughout the country (Taras, 2007; Sims, 2000).

Canada's labour movement historically has actively participated in the country's political life. The Co-operative Commonwealth Federation (CCF) (which in 1961 became the New Democratic Party) was born as an alliance between farm and labour interests. Through the CCF, which achieved electoral success in several provinces, unions were able to lobby for greater statutory protections (see Exhibit 2.5). The Canadian government finally gave workers the right to unionize and compelled firms to recognize unions in 1944, only after Prime Minister William Lyon Mackenzie King perceived that the CCF had gained sufficient momentum that it threatened his electoral chances. Many advances in statutory protections for unions can be attributed to the alliance between organized labour and the CCF/NDP (Bruce, 1989).

This tight alliance has frayed in recent years. Unions refused to support NDP Premier Bob Rae of Ontario in his efforts to introduce a "social contract" in 1993. Some unions withdrew formal support from the NDP. However, even without an overt partnership between labour and a particular political party, unions remain committed to making their presence felt on the political stage.

Exhibit 2.5
What Makes Canada Unique?

North American labour movements differ from those of other countries because of the emphasis on "business unionism"—the preoccupation with protecting and advancing the immediate economic interests of union members rather than engaging in direct participation in politics. However, the Canadian union movement has built a strong alliance with the New Democratic Party (formerly the CCF), making it more of a hybrid movement, practising business unionism in its collective bargaining relationships, but social activism and participation in political processes. Although the NDP has never attained power federally, there have been many instances where the NDP formed provincial governments or led official oppositions. Except for employees of federal undertakings, labour relations fall under provincial jurisdictions.

Unions try to shape public policy and legislation in other ways to benefit their members. Labour recognizes that its collective bargaining strength is strongly influenced by the laws, the policies, the general economy, and the social climate in which it is embedded. Moreover, union members' interests extend beyond the workplace so that unions must also concern themselves with issues like housing, taxation, education, medical services, the environment, and the international economy. Through mobilizing workers and forming coalitions with other advocacy groups, trade unions seek, among other things, to protect worker safety and health, to promote managed trade, and to ensure an adequate social safety net. Unions help workers see that they have common interests with fellow workers and make possible the collective action that can protect the vulnerable and improve conditions for all (Bernard, 1998). Sometimes Canadian unions have become active in international relations issues, seeking greater protection from open borders. For example, organized labour was a key player in the coalition of community, church, and farmer groups opposed to the Canada–U.S. Free Trade Agreement in 1988; again in 1991, labour led the fight against the North American Free Trade Agreement (Gindin, 1995).

One of the problems with this lobbying role is that union members sometimes do not support the same causes as their leaders. For example, although leaders in the Alberta labour movement fought the rapid deficit-reduction policies of Premier Ralph Klein, many members supported the Klein government and voted to ensure the Conservatives' electoral victory. Another example is provided by the CAW, which favours legislated gun control. However, considerable debate rages within the union as rank-and-file members disagree, often vehemently, with the positions taken by their elected leaders.[13] Some union members deeply resent the fact that the dues they pay to belong to a collective bargaining system are used to support social and political causes with which they personally disagree.

Some workers want unions to be organizations that mobilize workers to express themselves as part of a larger social movement. They expect unions to inform them about political issues and involve them in important causes. Although for a small subset of workers this role is vital, nevertheless, the Canadian evidence (reviewed later in this chapter) shows that most workers consider this to be the least relevant union function.

Voice: Organizational Involvement

For some workers, union activity provides an outlet for needs that are not being fulfilled in other facets of their lives. Groundbreaking early research by Leonard Sayles and George Strauss (1967) on the functioning of local unions identified the factors that caused certain workers to be attracted to a union and to become active in it while other seemingly identical workers were not. Their early field study findings, based on the in-depth study of more than 20 local unions, continue to be valid more than 40 years later.

People can be attracted to unions because of their level of idealism and discontent with the status quo. For many, the union is seen as a way to have influence not only over workplace issues, but also over larger political issues. Others are drawn to unions for more individual reasons. Many of those who are attracted to unions are highly competent in their current jobs and often find themselves at the top of their promotional ladders. The union offers them another outlet for challenge. Handling grievances, building political support, and solving workplace problems all provide people a chance to use creativity that may not otherwise be used on the job. Not only does such activity provide relief from the monotony of many industrial or menial jobs, but doing these things well provides people with a sense of achievement or accomplishment.

Union membership also offers people a social outlet. For many people whose jobs keep them physically tied to a specific workstation or area of a plant, the opportunity to interact with more people on a regular basis is a significant benefit. Further, union activity often requires time away from the job—work in the union hall, meetings with management, opportunities to travel and attend conventions or company-wide negotiations—which provides respite from the dreariness of everyday workplace life. Finally, others enjoy union membership because it provides them with an outlet for aggression—bored and frustrated by work, union membership allows them a means to vent.

Voice in the New Competitive Environment

The voice rationale has long been noted as an important impetus to unionization. However, with recent changes in the competitive environment, this function of unions has taken on even greater importance. Competition in many industries and sectors is now much more intense than in the past. Rapid and ongoing technological change, the

Photo 2.2

The Westray mining disaster led to the criminalization of employer negligence in safety and health matters.

Source: CP Photo/Andrew Vaughan

deregulation of formerly regulated markets, the reduction of trade tariffs, and the intensification of foreign competition have all combined to increase the pressure on Canadian firms. To succeed in an environment in which cost and quality concerns have come to dominate, some employers continue to neglect the health and safety of their workers. See the history of the 1992 Westray mining explosion, in which 26 miners were killed in Pictou County, Nova Scotia (www.littletechshoppe.com/ns1625/wraymenu.html).

Other employers who value flexibility, responsiveness, and innovation will turn to the types of high-involvement workplace practices described in Chapter 6. These practices work quite well in unionized settings. But many employers perceive the rigidities of a union contract as impediments to competitive success, and hence the drive to remain union-free continues to be a feature of the industrial landscape.

As a result, nonunion employers are becoming more sophisticated. In many sectors, they pay union wages and benefits and have put into place in-house grievance procedures (that sometimes include a worker majority on the panel). However, for precisely the same reasons that employers don't want to be burdened with union representation of their workforce, workers are increasingly seeking out union representation. Workers perceive the rapid changes in the competitive environment as increasing uncertainty, disrupting the wage–effort bargain, and leading to worksite changes that potentially can affect them negatively. These changes include the adoption of new technology; the reorganization of work, including broadening jobs, decentralizing decision making, and moving to team forms of work organization; and the implementation of quality- and productivity-enhancing programs with ramifications for employment levels. Workers, increasingly, despite their good pay, benefits, and access to a grievance process, want input over decisions such as these that are having dramatic effects on their daily work experience.

A case in point is the pre–"Framework of Fairness" experience of workers at Magna International's Integram plant. Despite union-level pay and benefits, Magna's "Charter of Rights" that guaranteed regular meetings between management and workers, "fairness committees" to hear worker grievances, and a hotline set up to field anonymous worker complaints, a majority of Integram workers voted in 1999 to be represented by the CAW.

In the words of one ten-year Magna employee, "We want a union so that as the environment of the workplace changes we can have solid input, not a 'façade' committee that never accomplishes anything without the OK of management" (Lippert, 1999: C8).

Clearly, what employees increasingly seem to be interested in gaining is a true voice in decisions that are going to have a direct impact on them on the job. Traditionally, unions have given control over the workplace to management, hence the dictum, "management acts and the union grieves." However, this is beginning to change. Increasingly, workers want their unions to speak up for them and to have input into these decisions before they are made.

UNIONISM AS A CONDITION OF EMPLOYMENT, STATUTORY AND "FORCED" UNIONISM

Not all unionized workers choose specifically to be represented by a union or choose a particular union to represent them. Rather, they simply begin working at a worksite that already has been certified by a union, and hence become subject to the pre-existing arrangements. These workers come to the union, not by choice, but by circumstance (see Exhibit 2.6). They might have been attracted to a unionized worksite because of higher pay or greater job protection, but they were not part of the original group of employees whose activities launched the unionization process. They may, or may not, be union supporters. Depending upon the "union security arrangements" (described in Chapter 11) they may be forced to become members of the union, or they may opt out of union membership but have to pay union dues regardless, or some other arrangement might exist. But whether or not they officially join the union, they are nonetheless considered part of a unionized worksite. The union's challenge is then to provide value to incoming workers in the long run, so that they feel attachment to the union. The Miracle Mart employee in Exhibit 2.6 may not feel much for the union at the start of his working relationship, but over time, and depending on how well the union meets his needs, perhaps he will someday.

Other employees may have been present during union organizing, but chose not to support the union. Nevertheless, once the majority of their co-workers supported unionization, the workplace became unionized, both for the supporters of the union and for those who opposed it. The only options available to these workers under Canadian laws are either to accept the union as their legitimate bargaining agent (regardless of their distaste) or to attempt to bring about a union decertification (an election held to vote the union out). Once unionized, however, employees who wish to get rid of their unions are a distinct minority. When asked in surveys, the vast majority of unionized workers would vote for the union again if given the opportunity. In an American survey (which we describe in a later section of this chapter), 90 percent of current private-sector union members would vote to keep their union, and they believe that a large majority of their colleagues would do the same (Freeman and Rogers, 1998).

Finally, there are anomalous situations in which workers are forced to unionize. Governments have passed statutes proclaiming that it is in the public interest for specified groups to engage in collective bargaining. For example, university professors in the province of Alberta must be represented by their faculty associations for the purpose of collective bargaining. Teachers' associations in some provinces are creatures of statute, as are some construction unions in Quebec. Sometimes, professional associations, which certify the credentials of their members, also act as bargaining agents. This is the case for public school teachers in Alberta, who must belong to their association (union) in order to be qualified to teach in the public school system.

Exhibit 2.6
Reflections on a Union-Joining Experience

I got my first real job when I was 17, working at a Miracle Mart store that had just opened in a mall near my high school in Montreal. I applied to work Friday nights and Saturdays and filled out the usual application forms. An employee from the personnel department interviewed me to find out where I could work (I ended up in the toy department) and to ensure that I spoke both English and French. She then told me that I had the job, but that I had to join the union before I could start. She showed me the union membership application and the form allowing union dues to be deducted. I said I was only working part-time, I didn't need a union, and I sure didn't want to pay union dues. I asked what would happen if I didn't sign. She said that the contract with the union required that all employees join the union and that if I didn't sign she couldn't hire me. I said, "Where do I sign...?"

Source: An anonymous colleague's first union experience.

Thus, the fact that 30 percent of Canadians are unionized does not mean that 30 percent of Canadians voted for or otherwise supported a union. Conversely, many Canadians who are not unionized may, at one time or another, have voted for a union. And still others would like to have a union but cannot convince the majority of their co-workers to support unionization. In a 1997 survey, union members and former members comprised just over one-half of all Canadians who expressed approval of unions, and the remaining support came from people who had never been members of unions (Bibby, 1997: 3). On the other hand, many Canadians who are part of unionized worksites never actually chose the union. And other workers became unionized through a government statute, or because their professional association provides both credentials and bargaining. As a result, the union density rate is a poor proxy measure of either the desire to unionize or support of unionization; the interpretation of unionization rates must be conducted with care.

WHAT WORKERS ACTUALLY WANT FROM COLLECTIVE REPRESENTATION

The chapter so far has discussed the reasons unions have come into being and the reasons why workers have joined them. In this section, we investigate what workers today (both union and nonunion) are saying about what they want unions to do for them (and by logical extension, the kind of union to which they would like to belong). We draw here on two recent surveys, one Canadian and one American. Despite being drawn from different populations operating in quite different labour relations climates, the results of the two surveys are startlingly similar. Traditional bread-and-butter economic issues continue to be important, but increasingly, voice on the job and influence over decisions at the workplace that affect people's working lives are seen to be valuable. These are what workers are demanding of their unions. We also include information from survey data on younger workers' willingness to join unions in Canada.

The Canadian Survey

The survey, conducted by John Godard in 1995, interviewed 341 employed Canadians from across the country, not including Quebec (Godard, 1997). Respondents were asked to rate the extent to which they valued each of 24 activities unions were known to undertake (including economic roles, democratic roles, and voice roles) and how effective they perceived unions to be at each of them.

The survey finds that workers desire high levels of activity by unions in what we would see as traditional union areas: protecting wages and benefits, protecting job security, pursuing grievances, pushing for stronger organizing laws, and supporting workers who elect to strike. And, at the same time, respondents report that unions have the most success in achieving their objectives in these same areas.

Godard also evaluates what workers believe unions ought to do. The issues perceived by Canadian workers to be most important include ensuring workers have a say in union affairs, finding positive solutions to workplace-based conflicts that arise, enabling workers to have a say at work, and representing workers' interests to management. These issues are not generally associated with the traditional bread-and-butter concerns of "business unionism." Rather, they are much more focused on the "voice" and workplace-democracy aspects of what unions can provide for their members. This Canadian survey appears to be telling unions that Canadian workers now expect different things from their unions if unions are to receive their support.

Such desires on the part of Canadian workers are consistent with the kinds of changes that are currently underway in the Canadian economy. Increasingly, narrowly defined jobs, rigid demarcations between jobs, and strict lines of seniority are dissolving as firms seek to gain competitive advantage. To compete in the current environment, firms are finding they require greater levels of flexibility and responsiveness from their workforce, more innovation, and more problem solving at lower levels in the organization. In the midst of this shift, workers are feeling vulnerable: What exactly is my job? Is my job secure? How does the shift to teams affect me? If I suggest productivity improvements, do I leave myself (or my co-workers) vulnerable to layoff? For these reasons, workers want their unions to devote more attention to negotiating over these, more intangible, changes with their employers, and to represent workers' interests in bargaining over new forms of work organization and the introduction of new technology. Workers want to have some input into how the workplace is being restructured. Increasingly, it appears, "the role of the union is to help workers find collective solutions to their work-related concerns" (Hurd, 1996).

The American Survey

Richard Freeman and Joel Rogers, of Harvard and the University of Wisconsin respectively, undertook a national survey of employees to hear from them their perceptions of the state of labour representation in American workplaces (Freeman and Rogers, 1999). The 1994 telephone survey involved speaking with 2408 employees: non-supervisory employees and low- and mid-level managers in private-sector establishments of 25 or more employees (a group that is representative of about 70 percent of the employed private-sector workforce in the United States). Freeman and Rogers' findings echo many of the themes found in Godard's smaller Canadian survey. Indeed, Freeman and Rogers also surveyed 1000 Canadian private-sector workers in November 1995 and found little difference between their American and Canadian results (Freeman and Rogers, 1995, 1999: 36–37).

Freeman and Rogers provide some informative background data. First, the data indicate that the vast majority of employees are sufficiently committed and loyal to their companies that they want to participate in workplace decisions. Second, at the same time, many employees are concerned about the quality of labour–management relations at their company and are not confident they can trust management. Well over half the respondents consider themselves to have "a lot of loyalty" to their firm. However, only 38 percent have "a lot of trust that the company will keep its promises to them and other employees." The third important finding is that many employees prefer dealing with management collectively. Some 57 percent agreed that they would "feel more comfortable raising workplace problems through an employee association rather than as an individual." Together, these responses tell us that American workers are committed to their firms, but that they do not entirely trust their employers, and prefer to deal with their employers collectively.

The survey then investigated three specific questions: (1) Do employees want greater participation and representation at their workplaces than are currently provided? (2) What do employees see as essential to attaining their desired level of participation and representation? (3) What solutions do employees favour to resolve any gap between their desired participation/representation and what they currently have?

The answer to the first question is a resounding "yes." Some 63 percent of employees, and fully 72 percent of those employed in manufacturing, want more representation and participation than they have now. In particular, these employees want to have input into decisions regarding work organization, scheduling, compensation, training, technology use, safety, and the setting of work goals. More than three-quarters of those surveyed believe that if workers did have input to decisions in these areas, their company would be "stronger against its competitors," "the quality of products or services would improve," and "employees would enjoy their jobs more" (Freeman and Rogers, 1999: 42).

Most workers surveyed welcome the adoption of "employee involvement" and other worker empowerment schemes by their employers. (These plans are discussed in greater detail in Chapter 6.) However, most do not believe these programs have gone far enough to encourage worker participation, and less than a third of respondents find these programs to be effective in improving productivity or quality. Overwhelmingly (82 percent of nonunion employees and 91 percent of unionized employees), respondents participating in employee involvement programs at their workplace believe such programs would be "more effective if employees, as a group, had more say in how these programs are run" (Freeman and Rogers, 1999: 43).

What solutions do employees propose for the problem of getting access to decision making at the workplace and having true empowerment on the job? Freeman and Rogers find that most employees want co-operative joint committees whose members are elected by other workers, and not appointed by management, and many want unions or union-like organizations.

The clear message is that most American workers want more involvement and greater say on the job. They want some form of workplace organization that provides them with collective (not just individual) voice and gives independent input into workplace decisions. Workers, for the most part, want influence on the issues that increasingly are affecting them on the job: new forms of work organization, the use of new technology, job safety, and training. They want to be able to select their own representatives to such a body and they clearly prefer co-operative relations with management to traditional conflictual or adversarial ones. If unions are able to adopt such roles and offer such workplace-based services to American workers, workers say they would be drawn to such organizations.[14] The challenge for unions is to achieve the gains that workers expect from them, but at the same time to develop methods of delivering gains without heightening conflict. The two goals are not comfortable bedfellows for most unions.

Young Workers and Unions

Three recent studies of the union attitudes and behaviours of young workers establish some important findings. While popular thought is that unions are not particularly relevant to today's generation of new workers, this sentiment is contradicted by empirical research. Lowe and Rastin (2000) analyzed data from a four-year panel study of school–work transitions in Toronto, Sudbury, and Edmonton. Samples of high-school and university students were surveyed at their graduation year in 1985. Then, 1605 of the respondents were contacted in 1986, 1987, and 1989 as they made their way into the workplace. It is clear that most young people begin with a "fence-sitting" attitude toward union support, but within three years, they develop solid positions. At the time of high-school graduation, 65 percent are neutral, and 20 percent report they are likely to join a union. After a few years on the job, support for unionization more than doubles, with 43 percent reporting that they are likely to join and 27 percent that they are unlikely to join. During the same period, the proportion of those who are not likely to join grows from 15 percent to 27 percent. For university students, the same phenomenon of moving

Photo 2.3

Collective action appeals to the younger demographic. Students are well known for their political activism.

Source: CP Photo/John Woods

from neutral to forming an opinion happens, but at the end of a few years only 34 percent are likely to join while 46 percent are unlikely to join. It is not unusual for graduate student teaching and research assistants, who are an especially vulnerable population, to want to unionize. Support for unions among students seems to grow after they have held four to six different jobs over four years, or after they've done part-time work when they would have preferred a full-time job. Labour market difficulties clearly are a factor in the growth of support for unions.

A second study, conducted in the U.K. by Waddington and Kerr (2002), further supports the notion that young workers are not inherently uninterested in union membership. The authors find that there is little ideological opposition to unions by young workers. Rather, unionization rates are lower among youth, they argue, because employers are more determined to resist unions in the service sector where many young people are employed, and unions have not been able to counteract management's anti-union tactics.

A third study, by Gomez, Gunderson, and Meltz (2002), supports the Waddington and Kerr (2002) U.K.-based findings. In Canada, Gomez et al. (2002) find the desire for union membership is actually higher among youths than it is among adults, and most of the greater demand reflects the stronger desire of youths to have unions deal with workplace issues on their behalf. The authors used the Labour Force Survey and the Labour Market Activity Survey, based on samples of approximately 50 000 households and 30 000 households, respectively.

Gomez and his colleagues also used the 1996 survey by Lipset and Meltz (1997) to compare 1057 adults with 147 youths. They found that 57 percent of youths expressed a preference to be unionized, compared to 50 percent of adults. Persons who have a union member in their family are much more likely to prefer unionization. The effect is strongest for youths, whose probability of favouring unions increases threefold if someone in the family is a union member. The influence of family and friends is stronger for youths than for adults. The desire among youths for greater political power and their significantly greater sensitivity to injustice at work causes them to be much more prepared to support unionization than are adults.

UNIONIZATION: PROPENSITY AND OPPORTUNITY

Given the findings from these in-depth surveys of North American workers, it appears that a considerable number of unorganized employees, including youths, are indeed interested in some form of collective representation. We will now assess the factors that influence whether or not those interests are translated into union membership. In particular, we will examine an individual's propensity to unionize as well as his or her opportunity.

Why do some workers join unions while others do not? Two issues are embedded within this seemingly simple question. As Gregor Murray (1995: 168–170) explains it, "a distinction should be made here between the propensity of an individual to join (the demand for union representation) and his or her opportunity to do so (the supply of union representation). Propensity refers to the individual preference, whereas opportunity concerns the context in which those preferences are exercised." For example, consistent findings since the 1970s coming from U.S. data sources show that between 30 and 47 percent of nonunion workers would join a union if afforded the opportunity, a figure significantly higher than the current 12 percent level of unionization.[15] Similarly, one-third of Canadians who are not currently unionized would vote for a union if an election were held tomorrow. So clearly, not all workers who approve of unions are currently union members. Table 2.1 reports the findings of the Lipset–Meltz 1996 survey that pertain to support for unions in both Canada and the United States.

Both propensity and opportunity are subjects that have received considerable research attention. Propensity to unionize can be explained by four factors (Buttigieg, Deery, and Iverson, 2007; Barling, Fullagar, and Kelloway, 1992; Piore, 1995).

1. *Job dissatisfaction*: Employees react to employer practices that are perceived to be unfair, substandard, or unpredictable. They want better treatment on bread-and-butter issues, greater job protection, and more voice.

2. *Perceived union instrumentality*: Employees are alert to opportunities to advance the terms and conditions of their employment. Employees act instrumentally by shopping around for the best deal and determining that a union can bring advantages. They see unions as attractive instruments because unions will provide countervailing power on behalf of worker interests.

3. *Preconceived views about unions*: Most employees have a general attitude toward unions as institutions. One of the important determinants of these views comes from whether or not a parent supports or is a member of a union, or whether the person has had prior experience with unions. Views about unions often are embedded within employees' larger political and ideological beliefs: If people have pre-existing beliefs that support class feelings, solidarity, and collective action, they are more inclined to support and join

Table 2.1 Canadian and American Workers' Views of Unions

	Canada (N=1495) (%)	US (N=1750) (%)
Workers who approve of labour unions	67	70
Workers who believe that as a whole unions are good	52	57
Workers who believe that unions have too much power	40	26
Nonunion employees who, if an election were held tomorrow, would vote for unionization at the workplace	33	47
Nonunion employees who would personally prefer to belong to a union	21	29
Nonunion employees who feel that unions are not needed since workers get fair treatment now	42	37
Nonunion employees who, when hearing of a labour dispute and before knowing all the details, would side with the union	40	57

Source: "Canadian and American Attitudes Toward Work and Institutions," *Perspectives on Work*, vol. 1, no. 3, by Seymour Martin Lipset and Noah Meltz. © 1998, IRRA, by permission.

unions. If people have an attachment to individualism and a distaste for collectivism, they will be quite reluctant to participate in a union.

4. *Self-image:* Three key points guide human behaviour: (a) people try to create and sustain work environments consistent with their identities; (b) people evaluate the notion of unionizing according to its compatibility with their self-conceptions; and (c) people support unions that preserve their identities, but fight against unions that do not match their self-conceptions. Unions face an enormous uphill battle when they try to unionize people (such as high-tech workers) who are drawn to an industry that values individual merit and personal flexibility when they also hold the stereotype of unions as being stodgy, inflexible, and anti-creative. In this situation, unions might be antithetical to, and possibly damaging to, a worker's sense of self (Milton, 2003; Piore, 1995). But a UFCW poster pitched to the self-image of young workers might reinforce the bond between self-image and unionization.

Such demographic variables as age, education level, and ethnicity have not been proven to be reliable predictors of union propensity. Apparently, there is no union profile.

Some implications follow from this conclusion. For example, over and above being ethically questionable, management attempts to ensure a union-free environment by excluding specific demographic groups would most likely be misguided. Also, it is both unnecessary and unwise for union organizers to target unionization campaigns for specific demographic groups (Barling, Fullagar, and Kelloway, 1992: 36).

Even assuming that a certain propensity to join unions can be measured and verified, there remains the issue of opportunity. The factors that affect the opportunity to unionize include the following:

1. *Type of industry and location of employment:* Some industries are more heavily unionized than others. Historically, it has been extremely difficult for unions to organize in the banking and finance sector, whereas unionization is relatively high in heavy manufacturing. There are also geographic differences in unionization opportunities. Workers in heavily unionized manufacturing centres are more likely to come into contact with unions than are workers in rural locations.

2. *Nature of the union that traditionally organizes the particular industry:* Some unions are aggressive in their organizing strategies and are willing to devote considerable resources to union organizing. These unions employ talented organizers who are willing to try novel strategies. Other unions may not be willing to expend valuable organizing resources on prospects that are poor because of a prior history of management opposition or knowledge that a large group of union opponents will make victory unlikely. We have been told by a senior union leader that his union is quite reluctant to commence any new organizing activities in Alberta, because the success rate for new certifications is quite low compared to that of other provinces.

3. *The public-policy setting:* We illustrate the importance of public policy with three points. First, Canadian public policy requires employers to take a "hands-off" approach to issues involving employees' decisions to unionize. Employees must be free to make a choice about joining a union without management interference. But public policy makes nonunion status the legitimate default mode of workers (Adams, 1999). Only concerted and sustained action by workers makes new union certifications possible. A

second and related issue involves majoritarian principles (those based on majority rule). Almost all worksites must achieve a threshold level of support of at least 50 percent plus one in order to be unionized. Thus, hypothetically, if the one-third of nonunion Canadians who would vote for a union were evenly distributed throughout all worksites, then no worksite would be unionized. Third, not all workers are eligible to belong to unions. For example, many labour codes across the country prohibit the unionization of domestic workers.

4. *Degree and expression of employer opposition:* Although there are many Canadian examples of employer interference in union organizing, the Canadian setting is relatively benign compared to that of the United States. There, a sizeable number of workers lose their jobs illegally each year as a result of employer interference in union organizing. American workers are often required to attend meetings in which they are told the negative consequences of organizing, have anti-union literature delivered to their homes, and can be shown propaganda films developed by a multimillion-dollar consulting industry employed by management to dissuade workers from joining unions. In these circumstances, the opportunity for union joining is severely curtailed despite evidence of high union-joining propensity.

Process of Unionization

What triggers unionization efforts among nonunion workers? What is the decision-making process used by employees as they make the transition toward unionization? Generally, unionization is initiated by employee dissatisfaction with pay, treatment, or a lack of voice on the job, or sometimes simply by the recognition that being unionized would provide a better arrangement. The model we present in Figure 2.3 begins with a gap between employees' expectations and their achievements. Awareness of this gap motivates activity leading toward unionization. Union supporters expect that the union can close this expectation–achievement gap.

The ultimate success of union organizing is moderated by the existence of inhibiting or facilitating conditions, including the emotional state of individual workers. Feelings of loyalty to the employer might inhibit union organizing and also prompt employees to give management a chance to solve problems without unionization. Fear of management reprisal might hinder some workers from seeking union support (as it surely does in the United States). Exhibit 2.7 discusses how new immigrants' memories of repressive regimes affect the organizing process. Some employees are wary of union methods (i.e., strikes) and dislike adversarialism. Facilitating conditions might include co-workers' positive sentiments about unions, a developing positive relationship with a union organizer, and anger at employer provocation.

The frustration that incites a search for a solution also heightens emotional intensity. The period of union organizing is a tense and difficult time for many workers. The worksite might be divided into pro- and anti-union camps, each vying for the support of unde-cided co-workers. Management actions, during both the union-organizing period and the many months or years leading up to the expectation–achievement gap, will be carefully scrutinized. Various unfair labour practices (described in Chapter 8) may be committed by management or the union. Making the unionization decision difficult in many worksites

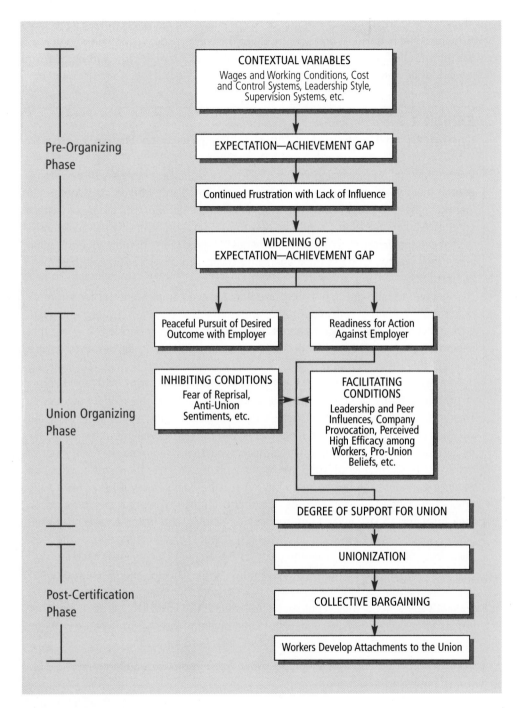

Figure 2.3 The Unionization Process

Source: Adapted from Wheeler and McClendon, 1991, p. 60; and Taras and Copping, 1998, p. 38.

is the knowledge that the vast majority of North American managers will see a pro-union vote as an act of betrayal. Workers worry about the consequences of bringing a union into their job site: Will relationships become even more adversarial? How will normal work interactions be restored?

Exhibit 2.7
Canadian and Immigrant Worker Response to Unionization

In a study of union organizing in workplaces with significant numbers of new immigrants, there were major differences between "Canadian" workers and workers in identical jobs with roots in Somalia, Vietnam, Iran, El Salvador, Honduras, or Eastern Europe. Workers raised in Canada tended to ask the more instrumental questions—"What can the union do to improve my wages?" —and didn't hesitate to join a union when they wanted to punish managers and owners for poor decisions or bad management style.

By contrast, the decision to unionize was a more complex one for recent immigrants from countries with more repressive regimes. Their social environment, work environment, and their concerns about the future shaped their decision. The fear that joining a union would lead to being fired accompanied by their desire to have a problem-free life in their new host community raised questions such as "Do we really need a union? Why can't we solve our problems without a union? What will happen to my family, to my children, if I join the union? Who will find me a job if I get fired?" Their cultural values played an important role too. Immigrant workers often felt indebted to the supervisors who hired them (who sometimes were from the same ethnic group), and anticipated that unionization would be interpreted as a major act of betrayal. "He is my friend!" one immigrant worker said; "He found me this job, he found me a house, he helped me a lot. What is he going to say if I say 'Yes' to the union?" Immigrant workers' spouses were also terrified of reprisal, put pressure on their husbands to stay away from trouble (i.e., unions), and in some cases they even begged union organizers not to do anything that would endanger their husbands' jobs. Their sense of vulnerability made the unionization decision much more emotional.

Union organizers had to be more sensitive to their needs, and different organizing tactics had to be developed. As one worker from Indonesia commented: "Maybe we don't speak good English but we are not stupid! We know what is going on. They [union organizers] are all nice people but I don't want to lose my job because of them. This may be our last chance and we worked really hard for this!"

Source: Tarik Timur and Fred Jacques, 2002, "Unionization in Ethnically Diverse Workplaces," unpublished study.

After the union is certified, collective bargaining begins, and over time many workers may develop a sense of having dual allegiances. They are attached to both their employing organizations and their unions. Sometimes these two loyalties can co-exist quite harmoniously, while at other times employees must make a choice.

A simplified version of the mechanics of initiating a union-organizing campaign is suggested in Exhibit 2.8. These steps are not always followed, and the sequence is sometimes different, but Exhibit 2.9 shows that union organizing can begin quite readily. After the union is assured that it enjoys majority support, it will apply for certification by a labour board. Some provinces require a secret ballot vote. Even so, the process can be dizzyingly fast for the neophyte manager. In Ontario, the Labour Relations Board tries to hold a vote within five days of the union's application. The complexities of certification and behaviours that are considered lawful, and those that breach the law, are described in detail in Chapter 8.

Exhibit 2.8
How Workers May Begin the Organizing Process

1. Call the Labour Relations Board in their province and obtain any relevant materials on certification procedures. (In the federal jurisdiction, call the Canada Labour Relations Board.)
2. Determine the appropriate union that has other bargaining units in their industry and/or seems to specialize in representing employees doing similar work.
3. Call the union offices and set up an appointment with an organizer. If the union agrees that the workers are "unionizable" under the law and of interest to the union, they should proceed to the next step.
4. Obtain a list of employees with addresses and phone numbers to help union organizing.
5. In consultation with the union, develop a local union-organizing committee to oversee the organizing effort.
6. Articulate the issues that would cause employees to support the union and develop a strategy to get the message out to employees. Follow the union's advice about how to notify the employer and the relevant labour board.
7. Become familiar with the relevant labour statutes and follow the steps (described in Chapter 8) to become certified and then to commence bargaining.

Exhibit 2.9
Tool Workers Vote for Union

Employees at one of Canada's largest independent tool and die shops have voted to be represented by one of Canada's largest independent trade unions.

In a vote conducted Monday by the Ontario Labour Relations Board, employees at the Superior Machine and Tool in Chatham voted 76 per cent in favour of representation by Local 519 of the Christian Labour Association of Canada.

Ed Bosveld, regional director in the Chatham CLAC office, said the vote was the culmination of a rapid organizing campaign.

"We were approached less than two weeks ago by employees," he said. "We applied for a certificate last Monday and this week the workers had the opportunity to make their decision."

Source: *Chatham Daily News,* January 30, 2002, p. 5. Copyright © Sun Media Corporation. Reprinted by permission of Sun Media Corporation.

CONCLUSION

As long as the employment relationship is based on an unequal balance of power, employees will likely desire some form of collective representation. This chapter demonstrates that the issues about which employees are most concerned have changed over time and with competitive circumstances. At the same time, unions have had to adapt to this turbulent corporate world with new strategies.[16]

Unions also must hear the message that is being delivered through a variety of surveys: that workers want more say in their work but less adversarialism in achieving it. If this is correct, perhaps the CAW's controversial "no-strike" pledge may actually have the effect of garnering more votes for the union. As union density is declining, even in Canada, unions must struggle to remain relevant and to satisfy the needs of their members. Clearly there is a strong demand for the functions provided by unions, but workers are not entirely convinced that unions are the most desirable vehicle. The next decade will likely test unions' capacities to innovate, to market themselves, and to win support from workers in an increasingly turbulent economy.

The bottom line as to what unions are all about and what attracts people to join them is their representation of collective interests. It is only through collective action that most workers have a chance of matching employers' levels of power. Whether the goal is wage and benefit increases, or increased voice on the job to gain say into the decisions that have fundamental impacts on employees' work lives, or a system of industrial justice to prevent unpredictable and unilateral managerial action, union representation is often the most established means of achieving it. Perhaps best expressing this sentiment directly is labour's anthem, *Solidarity Forever*:

> When the union's inspiration through the workers' blood shall run,
>
> There can be no power greater anywhere beneath the sun;
>
> Yet what force on earth is weaker than the feeble strength of one?
>
> Solidarity forever, for the union makes us strong.

Questions

1. When workers join unions for "more," what are some of the gains—both economic and non-monetary—that they are hoping to achieve?

2. What do the terms "taking wages out of competition" and "organizing to the extent of the market" mean? How are they interrelated? How do they affect business decisions?

3. Give additional illustrations of how the "wage–effort bargain" motivates employee behaviour in situations of wage rollbacks and periods of job insecurity.

4. Roughly 30 percent of Canadian workers are unionized. What does this figure tell us about the demand for unionization? Why is it a poor proxy measure for union demand?

5. What do modern workers want from unions? How can unions design organizing strategies to meet the desires of modern workers?

6. What is the difference between propensity to unionize and opportunity to unionize?

7. What types of issues trigger union organizing?

8. What factors make unions relevant today? What factors make them irrelevant? What is your view of unions?

9. Imagine if the law required that all workers in worksites employing more than 50 workers were required to be part of a union. Only if more than 50 percent of workers voted to leave the union would the workplace be union-free. How different would the world of work be if unionism was the default position of the law?

Weblinks

UFCW Canada:
www.ufcw.ca
UFCW's Local 401:
www.gounion.ca

Unions carefully monitor international events through such websites as:
Global Union News:
www.union-network.org
LabourStart:
www.labourstart.org
The International Labour Organization—see, for example, the International Programme on the Elimination of Child Labour:
www.ilo.org/ipec/index.htm

The following websites contain union campaigns on the Ontario auto policy, sweatshops, pay equity, the rights of agricultural workers, and the impact of the Kyoto Accord:
www.caw.ca/campaigns&issues/ongoingcampaigns
www.unitehere.org
www.psac.com/what/payequity/pay-e.cfm
www.ufcw.ca (and follow links to campaigns, then agricultural workers' rights)
www.cep.ca/policies/energypolicy_e.pdf

Chapter 3

Labour History and the Development of Modern Capitalism

Richard Marsden

Ignorance of the past is the other side of fatalism toward the future—the feeling that time moves through us, as if "the future is already . . . laid out and fully-formed . . . save that it is now awaiting the privilege of being experienced by us—in exactly the same way as the end of a movie is already completed halfway through its showing."

But this view is wrong. "We are not spectators in a completed scenario; we are actors, actresses, camera crew and stage-hands, making the film on location." An understanding of the past "can inform our understanding of the present and illuminate projects and strategies for a future, shaped but unmade" (Bhaskar, 1986: 219).

"Why did they build it so far from the parking lot?" complained a tourist, in all seriousness. He was visiting Stonehenge, a mystical and venerated circle of stone monoliths, approximately 3000 years old, England's most ancient historical monument. True or not, the anecdote is funny because it raises an uncomfortable truth: our headlong rush into the future is accompanied by a collective amnesia about our past.

History is often thought to be irrelevant to our experience of the present. Surely, by definition, the past is concerned with events that have gone by in time, are done with, and over? By this view, history is just a collection of facts about long-dead kings, queens, famous explorers, politicians, and military leaders. Opening a history book is like entering a musty museum: we find collections of dates, events, and artifacts from the past.

Most people form a view of the past not by reading histories or visiting museums, but by experiencing the marketing strategies of corporations and by watching television shows and movies. Witness the remarkable popularity of retro-products, a testimony to the effectiveness of companies that sell goods today by marketing a fantasy past—nostalgia. As never before, the past is commodified, sold, and consumed without having to be understood.

Our disregard for history is particularly prevalent among industrial relations practitioners, who are usually a pragmatic, hard-nosed bunch, preoccupied with the immediate problems of the here and now. An exception is a small minority of union activists, for whom memories of past struggles are as important as "the battle honours of a distinguished regiment . . . important reminders to union members of the courage and solidarity that built past gains and that may well be necessary again" (Morton, 1982: 95). Since management's power does not depend on solidarity to the same extent, its use of history to encourage or advise is less frequent and, with few exceptions, history is not seen as a useful preparation for a career in business.

But let us probe this conventional view of history. It assumes that time is a linear sequence of events, like frames in a film, moving in a straight line from past to future, like a movie stretches from beginning to end. This linear "arrow of time" approach also assumes that the present whizzes off into the past and disappears. But the past is still with us. We live among the monuments, social and material, of past generations. They constrain and enable how we act. It is for this reason that the object of history, like that of personal memory or recollection, is not the past, but the relationship between the past and the present. Industrial relations have a past, as well as a future. If we understand how they came to be as they are, we are in a better position to act on them.

MERCHANT CAPITAL DISCOVERS AMERICA

In the lagoon of the West Edmonton Mall sits an exact replica of the *Santa Maria*, one of the ships in which Christopher Columbus discovered America in 1492. It can be rented for functions and it displays the marketing ware of its latest sponsor. It is an ironic example of how commerce consumes its origins, for production relations in Canada grew from the chance discovery of America by merchant-adventurers from northern Italy, exploring business opportunities on behalf of Spain and England.

The notable character of northern Italy at the time of Columbus is that it was the centre of the earliest form of capital, "merchant (or trading) capital." Merchant capital can be defined as a form of profit made by traders or merchants by buying cheaply in one place in order to sell at a higher price in another. The strategic location of northern Italy in the Mediterranean allowed its merchants to grow rich on lucrative trade with India and the Orient, typically, cloth for spices (indeed, Columbus was the eldest son of a poor wool-weaver). Genoa, Florence, and Venice were centres of merchant capital much as today Tokyo, London, and New York are centres of finance capital.

Before merchants could trade cloth, they first had to get their hands on it. This led to the creation of the first "modern" employment relation. Cloth was produced by a handicraft system, often by families working in their homes using their own looms and raw materials. The man did the weaving, the woman and children the spinning, cleaning, and other chores, and they sold the cloth they produced at the local market. Producers were organized into trade guilds, associations of master craftsmen, journeymen, and apprentices exercising the same craft, for the purpose of protecting and promoting their common interests. There was no employee–employer

Photo 3.1

Much can be learned about merchant capital by studying occupational portraits of that age. Here is Jan Gossaert's *Portrait of a Merchant*, c. 1530.

Source: Gossaert, Jan (c. 1478–1532) *Portrait of a Merchant*, c. 1530, oil on panel, .636 x .475. National Gallery of Art, Washington. Ailsa Mellon Bruce Fund.

division as such. Notable about this guild or handicraft system is the control workers exerted over the creation and sale of the product; they had no intermediary between themselves and the market.

This community of interests was shattered first in Florence during the turn of the 14th century, when guilds based on the various skills involved in producing woollen cloth were disbanded and displaced by a Wool Guild dominated by an elite of merchants. Merchants used the new Guild as an employers' association, prohibiting workers from holding assemblies, keeping their wages low, and preventing them from buying and selling raw materials and finished goods. Wool workers were forbidden to trade and prevented from alleviating their powerlessness by organizing.

Merchants now controlled raw materials and finished products and coordinated each step in the production of woollen cloth, as materials passed from one place of work to another, from spinner to weaver to dyer. Under this "putting-out" system, merchants often employed thousands of men, women, and children working out of their homes or in workshops using their own tools and machines, paid not for their time, but by the piece. The merchant thus became a producer, a merchant-capitalist, coordinating and controlling the work of previously independent artisans, buying the wool and selling the cloth on the open market. Here the original meaning of "merchant" developed as "any trader in goods not manufactured or produced by himself."

For decades, workers resisted merchants' seizure of power in Florence by riots and strikes and demanded the right to organize themselves into self-governing bodies with a voice in Guild and communal affairs. Half a century of insurrection was crushed by an oligarchy of merchants in the 1380s, resulting in the death or exile of much of its leadership and rank and file. By the mid-18th century the putting-out system was prevalent throughout Europe.

The driving motive of merchant capital—profit through exchange—stimulated the extension of merchants' trading network via speculative adventures. Merchant-adventure was given an added incentive when the commercial supremacy of northern Italy was threatened by the fall of Constantinople (now Istanbul) to the Ottomans (Turks) in 1453, for they imposed high taxes and duties on goods in transit, which added to the already high transport costs of using the overland route to the spice and gem markets of the East. Merchants had a vested interest in cutting out the Ottoman middleman, and so interest grew in exploring alternative routes to the East.

In the race for the eastern spice markets, commercial interests vied for access to the latest in information technology to give them a competitive advantage. Today's information technology is computer technology, but then it was navigational technology. Navigators calculated their latitude using the astrolabe, and steered by compass; later, the chronometer allowed time to be measured accurately and longitude to be calculated. But the most important technology was the map, for maps revealed information on newly discovered territory and potential trade routes—vital to those looking to invest in new business openings (Jardine, 1996). Cartographers were the computer programmers of the 15th century; Florence was its Silicon Valley. What Columbus had going for him, apart from mercantile seafaring know-how, was that his brother was a cartographer who had managed to catch sight of a map by the Florentine cartographer Toscanelli. This map strongly suggested there was a western route to India. Commerce and information technology (the map) were intertwined from the very beginning.

Columbus, then, was exploring not so much unexplored territory as business opportunities. He aimed to forge a new trade route to the spices and gems of India. To his dying day, he thought he had landed on its east coast. This is why native Americans came to be known as "Indians." In this sense, it was the imperative of merchant capital, manifest in the lives of merchant-adventurers, that discovered America.

MERCHANT CAPITALISM IN CANADA

In Italy, merchant capital developed on the backs of sheep. In Canada, it developed on the hides of beaver. It was the growing market for the beaver felt hat in Europe, during the last quarter of the 16th century, that stimulated trade for beaver pelts in Canada, the origin of merchant capital within Canada (Ray and Freeman, 1978). Indian–European trade was facilitated by the Hudson's Bay Company (HBC), a new form of business organization: the joint-stock trading company, a privately financed but royally created monopoly, which evolved from the trading partnerships of medieval Italy and is the forerunner of the modern multinational corporation.

The HBC's charter was granted by Charles II in 1670, to the "Governor and Co. of Adventurers of England trading into Hudson's Bay." It controlled trade to, from, and within the area defined by its charter, which extended from Labrador to the Rocky Mountains. As a complex exchange system connecting a native trapping network with the fur markets of London, Paris, Leipzig, and Moscow, the HBC was as global as any modern transnational corporation. The nodes in this network were mercantile agents known as "factors," and in their "factories," or trading stations, beaver pelts were bartered for European goods.

Fur-trading companies were the only major employers in Canada until the middle of the 19th century. Settlement was confined to Ontario, Quebec, and the Maritimes and consisted of sparsely populated British colonies with economies based on agriculture, fishing, and the fur trade. The family farm was the main unit of production, and the rural village was the centre of economic activity.

Until the 1850s, those who worked for wages were the exception to the rule, but included men drawn from French-Canadian farm families and Irish immigrants who worked at logging and canal construction, domestic servants, farm labourers, seamen, and skilled craftsmen such as shipwrights and iron workers. Needs that could not be met by the household were satisfied in small, local workshops owned and managed by master craftsmen: saw and grist millers, carpenters, shoemakers, tailors, iron forgers, cabinet makers, distillers, brewers, tanners, and so on. These were generally small-scale concerns. The possibility of upward mobility, from apprentice to journeyman to master, fostered a community of interests reinforced by the close, direct, personal, and paternal relations typical of small-scale production. The main societal division was not between master and men, but between a mercantile elite and the farming and fishing families who were indebted to the marketers of their wheat and fish (Heron and Storey, 1986).

Merchants invested the money that they made through trade in staples (such as fish, fur, and, later, lumber and wheat) in manufacturing commodities for a growing urban market. Artisan workshops, characterized by handicraft techniques, were gradually mechanized to become the factories of the later industrial age. Mechanization increased the scale of production and also the cost of operating a business, and this limited self-employment to the small minority with capital (Palmer, 1992). At the same time, farmers were being forced off the land by mounting debt. These displaced labourers combined with the flood of southern Irish immigrants during the 1840s to form a pool of unskilled labour. They worked in the early factories and on railway, road, and canal construction, thereby establishing the transportation arteries that were to link isolated villages and forge a national market. By the 1850s, there was a workforce of primarily full-time wage earners (Palmer, 1992). The need for a physical infrastructure generated an urban workforce: the demand for houses, factories, and warehouses created the construction worker; the demand for tools and stoves, the foundry worker; and for boots and clothes, the shoemaker and tailor. Commerce and urbanization developed hand in hand.

These three causes—the development of workshops into factories, the displacement of labour from the land, and commercial growth of towns—lay behind the metamorphosis of merchant into industrial capital, the making of money by manufacturing commodities. This became possible only with the creation of an interrelationship between employers and employees: by trading the employer's money for workers' capacity to act (their time) and by ensuring that the exercise of that capacity created more value than that paid in wages. Modern industrial relations revolves around bargains over the price of both that capacity to act and its exercise ("time" and "work").

Industrialization

This movement from merchant to industrial capital entailed the displacement of one type of factory, a merchant company's trading station, by another type of factory, a building or range of buildings with plants for the manufacture of goods. The first factory workers were extremely dependent and subject to close supervision. In England, where manufacturing began, most of the first factory workers were women and children. Within Canada, "three-quarters of the workforce in Toronto's rising clothing industry were female" (Palmer, 1992: 83). In Halifax during the 1870s, "the percentage of children increased from roughly 9 to 22 percent of the labour force in baking," and "one in four boys aged 11–15 in Montreal worked for wages, where 42 percent of the industrial workforce in 1871 was composed of women and children" (Palmer, 1992: 99–100). Signalling an end to a way of life in which a measure of self-determination at work was highly valued, the introduction of factories often provoked riots and destruction (Clawson, 1980: 53). All things considered, people preferred the cottage or the homestead to the factory (Thompson, 1968). The first, and indeed subsequent, generations of factory workers did not have the luxury of deciding when and how hard to work. For them the choice was between working on the employer's terms or not working at all—which isn't much of a choice.

Subcontracting Management

In the first factories, employer-managers provided the premises, raw materials, and operating plant, and subcontracted jobs at a fixed price to skilled craftsmen acting as contractors, or piece-masters, who then employed and paid others to work on the job. Subcontracting was particularly entrenched in shipbuilding, mining, ironworks, and textiles. Managers concentrated on finance, marketing, and purchasing. It was contractors who managed labour, using a mixture of exhortations, threats, rewards, and outright coercion to get work out of workers. There was nothing subtle or hidden about 19th-century management. It was direct and personal rule (Littler, 1982).

The system of having subcontractors allocate tasks and organize work circumvented the problem of the employer possessing less technical knowledge and skill than his subordinates. It also avoided the need to maintain a large permanent staff in the face of fluctuations in demand. But it had the disadvantage, for employers, of protecting traditional craft skills, and the subcontractors' control over hiring and firing heightened their strategic importance (Nelson, 1975). Subcontracting was eroded by pressure from above and from below during the last quarter of the 19th century. Employers were under competitive pressure to minimize unit labour costs. Since contractors were paid by the piece or by the job, they guarded their profits either by substituting cheaper, semi-skilled labour in place of skilled labour, or by driving their workers harder ("speed-up"). Relations between contractors and workers deteriorated amid charges of "sweated" labour.

Employers, too, grew skeptical of the value of the intermediate layer of subcontractors, wary of the control they exerted and jealous of the profits they managed to make in this period of financial stringency. A particular problem was their control over hiring, a practice that proved inadequate in the face of increased demand for skilled labour during the 1880s and 1890s. To circumvent this problem, companies centralized hiring by establishing employment departments. This move seriously weakened the power of contractors, for with it they lost the ability to set entry-level wages.

Simply put, employers wanted more control, while increasingly organized workers wanted relief from sweated labour. The limits of the subcontracting system for extracting work had been reached, and it was replaced with a system of salaried foremen.

Salaried Foremen vs. Craft Power

Like contractors, foremen were responsible for how the job was to be done, the tools and often the materials to be used, the timing of operations, the flow of work, and the workers' methods and sequence of moves. While foremen (and those remaining contractors) were nominally in charge of production decisions, real control was more often than not in the hands of highly skilled craft workers. This was especially true in metal and metal-using industries, the core of the new "industrial revolution." The skill base of their power was supplemented by craft unionism (examined below), which tried to use collective strength to maintain jurisdiction.

Skilled workers in the 19th century exercised a great deal of power. Most unions of skilled workers did not deign to negotiate over wages, but unilaterally determined, and told management, the price of their labour. They felt they were the equal of the boss. The "right to manage," asserted as if it were a historical legacy, would have been incomprehensible to 19th-century craftsmen. Their control over the workplace was a natural counterpart of their skill and knowledge of the production process. When technological change threatened to undermine the skill basis of their power, they substituted the collective strength of the union, and the work practices of the artisan age became embodied in the union rule book—a defence against managerial control. Many strikes and lockouts of the 1880s and 1890s centred on the issue of control.

Early Craft Unions

Unions emerged spontaneously from informal social groups defending their customary practices and standard of living, both of which were under attack by Canada's developing industrial infrastructure. The first evidence of union organization in Canada is found in New Brunswick and Nova Scotia. "Starting with Halifax building tradesmen and shipwrights in 1798, and led by printers and carpenters, workingmen formed at least 45 unions in the years before 1850, establishing major centres of skilled labour in Saint John, Quebec, Montreal, and Toronto" (Forsey, 1982: 123). By the 1830s and 1840s skilled workers, particularly in the building, printing, clothing, and shoe trades, were forming trade unions and striking. Saint John, New Brunswick, was the trade union capital of British North America from the late 1830s to the late 1850s, with "more, bigger, stronger, and more respected unions than any other place in the North American colonies" (Williams, 1975: 9).

Early union membership was limited almost exclusively to male, skilled workers. While there was an obvious need for unions amongst the unskilled, the poorest, and weakest workers, they were vulnerable to employer sanctions and the law. Employers united in fighting unions. Activists often had to work in secret for fear of blacklisting. The power base of the craft union was the skill of its members. The unions' control over entry through apprenticeship put them in a position to unilaterally enforce work rules and rates. "When they could, unions in early nineteenth-century Canada set their rates and notified their employers, often in politely worded newspaper advertisements" (Morton, 1982: 96). Enforcement was simple: they would shun employers who flouted the rules. In their defence of the status quo, craft unions gradually developed an industrial relations function based on their unilateral control of the rules of the trade and rates of pay.

A second source of power was the solidarity derived from a collective sense of craft pride. Craft unionists associated with other "respectables," not with their fellow unskilled workers. Thus, from the outset, unions were exclusive and possessed a chauvinism that encouraged attachment to restricted and local priorities. The motivation to take collective action was a defence of privilege. Thus it was that hatters, printers, shoemakers, and carpenters "took steps to preserve their respectability by fighting against specialization, unlimited apprentices and hours, and wages that they judged to be inadequate compensation for their skills as well as insufficient for their needs" (Palmer, 1983: 34).

Finally, unions were small and usually restricted to one locale. Until 1859, "except for four Amalgamated Society of Engineers [ASE] branches, all seem to have been purely local, and very few seem to have any relations with other unions" (Forsey, 1982: 31). Distance and lack of mobility made communication between them difficult, fostering insularity and hindering solidarity.

The International Unions

The spread of the railway network beginning in 1850 linked discrete labour markets into a national and international labour market, so to control labour supply—a source of their power—unions had to follow suit. Although local unions continued to be formed until the end of the century, they were gradually supplanted by "international" unions, which made their first appearance in the 1850s and spread during the period 1860 to 1880.

The first international unions were not American, but British; skilled British immigrants brought with them their union consciousness and organizing skill. The British Amalgamated Society of Engineers established branches at Hamilton, Toronto, and Brantford during the 1850s, and others followed. Another British union, the Amalgamated Society of Carpenters and Joiners, established itself in Canada in 1871 with branches in Hamilton, Toronto, Kingston, and St. Catharines. American unions recruited in Canada later. The first to do so was the National Union of Iron Molders in 1861 (later named the Iron Molders' Union of North America), with members in Montreal, Hamilton, Toronto, London, and Brantford (Williams, 1975: 10). For American unionists, the close physical proximity between the two countries and their similar cultural, linguistic, and social roots created the potential for a single continental jurisdiction for each craft organization. By the 1860s and 1870s, central Canadian workers were part of a continental labour market, marked by large-scale movement back and forth across the Canadian–American border (Palmer, 1983).

The development of international unions illustrates the contradictory forces of unity and sectionalism at the heart of trade unionism. The extension of unionism from its local origins to an international basis was an expression of solidarity with workers in other regions; it was also a consolidation of sectionalism, for these predominantly craft organizations saw the unskilled as rivals for their jobs and a threat to the craft unions' monopoly over labour supply.

The Legalization of Trade Unions

Until the last quarter of the 19th century, workers' ability to combine and take collective action was severely constrained by law. Under the *Master and Servant Act*, for example, it was a criminal offence, punishable by imprisonment, for a worker to quit a job; a similar breach of contract by the employer—for example, a failure to pay wages—was only a civil offence. The British *Combination Acts* (imported into colonial Canada) prohibited collective organizations, and judges declared union activists liable for prosecution for criminal conspiracy in restraint of trade. While the law was used selectively rather than uniformly, its potent threat was one reason trade unionism was restricted largely to skilled workers, whose sense of common identity and craft pride sustained them through legal sanction.

Revision of the legal status of unions was stimulated by the Toronto printers' strike. The Typographical Union struck the Toronto *Globe* newspaper on March 25, 1872, in support of its demand for "a week's work to consist of 54 hours, $10 per week; 25 cents per hour overtime for job printers." The master printers used the common law to argue that unions were conspiracies in restraint of trade and obtained the arrest of the union's Vigilance (strike) Committee. At the subsequent pretrial hearing, the magistrate announced that since unions were illegal combinations, their actions must be unlawful. Before the strikers could stand trial, Prime Minister Macdonald, spurred by political expediency and public pressure, introduced into Parliament two bills: the Trade Unions Bill and the Criminal Law Amendment Bill. The *Trade Unions Act* legalized trade unions by freeing them from the common law liability of restraint of trade, limiting protection to unions registering with the Registrar General of Canada. The *Criminal Law Amendment*

Act gave a right to strike, but restricted the exercise of that right to peaceful actions that did not coerce the employer or prevent him from carrying on his business. Coercive acts were illegal, and a combination to carry out a legal act by illegal means was a criminal conspiracy. Trade unionists found these acts restrictive and, through intense political lobbying, succeeded in winning amendments in 1875 and 1876 that "narrowed the definition of criminal conspiracy for the purposes of trade combinations to the performance of acts expressly punishable by law" (Arthurs, Carter, and Glasbeek, 1981). The *Breaches of Contract Act* of 1877 provided that a breach of contract of service should no longer be a crime. These three acts—the *Trade Unions Act*, 1872, the *Criminal Law Amendment Act*, 1872 (as amended in 1875 and 1876), and the *Breaches of Contract Act*, 1877—provided the legal basis of freedom of association in Canada.

The Knights of Labour

Until 1859, "the only organizations of the unskilled were the two longshoremen's unions" (Forsey, 1982: 31). The unskilled lacked the common identity and organization to withstand employer and legal sanctions and form trade unions. Instead, they—most notably the rafters and canallers—expressed their discontent in less organized forms such as desertions or riots (Palmer, 1983: 39). Unskilled workers had to await the militancy and organizing boom of the 1880s to alleviate their disadvantage in bargaining. Its driving force was a very different form of international unionism from the craft unions: the Noble and Holy Order of the Knights of Labour. Originating in Philadelphia, the Knights of Labour aimed to be a worldwide labour body, organizing workers regardless of skill, gender, religion, or nationality: a form of industrial unionism. At its peak, the Order had 700 000 members— 12 000 of those in Canadian "assemblies"—scattered as far afield as Great Britain, Ireland, Belgium, Australia, and Hawaii. The first Canadian assembly was formed in Hamilton in 1867. Although Ontario was the Knights' stronghold, they spread through the industrial and railway towns of the Prairie provinces and British Columbia. By unifying workers across regions, industries, occupations, and crafts, the Knights formed the first mass working-class movement in Canadian history (Palmer, 1983: 103–104).

In the United States, the Knights were effectively halted by public reaction to the Haymarket bombing incident in Chicago in 1886. Implicated in the killing of seven policemen, four of their activists were hanged, and a fifth killed himself. But in Canada the Knights continued to operate normally, with their eventual downfall being caused by conflict with the international (American-dominated) craft unions. The cause was a basic philosophical difference, reflected in organizational strategies. The Knights advocated united concerns for all workers, whereas the international craft unions were oriented toward more exclusive interests.

Knights vs. Crafts The various industry trades and community labour councils, which developed from the 1860s, provided a forum for interaction between Knights and craft unionists. They were also the "local foundations for the creation of the Trades and Labour Congress of Canada (TLC), which first met in Toronto in 1883" (Palmer, 1983: 129). The TLC, Canada's first enduring national labour federation and the forerunner of the Canadian Labour Congress, became a forum for rivalry and conflict between the Knights and the craft unions. As supporters of industrial unionism, the Knights argued that craft unionism weakened class solidarity by contributing to jurisdictional disputes.

For this reason, they called for the TLC to devalue its concern with lobbying government in favour of organizing the unorganized. The mounting demands for an extension of industrial unionism, which entailed an organizational campaign that would go beyond craft boundaries, courted opposition from the craft unions (who had a vested interest in maintaining their exclusivity) and their central labour organization in the United States, the American Federation of Labor (AFL), formed in 1886. The increasingly frequent conflicts between the Knights and the craft unions came to a head in 1902 at the Berlin, Ontario (now Kitchener), Convention of the TLC, at which narrow craft triumphed over open reformist unionism, and the Knights were expelled. Women and the unskilled—the chief beneficiaries of open unions—"slipped back into a state of unorganized dependence on capital's mercy and the politician's benevolence" (Palmer, 1983: 133).

Taylorism

North America's depression of 1873–79 destroyed excess industrial capacity and provided a starting point for a round of new investment. It also marked the start of a 40-year struggle between employers who wanted to increase their profits by reorganizing work processes and craft workers who wanted to defend their power base.

Just one year before the end of the depression, Frederick Winslow Taylor began work at the Midvale Steel Company, where he worked until 1890. He was to develop a special interest in time and motion. Taylor discovered that the workers under his command were able to use their superior knowledge and skill to restrict output and to control their earnings. Taylor's strategy was to undermine the power of the workgroup, and thereby improve efficiency and profitability, by reducing a reliance on skill and transferring workers' knowledge to managers.

Taylor's objective was to be achieved by the following management practices (often described as the principles of Taylorism). The division of labour is increased by breaking jobs into their component parts—often referred to as the fragmentation of work. Work is simplified, standardized, and deskilled, making labour more substitutable. Less skilled and therefore cheaper workers are substituted for craftsmen, effectively reducing their power. The narrowly defined tasks are evaluated by time-and-motion study (symbolized by the stopwatch), which analyzes how a specific task can be completed in the shortest time with the fewest motions, providing a quantitative basis for monitoring and comparing worker performance, hence the term "scientific management."

Having been fragmented, the production process is reintegrated under the coordination and control of management. Managers, not workers, foremen, or subcontractors, now have knowledge of the production process and the ability to plan and direct work. This change marked the separation between the conception and execution of work, or between planning and doing, mental and manual labour. Instead of skilled workers telling management what was possible, management, through time-and-motion study, now determined the best sequence and time of operations and monitored worker performance. Knowledge that was previously the domain of workers became incorporated into management's own rules and practices.

This reorganization of work along Taylorist lines meshed with a concentration of corporate power. From the turn of the century, a wave of company mergers and takeovers began in the United States and swept over Canada, encouraged by the high tariffs on the import of manufactured goods established by the National Policy of the 1880s (introduced by Prime Minister Macdonald to encourage manufacturing in Canada). Those American firms establishing branch plants in Canada introduced this new method of managing labour, and Canadian firms often employed managers with American experience or hired American management consultants. By World War I, scientific management had a firm foothold in Canada. The development of the multinational corporation spread scientific management far afield. Ford and General Motors, for example, established subsidiaries abroad, thus allowing the transfer of techniques and machinery, and also of management techniques. By the mid-1930s, Taylorism had spread across Europe.

The Wobblies

Scientific management and technological change diluted skills and increased the need for cheaper, unskilled labour, thereby undermining the craft-dominated mode of production. This demand was met by a massive influx of immigrants early in the 20th century, drawn from the factories and fields of Europe. As foremen grappled with craft workers and their exclusive unions, these new, unskilled immigrant workers were being recruited by a successor to the Knights, the Industrial Workers of the World—popularly known as the Wobblies, supposedly following a Chinese restaurateur's mispronunciation, for whom IWW was "Eye Wobbly Wobbly."

Formed at a Chicago meeting in 1905, the IWW saw its purpose as the emancipation of the working class from capitalism, an objective to be achieved by action at the workplace, the locus of the employer's power. This belief affected the orientation of the Wobblies in two ways: first, economic action, particularly the general strike, had primacy over political action; second, the solidarity of the proletariat (the poorest class of working people) required that all workers in an industry be organized. As a form of industrial unionism, the IWW recruited from those ideologically opposed to the exclusivity of craft unionism: the itinerant, unskilled workers—loggers, harvesters, longshoremen, and construction workers. For this reason, it was the logging and railway construction camps of the West that provided conditions in which the radical industrial unionism of the IWW, and also that of the United Brotherhood of Railway Employees, the American Labor Union, and the Western Federation of Miners, could flourish. The Wobblies went out of their way to overcome the difficulties of organizing this itinerant, ethnically heterogeneous labour force; for example, they circulated propaganda in at least 10 different languages.

The IWW's decline was caused mainly by the loss of its membership base with the end of the railway building boom, which dispersed the construction labour force, its main constituency. By the start of the First World War, its membership was falling and its locals disintegrating.

The Wobblies are still with us; few in number, but big on hope, their banner is still likely to be found whenever labour takes to the streets in North America. Their campaign at Starbucks demonstrates their continuing will to organize at the workplace.

One Big Union and the Winnipeg General Strike

Workers in the Canadian West were radicalized by the Russian Revolution and, through their federations of labour, advocated workers' control of industry and general strikes to achieve political change. The year 1919 was a record one for strikes. The counterpart of the radicalism of western workers against employers was their antagonism to the conservative, eastern-dominated craft unionism. Out of this grew a split in the Trades and Labour Congress, in March 1919, and the birth of "one big union."

The One Big Union (OBU) succeeded the Knights and the Wobblies as an advocate of industrial unionism. Its ultimate goal was workers' control over essential industries; its intended means, the general strike. This philosophy found a receptive audience among the loggers and miners of British Columbia, where the OBU was endorsed by many local trade councils, and especially logging and mining unions. The most prominent incident associated with the One Big Union was the Winnipeg General Strike of 1919, seen by some as about collective bargaining and recognition rights, by others as a challenge to the capitalist system.

The strike is of interest here for what it reveals of the relationship between craft and industrial unionism. Although the immediate issues were modest—union recognition, an eight-hour day—employers cloaked them in revolutionary implications. The immediate stimulus to the general strike was a walkout of building and metal trades workers in support of their demands for wage increases and for employers to recognize the Metal Trades Council. Following a vote among its affiliates, the Winnipeg Trades Council ordered a general strike, and approximately 30 000 workers struck on May 15, 1919, effectively paralyzing the city of Winnipeg. The authorities took it to be a conspiracy to overthrow the government, rather than a simple attempt to obtain basic recognition and bargaining rights, and suppressed the strike. Strike leaders were arrested and charged with "conspiracy to bring into hatred and contempt the governments of the Dominion of Canada and the Province of Manitoba and to introduce a Soviet system of government." Following a year of trials, one of the leaders, R. B. Russell, was convicted and sent to the penitentiary for two years; five others received one-year sentences, one a six-month sentence, and one was freed (Bercuson, 1990).

What was the stance of the craft unions toward this all-too-brief and rare display of labour unity? The Trades and Labour Congress saw the OBU as a competitor for membership and, as a condition of support for the strike, required from the strikers a declaration of allegiance to the TLC, repudiation of the OBU, and assurances of adherence to the constitutions of international unions—terms unacceptable to the Winnipeg strikers (Williams, 1975: 133). Most officers of the international unions were opposed to the strike and shed no tears at its defeat. Attempts to establish industrial unionism were stopped dead in their tracks, union membership fell, and militancy declined. As for the OBU, it experienced a further setback in the Crowsnest Pass coal strike in 1919, then declined.

"Fordism" and Mass Production

As efficiency-conscious employers restructured work along Taylorist lines, subdividing tasks, accelerating the pace of work, and intensifying operations, workers fought back, defending against the erosion of their skills and hence their power in the workplace. This encouraged the design of machines and plant that would circumvent this resistance to management control: continuous-flow production. Since Henry Ford perfected the flow-line principle of assembly work, it is commonly referred to as Fordism.

The Ford Motor Company was founded in 1903 in Detroit. In its early years, Ford was dependent on skilled labour "because the imperfect and unstandardized parts had to be drilled, milled, ground, planed, and bored before they would fit together satisfactorily" (Gartman, 1979: 195). The assembly procedure was stationary; the team worked together to construct the entire car, which was placed on a wooden horse on the shop floor. Much time was consumed transporting the various components and tools. As production grew, this process multiplied "until the whole shop floor was filled with long lines of stationary positions, a few workers at each" (Gartman, 1979: 195). Ford's innovation, introduced in stages, was to turn this process on its head. Instead of workers moving from job to job, parts were brought to them by conveyors and transporters, eliminating the need to move around the workshop, in effect rooting workers to the spot. It was the assembly line, not the worker, that now determined the sequence of operations and the pace of work.

In effect, Ford pushed Taylor's job fragmentation to its logical conclusion and combined it with technical devices for moving material past successive workstations in a continuous flow. These mass-production techniques integrated the production process in a way that allowed a small group of strategically placed workers to shut down an entire plant if they stopped work. This strategic advantage, combined with an increasingly homogenized workforce, created the conditions for establishing industrial unionism within these car plants.

Industrial Unionism Becomes Permanent

As we have seen, industrial unionism has a long history. Most prominent are the Knights of Labour of the 1880s, the IWW, and the OBU, but both the Western Federation of Miners and the United Mine Workers of America, in accepting everyone regardless of level or craft, were effectively industrial unions. Since the conflict between the exclusivity of craft unionism and the breadth of industrial unionism is a recurrent theme in Canadian union history, it is worth reiterating the philosophical differences over the purpose of trade unionism that lay behind jurisdictional disputes. Central were the different sources of power of the two types of unions. The power of craft unions lay in eliminating competition between their members and controlling the supply of labour, primarily by regulating the rules governing apprenticeship, the means of acquiring craft skills. To maintain this power base, it was essential to resist mechanization, which eroded the skill component of their work, and to defend their jurisdiction against the encroachments of other workers, skilled and unskilled. The power of industrial unions, in contrast, lay in strength of numbers. Hence the necessity to recruit widely, and their regular clashes with craft unions. The conflict between exclusivity and breadth continued throughout the 1920s and 1930s, and was resolved only by an institutional split in the labour movement in both the United States and Canada.

In the United States, workers in the mass-production industries were organized by the Congress of Industrial Organizations. The CIO began as a committee of industrial union representatives within the craft-dominated AFL; it became a separate federation in 1937 when jurisdictional disputes with craft unions led to the expulsion of its unions from the AFL. In Canada, the new industrial unions were at first coordinated by a committee of the CIO. Under pressure from the AFL, the TLC expelled these CIO affiliates in 1939. Together with several industrial unions already outside the TLC, the CIO unions in Canada formed the Canadian Congress of Labour (CCL) in 1940. In this fashion, the union movement in the United States and Canada was split in two: craft (AFL/TLC) and industrial (CIO/CCL). In 1955, the AFL and CIO merged to form the AFL–CIO, and a year later the TLC and CCL merged to form the Canadian Labour Congress (CLC).

The increasingly costly conflicts between industrial unions and employers over recognition encouraged development of procedures for institutionalizing this conflict. In the United States, the *Wagner Act* of 1935 recognized the rights of workers in the private sector to belong to a union of their choice, prohibited certain "unfair labour practices" often used by employers to thwart unionization, and required employers to bargain in "good faith" (see Chapter 8). Since industrial unionism in the United States was stimulated by the *Wagner Act*, Canadian union leaders lobbied for similar legislation. Eventually, the Wagner principles were introduced in Canada through the temporary wartime Privy Council Order 1003, the National War Labour Order, in 1944.

This temporary order became a federal statute in 1948, which was modified and adopted by all 10 provinces. Canada had its legal framework for trade unionism and collective bargaining, setting the stage for a sustained period of union growth that continued into the 1990s. The merger of the Trades and Labour Congress and the Canadian Congress of Labour heralded the end of the bitter feud of craft versus industrial unionism. Both kinds of labour organization could flourish within a unified house of labour, which also would welcome public-sector employees in record numbers in the 1970s. The industrial relations system enjoyed a period of relative stability as employees, through their unions, were able to share in a rapidly expanding economic pie.

Fordism–Keynesianism

For most of the post–Second World War period, Fordism dovetailed with the institutional framework of collective bargaining and Keynesian management of the economy: stimulating consumer demand through monetary and fiscal policies, investing in industry and social welfare programs, and expanding the public sector. The mass production of Fordism meshed with a mass-consumer society. The aim of the first, to keep costs of production down, complemented the aim of the last, to keep levels of consumption up. In Canada, "not a single serious recession was experienced during the first 35 years following the end of World War II. In per-person terms, real GDP grew by 2.8 percent per year, providing a real foundation for the greatest increase in living standards ever experienced in Canada" (Stanford, 1999: 189). The difficulty, however, with deficit financing and other measures to maintain consumption is that employers will increase productive investment only if there is a reasonable expectation that it will increase their profits. In the face of a global crisis of stagflation (slow economic growth coupled with a high rate of inflation and unemployment) during the early 1970s, this precondition disappeared. It was a stark reminder: for compromises to be possible in industrial relations, there must be something to bargain over.

Restructuring Workplaces and Marketplaces

By the 1970s, Fordism–Keynesianism had reached the limits of its possibilities. This was manifest in a long deterioration in the profitability of private business in Canada and other industrial economies, and the co-existence of stagnation and inflation as stagflation, once thought by Keynesians to be impossible. Management's response was to reorganize labour to raise productivity. In the era of industrial capital this reorganization was done via Taylorism and Fordism. Now it would be done via re-engineering business processes and by what is known as the McDonaldization of work (Ritzer, 1996).

Re-engineering sped up production as companies began to use information technology to link the knowledge held by individuals, remote in space and time, within and across organizations. The McDonaldization process called for the redesign of jobs according to criteria of efficiency, calculability, and predictability. While we associate it with the fast-food industry, it is rooted in Fordist assembly-line techniques. It spread from industry to industry, turning workplaces into factories (McUniversity, McHospital). Within service industries, these techniques were extended from what workers do to how they look, speak, and feel—emotion itself became a job duty, the "heart" managed (Hochschild, 1983). McDonaldizing has also spread to other countries, turning them into replicas of America. In the 1930s and 1940s these techniques homogenized workers; now they homogenize societies. We are heading for McPlanet.

The techniques for speeding up production complemented techniques for speeding up response to markets. Just-in-time inventory systems minimized carrying costs and enabled firms to adjust more quickly to changing market conditions. Flexible labour processes and labour markets created the just-in-time workforce: a small core of permanent, full-time employees and a large periphery of part-time, casual, on-call, temporary, and subcontracted workers. The same information technology that makes all this possible gathers information about employees and deposits it in human resource information systems, where worker performance is measured, described, evaluated, examined, and compared (Menzies, 1996: 109–130).

The ultimate in flexibility is the virtual organization, unencumbered with physical infrastructure, perfectly responsive to the changing needs of the market. Like the commodities they produce, virtual organizations are disposable. These, and other techniques, replace homogeneous products for mass markets with adaptable products for niche markets, large-scale with small-batch production.

Corporations no longer produce commodities and advertise them; they buy products and brand them. Branding is about creating synthetic emotions to sell commodities. They subcontract production to wherever costs are lowest, and this usually means a Third World country where unions are weak or non-existent.

Privatization, deregulation, and freer trade were the backdrop to these developments, making them possible by reducing the power of unions to resist. This was an effect of the Free Trade Agreement (FTA) between Canada and the United States and the North American Free Trade Agreement (NAFTA) among Canada, the United States, and Mexico, and the creation of the World Trade Organization (WTO) in 1995, a free trade club of 146 nations. Free trade tips the balance of power in favour of employers.

The Global Challenge

What are the key lessons of this review of Canadian labour history?

First, at the core of trade unionism is a tension between two contradictory tendencies: breadth, unity, and solidarity versus parochialism, sectionalism, and exclusiveness (Hyman, 1975: 41). This is true of each country's trade union structure; the differences lie in the forms this tension takes and how it is negotiated. Tension is evident today in the relationship between Canadian social unionism and the tradition of business unionism of U.S.-based international unions. The formation of the CAW, now Canada's largest private-sector union, in September 1985, through divorce from the United Auto Workers (UAW) is a good example of this. The CAW thinks of itself as a new form of unionism, not just a new union.

Second, there is a tension within capital: it atomizes as it organizes, it represses as it empowers, it creates poverty as it creates wealth (Marsden, 1999). The way that capital expands is through a process that the German sociologist Max Weber called "rationalization": the elimination from business of those human, emotional elements that escape calculation. Rationalization increases efficiency, but it also dehumanizes. McDonaldization is a good example of this. Unions, of course, have done much to alleviate the worst excesses of dehumanization, but a larger problem remains. Business "without regard for persons" creates social distance between causes and effects, intentions and consequences, rulers and ruled. This is an issue because the more rational the organization of action, the greater the social distance, and "the easier it is to cause suffering—and remain at peace with oneself" (Bauman, 1989: 155). As an example of moral blindness, "think of the workers of an armament plant who rejoice in the 'stay of execution' of their factory thanks to big new orders, while at the same time honestly bewailing the massacres visited upon each other by Ethiopians and Eritreans; or . . . think how it is possible that the 'fall in commodity prices' may be universally welcomed as good news while 'starvation of African children' is equally universally, and sincerely, lamented" (Bauman, 1989: 24).

Third, there is nothing new about globalization. Although it is true that we have recently experienced a wave of "space–time" compression (Harvey, 1989), capital has always used speed to tear down spatial barriers to commerce. Unions have always faced a highly mobile adversary—only the scale of their challenge changes. Globalization came to public attention, not because it was new, but because of the nature and degree of *opposition* to it, beginning, most evidently, at the third WTO Ministerial Conference, held in Seattle in December 1999.

Let me link together the contradictory tendencies of trade unionism, the moral dilemma posed by capital, and globalization. Think of the anti-globalization movement as a refreshing wave breaking against trade union structure, forcing and forging connections among remaining islands of sectionalism. It meshes with social unionism and direct action; a harbinger perhaps of a revived Wobbly movement in Canada and the United States.

It is significant that many anti-globalization activists are modernity's "emotional revolutionaries"—women (Giddens, 1992). They give flesh to Carol Gilligan's argument regarding women's "ethics of care": a different way of thinking about and acting on moral conflicts. Simplifying: where men see a hierarchy of rights and an injunction not to interfere with the rights of others, women see a web of relationships and a moral responsibility to discern and alleviate the real troubles of the world (Gilligan, 1982).

It is these activists who are forcing us to confront the connections between First World causes and Third World effects. Consider, for example, this from Naomi Klein: "for the [branding] system to function smoothly, workers must know little of the marketed lives of the products they produce and consumers must remain sheltered from the production lives of the brands they buy" (Klein, 2000: 347). Increasingly, in this information age, this is not the case. We can compare the image of the brand with the realities of production, the emotions of Western consumers with the emotions of Third World producers. There are no more excuses for moral blindness toward the needs of strangers. Globalization, Klein argues, citing Lorraine Dusky, "means that we are all our sisters' and brothers' keepers" (Klein, 2000: 349).

Questions

1. Describe the origins of merchant capital in Canada.
2. Describe the origins of the early unions in Canada.
3. Outline the events surrounding the Winnipeg General Strike.
4. Distinguish between craft and industrial unions.
5. What was the impact of Taylorism on union development?
6. Explain what is meant by the "McDonaldizing" of work.
7. What strategies might unions adopt to appeal to workers in the economy of the early 21st century?.

Weblinks

National Library of Canada Guide to Canadian Labour History Resources:
www.nlc-bnc.ca/2/26/h26-201-e.html

Canadian Committee on Labour History:
www.mun.ca/cclh/llt

Hudson's Bay Company Archives:
www.gov.mb.ca/chc/archives/hbca

Frederick Winslow Taylor (Stevens Institute of Technology Collection):
www.stevens.edu/library/collections/taylor/.html

Sam Gindin's *The Canadian Auto Workers: The Birth and Transformation of a Union*:
www.caw.ca/whoweare/ourhistory/cawhistory/index.html

Peoples' Global Action:
www.nadir.org/nadir/initiativ/agp/en/index.html

Industrial Workers of the World:
www.iww.org

Global Unions
www.global-unions.org

Union Network International:
www.union-network.org/UNIsite/dhtml/menu.html

International Confederation of Free Trade Unions:
www.icftu.org

Chapter 4

Unions: Membership, Structures, Actions, and Challenges

Gregor Murray

Consider three scenarios:

Union A is approached by a number of young nonunion workers from the local branch of a well-known hamburger chain. They are dissatisfied with working conditions, particularly the arbitrary allocation of shift schedules and the macho managers that the new franchise owner has brought in. Union A's leaders know that this is a good opportunity to break into an industry with a low level of unionization, high usage of temporary and part-time workers, minimum wages, and poor benefits. Yet they are wary of squandering scarce organizing resources, especially in the light of complaints from some of their union locals about the diversion of attention and funds away from existing bargaining units. The union leaders anticipate a fight to the finish. The hamburger chain has a history of opposing unionization, and the franchise owner could probably stall the process long enough for these young workers to lose interest in an industry where they are bound to work only a brief time. Further, the costs to Union A of servicing the needs of this small potential bargaining unit might never be matched by the union dues collected from these workers. The union is caught between a rock and a hard place: seeking to *organize the unorganized*, who really do aspire to a higher degree of dignity at work, but faced with poor prospects for meaningful success in the current legislative and social climate.

Union B is rocked by profound structural change. Only a decade ago, almost all of its members were covered by a single agreement in the public sector. Government cutbacks, restructuring, and privatization, as well as its own dynamism in reorganizing the members it has lost from the public sector, have transformed this landscape. Union B's members are now covered by multiple agreements in newly privatized agencies such as licensing companies, homecare workers, and a host of not-for-profit agencies. There are many more calls from members requesting advice and representation, and Union B's staff seems often on the verge of revolt because its servicing load is so heavy. Although the union has more than weathered the storm, it is looking at how to reorganize itself for this new economy. Should it decentralize the way that it serves its members by educating a new generation of workplace delegates or stewards to offer basic union services in the workplace? Or should it develop a call centre to offer instantaneous help and advice to all of its members, at the risk of losing its collective capacity in the workplace?

Union C's members are employed by multinational firms in manufacturing. Their jobs are threatened by possible company offshoring, some to lower-wage plants in Mexico, others to China. This problem is hardly new but the appreciation of the

Canadian dollar has made it more acute. Union C advocated a proactive policy to protect jobs and working conditions. In the 1990s, it championed RRSP-type worker investment funds to promote employment in its core industries. It pioneered worker retraining and participated in government-sponsored sector training councils. The union also was highly receptive to worker participation in new forms of work organization and had many successes in this regard. Yet there is a membership backlash, as high-involvement worksites are often *lean* and sometimes quite *mean*. Union C has many fewer members than it did a decade ago, and its members made wage concessions on several occasions in order to gain job security provisions and more involvement in workplace decisions. A new leadership is coming of age and, at the possible risk to future investments, its supporters want it to take a much more militant stance on wage increases and job security.

The three scenarios above are snapshots of the challenges faced by Canadian unions. Servicing the needs of existing membership is an urgent matter, but the long-term survival of unions depends on their ability to recruit new members. There is considerable stress on union structures that appear out of sync with the new economy. There are strategic conundrums in the search for the right blend of short-term defensive goals to protect working conditions and wages of current members and the advocacy role of promoting policies for better workplaces and communities. Like so many organizations, unions have multiple mandates but limited resources.

There are approximately 4.2 million union members in Canada, distributed among roughly 1500 union locals. These union members represent 29.7 percent of non-agricultural paid workers (excluding self-employed and unemployed). They negotiate the terms and conditions of employment of these workers and undoubtedly exert spillover influence on the employment conditions of many other workers. Union representatives are present in a wide variety of public and private bodies in Canada concerned with labour market and social questions, ranging from health and safety at work to pay equity, training, pension management, and economic adjustment. Unions are among the more important social actors in the Canadian labour market.

This chapter describes union organizations and their actions, while highlighting both the great diversity of Canadian unions and the challenges they are currently experiencing. The first part concerns the different dimensions of union membership: growth trends, international comparisons, distribution of union members, and pressures on union membership. The second part of the chapter looks at the structure of unions and their internal governance. The final part reviews union actions, both economic and political.

UNION MEMBERSHIP AND COLLECTIVE BARGAINING COVERAGE

Faced with significant structural adjustments over the last three decades, unions represent a diminishing proportion of the labour force in many industrialized Western economies. The recent history of Canadian unionism both confirms and confounds this trend. In relative terms, union membership in Canada grew more quickly than the non-agricultural labour force from the mid-1960s to the mid-1980s.

This trend stabilized in the last half of the 1980s and reversed in the last half of the 1990s, resulting in a decline in union membership density, expressed as a percentage of non-agricultural paid workers (see Table 4.1). The Canadian pattern is particularly remarkable when compared with declining fortunes of the neighbouring U.S. labour movement: Canadian unions have performed well in comparison to their U.S. counterparts. However, this should not negate the significance of the pressures—many featured in the opening vignettes—currently operating on union membership.

Union membership and relative union presence is estimated using two key measures: union *membership* and collective bargaining *coverage*. The former refers to the number of individuals who are members of a union, the latter to all persons whose terms and conditions of employment are determined by a union through collective bargaining and who may or may not be union members. Collective bargaining coverage tends to be a couple of percentage points higher than the membership rate.

Several sources of such information depend on different methods of data collection and reporting periods. This chapter draws on the two principal sources of information. First, Human Resources and Social Development Canada (HRSDC), formerly known as Labour Canada, conducts an annual survey of union membership (HRSDC and Labour Policy and Workplace Information). Unions' reports of their own level of membership are compiled to give an overview of union membership as a whole (see Table 4.1). This series provides a good historical overview as well as more detailed information on each of the reporting union organizations. However, it is subject to the problems of self-reporting. Second, since the beginning of 1997, Statistics Canada has included questions on union membership and bargaining coverage in its monthly Labour Force Survey (LFS). This is a principal data source because it uses a detailed survey of individual experience in the labour market also used to provide estimates of employment and unemployment (see Akyeampong, 1997, 1999; Statistics Canada, 2007). While this kind of survey can provide only an estimate, the survey is reputed to be accurate and also permits more detailed breakdowns by regional, economic, and socio-demographic characteristics. Some provinces also produce data on provincial union movements based on analysis of collective agreements or surveys of unions.

Thus union membership figures vary according to the type of measure and the source of data. Readers should be aware that this is also the case in this chapter and throughout this book. The key distinction in measuring union membership is between *absolute levels of union membership* (how many individuals the unions represent), and the *relative levels of union membership* (the proportion of represented workers in relation to some measurement of all workers).

The absolute measure poses three problems. First, the surveys generally exclude small, independent local organizations, and they sometimes exclude professional groupings, such as police and firefighters' associations, that perform union functions. Second, the absolute number does not include workers who are not members of a union but on whose behalf a union negotiates. In 2007, for example, it was estimated that actual union membership accounted for 93.4 percent of persons covered by collective agreements (calculated from Statistics Canada, 2007). Third, union reporting may create problems because not all unions have accurate membership-tracking systems. Union membership can fluctuate during the course of a year. Further, unions may under- or over-report their membership in order to increase their importance or reduce their financial obligations in affiliation fees.

Table 4.1 Canadian Union Membership, 1911–2006

Year	Membership (thousands)	Membership as a Percentage of Non-agricultural Paid Workers
1911	133	—
1916	160	—
1921	313	16.0
1926	275	12.0
1931	311	15.3
1936	323	16.2
1941	462	18.0
1946	832	27.9
1951	1029	28.4
1956	1352	33.3
1961	1447	31.6
1966	1736	30.7
1971	2231	32.4
1976	3042	36.9
1981	3487	36.7
1986	3730	37.7
1991	4068	36.3
1996	4033	34.3
2001	4111	30.9
2002	4174	30.6
2003	4178	29.9
2004	4261	29.9
2005	4381	30.3
2006	4441	30.0

Note: Data on union membership for the years 1911 to 1946 are as of December 31. Thereafter, they refer to January 1 of each year.

Sources: 1911 to 1966: Dion, 1986; 1971 to 1986: Labour Canada, 1994; 1991 to 2006: Workplace Information Directorate, HRSDC, 2007.

The relative measure of union membership, usually referred to as *union density*, expresses the proportion of the labour force that is unionized. If expressed as a proportion of the total civilian labour force, which includes all of those persons who are either employed, self-employed, or seeking employment, then the rate of unionization is lower than if expressed as the proportion of paid workers (LFS survey) or non-agricultural paid workers (HRSDC survey). Union density usually is expressed in terms of the latter two measures to facilitate comparisons between countries with varying degrees of industrialization, and because they provide a more accurate gauge of potential union membership. However, density is still not entirely accurate since most Canadian jurisdictions restrict certain categories of employees from unionizing (e.g., managers and supervisory personnel). At the beginning of 2006, HRSDC numbers estimated that 30.0 percent of paid non-agricultural workers were union members (Table 4.1). The LFS survey found that the rate of collective bargaining coverage in 2007 was 31.8 percent of paid employment with a union membership rate of 29.7 percent (Statistics Canada, 2007).

Absolute membership figures reflect the relative health of unions, especially in terms of dues income and levels of organizing. Indicators of relative union membership are especially useful for understanding the penetration of unions in different industries and occupations. These two measures should be understood as complements because they express different aspects of union membership activity (Bain and Price, 1983: 4). For instance, as sometimes occurs during downturns in economic activity, union density might actually increase while union membership declines or remains stable.

When we compare Canadian union growth with that of other industrialized economies, only the union movements in Ireland, Norway, the Netherlands, Belgium, and Spain also registered an absolute growth in union membership in the 1990–2003 period. The aggregate membership performance of Canadian trade unions thus contrasts markedly with the more significant declines in countries such as Australia, Japan, the United Kingdom, the United States, and a variety of Eastern European states (Visser, 2006).

What about variation within Canada? Absolute union membership in all provinces increased significantly over the last two decades, but there are significant differences from one province to another (Table 4.2). At one end of the scale, the province of Newfoundland and Labrador consistently exhibits the highest union density (36.6 percent), followed by Quebec (35.8 percent). Alberta has the lowest union density (22.3 percent).

Three explanations might account for these differences. First, differing industrial structures exist. Employment in Newfoundland and Labrador, for example, is concentrated

Table 4.2 Union Density by Province, 2007

Province	Union Density (%)	Province	Union Density (%)
Newfoundland and Labrador	36.6	Ontario	26.8
Prince Edward Island	29.5	Manitoba	35.9
Nova Scotia	28.9	Saskatchewan	33.4
New Brunswick	27.1	Alberta	22.3
Quebec	35.8	British Columbia	31.0

Note: Union density is calculated on the basis of union membership and the number of paid workers.

Source: Adapted from Statistics Canada, *Perspectives on Labour and Income*, Catalogue 75-001 XIE, August 2007, vol. 8, no. 8.

in strongly unionized industries. Second, expansion and contraction of regional labour markets also plays a role. In Ontario, the aggregate union membership growth has not kept pace with the rapid expansion of the labour market. Finally, there are important differences in community attitudes to unionism that, despite initial differences in industrial structure, spill over into assessments of the acceptability of unionism. The rate of unionization in large metropolitan areas varies greatly from one area to another. While industrial structure clearly explains some variation, differences in community attitudes about the benefits of unionism also play a role. (For a study of this phenomenon in Edmonton and Winnipeg, see Krahn and Lowe, 1984.)

Canadian vs. U.S. Union Membership

The contrasting fortunes of trade unions in Canada and the United States over the last two decades have sparked considerable research comparing the circumstances of the two labour movements (Godard, 2003).

Table 4.3 gives an overview of the post–World War II evolution of union membership in the two countries. Whereas they displayed similar patterns of growth throughout the first half of the 20th century, they began to diverge sharply in the mid-1960s. Union membership in the United States has diminished in both absolute and relative terms over the past three decades, falling from over 20 million (29.1 percent density) at the beginning of the 1970s to 15.4 million (12.0 percent density) in 2006. Union density in Canada is now considerably more than twice that of the United States. Moreover, there is a substantial differential in the rate of unionization in all sectors.

The explanation for this divergence appears related to supply rather than demand factors. On the demand side, there is increasing evidence that a substantial minority of nonunion workers in both the United States and Canada indicate an interest in joining a union. In a 1996 comparative survey, Lipset and Meltz (1997) found that 47 percent of nonunion workers in the United States and 33 percent of nonunion workers in Canada would vote for unionization at the workplace. On the supply side, there is considerable evidence that Canadian workers have, for a variety of reasons, easier access to unionization. Many American scholars and union leaders point to contrasting public policies as one of the principal explanations for the union density differences. They argue that the revival of trade union fortunes in the United States is contingent on securing substantial changes in public policy (Weiler, 1984; Block, 1993). It also has been suggested that Canadian unions have been more innovative (Kumar and Schenk, 2006), pursued new organizing with more vigour than their American counterparts (Rose and Chaison, 1990), achieved political change and favourable public policy more effectively (Bruce, 1989), and pursued a broader social agenda over a longer period (Piore, 1983; Robinson, 1998). However, aggregate union membership in the United States recorded a very slight increase from 1996 to 2001 (see Table 4.3)—the first in the past several decades—but has continued to decline in most years since then. This change, however modest, might be associated with a new emphasis on the importance of organizing new members as opposed to servicing existing members (see Bronfenbrenner et al., 1998; Nissen, 1999). This new emphasis is one of the tensions, moreover, that led to the creation in 2005 of a breakaway of seven major affiliates of the AFL–CIO to create a new central labour body known as "Change to Win" (Masters et al., 2006).

Table 4.3 Union Membership and Density in Canada and the United States, 1946–2006

Year	Canada		United States	
	MEMBERSHIP (THOUSANDS)	PERCENTAGE OF NON-AGRICULTURAL PAID WORKERS	MEMBERSHIP (THOUSANDS)	PERCENTAGE OF NON-AGRICULTURAL PAID WORKERS
1946	832	27.9	12 254	30.4
1951	1029	28.4	15 139	31.7
1956	1352	33.3	16 446	31.4
1961	1447	31.6	15 401	28.5
1966	1736	30.7	18 922	29.6
1971	2231	32.4	20 711	29.1
1976	3042	36.9	22 153	27.9
1981	3487	36.7	20 647	22.6
1986	3730	37.7	16 975	17.1
1991	4068	36.3	16 568	15.3
1996	4033	34.3	16 269	14.5
2001	4111	30.9	16 387	13.4
2002	4174	30.6	16 145	13.3
2003	4178	29.9	15 776	12.9
2004	4261	29.9	15 472	12.5
2005	4381	30.3	15 685	12.5
2006	4441	30.0	15 359	12.0

Source: HRSDC and BLS (annual).

Some authors suggest that, because of the increasing integration of the Canadian and U.S. economies, there will be increasing pressures to bring Canada's favourable legislative climate for unions more in line with the American treatment (Robinson, 1994). One such example was the unsuccessful attempt to bring American-style right-to-work legislation to the province of Alberta in the mid-1990s (Ponak and Taras, 1997). It has also been argued that the cohesive labour relations associated with high levels of union density in many small nations, for example, in Scandinavian economies, can be a source of competitive advantage (Freeman, 1990).

Minority views in this Canada–U.S. convergence–divergence debate should be noted. Troy (2000), in particular, has argued that the divergence between the American and Canadian union movements has been greatly exaggerated by the failure to take into account the greater size of the public sector in Canada and the fact that union movements in both private sectors are in decline. Although this effect is difficult to disentangle fully, Riddell (1993: 133) has estimated that only 7 percent of the gap between U.S. and Canadian unionization rates is accounted for by the greater proportion of the Canadian workforce in the public sector, and Godard (2003) has written a full rebuttal of Troy's position. Moreover, the differences in union density between the United States and Canada are just as great in the private and the public sectors.

Distribution of Union Membership

Union membership is not evenly distributed throughout the economy. There are significant variations by socio-demographic characteristics, industry, occupation, firm size, and employment status.

A first source of variation is by sex (see Table 4.4). Historically, the rate of unionization among women was less than that among men. However, this trend has been reversed. Currently, 30.0 percent of women, as opposed to 29.3 percent of men, were union members in 2007. This represents a significant change since the 1960s. In 1962, women

Table 4.4 Union Membership and Collective Bargaining Coverage by Sex, Age, Employment Status, and Establishment Size, 2007

	UNION MEMBERSHIP (PERCENTAGE)	COLLECTIVE BARGAINING COVERAGE (PERCENTAGE)
Sex		
Male	29.3	31.7
Female	30.0	32.0
Age		
15–24	13.3	15.0
25–44	29.8	32.1
45–54	38.3	40.7
55 and older	35.1	37.4
Employment Status		
Part-time	22.9	24.6
Full-time	31.2	33.5
Establishment Size		
Less than 20 employees	13.1	14.7
20–99 employees	30.0	32.3
100–499 employees	41.1	43.8
500 or more employees	51.2	53.8
Total	29.7	31.8

Source: Adapted from Statistics Canada, *Perspectives on Labour and Income*, Catalogue 75-001 XIE, August 2007, vol. 8, no. 8.

constituted only 15.4 percent of all union members. This percentage increased steadily: to 23.5 percent in 1971; 31 percent in 1981; 40.6 percent in 1991; and slightly more than 50 percent in 2007. Moreover, while male union membership has grown very slowly over the last two decades, female union membership has increased substantially. For example, from 1983 to 1995, male union membership increased by only 1.5 percent, while female union membership increased by 41.9 percent (calculated from Mainville and Olineck, 1999). Thus, underlying a relative stability in union membership is an increasing feminization of the union movement that has significant implications for the character of unions in Canada (see White, 1993; Briskin and McDermott, 1993; Yates, 2005).

Considerable variations also exist in the degree of unionization by industry (see Table 4.5). According to 2007 Statistics Canada figures, workers in the education sector have, by far, the highest union density (67.8 percent). They are followed by other industries characterized by a high degree of public ownership or regulation: public administra-

Table 4.5 Union Density by Industry and Sector, 2007

INDUSTRY	ESTIMATED MEMBERSHIP (THOUSANDS)	UNION DENSITY (%)
Goods-producing	1009	30.4
Agriculture	4	3.5
Natural resources	58	20.2
Utilities	87	66.7
Construction	222	30.6
Manufacturing	535	27.5
Service-producing	3274	30.1
Trade	304	12.9
Transportation and warehousing	281	41.7
Finance, insurance, real estate, and leasing	85	9.7
Professional, scientific, and technical	32	4.3
Management, administrative, and support	67	12.9
Education	797	67.8
Health care and social assistance	855	53.3
Information, culture, and recreation	161	25.1
Accommodation and food	71	7.4
Other	50	10.3
Public administration	567	67.6
Total	4184	29.7
Sector		
Public	2335	71.7
Private	1841	17.0

Note: The totals are variable because of the estimating procedure.

Source: Adapted from Statistics Canada, *Perspectives on Labour and Income*, Catalogue 75-001 XIE, August 2007, vol. 8, no. 8.

tion, utilities, and health care and social assistance. The private service industries remain little unionized (accommodation and food, for instance, with only 7.4 percent).

Manufacturing, which traditionally has been highly unionized, has experienced both an absolute decline in union membership and a relative decline in union density over the last two decades, falling from 44.3 percent in 1982 to 38.4 percent in 1995 (CALURA) and 27.5 percent in 2007 (LFS). Indeed, the most significant change in union composition over the past two decades has been the declining proportion of union members in manufacturing and the increasing proportion of public-sector workers in the union movement. In 2007, 12.8 percent of union members came from manufacturing, while 55.8 percent were in public services such as health, education, and public administration.

The least unionized industries include those that have been growing most quickly. Thus, only 12.9 percent of wholesale and retail workers are unionized, and union density falls to 9.7 percent in the finance sector. It should be emphasized that the degree of unionization in these two sectors has increased steadily over the past two decades, but the penetration of unions remains extremely weak. This poses a significant challenge for the labour movement because its areas of relative strength seem to be those that are now either in relative decline (manufacturing, primary industries) or facing cutbacks (the public sector). As the employment structure continues to shift toward private services, the future of the Canadian union movement, in many ways, hinges on its ability to navigate this change.

These sectoral differences in the degree of unionization of industries also are apparent by occupational category. Much higher percentages of union members occur in some occupations than in others. Traditional jobs in manufacturing, construction, and transport tend to be highly unionized. Unions also have significant presence among professional and technical job categories in the public sector. For example, 86.8 percent of elementary and secondary school teachers, 81.2 percent of nurses, and 56.5 percent of technical staff in health services are unionized. By contrast, only 8.3 percent of managerial employees, 7.8 percent of food and beverage employees, and 12.3 percent of retail food employees are members of a union (Statistics Canada, 2007).

Firm size also matters (see Table 4.4). While the overall level of collective bargaining coverage was 31.8 percent of paid workers in 2007, this figure was only 14.7 percent for firms with less than 20 employees, gradually increasing with firm size to a high of 53.8 percent for establishments with more than 500 employees. Fully 51.5 percent of workers covered by a collective agreement worked in firms of 100 or more employees, even though only 34.4 percent of paid employees worked in such firms. It is well known that unions have a more difficult time, or less interest, in securing their presence in smaller firms.

Employment status also exerts an important effect. More full-time workers (those working more than 30 hours per week) tend to be unionized than are part-time workers. Collective bargaining coverage for full-time workers was 33.5 percent in 2007, as opposed to 24.6 percent for part-time workers (Table 4.4). This differential constitutes a challenge for unions because part-time employment accounts for an increasingly important share (18.5 percent) of overall employment in Canada.

Pressures on Union Membership

If Canadian unions have performed fairly well relative to other labour movements, the pressures operating on them are nonetheless very intense. Employment areas in which unions traditionally have been most representative are shrinking, while the areas in which unions have only a tenuous foothold are growing.

There is considerable evidence that the Canadian union movement has been highly adaptable and fairly inventive over the last decade. Several indicators point in this direction: the overall growth in aggregate union membership, continuing high levels of recruitment activity, the entry of women into the unionized labour market, and some limited successes in obtaining changes in provincial labour laws that facilitate organizing. However, there is also some evidence of a drop in the rate of organizing in the context of less favourable provincial labour laws (for example, in Ontario; see Yates, 2000) and a move to less favourable organizing provisions in some other provinces (for example, in Saskatchewan). The national campaign to unionize Wal-Mart stores in Canada illustrates some of the difficulties inherent in the organizing climate as local success in securing certifications, notably in Quebec, has encountered determined employer resistance and a capacity to exhaust a wide variety of judicial avenues (see Adams, 2005).

UNION STRUCTURE

Union structure is composed of several basic building blocks: the certification unit, the union local, the national or international union, the central labour body or congress, and affiliations to international labour organizations by any one of these other levels of union structure.

Components of Union Structure

The cornerstone of all union structures in Canada is the *certification unit* or *appropriate bargaining unit*. This is the defined group of workers for which a labour board or other similar administrative body grants exclusive bargaining rights to a designated agent (a union), after a majority of those workers have indicated support for union representation. (See Chapter 8.) Bargaining units in Canada generally are quite small, and bargaining is highly decentralized. With the notable exception of the public sector, the norm is the negotiation of a single agreement between an employer and a union for a single site. The focus of union activity usually is at the level of the certification unit, unlike many European unions that engage in national-level, centralized bargaining.

Canadian decentralization is further exacerbated by the division of powers over labour matters within the Canadian federation. Roughly 8.4 percent of Canadian workers fall under federal jurisdiction. The other 91.6 percent are subject to different provincial jurisdictions whose labour codes may vary considerably (Arthurs, 2006: 8).

Despite this decentralization, the certification unit is most frequently also part of a larger union structure. A *union local* may be made up of one or more such certification units. There were roughly 15 500 such locals in Canada in 2006. Union locals in industries such as construction typically are made up of multiple certification units. In large manufacturing establishments, on the other hand, a union local generally consists of a single certification unit. Union locals have their own form of governance with bylaws, rules of procedure, and periodic elections.

Some locals are highly autonomous. Indeed, there are many independent union locals in Canada that have no form of affiliation. Approximately 3.6 percent of union members belong to such locals (HRSDC, 2007). Typical examples would include the

Sunoco Employees' Bargaining Association, the Lethbridge Police Association, and the West Vancouver Municipal Employees' Association.

Most union locals are part of a larger structure (see Table 4.6). A union local typically is chartered by a *national* or *international union organization* from which it receives its name and its statutes. For example, Local 444 of the Canadian Auto Workers Union (CAW) organizes Chrysler employees in Windsor. It is a constituent unit of the national union and is governed in accordance with the national union's constitution.

National and international unions organize and charter locals in the industries or professions defined by their constitutions or policies. This is known as a union's *jurisdiction*.

For example, the United Steelworkers of America organized workers in mining, metal transformation, and some areas of manufacturing across North America. The United Brotherhood of Carpenters and Joiners of America organized carpenters in the building trades. The Canadian Union of Postal Workers organized workers of Canada Post. As we will see below, these well-defined jurisdictions are blurring as unions seek to diversify their membership base. There were 246 national and international unions operating in Canada at the beginning of 2006 (HRSDC, 2007). In 2006, the 15 largest (those totalling more than 55 000 members) accounted for 59.2 percent of all union members in Canada (see Table 4.7).

Most, but not all, of these unions are, in turn, affiliated with *central labour bodies* or *congresses*. For instance, the Canadian Auto Workers Union, a national union, is affiliated with the Canadian Labour Congress (CLC). The United Brotherhood of Carpenters and Joiners of America, an international union, is affiliated with Change to Win (CTW) in the United States and with the CLC in Canada. The Steelworkers is affiliated with the AFL–CIO in the United States and with the CLC in Canada.

Table 4.6 Union Membership by Congress Affiliation, 2006

	LOCALS	MEMBERSHIP	PERCENTAGE OF MEMBERSHIP
Canadian Labour Congress (CLC)	11 640[a]	3 197 600	72.0
Confédération des syndicats nationaux (CSN–CNTU)	1850	284 280	6.4
Centrale des syndicats du Québec (CSQ)	314	123 510	2.8
Centrale des syndicats démocratiques (CSD)	100	59 160	1.3
AFL–CIO only	39	74 650	1.7
Confederation of Canadian Unions (CCU)	25	9390	0.2
Unaffiliated national unions	1503	531 720	12.0
Unaffiliated international unions	8	2150	0.0
Independent local organizations	269	158 085	3.6
Total	15 479	4 441 000	100.0

[a] CLC includes 3663 locals with both CLC and AFL–CIO affiliations.

Source: Published in "Union Membership in Canada–2006," Human Resources and Social Development Canada, 2006. Reproduced with permission of Minister of Public Works and Government Services Canada 2008.

Table 4.7 Largest Unions in Canada and Their Affiliations, 2006

RANKING (SIZE)	UNION ORGANIZATION	WEBSITE	MEMBERSHIP (thousands)	(as % of total union membership)
1	Canadian Union of Public Employees—CUPE (CLC)	www.cupe.ca	548	12.3
2	National Union of Public and General Employees—NUPGE (CLC)	www.nupge.ca	337	7.6
3	United Steel, Paper and Forestry, Rubber, Manufacturing, Energy, Allied Industrial and Service Workers International Union—(AFL–CIO/CLC)	www.uswa.ca	280	6.3
4	National Automobile, Aerospace, Transportation and General Workers Union of Canada—CAW—CANADS (CLC)	www.caw.ca	265	6.0
5	United Food and Commercial Workers Canada—UFCW (CLC)	www.ufcw.ca	233	5.2
6	Public Service Alliance of Canada—PSAC (CLC)	www.psac.com	162	3.6
7	Communications, Energy and Paperworkers Union—CEP (CLC)	www.cep.ca	150.0	3.4
8	International Brotherhood of Teamsters—IBT (AFL–CIO/CLC)	www.teamsters.ca	120	2.7
9	Fédération de la santé et des services sociaux—FSSS (CSN)	www.fsss.qc.ca	114	2.6
10	Service Employees International Union—SEIU (AFL–CIO/CLC)	www.seiu.ca	85	1.9
11	Fédération des syndicats de l'enseignement—FSE (CEQ)	www.fse.qc.net	82	1.8
12	Laborers' International Union of North America	www.laborersinternational.net	72	1.6
13	Elementary Teachers' Federation of Ontario—ETFO (IND.)	www.etfo.on.ca	69	1.6
14	International Brotherhood of Electrical Workers—IBEW (AFL–CIO/CLC)	www.ibew.org	57	1.3
15	Fédération interprofessionnelle de la santé du Québec—FIQ	www.fiqsante.qc.ca		
	Total of the largest unions (55 000 or more members)		2630	59.2
	Smaller unions (fewer than 55 000 members)		1811	40.8
	Total of all unions		**4441.0**	**100.0**

Source: Published in "Union Membership in Canada–2006," Human Resources and Social Development Canada, 2006. Reproduced with permission of Minister of Public Works and Government Services Canada, 2008.

These central labour bodies have both a national presence and, in the case of the CLC, a significant provincial and territorial presence in the form of 12 provincial and territorial federations of labour. Provincial federations organize congress affiliates in their provinces and represent union interests at the provincial government level (which, it should be recalled, is capable of passing labour legislation covering 90 percent of Canadian employees). In Quebec there also are several autonomous central labour bodies or confederations, notably the Confédération des syndicats nationaux (CSN) and the Centrale des syndicats du Québec (CSQ).

Labour congresses or confederations also are present at district or regional levels. In the case of CLC affiliates, 136 *district* or *local labour councils* coordinate the activities of congress locals in a particular district, for example, the Peterborough and District Labour Council or the Saskatoon and District Labour Council. In Quebec, the Conseils centraux play a similar role for CSN affiliates.

These central labour bodies, as well as many of the national and international unions associated with them, generally maintain *international affiliations*. Both the Canadian Labour Congress and the Confédération des syndicats nationaux are affiliated with the International Trade Union Confederation (ITUC), a grouping of 305 national trade union centres and affiliated organizations in 153 countries and territories. Note that the ITUC was created at its founding congress in Vienna in November 2006 when two previously rival organizations (the International Confederation of Free Trade Unions and the World Confederation of Labour) overcame longstanding differences to create a single global labour confederation that represents most national labour organizations in the world. National and international unions also are affiliated with various international labour federations that operate in particular industries or sectors. For example, many of the public-sector unions in Canada, such as the National Union of Public and General Employees (NUPGE), are affiliated with the Public Services International (PSI).

International labour linkages are increasingly important. National union leaders now coordinate their own meetings to coincide with the G-8 summit meeting of the eight largest industrial nations, and union representatives are active participants in coalition meetings held to coincide with regional and international free trade issues. Similarly, the international labour federations, or what are increasingly being called global union federations (GUF), play a more active role in international labour solidarity issues affecting particular industries. This can take the form of cross-border support for strike action in some part of a multinational or transnational firm. Global unions also are interested in negotiating framework agreements that set out core labour standards and principles, such as those promoted by the International Labour Organization, that apply to all of the locations of a particular company throughout the world and sometimes even to its suppliers (Hammer, 2005). For example, after a long campaign by an alliance of national and international unions in its core industry, Quebecor World, a global printing company headquartered in Montreal, signed such a framework agreement with Union Network International (UNI) in May 2007.

The next sections focus in more detail on the three most important levels of union structure: labour congresses, national and international union organizations, and union locals.

Central Labour Congresses

The Canadian Labour Congress (CLC) is the principal central labour congress in Canada. It represented 3.2 million members at the beginning of 2006, approximately 72.0 percent of Canadian union members. There were 98 national and international unions affiliated with the CLC, each paying affiliation fees to the CLC on a per-member basis. The CLC also has a very small number of directly chartered locals, but the major form of affiliation is still through national and international labour organizations. It is the unions and not the CLC or its provincial federations that provide the bulk of direct services to members. Although the CLC experimented with recruitment in the financial sector in the 1970s, labour congresses usually do not negotiate for their members or recruit new members. That is the role of their affiliated organizations.

Labour congresses thus focus on policy-making activities in the social, economic, and political spheres. CLC representatives participate in a number of national and international bodies to deal with issues such as training, unemployment insurance, and social policy. Provincial federations do likewise at the provincial level. Only the Quebec Federation of Labour, whose distinct status within the Congress was first recognized in 1974 and further clarified at the 1994 CLC convention, tends to assume other roles normally reserved for affiliates, such as the coordination of sectoral bargaining in the Quebec public sector and construction industry.

Affiliated unions zealously maintain their autonomy, and the CLC has very weak formal authority over the activities of its affiliates. Given this weak integration and the Congress's relative lack of financial resources, coordination between the Congress and its principal affiliates depends on consensus building on policy issues and on persuading the affiliates to commit resources to particular campaigns. However, because of increasing conflicts among affiliates involving jurisdictional issues, the CLC has bolstered its disciplinary powers. It has become more difficult for a union local to switch its allegiance from one national or international union to another. This change was driven particularly by a bitter dispute in the Maritimes' fishing industry between the United Food and Commercial Workers Union (UFCW) and the CAW over the decision of how many UFCW certification units to transfer to the CAW. There have been many other inter-union conflicts over jurisdiction.

The CLC is governed by an executive council that is elected at the triennial convention by union local delegates. The president, two vice-presidents, and the secretary-treasurer hold full-time positions. Kenneth Georgetti, who previously had been president of the British Columbia Federation of Labour, was first elected president in 1999 and re-elected in 2002 and 2005. Other members of the CLC executive usually are senior officers of major affiliated unions. Several positions are reserved for women union leaders and representatives of visible minorities. The executive and its subcommittees meet at regular intervals between triennial congresses to formulate and implement CLC policy.

The Confédération des syndicats nationaux (CSN) is the second-largest congress. Formerly a confessional or Catholic union movement, but fully secular since the early 1960s, its membership is largely from Quebec. It recently integrated a significant unit of almost 6000 correctional officers who work throughout Canada. As a rule, and unlike for many CLC affiliates in other provinces, certification is vested solely within the union local (Verge and Murray, 1991: 62). Union locals then affiliate directly to the CSN as well as to one of its nine industrial or sectoral federations and to one of its regional councils (Conseils centraux). That means union locals are free to re-affiliate with other labour centrals should they become dissatisfied with their representation or services. Particularly in the public sector, there is considerable movement back and forth between different affiliations at the beginning of each bargaining round.

Like the CLC, the CSN is administered by a number of full-time executive officers elected at a triennial congress. Its industrial federations do likewise. Unlike the CLC, but like some of the continental European labour congresses, the degree of vertical and horizontal integration of locals within the CSN is highly developed, with meetings bringing together different affiliates at regular intervals.

The Canadian union movement became increasingly fragmented in the 1980s and early 1990s. This was the result of two factors: first, continued increases in membership of non-affiliated unions, particularly those representing professionals in the health and education sector; and, second, the 1982 breakaway from the CLC of a number of U.S.-based affiliated unions, especially in the construction trades, to form the Canadian Federation of Labour (CFL). The CFL took a more conservative approach to union political involvement and social change than that developed by the CLC. At its peak, the CFL represented roughly 200 000 members. Faced with continued membership and financial pressures, it ceased its activities in 1997, and many of its former affiliates have rejoined the CLC. At the same time, faced with continued public-sector restructuring, a number of unaffiliated public-sector unions have affiliated with the CLC and its provincial labour federations both out of a sense of common cause with other public-sector unions and to become more visible publicly. Thus the increasing fragmentation of central union structures has largely been reversed.

Other labour congresses in Canada include the Centrale des syndicats du Québec (CSQ), a confederation of Quebec public-sector unions located primarily in the field of education; the Centrale des syndicats démocratiques (CSD), a small grouping of Quebec unions that broke away from the CSN in the early 1970s; and the Confederation of Canadian Unions (CCU), a loose grouping of independent local Canadian unions with a specific nationalist perspective.

National and International Unions

In terms of the organization of resources and the development of strategies, national and international unions undoubtedly are the most significant organizational level. Major decisions about bargaining, recruitment, and political activity are made here. As befits the decentralization of the Canadian labour movement, national and international unions in Canada are highly diverse in their structures and policies.

Table 4.7 lists unions with more than 55 000 members at the beginning of 2006, as well as their affiliations and websites. By far the largest is the Canadian Union of Public Employees (CUPE) with roughly 548 000 members in a wide variety of public-sector occupations in municipal employment, public and private transport, and health and education. This is a complex organization with a national office, provincial and often district offices, a national executive board and several full-time executive officers, hundreds of union employees including support staff, a wide range of specialists at its Ottawa headquarters, and a large number of field staff.

The National Union of Public and General Employees (NUPGE) is the second-largest union. Unlike other large national and international unions that provide the bulk of services to their members, NUPGE is, in fact, a federation of highly autonomous provincial government employees' unions. The Public Service Alliance of Canada (PSAC) is the sixth-largest union and represents federal government employees. The United Steel, Paper and Forestry, Rubber, Manufacturing, Energy, Allied Industrial and Service Workers International Union and the United Food and Commercial Workers Canada are the two largest international unions in Canada. Both organize primarily in the private sector. The Canadian Auto Workers (CAW) and Communications, Energy and Paperworkers Union (CEP) are the largest private-sector national unions.

By international standards, one of the peculiar features of Canadian unionism has been the interpenetration of Canadian and American union structures. Indeed, among industrialized economies, only Ireland and Britain contain this same tight linkage of union structures. The high Canada–U.S. economic integration created spillovers of both craft (AFL) and industrial (CIO) unionism from the United States to Canada. A large proportion of Canadian union members once belonged to such "international" unions. An important trend has been the relative decline in the proportion of international or American unionism. At the beginning of 2006, only 28.5 percent of Canadian union members belonged to U.S.-headquartered unions (HRSDC, 2007). By contrast, in 1969, 65 percent of Canadian union members belonged to U.S.-based unions. Thus, the importance of international unionism in Canada has experienced almost a complete reversal.

National unions have been growing faster than international unions, particularly because of the spread of unionization in the public sector, where almost all union members belong to national unions. There also have been significant breakaways from parent U.S. unions, for example, the CAW's dramatic 1985 split from the United Auto Workers. The move toward greater Canadian autonomy also occurred in other industries, notably in communications and paper in the 1970s and in breweries, woodworking, and energy in the 1980s.

The Canadianization wave has not always resulted in secession by Canadian affiliates from American unions. The trend has been toward more self-governance by Canadian members of international unions (Thompson and Blum, 1983). From the early 1970s, the CLC adopted a set of minimum standards for the governance of Canadian union members by Canadians. These included provisions on the election of Canadian officers by Canadians, the right to determine policies that deal with national affairs and to speak for their unions in Canada, separate affiliations with international union bodies, and freedom from constitutional or policy constraints to full participation in the Canadian community.

International unions remain a significant feature of Canadian union structure. Of the 15 largest unions listed in Table 4.7, six are international and nine are national. As workers strive to construct cross-border alliances to deal with common problems in the context of the internationalization of production and services, not only are many forms of international unionism likely to endure but new forms are emerging as unions, both national and international, engage in increased contacts with unionists in other countries. For example, three unions, including the Steelworkers (USWA) present in both the United States and Canada, and Amicus and the Transport and General Workers Union, which are both major unions in the UK, announced their intention to form a first major transatlantic superunion in April 2007.

Unions have a wide variety of internal structures that reflect the evolution of partic- ular visions of territorial, occupational, and industrial solidarities as well as administrative arrangements for providing services to members. The great historical conflict was, of course, between craft unionism, which favoured occupational solidarities, and industrial unionism, which sought to organize workers on the basis of industries. Most unions con- tinue to be based on either an occupational or industrial principle. For most unions, how- ever, these organizing jurisdictions have become increasingly blurred over time. Changes in the sectoral distribution of employment have had profound effects on these organizing principles. A significant modification in union structure is thus underway.

First, many previously single-industry unions are involved in mergers. In 1992, for example, three major industrial unions—the Canadian Paperworkers Union, the Communications and Electrical Workers of Canada, and the Energy and Chemical Workers Union—merged to create a single new union: the Communications, Energy and Paperworkers Union of Canada (CEP). The Canadian Auto Workers has been extremely active, merging successively in the 1990s with several unions: the Canadian Association of Industrial Mechanical and Allied Workers; the United Electrical, Radio and Machine Workers of Canada; the Marconi Employees' Union; the Canadian Division of the Brotherhood of Railway Carmen; the Canadian Textile and Chemical Union; the Canadian Brotherhood of Railway, Transport and General Workers; the Canadian mem- bers of the Retail, Wholesale and Department Store Union; and various affiliates of the Confederation of Canadian Unions (CCU). Likewise, the Steelworkers in Canada merged with the International Woodworkers Union in 2004. Thus, the merger-mania in the corporate world throughout the previous two decades was matched within the union movement.

Second, many of the international unions in manufacturing have faced declining membership and diminished opportunities for new recruitment activity in their tradi- tional jurisdictions. This has prompted some unions to diversify their areas of recruitment. A striking example of this phenomenon is the Steelworkers, which increasingly recruits in the service sector. Seeking to compensate for significant membership losses in mining and manufacturing, the Steelworkers began organizing security guards, hotel and restau- rant workers, and even university employees. Public-sector unions have been recruiting in the private sector. The former National Union of Provincial Government Employees is now the National Union of Public and General Employees (NUPGE, and even further abbreviated to the National Union) to better reflect the change in focus. The British Columbia Government and Service Employees' Union (a NUPGE component union), which was greatly affected by successive waves of public-sector privatization implemented by the Social Credit government, became particularly active in recruiting members out- side the public sector.

Thus, industrial unionism is giving way to new varieties of general unionism. In the past, there were a few unions that organized in a wide variety of sectors. Such *general unions* were based on neither craft nor industrial jurisdictions. The International Brotherhood of Teamsters, though concentrated in trucking and warehousing, organized in almost any sector and grew to be one of the largest unions in North America. The search for appropriate union structures that can take root in the new service sector is likely to accelerate this transformation of industrial and craft unions into modified forms of general unionism (see Murray, 1998, Yates, 1998).

At the same time, there is a reaction to this trend. In particular, a large number of unaffiliated national unions that typically represent professional groups in the public sector, such as nurses and teachers, opted not to affiliate with a central labour body. They have been wary of political associations, and they prefer not to lose their sharp sense of occupational attachment. In an era in which jurisdictional lines are becoming muddled, the clearer professional focus of some of these unions, especially in health care, has proved to be an impetus for growth. Yet, at the same time, continued pressures to reorganize the public services have prompted some unaffiliated professional associations to consider joining other unions and affiliating with central labour congresses. Whereas the nurses' union in Quebec sought to do this but could not reach any internal consensus, the Health Sciences Association in Alberta voted to affiliate with NUPGE and the CLC in 2003.

Union Locals

The decentralization of Canadian union structure gives many union locals a high degree of autonomy. Union locals tend to reflect either their craft or industrial union servicing traditions. The craft tradition tends toward a very autonomous union local that organizes a large number of certification units on a regional basis. All dues are paid to that local. It generally has a full-time president who employs business agents to carry out basic servicing activities. The union local is affiliated with a national or international union to which it pays dues on a pro rata (proportional) basis. With the growing demands on union services centrally, unions organized along this model have tried to add centralized services but their effectiveness is weakened by union local autonomy, in tandem with the financial control retained at the local level.

The industrial tradition is more centralized. The union local usually consists of one certification unit. Union locals usually have part-time presidents who do not draw their salary from the union, but the locals are serviced by a cadre of full-time officials employed by the national or international union. Some portion of these dues, in conformity with the prevailing constitutional provisions of the organization, is then allocated to the union local. The proportion of dues accruing to the local level varies considerably. The central union body or head office generally develops specialized services delivered by field staff. Steelworkers and CAW are examples of this industrial tradition.

Many of the newer public-sector unions tend to adopt some variation of the industrial union model. Most evolved from government-employee staff associations whose high centralization reflected their employer's structure. While public-sector unions might organize a broad range of employees for a particular government employer, their internal organization, unlike that of industrial unions, is sometimes based on professional category rather than location or administrative unit. They have tended to develop expert services at the head office and have fairly weak local structures. As could be seen in the vignette describing Union B at the beginning of this chapter, decentralization and privatization are exerting increasing pressures on this distribution of responsibilities.

There is considerable pressure on all of these models because of changes in industrial structure. Some models are better suited to the characteristics of the new service economy than others. The changing organization of the firm and larger trends in the labour market have had a marked, if highly differential, impact on the structures and strategies of union locals. Most notably, the declining size of existing bargaining units and the small size of many new certifications have prompted some unions to amalgamate different certifications into larger, composite locals.

This is evident in many of the older unions that are characterized by a craft structure and that have traditionally organized a multiplicity of units within a single local and built their servicing structure around this arrangement. In the case of the United Food and Commercial Workers Union (UFCW), there are new hybrid models in which union locals maintain autonomy, but also use full-time officials paid by the national union for basic services and policy coordination. Local 175 and 633 of the UFCW Canada is a single local with more than 50 000 members across Ontario. It is more akin to a region or district in many unions.

The local structures of industrial-model unions, such as the Steelworkers, also are changing (Murray, 1998). With the infusion of smaller certification units, particularly in private services, the Steelworkers gradually altered its local structures, with the average number of certifications per local increasing. This represents a conscious organizing and servicing strategy designed to better meet the needs of new membership groups both in the service sector and in small manufacturing units. Indeed, this strategy aims to create union locals that can adjust to the small size of new units being organized. It also allows the union to achieve a financially viable servicing strategy. At times, the union trains full-time lay representatives to perform the functions of professional business agents and servicing staff. The increased importance of amalgamated locals naturally pushes unions organized on the industrial model toward greater decentralization in the distribution of services. In the U.S. labour movement, such an approach is labelled the "organizing model," a term that is increasingly popular in Canada. The objective is to revitalize union recruitment through reallocating resources and energies toward recruitment and defence of new groups of workers.

Services and Dues

Canadian unions face increasing demands from their members to provide a wide range of sophisticated services. Basic services include the negotiation and application of collective agreements. While these services might be provided by a lay official such as a union local president or shop steward, or by a full-time official working for either the national or local union, larger certification units generally require complex backup services, such as research and legal assistance. The wider the range of issues dealt with in the collective agreement, the more complex is the range of services required. Thus, in recent years, most unions have added health and safety, pension, and pay equity specialists. Demand is increasing for information and advice on company finances, work reorganization, new technologies, and environmental regulations. Many unions provide supplementary services. Unions began as mutual insurance societies to provide benefits to craft workers in times of hardship. Strike pay and supplementary health and insurance schemes are examples of such benefits. Some unions have expanded into other types of individual services such as legal, financial, counselling, and employment advice to members. Other unions have developed collective instruments, such as investment funds, to safeguard and promote employment in particular workplaces.

Whereas most unions used to charge dues on a flat-rate basis, they switched to a percentage basis during the inflationary period of the 1970s. Union dues typically are 1 to 2 percent of salary. For example, monthly dues of Steelworkers are established by the international constitution at 1.3 percent of total salary with provisos for minimum and maximum contributions. The constitution also indicates the percentage distribution of this revenue among different levels of the union. Both the union local and international union receive 44 percent of dues; 7 percent goes to the international strike fund, and smaller amounts are allocated to education (1 percent), political action (1 percent), and organizing (3 percent). Unions with more decentralized traditions, such as the UFCW, have more variable arrangements, since the union local is free to fix its own level of dues from which it then must pay per-capita affiliation fees, often on a flat-rate basis, to other levels of the union. Flat-rate dues are a particularly contentious issue for many part-time workers who feel that they are unduly penalized in having to pay a higher percentage of their income in union dues than do full-time workers. This is why a number of unions seeking to attract part-time members have moved away from this kind of dues structure.

As the demand and need for services increase, the capacity to pay for them decreases. In particular, structural changes in the labour market—such as static incomes, or the growth of part-time work—have resulted in reduced real dues income per member (Murray, 1998). As was the case with Union B in the chapter's opening vignette, these trends have increased the pressures and led to a rethinking of the role of full-time staff in some unions, and especially of the relative division of labour between staff and activists and the role of education and self-empowerment in the provision of services by activists. Some unions are developing extensive education programs in an effort to upgrade the skills of their steward or delegate representatives so that they might provide basic services to their members. Other unions are experimenting with alternative forms of service delivery such as call centres to answer member queries and help resolve workplace problems.

Union Governance and Democracy

The union as an organization is characterized by a certain ambiguity, for it is both collective and democratic. It is necessarily collective because its power is derived from its capacity to coordinate the actions of its members to achieve common objectives. But if a union is to exercise a degree of power for its members, it invariably exercises a degree of power over them (Hyman, 1975: 65). Craft unions were traditionally illustrative of this point because their power vis-à-vis the employer depended on their control of entry into the trade and their disciplinary powers over those exercising the trade (Clegg, 1976: 30).

Unions also are democratic organizations with constitutions that ensure the protection of individual members and guarantee the right of members to participate in the selection and application of policies and to choose their leaders. The power of the collective over the individual is thus limited by the democratic character of the union as well as by certain legislative and *Charter of Rights and Freedoms* provisions regarding union elections and strike votes, the ratification of collective agreements, the union's duty to represent members fairly, and the observance of principles of natural justice.

Even if participating in the economic life of their workplace and their country is sometimes an important motive for workers to become union members, it probably is safe to say that the primary objective of most union members is not to enjoy the experience of democracy. Rather, the democratic character of the union is a way of controlling the pursuit of collective goals. Moreover, the attainment of such goals invariably depends on the willingness of individual members to forgo individual prerogatives in favour of democratically agreed-upon collective objectives. The dilemma for union democracy, therefore, is the choice between a stable leadership and efficient organization, on the one hand, and the right of opposition, with all the attendant risks of fragmentation and disorder, on the other (Hemmingway, 1978: 2).

This tension between collectivism and democracy is central to the union organization and affects much of its internal life. Drawing on what a famous observer of life in voluntary organizations labelled the *iron law of oligarchy* (Michels, 1962), a pessimistic vision of union democracy suggests that, sooner or later, leadership ends up concentrated in the hands of a small elite that is not easily removed from power. The concentration of power can lead to abuse. The image of certain union bosses connected to underworld racketeering in the United States readily springs to mind, and there are cases of such abuse in Canada (see, for example, Kaplan, 1987, on the Seafarers International Union in the 1950s and 1960s). More typically, full-time officials in many unions exercise a tremendous influence on policy outcomes and application.

A more optimistic vision suggests that unions are constantly subject to democratic renewal. Union leaders cannot ignore the real and democratic limits of their power. While such limits are formally part of the governance of the union, they also are highly practical. The constant possibility of election defeat, the potential emergence of organized opposition within the union, the obligation for union officials to account for their actions, and, ultimately, the need to mobilize union members in the pursuit of collective goals while maintaining their satisfaction with union representation—these are all factors that limit the power of union leadership. Most union leaders are preoccupied with the problem of ensuring membership participation. Many have altered their internal union structures to facilitate membership participation, especially that of women and visible minorities, and to better respond to members' needs. Drawing on the traditions of its former parent union in the United States, the CAW constitution provides for a type of ombudsperson procedure, where an independent panel made up of impartial individuals from outside the union will hear any membership complaint about improper internal procedures not resolved through the internal appeal procedure of the union.

Several possibilities are available for membership participation within the union. The most typical form of participation, and the one that generally stimulates high member involvement, is membership input on collective bargaining. Members are asked for input on the objectives of particular bargaining rounds, and they can participate in meetings that frame issues. In addition, the law generally obliges members to formally ratify a decision to accept a collective agreement or strike.

Members also can take on tasks related to the life of the collective agreement or the representation of union members within the establishment. Stewards or workplace representatives are concerned with the application of the collective agreement and the expression of grievances. Workplace health-and-safety representatives are concerned with this aspect of union work. Increasingly, there are other new channels for membership participation and activism on issues such as pay equity and training.

Members also play a role in the administration of the union. The most typical form of participation involves attendance at union local meetings; although, aside from during the most intense periods of collective bargaining, the rate of membership attendance at routine meetings remains very low. Union members also elect their local leaders. The union local must also be represented at other decision-making bodies within union structures. While the number and level of such bodies vary from one union to another, the final decision-making authority in almost all unions is some form of convention or congress to which union locals send voting delegates on the basis of their membership. The frequency of such conventions varies from one to five years or more. Most unions elect their leadership at such conventions, a form of indirect membership elections. Some unions, notably the Steelworkers, elect their leaders by direct membership postal ballot.

Between conventions, most unions provide for other decision-making bodies to deliberate on the implementation of policy. Sometimes, this involves a small number of full-time elected executive members. Sometimes, it involves some form of representative council at which most major locals or territorial or professional groupings would be present. Some unions, for example the Auto Workers, have both an executive and a council meeting every four months to which all locals are requested to send delegates. Many unions also have regional or industry structures that might duplicate these arrangements. In particular, this is the case with the Quebec sections of many national and international unions. Over the past three decades, they have developed forms of self-governance that recognize the *distinct* character of their Quebec membership within the larger union structure. Union locals also send delegates, in principle at least, to the conventions of their national and provincial central labour bodies.

The degree of membership participation in the administration of the union tends to be less than that in the bargaining activities of the union. Most unions nonetheless depend almost entirely on the activism of their members to ensure their daily operations. The dynamism and the influence of a union ultimately depend on the participation of the membership. Most unions invest heavily in membership education in order to train members to administer their organizations. They also seek to ensure that members do participate and to solve the perpetual participation problems that seem to characterize most voluntary organizations. As for individual union members, participating in the democratic life of their unions can be a training ground for experiencing democracy in the larger society as well as an occasion for developing their own abilities. Many union activists speak glowingly of the tremendous influence that union participation has had on their personal development and of how it has enriched their understanding of society (see, for example, Martin, 1995).

Challenges for Union Structure and Governance

A number of common structural adjustments are taking place in Canadian unions to reflect the changes in membership composition, the movements in corporate structure, the rise of new social identities at work related to age, gender, ethnicity, and education, and the real problems of organizing new groups of workers into unions, especially in private services.

With women participating in the labour force in growing numbers, unions have had to focus on ensuring that women enjoy a more active role in organized labour. The unionization of the public sector brought large numbers of women members into the ranks of unions. Moreover, the growth of private-service-sector employment suggests an even greater potential for union membership growth among women in the future. However, many women members have charged that unions do not reflect their concerns or accommodate their needs by allowing them to participate in official roles within their unions.

Thus, through the 1980s and 1990s, there was a continuing debate as women sought to introduce issues such as sexual harassment, child care, maternity leave, employment equity, and pay equity to union agendas. Debate also has surrounded attempts to ensure that women were adequately represented in elected positions and in the different parts of their unions, as well as attempts to eliminate barriers to women's active participation in the life of the union (Briskin and McDermott, 1993: 5). Indeed, women's groups and the feminist movement more generally have been major sources of renewal for many unions. Some union leaderships, for example that of CUPE, now reflect their formative experience in union women's committees and in coalition activity with other feminist groups.

The relative success of women in this endeavour has served as an example to other groups, such as visible minorities, to claim equivalent recognition within the political channels of their unions. Thus, many unions have adopted a variety of employment equity measures to ensure the greater participation of different membership groups. Special internal structures based on specific identities, such as gender, ethnicity, or sexual orientation, also have provided a focus for new activism (Yates, 2005; Hunt and Haiven, 2006). Union leaders are sometimes confronted with the potential clash between new activists and traditional membership groups who are nostalgic for an older, more homogeneous industrial structure.

At the local level, the rise of the composite or amalgamated local has been a response to the importance of smaller unit size in both manufacturing and services. At other levels, as could be seen in the opening vignette, there is the question of how to create effective coordinating mechanisms in an effort to organize the new groups into viable structures and make links between core and peripheral workers. This is an enduring problem in a large number of unions. Thus, the challenge of fostering participation and giving a sense of ownership to the various diverse groups in the organization will continue to be a major preoccupation of unions.

UNION ACTION

The choice traditionally available to a union is either economic or political action. If its objectives were defined largely in terms of improvement in terms and conditions of employment of its members, a union might rely exclusively on collective bargaining and, ultimately, on recourse to sanctions such as strikes. Alternatively, it might employ various forms of political action, be it through lobbying, the creation of a political party, or even a mass movement, to pursue the same objectives. Moreover, a union might define its objectives more widely, seeking to represent its members not only as wage earners, but also as citizens (Murray and Verge, 1999). Indeed, central union bodies often aspire to be the voice for all workers.

Nature of Union Action

Why do particular union movements emphasize one type of action rather than the other? Many explanations point to the lasting imprint of the formative period of the union movement in a particular country. Did workers already enjoy universal suffrage and was the labour market characterized by shortages or an excess supply of unskilled labour? If a particular country's labour movement played a key role in obtaining the vote, for men at least, it was likely to continue this political role. If there was a shortage of unskilled labour, then the union movement would rely on economic action or collective bargaining. However, if an excess supply of unskilled labour existed, then political action was more likely to improve the lot of the vast majority of unionized workers. In North America, where the market was expanding rapidly and labour shortages were common, and the right to vote came independently of the formation of the labour movement, early unions were typically characterized by the label *bread-and-butter unionism* since they concentrated their efforts in the collective bargaining realm.

The creation of industrial unions was characterized by a period of political ferment leading to the formal obligation on the part of employers to recognize unions where a majority of workers favoured such representation. The consolidation of our current industrial relations regime in the immediate aftermath of World War II, however, tended to emphasize the narrow, economic or industrial character of union representation to the detriment of a broader civic or socio-political role. Increasingly, the Canadian union movement tends to rely on some combination of both economic and political methods.

Collective Bargaining

The classic method of union action is collective bargaining, a subject treated in detail in Chapter 10. It should be emphasized that Canadian unions have long pursued a strategy of wage militancy. Indeed, even during the recession of the early 1980s, the CLC adopted a "no-concessions" policy.

However, current shifts in corporate strategy and organization place traditional collective bargaining under severe pressure. At root here is the social reorganization of production at the workplace, which is particularly evident in the use of new transnational production systems and the reorganization of internal labour markets. This results in a dual, and often contradictory, process of *integration* and *differentiation*.

Integration is the ideological reconstruction of the workplace around new production systems and management techniques that seek to mobilize employee enthusiasm and knowledge to achieve greater productivity and competitiveness (Lewchuk and Wells, 2006; Murray et al., 2002). At one end of the continuum, this might be yet another fad in a never-ending series of managerial initiatives. Alternatively, it might be a complete reformulation of the social system of the firm that can seek to integrate (or exclude) certain forms of participation and workers' representative mechanisms into the very culture of the firm. This can involve a range of new managerial practices, including total quality management, quality circles, variable compensation systems, and new forms of worker participation (see Chapter 6 on employee involvement). Whatever its orientation, which certainly varies greatly from one firm to another, this integrative process opens up a range of strategic questions for union organizations, particularly, as could be seen with Union C in the opening vignette, the extent to which a workers' representative organization can ally its objectives with those of the firm without compromising its watchdog role in the defence of working conditions.

At the same time, there also is a process of differentiation whereby firms seek new levels of *flexibility* by transforming traditional full-time, secure jobs into other categories of employment. These can include part-time, contractual, temporary, or subcontracted work. Also, the firm can identify different profit centres and reorganize production and services into smaller, more highly differentiated units, or it can forgo employment relations altogether in favour of outside contractors, sometimes at vastly reduced cost through offshoring activities to locations outside of Canada (for example, call centres in India or manufacturing in Mexico or China). Some employers have sought to disconnect or reorganize traditional wage comparisons between firms and units through this same differentiation philosophy. In the retail food sector, for example, numerous franchising activities have resulted either in de-unionization or increased differentiation among contracts. Similarly, large hotels have subdivided their different activities (reception, catering, cleaning, etc.) into distinct businesses, often with different employers. Moreover, as could be seen in the case of Union B at the outset of this chapter, this is far from being strictly a private-sector phenomenon. Public agencies emulate differentiation strategies both in the organization of services and in the wages and working conditions of their direct employees or contracted workers.

Pattern bargaining, the coordination of bargaining objectives and tactics within a particular sector, previously tended to alleviate the effects of this decentralization. The kinds of comparative linkages previously associated with such patterns are difficult to maintain in more competitive product markets, however. Various new union strategies exist to deal with these developments. Unions are building broader-based bargaining structures to obtain greater bargaining power in order to create viable servicing structures. While some unions have also supported new forms of co-operative bargaining techniques, such as interest-based or mutual gains bargaining, others, as was the case for Union C in the opening vignette, are advocating a return to increased militancy to secure a greater share of productivity gains for their members. Increasing demographic pressures are likely to accentuate this phenomenon where labour markets are tight and labour shortages are in evidence. In terms of a bargaining agenda, in addition to traditional and ever-present concerns over job security and remuneration, unions have made some effort to enlarge their bargaining strategies to reflect the changed political economy, the pace of workplace change, and the preoccupations of new groups in the labour market.

In a study of national union bargaining priorities and success in Canada, Kumar and Murray (2002) identified four areas around which union bargaining agendas are currently structured. In order of importance, they are: (1) protecting current wages and benefits; (2) pursuing an active union and worker role in workplace change, particularly on issues such as consultation and training; (3) limiting the effects of workplace flexibility on workers, in particular on such issues as contracting out and regulating workloads; and (4) promoting a progressive agenda on gender, family, and working-time issues through the negotiation of items such as employment equity and time off work for family reasons. In analyzing the degree of success achieved by national unions on these items, Kumar and Murray found that unions were achieving a fairly high degree of success on the traditional bargaining agenda (protecting current wages and benefits), but much less success on new items, particularly the effects of workplace flexibility. Unions were, however, able to achieve a high degree of success on gender, family, and working-time issues, but only if these issues were prioritized during negotiations. The strategic challenge for unions is how to strike the appropriate balance between the necessary defensive agenda, driven by employer responses to environmental change, and the more proactive agenda that seeks to connect with both worker concerns to have a voice in their workplaces and the concerns of the new constituencies that unions must organize if they are to maintain and enhance their role in the workplace and in society.

Workplace Reorganization

Considerable debate takes place within the labour movement over the challenges of workplace reorganization. The new *co-operative* union strategies that focus almost exclusively within the individual firm to the detriment of larger labour market solidarities are particularly contentious. Some unions are tempted by the appeal of enduring, co-operative, strife-free relationships with employers. This kind of new *enterprise unionism* is currently being promoted in a number of countries. Moreover, the threat of unemployment in an era of restructuring and global competition pushes many union leaders toward more collaborative relationships with employers. Most unions have some kind of policy response. Some, such as the CEP and CSN, have actively promoted a co-operative approach to change in the workplace in the past, notably the CSN, which pioneered long-term collective agreements with employers in order to secure assurances of greater employment security in the context of stable industrial relations. Others, notably the CAW, have traditionally taken a more critical approach. This tradition made CAW's October 2007 Framework of Fairness agreement with Magna, a Canadian-controlled multinational auto parts firm, all the more surprising (CAW–Magna, 2007). This agreement provides an avenue for the unionization of a company that had successfully avoided most attempts at unionization (Lewchuk and Wells, 2006). It also clearly abandons many of the adversarial aspects of the traditional labour–management relationship in favour of a model of employee relationship closely aligned with company objectives.

The new forms of work design often challenge traditional *Taylorist* forms of work organization (see Chapter 3), with profound implications for union operations (Kumar, 1995; Rinehart et al., 1997). Certainly, collective agreement provisions are reflecting changes in work organization, for example, with more evidence of variable pay, training, and multi-skilling (see Chapter 6 for details). However, there is also much evidence of acute problems of sustainability in such arrangements (Murray et al., 2002), as corporate restructuring and pressures for short-term financial gain can trump efforts by local union leaders and managers to develop new labour relations models. In essence, the very conditions that should support these efforts are undermined elsewhere in the company, and unions are caught between a "rock and a hard place."

There is increasing evidence that a union local able to draw on its own internal and external resources is in a better position to play an active role in workplace change (see Frost, 2000, and Lévesque and Murray, 2002). Internal resources include a network of union delegates, time off to take care of union business, and, most importantly, a high degree of membership participation in and support for the union. External resources include the capacity to draw on information and expertise, notably from the larger union with which the union local is affiliated, and coordination and solidarity from a wider network of local unions experiencing such change. It is therefore especially important for national unions to develop support mechanisms and training for their union locals on workplace change (Kumar et al., 1998).

Economic Restructuring Beyond the Workplace

In the context of current socio-economic transformations both within and beyond the firm, representation beyond the firm is increasingly important. The creation of consultative and representative forums and institutions to deal with such issues as training, sectoral adjustment, productivity, pay equity, and regional economic development is an example of this trend. The severity of the recession in the early 1980s prompted many union leaders to diversify union action in the economic sphere. Labour came to define the representation of economic interests more widely, and governments, to a limited degree at least, came to recognize the legitimacy of such representation. This was the case, for example, with the 1984 creation of the tripartite Canadian Labour Market and Productivity Centre (CLMPC) to promote more and better-quality jobs, with representatives from business, government, and labour (CLMPC, 1992). Subsequent efforts to pursue this type of initiative have slowed markedly with the dissolution in 2006 of the Canadian Labour and Business Centre, a bipartite employer–union organization, due to federal government funding cutbacks for its activities.

At the national level, the labour movement continues to play some role in the administration of certain labour market social programs such as employment insurance. For example, one of the four representatives on the Employment Insurance Commission, which is responsible for the system of employment insurance, is appointed only after consultations with the labour movement. Although the CLC's relations with the federal government ebb and flow with changes in government, notably deteriorating since the election of a minority Conservative government in 2006, the overall level of consultation between the central labour body and the national government is very weak when compared with European models.

There has also been a proliferation of sectoral initiatives to deal with issues of restructuring and training in particular industries (Gunderson and Sharpe, 1998). One of the most visible is in automobile manufacturing. Moreover, these consultative bodies have, to varying degrees, been replicated at the provincial level. Some of these, notably in Quebec and Ontario (see Charest, 1999; Murray and Verge, 1999), are fairly extensive, but they are vulnerable to the shifting orientations of different governments.

Another type of economic action concerns new labour vehicles for effecting economic change and protecting jobs. The Quebec Federation of Labour was a pioneer in the creation of its Solidarity Fund in 1984. Operating as a registered retirement savings plan (RRSP), this multibillion-dollar worker investment fund, which benefits from both federal and provincial government tax credits, channels worker investment into the safeguarding and creation of jobs, primarily through the provision of risk capital to firms in Quebec (Fournier, 1991). The Working Ventures funds and the Fondaction (CSN) funds share similar objectives. Several provincial governments have granted special tax recognition to such funds.

Political Action

Political action concerns the defence of the worker both as a wage earner and as a citizen. The importance of political activity as a dimension of union action was confirmed in the Supreme Court of Canada's 1991 landmark decision (*Lavigne v. Ontario Public Service Employees Union* (1991) 81 D.L.R. (4th) 545 (S.C.C.)).

Unions exhibit varying attitudes to the role of the market and the need for social change. On the one hand, there is a commitment by some to *bread-and-butter* or *business unionism*: seeking the best deal possible for their members. On the other hand, many union leaders express a critical view of the workings of the market and argue for the promotion of social and political change as an integral part of union activity. Here we might distinguish between *social* and *social movement unionism* (Kumar and Schenk, 2006; Kumar and Murray, 2006; Robinson, 1994, 1998). As opposed to business unionism, both social and social movement unionism embrace a much wider definition of solidarity, i.e., that unions should defend all workers and not just their members. Moreover, both seek to promote the interests of the worker as citizen as well as wage earner and, in so doing, emphasize the importance of unions' political activity. However, the politics of social unionism, deeply rooted in the traditions of industrial unionism in Canada, are more likely to be expressed through a privileged relationship with a social democratic political party, such as the New Democratic Party (NDP), while the politics of social movement unionism are more typically outside of parliament, for example, public protests in coalition with social and community groups. Advocates of social movement unionism are likely to be critical of a narrow emphasis on electoral support for parliamentary social democratic parties and to accentuate the transformative potential of political conflict and public protest. All of these strains of thought co-exist within most Canadian unions in one way or another but, at any given time, they will find particular expression so that a union comes to be known as more or less radical in its political activities. Union political involvement varies from no political activity at all to pressure-group tactics to influence the parliamentary or governmental process, direct partisan political action in favour of a particular political party, and coalition activity designed to work with other social groups toward common objectives.

Although most independent unions tend to reject partisan political activity, public-sector cutbacks have sparked many to engage in a much more public political role as increasingly severe restraints have been placed on their ability to bargain collectively (Panitch and Swartz, 2003). Indeed, the affiliation of some formerly independent unions to the CLC, notably the Ontario Secondary School Teachers' Federation in 1998, also highlights this trend. Nowhere is this increased emphasis on political activity more apparent than in the health sector, where nurses' unions have proved to be among the most militant unions in the country (see Haiven, 1995). Similarly, the CSN in Quebec is engaged in a wide variety of political activities even though its statutes expressly forbid it to support a particular political party.

In contrast, many CLC affiliates have long maintained a close relationship with the New Democratic Party (NDP) of Canada and its predecessor, the Co-operative Commonwealth Federation (CCF). From the election of 1979, the CLC became increasingly allied with the NDP. Indeed, this process was facilitated when some of the more conservative, business-oriented unions left the CLC to form the Canadian Federation of Labour at the beginning of the 1980s. Many, but not all, CLC affiliates are organically linked to the NDP. The NDP constitution provides for both individual and affiliated membership. Affiliated membership is available to organizations such as unions, farm groups, co-operatives, and women's organizations, and the cost of affiliated membership is generally lower than individual membership. Affiliations give organizations direct representation on the different decision-making bodies of the NDP. Leaders of affiliated organizations such as the Steelworkers participate actively in policy debates and the selection of leaders.

Both the NDP's distance from government at the federal level and its experience of government at the provincial level have put strains on the relationship between labour and the NDP that are similar to the problems observed between labour parties and union movements in many other countries. The continuing inability of the NDP to form a national government has led some union leaders to query whether a strong identification with the NDP is really an asset for representing their members' interests. Conversely, some in the NDP have wondered whether its alliance with the union movement translates into votes and have promoted an alternative "Third Way," or middle-ground politics.

The experience of the NDP government in Ontario in the first half of the 1990s and its implementation of social-contract legislation provides an especially good illustration of the tensions inherent in the relationship between organized labour and the NDP, as well as the gap that separates advocates of social and social movement unionism. The Ontario NDP government suspended free collective bargaining and enacted wage-restraint legislation in the public sector, causing many unions, including the CAW, to withdraw support. Indeed, the tensions over this particular episode spilled over into the rest of the decade and largely coloured the sometimes acrimonious discussions among Ontario union leaders about appropriate protest strategies against the policies of subsequent Conservative governments. Nor are such strains unique to the NDP. Similar tensions were observed between Quebec labour unions and the Parti Québécois (PQ) government of the 1970s and early 1980s—these tensions continued through the two mandates of the PQ government from the mid-1990s until the spring of 2003 when the PQ left power.

Unions in Canada also form coalitions with other social groups in an attempt to influence public debates on a range of issues (Kumar and Schenk, 2006). Significant examples of union activism, in tandem with other social groups, occurred over the free trade agreement with the United States and the North American Free Trade Agreement (NAFTA) (Robinson, 1994). Similarly, some unions have shared platforms on questions such as the environment, equal rights, and international solidarity. A number of unions have also created special funds to assist their work in this domain. Steelworkers created their Humanity Fund to assist international development projects. The CAW's Social Justice Fund promotes worthy projects both in Canada and abroad. Many unions have, of course, long maintained an active civic and community role in philanthropic work such as the United Way. To cite but one of many examples, the UFCW invests considerable organizational resources in an annual fundraising campaign for research on leukemia.

CONCLUSION

This chapter has sought to portray the changing character of unions in Canada. Unions are obliged to come to terms with market changes, but the extent and the direction of adaptation is quite different from one union to another because of the emphasis on different goals.

These changes have been made in a context of relative success. Not only has overall union membership in Canada increased or held fairly stable, but the labour movement has sought, however imperfectly, to adapt to the major challenges of a rapidly changing global economy. Its strategies have included increased emphasis on organizing the unorganized, notably through the shift of resources to organizing; the expression of new labour market identities, be they gender, ethnicity, sexual orientation, or otherwise, in policies and bargaining agenda; experimentation with new local structures that take better account of the changing nature of the workplace; attempts to equip union locals to deal with the challenges of workplace change through activist education and new specialist resources; increasing use of new technologies to communicate with members and the general public; and an increasing public profile on political and social issues.

These developments point to a movement toward new union forms that take account of the broader trends in the economy and society. Just as we can now look back on the decline of craft unionism as the passing of an exclusive but effective organizational form, so too can we increasingly discern the limits of the industrial union model, which diffused in a wave of CIO-based organizing throughout Canada in the years of post-war industrial expansion. This model protected its particular membership, primarily male, mass-production workers, through the elaboration of collective agreements. These agreements regulated aspects of the job, while leaving broader questions of work organization in the realm of managerial prerogative. The jurisdiction of the industrial union model was restricted to particular industries, and its organizational form was focused on particular units, generally one agreement per local, with external solidarities being extended only as far as pattern bargaining required some kind of linkage with other units.

The real importance of the new service sector, the significance of workplace reorganization, the changes in union membership and practices, and the continuing mutations of previous organizational forms all point toward the emergence of new union structures. The future of Canadian unions very much depends on the development of these new models, their appeal to an increasingly heterogeneous workforce, and their success in dealing with the problems encountered by workers in their workplaces, their communities, and beyond.

Questions

1. Why did union membership in Canada grow so much until 1990 and then stagnate and decline thereafter? What is the significance of the differences in absolute and relative membership trends?

2. Discuss the growing divergence in union density between Canada and the United States. Is it likely to continue?

3. Describe the sectoral differences in the degree of unionization by industry in Canada and the challenges that these pose for unions.

4. How do changes in the larger economy have an impact on the definition of union jurisdictions?

5. What are the different possibilities for a union member who wants to participate in the life of the union? Is the union inevitably an oligarchy (government by few)?

6. How do you explain the bargaining priorities of national unions and the degree of success achieved?

7. Discuss different ways that Canadian unions have responded to economic restructuring and workplace organization, and the problems that might arise within union locals over the different approaches that they might adopt.

8. Why do unions become involved in political activity? Discuss the relative merits of a partisan as opposed to a non-partisan approach to political activity. Contrast business unionism with social unionism and social movement unionism.

Weblinks

Human Resources and Social Development Canada Labour Information:
www.hrsdc.gc.ca/en/lp/wid/info.shtml

Canadian Labour Congress:
www.clc-ctc.ca

AFL–CIO:
www.aflcio.org

International Trade Union Confederation:
www.ituc-csi.org

Confédération des syndicats nationaux (CSN):
www.csn.qc.ca

Centrale des syndicats du Québec:
www.csq.qc.net

Bureau of Labor Statistics (U.S.):
www.bls.gov

Chapter 5

The Management of Industrial Relations

Mark Thompson[1]

Is it possible for a company and union to transform their relationship from deeply acrimonious to a model of co-operation and trust, while also closing plants and enduring business turbulence? Here is the story of an inspiring transformation.

In the 1990s, the British Columbia pulp and paper industry had a well-earned reputation for some of the most bitter labour–management relations in Canada. Following a difficult 1997 strike, Fletcher Challenge's labour relations on the West Coast were among the worst in the forest industry.

But when Norwegian paper giant Norske Skog bought Fletcher Challenge in 2000, which in turn bought Pacifica Papers, the merged entity known as NorskeCanada (which has since been renamed Catalyst Paper) encouraged a strong, values-driven management and co-operative relationships with workers and unions.

NorskeCanada's new senior management team knew fresh leadership would be essential at their Powell River plant. Between 1980 and 2000, Powell River's fortunes had declined dramatically. The plant went from 10 paper-making machines to 3 and from 2100 employees to 1000. Layoffs, combined with an autocratic, command-and-control style of mill management, gave Powell River, then owned by Pacifica Papers, a B.C. reputation as the worst mill in the worst company in the worst industry.

In September 2001, CEO Russ Horner made a trip to Powell River to announce that the obsolete kraft pulp mill, which was part of the Powell River complex, was closing. Of the 1000 employees at Powell River, 300 would be laid off, all from Local 76 of the Communications, Energy and Paperworkers Union of Canada (CEP).

Union workers had become resigned to similar messages, but they didn't expect Horner's promise: "Every employee of the mill will have a job or will have a package that they accept."

There would be no involuntary layoffs. Instead, workers would either relocate to another mill, accept an early retirement or severance package, join an apprenticeship program, or retrain for forestry or other industries.

The union leaders at Powell River were long-time employees Mike Verdiel and Gary Thorsell. "NorskeCanada had done their homework. They did it as painlessly as possible," said Thorsell. Local 76 leaders proposed another idea to management: if members throughout the entire plant went to a 37.3-hour workweek, they could save another 18 jobs. Every third Friday was taken off as a designated averaging day to reach 37.3 hours.

Ironically, the closure of the Powell River kraft mill represented a real turning point in labour relations. "The union was waiting to see the true colours of the company, but with the way the downsizing was handled, involving the union and demonstrating a different philosophy, members were convinced," said Thorsell.

Goodwill would be further strengthened as the company's attention turned to safety. Two slogans were adopted: "all injuries can be prevented" and "safety has overriding priority." Lost-time injuries dropped from 36 in 2001 to 8 in 2002. In July 2004, Powell River achieved a new record of six months without a lost-time injury and finished the year with only four lost-time injuries, another record.

These positive concrete results opened the way for co-operation in collective bargaining. As the collective bargaining agreement was set to expire in 2003, some major customers began warning NorskeCanada they would not renew their contracts because of the risk of a strike. NorskeCanada management took the problem to union local presidents and to Dave Coles, western region vice-president of CEP (now national president). The union was persuaded that opening bargaining early would secure labour peace. Certainly, the loss of customer orders would have a crippling effect on NorskeCanada's operations and workers.

Management offered a guarantee they would not ask for concessions from the union during the bargaining process, but that it was "now or never" for negotiations. With the "no clawbacks" commitment, the union was prepared to bargain early, but only if all 125 union local pulp and paper representatives from across the province were in the room to ensure transparent bargaining. The company agreed to this unusual condition.

The union, led by Coles, and management, led by Buchhorn, jointly and within their own caucuses spent weeks narrowing down the bargaining items. As a result, it took only nine days of negotiation in September 2002 to reach a five-year deal. The success amazed both sides.

For the first time in memory, families of the plant workers could plan vacations and house purchases under the security of a lengthy labour agreement. In addition, customer concerns over security of supply were erased and orders were renewed.

The remarkable turnaround in labour–management relations at NorskeCanada can be attributed to three groups of practices: interdependence, involvement, and operational excellence.

Labour and management understand their interdependence in attaining common objectives of plant profitability and job retention. Those common objectives drive the sharing of information. With increased involvement, union and management jointly raise operational productivity, which in turn justifies the interdependence. The cycle builds upon itself.

In moving from a highly directive organization with previous owners to a high-involvement organization with NorskeCanada, the key was having open communication through which people share knowledge on plant operations and ideas for improvement. Management does not hesitate to ask union workers to represent the mill by visiting customers to discover better ways to serve customers. Reciprocally, workers expect management to honestly disclose profitability and operational problems and to involve workers in developing solutions to future challenges. Union leaders are invited by the site vice-president to all the regular meetings of the senior management team. Thorsell and Verdiel point out that the high level of co-operation does not lead to co-optation.

Will this co-operative relationship stand the test of time? In 2007, both the CEO and Chief Financial Officer left the company. The Canadian dollar rose to unprecedented heights, jeopardizing firm profitability. Only one week after announcing its intention to raise $200 million in private placement offerings, the company withdrew its plans due to "adverse capital market conditions." The share price plummeted from over $4.00 to under $1.50. The company laid off 350 workers, including 100 Powell River mill workers.

Yet both company and union remain committed to co-operative, respectful relations, and continue to work together through hard times. The company continues to proclaim in its official statement of "What We Stand For" that it wants to be regarded as a partner to the union, and a leader in labour–management relations.[2]

The labour movement and the role of government in Canadian industrial relations have been studied widely. Yet little attention was paid to the third actor in industrial relations—the employer. This omission has been remedied in more recent scholarship. As the opening vignette illustrates, management has many strategic options for carrying out industrial relations functions, and it can be proactive rather than reactive. This chapter provides an overview of the industrial relations policies and practices of unionized private-sector Canadian companies, relying on data collected since interest in the role of management became more prominent in Canadian industrial relations.

Managers in any organization must deal with many issues, ranging from the basic strategy of the organization to the implementation of decisions by directors or senior executives. When employees are unionized, or unionization is probable, labour relations problems must be addressed. Despite their importance to the organization, industrial relations issues are normally missing in the literature of management. Company industrial relations statements tend to be vague and invariably positive, dominated by sentiments such as, "People are our most important asset," or "We are firm but fair with our unions," without providing any specifics on management's intentions. These statements cover a wide variety of management policies, ranging from open and vigorous hostility to unionism to acceptance and co-operation with labour organizations. The frequency of mass layoffs in both unionized and nonunion companies in the 1990s through the early years of the 2000s undermines the claims that firms value highly the contributions of their employees. Unions in the past decade concentrated most of their energies in trying to maintain jobs and conditions of employment, not in making major improvements to terms and conditions of employment. However, where there are pockets of astonishing prosperity—as in Alberta's oilsands—companies have had to make dramatic increases to compensation packages in order to recruit and retain workers.

Canadian industrial relations policy emerged after World War II. Between the 1940s and 1980s, the combination of steady economic growth, the expansion of the welfare state, and relatively low unemployment all strengthened labour's bargaining power and encouraged worker militancy. When confronted by a union organizing campaign, most employers initially concentrated on defeating the union. When labour succeeded in winning bargaining rights, management's role was to resist union demands in negotiations. Above all, however, management of the industrial relations function concentrated on maintaining labour peace—by granting concessions to unions when necessary. Other firms concentrated on building positive relations with their unions, usually based on stable employment at competitive rates of pay. Consultation and frequent training opportunities also contributed to a positive industrial relations climate. Some employers never achieved peace, or did not see labour peace as a particularly important goal, and resisted union demands, endured frequent stoppages, and sought legislative changes to weaken unions.

With some exceptions (Jacoby, 1997), management produced few innovations in the employment relationship. Instead, labour maintained the initiative. Unions negotiated the first pensions for non-managerial employees; they raised wages substantially in many industries, promoted occupational health and safety, shortened hours of work, secured medical insurance before government plans appeared, and introduced principles of justice into workplaces. Ironically, many of these policies became pillars of progressive human resources management.

After the recession of the early 1980s and a decline in the rate of economic growth, the balance of power between labour and management shifted. In an increasingly market-driven economic climate, many Canadian firms found themselves to be high-cost producers compared with their foreign (or nonunion Canadian) competitors. The arrival of Wal-Mart in Canada was an example of the changing business climate. Aggressively anti-union, this American firm put pressure on both the nonunion and unionized elements of the retail sector. In addition to reducing overhead costs, eliminating less profitable operations, and refocusing their business strategies, many companies looked for a competitive advantage in their management of human resources. Senior managers wanted to integrate human resource strategies with the firm's general business strategy; management was less likely than previously to merely react to labour's initiatives.

These developments focused attention on labour relations as a source of competitive advantage (or disadvantage). During the 1990s, for example, General Motors in both the United States and Canada endured several strikes, while Ford, its largest competitor, enjoyed harmonious labour relations. Ford operated profitably partly because of its success with labour relations, which gave it a competitive advantage over General Motors.

By the 2000s, a large proportion of Canadian unionized firms concentrated on reducing labour costs, including concessions from their workforces. Telus, for example (at this writing Canada's second-largest telecommunications provider) orchestrated a long work stoppage to reduce many entitlements in an existing collective agreement, especially the scheduling of work and fringe benefits (but not wages). When a B.C. forest products strike was settled in 2003 through arbitration, the arbitrator increased managerial authority to schedule work, especially overtime. The union struck again in 2007 to reduce management rights.

INDUSTRIAL RELATIONS AND MANAGEMENT DECISIONS

Industrial relations considerations affect strategic management decisions in a variety of ways. In general, the impact of industrial relations is smaller than public comment and political rhetoric indicate. Overall, industrial relations linkages to specific corporate decisions are strongest in investment in new plants. Research has shown that about half of unionized companies consider industrial relations an important or dominant factor in determining the level of investment and choice of location. For another quarter of companies, labour matters have no impact, and for the remainder, industrial relations come under consideration but are not deemed significant.

These data must be considered in the broader context of business decisions. The dominant factors for locating new plants in resource industries, for example, are first the location and quality of a resource (e.g., mineral deposits), followed by the financial structure (commodity prices and taxes). Firms in the service sector, such as large retailers, locate their operations near their markets, but industrial relations clearly can play a role. Manufacturing companies, which often have the ability to choose among locations for new plants or the expansion of current operations, are often quite careful in their analyses of industrial relations issues. In deciding whether to invest in a new plant, rather than upgrade an existing plant, factors include the current industrial relations climate in the plant, the collective agreement provisions there, and the attitude of the union. Plants in which industrial relations are perceived to be poor are clearly at a disadvantage in attracting new investment from their corporate owners. Alternatively, companies build new facilities in rural areas partly because they expect that people in rural areas are less likely to be attracted to unions than their urban counterparts. In practice, however, this strategy is relatively rare outside of Ontario, as Canadian manufacturing is concentrated in urban centres.

On the other hand, industrial relations issues are significant in major corporate decisions such as the adoption of new technology or corporate reorganization, presumably because management is confident in its ability to deal with these matters successfully through existing procedures. One-third of the companies surveyed stated that labour relations are significant in these types of decisions.

MANAGEMENT INDUSTRIAL RELATIONS STRATEGIES

Few Canadian companies that engage in collective bargaining have formal "industrial relations strategies," in the sense of well-articulated policies governing organizational decisions. Instead, employers operate with distinctive sets of principles that guide management policies and behaviours (Purcell, 1987). Although a company's principles may not be stated in writing, industrial relations managers know them quite well and are able to relate specific decisions to the firm's general position. For convenience, the combination of principles that guide an employer's industrial relations functions will be called a "strategy."

Firms vary enormously in the extent to which they use industrial relations strategies within their broader human resources policies and larger corporate strategy. Corporate industrial relations strategies typically evolve over time. Historically, most employers have reacted negatively to the possible unionization of their employees. The degree of opposition to unionization can be related to the basic human resources position of the firm or industry, experience with unionization, or the ideology of controlling shareholders. But after unions are established, employers must determine how they want to manage their relationship, which leads to the development of a "style" for industrial relations that is very similar to a policy. In a well-managed organization, this policy supports the company's overall business strategy.

Thus, most employers in the fast-food industry hire young workers with limited skills, set starting pay at or near the minimum wage, and expect high employee turnover. The introduction of a union would upset this system, as organized workers would press for higher wages, job security, and other possibilities to improve their situation. It is not surprising that McDonald's and Tim Hortons, for example, vigorously resist unions whenever they appear in one of their franchises (Skogan, 1999). Large retail chains follow similar strategies. While their employees are more mature, the corporate objective is to minimize the number of full-time workers and to maintain the maximum control over hours of work. Wages are regarded as one of the employer's largest controllable costs, although they are not a large percentage of the total cost of goods sold.

Public utilities have a much different environment. They employ highly skilled workers who must provide service under all conditions. High skill levels and stable employment fit well with a well-paid unionized workforce. For other firms, the philosophy of management is a factor. U.S.-based automakers accept unions in their assembly plants (they had resisted unionism in the 1930s). In fact, their production strategies may include consultation with unions as a normal management process.

Determinants of Management Strategies

According to management theories, senior managers are presumed to have considerable latitude in establishing or changing their strategies in most fields, constrained principally by markets or legal regulation. The same flexibility does not always exist for industrial relations. The Canadian industrial relations system is embedded in legal protections and supervised by labour relations boards. Thus, managers are not free to act unilaterally when they make many decisions. Instead, they must persuade their employees' representatives that corporate policies that affect employees are desirable or necessary. Because unions are relatively independent organizations, they have the resources to challenge management policies. Many managers find this exercise of workplace democracy undesirable or stressful. Even nonunion firms must carefully assess the union threat posed by any strategy that disadvantages employees. Employees may join a union to protect themselves against what they see as unreasonable changes in their wages and conditions of work, especially in industries or regions where unionism is well entrenched.

Unionized firms have to work within the limits of their collective agreements because these contracts cannot be altered without the consent of the union. For example, a firm seeking to reduce wage levels or displacing workers to adopt a low-price strategy requires agreement from its union. A union might agree to some of these changes, but usually in return for other protections for its members. Canadian unions vary in their willingness to co-operate with management plans. On balance, well-managed firms have been able to achieve most of the changes they sought, although not always at the price they preferred.

In personal interviews, many Canadian industrial relations executives referred to major strikes as turning points for industrial relations in their firms. Some disputes caused managers to re-examine their positions and promote improvements in labour relations; in other words, labour resistance caused employers to adopt new strategies to avoid labour discord. For example, Manitoba Telephone and its union endured a 103-day work stoppage in 1999. Determined not to repeat this experience, the parties established a negotiations protocol for the next round of bargaining. In 2001, they reached a collective agreement in record time, before the expiry of the old collective agreement.

Management's industrial relations policies are shaped by the political environment in which the firm operates. Where a pro-labour party (usually the NDP) is prominent in provincial politics, employers must consider the political effects of their policies. Anti-union policies that go beyond the range of acceptability in local politics may provoke legislation that could restrict future management actions.

The degree to which unions are established in a firm also is a significant factor in management's attitude toward industrial relations. For example, Petro-Canada, formerly a federally owned company, purchased a number of unionized facilities in its early years. Although many other firms in the petroleum industry operate without unions or have employee committees that fulfill some roles of unions, Petro-Canada built its policies around the acceptance of unions in the unionized locations it purchased (Taras and Ponak, 1999). When Stelco reduced the scale of its operations, it sought to work co-operatively with the United Steelworkers (which represented almost all of its hourly employees) and succeeded in most cases (Frost and Verma, 1999). By contrast, several manufacturing firms—Honda, for example—have built new plants in rural areas, where union influence traditionally is weak. They operated on a nonunion basis, relying on human resource practices that mimic unionized plants and skilful managers to remain nonunion. Employees at a number of these plants eventually were unionized. Firms with a history of dealings with unions accepted this change, while Japanese firms, unaccustomed to dealing with truly independent unions, have resisted unionization virtually everywhere in North America.

A major factor in determining the ability of an employer to act strategically is the relative bargaining power of the parties. Beginning in the early 1990s, the balance of power at the bargaining table clearly shifted toward management. High rates of unemployment, a decline in labour militancy, plant closures, deregulation, and free trade agreements with the United States and Mexico all combined to increase the ability of employers to obtain their own objectives in collective bargaining. In such an environment, managers were able to negotiate wage freezes or even reductions.

In summary, the determinants of industrial relations strategy include

- management business strategy
- union power
- union co-operativeness
- union militancy, especially strike propensity
- the degree of unionization within the firm
- labour laws
- collective agreement provisions

ELEMENTS OF AN INDUSTRIAL RELATIONS STRATEGY

An examination of our survey data and secondary sources shows that the common elements of most strategies are management attitude toward unions, compensation, and workplace practices (Kochan, McKersie, and Capelli, 1984).

The first element is the employer's attitude toward the unionization of its employees, both in terms of existing relationships with labour and the organization of new units.

Is there a strong hostility toward unions? If so, the firm is unlikely to share information with unions, develop consultative mechanisms, or conduct joint union–management initiatives. The firm might even resist unionization of unorganized plants or try to remove unions where they exist. If the attitude is more accepting of unions, then greater potential exists for maintaining harmonious relationships.

A second element relates to compensation and how wages and employee benefits compare with those of other firms. Some firms are leaders in the labour market and, presumably, find that this position enables them to hire more selectively, avoid labour strife, and retain their workforce. A stable labour force in turn makes investment in training workers feasible. Others prefer a low wage rate and choose to accept high turnover. Training is minimal in these firms, although management may cultivate an image of caring for employee welfare in order to legitimize management authority (Purcell, 1987).

Third, a strategy can be discerned by the manner in which a firm conducts its affairs in the workplace. Has management sought a constructive relationship with its union, has it ignored the union at this level, or has it tried to limit or undermine the union's influence? While most managers have a preference to run union-free workplaces, the issue is whether the firm is translating this preference into managerial practices.

Four Strategies Toward Unions

Four general strategies for dealing with unions apply to most companies.

1. The *union-acceptance* strategy means that the company accepts the inevitability of unionism and collective bargaining for some or all of its operations. These companies may prefer not to have unions, but remain neutral when a union attempts to organize one of their nonunion operations, partly for philosophical reasons, but also because of their broader strategy of working viably with unions. Within the framework of collective bargaining, the company seeks to negotiate the most favourable settlements possible.

2. The *union-resistance* strategy exists in partially unionized firms that seek to limit the spread of unions to the unorganized parts of their workforce, although they accept the legitimacy of their existing unions. They vigorously oppose union-organizing campaigns within their organizations. They normally extend terms and conditions of employment negotiated by unions to nonunion employees. This tactic discourages the spread of unionism. Employees may see improvements in employment coming from management, not union pressure.

3. A third strategy can be called *union removal*. The basic goal of companies using this strategy is to eliminate unions where they exist in their operations. These employers resist negotiating any collective agreements that give unionized employees better conditions than are already provided for nonunion workers. They do this to emphasize the minimal role a union can play. They engage in extensive and ongoing campaigns to discourage union activity among their workers and resist unions' organizing.

4. Companies that are not unionized but fear that a union may gain a foothold in their organizations may follow a *union-substitution/avoidance* strategy. They establish their own forms of representation, designed to make their employees regard unions as unnecessary or inferior to management-sponsored bodies.

Union Acceptance Where unions already exist, the majority of Canadian companies practise the union-acceptance strategy. A survey of 106 private-sector companies with some unionized employees found that 71 percent regarded negotiating the best possible collective agreement as the primary objective of their industrial relations policy (Thompson, 1995). Only 9 percent reported that they concentrated on limiting the influence or spread of unions where they existed. The remaining companies had multiple goals, the most common combination being to negotiate the best possible agreements and to limit the influence or spread of unions. No company reported that its primary goal was to remove existing unions, and only 3 percent of the companies included the removal of unions with another goal (Thompson, 1995). Another survey of 161 unionized private-sector firms conducted between 1992 and 1994 found similar results. A majority of employers reported that they had taken a tough stance in bargaining in the past decade. About 20 percent reported that they had obtained reductions in wages, benefits, or negotiated restrictions on their authority (Godard, 1997).

Inco was one example of the union-acceptance strategy. The company had little choice. All of its major production facilities were unionized by militant unions. Nonetheless, Inco was able to reduce its employment sharply, by 55 percent between 1980 and 1985, while making substantial improvements in the conduct of labour relations. Co-operation between the parties increased. Joint consultation grew in scope and importance. Consultation over job security was incorporated in the collective agreement (Chaykowski, 1999). Stelco is another heavily unionized company that practises union acceptance. Stelco built a new plant in the 1980s and recognized the United Steelworkers, the union at its other operations, before construction was completed. The company did insist, however, on negotiating a new collective agreement for the plant (Frost and Verma, 1999). At Canadian Pacific Railway, significant technological changes were introduced that resulted in major job losses. The changes were negotiated with the company's unions; employees who lost their jobs received payouts, education and retraining, and early retirement packages (Timur and Ponak, 2002). ABB, a Swedish multinational manufacturer of electrical equipment that operates in 17 countries, introduced numerous changes in the organization of work at its two Canadian plants in the 1990s. Union influence was much stronger at the Quebec location than at Guelph, Ontario, but management implemented the new practices successfully at both locations (Bélanger, 1999).

Union Resistance Nevertheless, few Canadian companies are enthusiastic about unions. In the survey of 106 companies, 71 percent preferred not to have a union or actively opposed unionization during an organizing campaign. Another survey in 1996–1997 found that between 60 and 80 percent of Canadian employers engaged in some form of overt resistance to unionization. Between 10 and 20 percent acknowledged that they engaged in illegal tactics to defeat a union organization campaign. Yet some companies hired consultants who apparently counselled management on establishing a successful relationship with a new union (Bentham, 2002). When a union campaign is not underway, most employers state their policy as: "We try to manage well enough to make a union unnecessary, but we respect our employees' choice if they select one." Companies often attempt to keep unions at bay and attribute any union organizing victories to managerial errors, or local conditions. A major forest products company in British Columbia made a point of attempting to operate new plants outside the province on a nonunion basis and publicly boasted about its success, although it had no alternative to dealing with its unions in the province. Exhibit 5.1 illustrates an example of a company determined not to have a union.

Exhibit 5.1
Eaton's: Keeping Unions at Bay

In the early 1980s, six branches of Eaton's Department Store in Ontario unionized after a 26-month wage freeze and substantial layoffs. Management engaged in an advertising campaign, urging its employees to reject union representation. It asked its employees if they wanted the same reputation as the Auto Workers or Canada Post. When the company refused to negotiate a first collective agreement, a six-month strike followed. One of the four Eaton brothers who owned the chain crossed the picket line to encourage workers to follow his lead. After six months, the union capitulated. It accepted a first agreement with the same wage increase the company had unilaterally granted to its other employees. Eaton's obtained the result it wanted. Employees in all six stores abandoned their union. In Manitoba, the labour relations board imposed a first contract for a Brandon store. The company then dismissed half of the employees and demanded concessions from the union. By the end of the decade, this bargaining unit, too, had decertified (McQueen, 1998; Palmer, 1992).

Canadian corporate policies differ from those of American companies. Most American firms probably fall into the union resistance or removal categories. Which path do American companies operating in Canada follow? It is frequently assumed that American companies retain their industrial relations policies when they operate in Canada. In fact, Canadian data show that the aggressive anti-union practices that are so popular in the United States are rarely imported into Canada by unionized companies.

Consistent with practices in other countries, most industrial relations executives of foreign-owned firms report that their head offices have little or no influence on Canadian activities. Management at the foreign headquarters wants to be informed of major events, such as strikes, but seldom dictates policies or practices in its Canadian affiliate. Industrial relations managers normally report to senior management in Canada. General Motors of Canada, for example, has a Canadian board of directors, including outsiders and senior managers. The vice-president of personnel reports to the board of directors in Canada (Kumar, 1999). The manager of another American-owned firm that is almost entirely nonunion in the United States but about 35 percent unionized in Canada declared, "We play by the rules where we operate. In the United States, there are no rules. Here rules exist, and we follow them." No significant differences in industrial relations vis-à-vis the nationality of the parent company appeared either. In other words, for unionized companies, U.S., British, and European owners tend to follow much the same policies as their Canadian counterparts (Thompson, 1995).

A case study of ABB, the Swedish multinational enterprise discussed previously, reinforces these findings. The company respects national differences in its employment relations. Increased competition in the product market has caused ABB to adopt central policies on common computer software, improved design, and common production methods. Employment relations, however, including the role of employee committees,

Union Removal While none of the large unionized companies surveyed for this chapter had a union-removal strategy, there was evidence of this strategy in other firms. The most common employer tactic is to drag out negotiations for its unionized operations. While bargaining is going on, nonunion workers receive wage increases. The employer then informs the unionized bargaining units of the corporate "pattern" and, in negotiations, refuses to offer any terms superior to those already in place. When the number of unionized employees is small, a large employer can hold out in bargaining and through a strike to achieve its ultimate objective, the removal of its union. Starbucks, a well-known coffee chain, paid the father of one of its employees to hire a lawyer to lead a decertification campaign (BCLRB, 2003).

Aided by the small size of individual branches and high turnover of union supporters, chartered banks had such a strategy from 1979 to 1983 (Brody et al., 1993). The CIBC had set the tone of industrial relations for its employees when it engaged in a massive propaganda campaign against unionism. The Canada Labour Relations Board found the employer had engaged in so many unfair labour practices that the president of the bank was required to write a letter of apology to each employee and express the bank's willingness to abide by the law. Despite such measures, unionism has essentially disappeared from the banking industry.

Other large multibranch companies follow similar strategies. Retail chains, anxious to preserve a largely part-time labour force and managerial control over work schedules, proactively practise a union removal strategy. Bargaining for unionized units normally follows compensation adjustments for nonunion units, and the company typically refuses to improve on changes implemented unilaterally for nonunion employees. Workers at a unionized location know that their employer has dozens of other stores that will continue to operate if they strike, leaving them little bargaining power.

The first McDonald's franchise to unionize in North America was in Squamish, British Columbia, in 1998. Two grade 12 students led the organizing drive, aided by the Canadian Auto Workers. The labour movement hailed the McDonald's unionization victory, but it was short lived. The employer launched three separate legal challenges after the union arrived, two of them asserting that workers 19 years of age or less (a majority of McDonald's employees) were "infants" under the law and could not apply for union membership or authorize collection of union dues.[3] In the third challenge, anti-union employees, most making slightly more than the minimum wage, also appeared before the board, represented by a lawyer, to contest the union's application for certification. The union was successful before the labour relations board, but ultimately lost the support of its members. After 10 months, the CAW Union was unsuccessful in negotiating a collective agreement. Some supporters had resigned their jobs. A majority of the remaining workers voted to decertify the union. The identity of the party who paid for the lawyer to represent the "anti-union employees" was never revealed.

Union Substitution/Avoidance While data on the extent of union-substitution policies are not readily available, a handful of published accounts describe this strategy. The petroleum industry has several examples of these policies. Imperial Oil has relied upon "joint industrial councils" (JICs) as part of a general strategy to discourage unionization since 1919. Other elements include slightly higher wage scales and generous employee benefits—which are not negotiated with unions at any locations (Taras, 1997). William Lyon Mackenzie King, Canada's first minister of labour and later prime minister, introduced JICs to the Canadian oil industry. The councils consist of equal numbers of managers (selected) and employees (elected by their peers) who meet regularly to discuss health and safety, recreation, production issues, and occasional grievances (Taras, 2000; Boone, 2000).

Petro-Canada has "Employee–Management Advisory Committees" (EMACs) at several of its nonunion operations. These joint committees meet semi-annually to discuss grievances and production issues. Employees receive an information booklet outlining the structure and the powers of the EMAC and containing several other substantive provisions commonly found in collective agreements, with the notable exceptions of procedural subjects such as seniority rights, promotion criteria, job security, and formal grievance procedures (Taras and Ponak, 1999).

Roughly 30 percent of employees in the petroleum industry are covered by formal nonunion representation schemes. Despite this substantial presence, the policy has drawbacks. Systems such as JICs consume a great deal of management time and make the employer vulnerable to minor employee pressure tactics and the union threat. One study of nonunion systems in three different industries found that if nonunion workers holding leadership positions in the nonunion systems become dissatisfied with management policies or style, they actually use their leadership skills to support union organizing, and then become key figures in running the union local (Timur, 2005). The nonunion systems can be turbulent at times. Imperial Oil unilaterally cancelled one JIC, and its workers cancelled another at a second location. At Petro-Canada, EMACs have been the basis of successful union certifications (Taras, 1994), and at Imperial Oil an important site located in Norman Wells, near the Arctic Circle, rejected the JIC in favour of a large national union (Taras and Copping, 1998). In 2007, however, the Norman Wells workers decertified the union and were welcomed back into the JIC fold.

Beginning in the 1930s, Dofasco, a steel producer located in Hamilton, Ontario, used a human resources strategy designed to prevent unionization by the United Steelworkers, which had organized the other major steel producers in Hamilton and elsewhere. Dofasco does not have a formal collective representation mechanism for soliciting employees' views. However, it matches the wage rates negotiated by the United Steelworkers at nearby Stelco and adds a profit-sharing plan. It also sponsors social events and recreational activities for its employees. Dofasco makes a concerted effort to foster a sense of community among employees and makes heavy use of employee involvement plans (Storey, 1983; Harshaw, 2000). In 2007, a foreign company purchased Dofasco and granted the Steelworkers access to its operations for the purpose of gaining certification. The initial attempt in 2008 failed. It is highly likely that the Steelworkers will launch another sign-up campaign.

These examples of union-substitution strategies, combined with survey results of unionized firms, demonstrate that most Canadian companies would prefer to operate without a union. An equally significant conclusion is that once a union is certified and established, most large employers experienced in labour relations seek to negotiate the best collective agreement possible and have found that they can operate successfully in a unionized setting. Data discussed in Chapter 14 show that unionized firms are often more productive than nonunion firms. For large Canadian employers in this situation, the dominant strategy for dealing with unions is union acceptance.

Relative Compensation

All employers must be aware of labour market realities when selecting compensation levels for their employees. Firms whose wages fall below normal levels for the region in which they operate can expect to experience high turnover, employee dissatisfaction, and difficulties in recruiting. For some companies, the savings realized by holding wage costs down offset the disadvantages, especially when the labour force is unskilled and tightly controlled. High-wage strategies offer the opposite benefits and costs. High-wage firms are preferred employers in many localities, so they have no difficulty in recruiting staff with strong qualifications. Turnover usually is low, although employee dissatisfaction can still be a problem if other elements of the employment relationship are deficient.

Unionized employers have difficulty pursuing a low-wage strategy, and even nonunion employers in an industry where unions operate also face problems with this policy. Nonetheless, low-wage firms do exist with and without unions. Where unions are present, workers can easily compare wages, and union members expect their unions to negotiate better compensation. Apart from their bargaining power, unions bring information on wage levels at other firms to their members' attention, thereby introducing additional market pressures on management in wage determination. In the nonunion environment, employers share compensation data with each other, but typically conceal this information from their employees.

Unsurprisingly, compensation issues are important to managers. In a survey of unionized companies in the 1990s (see Thompson, 1995), senior industrial relations executives were asked with which other firms they compared their wages and fringe benefits. Overwhelmingly, these companies compare their compensation to other firms in the same industry or sector. For example, manufacturing firms in Ontario look to other companies in the region facing similar labour market conditions when deciding the appropriate compensation levels for their employees. Naturally, their unions make similar comparisons, reinforcing industry wage patterns. A small proportion of firms compare their wages to other industries, in part because appropriate firms in the same industry may not be available or a single large firm dominates the industry in a region. No firms reported making foreign country comparisons. Unless wage levels determine the ability of a company to operate successfully, management decisions on appropriate wage rates are based on a combination of the firm's cost structure and the wages other firms pay in the same industry, especially their product market competitors.

Large unionized firms generally have compensation packages above the average for all firms in their region. Two effects are at work: size and unionization. Overall, large firms pay higher wages than smaller ones, and unionized firms generally pay wages about 8 percent higher than do nonunion firms. Interestingly, the 1990s survey found that only 40 percent of the firms believed that their compensation was higher than the average for their relevant comparison group in the same industry or region. Almost 55 percent believed their wages and fringes were average compared to other relevant employers. This suggests that unionized employers accept wages at or above the average for their industry unless strong competitive pressures emerge. Traditionally, bargaining objectives have not included reducing wages below the levels of domestic competition.

Air Canada is a prominent example of a company's responding to financial pressures (see Chapter 11's opening vignette). The company was beset by nonunion competition, declining revenues from the September 11, 2001, terrorist attacks and the 2003 Toronto SARS outbreak, and reductions in business travel. It sought, and received, wage cuts and changes in work rules to enhance productivity (and reduce employees' quality of work life). As another example, a number of companies in the supermarket industry responded to competition from large retailers by obtaining wage cuts in the 1990s and into the next decade. The expansion of Wal-Mart into food sales is likely to produce similar results. Unionized employers in these industries realized that they had to address their competitive issues through collective bargaining. Judges controlling corporate restructuring under the threat of bankruptcy also respected existing labour–management relationships.

The supermarket industry experienced substantial changes in the 1990s and first decade of the 2000s. Faced with competition from low-cost rivals—primarily Wal-Mart— many unionized companies negotiated two-tier wage systems, combined with buyout packages for the current (senior) labour force. The net result was that senior workers were rewarded for resigning and were replaced by new employees making substantially lower wages. In addition, full-time positions were replaced with part-time jobs, again at lower wages and with reduced fringe benefits (Kainer, 1998).

Workplace Practices

Canadian employers initiated significant changes in their operations during the 1990s. Large surveys have shown that almost half of unionized firms engage in some form of employee participation or consultation. Quality- and performance-related programs also are popular (Betcherman et al., 1994; Smith, 1993). Profit sharing is used less often by unionized companies for employees represented by unions (Betcherman et al., 1994). New initiatives took place alongside traditional and long-standing union–management consultation in such matters as health and safety and technological change. A 1995 survey of over 200 Canadian firms, both unionized and nonunion, found that two-thirds had implemented some form of workplace reform (Godard, 1998).

Definitions of workplace change vary, so direct comparison across firms is difficult. A common employer practice to improve productivity was to reduce the number of job classifications, giving management the right to assign work more flexibly. Job classifications, i.e., rates of pay connected to specified responsibilities, originated as a management technique to control workers. In the changing workplaces of the 1990s, however, detailed descriptions of employees' duties became a barrier to efficiency, at least from the employers' perspective. Inco was a typical case. The company reduced the number of job classifications, and employees were trained to assume additional duties in the enlarged classifications and received higher pay to reflect their new status (Chaykowski, 1999). General Motors agreed to create new job classifications to introduce "multi-tasking," i.e., the amalgamation of job responsibilities, through local bargaining.

New job classifications typically involved a wage increase to reflect added responsibilities (Kumar, 1999). Canadian Pacific Railway won the right to assign workers outside of their classifications for temporary assignments of increasing duration (Coates and Downie, 1999).

When asked what initiatives they had taken to improve labour relations and productivity, managers' most common response (35 percent) was improved communications with their unions and their employees, most often with respect to the operations and financial status of the firm. The focus on production and financial issues was deliberate. Improved communications with unions and employees clearly was intended to demonstrate to union leaders and their members the employer's financial, competitive, and production issues. Employers believed that they would enjoy a smoother acceptance of changes in their operations if unions understood the reasons for their decisions and the pressures the firm faced. Deliberate efforts were made to steer discussions away from industrial relations issues (e.g., grievances or potential collective bargaining demands).

At Stelco, local management began sharing financial and business information with its local unions, going beyond traditional health and safety issues. One topic was a joint effort to reduce the reliance on outside contractors. The parties also administered training programs to prepare workers for changes in the firm's product line (Frost and Verma, 1999). Bell Canada initiated regular "forums" with senior union leaders to share information on a wide range of subjects (Verma, 1999).

Line management rather than industrial relations staff typically represented the employer. A common format was regular meetings with union officials to discuss production matters, such as the volume or quality of production. Union representatives had the opportunity to comment or ask questions, but management typically saw these meetings as forums for providing information, not as a form of consultation. Meetings with union representatives enabled management to exchange views with its unions and to discuss issues of mutual concern without at the same time yielding any of its authority to make decisions on matters not covered by the collective agreement. Unions have not become involved in management strategic decisions through these meetings (Wagar, 1994).

Another common employer initiative is to encourage employees to take more responsibility for improving productivity and product quality. About 20 percent of employers instituted formal programs to improve quality. These programs have several names: "quality circles," "total quality management," or "quality improvement" systems. While these programs differ in many important details, they normally include teams of employees, supervisors, facilitators, and technical advisers charged with making specific improvements in the quality of the product or service for which they are responsible (see Exhibit 5.2).

Employee-involvement programs are another way for management to change the workplace (see Chapter 6). These programs are designed to solicit employee suggestions on production issues, work schedules, and other workplace problems. These normally involve "mixed" teams of employees (union members) and supervisors. Unions may be wary of employee-involvement programs, which are initiated and controlled by management. Unions see them as a potential threat to their role as employees' exclusive representative in the workplace. Privately, some employers have tacitly admitted that they expect employee-involvement programs to weaken the militancy of their workers, so labour's concerns may be justified.

The troubled history of the B.C. paper company Catalyst was described in the opening vignette. It went through three major ownership changes and is struggling to remain profitable. It built union–management trust through employee-involvement programs at each location to cut costs without cutting jobs, and a bonus was introduced based on the price of newsprint. Money from the bonus would allow the union to enhance early retirement benefits in the pension plan. The company and union seem to be trying to retain their commitment to co-operative relations even in the midst of significant strains in the business environment.

An interesting aspect of the Catalyst story is the response of other B.C. pulp and paper companies. Instead of following Catalyst's lead, they were surprised and some were even dismayed by Catalyst's model of union–management co-operation. Catalyst's initiative caused an employer association to disband. No other companies have started employee-involvement programs of the same type. Other unions in the forest products sector are suspicious of the Catalyst package (personal interview, June 2003).

In summary, the most common labour relations response of unionized Canadian employers to increased competitive pressures was to co-operate with unions and seek assistance from their workers. It is noteworthy that in adopting these strategies, most employers rejected other, more confrontational approaches. Only two companies stated that they chose to confront their union or to regain management rights that were constrained by the collective agreement. Concession bargaining, i.e., demanding reductions in existing terms and conditions of employment, also occurred when the employer experienced serious difficulties. Many firms relied on changes to their collective agreements to improve productivity, and companies in some cases had traded new clauses in collective agreements for job security or other benefits to workers. However, most large unionized Canadian companies chose co-operation over confrontation (see Exhibit 5.3).

Taken collectively, these initiatives are called "high-performance" workplace systems. These practices often have a short life expectancy. At any given time, a minority of Canadian firms are actively pursuing these policies (Godard, 2004). Based on the interviews conducted for this chapter, it is likely that firms will try new forms of work organization in collaboration with their unions, even if previous efforts have not endured.

Exhibit 5.3
Changes in Workplace Practices

- reduced job classifications combined with employee retraining to increase skills
- enhanced communications with employees and unions with focus on financial and operational issues
- quality improvement programs
- employee involvement
- union–management consultation

INDUSTRIAL RELATIONS STAFF

Corporate headquarters is directly responsible for major industrial relations policy decisions in the majority of Canadian companies. Some divide the responsibility between headquarters and other levels of authority. Routine approval of decisions by headquarters is rare, except for decisions on the settlement of grievances where authority is widely dispersed. Even in areas where corporate managers do not have operational responsibility, for example in the monitoring of labour relations, they have significant influence on the formulation of the policies under which lower-level managers will operate.

The high degree of centralization of authority for key industrial relations decisions and policies, especially decisions connected with collective bargaining, indicates that the importance of these decisions, their complexity and political character, and the uncertainty of the business environment outweigh the decentralizing tendencies of the Canadian industrial relations system.

Industrial relations is not purely a staff function. Line managers in most firms have some responsibility for industrial relations activities, supported by industrial relations staff. Because many industrial relations processes can be highly technical and complex, organizations must assign technically competent staff to assist line management and to conduct many specialized functions.

CONCLUSION

After more than two decades of employer initiative in industrial relations, several features have emerged. Firms that have adopted industrial relations strategies tied to their business strategies generally are satisfied with their policy. Industrial relations considerations influence a small number of business decisions heavily. It is not clear whether the limited influence of industrial relations is due to the importance of other factors (such as access to the market or raw materials costs) or the confidence of senior management that they can operate successfully within the general context of Canadian industrial relations.

The hardline approach of American employers toward their unions and employees meets with little acceptance in Canada. Although most Canadian employers would prefer not to have a union, large unionized firms accept that employees chose to be unionized. Companies work to maximize their position within the framework of collective bargaining. Most large firms are resigned to paying above-average wages and employee benefits, and they accept that collective bargaining raises their visibility in the labour market. When faced with competitive pressures, a number of firms have negotiated substantial wage reductions, although this was not the norm for the economy. Unionized firms did not believe that collective bargaining was a serious barrier to their commercial success. Nonetheless, traditionally nonunion firms continue to vigorously resist unions.

In the face of strong competitive pressures, unionized firms emphasize communication with their unions. They rely on existing arrangements for union–management consultation to prove to their unions and employees the economic realities of product markets and to solve operational problems jointly where wage reductions are not feasible. Labour–management consultation is especially common on the subjects of occupational health and safety, production problems, employee assistance, and technological change. Authority for bargaining decisions is highly centralized, despite decentralized bargaining structures and the shift of responsibility toward line management for some industrial relations processes.

By 2007, a pattern of more adversarial bargaining had emerged, without challenging the legitimacy of collective bargaining as an institution. As described above, Telus locked out its employees for several months in 2006 to achieve substantial changes in its collective agreement. Teck Cominco had a long strike earlier in the decade when workers demanded higher wages as mineral prices rose and the company had $6 billion in cash. In both cases the employer was successful, and normal labour relations processes resumed after the stoppages.

This chapter is based on a data set of in-depth interviews with senior industrial relations officials in 106 unionized Canadian companies during the 1990s (see Thompson, 1995). Since those interviews, over 25 percent of those companies have ceased to exist. Some firms were absorbed by larger competitors. The number of Ontario and Quebec supermarket chains fell, for example. Consolidation of forest products companies occurred across all regions. Other Canadian business icons, including Molson, Dofasco, Inco, Seagram, and Alcan, were purchased by foreign companies. The effects of these changes on industrial relations policies are unclear. Where one Canadian company purchased another, perhaps policies of the purchasing company will continue. In the original sample, there was no pattern of foreign owners imposing policies on Canadian subsidiaries. But these old assumptions have not been tested in this new century.

In many respects, the unionized segments of the Canadian economy have performed well without having to remove or severely weaken either the unions or the collective bargaining process. Unionized companies compete successfully in international markets. Productivity and product quality are high. Public policy has played a minor role in the recent initiatives of Canadian employers. But market pressures, fed by international competition, free trade agreements, changing technology, and deregulation, will continue to challenge existing strategies and practices.

Questions

1. What are the constraints on management's industrial relations strategies?
2. What industrial relations issues face a firm wishing to pursue a low-wage compensation strategy?
3. Distinguish among the strategies of union acceptance, union resistance, union removal, and union substitution/avoidance.
4. What employer initiatives might improve productivity and industrial relations?
5. What factors would lead to the decentralization of authority for management industrial relations decisions? What factors lead to the centralization of authority?
6. Do you think the Catalyst model can survive in the longer term? Is it truly embedded, or does it remain fragile? What factors might tip it in one direction or the other?

Weblinks

Construction Labour Relations Association (Alberta):
www.clra.org

A pro-management website:
www.labourwatch.com

Canadian HR Reporter:
www.hrreporter.com

Canadian Labour and Business Centre:
www.clbc.ca

Chapter 6

Managing the High-Involvement Workplace

Anil Verma and Daphne G. Taras

Deregulation throughout the 1980s and 1990s has created serious disruptions to some large and otherwise stable companies. In this vignette, the iconic Canadian company Canadian Pacific Railway (CPR) uses employee involvement as part of a larger strategy of union co-operation to keep some of its peripheral railway lines open.

The Canadian Pacific Railway (CPR) was built in the 1880s to bind the nation. Today it is a publicly traded, Class 1, North American railway providing freight transportation services over a 14 000 mile network. The CPR workforce, comprised of 15 000 employees in the mid-2000s, is less than half of the size that it was in the 1980s. New technology is the main reason behind the smaller workforce, but there has also been downsizing from track closures and the sale of branch lines.

Closure of lines was highly disruptive to workers' jobs and their lives. Having seen the dislocations that had taken place, and sensing that more upheaval was on its way, the United Transportation Union (UTU, representing conductors and train service employees) and the Brotherhood of Locomotive Engineers (BLE, representing engineers) approached management asking for a joint study. The study's goal was to examine other operations in Canada and the United States to see if solutions could be found to keep marginal branch lines within CPR. They focused on branch lines that could be turned into internal, semi-autonomous profit centres, or short line railways, as they are known in the industry.

Supported by a government grant, the two unions and CPR management launched the study in 1994. The study revealed that selling branch lines often led to nonunion worksites and reduced wages, benefits, and pensions for employees. Even then, once these changes were implemented and accepted, short lines were often abandoned within five to ten years. The study recommended that establishing an internal short line labour agreement would reduce labour costs by about 30 percent. At the same time, the union wanted to maintain pensions, benefits, vacations, seniority, and wage levels at relatively the same levels.

To reduce labour costs by 30 percent while keeping employee wage rates and benefits at current levels, revolutionary changes would have to be made to workplace governance at the rescued branch lines. The new system of "co-determination" would allow employees to jointly manage the new internal short line with management.

Co-determination meant senior labour–management participation on an advisory board overseeing the business. Local self-managed work units of unionized employees work with a reduced core of management to run the day-to-day operation. Work rules were to be "reduced to a minimum," and unionized workers would break out of their traditional work roles to engage in multi-tasking ("flexible specialization"). A new pay structure would be comprised of a salary and a profit-sharing plan. The short line organizational culture was to have an "entrepreneurial spirit" with a mission: "innovative customer rail service through an involved workplace."

These changes were set against 100 years of tradition that included a hierarchical management structure and sharp job demarcations. However, with the assistance of Mike DeGirolamo championing the initiative, these bold suggestions were accepted by the CPR executive committee. The potential benefits to the core CPR business included retaining feeder rail traffic from the two routes and not introducing a competitor into the market. The executive committee authorized management to negotiate short line agreements for the two marginal branch lines that would otherwise be sold or simply abandoned—Kawartha Lakes Railway (KLR) in central Ontario (Peterborough area) and Kootenay Valley Railway (KVR) in the interior of British Columbia (Nelson area).

As a start, they set the collective bargaining agreement aside and agreed to treat the creation of the new short lines as a greenfield site.[1] They would revisit the collective agreement once they had agreed on a new structure and operational procedures. The first step was for management to establish a unique profit centre for each short line so its performance could be measured and tracked independently from the rest of CPR, a first within the company. There was a full sharing of all financial and commercial information with the unions, and, by extension, the employees. Armed with this information, employees challenged 100 years of history by "sitting down and saying—ok, we have to find a better way to do our jobs, we have to figure it out and we have to operate the line ourselves."

Each employee would have to be a multi-tasking, multi-purpose worker within his or her own general skills and trade. For example, a conductor or a running trades employee would perform multiple tasks within the running trades but would not cross over to perform maintenance functions. This flexible approach fit well with the new concept of group decision-making. Unionized employees on site at the short line would meet at least monthly as a group with management to make decisions by consensus on key operational matters.

The number of managers would be greatly reduced. In the past, a short line would have had up to four managers. Now, each short line would have only one manager who would act more as a facilitator or leader. A joint union/management committee selects the sole manager for each short line property; in other words, unions hold a veto over who becomes the short line manager.

The new arrangement succeeded in creating an entrepreneurial spirit among the workers. Knowing they could design and run their own operation, they scrutinized the short line, and delivered significant cost-savings by making sensible changes to operations, work rules, seniority and staffing. Wage rates remained constant but the overall result was a drop in employees' regular take-home pay. To compensate for that, and in alignment with the entrepreneurial spirit, profit sharing (that included also a gainsharing component) was added to the employees' benefits. The new system would provide a payout based on financial and safety performance targets set jointly by employees and the site manager (and approved by the advisory board) at the beginning of each year.

The next task was negotiating a collective agreement for each short line start-up, to formalize the intentions of management and union. The changes from the core CPR collective agreement would be dramatic. The parties understood that a lengthy and detailed agreement similar to the main line agreement would not work for the short lines. Instead, the new collective agreement simply had a number of guiding principles and lacked the detailed work rules of the core agreement. In the end, the agreement was a "pretty thin, little book." CPR agreed to keep the line running and not sell it for the duration of the five-year contract.

The newly appointed manager of the short lines observed "there is no one that is better equipped to find ways to eliminate waste than the men that work day to day on the property." Now workers' ideas were not only brought forward, but also enthusiastically acted upon. Each operation established committees to focus on specific areas: finance, engineering, safety, operations, and property. These committees have made recommendations to the whole group of employees and the manager for decision and action.

The payoff for union workers is clear. They remain a part of their communities and have retained secure jobs. To encourage younger employees to remain, senior employees voluntarily gave up their right to take all their vacation time in the summer. This allows junior employees with young families to vacation in prime periods.

According to DeGirolamo, both lines have a "tremendous safety record" that is coupled with a "very high level of customer service." Grievances and arbitration have fallen dramatically. Since their establishment, both short lines have been profitable.

A major ingredient in the success of both short lines is the commitment of the employees. For example, KVR lost their main customer with the closure of a large Cominco smelter. The result would normally be layoffs. Instead, the KVR team used a reduced hauling schedule, vacation time, voluntary layoffs, and juggling of staff to achieve a reduction in labour costs that matched the revenue losses.

Management now clearly sees the potential of engaging employees in the process of running the railways. In fact, many of the innovations at KLR and KVR have been rolled out elsewhere in the CPR properties. This includes multi-tasking, hourly rates, and the positive performance system that defines the profit sharing for employees.[2]

In this chapter we address the development of contemporary high-involvement workplace practices and their diffusion. We examine their impact on performance and satisfaction, and review the legal status of employee involvement in both nonunion and unionized workplaces. Finally, we discuss the effect of employee involvement on employer–employee and union–management relations.

MANAGEMENT OBJECTIVES IN THE WORKPLACE

An understanding of workplace practices requires a consideration of managerial objectives for those practices. When a company like CP Rail (CPR) undertakes the type of effort described in the opening vignette, what does management want from the workplace and how does management reach its goals? Classical management and economic theory posits that management's overall objective is to maximize profits or shareholder value. CPR is interested in running short lines to make money. Often, firms simply cannot influence the price of their goods, as there is too much competition from rival firms, and the only way to maximize profits is to minimize costs. The railroad industry has become very competitive since deregulation, and any firm whose costs are higher than the competition's will not survive for long. CPR might concentrate on being an efficient producer and having a smooth-running operation, free from downtime caused by labour frictions, accidents, and lack of employee effort. Such an economic approach to thinking about management goals leads us to the concepts of *maximizing efficiency and productivity* in the workplace as the first management objective. The concepts of efficiency and productivity, even though initially derived from notions of profit maximization, apply equally well to public-sector and other not-for-profit organizations where there are limited budgets and competing demands for resources among rival agencies and uses. Under this efficiency imperative, management will seek to reduce or eliminate any threats to efficiency, and enhance efforts that lead to improvements in productivity.

A second managerial objective in the workplace, namely that of exercising *control*, derives from the history of labour–management relations over the last century (Bendix, 1956). This argument holds that managerial control of the workplace is as important as— if not even more important than—the need to maximize efficiency. Hence, CPR's workplace initiatives are risky because they require that managers give workers much more autonomy than they had in the past.

Why is control of the workplace so important? One reason often mentioned by experts is the need to manage uncertainty and ambiguity. The organizational context is characterized by uncertainty and ambiguity. Management's goals are difficult to achieve consistently and predictably in such an environment without complete control of the workplace and workplace decisions. Accepting unions or ceding authority to employees reduces the nature and extent of managerial control.

Another reason for management to want control may be purely ideological: a fundamental belief that it is management's right to govern the workplace and that any dilution of that role will not be acceptable. Ideology can play out at the societal, organizational, or individual level. Karl Marx articulated societal-level conflict between capital and labour as a clash of two *classes* within society in which each class attempts to dominate the other. Capital protects its interest by dictating its terms to workers in the workplace, while labour works to overthrow the capitalist class from power and achieve full access to the fruits that derive from work. While the Marxist appeal is best played out at a societal level, similar ideologies at the organizational and individual levels frequently guide management policies at the workplace. One such ideology derives from the concept of property rights. In this view, managers act as representatives of the owners who possess a fundamental right to govern the workplace. Although the application of property rights to the employment context has undergone considerable modification in Canadian law in the last century, managers generally claim "residual" rights, i.e., rights not specifically modified by law, to govern the workplace.

Yet another form of managerial ideology played out at an individual level is a deeply held belief among many managers that employer–employee relations are best handled on a bilateral basis. In this view, any form of representation, in the form of unions or other types of employee organizations, is unwarranted and wasteful. The belief in the efficacy of the "open-door policy" is typical throughout industry. Managers generally believe that they have, or can easily obtain, good knowledge of employee needs and the needs of the organization. They believe that a progressive management team can devise workplace policies to meet employee needs fully and adequately. They argue that the presence of a "third party" that has a poor understanding of business and employee needs can only make matters worse, not better. When the workforce grows too large to handle based on interpersonal relationships, some managers will advocate in-house collective forums for workers, but only very cautiously, and only with proper employee socialization and training so that managerial authority is not threatened. Later in this chapter we shall examine the implementation of high-involvement practices, such as those at CPR, in unionized and nonunion workplaces.

In summary, management is most concerned with issues of efficiency and control in the workplace. Some management practices achieve both goals at once. Sometimes, achieving efficiency goals might be at the expense of control. To fulfill or balance these goals, managers have experimented with a variety of approaches and policies in the course of the last century. What follows is a brief review of managerial workplace practices. Our objective in providing this review is to help the reader develop a better understanding of contemporary workplace practices.

A HISTORICAL OVERVIEW OF WORKPLACE MANAGEMENT

Throughout the 20th century, work tended to be organized in a top-down, "command and control" system. At the top of the pyramid were high-level executives who designed strategy and approved company policy. The middle held gradations of staff and management who executed policy, supervised shop-floor employees, and reported operational results back up the chain of command. At the bottom was the mass of employees who followed orders and produced goods and services. This traditional mode of organization is widely practised, even though it has attracted many critics who argue that it is anachronistic in an era of heightened global and domestic competition, shortened product and technology life cycles, and greater employee expectation of involvement and satisfaction at work.

In this section, we discuss important developments in the philosophy of management. First, we provide a brief overview of Taylorism, which made its mark in the early 20th century as a system of efficient production. This is followed by brief descriptions of the human relations school of the 1920s that sought to modify Tayloristic practices by emphasizing the contribution of social systems to productivity in the workplace. (This review reiterates some of the historical summary provided in Chapter 3, but places management developments in the context of workplace practices.) Both of these movements continue to guide contemporary organizational practice, and both influenced the growth of high-involvement workplaces described in sections to follow.

The Efficiency and Productivity Imperative: Taylorism

Of all the developments that attempted to reduce workplace chaos and bring a more systematic approach to managing workers, Taylorism is the most famous. One of the most influential, controversial, and perhaps most misunderstood management pioneers of the industrial age was Frederick Winslow Taylor (1865–1915). He believed that the key to productive efficiency was to simplify work by dividing the total production process into infinitesimally small and simple tasks (Taylor, 1911; Kanigel, 1997). Each task would be performed repetitively. The worker would be easy to train and replace because the skills needed to do the job would be very simple. This "one best way" to organize production would be determined by experts following carefully laid-out principles of work division and simplification, the length of work and rest periods, and the specialized tools needed to perform the tasks. Once management had devised the optimal way of doing the job, the worker was to follow these scientifically derived instructions. Taylor also advocated monetary incentives as the best way to motivate workers. Taylor's ideas shaped production systems in fast-growing mass manufacturing sectors such as auto and steel, leading to the development of fields of study such as industrial engineering and ergonomics, and practices such as time-and-motion studies and piece-rate incentive systems. Although the scientific management movement has undergone many modifications since it was first proposed, many of Taylor's ideas continue to make a huge impact on the way industrial societies organize production.

A key principle of scientific management was to separate worker and manager roles. Managers did all the "thinking" by hiring experts and developing the most efficient production process. Workers were responsible for "doing." Workers were not to do any thinking about the production process lest they tamper with the most efficient way of doing the job. At one point, Taylor argued that any involvement of the worker with the production process might be fatal to success.

Other workplace conditions such as growing unionization also helped institutionalize Tayloristic practices. For example, industrial unions responded to scientific management by negotiating written collective agreements that clearly specified divisions of responsibilities and the types of rigid work rules most appropriate to repetitive work in factory settings.

Taylorism is essentially a "technical" system of organizing work for mass production. It has its strengths but also several weaknesses. To learn from this system and to adapt it for future use, organizations need to understand two aspects of Taylorism: why it has been so influential, and what its key deficiencies are in meeting organizational and individual needs in the current context.

Taylorism as a process of work division and work simplification can be very efficient for firms that mass produce standard products for growing markets. By adopting Taylorist principles, the Ford Motor Company was able to produce the best-selling Model T as an inexpensive car for the average American. The engine, transmission, and chassis of the Model T when it was phased out in 1927 had not changed from those of the original Model T made in 1908. The success of the Model T can be attributed in part to cost efficiencies derived from low training costs, simple repetitive tasks that reduce chances of error, and economies of scale in mass production.

Even as Taylorist ideas spread throughout all segments of industry, its weaknesses were evident, although not significant as long as products and technology remained relatively stable. Taylorism in general discourages employee involvement or empowerment. It is best suited to low investment in training and very simplified tasks. Also, it views efficient production as combining the *individual worker* with the *technical production system* of equipment, materials, and production methods. However, in practice, people are also social beings whether they are at home or at work. Taylor essentially disregarded the role of the social context at work.

Even today many workplaces continue to be organized along Taylorist principles. The traditional time–motion efficiency emphasis of Taylorism can be found today in Canada Post's letter sorting, in major grocery chains that train cashiers to pass 30 items per minute across electronic scanners, and in all assembly-line work such as automobile assembly. Taylorism continues to be popular because it meets management's dual goals of efficiency and control.

A major management technique that borrows heavily from Taylorism and that made a considerable impact in the 1980s and 1990s is *lean production*.[3] Lean production concentrates on improvements in operational management so that costly inventories of supplies and finished products can be reduced. The movement was associated with just-in-time (JIT) management. Some people would argue that this required workers who could solve problems, respond quickly and knowledgeably to production demands, and feel fully engaged in their workplace. Others argue that lean production tended to alienate workers, intensify their work, and speed up production without adequate attention to the impact on people. The Canadian Auto Workers (CAW) sponsored a number of studies on the lean production technique, arguing that lean production is designed to reduce both production time and labour cost. The CAW found that the primary efficiency advantages of lean production came through its negative effects on labour interests: outsourcing (contracting out), lowering wages, and intensifying work.

The Human Imperative: Welfare Capitalism, the Hawthorne Experiments, and the Human Relations School

A small number of companies have always practised a form of paternalistic management that recognized the needs and aspirations of workers. To these companies, proper management would help assimilate immigrants, develop the North American economy, build a moral and upright society, and eliminate the abuses of hard-edged capitalism. These companies that practised *welfare capitalism* paid attention to personnel practices, adopted health and safety practices well in advance of the industry norm, and were sympathetic to the needs of employees for education, insurance, health, and death benefits (Jacoby, 1997). Some Canadian examples are Dofasco, Imperial Oil, and Magna—although each has received criticism for using welfare capitalist precepts to avoid unionization (Grant, 1998; McCallum, 1990; Taras, 2003; Lewchuk and Wells, 2006). Pure paternalism didn't really satisfy either of the management goals of efficiency or control, and therefore was never very popular among employers.

Even as Taylorist ideas shaped industrial production in the first two decades of the 20th century, there were problems that this system could not fully address. In 1924, Dr. Elton Mayo from the Harvard Business School was hired by Western Electric (a subsidiary of the American Telephone and Telegraph Company) to investigate quality and morale problems at the plant in Hawthorne, Illinois. This plant had employed the best Taylorist practices of its time without success in achieving high productivity, quality, or morale. Mayo found that productivity increased when the workers, mostly women assembling radio relays, received attention from the researchers and managers. As their work methods and physical environment were improved, their productivity increased. However, productivity rose even when these conditions were made worse! Apparently, workers became more productive when their social needs were met. This led Mayo to conclude that "the group unquestionably develops a sense of participation in the critical determinations and becomes something of a social unit."[4]

The work of Mayo and others laid the cornerstone for a new movement called the *human relations school* of managerial thinking that grew in response to Taylorism. Where Taylor emphasized the individual, the human relations school emphasized the need to foster the social system in the workplace. Many companies formed human relations departments for the first time during this era. This movement helped humanize the Taylorist system that remained ever more influential but in a slightly modified form. Although Mayo and later Peter Drucker (1954) urged managers to increase employee involvement in decision making, the human relations school did not make great strides in this direction. Most practitioners focused on the need to increase employee satisfaction by attending to their social needs rather than increase involvement in decision making and self-motivation for higher performance.

Many companies today argue they are trying to increase employee involvement, but their efforts do not in any way weaken management control of the enterprise or give employees greater say in how work is done. These companies may have specialized human resource departments that, in addition to the usual HR functions, also design elaborate ceremonies and rituals for employee recognition (e.g., giving clocks to 15-year employees and gold watches to 25-year or retiring workplace veterans), produce in-house newsletters to foster a culture of information sharing, sponsor fitness activities, and encourage interesting hobbies. To build morale and shared experiences, some companies send employees to wilderness retreats, have them walk through hot coals, and participate in team-building days. Surveys are also conducted on the quality of working life. While these may (or may not) be worthwhile activities for social reasons, there is little linkage to production.

Post–World War II Developments Developments in markets, technology, and later in workforce demographics continued to create conditions for greater involvement of the worker in workplace decisions. Collective bargaining grew as a form of participation and representation. At the individual worker level, a series of experiments in Norway, Sweden, and the U.K. pioneered the concept of greater employee involvement as a way to improve performance. Eric Trist at the Tavistock Work Research Institute in England introduced the concept of combining the technical and social systems of production in a synergistic way, an approach that came to be known as the *socio-technical systems* approach. This approach introduced the concept of work teams as an alternative to individualized production. They argued that teams can be more resourceful and productive than individuals, if given the right training, tools, and incentives. Teams later became the building block of various efforts to reinvent the modern workplace. The Quality of Work Life (QWL) movement of the 1970s, the quality circle (QC) thrust in the 1980s, and the Total Quality Management (TQM) and re-engineering efforts of the 1990s all embraced team concepts and placed greater employee involvement at the core of their respective designs.

Conclusions Greater employee involvement as a guiding principle for managing the workplace has a long and checkered history. At one end is the Taylorist system that discourages, almost forbids, any employee involvement in the production process. The other end would see a system in which a very flat organization is run through a system of participative decision making without much organizational hierarchy. While we have not yet reached a stage when organizations can do away with hierarchies of power, authority, and accountability, we have moved well beyond early Taylorist formulations. This change has come about gradually with the help of a great deal of experimentation. But the direction of change is unmistakable: the more involved employees are in their jobs, the more likely they are to meet the needs of dynamic markets and ever-changing technology.

THE HIGH-INVOLVEMENT PARADIGM

High-involvement workplaces have the following characteristics:

- a conception of employees as assets of the firm rather than merely as interchangeable factors of production;
- use of a combination of personnel practices, including job and workflow redesign, and innovative compensation practices;
- belief that the interaction of employees on teams leads to better problem solving and enhanced performance;
- an attempt to reduce or eliminate close supervision;
- willingness to provide training to enhance the skills and knowledge of workers.[5]

A confusing proliferation of terms is used to describe modern management practices: "Variously designated as high-commitment, high-involvement or simply innovative work practices, the term high-performance practices is increasingly being used to label them, as if their performance-enhancing qualities can be taken for granted. . . . " (Wood, 1999: 368). Hence, in this chapter we favour the term "high involvement" rather than "high performance."

The modern high-involvement approach emphasizes bottom-line results: Has productivity actually improved? Are costs being managed and reduced? These modern workplace practices are being implemented not because they make workers happier or the workplace more democratic (although those may be beneficial side effects), but because they might well make good business sense.

Even though articulations differ as to what constitutes a high-involvement workplace, in general there are *four sets of practices* that appear in most formulations. These are (1) training, (2) sharing through innovative compensation, (3) flexible work organization and job redesign, and (4) employee involvement at an individual or group level. For a high-involvement system to be evident, there needs to be a combination of several or all of these practices. In the workplace, employee involvement by itself and without the supportive role of other workplace practices has been found to be ineffective in creating a high-involvement workplace.

Although we will briefly review and incorporate all four of these elements into much of our discussion, the main focus will be on employee involvement (EI). This is defined as the "various means and processes by which workers take part in decisions concerning the use of their skills and resources in the production process" (Bélanger, 2001: 65). EI poses particular challenges for employment relations in both union and nonunion settings.

We take the view that, although EI can be promoted as a humane way to organize work, its diffusion in the workplace is driven by changes in the marketplace. Under conditions of increasing competition and flexible technologies, workforces would have to become highly skilled and trained, involved with the production process, and flexible and adaptable to shifting market conditions. In the following paragraphs, we draw a theoretical link between changes in the marketplace that are driving the demand for high-involvement workplaces. These pressures then lead to the bundle of practices collectively known as the high-involvement workplace. Figure 6.1 draws the impact of external pressures on the internal practices of firms.

What kind of workforce could cope with these demands for high involvement and engagement?

First, the creation of a highly skilled workforce requires that firms invest more resources in *training*. The emphasis on quality and innovation within the differentiation strategy also means that firms must involve their workers more in the production process. Hence, a greater emphasis on participation may be expected. If management is spending resources on training, it will take steps to ensure that the right kinds of employees are being selected for jobs. In unionized companies undergoing transformation toward employee involvement, management must work with the existing workforce. But in nonunion companies, and in start-up companies, the careful screening of employees is vitally important to ensure that only those whose values would support the company's vision are hired. For example, in the company Lauralco, for every worker hired, the company rejected roughly 32 applicants (Dompierre et al., 2003). Once employees are highly trained, they are more valuable to the firm, and steps might be taken as well to try to retain them—to prevent them from quitting.

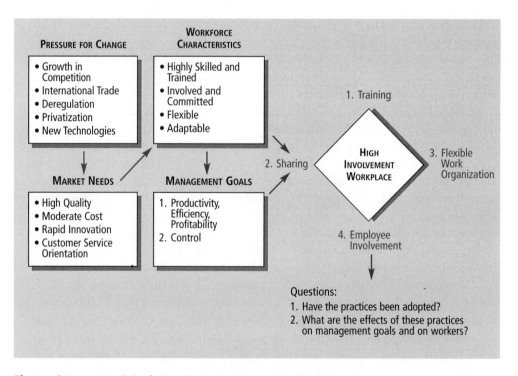

Figure 6.1 A Model of the High-Involvement Workplace

Second, high-involvement policies and programs are unlikely to be effective unless they are complemented with a set of policies that promote *sharing*. Sharing profits or gains with workers according to a pre-set formula is one way of conveying to workers that they will get an equitable return on their efforts. Employee ownership is yet another method that has gained some currency in recent years. Sharing need not be confined to financial matters alone, e.g., a profit-sharing or gain-sharing compensation program. Sharing can also refer to information dissemination. To promote employee involvement, many organizations in the 1980s began to share information widely with all levels of employees. Sharing can also be extended to privileges: removal of hierarchical privileges such as preferential parking, cafeterias, and washrooms for managers can also promote the perception that workers are equal partners in the enterprise. *Equity theory* suggests that people are motivated to seek equitable rather than maximum rewards, i.e., the same rewards that other people with comparable skills and experience receive. *Expectancy theory* suggests that people are motivated only when they believe that expended efforts will generate commensurate rewards. Put together, these two theories imply that, unless workers share in the fruits of their labour and perceive fairness in the organization, they are unlikely to expend maximum effort.

Third, as competition forces firms to move to higher value-added products and greater investment in skills, there will be greater pressure to move away from Tayloristic to more *flexible forms of work organization* (Gerwin and Kolodny, 1992). Greater employee involvement requires broader multi-skill training. Team-based work organization, in which workers have multiple skills and greater responsibility for decentralized decision making, is much more compatible with a high-value-added workplace that is competing on the basis of high quality and innovation.

Fourth, by organizing work with highly trained employees who expect sharing and engage in flexible forms of work organization, workers will naturally desire more input into and engagement in what they are doing. The creative talents of knowledgeable workers could benefit the enterprise. Whether the organization asks for greater physical work effort done willingly, or for more mental effort through problem solving and creativity, there is an underlying expectation that workers will perform better if they feel involved.

The preceding discussion shows that the pressures leading firms to explore the implementation of high involvement have a great deal to do with productivity, flexibility, and competition—management's agenda—and less to do with workers' desire for a stronger voice in the operations of the worksite and better terms and conditions of employment. Contemporary surveys of workers' attitudes (described extensively in Chapter 2) show that modern workers expect greater participation at work and want more open communication and less adversarial relations with management. By introducing EI practices and meeting the employer agenda, firms are also in the happy position of being able to deliver greater voice to workers.

Yet, despite its intuitive appeal and its compatibility with demands for higher quality and innovation, the diffusion and effective implementation of EI remain elusive. Managers routinely underestimate the difficulties of making the transition from traditional to high-involvement workplaces. Despite the failures, high-involvement rhetoric has continued to grow in popularity. Many elements of the high-involvement philosophy are being adopted, but few firms are willing to implement fully the package of practices that lead to high involvement. Some practices can be brought quite easily into existing organizational structures and processes, while other initiatives require substantial organizational redesign.

In particular, employee involvement seems to be the vaguest element of the high-involvement workplace. The next sections of this chapter tackle the issues of employee involvement in greater depth.

A GENERAL THEORY OF EMPLOYEE INVOLVEMENT (EI)

The adoption of EI in practice has been driven more by its intuitive appeal than by scientific evidence of its benefits. Yet if employee involvement is to become widespread in practice, a theoretical framework must be developed to guide policy and research. In this section, we provide a brief overview of the principal theoretical ideas found in the EI research. We examine the theoretical foundation for the efficacy of EI, the factors that influence its adoption, the consequences of EI, and issues arising from EI implementation in unionized environments.

Theoretical Foundations for Employee Involvement

Employee involvement is crucial because, to a large extent, a worker's effort remains discretionary. One employee can work hard, make excellent contributions to the morale of the workplace, and implement measures that improve individual and group performance. Another employee can put in a minimum amount of work, decline opportunities for training, and withhold valuable suggestions. For management, the issue is how best to motivate employees to give their best efforts and ideas to the job. As discussed earlier, Frederick Taylor's scientific management improves productivity by strict management control and the removal of employee discretion. So will bringing back discretion to the employee improve performance?

At the policy level, the introduction of EI has been driven by two distinct underlying philosophies. The first approach is derived from a moral, ethical, and socio-cultural base. Its main precept is that greater say in decision making is crucial for those who are affected by these decisions, an ideal that is as pertinent to the workplace as it is to democratic societies. The European notion of industrial democracy and the systems of co-determination that exist in Germany and several other countries in Western Europe are good illustrations of this approach. It should be noted that most instances of industrial democracy in Europe have taken the form of legally mandated worker representation vehicles such as works councils, rather than the more voluntaristic and production-oriented high-involvement initiatives.

The second approach, championed by Japanese and North American firms, derives from the utilitarian principle that innovative workplace practices (such as employee involvement) are a means to other important ends such as improving quality and productivity. In this view, employee participation leads to better outcomes for all parties because it improves productivity and creates more satisfied and energized workers.

There is no single theory of why employee involvement would produce positive outcomes. Rather, a number of theories, such as expectancy theory, attribution theory, and equity theory, among others, have been combined to develop models that predict the outcomes of EI (Cotton, 1993). The relationship between discretionary effort and the organization of work is reviewed by Appelbaum and her colleagues (2000). They argue that three components are needed: motivation, skills, and opportunity for participation. A selected number of models are reviewed here, very briefly, to show how and why positive effects of participation on productivity and affective responses such as job satisfaction may be expected.

Sashkin (1976) suggested that the psychological and cognitive effects of employee involvement are likely to produce "ownership" of decisions. In this model, EI is also seen as leading to shared norms and greater information flow. These outcomes, in turn, will lead to increased commitment, higher quality, and a greater capacity for adapting to change. Locke and Schweiger (1979) argue that employee involvement may increase productivity through two different mechanisms: cognitive effects such as better communication and better understanding of the job, and motivational effects such as greater "ownership" from ego involvement and increased trust.

In other models, employee involvement is seen as reducing role conflict and role ambiguity (Schuler, 1980). Employee involvement may also strengthen expectancy links between performance and rewards because the employee will know more about the behaviours that are rewarded (Lee and Schuler, 1982). Conger and Kanungo (1988) modelled participatory effects through increased self-efficacy information such as enactive attainment, vicarious experience, verbal persuasion, and emotional arousal. These effects lead to a strengthened belief in personal efficacy, which in turn leads to behaviours necessary to accomplish task objectives.

Lastly, some scholars have modelled effects of participation within the structural context of groups. Tjosvold (1991) proposed that participation leads to more opportunities to discuss problems, thus creating constructive interactions in the form of a co-operative context and productive controversies. These interactions, in turn, lead to effective problem solving, which can be expected to result in high productivity and morale.

Photo 6.1

An example of increasing importance: employee involvement in the Port of Santos, Brazil's largest shipping port. Such work is highly productive (few people), capital-intensive, and one that needs high EI to succeed.

Source: Photo by Anil Verma, 2007

Why Do Firms Adopt EI?

One of the more striking findings in the EI literature is that practices are considerably diverse among establishments—even of similar sizes and within the same industries. The pace of diffusion is difficult to assess (Gittleman, Horrigan, and Joyce, 1998: 113). However, sufficient case studies exist that allow for the classification of five categories of triggers for EI adoption (Verma, 1990; Jackson and DiGiacomo, 1997).

Threat to Firm Survival External shocks, such as recessions, deregulation, and so on, that threaten a firm's profits or markets induce the vast majority of firms to adopt greater EI. A manager at NBTel observed, "We used to have slow, infrequent change. Now we have daily wrenching change. . . . Revenues are a monthly adventure!" Given regulatory and technological change, and rising customer expectations, the company "had no chance of surviving with a hierarchical bureaucracy." When asked why NBTel decided to restructure workplace practices, he declared that "survival, survival, survival are the three main reasons!" (DiGiacomo, 1997).

Implementation of EI involves its own costs, which can be quite high. A crisis, therefore, is a double-edged sword when it comes to introducing EI. On the one hand, the crisis provides an incentive for change but, on the other hand, implementing EI requires resources that may be scarce during a crisis. Experience seems to suggest that a crisis of moderate proportions provides the best combination of conditions for successful implementation. A firm careening into bankruptcy is unlikely to have the resources to invest in EI.

Crisis in the Labour–Management Relationship In a smaller number of cases, EI adoptions take place in the aftermath of labour–management crisis. Some adversarial relationships in a downward spiral keep getting more conflictual until they are dysfunctional to both parties. At this point, the parties initiate positive change, and EI can be a part of that effort. For example, the turmoil caused by a nationwide strike in 1969 in the Canadian petroleum industry led the parties to develop their own mutual gains approach to bargaining, long before this approach was adopted by professional negotiators.

Workplace Problems In some cases, certain crises specific to the workplace account for the need to adopt greater EI. Manitoba Telephone Systems and the CEP used EI to reduce stress on the job (Verma and Cutcher-Gershenfeld, 1993). At Abitibi-Price's paper plant in Alma, Quebec, in the 1980s, between 150 and 200 grievances were submitted yearly among 900 workers, and Alma had the poorest-quality products and largest accumulated number of days lost to strikes of any Abitibi-Price plant. Labour relations were so acrimonious that the company considered plant closure. Against this backdrop, the union and management came together in the early 1990s, and, after consulting with numerous small groups in the plant, developed a "Vision 2000" statement (reproduced in Exhibit 6.1). Between 1991 and 1996, only one grievance was recorded, client satisfaction increased by three to six times the previous levels, and production costs were reduced.

Emulation EI professionals communicate with each other through extensive networks. Word about cutting-edge practice is thus passed from one organization to another. Some companies, especially those that benchmark themselves against the best methods, adopt EI simply because they find that EI has won acceptance among leading-edge firms. The introduction of EI programs in the Canadian oil industry follows this pattern (Taras and

Ponak, 1999). The internet makes available a number of websites through which managers submit and receive information.

Exhibit 6.1
Abitibi-Price Alma Paper Plant "Vision 2000" Statement

- ■ Each employee acts and thinks as if the plant was his.
- ■ Each employee decides and goes ahead, with no need for approval from his boss.
- ■ Each employee has enough information to allow him to participate efficiently in the success of his team and his enterprise.
- ■ Each employee is responsible for the work of his team, and knows the impact of his actions on the other members of the team.
- ■ All know and act in function of the concept "supplier/client." This concept is omnipresent in everything we are undertaking up to the user of our products and/ or our services.
- ■ Criteria for success are clear, known, and requested by all and everyone: unionized employee, manager, supplier, client.
- ■ Total quality is a predominant concern and a way of life.
- ■ Recognition of one's worth is based on performance and excellence.

Source: Quoted in Chamberland (1997). Reproduced with the permission of the Minister of Public Works and Government Services, 2000.

Proactive Adoption Another small group of firms adopt EI because they anticipate problems they are likely to face in the future and they want to be prepared. These organizations truly believe that EI is a better way to manage and to compete. These are typically large companies or members of large conglomerates such as Boeing, Bell Canada, and Motorola. Often, innovative workplace practices are initiated by senior management in a top-down fashion, but there is a general preparedness at the most senior levels of companies to provide training, incentives, and organizational environments that encourage innovation (Jackson and DiGiacomo, 1997).

New Work Practices and Employee Involvement

Employee-involvement initiatives can be classified in a number of dimensions. Practice is remarkably diverse. We observe differences in the forms, functions, topics, representation modes, and degrees of power. Exhibit 6.2 illustrates five dimensions that could be used to describe and sort employee-involvement initiatives, and the discussion that follows simply highlights a few examples listed in Exhibit 6.2.

1. **Forms** The literature is filled with examples of EI forms and structures. Some are ad hoc or informal, and other types are long-standing and quite complex. Exhibit 6.2 provides a list of EI vehicles that allow employees to provide input into firm activities. Sometimes firms solicit employee involvement through the creation of committees or advisory groups. Sometimes workers themselves initiate and coordinate their own

groups, and here would fit many identity-based groups that help workers lobby for positive changes from management. For example, minorities might form self-help groups to advance their interests at work and prevent discrimination. Of course, a union also could be considered a form of employee involvement, since it engages the interest of workers in finding solutions to worksite issues.

EI programs sometimes are small in scope and self-contained. Suggestion systems have little impact on the structures of the firm. Other more complex types of EI have cascading effects on work processes within the firm (Cutcher-Gershenfeld, Kochan, and Verma, 1991). The implementation of complex forms of EI requires a high degree of integration with, and impact on, the organization. A host of changes in organizational structures and procedures are required. Autonomous work groups, in their very design, are intended to challenge the traditional hierarchical structure of authority. Because their impact on the organization is substantial, such forms require a large investment of funds and effort and are more difficult to implement. This explains, in part, why the diffusion of these forms has remained well below that of the simple, more contained type of EI program.

2. **Functions** Employee involvement can serve many interests. Certainly, one of the most common reasons that firms give in support of their EI is to improve the communication flow between workers and managers so that improvements can be made to firm processes. EI initiatives can support other high-involvement activities such as training and information sharing and the design of flexible work systems. Sometimes, nonunion firms create EI structures to prevent unions from making organizing gains within the firm: hoping to satisfy workers' desires for input internally, firms try to limit the allure of unions. Chapter 5 described this as a strategy of union substitution or avoidance.

3. **Topics** The third dimension of participation is the substantive content of decision making, i.e., the set of issues over which decision making is exercised. Issues may be limited to a small cluster such as the administration of training programs, health and safety concerns, or quality control. Issues may also be broadened to include those arising from the terms and conditions of employment, or the entire production process. In some cases, participative forums may have an open-ended mandate to consider any relevant workplace issues.

4. **Representation Modes and Characteristics** Forms and methods of employee involvement forums vary considerably. Many EI programs, such as quality, productivity, and cost, are run by management to focus primarily on issues of interest to the firm. Other programs provide opportunities to workers to focus on issues of primary interest to them, e.g., safety, voice, and fairness at work. Representation can take many forms. First, there is the issue of *direct* versus *indirect* forms of participation and influence. Do workers make their needs and views known to management directly, or do they channel their sentiments indirectly through an agent who speaks to management on their behalf? Suggestion systems, quality circles, focus groups, and some types of committees all expect workers to speak out directly, without filtering messages through an intermediary. The individual is personally involved. Direct involvement can be at the *individual* or the *group level*. Suggestion schemes are a mild form of involvement at the individual level. A quality circle is an example of group participation.

Exhibit 6.2
Examples of Diversity of Employee-Involvement Plans

1. Forms	2. Functions	3. Topics	4. Representation Modes and Characteristics	5. Degree of Power
Ombuds	Communication & Information Flow	Benefits, Including Pensions and Health Insurance	Direct or indirect representation	Scope of power, e.g., single topic or broad authority
Joint Safety Committees	Production and Organizational Coordination	Safety/Health	Internal to the firm, e.g., elected representative from among workers in the group	Informal consultation
Dispute Resolution Panels	Employee Input into Recruitment and Selection	Working Conditions	External to the firm, e.g., players' agents in sports	Advisory groups
Scanlon Plan & Gain-Sharing Committees	Employee Morale & Esprit de Corps	Grievances/Dispute Resolution	Representatives appointed by management	Decisions made by consensus only
Special Project Teams	Education and Training of Employees	Management Problems	Representatives elected by workers (secret ballot)	Preparation and presentation of workers' formal position
Departmental Production & Coordination Committees	Employee Relations and Disposition of Irritants	Employee Relations Climate	Degree of independence of representation (e.g., budget and resources; reporting relationships; ability to meet independently from managers, etc.)	Chairing or co-chairing meetings
Autonomous Work Groups	Employee Involvement	Recruitment and Selection	Ability to seek professional expertise outside the firm (e.g., lawyers, actuaries, etc.)	Developing the agenda
Quality Improvement Committees	Corporate Culture	Production Issues		Negotiating
Quality Circles	Co-operation & Common Purpose	Equipment/Capital Issues		Distribution of minutes and positions
Gender/Ethnic/Sex Identity Groups	Management & Employee Development	Customer Service		Ability to take actions to promote positions
Employee–Management Advisory Committees	Union Avoidance	Quality of Products and Production		Vote-taking in which the majority wins
Cross-Divisional Council for Employment Issues	Lobbying Government	Business Strategy		Worker veto power over change
Plant Councils		Wages and Other Terms and Conditions of Employment		
Company Grievance Review Boards		Status of the Occupation		
Employee Committee on Board of Directors				
Company-Wide Representation Systems such as JICs				
Staff Associations				
Professional Advocacy Groups				
Unions				

Source: D. Taras and B. E. Kaufman. 2006. "Non-union employee representation in North America: diversity, controversy and uncertain future," *Industrial Relations Journal* 37, No. 5, pp. 513-542. Table 1 on p. 518.

Some workplaces allow workers to select representatives from their work groups who join in higher-level committees or review teams. Representatives often are engaged in the same work as the colleagues they represent. In the petroleum industry, for example, roughly one-third of "rank-and-file" workers in the gas fields and refineries select worker representatives who engage in discussions with management to resolve various work-related issues.

Most nonunion EI is enterprise-based. Thus, the representatives come from within the firm's workforce. There are, however, cases in which representatives are external to the firm. For example, professional associations may provide agents or experts to help advance their members' interests in interactions with employers (e.g., in disciplinary hearings or in contract negotiations).

Collective bargaining and the legislative process use elected representatives and hence participation is indirect. Indirect forms of participation often involve representatives from outside the firm. For example, doctors at hospitals are represented by their medical associations; engineers and other professionals have province- or nationwide associations to advance their interests and uphold their professional standards. Unions offer shop stewards and business agents, and are properly classified as an indirect system.

Some representatives have budgets and access to professional advice from experts outside the firm, but this is rare except in unionized environments. In most nonunion EI systems, workers have limited resources.

5. **Degree of Power** The final dimension is the extent to which participation is allowed. *Consultation* is a milder form of participation because it does not imply decision-making authority. *Equal say* in decision making for all parties and the power to implement decisions are much stronger forms of participation. Some highly participative forums may also contain a mechanism to resolve any disputes among the parties participating in decision making.

In nonunion settings, management is inclined to adopt the types of EI initiatives that involve harmonious relations between workers and managers. Joint problem solving, "win–win" solutions, and decision making by consensus are preferred over the more adversarial approaches. Since workers have limited power in nonunion workplaces, they are more effective at achieving their goals with management through persuasion rather than confrontation. When necessary, nonunion worker representatives try to use the techniques of persuasion to increase their power: they document the needs of their co-workers, articulate the rationale for change, frame their requests as reasonable in the context of the employers' business strategy, and occasionally even use the threat of unionization. However, as nonunion systems are rarely adversarial, power-enhancing tactics are less a feature of these systems than are the voice-enhancing elements (see Chapter 2). Thus, the ability to arrive at decisions through consensus is stressed. Votes are very rare, as they tend to polarize positions and undo the carefully constructed features that stress joint problem-solving and the mutuality of interests. Also, while North American union–management relationships have fairly narrow windows of opportunity for bargaining and approving formal collective agreements, ongoing forms of nonunion systems engage in constant communication and information exchange.

When we examine the types of EI systems available in the Canadian industrial relations landscape, it is clear that most of our knowledge about employee interests has relied on studies of indirect participation through unions, collective bargaining, and grievance procedures. How does the introduction of direct and nonunion forms of participation affect relations among the actors within the industrial relations system? Is direct participation compatible with indirect participation or does it, as is often alleged, supplant the need for indirect representation? Is EI capable of meeting employees' needs for economic advances, fairness and equity, countervailing power, and voice (see Chapter 2) without unions? To what extent might EI be used in managerial strategies of union avoidance, substitution, or replacement (see Chapter 5)? Are enterprise-specific forms of EI sufficient, or do workers also need information about other employers in order to make informed choices? While unions are active lobbyists on the political stage, are viable umbrella organizations available to enhance the voice of nonunion workers? These are troubling questions.

For examples of corporate information on EI, see if it is possible to use the five components of EI to classify actual EI initiatives by locating company websites. It is interesting that most of the internet information posted by companies about their own EI initiatives tends to describe charitable events, community-relations activities by employees, and morale building. There is little sharing of power or diffusion of control. These types of activities fit well within the welfare capitalist and human relations schools that we described earlier. But a website search also will reveal that attention has turned quite sharply from EI (quite popular on North American websites only a few years ago) toward "corporate social responsibility" and "sustainability" as the new website mantras. Perhaps EI is now being taken for granted, no longer a novelty, or perhaps it has been superceded by more socially compelling and market-driven trends.

First Major Question: What Is the Diffusion of EI and Other High-Involvement Practices?

Information on the extent of EI and other innovations in Canadian workplaces was scant up until 1999 when Statistics Canada began to conduct the Workplace and Employee Survey (WES). For data prior to 1999, readers can consult the 1993 Human Resource Practices Survey (HRPS) which was limited to four industries (wood products, fabricated metal products, electrical and electronic products, and business services) across 714 establishments (Betcherman et al., 1994). Another survey, the Working with Technology Survey (WWTS), was conducted in 1985 (Long, 1989; Betcherman and McMullen, 1986) and repeated in 1991 (Betcherman et al., 1994). Measures used by these surveys are not all identical and, therefore, not directly comparable.

Adoption of High-Involvement Practices in Canada Table 6.1 shows a snapshot profile of employee-involvement practices in Canadian workplaces with 10 or more employees. These numbers are based on a total sample of 6351 workplaces in 1999 and 6223 workplaces in 2001 included in the Canadian Workplace and Employee Survey (WES). The number of workplaces with fewer than 10 employees was not disclosed by Statistics Canada.

The most popular practice, information sharing with employees, was reported by nearly half of the workplaces. Roughly a third of the workplaces offered flexible job designs and slightly fewer (31 percent) offered a formal employee suggestion program to

Table 6.1 Percentage of Canadian Firms with Selected Work Practices

Organizational Practice	% of workplaces					
	1999					2001
		by number of employees				
	Overall	11–19	20–99	100–499	500+	Overall
Information-sharing with employees	49.5	47.2	49.8	60.3	68.0	43.7
Flexible job design	31.9	37.2	28.1	20.7	28.6	18.5
Employee suggestion programs	31.0	28.5	32.3	38.3	39.0	33.2
Problem-solving teams	25.7	22.6	27.3	32.3	53.3	22.1
Joint labour–management committees	20.0	11.6	23.9	44.6	71.8	16.1
Self-directed work groups	10.3	8.0	11.4	15.7	27.8	8.7

Note: Workplaces with 10 employees or fewer were not asked these questions.

Source: Adapted from Statistics Canada, Workplace and Employee Survey Compendium, 1999 and 2001, Catalogue 71-585-XIE.

their employees. Problem-solving teams were reported by nearly one-quarter of all workplaces while self-directed work groups were used by only 10.3 percent of the workplaces. Lastly, joint labour–management committees were reported by one-fifth of all workplaces.

When the incidence is examined by workplace size, as measured by the number of employees, larger workplaces are generally more likely to report each of the practices, with the exception of flexible job design. Information sharing and labour–management committees were the most prevalent in the largest workplaces. The incidence of flexible job design was highest in the smallest workplaces, declining slightly in larger workplaces.

Questions about employee-involvement practices were asked in the WES every second year. Comparable figures from the 2001 WES, shown in the last column of Table 6.1, suggest that the reported incidence of these practices did not grow over the two years. In fact, the reported incidence was almost the same or had declined slightly. Although it is not clear what factors may account for this flattening out of the popularity of these practices, it is also likely that many of these practices introduced earlier as innovative new programs are gradually being absorbed into everyday practice. Thus, over time they fade away as formal programs but their effects are nonetheless present in workplace practices and norms.

When the data in Table 6.1 are put into bundles of practices, less than 5 percent of firms practise a combination of teams, flexible job designs, and profit or gain sharing. Only 2.1 percent of firms have adopted all three of these practices plus teamwork-related formal training.[6] If particular workplace practices can be demonstrated to blend well, then practices should be selected that work in conjunction with each other. We would expect to capture synergies this way. But high-involvement practices are rarely adopted in a coherent manner; rather, only one or two elements are championed. If companies claiming to practise high-involvement management select only those practices that are easiest to implement or are most immediately pleasing, the companies may not be reaping any particular benefits from the newer management philosophy.

Why is it that so few companies practise EI in a comprehensive way? First, it may be easier to implement EI in new sites than engender the "switching costs" of transforming existing workplaces. One of the most famous Canadian examples of a high-involvement workplace is the Shell plant in Sarnia, Ontario. Management and the union jointly developed a new way of operating while the plant was being constructed. Hundreds of workers were hired into this "socio-technical system," and the company used the Sarnia site to learn how to manage in a high-involvement environment (Rankin, 1986). Taking the ideas from this experiment into an existing worksite at the East Montreal refinery was much more difficult and required a significant investment of time and effort by managers, the union, and individual workers. Second, managers don't necessarily wish to fully implement EI because it means a significant dilution of their control over the workplace: "Many employers are still worried that making their production system too dependent on employee involvement would make the production systems more vulnerable and open the employers' decisions to more discussion" (Bélanger, 2001: 75). Third, unions and workers may resist new workplace initiatives that demand more of workers without a quid pro quo from the employer. It is quite natural for workers to ask, "What's in it for me?"

Second Major Question: What Are the Effects of EI and High-Involvement Practices?

Changes occur in many areas following the introduction of high-involvement practices. For the sake of brevity and focus, three areas which feel the impact the most are considered below. These areas also need the most attention in the formative period when the foundation for high-involvement effectiveness is laid.

Training As discussed earlier, one of the most important requirements is training. The traditional organization invests only a modest sum in training, and most of that is directed at management or at training in technical and functional skills. Effective implementation of high-involvement practices requires that training be increased in both magnitude and scope. Training in problem-solving skills and team-based skills is a must. Notably successful companies in Canada appear to be investing roughly five to seven days of training per employee per year on an ongoing basis (Verma and Irvine, 1992).

Successful companies use training in the context of high involvement for three distinct purposes. First, training is used to inform and socialize employees into appreciating the value of employee input and the organizational need to improve quality and productivity. Firms have been generally quite successful in raising awareness of EI and in getting employees to identify with strategic goals of the business. The second task for training is to provide employees with a set of basic skills in problem solving so they can begin to get involved. Finally, training is used to upgrade skills, to disseminate information about the firm's strategic direction, and to renew interest on an ongoing basis.

First-Line Supervision First-line supervisors are among the first managers directly affected by the implementation of high-involvement practices (Klein, 1988; Klein and Posey, 1986). Experience shows that if EI is to be meaningful, certain changes must occur in the quality and quantity of first-line supervision.

In many organizations, high involvement has been followed by a decrease in the amount of direct supervision and by the redefining of the role of a supervisor from monitor to coordinator and facilitator (Klein, 1988). If high-involvement practices are effective, workers do not need much supervision. Organizations have terminated the employment of cadres of supervisors, making employee involvement an immediate and measurable contributor to the corporate bottom line.

The supervisors who remain on payroll must dramatically alter their expectations and job duties. Workers learning problem-solving skills need a different kind of support. Supervisors are becoming "coaches" and "facilitators" whose skills are used for employee training, promoting communication flows with other parts of the organization, developing benchmarks, and assisting with the acquisition of information. Often, supervisors who were selected for traditional organizations and who are accustomed to "command and control" styles are unable to make the difficult transition to high-involvement work settings. They become casualties of the new workplace designs. Given the threats to their traditional ways of managing and even to their job security, it is understandable that first-line supervisors are quite resistant to employee involvement.

Information Flow The medium- to long-term consequences of EI for the organization are in the areas of information flow and access. A hierarchical organization is characterized by a protocol for information flow both horizontally and vertically. The introduction of EI creates a demand for information that severely tests the old protocol in which employees at progressively lower levels of the organization had access to less and less information.

Organizations have developed a wide variety of ways to deal with increasing demands for access to information. In some companies, employee teams include staff representatives from support departments such as accounting, engineering, and maintenance. Support staff members become a link between the team and other departments for access to information. But usually there are not enough of such personnel to allow them to be assigned to every employee team. In many situations, it becomes problematic for non-managerial employees to request and receive technical or cost data from other departments. Yet the need to increase flow of information is urgent if EI is to be effective and successful.

The Effect of EI on Productivity and Satisfaction

Numerous studies have been conducted to measure the effects of participation on individual and organizational outcomes since the 1950s.[7] Recall that the move toward EI was driven, in large part, by an assumption that adopting innovative work systems would affect productivity positively. We don't really have a strong grasp on how this relationship actually works, or on the magnitude of the effect. There are a number of explanations for improvements in productivity:

- greater motivation among employees—"working harder"
- elimination of extraneous tasks—"working smarter"

- reduction of inventory costs, storage, and processing costs

- policies that foster a higher quit rate among less productive workers, or higher retention of more productive workers

- greater attention to screening, and hiring more productive workers

- reduction in the total number of production workers

- reduction in the number of supervisors needed to oversee the work

- other factors happening at the same time as EI policies, e.g., adoption of new technologies, closure of obsolete plants, etc.

Studies over the past decade have closely examined the effects of EI on productivity (Appelbaum et al., 2000; Becker and Huselid, 1998; Ichniowski, Shaw, and Prennushi, 1997; Wood, 1999). They conclude that a bundle of practices together form a high-involvement workplace. Most companies that say they practise EI actually implement only a small number of practices, and experience only limited productivity gains. As Bélanger (2001: 72) put it, "a clear and recurrent research finding is that single workplace practices have little effect but that a combination of such practices really makes a difference when these operate in a complementary way." When companies have comprehensive and internally consistent bundles of practices, these interact with each other in complementary ways, producing demonstrable effects. In a study of 36 steel finishing lines in the United States, innovative human resource management practices raised worker productivity by about 6.7 percent (Ichniowski, Shaw, and Prennushi, 1997). Another study of 44 U.S. plants in many different industries showed consistently positive results because workers voluntarily raised their discretionary effort level in order to reduce waste, solve problems, better control the pace of their work, and generally work smarter (Appelbaum et al., 2000).

Comprehensive studies summarizing dozens of research studies conclude that it has not always been possible to show a direct, significant, and positive impact of EI on bottom-line measures of cost and productivity (Godard, 2004; Cotton et al., 1988; Locke and Schweiger, 1979; Miller and Monge, 1986). While a majority of studies do show a positive impact, the effects frequently vary, and a number of studies have found no effect. The positive effects of participation are more clearly observed in the case of job satisfaction where the evidence suggests a small but positive impact. Case studies in the automobile industry of the effects of lean production on worker outcomes such as empowerment, work pace and workload, and health have found negative results (Graham, 1995; Lewchuk and Robertson, 1996). In the American steel industry, practices that link pay to performance, share information with workers, provide employment security, or involve workers in decisions do not affect job satisfaction. Rather, job satisfaction in this mature, male-dominated industry was influenced by good employee–management relations and flexible practices that helped balance work and family (Berg, 1999).

Case studies also have provided evidence of positive effects, and some are glowing testimonials for EI programs. It is hard to interpret this evidence. For example, the vast majority of reported cases involve success stories. Rarely does the case-study literature touch on cases that have failed. There are no reliable estimates of the failure rate among EI programs. However, anecdotal evidence places the attrition rate as high as 40 percent in the first two or three years following introduction (Rankin, 1986), possibly indicating that organizations are still at an early stage in the learning curve for EI implementation.

Many case studies are written by those who are directly involved with the initiative, such as the managers or consultants responsible for design and implementation. Thus, many case studies suffer from lack of objectivity and so do not meet the rigorous standards for scientific investigation.

Although there is evidence that high involvement, when applied as a comprehensive set of practices, is good for meeting management objectives, what impact does it have on workers' welfare? Debate occurs within labour relations circles about negative consequences to workers, but the data are not yet clear. In Britain, one major study found that despite a marked trend toward upskilling, the restructuring of the employment relationship has actually reinforced traditional lines of division in the workplace (Gallie et al., 1998). There also is concern about work intensification—that workers are working harder but not reaping any benefits. For example, many Canadian hospitals have responded to government calls for cost containment in ways that have increased the level of care needed by the patient mix and hence the demands on nursing staff. For example, many years ago a woman giving birth or a man having gall bladder surgery would have stayed in the hospital for a week, but now a two-day stay is quite normal. Nurses working in these circumstances might be tending to the same number of patients as in the past, but the chances are that each bed contains a patient who is sicker, needier, and more fragile than was the case 15 years ago.

Not all employees are unhappy about having to work harder. There is a "disciplined worker thesis" that posits, with confirming evidence, that workers will increase their workload provided that the workplace is well managed (Edwards, Collinson, and Rees, 1998) and they are treated with respect. Appelbaum and her colleagues (2000) found that workers' welfare was not jeopardized when there was sufficient trust in management and the employee-involvement practices were soundly implemented. But the literature is still at an early stage of development, and we definitely need to see more long-term studies on the impact of employee involvement on workers' welfare.

Outcomes for workers may be negative in the following types of circumstances:

■ EI practices are implemented in a piecemeal, flavour-of-the-month manner, with little long-term commitment;

■ employees are asked to increase their amount of work effort, but are not adequately compensated for it, or their extra efforts are not acknowledged with respectful treatment;

■ managers raise employee expectations but do not follow through on promises.

There is also the possibility that moderate levels of adoption of EI techniques can improve workers' outcomes (such as the feeling of belonging and work satisfaction) whereas higher levels of adoption might worsen workers' outcomes (by intensifying the pressure to perform at high levels and increasing stress) (Godard, 2004).

Methodological problems exist in isolating the precise contribution of high-involvement programs as distinct from the effects of technology or markets or other changes that happened simultaneously with high involvement. As a rule, positive impacts are reported when concurrent changes take place in technology, products, markets, processes, materials, or even staffing.

Critics of impact studies argue that precise measurement of EI programs is flawed for three reasons. First, the benefits of greater employee involvement will show up in individual as well as group activity, and few of these studies measure group outcomes such as the launch of a new product or effective implementation of a new system. Further, some impact of EI may be observable only when organizations go through sudden and unexpected change such as technological change (e.g., EI may make employees more amenable to technological change), downsizing (e.g., employees may identify more strongly with the strategic goals of the business), or the introduction of new markets or products (e.g., EI may aid in the development of a more flexible and agile organization). Most studies in the past have not measured such effects because of the problems inherent in such measurement.

Second, critics charge that measuring EI outcomes in a narrow, short-term frame will hurt the very process the study is designed to measure. The EI process would change once the fact of measurement became known to the participants, who would be likely to experience some anxiety as a result of being monitored. Consequently, in many firms managers have decided not to measure the outcomes of EI, at least in the short run.[8]

Third, in field studies, it is difficult to measure the factors separate and independent of EI that are often introduced along with other workplace changes and innovations.

In practice, the decision to introduce greater employee involvement is not always made contingent upon a quick demonstration through hard data of a positive impact of EI. Often, quantitative assessment of EI and its impact on performance is made only after the program has had some time to become absorbed, in whole or in part, into the organizational culture. Many organizations adopt EI as matter of faith, hope, and optimism about human nature.

EI in Unionized Environments

It is in the unionized context that EI poses the deepest challenges for all actors in the industrial relations system. Implementation of EI in a union environment is problematic because EI is an ideologically loaded intervention in the employment relationship. Many unions fear that employee involvement is a potent socialization tool through which employers can co-opt employees into a managerial agenda and, thereby, weaken collective bargaining and the union. These fears have been fuelled in part by the growth of the nonunion sector in the United States, where employers have successfully resisted unionization in new nonunion plants by implementing, among other policies, greater employee involvement (Verma and Kochan, 1985).

The vast majority of unionized workplaces have experienced difficulties in implementing EI, and not only for the reasons stated above. The introduction of EI requires a drastic change in the traditional labour–management relationship, conventionally characterized by a separation of management and labour roles and the associated mutual distrust and adversarial bargaining. On the other hand, there is some evidence that unions play a positive "watchdog" role in ensuring that the employee-involvement initiatives that come to fruition are well reasoned, implemented with care, and fair from the employees' perspective.

Impediments to EI Adoption and Implementation Two impediments to the introduction of EI in unionized workplaces have been identified in the literature.

1. **The History of Labour–Management Relations** Many companies that began to introduce EI in the 1980s discovered that their enthusiasm was not universally shared. Quite often, unions were not nearly as excited at the prospect of introducing

EI. Part of the reason lay in the history of adversarial relations, which had taught the parties to be cautious, if not distrustful, in dealing with the other side. Thus, the initial call for collaboration for mutual benefit has been generally obscured by the shadow of the past.

In cases where EI has had a more successful start, the introduction has generally been preceded by a series of activities whose intent and effect has been to build the relationship up from its adversarial past. In general, the following sequence may occur at a site where EI is being introduced.

a. Teams of employees, both from management and the union, visit other organizations where EI has proven to be successful.

b. EI experts speak at company training sessions. Some of these sessions are attended by union and management representatives.

c. The company and union agree to attend an off-site workshop designed especially to discuss mutual interests.

d. Union and management agree to expand the traditional bargaining agenda by removing obstacles such as a large backlog of unresolved grievances.

e. Both sides agree to form a joint steering committee to oversee the design and implementation of the EI program.

Where the parties do not invest in such prior relationship building, the results are generally unfavourable. In some cases, the union refuses to discuss the EI issue, forcing management either to implement it on its own or to drop the initiative altogether. In other cases, EI has a very slow start and proves ineffective despite several years of costly investments. Eventually the effort is either formally cancelled or it dies slowly through lack of interest.

2. **The Knowledge Gap** Another impediment to effective introduction of EI lies in unequal knowledge of and expertise in EI matters on the part of labour and management. Management, in most cases, has had a head start on learning about the nuts and bolts of EI in the 1980s, by working closely with behavioural scientists and other experts and by using organizational resources to hire experts and to train its own personnel.

Labour, on the other hand, has lagged in educating itself and its membership on these concepts. This gap was glaring in the early and mid-1980s. Although the knowledge gap narrowed a great deal in the 1990s, it remains an important hurdle that must be overcome if EI is to be diffused widely throughout the unionized sector.

The key decision for these unionized firms is the extent or scope of union involvement in EI initiation, implementation, and evaluation.

Extent of Union Involvement

The extent of union involvement can be described in terms of the following five levels. Under *unilateral management decision making*, management makes all the decisions and there is no role for the union. Management argues that it has the exclusive right to manage the workplace. Under *managerial information sharing*, management informs the union of its plans and actions, and the union may have the right to request information. This does not allow for any direct input into decision making but it does provide additional resources (i.e., information) to the union to represent its interests through traditional channels. Under *consultation*, management provides information and solicits union input with no promise of acting on the input. The power of decision making remains with management, which becomes better informed about the needs of the union as a result of the consultative process. Progressive managers would try to accommodate union needs as often as possible. Autocratic managers or militant union leaders could, however, defeat the process by making consultation irrelevant to decision making. Under *decision making by consensus*, both sides make decisions jointly but agree to rule only by consensus. Legal authority remains with management but formal authority is delegated to a joint forum. There is no dispute resolution mechanism. In the event of a dispute that cannot be resolved, authority reverts to its traditional owner, management. Finally, under *joint governance*, decisions are made jointly by both sides; a dispute resolution procedure is used if the two sides cannot agree (Verma and Cutcher-Gershenfeld, 1993).

Some unions have developed policies with regard to their role in workplace change interventions. Exhibit 6.3 excerpts the CEP's requirement that programs be negotiated with the union's full participation and receive union membership approval.

Exhibit 6.3
CEP Policy on Employee Involvement and Participation

CEP will enter into discussions at the sectoral or workplace level with a view to conclude agreements that enhance employment and income security and enhance productivity based on investment in the labour force and strategic investment in the enterprise or industry.

CEP will work with industry and negotiate particular programs providing that CEP is a full participant in the design, implementation, and continuous development of these programs.

Sectoral or workplace agreements may address training programs, workplace restructuring, and particular investment and production plans.

Any such agreement shall be properly negotiated, and must be subject to membership debate and approval.

Source: CEP. 1994. *New Directions: CEP Policy on Workplace Reorganization.* Toronto: Communications, Energy and Paperworkers Union of Canada. Available at www.cep.ca/policies/policy_906_e.pdf.

Scope of Union Involvement Unions can be involved in various stages of EI—idea, design, and implementation. In the vast majority of cases, unions are brought into the picture only at the implementation stage. This sets up a dysfunctional dynamic between the parties right from the start because unions feel that by the time they are involved, most of the major parameters of the EI program have been set. Unions frequently are put into the position of either agreeing to a package designed unilaterally by management experts, or rejecting it completely.

Union Concerns About EI Unions have articulated their concerns about EI in a variety of ways, ranging from the ideological to the practical. Apart from some ideologically driven hardline opinions, most union concerns have to do with the potential impact of EI on the collective bargaining process. If union leaders perceive that EI will weaken collective bargaining and the union, they are generally opposed to it. They worry that EI may co-opt workers into a managerial agenda (i.e., to improve quality and productivity) to the extent that workers will begin to see the union as irrelevant to their welfare.

Unions also worry that some employers will use EI meetings to promote anti-union sentiments among workers to the point that workers will be ready to decertify their union.

Case evidence is strongly suggestive of EI's potential to thwart union interests (Verma and Kochan, 1985). But there is no evidence to indicate that this potential is innate to EI or that it is inherent in EI's dynamic as an organizational process. Rather, the evidence suggests that, like any other instrument, EI can be used for a variety of purposes, both functional and dysfunctional. Research shows that if EI is supported by the union, its outcomes are generally positive toward union as well as company goals. On the other hand, lack of union involvement leads to a perception that the union's contributions are marginal, which in turn leads to outcomes less favourable to the union.

Union leaders are concerned about EI programs because they socialize workers with pro-company and, possibly, anti-union views. Not all employers use EI as a forum to reinforce anti-unionism, but almost all programs do conduct training and provide information on a firm's competitive position as well as on the need to improve productivity and upgrade technology. Some studies have found that EI has a positive effect on the extent to which workers identify with company goals (Lischeron and Wall, 1975; Verma and McKersie, 1987)—termed a *program effect* (Verma, 1989).

A second concern for unions is the possibility that EI programs attract workers with anti-union views. In other words, EI programs result in a sorting of workers by their affinity to the union—pro-union workers stay away while anti-union workers tend to volunteer for participation in the program. This has been called the *selection effect* (Verma, 1989). Of course, the selection effect is much stronger when management deliberately screens and hires workers who are unlikely to find unions appealing. Selection questionnaires might include subtle items such as "If I run into trouble at work, will I confide in my manager?" or "Do I believe that workers and managers have different interests?"—a "yes" for the first question and a "no" for the second question would be the most desirable answers from the management perspective.

Empirical studies suggest that a union's own involvement may determine whether the program and selection effects are positive or negative. Where unions support EI programs, the program effect is positive and the selection effect zero or absent (Verma, 1989; Thacker and Fields, 1987). On the other hand, when a union is not involved in EI, there is evidence of a negative selection effect (Verma and McKersie, 1987). These results suggest that by withdrawing from EI efforts, unions may be creating a self-fulfilling prophecy, i.e., lack of union involvement may create the very effects unions fear most.

The extent to which union fears may be justified also depends on management's intent. EI can be used to undermine as well as reinforce and reform the labour–management relationship. One research study that monitored EI developments in companies like Boeing, Cummins Engine, General Motors, Xerox, Western Airlines, Alcoa, Budd, Boise Cascade, and Goodyear over a number of years found that EI tended to reinforce collective bargaining in cases where its principles were used to address external shocks such as restructuring due to recessions and other crises (Cutcher-Gershenfeld, Kochan, and Verma, 1991). On the other hand, in cases where EI principles were suspended or bypassed during these critical incidents, EI tended to either disappear or undermine the collective bargaining process.

Unions often negotiate quid pro quo conditions for their participation. For example, before agreeing to a work redesign at NBTel, the CEP demanded a written agreement from management that the initiative was not intended "to reduce the workforce, reduce the level of bargaining unit work, or lower any standards of living or wages" (quoted in DiGiacomo, 1997). The union often wins job security provisions in exchange for the removal of restrictive work rules.

The Consequences of Non-Involvement of Unions Management faces a series of choices about its relations with the union. The question is whether to implement EI without any involvement of the union as well as to consider the *implications* of implementing EI without any involvement of the union.

Many managers believe that they can make decisions about and also implement EI without the union. This is natural given the EI expertise that management usually can marshal on its own. Moreover, many managers feel that EI is largely a bilateral matter between their employees and them, and that the union as a third party has no role, expertise, or contribution to make. Research shows that non-involvement of unions in the EI process can lead to a number of potential problems that managers must anticipate (Verma and McKersie, 1987).

First, lack of union involvement may be viewed by some employees as an ambiguous signal. Most employees trust the union more than management to safeguard their interests. They may wonder why the union is not talking about EI. This potentially disruptive effect, while discernible in some surveys, is clearly not a great threat, at least in the near term (Verma, 1989). But the lack of union involvement can also be viewed as a missed opportunity for management to marshal the union's support in making EI more effective.

Second, if the union chooses to oppose the EI program, it can very effectively compromise the program's impact on the workers. Unions have threatened and carried out anti-EI campaigns with some success. At BC Tel (now Telus), the union opposed quality circles and, to make its opposition effective, conducted an education campaign to render quality circles ineffective. Other unions, including the United Steelworkers and the Communications Workers of America, have stated that if they were not allowed to be involved, they would carry out a campaign against EI efforts. Unions can file unfair labour practice complaints against companies, arguing that management is attempting to bypass the employees' legitimate bargaining agents, thereby preventing management from making any unilateral changes in terms and conditions of employment that would bolster the EI effort.

An active opposition campaign by the union sends confusing signals to workers who are not sure whom they should believe—union leaders or managers. Employee surveys at many companies, including Boeing and Xerox, have documented the fact that workers tend to separate into different factions when they hear these conflicting messages about EI (Verma and McKersie, 1987; Cutcher-Gershenfeld, 1988). Those who are active in the union tend to view EI in negative terms, while those who are less interested in, or are opposed to, the union tend to view EI in positive terms. Clearly, these divisions do not bode well for a successful EI effort.

Should management decide to involve the union, it would have to make choices about the extent and scope of union involvement. Systematic research has not been conducted on the pros and cons of the different choices managers make in this regard. There is, however, much case and anecdotal evidence. The rule of thumb is to involve the union

as early in the process as possible, perhaps at the idea stage. The evidence also points to an active rather than a passive union role as the key to effectiveness.

Canadian Unions and Direct Participation When Canadian firms began to introduce direct participation processes such as quality circles, work teams, and other such forums, a number of unions saw them as an employer ploy to gain the upper hand in industrial relations. Several unions warned of the dangers of direct participation forums and urged opposition to such managerial initiatives. Many other unions, as well as the Canadian Labour Congress, issued statements of caution and provided guidelines on the conditions under which a union could get involved in such efforts.

By the end of the 1980s, a number of unions had developed their expertise in such matters, and they began to join with a small number of companies in exploring and implementing worker participation in the context of workplace reorganization. Notable among these unions were the Communications Workers of Canada (later the Communications, Energy and Paperworkers), who adopted a policy at their annual convention in 1992 (CEP, 1994), and the United Steelworkers of America, who held a major policy conference on restructuring in 1991. Both of these unions released statements that endorsed the idea of proactive union involvement in introducing innovations such as direct worker participation through joint efforts with management. Recent examples of the implementation of EI initiatives in unionized Canadian workplaces are available, and most report quantifiable gains as a direct result of EI.[9]

The lack of enthusiasm for EI programs on the part of some unions can be argued to have slowed down the diffusion of EI in workplaces represented by these unions. However, it would be misleading to suggest that the examples of union opposition cited above have completely blocked the adoption of EI. Given the decentralized nature of the Canadian industrial relations system in which the power to sign collective agreements rests with union locals rather than with union centrals, a number of workplaces have adopted EI programs despite union policy statements critical of them. For example, the CAMI auto-assembly plant in Ontario, a joint venture between General Motors and Suzuki, has adopted a team-based production system in agreement with its local of the CAW.

THE SUSTAINABILITY OF EMPLOYEE-INVOLVEMENT PROGRAMS

The practice of employee involvement has seen many innovations and, some would say, fads over the past 15 years. As mentioned previously, in the 1970s, the Quality of Work Life movement was very strong, and a number of significant EI programs were launched under its banner. In the 1980s, quality circles (QCs) became very popular. The 1990s saw a major growth in Total Quality Management (TQM) programs. The shifting sands of management fads and fashions raise a fundamental question about employee involvement: what factors sustain such innovations over time?

Although few empirical studies of the sustainability issue have been conducted using large random samples, the case-study literature suggests a number of generalizations. First, as discussed earlier in the section on EI's organizational consequences, sustainability is facilitated by access to information and communication within the organization, and by corresponding changes in training and work organization. Second, a number of theorists have argued that, in unionized organizations, the support and co-operation of the union would enhance the effectiveness and sustainability of EI (Kochan, Katz, and Mower, 1984).

Further, as discussed earlier in the section on emergent types of EI, there is a link between sustainability and the type of EI: the narrow self-contained type such as quality circles or the integrated form such as autonomous work groups. The first type may be easier to introduce because its implementation requires relatively minor changes in the organization, but it is harder to sustain (at least in the North American setting) given its narrow scope. The second type is harder to implement given all the changes that need to be made, but easier to sustain because of its wide scope (Lawler and Mohrman, 1985; Cutcher-Gershenfeld, Kochan, and Verma, 1991).

Running successful nonunion employee-participation plans requires a change in management style and a great deal of forethought. In Exhibit 6.4, the senior manager in charge of Imperial Oil's upstream operations' joint industrial council plan for worker representation analyzes the key elements that require management commitment. This plan is noteworthy because it involves *indirect* representation (workers are represented by elected worker delegates) and has an open mandate to advise—but not bargain—on matters normally falling within the purview of a union. Very few firms are willing to "walk the talk" on formal, nonunion representation plans. In particular, autocratic management styles, found in the "command and control" structures embedded in most firms, are incompatible with the principles necessary to run nonunion plans.

Exhibit 6.4
Operation of the Production District Joint Industrial Council, Imperial Oil

1. MANAGEMENT VALUES, PRINCIPLES, LEADERSHIP STYLE

The values and principles of senior management are critical. Delegates and employees are sensitive to such questions as:

- Does the management team believe that employees have a role to play in influencing and setting policy?
- Is open, honest communication valued?
- Is constructive criticism welcomed?
- Are different perspectives respected and valued?
- Do the leaders do what they say they will do?

The values of the company and its leaders/managers translate into behaviours and a management "style" that can make or break the success of any form of representation, but it is especially key for nonunion representation in which there is no veil behind which management can hide.

Imperial takes care to appoint leaders/managers who demonstrate the ability to work well with a diverse workforce and have a proven track record in maintaining positive employee relations. We build this expectation into our management succession planning.

2. THE COMPETITIVENESS OF EXISTING WAGES, BENEFITS, AND WORKING CONDITIONS

It is important that a process exist to ensure we remain competitive in our wages, benefits, and working conditions. Let's not be naive. If our compensation package is not competitive, then a nonunion form of representation can break down very quickly. If employees feel they are being given fair and equitable treatment and their issues in these areas are being resolved, they typically see less value in injecting a third party such as a union into the process.

3. IMPACT AND ABILITY TO INFLUENCE

A representation vehicle that has (and is perceived to have) influence over matters within its mandate is more likely to succeed. . . . Responsiveness is valued and expected. We keep a log of issues to ensure that response time is tracked. Delays without reasonable explanation are flagged for discussion and action.

4. HAVING BOTH FORMAL AND INFORMAL ISSUE RESOLUTION PROCESSES

The presence of formal and informal issue resolution processes is valued and the perception as to whether or not they are effective is important to monitor. The existence of a grievance procedure often is cited by people as an advantage of unions and there is a message in this for nonunion forms of representation. We have provided training for our delegates into how grievances are best handled. . . . Equally important is a working environment where issue resolution can take place and employees are free to voice their opinions without fear of reprisal. . . . It is most important that we "walk this talk."

5. EXTERNAL LABOUR RELATIONS AND LEGAL/HUMAN RIGHTS ENVIRONMENT

Our company does not operate nonunion representation in a vacuum. In other words, union actions, whether they be contract settlements, job actions, or grievance/arbitration decisions have some residual effect in nonunion areas.

In addition, legal or human rights rulings that affect the workplace require clear understanding by our delegates. Things like alcohol and drug policy implementation have been a hot topic for us. The key in all of these areas, from my perspective, is to ensure that we have frank, open discussion of these matters. . . .

6. THE WILL TO MAKE IT HAPPEN AND THE ABILITY TO EVOLVE

[We] press for continuous improvement in the Joint Industrial Council processes. If this evolution had not occurred, there is no doubt that JIC would not have survived to see its 50th anniversary in Imperial Oil's upstream.

A key area for long-term success of employee involvement in any organization, but especially a unionized one, is the issue of employment security. Since job security is fundamental to employee interests, it is only natural for employees to wonder about the effect on their own jobs of EI programs that seek to improve productivity and quality. Few people would be willing to help eliminate their own jobs. Hence, EI programs must create an implicit, if not explicit, guarantee that participants in the program will not become victims of their own success. In some organizations, such as Xerox and Saturn, explicit employment guarantees have been made. In others, implicit guarantees often accompany successful implementation.

In several documented cases, the loss of employment through major layoffs has often derailed EI programs. In firms such as Budd, Cummins Engine, U S West, and even the Edmonton hospitals, large-scale layoffs have led to a pulling back of labour–management co-operation or cancellation of the program or both. This is not to say that EI programs cannot be sustained in firms that are going through external shocks such as downsizing, restructuring, or market upheavals. However, attempts to implement EI during downsizing can have counterproductive results (Lam and Reshef, 1999). In a small number of cases, when the EI process is used to inform people about important business decisions, even those with negative outcomes for employees, the trauma reinforces the EI process. At Xerox, when key business decisions such as subcontracting and location of a new plant were made through the EI process, that process was reinforced. On the other hand, when key decisions bypass the EI process, the effect is to undermine employee involvement.

Table 6.2 summarizes the factors that help and hinder effective employee involvement at the idea, design, and implementation stages. But underlying the specific factors listed in Table 6.2 might be a general construct relating to the tone of the relationship of workers and managers within the firm. A recent study of a Vancouver-based lumber co-operative proposed that *how* employees and managers interact and discuss issues

Table 6.2 Successful and Unsuccessful EI Initiatives

STAGE OF EI	FACTORS THAT HELP EI	FACTORS THAT HINDER EI
Idea Stage	• Consultation with employees and their employee representatives. • Assessment of EI readiness. • Commitment from senior managers. • Analysis of the HRM and IR systems that would need modification, including the need for change in the organization's culture.	• No consultation or advanced indication of intention to introduce EI. • No commitment of senior managers, or high rate of turnover of managers such that no EI "champion" is sustained. • Thinking about EI as a practice without ripple effects throughout the employment practices and culture of the firm.
Design Stage	• Input from employees or their representatives. • Training in skills needed for EI design. • Redefinition of the new role of supervisors. • Renegotiation of terms and conditions of employment so rewards from EI are allocated appropriately.	• No input from workers, unions, or supervisors. • No training in design skills. • No coordination with line managers in integrating EI with work itself.
Implementation Stage	• Organization-wide communication on EI goals and methods. • Training for all employees in "soft" skills. • Redefinition of supervisory role as coach and mentor. • Appropriate incentives for EI efforts. • Tie-in of EI efforts with organizational goals. • Incentives for line managers to adopt EI.	• Insufficient autonomy for EI efforts. • Insufficient communication about EI to all employees. • Involuntary participation in EI. • Lack of funds to start EI. • Lack of focus on outcomes of interest to workers, e.g., safe jobs, more interesting jobs, job security, enhanced compensation.

significantly impacts on the success of employee involvement. People with co-operative goals who discuss problems openly and constructively are more likely to experience success with EI than those who have competitive goals that result in avoidance or escalations of conflict, in low productivity, and in low morale (Tjosvold, 1998).

In general, EI initiatives challenge the comfort zone of employees and managers, who are accustomed to a certain "wage–effort bargain." Suddenly, people are being asked to work harder, or work "smarter," or communicate with each other in ways that were never required in the past. Psychological theories of motivation suggest that, in exchange for more effort, employees anticipate additional compensation from the corporation. Firms should acknowledge employee expectations of greater wages, benefits, and job security; satisfying training opportunities; respectful treatment; more collegial management styles; and other conditions of employment. EI will have spillover effects on many aspects of the firm, and successful interventions are those that anticipate and plan for such challenges, all within a more co-operative style of interaction.

THE LEGALITIES OF EMPLOYEE INVOLVEMENT

In this final major section of the chapter, we briefly turn to the legal issues that surround the high-involvement workplace. Although a variety of government policies has promoted employee-involvement practices, such activities are voluntarily adopted by the affected parties, and government compulsion is rare. Canadian public policy generally has taken a non-interventionist role, and allows the parties to handle EI on their own. Labour and management are free to devise their own responses to workplace challenges, which might include restructuring, technological change, EI, and so on.[10]

Given the hands-off approach by government, to what extent do legal constraints exist around new worksite practices? Is this truly uncharted terrain, or are there ground rules? For example:

- Is it lawful for employers to create teams, groups, and worker participation plans (particularly if these behave like unions)?

- What is the difference between employee participation in unionized versus nonunion workplaces?

- Can employers use employee participation plans to avoid unionization?

- How far can managers and nonunion employees move in the direction of formalized representation systems without incurring legal roadblocks?

- Can employers implement employee participation plans in unionized worksites? What if the union objects?

Nonunion Workers and EI: The Canadian Approach

To this point, we have focused on EI systems based primarily on meeting managerial objectives. But EI also brings opportunities for workers to group together, increases their ability to exert some influence on decision making, and generally makes them feel more effective. In these conditions, workers might be interested in collective representation of their own agenda, i.e., improving the terms and conditions of their employment. The ability of nonunion employees to seek a collective voice mechanism where unions have not proven to be a viable option is of considerable interest. After all, over 70 percent of Canadian workers are not unionized.

The Canadian policy approach is that all nonunion forms of employee representation are lawful (Taras, 1997). There is no ban or limitation on nonunion employee representation, so long as a company is not setting up a nonunion system for the purpose of thwarting the workers' statutory right to choose to be represented by a union (Taras, 2006). Using EI to oppose union organizing is an unfair labour practice. (By contrast, the American approach greatly restricts both the form and scope of nonunion plans. See Kaufman and Taras, 1999.)

Where does EI and nonunion representation exist in the legal web of rules governing Canadian employment? The simple answer is "nowhere." Aside from some statutes that compel larger companies to set up health and safety committees within union and nonunion worksites, there is no overt recognition in Canadian public policy of nonunion employee representation and participation systems.

Dissatisfied workers in an EI plan cannot simply transform themselves into a union because no labour board will certify a group of employees as a union when management has participated in, interfered with, or dominated their attempts to form a collective entity. That is, labour boards will not consider a management-dominated group to be appropriate for the purposes of collective bargaining. Almost all nonunion groups involve substantial management participation. Often, the nonunion plans are encouraged or even established by management. Workers meet with managers in order to exchange ideas, usually on paid time and on company premises. Management has considerable input into the agenda and guides the discussion. Workers rarely have access to independent resources or expertise, but instead rely on information provided by management. Workers rarely pay any type of dues or charge for their participation in nonunion plans, as these plans are usually funded entirely by management. Because of the extent of management presence in these nonunion plans, the plans cannot be certified as unions, and thus they exist outside collective bargaining laws.

Though EI is not protected by laws, neither is it banned or interfered with by any laws. In Canada, managers and workers are free to establish whatever types of plans and vehicles they desire in nonunion worksites. Thus, in Canada, the issues involving employee participation rarely touch on legality, but more often involve implementation. The success and failure of nonunion plans depend on their design, the integrity of management, whether the workers trust that management will hear them, and the company's long-term commitment to employee participation.

Employee-Involvement Plans and Unions: The Legalities

The legal situation is more complex in worksites that involve the co-existence of EI and collective bargaining arrangements. Canadian laws grant exclusive bargaining rights to unions that achieve certification. With the Supreme Court of Canada's 2007 *Health Services* decision (described in Chapters 1 and 8), collective bargaining must be respected as a fundamental right, protected by the provision within the *Charter of Rights and Freedoms* for freedom of association. While nonunion employers may freely communicate with employees, the situation is more complex in unionized settings. Employers' communication with unionized workers is constrained as follows:

- There can be no promises of reward, intimidation, threats, or coercion to interfere with, undermine, or derogate the union.

- Employers may not negotiate directly with workers on matters within the purview of the collective bargaining relationship. No "side deals" are permitted.

- The union must not be maligned or demeaned by the employer.

Canadian labour relations boards have sufficient powers, under the various labour relations statutes, to safeguard the role of unions. Employers cannot use consultative programs to "subvert, circumvent, or replace the union in its legitimate role as exclusive bargaining agent."[11]

Thus, to introduce and operate high-involvement systems in unionized worksites requires a great deal of communication and collaboration with the union. It often is argued that unionization is a formidable barrier to the type of flexibility needed to run sophisticated employee-involvement plans. The flip side of this assertion is that if a union accepts and oversees the implementation of such a plan, the plan is more likely to be well conceived and of lasting impact.

LOOKING BEYOND—THE FUTURE FOR HIGH INVOLVEMENT

Although the idea of greater say for workers has been accepted in principle, its implementation continues to be fraught with ambiguity and uncertainty. Battles, both ideological and tactical, continue around the scope, the extent, and the form that participation is to take within the organization.

In the past few years, management has been seeking greater evidence of the costs and benefits of different types of practice. While the high-involvement paradigm became popular because of the *hope* of reaping improvements in productivity, simple faith is no longer viewed as sufficient justification for the large investment in moving toward a high-involvement workplace. The latest managerial trend is to establish benchmarks and measures. This is part of a larger movement that promotes measurement of a host of indicators of firm performance, of which productivity and efficiency are subsets. In a turbulent world consisting of vigorous competition and great uncertainty, it is not surprising that managers are using the modern technologies at their disposal to more closely monitor the activities of their workplaces and industry. Examples of conventional benchmarks used to monitor the labour–management relationship are the rate of absenteeism, worker quit rates and turnover, grievance filing rates, and so on.[12] The move toward employee involvement requires the development of additional measures, including work climate or quality of work life scores, employee commitment, satisfaction with training and skills, as well as measures of productivity such as amount of downtime versus productive work, quality of goods and services, customer satisfaction, and the impact of cost cutting.

Although workers in a high-involvement work setting may have the sense that they have been given autonomy over how the work is getting done, there is little doubt that their efforts are being carefully scrutinized and evaluated. The movement toward benchmarking allows managers to feel they are meeting the dual objectives of efficiency and control.

Questions

1. What advantages and disadvantages do high-involvement systems offer over purely Tayloristic forms of work organization?

2. Debate the proposition that EI should be implemented *only* if it improves productivity and efficiency.

3. Identify key organizational and external factors that will make a company more likely to adopt greater EI.

4. Identify individual, group, organizational, and external factors that cause many EI programs to fail.

5. Why are high-involvement practices not more widely adopted?

6. Is EI more likely to be adopted in a unionized organization? Less likely? Why?

7. Do EI programs have the potential to destabilize labour–management relations? How can managers make EI a positive intervention in labour–management relations?

8. How can labour boards tell the difference between EI initiatives that are lawful and those that are considered unfair labour practices?

9. Discuss the role of various management levels and functions in the successful implementation of EI: top management, middle management, first-line managers, HR/IR managers, and line managers.

Weblinks

Principles of Scientific Management:
http://melbecon.unimelb.edu.au/het/taylor/sciman.htm

Biography of F. W. Taylor and links to his works:
www.ideafinder.com/history/inventors/taylor.htm

Employee Involvement Association:
www.eianet.org/

Chapter 7
Social, Political, and Economic Environments

Frank Reid and Rafael Gomez*

Until the late 1980s and early 1990s, the normal pattern in most car manufacturing plants was a rotating shift schedule of two weeks on the day shift alternating with two weeks on the afternoon shift. The General Motors truck plant in Oshawa, Ontario, was no different in this respect. In 1993, however, when the plant added a night shift, becoming the first automotive assembly operation in North America to run 24 hours a day, it gave employees the opportunity to *volunteer* to work steady nights at a premium wage and reduced hours. The Canadian Auto Workers union, despite its expressed role as an advocate for economic equity at the workplace, supported the idea and agreed to a change of work rules to accommodate the new option.

The 700 employees at the GM truck plant who volunteer to work a steady night shift earn a 10 percent wage premium and work only 7.5 hours while getting paid for 8 hours, effectively adding another 6.7 percent premium to the hourly wage.

Employees find the steady night shift much better than the rotating shifts, which can be even more disruptive to sleeping and eating patterns. Few have elected to go back to the normal rotating shifts pattern, and for those who do, employees on a waiting list are ready to take their place.

General Motors is also pleased with the volunteer night-shift option because the company has saved the enormous cost of building a new plant. The quality on the night shift equals that of the other two shifts, and the night shift has met its production targets.[1]

This innovation by GM and the CAW is an example of what economists would call a compensating wage differential to allocate labour. Compared to the alternative of simply assigning shifts on a rotational basis, using wages to induce voluntary changes in behaviour can be a win–win alternative (i.e., it can make some people better off and make others no worse off—what economists call an increase in Pareto efficiency). It can also be more equitable.

The social, political, and economic environments are fundamental determinants of decisions by the three actors in the industrial relations system—workers and their representatives (generally in the form of trade unions), management, and government. The purpose of this chapter is to discuss the impact of each of these environments on the actors, and through them, on the outcomes of the industrial relations system. While we focus primarily on the impact that the environment has on the actors, we also observe that the actions of the actors can affect the environment. Both unions and management consciously attempt to change the political, social, and legal environments in order to influence the laws that are put in place to regulate and enforce standards in the labour market and in the industrial relations system. Our discussion begins with the social environment because that represents the attitudes and values of the population, which in turn affect the political environment and the perceived role that government should play inside the workplace and in the labour market as a whole.

The political environment represents the vehicle to translate social attitudes into legislation and the mechanisms for its enforcement. In any country, it reflects the diverse social views of the population. However, the political environment is not simply a passive response by political parties representing the various views in society. The process is much more complicated. Each political party tries to attain a mandate from a much wider constituency than the formal membership in the party. The parties try to broaden their representation by appealing to as wide a following as possible, and several political parties in Canada have formal ties with the union movement.

The economic environment sets out the limits within which the actors can press for economic improvements in compensation and benefits for employees, and for reduction in labour costs and improvements in productivity and profits for employers. The forces that underlie the operation of the labour market are supply and demand. How these interact, together with the impact of government, are essential components to understanding the industrial relations system.

In discussing each of these environments, we will compare and contrast the situations in the United States and Canada. For unions, on the surface, we should see similar behaviour since many of the same unions bargain in both countries, sometimes with the same companies. We include inter-country comparisons in our discussion of each of the environments since those kinds of comparisons help illuminate the role of social, political, and economic forces on the outcomes of the industrial relations system.

THE SOCIAL ENVIRONMENT

The social environment represents the combination of attitudes and values of the population toward the institutions and collective goals of society. Seymour Martin Lipset and Noah M. Meltz published a book in 2004 called *The Paradox of American Unionism*, comparing the views of Americans and Canadians on such topics as trust in government, unions, and corporations. One of the major contributions of that book was the commissioning of a survey that, among other things, compared the percentage of employees in the two countries who had either "a lot" or a "great deal" of confidence in the three institutions with the percentage who had "very little" confidence. In each country there were fewer people of the former persuasion and more who had very little confidence in the government, unions, and corporations. Those in the in-between group, who had "some" confidence, represented about half of the workforce. People in both Canada and the United States seem to have similar feelings toward these institutions.

Major differences emerged between the two countries in attitudes toward the role of government. As indicated in Table 7.1, there is overwhelming agreement in both countries that the gap between rich and poor is too wide, 87 percent in Canada and 84 percent in the United States. However, when asked what role the government should play in narrowing the gap, almost one out of every two Canadians (45 percent), compared with

Table 7.1 View of Government

SURVEY RESPONSE	PERCENTAGE OF TOTAL EMPLOYED	
	Canada	United States
Workers who say that the gap between the rich and the poor is too wide	87	84
Workers who feel that it is the responsibility of government to reduce the difference between incomes	45	31
Workers who agree that it is a responsibility of government to ensure the well-being of all citizens	83	72
Workers who feel that it is a responsibility of government to preserve society's morality	73	53

Source: "Canadian and American Attitudes Toward Work and Institutions," *Perspectives on Work*, vol. 1, no. 3, by Seymour Martin Lipset and Noah Meltz. © 1998, IRRA, by permission.

only 31 percent in the United States, felt that it is the responsibility of government to reduce the difference between people earning high and low incomes. Canadians also are much more strongly committed (73 percent) to the government's taking responsibility to preserve society's morality than are Americans (53 percent).

In terms of attitudes toward work, Table 7.2 shows that Canadians and Americans have remarkably similar attitudes. The vast majority take pride in their work, are satisfied with their job, would do their best regardless of pay, and think they are paid fairly.

Differences appear when employees in the two countries are asked specifically about how people should be treated in the workplace. In answer to virtually every question that deals with the balance between equity (fairness) and efficiency, Canadians are more supportive of fairness than are Americans, even though both countries support equity in the workplace. For example, as shown in Table 7.3, fewer than half of the workers in Canada (45 percent) think that it is very fair to pay more efficient workers higher salaries, while a majority (57 percent) of Americans support such an idea.

Table 7.2 Employee Views of Work

SURVEY RESPONSE	PERCENTAGE OF TOTAL EMPLOYED	
	Canada	United States
Workers who are somewhat or very satisfied with their job	86	85
Workers who think they were paid fairly in the past year for their main employment	73	74
Workers taking some or a great deal of pride in their work	97	99
Workers who agree that they would do their best regardless of the pay	77	75

Source: "Canadian and American Attitudes Toward Work and Institutions," *Perspectives on Work*, vol. 1, no. 3, by Seymour Martin Lipset and Noah Meltz. © 1998, IRRA, by permission.

Table 7.3 Work-Related Values

Survey Response	Percentage of Total Employed	
	Canada	United States
Workers who believe that it is very fair to pay more efficient workers higher salaries	45	57
Workers who feel that freedom is more important than equality	55	63
Workers who agree with the statement that job security is more important than career advancement	67	61

Source: "Canadian and American Attitudes Toward Work and Institutions," *Perspectives on Work*, vol. 1, no. 3, by Seymour Martin Lipset and Noah Meltz. © 1998, IRRA, by permission.

These tables demonstrate that, while there seem to be similar limited levels of confidence in most institutions in the two countries, where the Americans and Canadians part company is on their attitudes toward equality (and fairness) versus freedom and efficiency. Canadians are more supportive of equality and equity than are Americans. As well, more than Americans, Canadians expect government to play an activist role in the workplace and in society. This has implications for the political environment.

THE POLITICAL ENVIRONMENT

The political environment has a major impact on the legislative environment, which in turn affects the actors in the industrial relations system. As well, the actors attempt to influence the political and legal environments. How the political impacts occur is a complex process, very dependent on the institutions themselves and the political parties that interact and react within these institutions. The differing patterns of trade union stability in Canada and decline in the United States provide a good example of the influence of political institutions. Recently, democratic institutions have had very different effects on the actors in the industrial relations system in the two countries. In the United States, labour policy reform has stalled despite intensive efforts on the part of unions. Canada continues to make perhaps small, but continual, adjustments to labour laws in both the federal and provincial spheres.

The political environment in Canada is based on a parliamentary system, in which the party (or parties if there is a coalition) with a majority or plurality of the elected representatives forms the government. In the United States, the congressional system is one of checks and balances with a separately elected president (executive branch), congress (the Senate and House of Representatives), and judiciary. A Democratic president can be rendered ineffective by a Republican congress, and vice versa. In a parliamentary system, a governing party has a greater chance of attaining its objectives. This makes it relatively easier for governments in Canada to pass pro- or anti-union legislation. In the United States, with the exception of the New Deal period during the Great Depression of the 1930s, it has been much harder for the president to pass labour legislation that is supportive of unions.

The Historical Context: 1900–1949

The political environment for union–management relations has experienced swings during the past century, moving from laissez-faire and even pro-management/anti-union to pro-union and then to lesser support for unions. Prior to the 1940s, with the exception of the First World War, the political environment was not supportive of organized labour. At the beginning of the 1900s, the federal Liberal government passed the *Industrial Disputes Investigation Act* (1907), which gave a form of recognition to unions by requiring a suspension of a strike and the appointment of a conciliation officer—and later, if necessary, a conciliation board—to inquire into the causes of strikes and to recommend terms for an agreement. The recommendations were not binding, and the parties were permitted to resume a strike or lockout after the board's report was made public. There was no protection for employees to form unions.

It was again a federal Liberal government that in 1944 enacted sweeping legislation—PC 1003—that provided for the rights of employees to join unions and introduced a mechanism to enforce the legislation, the Canada Labour Relations Board. This legislation, by virtue of the wartime situation, was deemed to apply not only to workers under the federal jurisdiction, but also to employees under the provincial jurisdiction (approximately 90 percent of all Canadian employees). In 1948 responsibility for labour legislation was returned to the provinces, and PC 1003 for the federal jurisdiction was formally titled the *Industrial Relations and Disputes Investigation Act*.

The political environment in 1944 was crucial for the passage of union-supportive legislation. The Americans had passed similar legislation in 1935, the *Wagner Act*. What gave a push to the passage of such legislation in Canada was the victory of the socialist CCF (Co-operative Commonwealth Federation) Party in Saskatchewan in 1944, and polls showing that in Ontario the CCF was almost even with the Liberals in popular support going into the elections that were expected to take place in 1944. In the same year, the CCF government in Saskatchewan passed legislation that gave both private-sector and public-sector workers the right to organize, bargain, and strike. The federal government passed not only the collective bargaining legislation, but also legislation providing for unemployment insurance and "baby bonuses." Partly as a result of these initiatives, the Liberals were able to co-opt the votes that might otherwise have gone to the CCF, and they were again able to form a majority government.

The Post-War Years: 1950–1979

Changes in the political environment in the 1960s and 1970s were responsible for the next major changes in labour legislation in Canada. The Quiet Revolution in Quebec, which began in 1960 with the election of a Liberal government to replace the Union Nationale, led to the passage in 1964 of legislation similar to Saskatchewan's permitting collective bargaining and the right to strike by public-sector employees (government employees, teachers, health care workers).

At the federal level, in 1967, the Liberal government passed the *Public Service Staff Relations Act* (PSSRA) giving public-sector workers under federal jurisdiction the right to bargain and, under certain circumstances, to strike. In the next few years, most of the provinces passed legislation supporting some degree of public-sector collective bargaining. These governments were made up of Conservative (Ontario), Liberal, and, later, NDP (successor to the CCF) governments. The changes in legislation, and the different political parties that introduced them, occurred in a political environment that was moving toward supporting the right of employees in all sectors to form unions and to bargain.

This right was somewhat abridged for three years (1975–1978) when the Liberal government of Pierre Trudeau introduced wage and price controls, even though it was elected in 1974 on a platform opposing the proposal for price controls by the federal Progressive Conservative party. The Anti-Inflation Board (AIB) imposed steadily lower guidelines for wage settlements over the three years of the program and, in conjunction with a restrictive monetary policy, helped to bring down the inflation rate. The AIB was perhaps the most dramatic government intervention in the Canadian collective bargaining process in the post-war period.

The Last Quarter Century: 1980–Present

From 1980 until the early years of the 21st century, the direction of change in the political environment was not as clear as in earlier periods. Some of the changes were away from union support, some were toward more union support, and in some cases, particularly in British Columbia and Ontario, the political environment moved back and forth. In the period 1982–1984, the federal government introduced limitations on the increases in public-sector wages (the so-called 6 and 5 program, indicating the percentage increases in wages that were permitted to federal public servants). Ontario followed suit with a program of 9 and 5, and some other provinces such as British Columbia introduced similar programs, all aimed at containing wage increases in the public sector that might spread to the private sector, or so it was feared.

In the early 1990s there was first a swing toward the NDP and more liberal labour legislation, then a partial swing back, especially in Ontario. NDP governments were elected in Ontario (1990), British Columbia (1991), and Saskatchewan (1991). The first two introduced major changes in labour legislation, with Ontario totally banning the use of strike replacement workers, and B.C. partially banning their use. Earlier, the province of Quebec had also introduced limitations—though not as encompassing as Ontario's—on the use of replacement workers (see Chapter 16 on Quebec's industrial relations).

The Ontario NDP then reversed direction because of the continuing recession, and in 1993 introduced what was called the Social Contract, which for 3 years forced a 5 percent reduction in public-sector wage costs by imposing unpaid reductions in work time. The labour movement in Ontario split over the Social Contract. The public-sector unions and the Canadian Auto Workers (CAW) opposed the NDP policy and refused to support the NDP in the next election. The private-sector unions, with the exception of the CAW, supported the government's action, on the grounds that a 5 percent temporary cut in work time was better than the layoff of 13 000 public-sector employees. The split in labour's ranks, along with a general dissatisfaction with the NDP and a strong Progressive Conservative platform (the Common Sense Revolution), combined to produce a massive NDP defeat in Ontario in 1995. The political environment had changed again in central Canada. Upon assuming power, the Tories immediately reversed the union-supportive changes that had been put in place by the NDP. A subsequent Liberal electoral victory in 2003 has not done much to alter the major changes of the 1990s.

Currently, no federal or provincial political party seemingly has any appetite for major labour reform, perhaps in keeping with the previous history of progressive rather than revolutionary legislative change in Canada.

The political environment must therefore be seen as a factor affecting the bargaining strengths of the actors in the industrial relations system and, ultimately, the outcomes at the bargaining table. Of course, bargaining between unions and management takes place within an economic context. That context in itself exerts a major force at the bargaining table. To understand the impact of economic forces, we have to explore what makes up the economic environment and how it affects the industrial relations system.

THE ECONOMIC ENVIRONMENT

The economic environment sets the limits within which employees can press for economic improvements in compensation and benefits, and employers can press for a reduction in labour costs and an increase in profits. Although supply and demand constrain what occurs in the labour market, constraints also result from government legislation and the accompanying rules and regulations, such as employment insurance, pay equity, minimum wage, and other employment standards legislation.

The Theory of a Competitive Labour Market

In this section, we explore what we call the "theory of a competitive labour market"; i.e., what makes a labour market tick?

How Competitive Markets Are Supposed to Work Competitive labour markets are assumed to be characterized by a large number of employers and employees of each type of labour so that no single employer or employee exerts a significant influence on the market wage rate. It is also assumed that there are no artificial barriers to entering any occupation. In a competitive market, each employer is a *wage-taker*, that is, the employer takes the wage as given by the market and decides how many employees to hire in order to maximize profits, given product market conditions and the state of technology.

The supply of labour to any particular occupation (that is, the number of persons who want to work in that occupation) depends on numerous factors, including the wage rate for that occupation; the required levels of skill, training, and experience; working conditions; the status of the occupation; and the preferences of labour force members. For any fixed level of the other factors that affect labour supply, an increase in the wage rate for one occupation will make that occupation more attractive, resulting in an increased number of persons who want to work in that occupation.

The demand for labour—that is, the number of persons in each occupational group whom employers want to hire—depends on factors such as the wage rate for the occupation. The demand for labour is a derived demand; i.e., it is derived from the amount of output the employer wants to produce, along with technological considerations. For any fixed level of the other factors, a wage increase will tend to reduce the amount of labour employers wish to hire (the number of persons or the number of hours). This reduction occurs for two reasons: the *substitution effect* and the *output effect*. First, for any given level of output, in the long run, employers will tend to substitute capital or other less expensive types of labour for the type of labour that has become relatively more expensive (the substitution effect). Second, an increase in wage costs will increase unit costs and the price of the product being produced, resulting in a drop in sales and a reduction in the derived demand for labour (output effect). Both effects work in the same direction, leading to a reduction in the demand for labour as wages increase (i.e., labour demand curves slope downwards).

In the classic competitive labour market model, there is a particular wage rate, known as the *equilibrium wage*, at which the supply of labour and the demand for labour are equal. At the equilibrium wage, no one would be unemployed; that is, everyone who wanted to work at that wage rate would be able to find work. In other words, the labour market would clear. This simple model can be easily modified to allow for frictional unemployment due to employee turnover in a dynamic labour market. Although unfilled jobs and unemployed workers could co-exist in this model, there would be no overall shortage of jobs at the equilibrium wage.

At any wage rate above the equilibrium wage, the supply of labour exceeds the demand for labour, resulting in downward pressure on the wage rate. Conversely, at any wage rate below the equilibrium level, the demand for labour exceeds the supply of labour, resulting in unfilled job vacancies and upward pressure on the wage rate. Consequently, in a competitive labour market, compensation tends toward the equilibrium wage where the quantity of labour supplied equals the quantity demanded.

How Wages Allocate Labour: Compensating Wage Differentials An implication of competitive labour markets, which can be traced back to the work of Adam Smith more than 200 years ago, is that, in the long run, the equalization of the net advantage in each occupation results in compensating wage differentials that offset undesirable non-wage aspects of the job. For example, a job that is dirty or dangerous or requires a long period of training or unduly long hours of work would receive a higher wage that would be just sufficient to offset these disadvantages for the marginal employee. Such differentials serve two economic functions in allocating labour. On the supply side, they attract workers to undesirable occupations and compensate them for tolerating unpleasant working conditions. On the demand side, compensating wage differentials also provide an economic incentive for employers to eliminate undesirable working conditions, provided the cost of eliminating them is less than the cost of paying the compensating wage differential.

The principle of compensating wage differentials can be applied to the use of shift premiums (see the opening vignette). For simplicity, suppose that initially there were equal numbers of employees working a day shift and a night shift, all employees were required to alternate shifts every two weeks, and there was no shift premium. It can be shown that some employees can be made better off, and no one worse off, if the shift premium is widened sufficiently to induce the required number of employees to volunteer for regular night shift. To ensure that the employer is also not made worse off, assume that the shift differential is created by raising the night-shift wage and lowering the day-shift wage by equal amounts so that labour costs are not increased. Also assume that employees are given the option of continuing to alternate shifts every two weeks, in which case they would earn the same amount over a four-week cycle as they would under the old system. This option guarantees that no employee would be worse off.

For some employees, their personal situation may be such that the extra money from working straight nights is more important to them than the inconvenience of night shift. A few employees may even have reasons to prefer night shift to day shift. The point is that any employees who voluntarily choose to work continuous night shift at the higher wage must be better off, otherwise they would not choose that option over the option of continuing to rotate shifts. Similarly, other employees in different personal situations may find the opportunity to work a continuous day shift so appealing that they are prepared to accept the lower day-shift wage. Again, these employees must be better off, otherwise they would not choose a day shift over the option of continuing to rotate shifts. Thus, some employees are made better off and no employee is made worse off by using a compensating wage differential to allocate employees between shifts, rather than relying on the more traditional approach of requiring all employees to alternate shifts. This example illustrates the win–win possibilities of applying economic rationale to solve workplace problems.

What Happens When Competition Is Not Perfect? Most labour markets differ from the perfectly competitive ideal in several important respects. First, although wage rates are influenced by economic forces, these rates generally do not adjust rapidly enough to equate supply and demand as predicted by the competitive model. Actual labour markets are often characterized by substantial periods of labour surpluses (unemployment) or, occasionally, periods of labour shortages (job vacancies) even in the absence of institutional factors that impede adjustment such as minimum wage laws, equal pay legislation, or unions. In particular, a reduction in demand for labour often leads to involuntary terminations (layoffs) rather than a lowering of the wage to the equilibrium level. Attempts to explain why wage adjustments do not clear the labour market in a satisfactory period of time have been the source of considerable controversy and will be discussed below in the context of barriers to labour market flexibility.

The second reason why actual labour markets differ from the competitive ideal is that many employers are "wage-setters" rather than "wage-takers" as assumed in the competitive model. Being a wage-taker implies that the employer can hire any desired amount of labour at the given market wage, but that at a slightly lower wage the employer would not be able to attract any employees because they would move to a competing firm offering the market wage. Typically, however, employers recognize that if they reduce the wage rate, there may be some reduction in the supply of labour to the firm (or an increase in turnover rates), but they will not lose their entire workforce as assumed in the perfectly competitive model. In fact, survey evidence indicates that teenaged workers would require a wage that is 26 percent higher than their current wage to induce them to move to a similar job with a different employer in the same area (Card, 1992: 53). The size of this differential presumably reflects the substantial psychological and economic costs of changing employers, thus giving employers a substantial role as wage-setters.

Employers who are wage-setters rather than wage-takers are said to possess some degree of *economic power* to affect flows in and out of the company (known as *monopsony power* in labour economics) and it can be shown that, in exercising their economic power to maximize profits, they will not pay equilibrium or market clearing wages as would an employer in a perfectly competitive labour market (Manning, 2003). The extreme case of economic power is a situation in which there is only one employer of a particular type of labour in the market, such as a school board that is the only employer of teachers in a community, or a hospital that is the only employer of nurses.

Employers with some degree of economic power can also affect the amount of labour supplied to their establishments through their recruiting, promotion, and training procedures as well as through changes in their wage structure or the redesigning of jobs.

The Demand for Labour

In this section, we first consider the magnitude of the employment reduction in response to a wage increase, then examine the case of a minimum-wage increase, and finish with a discussion of the issue of deindustrialization.

How Much Does Employment Fall When the Wage Rate Increases? Elasticity of Demand

Many of the changes implemented or proposed in the industrial relations field increase labour costs. Examples include an increase in minimum wages, an increase in wages of female employees through pay equity legislation, an increase in payroll taxes such as Canada Pension Plan premiums, and an increase in pension benefits directly or by indexing benefits to inflation. In the context of a competitive labour market, an increase in labour costs will result in a reduction in employment as discussed previously. In order to make an informed assessment of the potential employment impact of changes in labour costs, it is, however, often necessary to know by *how much* employment will be reduced in response to a given cost increase.

The concept used to measure the responsiveness of employment to labour costs is the *elasticity of demand for labour*, defined as the percentage reduction in employment in response to a 1 percent increase in wages in a particular job (for a given level of wages and prices for the economy as a whole). The percentage reduction in employment associated with a wage increase will be larger under the following circumstances:

- if the firm can easily substitute capital or other types of labour for the type of labour that has increased in cost;
- if a price increase induced by a wage increase would cause a substantial drop in the firm's sales; or
- if labour costs are a substantial portion of total costs so that a wage increase would have a substantial impact on unit costs.

The employment effect will also be greater the longer the time allowed for adjustments to take place.

A review of the empirical evidence suggests that, on average, over a one-year time horizon, employment is reduced by about 3 percent for each 10 percent increase in labour costs (Hamermesh, 1993). In situations where employment is particularly sensitive to labour costs, the employment impact could be twice as large, and in situations where employment is less sensitive to labour costs, the impact may be virtually zero. The evidence also indicates that, on average, the cause of the employment reduction is divided roughly equally between the replacement of the more expensive labour by capital or other types of labour (the substitution effect) and a drop in sales due to the higher price of the output (the output effect).

The Impact on Employment of Raising the Minimum Wage

One goal of a minimum-wage policy is to improve the equity of the distribution of income. In competitive labour markets, setting a minimum wage above the equilibrium rate may result in employers' reducing the number of minimum-wage jobs. For an employer with economic power, however, it can be shown that it is theoretically possible for a moderate increase in the minimum wage to increase employment (Manning, 2003). The theory is that the minimum wage can cause the employer with economic power to become a wage-taker instead of a wage-setter (although in this case the wage is determined by legislation rather than by the market). As the minimum wage increases toward the wage that would have been determined in a competitive market, then employment also increases toward the competitive level. In effect, the legislative intervention offsets the tendency of employers with economic power to pay wages below the competitive wage and to hire fewer employees than in a competitive market.

The conventional wisdom that an increase in the minimum wage causes a reduction in employment has been challenged in some important work in the early 1990s by David Card and his associates using American data.[2] An alternative, quasi-experimental methodology assessed minimum-wage increases in one U.S. state by comparing employment levels to those in another state where the minimum wage did not rise. The second state served as a "control group." Card found no evidence of negative employment impacts, which led him to conclude that more attention should be given to non-competitive models of the labour market.

This conclusion has, however, been challenged by other economists (e.g., Baker, Benjamin, and Stanger, 1999; Campolieti, Fang, and Gunderson, 2005; Campolieti, Gunderson, and Riddell, 2006; Yuen, 2003) based on Canadian data, and the topic remains highly controversial. In those studies, minimum wages were associated with reduced employment opportunities for youths. The magnitudes are such that a 10 percent increase in the minimum wage is associated with approximately a 3 to 6 percent reduction in the employment of youths. These findings are important as Canadian data is generally regarded as better than the U.S. data for testing for the impact of minimum wages, since there has been more variation in minimum wages across provinces and over time in Canada.

On the other hand, in 1997 Britain went from having no minimum wage under the previous Tory government to a brand new minimum wage that was increased several times under New Labour. The most recent assessment by David Metcalf of the British Low Pay Commission—whose remit was to guide government policy on the setting of the minimum wage—is that there were no adverse employment effects. If anything, income inequality was reduced and more net jobs were created in Britain than in any other period in its post-war history (Metcalf, 2007).

Deindustrialization and Business Offshoring Deindustrialization refers to a shift of employment away from manufacturing and other goods production toward employment in the service sector. This trend is an issue of perennial concern to trade union members and others since many of the jobs in the goods sector are higher-paying, unionized, blue-collar jobs and many of the service-sector jobs are lower-paying and often nonunion.

Three fundamental economic forces related to the demand for labour account for the long-term decline in Canadian manufacturing employment as a percentage of total employment. First, as living standards have risen over time, there has been an increase in the consumption of both goods and services, but consumers' preferences for services have increased faster than their preferences for goods. Second, productivity growth has generally been higher in goods industries than in service industries. Service industries require greater numbers of workers who are less easily replaced by technology. Third, the demand for labour in Canadian manufacturing has declined as production has shifted to Third World countries with lower compensation costs.

Foreign competition affects manufacturing more than services since services cannot be transported and traded as easily as manufactured goods. Growth in the service sector occurred primarily in the form of a shift in the production of some services and commodities from within manufacturing toward the service sector itself. This has occurred, for example, in many business services (financial, accounting, marketing), security and cleaning services, and cafeteria services. In addition to this shift toward purchasing from within the service sector itself, the demand for services has grown in general.

Within the service sector, which contains almost 70 percent of the workforce, there are enormous differences in employment trends, wage rates, and the extent of unionization. Government employment growth slowed markedly from the 1980s onward after increasing in the 1960s and 1970s. Employment in transportation, storage, communications, and utilities also did not keep up with the overall growth. In contrast, absolute and relative increases occurred in business services, retail trade, consumer services, and education and health. Earnings and the degree of unionization are high in utilities, transportation, storage, communications, government, education, and health, and low in wholesale and retail trade and consumer services. Earnings are high and unionization is low in business services.

Labour markets have faced severe adjustment challenges associated with trade liberalization and globalization. The newest challenge, in this respect, is *offshore outsourcing*, a phenomenon driven by the conflux of three technological developments: undersea fibre optic cables that provide internet bandwidth at almost zero marginal cost; the proliferation of personal computers; and the rise of software applications for global networking via personal computers and the internet (Blinder, 2006).

Earlier offshore outsourcing involved the outsourcing of manufacturing from developed high-wage countries to developing low-wage countries. This led to wage polarization in the developed countries as generally well-paid jobs in manufacturing were lost (Yan, 2006). Workers who lost such jobs generally could not move to the higher-paying business, professional, and managerial services that were also being created. Rather, they often could obtain jobs only in the lower-paying service sector, with their supply influx further lowering wages in that already low-pay sector.

The next wave of offshore outsourcing, however, is in business services, fostered by the decrease in the costs of communicating across the internet. Such costs are likely to continue to fall while at the same time the quality of services is likely to increase. The positive trend is therefore both an opportunity and a cause of concern for labour.

The issue of deindustrialization and offshoring, therefore, is more complex than simply moving from situations of extensive unionization and high wages to situations of low unionization and low wages. Even if the degree of unionization remains unchanged, the long-term trend toward the service sector (and the resulting shifts of certain service-sector occupations offshore) will produce mixed results in terms of its implications for both unionization and wage rates.

Supply of Labour

The supply of labour to individual occupations depends on the net advantages in each occupation, as discussed previously, but the supply of labour to the labour market as a whole requires a somewhat different analysis. Labour supply has both quality and quantity dimensions. The quality dimensions refer to education and training (subjects that have been analyzed within the context of human capital theory) as well as such factors as motivation and alienation (subjects within the purview of human resource management and organizational behaviour).

The quantity dimensions of labour supply are numerous, basically involving the size of our population (births less deaths plus net immigration), the extent to which the population participates in labour market activities (labour force participation), and the hours worked by those who participate in the labour market. The economic determinants of these various components—births, net immigration, labour force participation, and hours of work—have been the subject matter of considerable research.

Labour Force Participation and Hours of Work The theoretical framework used by economists to analyze employee preferences for hours of work and labour force participation decisions is the "income–leisure choice model," which treats the purchase of "leisure" (a catch-all word for all non-work activities) the same as the purchase of any other commodity. The individual has a fixed amount of time that can be allocated to leisure or to earning income through work. The wage rate indicates the amount of goods and services that can be purchased by giving up one hour of leisure.

In the income–leisure choice model, an increase in the wage rate influences the number of hours the employee desires to work through two effects operating in opposite directions: a *substitution effect* and an *income effect*. On the one hand, the substitution effect of a higher wage means the employee can earn more income and purchase more goods and services for each hour of leisure given up, inducing the employee to work more. The higher wage makes leisure relatively more expensive; leisure forgoes more goods and services to consume it. The substitution effect means that at a higher wage, the employee will prefer to work longer hours. On the other hand, the income effect of a higher wage means the employee is wealthier and can afford to consume more of both goods and leisure (i.e., work fewer hours).

The empirical evidence suggests that, on average, the income and substitution effects are of roughly equal magnitude—that is, they tend to offset each other. This implies that a wage increase will normally affect desired hours of work only slightly or have no impact for males. For women, the substitution effect is slightly dominant, so it induces a small increase in the labour supply of females.

The income–leisure choice model sheds light on several issues that are significant in union–management relations. The standard workweek in Canada has declined dramatically over the last century, influenced by both collective bargaining and employment standards legislation. In Canadian manufacturing, the standard workweek has declined from 64 hours per week in 1870 to under 40 hours per week at beginning of the 21st century. In the post-war period, the reduction has been in the form of longer vacations and more holidays, that is, a shorter work year, rather than reduced hours-per-week, in part because the fixed costs of commuting make the reductions in hours-per-week less economical than a longer vacation. The income–leisure choice model suggests that, as productivity and real wage rates have increased over time, the income effect of the wage increase outweighed the substitution effect, resulting in a desire for more leisure and shorter work hours as the wage rate increased.

The income–leisure choice framework also illustrates how various income maintenance programs (e.g., welfare, employment insurance) can reduce work incentives. This occurs because they provide income and hence reduce the need to work (the income effect), and also because they often tax labour market earnings, usually implicitly by requiring the recipient to forgo all or some of the transfer payment if he or she works (the substitution effect).

The Aging of the Population The last decade has seen a continuation of fundamental changes in the demographic composition of the labour force that have important implications for union–management relations. One of these changes is that in 2006, the front end of the large baby-boom generation (those born between 1946 and 1956) had moved solidly into near retirement (50-plus) and the rest (those born between 1957 and 1965) moved into middle age (40-plus years of age) (Foot and Stoffman, 2000).

Foot and Venne (1990) argue that the movement of the large baby-boom generation into middle age can create a mismatch between the typical organizational structure of the 1960s and the demographic structure of the labour force. In the past, the rapidly growing labour force resulted in a "population pyramid" (with a younger population base and fewer persons at the apex in the older age groups), which roughly mirrored the typical pyramidal structure of most organizations (with fewer positions at the higher levels). The population pyramid was transformed, however, as the baby-boom generation was followed by the relatively small baby-bust generation. The result was a mismatch in which the traditional upward career movement was blocked by a lack of senior positions for the baby boomers. Foot and Venne indicate that the degree of mismatch declined during the 1960s and early 1970s, but increased during the 1980s and the 1990s.

In terms of implications for human resource management, Foot and Venne suggest that the "flattening" of the corporation that occurred in the 1990s—whereby conventional linear career paths that moved up the traditional hierarchical organization were replaced by managerial downsizing and a spiral path that combined both lateral and vertical movements—was a consequence of this demographic shift. Such changes naturally produce new challenges for employees, as well as greater emphasis on planning and retraining. Workforce aging may also call for complementary policies, such as increased study leaves or sabbaticals and modified compensation structures in which success is related not just to the levels of the positions held in the organization, but also to their variety.

Differences between age groups are also important. For example, middle-aged workers tend to be more stable in their attachment to their employers than are younger workers. The aging of the labour force can be expected to reduce voluntary turnover, and this in turn can make unionization a more attractive option. The longer a worker intends to remain with an employer, the more appealing is the investment of effort and money in forming and nurturing a union. In other words, for the greying labour force, the use of "voice" (unionization) becomes more attractive relative to the use of "exit" (quitting) as a way of improving the work environment.

As individuals approach retirement, their preferences in collective bargaining tend to shift toward pension and related benefits and away from an emphasis on wages. Sharp differences can be seen within a bargaining unit between younger workers with families to support, who are interested in the amount of take-home pay, and older workers who are prepared to accept reduced take-home pay in favour of putting more money into a pension plan. Workers of different ages with differing family responsibilities may also place different emphasis on such factors as health and safety, medical benefits, and seniority and work-time practices including flexible work-time arrangements. Although workers of all ages are interested in job security, this is especially true of middle-aged workers.

The aging of the labour force has also been accompanied by an increasing emphasis on the issue of age discrimination in employment. In almost all Canadian jurisdictions, it is illegal to use age as a criterion in employment decisions such as hiring, promotion, or layoffs. Of course, exceptions typically occur related to issues of public safety or where the employer can demonstrate that an age restriction is a bona fide requirement of the job (see Exhibit 7.1).

Exhibit 7.1
Age Discrimination and Mandatory Retirement

- Mandatory retirement refers to a personnel practice of an employer requiring employees to retire at a fixed age (typically 65 years).
- Mandatory retirement constitutes a form of age discrimination, and as a result has been prohibited by legislation in some provinces (such as Quebec, Manitoba, and Ontario) and in the United States.
- The Supreme Court of Canada, in a 1990 *Charter of Rights and Freedoms* case, ruled that, although mandatory retirement was a form of age discrimination, and age discrimination is prohibited under the *Charter*, it was reasonable for the Ontario government to allow mandatory retirement because its abolition might have wide-ranging impacts on the industrial relations system.
- Basically, the Supreme Court decision means that any decision to prohibit mandatory retirement will be a political decision made by the provincial legislature rather than by the Court.
- Most provinces are slowly moving to ban mandatory retirement. In Ontario, a "cap" of 64 years on the age discrimination provision in the *Ontario Human Rights Code* allowed mandatory retirement by removing protection from age discrimination for employees over age 64. The Ontario Liberal government first proposed removing this cap upon taking office in 2003, and as of December 12, 2006, mandatory retirement in Ontario was effectively banned.

The public and legal debate over the issue of mandatory retirement has been extensive in Canada, and this debate provides information for other countries dealing with the issue. The extent to which mandatory retirement exerts a constraining influence on transitions into retirement is therefore an extremely important question, especially in the context of an aging population. Empirical evidence generally indicates that only a small proportion of the retired workforce attribute their retirement decision to a mandatory retirement policy at work. To the extent that mandatory retirement is an intricate part of the compensation and human resource function of firms, however, banning it can have significant implications for those functions and, in turn, for the transition of workers into retirement. In the context of an aging and longer-lived workforce (relative to a smaller working-age population), the importance of issues associated with workforce aging will likely continue to grow (Gomez, Gunderson, and Luchak, 2002).

Increasing Importance of Women and Ethnic Diversity in the Labour Force
Another important demographic change is that during the last two decades, the Canadian labour force has been transformed from one that was predominantly white and male to one approaching an equal balance between men and women, and in major urban centres such as Toronto, Montreal, and Vancouver, the labour force is becoming predominantly non-white and foreign born.

In 1970, men constituted 66 percent of the labour force, double the proportion of women, who constituted only 34 percent. By 2006, however, 52 percent of employees were male and 48 percent female, not far from a 50/50 ratio.[3] In terms of diversity, while Canada's working-age population as a whole is still mostly native born (only 18.8 percent of Canada's working-age population was foreign born in 2006), in two of its major urban centres—Vancouver and Toronto—the number of foreign-born persons was 44 and 38 percent respectively. In terms of ethnicity and the preponderance of visible minorities as part of the working-age population, the figures are more striking. According to the 2006 census, 46 and 54 percent of Toronto and Vancouver's population were visible minorities, whereas in Canada as a whole, that percentage was only 15.6 percent.

The change in the gender composition was primarily due to a sharp rise in the labour force participation rate of women, mainly reflecting a rise in the participation rate of married women, especially those with children. As well, the male labour force participation rate has declined slightly, largely reflecting a trend toward earlier retirement.

The increase in foreign-born and visible minorities was due to a mixture of policy changes and homegrown demographic shifts. The fall in fertility rates since the late 1960s and the steady inflow of immigrants from non-European countries (especially East Asia and the Caribbean) in and around the same time period has meant that Canada's labour force is much more diverse today than it was three decades ago. However, since most immigrants cluster in specific urban centres, that diversity is manifested more strongly in Canada's three largest cities than in the nation as a whole.

The growth of immigrants and women in the labour force has been accompanied by increased concern about the ratio of immigrants' and women's earnings to native-borns' and men's earnings respectively. This rise in the number of working immigrants and women has brought about important changes in legislation governing their pay and working conditions. The gender pay gap has narrowed over time as women's earnings (for full-time, full-year work) rose slowly from about 60 percent of men's earnings in the mid-1970s to just over 72 percent in the year 2000 (Statistics Canada, CANSIM Table 202-0102).

In terms of the relative wages of immigrants with respect to native-born workers, there has been considerable concern as to whether entry-level earnings and the assimilation rate (the speed at which immigrant wages catch up to native-born wages) have fallen in recent years. The evidence seems to indicate that immigrants are earning less relative to native-born workers than they did 30 years ago and that the speed at which they are catching up is slower (Abdurrahaman and Skuterud, 2005) There are a few possible reasons for this: the higher quotient of visible minorities among immigrants where discrimination may be more prominent; language differences and credential recognition problems; the increase of the family reunification criteria whereby immigrants are granted immigration into the country based on pre-existing family ties in Canada as opposed to skills or language qualifications; and the possibility that recent immigrants are entering the labour market under less favourable economic conditions and when middle-wage manufacturing jobs are no longer there, as discussed previously in this chapter.

In terms of legislation, *equal pay for equal work* legislation (which requires women to be paid the same wage as men if they are doing substantially the same job) was generally replaced with *pay equity legislation*. The latter requires that female-dominated jobs be paid the same as male-dominated jobs if the jobs are of equal value, based on a composite of skill, effort, responsibility, and working conditions. Gender-neutral job evaluation techniques are used to compare the value of jobs that might be in quite different occupations, such as a secretary and a truck driver.

Increasing Importance of Part-Time and Contingent Work In 2002, almost one in five employees was a part-time worker, defined by Statistics Canada as someone usually working fewer than 30 hours per week at their main job.[4] The part-time employment rate (i.e., part-time employment as a percentage of total employment) increased steadily from approximately 4 percent in the mid-1950s to 19 percent in 2002.[5]

The rise in part-time work reflects several of the labour market trends already outlined. On the supply side, the rise in the labour force participation rate of women, particularly married women, resulted in an increase in the proportion of employees desiring to work part-time. Over two-thirds of part-time employees are female. Statistics Canada data indicate that normally about three-quarters of part-timers work part-time voluntarily, although in recessions the amount of involuntary part-time work typically increases. On the demand side, since services cannot be stored as easily as can goods, the increasing importance of the service sector in the economy resulted in an increase in the demand for part-time employees to meet peak periods of demand.

The federal government's Commission of Inquiry into Part-Time Work (1983) found that the productivity of part-timers is generally equal to or higher than that of full-timers, although the compensation of part-timers is often substantially less than that of full-timers doing the same work. To address this inequity, the Commission recommended employment standards legislation to provide equal pay for work of equal value for part-timers and full-timers, with benefits for part-timers pro-rated according to the number of hours worked. However, employer opposition to such recommendations is substantial. In Saskatchewan, the government introduced, then withdrew, legislation designed to pro-rate part-time benefits. Similarly, the British Columbia government chose not to follow the advice of an independent employment review commission, which had recommended pro-rated benefits for part-time employees.

Unions have often strongly opposed the use of part-time workers, and in many strikes a major issue has been the union's opposition to management proposals to increase the use of part-time employees. The reason for union opposition is that the poor compensation of part-timers is seen as a threat to the employment and compensation of full-time employees. As well, part-time workers are often more difficult to organize. Many employees do prefer part-time work, however, and if the compensation of part-timers is made comparable to that of full-timers, union opposition may diminish. Even in the absence of such legislation, unions have increased their efforts to organize part-time workers, partly as a result of the increase in their numbers.

One of the other reasons for the disadvantage faced by part-time employees is that the Ontario Labour Relations Board, for example, tended to place part-time and full-time employees in separate bargaining units, on the assumption that they do not share a "community of interest." The effect of this was to exclude many part-timers from collective bargaining. Modifications to the *Ontario Labour Relations Act* (see Exhibit 7.2), introduced by the NDP government in 1992, remedied this situation by directing the Ontario Labour Relations Board to place part-timers and full-timers in the same bargaining unit, unless doing so would cause the certification application to fail. This provision was, however, repealed by Ontario's Conservative government in 1995.

Exhibit 7.2

Provisions for Part-Time and Full-Time Bargaining Units
Ontario Labour Relations Act (Bill 40 Amendments)

7. (1) Section 6 of the Act is amended by adding the following subsections:

(2.1) A bargaining unit consisting of full-time employees and part-time employees shall be deemed by the Board to be a unit of employees appropriate for collective bargaining.

(2.2) Despite subsection (2.1), the Board shall determine that separate bargaining units for full-time and for part-time employees are appropriate if it is satisfied that less than 55 percent of the employees in a single unit of full-time and part-time employees are members of the trade union on the date the union applies for certification or have applied to become members on or before that date.

Source: Copyright © Queen's Printer for Ontario, 1992.

In addition to the growth of part-time work, there has also been an increase in the use of contingent work, i.e., casual, term, contract, temporary, and seasonal jobs. According to Statistics Canada's 1995 Survey of Work Arrangements, non-standard work (part-time and contingent work) now comprises about one-third of employment in Canada (Payette, 1999: 116). Managers report that the main reason for using contingent workers is to provide flexibility to respond to fluctuations in demand. Union representatives suggest that, in addition to providing flexibility, contingent work helps employers to reduce benefit costs and avoid unionization. Union response to contingent work has included resistance strategies (such as prohibiting contingent work and contracting out), accommodation strategies (negotiating work rules and due process for contingent workers), and proactive strategies (such as using union hiring halls for hiring contingent workers and managing pension and benefit plans) (Payette, 1999).

The Brain Drain and Immigration In the late 1990s, a controversy arose concerning the issue of the *brain drain*, i.e., the emigration to the United States of highly skilled Canadians, particularly engineers, computer scientists, doctors, nurses, professors, and managers. Higher earnings and lower taxes in the United States have been suggested as important causes of the brain drain, prompting the minister of finance in 1999 to cite concern about the brain drain as one of the factors motivating his proposal to reduce taxes for the middle class in his next budget.[6]

A Statistics Canada study in 1998 concluded, however, that "there is little evidence in support of a large-scale exodus of knowledge workers from Canada to the United States. . . . The brain drain was found to be small in a historical sense, small relative to the stock of workers in these disciplines, and small relative to the supply of new workers in these disciplines" (Statistics Canada, 1998: 1). In March 1999, HRDC, in co-operation with Statistics Canada, undertook a special survey of Canadian university graduates of 1995 who had moved to the United States. The results of the survey substantiated the conclusion that the brain drain to the United States is small—only 1.5 percent of the 1995 graduating class. Emigrants did, however, tend to be above average—almost half ranked themselves in the top 10 percent of their graduating class (HRDC, 1999: ix–x). Helliwell (1999) also found the brain drain to be of small magnitude in his analysis of U.S. census and current population survey data on the number of Canadians living in the United States. Furthermore, these studies showed that Canada gains about four times as many highly skilled workers through immigration from the rest of the world as it loses through emigration to the United States.

In spite of this evidence, some writers (Devoretz and Laryea, 1998; Iqbal, 1999) argued that the brain drain is important for three reasons: first, the quality issue—those that Canada lost may have been the "best and brightest." Second, the *churning argument*—Devortz and Laryea argue that replacing emigrants with immigrants is still costly because of administrative and settlement costs and because, at least in the first few years, immigrants earn less than their Canadian counterparts, possibly reflecting a lower productivity level. Third, the data showing a relatively small brain drain focused on Canadians who are permanent residents of the United States, but did not count Canadians temporarily residing in the United States who may become permanent residents in the future.

A further issue is that in many cases there seem to be artificial barriers to the recognition of the qualifications of highly skilled immigrants to Canada. If such barriers reflect an artificial restriction on the supply of labour in these occupations, rather than an appropriate evaluation of skills, then Canada may be failing to take advantage of the high levels of skills that many immigrants bring to the country.

Interaction of Supply and Demand for Labour

Market forces of supply and demand set the general boundaries for the employment and wage-rate decisions, but earnings are also affected by collective bargaining and by government regulations such as minimum wages, training, and education requirements.

Earnings Differentials and Efficiency Wages Empirical studies indicate that earnings differ substantially among *occupations*, even after controlling for years of schooling, experience, and other factors. For example, managerial/business professional occupations earn about 30 percent more than tradespersons with equivalent qualifications whereas child care occupations earn about 35 percent less (Benjamin, Gunderson, Lemieux, and Riddell, 2007: 297). Evidence also indicates the existence of substantial wage differentials by *industry*, beyond what appear to be required as compensating differentials to reflect variations in qualifications and working conditions. For example, "high-wage" industries, such as tobacco products and petroleum manufacturing, appear to pay 20 to 30 percent above the competitive norm, whereas "low-wage" industries, such as accommodation and food services, tend to pay 20 percent below the competitive norm (Gera and Grenier, 1994). These inter-industry differentials appear to be relatively stable over time and across countries.

A possible explanation for such inter-industry wage differentials is the notion of "efficiency wages"; i.e., employers in some industries may find it profitable to voluntarily pay above the market clearing wage if the higher wage results in higher productivity through mechanisms such as greater work effort, improved morale, and lower turnover. Empirically, however, it is difficult to determine if the observed inter-industry differentials reflect efficiency wages or simply other economic factors such as employees' benefiting from the employer's monopoly power in the product market. As discussed later in the section on barriers to labour market flexibility, efficiency wages can also result in unemployment by preventing the labour market from clearing.

Increased Earnings Inequality During the 1990s and the first five years of the 21st century, the degree of inequality of family market incomes in Canada increased substantially. Although government transfer payments and the progressive income tax offset some of the rise in inequality of market incomes, after-tax income was more unequal in the post-2000 period than at any other point since 1976 (Heisz, 2007: 6).

The overall tax system in Canada also became less progressive over the period from 1980 to 2005 as regressive taxes (such as sales, property, and payroll taxes) offset much of the progressivity of the income tax. As a result of a drop in tax rates for those with highest incomes, by 2005 the richest 1 percent of families paid a slightly lower rate of tax than the poorest 10 percent of families (Lee, 2007: 9).

The Information Revolution and the Productivity Paradox The proliferation of computers and spread of information technology (IT) during the past three decades would generally be expected to boost the rate of growth of labour productivity (output per person-hour). Instead, annual productivity growth in the 1989–1996 period averaged only 0.7 percent in the Canadian business sector, the lowest rate in any decade going back to the 1960s (Sharpe, 1997: 35). Furthermore, a cross-sectional analysis indicates that those sectors that invested more in information technology have, on average, shown lower rates of productivity growth. This productivity paradox is not unique to Canada—it has occurred in a wide range of OECD countries (Sharpe, 1997: 43–44).

Andrew Sharpe has offered three explanations for the paradox that investment in IT has not produced the expected benefits in terms of increased productivity growth. The first explanation is the mismeasurement hypothesis (which he labels "the benefits are here"). This suggests that the methods used to measure productivity at the national level do not adequately capture the impact of computers. For example, measurement of output in the service sector is problematic. In addition, much of the benefit of computers may be in terms of qualitative change, such as more convenient access to services, rather than an increased quantity of services.

Sharpe's second explanation is the lag hypothesis ("the benefits are coming"). The suggestion is that computers have the potential to increase productivity, but this potential will be realized only with improved organizational structure, more training, and improved computer design.

Sharpe's third hypothesis is that "the benefits are never coming." There are several arguments in support of this hypothesis. One is that, in spite of the prevalence of computers in the workplace, the actual magnitude of investment in information technology is a relatively small fraction of total investment, so it should not be expected to have a substantial impact on overall productivity growth. Another explanation is that the benefits of computers are largely offset by their costs in terms of never-ending upgrading, crashes, incompatibility problems, and viruses—problems that are unlikely to be eliminated in the future. Sharpe suggests that all three hypotheses probably have some validity, but he feels that the third hypothesis (the benefits are never coming) is closest to the mark.

The newest empirical evidence, however, shows accelerated productivity growth since the mid-1990s (after Sharpe's study ended) and suggests that new IT may be responsible for a substantial part of the accelerated productivity growth since the mid-1990s (Jorgenson, Ho, and Stiroh, 2005). The new empirical analysis reveals three main results that highlight how the adoption of new IT involves much more than just the installation of new equipment on the factory floor. First, adopters of new IT–enhanced equipment also shift their business strategies and begin producing more customized products. Second, new IT investments improve efficiency of all stages of the production process by reducing setup times, run times, and inspection times. The reductions in setup times are potentially important because they make it less costly to switch production from one product to another, and support the change in business strategy to more customized production. Third, adoption of new computer-based IT coincides with increases in the skill requirements of workers, notably technical and problem-solving skills, and with the adoption of new human resource practices (Bartel, Ichniowski, and Shaw, 2007).

THE MACROECONOMIC ENVIRONMENT

The overall state of the economy, known as the macroeconomic environment, significantly influences many aspects of union–management relations. An expanding economy, for example, leads to higher wage settlements and more strike activity; the latter also tends to increase in periods when there is uncertainty about high levels of inflation. An expanding economy may also facilitate the attainment of broader social goals such as occupational health and safety, pay equity, and equal employment opportunities for women. It is also associated with a higher rate of growth of unionization and greater success for unions in certification and decertification applications at the labour relations boards.

In periods when the economy is in recession and temporary layoffs are more prevalent, provisions for seniority in layoff and recall assume a greater importance in both the negotiation and the administration of the collective agreement. In cases of permanent layoffs or complete plant shutdown, negotiations about severance packages become more prominent. The overall state of the Canadian economy also affects the courts' interpretation of the length of "reasonable notice" required in wrongful dismissal cases under the common law—the notice required is about three and one-half months more when the economy is in recession than when it is booming (McShane and McPhillips, 1987).

Uncertainty about high rates of inflation tends to result in higher wage settlements and a greater prevalence of cost-of-living adjustment (COLA) clauses in collective agreements. On the other hand, a reduction in uncertainty about the macroeconomic environment can partly explain the significant increase in average contract duration during the 1990s (from under 2 years in 1990 to 2.75 years in 2001).[7]

Swings in the Unemployment Rate Since the unemployment rate is by far the most prominent measure of the state of the macroeconomic environment, actors in the industrial relations system were greatly concerned when the Canadian unemployment rate rose to double-digit levels during the recessions of the early 1980s and early 1990s.

Unemployment is measured in Canada by a monthly labour force survey covering about 52 000 households. Since Statistics Canada recognizes that there is some ambiguity about the appropriate definition of unemployment rates, it publishes a range of eight unemployment rates with alternative definitions, designated R1 to R8 (Statistics Canada, 2007). For example, in 2006 when the "official" unemployment rate (R4) was 6.3 percent, its most restrictive definition, the rate for those unemployed for one year or more (R1) was only 0.5 percent, and the rate comparable to the U.S. definition of unemployment (R3) was 5.5 percent. Adding discouraged searchers increases the unemployment rate to 6.4 percent (R5); adding persons waiting for long-term recall and long-term future starts raises unemployment to 7.0 percent (R6); while including the full-time equivalent of those underemployed, i.e., involuntary part-timers, raises the rate to 8.2 percent (R7). The most comprehensive measure of unemployment, which includes all three of these categories, was 9.0 percent (R8).

Analytically, it is useful to distinguish deficient-demand unemployment, which refers to an overall lack of jobs in the labour market, from structural and frictional unemployment. Structural unemployment occurs when unemployed persons and vacant jobs do not match in terms of such factors as geographical location, occupation, or experience. Frictional unemployment occurs when, due to turnover and the fact that it takes time to locate a job, unemployed workers and suitable vacant jobs co-exist in the same labour market. New entrants to the labour market can also experience frictional unemployment. The distinction is important because policies to deal with deficient-demand unemployment (e.g., stimulation of the economy through monetary policy or government spending and taxation) differ from policies to deal with structural or frictional unemployment (e.g., education, training, relocation). The distinction is also important for union–management relations because the level of deficient-demand unemployment indicates the overall state of the labour market and affects strike activity, wage settlements, and the other aspects of labour–management relations discussed above (also see Exhibit 7.3).

Barriers to Labour Market Flexibility The pressure of international competition has resulted in increased calls for flexibility in the labour market. A difficult question is why the labour market, and wages in particular, responds so sluggishly to changes in economic conditions. The answer is the subject of considerable controversy.

Keynes (1936/1967) argued that during periods of unemployment, employees are reluctant to accept wage cuts to preserve jobs because inequities would result if reductions are not being spread equally over the whole labour force. Another explanation, given in the context of *efficiency wage models*, is that wage reductions may reduce employee morale and productivity. This argument suggests that it may not be sensible for employers to force wage reductions during periods of unemployment, even if they have the power to do so.

Another explanation for the failure of the labour market to clear is that employers in both union and nonunion establishments have an understanding or an *implicit contract* with their employees in which they agree not to reduce wages during economic downturns. The purpose of implicit contracts is to insure risk-averse workers against wage fluctuations in exchange for a slightly lower average wage over the business cycle or to prevent quits by experienced workers in whom the employer has an investment in terms of training.

Exhibit 7.3
The Mystery of the Canada–U.S. Unemployment Rate Gap

A four-percentage-point gap between the unemployment rates in Canada and the United States emerged during the 1990s, but the gap declined to 1.65 percentage points by 2006.

The Canadian unemployment rate was only slightly (0.5 percentage points) higher than the U.S. unemployment rate during the 1970s, but it was almost two percentage points higher during the 1980s and almost four percentage points higher in the 1990s. Riddell and Sharpe (1998) outlined the reasons for the emergence of the gap, summarizing the results of several papers presented at a conference devoted to the issue.

First, about 0.7 percentage points of the gap was due to different definitions of unemployment used in Canada and the United States. Individuals whose job search consists only of looking at job ads are defined as unemployed in Canada but out of the labour force in the United States.

Second, during the 1980s, employment grew by a similar amount in Canada and the United States. The two-percentage-point unemployment rate gap that appeared in the 1980s was due to a relative rise in the labour force attachment of the non-employed, i.e., more people remained unemployed in Canada whereas in the United States they were not in the labour force (Card and Riddell, 1993).

Third, the further two-percentage-point increase in the unemployment gap in the 1990s was simply due to a rise in deficient-demand unemployment—the recession of the early 1990s was more severe in Canada and the recovery weaker (Fortin, 1996).

Some economists have suggested that the wage system could be made more flexible and macroeconomic performance enhanced by the use of bonuses paid through profit-sharing or gain-sharing plans. Gain-sharing plans (e.g., the Scanlon Plan) are based on cost savings or increased production relative to a base period. Profit-sharing is based on increased profits. Gain-sharing plans are more closely related to employee effort than are profit-sharing plans because profits can be affected by a wide variety of external developments that are not subject to employee control. Profit-sharing and gain-sharing plans have long been advocated as means of improving productivity but, more recently, potential benefits for macroeconomic performance also have been suggested. Since bonuses paid are not built into base salary, they increase flexibility in the total compensation package. Profit-sharing is more effective than gain-sharing in enhancing macroeconomic flexibility because profits tend to increase in booms and decrease in recessions, but, for the same reason, gain-sharing is more effective than profit-sharing in enhancing employee effort and productivity.

The Impact of the Macroeconomic Environment on Wage Settlements

The wage settlement in any particular set of negotiations will be greatly affected by the magnitude of the average wage settlement in the economy at the time of negotiations. For example, wage settlements in major collective agreements averaged over 5 percent in 1990, then dropped to 0.3 percent in 1994, and slowly increased to roughly 3 percent by 2002.[8] More dramatically, wage settlements that averaged approximately 15 to 18 percent in the mid-1970s (just prior to the introduction of the AIB wage controls) fell below 4 percent by the early 1980s. What accounts for such changes? (See Exhibit 7.4.)

When the labour market is in balance, the overall supply of labour equals the overall demand for labour, and the economy will experience frictional and structural unemployment but not deficient-demand unemployment. The amount of frictional and structural unemployment at this position is also known as either the "natural unemployment rate" or by the more neutral term, the "non-accelerating inflation rate of unemployment" (NAIRU). The latter name reflects the idea that at such an overall equilibrium position, there would be no labour market pressure for the rate of wage or price change to increase or decrease.

Labour Market Impacts of Free Trade and Globalization One of the most significant changes in the Canadian economic environment in the 1990s was the increasing international competition resulting from a series of trade agreements. The bilateral Free Trade Agreement (FTA) with the United States, which took effect in 1989, was followed by the trilateral North American Free Trade Agreement (NAFTA) with the United States and Mexico, which took effect in January 1994. In 1994, in a new round of negotiations under the General Agreement on Tariffs and Trade (GATT), which is now the World Trade Organization (WTO), Canada also agreed to a reduction of tariffs in its global economic trade with countries such as India, Brazil, Turkey, Indonesia, and Malaysia.

Exhibit 7.4
The Overall Rate of Wage Change

Empirical work on the determinants of the overall aggregate rate of wage change, known as the *Phillips Curve*, has established two basic propositions (Wilton and Prescott, 1992):

■ for any given level of expected inflation, wage settlements are high when the rate of deficient-demand unemployment is low (i.e., when the labour market is in a boom); and

■ for any given state of labour market conditions, wage settlements fully reflect changes in the expected inflation rate.

The fluctuations in overall wage settlements in Canada reflect these factors—the decline and subsequent rise in wage settlements in the 1990s reflected a sharp rise in the unemployment rate in the recession of the early 1990s and the boom of the late 1990s.

The reduction in wage settlements between the mid-1970s and the early 1980s reflects both a rise in unemployment during the recession of the early 1980s and a decline in expected inflation.

A question of great concern to many Canadians is how Canada can be expected to compete against countries with much lower wage costs and employment standards. For example, countries such as Mexico and Hong Kong have average hourly compensation costs that in 1999 were less than one-third the cost in Canada.[9] The answer is that unit labour costs (dollars/unit) are determined by compensation (dollars/hour) divided by productivity (units/hour). If low wages generally reflect low productivity, then unit costs of production are not necessarily lower in low-wage countries. Indeed, some of Canada's toughest competition internationally comes from high-wage, high-productivity countries such as Japan (which in 2003 had compensation costs that were slightly *higher* than Canada's) and Germany, with compensation costs about 60 percent higher than Canada's (Benjamin et al., 2007: 173). The concern is, however, that many of the low-wage countries are moving up the productivity spectrum and will become low-wage, *high*-productivity countries, at least until their wages adjust to reflect their increased productivity.

Why has Canada (and most other countries) moved toward free trade in the last few years? The basic argument in favour of free trade is that by allowing production to be located where it is most efficient, costs can be reduced and, in the long run, citizens of all countries can potentially benefit from an increase in their real income. Increased efficiency arises from comparative advantage (which takes advantage of geographical differences in relative ability to produce goods) and economies of scale (which take advantage of longer production runs to use mass-production techniques).

The estimated size of the increase in real income resulting from trade liberalization was, however, quite modest. For example, following a review of empirical studies, the Royal Commission on the Economic Union (1985: 331) indicated that real incomes of Canadians could be increased from 3 to 5 percent on average by free trade with the United States. The benefits could be larger if free trade prevented a reduction in Canadian incomes resulting from protectionist trade restrictions that otherwise may have been imposed by the United States. By removing tariff barriers and other trade impediments, free trade may also lead to a dissipation of inefficient market structures, regulatory regimes, and work practices that require protection from the forces of competition in order to survive. These *dynamic* gains from trade can enhance the conventional static gains arising from cheaper imports and increased exports.

Critics of free trade point out that the reallocation of labour and capital to achieve a more efficient outcome in the long run involves a substantial economic dislocation in the short run. If increased efficiency is to be attained, some industries and firms will be put out of business and others will expand. In the short run, layoffs, plant shutdowns, and a rise in structural unemployment are likely to result. Although these adjustment costs can be lessened by policies to facilitate relocation and training (and the benefits of free trade should provide the means for such compensation), it is unlikely that there will be complete compensation to the firms and workers bearing the costs of the adjustment.

Equally important, critics have suggested that free trade may lead to a *harmonization* of tax policies, employment standards, and labour relations legislation down to the lowest common denominator as a result of inter-jurisdictional competition for investment and jobs. Gunderson (1998) has argued, however, that there also may be pressure toward upward harmonization by governments (through agreements on minimum standards, such as the Social Charter in Europe) and by union and consumer boycotts against practices such as child labour. Pressure for upward harmonization can also occur when social policies are more cost effective, such as Canada's public health-care system compared to the American private-sector model. Individual employers in Canada may have lower costs of production vis-à-vis the United States since major employers in the United States usually pay more toward health care and pensions than those in Canada. As a result, these components of labour costs are lower in Canada than in the United States. This factor has often been cited as giving an advantage to Canadian automobile plants. On the other hand, these benefits are financed out of taxes, which are higher in Canada.

The same concern is expressed when Canada trades with low-wage countries such as Mexico, which also have lower labour standards. The concern here is that plants will relocate and capital will flow into such countries given their lower labour costs. To stem this loss of business and of the associated jobs, Canadian governments may be pressured to lower their labour standards until they are more in line with those that prevail in the low-cost countries. Whether free trade will lead to a "race to the bottom" in terms of lower standards and regulations, or simply put pressure on excessive regulations for which the benefits do not exceed the cost, is an interesting question that merits additional analysis.

Although Canada has now had several decades of experience under the FTA and NAFTA agreements, measuring the actual impact of the agreements is difficult because the changes were phased in over a number of years, and because the impacts have been confounded with the effects of other developments such as the federal government's implementation of the GST, the recession of the early 1990s, exchange-rate fluctuations, and most recently energy price increases (see Exhibit 7.5).

On the legislative side, there does not yet appear to be a widespread dismantling of Canadian employment law to harmonize with that in the United States (Gomez and Gunderson, 2005). Ongoing assessment of the impacts of Canada's various trade arrangements will no doubt be an important topic of future research.

Exhibit 7.5
Impact of Free Trade on Employment and Wage Structures in Canada

A study of the short-run employment impacts of the Free Trade Agreement by Gaston and Trefler (1997) showed that between 1988 and 1993, employment losses in high-tariff industries averaged 24 percent compared to employment losses of 15 percent in low-tariff industries.

The nine-percentage-point differential between these two figures provides an estimate of the impact of job losses due to the FTA because both the high-tariff and low-tariff industries were affected by the recession and other factors affecting employment.

While the employment loss in those industries most affected by the FTA is substantially higher than the industries in the control group, Gaston and Trefler point out that the loss is still small relative to the job losses attributable to the recession in the early 1990s.

In a more recent study, Lemieux (2005) compared average wages and wage differentials of comparable workers between Canada and the United States in 1984 and

2001 (before and after the implementation of the FTA and NAFTA). The goal was to see whether economic integration led to a convergence of wage outcomes in the two countries.

The main finding is that there has been, if anything, a divergence between wage structures in Canada and the United States over the last 20 years, with Canadian wages falling substantially relative to average wages in the United States. Where Canada did relatively better than the United States, post–free trade, was in lessening the dispersion of wage outcomes among workers.

Labour Market Pressures Emanating from Global Standard Setting

Finally, apart from free trade agreements, more broad-based international pressures have emerged. It has become commonplace to refer to these pressures as the forces of *globalization*. However you refer to them, one thing is certain—though such pressures are much harder to measure than a tariff reduction, they can still affect Canada's labour market in important ways. Take, for example, the recent controversy surrounding the reduction of greenhouse gas emissions. Canada and its two NAFTA partners, Mexico and the United States, all agreed to the basic concepts laid out in an emissions reduction document signed in Kyoto, Japan, in December 1997. The document, now known as the Kyoto Protocol, sets targets to reduce greenhouse gas emissions by at least 5.2 percent before 2012. It also describes several options available for signatories to meet the targets. According to the United Nations Framework Convention on Climate Change, Canada needs to reduce emissions by 33 million tonnes by 2010 to fulfill its Kyoto target. This would represent a 26 percent reduction from projected 2012 levels. The problem is that in 2001, Canada had already surpassed its 1990 levels by close to 20 percent. What implications could complying with this multilateral agreement have on Canadian workers? The answer depends on where you stand.

Alberta's oil and gas producers estimate heavy job losses, while in British Columbia companies such as Ballard Power Systems, Inc.—whose fuel cells produce no greenhouse gas emissions and which are now powering clean-burning motors around the world—see a potential doubling in sales and corresponding employment. The potential upside of such environmental standards has led some, like Michael Porter, to argue that the conflict between environmental protection and economic competitiveness is a false dichotomy, based on a narrow view of the sources of prosperity and a static view of competition.

Strict environmental regulations do not inevitably hinder competitive advantage against foreign rivals; indeed, according to Michael Porter, they often enhance it. Tough standards can trigger industrial innovation and upgrading. In Porter's 1998 book *The Competitive Advantage of Nations*, he found that the nations with the most rigorous requirements often lead in exports of affected products. Porter and his colleague Dan Esty have even argued that companies not only complying, but taking the lead, in environmental standards will enjoy sustained competitive advantages. In a labour market context, such advantages should produce higher-paying and more secure employment far into the future (Porter and Esty, 1998). The explosion in Green-related public interest around the globe in 2006 and 2007—culminating in the Earth Day concert celebrations on all seven continents in April 2007—perhaps validates Porter's assertions of the late 1990s. Green consumer and corporate demands will engender labour opportunities for those with well-placed skills and interests.

CONCLUSION

This chapter has documented ways in which the social, political, and economic environments constrain the various actors—labour, management, and government—and influence the outputs of the industrial relations system. Although we have discussed a wide range of factors, including demographic trends, legislative changes, deindustrialization, and the macroeconomic environment, our review has only touched on the rich and diverse array of research in this field.

Questions

1. Explain each of the following terms: compensating wage differential; equilibrium wage; wage-taker.

2. Discuss why actual labour markets differ from the competitive ideal.

3. Explain why the economic theory of competitive labour markets predicts that the imposition of minimum wage rates will reduce employment. In light of this expectation, what are the possible explanations for Card's finding that the raising of the minimum wage had no negative effect on employment?

4. Describe the different types of unemployment that researchers have identified and discuss why the distinctions are important for the purposes of public policy.

5. Describe the income–leisure choice model and explain how it can be used to shed light on significant issues in labour–management relations.

6. Discuss how the projected aging of the labour force will affect both industrial relations and human resource management practices.

7. What is the magnitude of Canada's "brain drain" and what policies, if any, would be appropriate to alleviate this problem?

8. Outline the magnitude of the gap between the unemployment rates in Canada and the United States and explain the reasons for the gap.

9. Explain the "productivity paradox" and the alternative hypotheses to resolve the paradox.

10. Outline the expected impacts on the industrial relations system of free trade policies.

Weblinks

Human Resources and Social Development Canada (Canada's federal department of labour):
www.hrsdc.gc.ca

Statistics Canada:
www.statcan.ca

U.S. Department of Labor, Bureau of Labor Statistics:
www.bls.gov

Canada and the Kyoto Protocol (and search for "Kyoto Protocol"):
www.canadiansolution.com

Centre for Industrial Relations and Human Resources, University of Toronto:
www.chass.utoronto.ca/cir

The End of Mandatory Retirement in Ontario:
www.ontario.ca/mandatoryretirement

Chapter 8

Collective Bargaining Legislation in Canada

Sara Slinn

In September 1996, the Canadian Auto Workers union (CAW) certified (unionized) some 60 employees at a group of five Starbucks stores in Vancouver, British Columbia. At that time there were 91 Starbucks coffee shops in the province. Triggers for unionizing included employee concerns over the low starting salary of $7 an hour, desire for more control over shift scheduling and for clearer job duties.

Starbucks objected to the CAW's certification application, claiming that the union had applied to certify an inappropriate group of workers (called a "bargaining unit"). It argued that the CAW should organize each store individually, not a group of stores. On the day of the British Columbia Labour Relations Board (BCLRB) certification hearing, Starbucks took out a full-page advertisement in a Vancouver newspaper heralding the benefits of Starbucks employment. The CAW claimed the advertisement was an attempt to influence the certification drive, but Starbucks said the timing was purely coincidental. The Board granted the CAW's certification application, grouping employees from the five stores as a single bargaining unit.[1]

In September 1996 the CAW notified Starbucks that it was ready to begin collective bargaining. That fall the parties met to negotiate a number of times, but bargaining did not progress well.

In December 1996, the union applied to have a third-party mediator assist it and the company with the negotiations, and the parties and mediator met several times thereafter. When spring arrived and no agreement was in sight, the CAW held a strike vote. Ninety-two percent of the unionized Starbucks employees supported striking.

In April 1997, shortly after this vote, Starbucks announced the closure of a distribution centre employing nine of the now approximately 100 workers covered by the CAW's certification. The CAW filed an unfair labour practice complaint with the BCLRB, claiming the closure was an intimidation tactic intended to interfere with bargaining. Starbucks claimed the timing was coincidental, would have no effect on negotiations, and that it was acting in good faith at the bargaining table.

Mediation broke down shortly after this closure was announced, and the CAW began a legal strike on May 16, 1997. The strike was over a month old when the BCLRB released its decision on the unfair labour practice complaint. The BCLRB held that closing the distribution centre was not an unfair labour practice, nor was Starbucks bargaining in bad faith.[2] The BCLRB recommended that the parties resume negotiating and make every effort to reach an agreement.

Starbucks and the CAW eventually reached a collective agreement, and two subsequent agreements were negotiated over the next 10 years. But the union was not able to organize more workers, and without much bargaining power, it was not able to achieve major improvements in conditions for Vancouver's unionized Starbucks workers. Wages and benefits at the unionized stores did not substantially differ from those at nonunion shops. Starbucks tended to provide the same salary increases to employees in the uncertified shops. Some unionized workers then saw paying union dues as putting them at a financial disadvantage compared to nonunionized Starbucks workers earning the same hourly rate and not paying dues. Starbucks' efforts to maintain the status quo at the bargaining table largely succeeded, with the exception of minor improvements in shift scheduling and job language.

Unionized stores began losing interest in the CAW. In addition, turnover within the group that initially certified posed difficulties in maintaining union support.

Eventually, and after many hard-fought legal battles between 2001 and 2007, all five of the B.C. Starbucks outlets were decertified.

This vignette about the unionization and ultimate decertification of Starbucks stores in British Columbia demonstrates some of the difficulties young workers in the service sector encounter in obtaining and maintaining union representation, and in achieving collective agreements. It deals with such important legal issues as certification, appropriateness of the bargaining unit, unfair labour practices (ULPs), bargaining in good faith, and strikes. It offers insight into the fact that gaining union representation is only a first step for employees, who then must also enter into negotiations with their employer. It also shows that union representation is not permanent, and that continued employer resistance can wear down union support and lead to decertification.

DEVELOPMENT OF LABOUR RELATIONS LAW IN CANADA

Canadian labour relations law regards representation of workers by unions and collective negotiations of terms and conditions of work as a desirable way to order the workplace and allow employees a voice in their workplace. As we examine Canadian labour legislation, we will see two themes throughout the law: an interest in encouraging collective bargaining, and an interest in discouraging industrial conflict and work stoppages such as strikes and lockouts (a lockout is like a strike but, instead of workers refusing to work during a labour dispute, the employer bars employees from working).

Until the early 20th century, there was no specific labour relations law, and no laws to support or protect workers acting collectively. Rather, civil and criminal laws, such as prohibitions on conspiracies, were used by employers to punish, suppress, or prevent collective employee action. By the early 1900s, these laws had been removed, or made inapplicable to union activities. However, it was much later that laws that actually supported or protected union activities were created.

In the early 1900s, a series of strikes by railway, mining, and public utility workers prompted the federal government to pass the 1907 *Industrial Disputes Investigation Act*

(IDIA) to address this industrial unrest.[3] The crucial mechanism introduced by the IDIA—and which characterizes Canadian labour legislation today—is compulsory third-party intervention as a precondition to a legal strike or lockout when collective bargaining breaks down. Under the IDIA, parties were required to meet with a "conciliation board" made up of representatives of labour, management, and a neutral party. The purpose of the conciliation board was to investigate the facts of the dispute and to publicly report its assessment of the situation and its recommendations for resolution and settlement of the dispute. The intent of this was to use public opinion to pressure an unco-operative party to compromise and settle.

This is described as one of the "paradoxes" of Canadian labour law: on the one hand, our system of labour law accepts that union–management relations will include conflict and that work stoppages may occur. Indeed, the system establishes work stoppages as the economic threat underlying bargaining. On the other hand, our labour law system is characterized by regulations, procedures, and other obstacles to such expressions of conflict. For instance, as central as work stoppages—or the threat of them—are to the collective bargaining system, our laws strictly prohibit strikes or lockouts during the life of a collective agreement (the contract containing the terms and conditions of work for employees represented by the union in a particular workplace). Collective agreements must have a term of at least one year; most terms are two years, and some are much longer. This means that, except for brief periods every few years when a collective agreement has expired, unions and employers are barred from engaging in work stoppages, and even then legislation demands additional requirements before the strike or lockout can occur (see Exhibit 8.1, and material later in this chapter).

Exhibit 8.1
Work Stoppages

Labour legislation throughout Canada states that work stoppages (either strikes or lockouts) are illegal while a collective agreement is in force. In Ontario, for example, a work stoppage is illegal except under the following circumstances:

- the collective agreement has expired (if there was one);
- a conciliator has investigated the dispute and issued a report, or the parties have engaged in mediation (where a third party works with the parties to reach agreement).
- In the case of a strike, employees have voted in favour of striking.

Following are the requirements needed before a "strike vote" can be held:

- if the collective agreement has not expired, then the vote cannot be held more than 30 days before it expires;
- if the collective agreement has already expired, then the vote cannot occur before a conciliator is appointed.

Not all jurisdictions require conciliation or mediation, or strike votes. Some only require the union or employer to give advance notice of a work stoppage. In B.C., for example, a union or employer must give at least 72 hours' notice to the other party and to the labour relations board.

Perhaps the greatest single influence on Canadian labour legislation is the U.S. *National Labor Relations Act* (NLRA or the *Wagner Act*, named after Senator Wagner who supported the legislation), passed into law in the United States in 1935.[4] The *Wagner Act* was part of President Roosevelt's New Deal plan to combat the Great Depression. The *Wagner Act* had both a social and economic purpose: by providing legal rights for employees to unionize, and protection for collective bargaining activities, the Act would increase workers' purchasing power which, in turn, would help support the economy. Key elements of the *Wagner Act* included explicit legal protection for union recognition and organizing, and establishment of specific unfair labour practices (ULPs) (set out in Exhibit 8.2). ULPs are defined as employer conduct that, in Congress' view, had to be prohibited in order for employees' right to organize to be effective.

Before the *Wagner Act*, it was difficult, dangerous, or impossible for workers to obtain union representation. For example, in the absence of laws compelling employers to recognize the union as the workers' representative, the only tool available to employees was to strike (called a *recognition strike*). However, there was nothing to stop the employer from simply firing and replacing the striking workers, and continuing to refuse to deal with the union. Employers could also create *company unions* (also called *employer-dominated unions*), which, instead of being a real union, were made up of employer-friendly employees who supported the employer rather than representing employee interests. Employers could also engage in all manner of blatantly anti-union conduct, including planting spies in the workplace to report on any union activity, and firing union sympathizers. Employers also compelled workers to enter into *yellow-dog contracts*, which made it a condition of the worker's employment that he or she not join a union.

Against this background, the legal recognition and protections of the *Wagner Act* were tremendously important to workers and unions and marked a turning point for labour relations. The *Wagner Act* was the model for labour legislation that was soon adopted throughout Canada.

Exhibit 8.2
Wagner Act: Unfair Labour Practice Prohibitions

The *Wagner Act* identifies the following as prohibited ULPs:

1. interfering with employees' right to organize;
2. employer domination of a labour organization;
3. discriminating against employees for union activity;
4. retribution against employees for seeking to enforce their rights under the Act;
5. failing to bargain in good faith.

The first comprehensive labour relations legislation in Canada was passed by the federal government in 1944. Using its wartime emergency powers, the government enacted the *Wartime Labour Relations Regulations* (known as PC 1003), which extended to industries that would normally be under provincial jurisdiction.[5] PC 1003 closely followed the *Wagner Act*, and also represented a balance between recognition and legal support for unions and ensuring stability and labour peace for employers. Core features of PC 1003 included

- requiring employers to recognize and bargain collectively in good faith with trade unions chosen by workers as their representatives;
- prohibiting specified ULPs;
- prohibiting strikes and lockouts during the term of a collective agreement;
- requiring parties to resolve differences arising during the term of a collective agreement without a work stoppage, generally by arbitration;
- creating a labour relations tribunal to administer PC 1003.

After the wartime emergency ended, PC 1003 was replaced with federal labour legislation and individual provincial labour statutes, all of which were closely modelled on PC 1003 and the *Wagner Act*. Elements of these models are apparent in Canadian labour legislation today.

These *Wagner Act* origins are evident in several parts of our modern labour legislation: exclusive representation rights for unions; procedures for union representation rights; and ULP prohibitions. However, Canadian labour legislation differs from the *Wagner Act* in two key ways. First, it puts more emphasis on conciliation and on reducing and discouraging work stoppages than the *Wagner Act* does. Second, most labour relations in Canada is the responsibility of the provinces; in the United States, the reverse is true: most labour relations falls within federal jurisdiction.

Federal and Provincial Labour Relations Responsibility

Originally, labour relations in Canada was seen as a central responsibility of the federal government. However, the 1925 *Toronto Electric Power Commissioners v. Snider* decision changed this.[6] This decision determined that, in terms of labour law, only certain industries fall under federal jurisdiction. The remainder is the responsibility of the provinces. As a result, existing federal labour statutes were amended to clarify that they applied only to industries under federal authority, and the provinces began emulating this federal legislation to regulate labour relations for the industries they are responsible for.

The Canadian Constitution sets out which matters are the responsibility of the federal government (and therefore under the *Canada Labour Code*, the modern federal labour legislation), and which fall under provincial jurisdiction (and therefore under provincial labour legislation).[7] As Exhibit 8.3 shows, where responsibility falls for labour relations is based on the industry involved, rather than the geographic location of the company. As a result, most employees are under provincial rather than federal jurisdiction.

Exhibit 8.3
Federal and Provincial Labour Relations Jurisdiction

Labour relations in the following industries falls under federal jurisdiction:

- Aeronautics
- Air transportation and airports
- Cross-border transportation
- Most railways
- Shipping and navigation
- Grain elevators
- Telecommunications
- Television and radio broadcasting
- Banking
- Customs
- Postal service
- Atomic energy

In addition, labour relations for the following is a federal responsibility:

- Federal civil service employees
- Employees of federal Crown corporations
- The Yukon, Northwest Territories, and Nunavut.[8]

Labour relations for all other industries falls under provincial jurisdiction.

Some examples of how decisions are made about whether a company's labour relations falls under federal or provincial labour law illustrate the potential difficulty of this question. For example, though Starbucks is a national and international operation, employing workers at almost a thousand outlets across North America at the time the B.C. stores unionized, it fell under provincial labour legislation. This is because the economic activity involved—retail sales—is not one of the industries within federal jurisdiction. In contrast, a telephone company operating only within Ontario falls under federal, rather than provincial, labour laws because the telecommunications industry is a federal responsibility. It can be very difficult to determine which laws apply to companies such as trucking or taxi operations where some—but not all—of their business includes crossing provincial or international borders. The question in these cases becomes whether this part of the business is sufficient to characterize the whole operation as within the cross-border transportation industry and, thus, a federal responsibility.

Labour relations legislation and the constitutional division of powers provisions are the central, but not only, statutes affecting labour relations. The *Charter* and other legislation such as human rights, equity, and privacy legislation are gaining increasing importance in the workplace. The influence of these other types of legislation is discussed later in this chapter.

LABOUR TRIBUNALS

Labour legislation is primarily interpreted and enforced by *labour tribunals* instead of courts. Labour tribunals are specialized tribunals with decision makers who have labour relations expertise. As a result, labour tribunals have two key advantages over courts. First, this expertise may lead to more creative, effective, and appropriate solutions than a court might craft. Second, historically, the courts had shown great dislike for labour, helping employers and owners use the law to suppress workers' collective actions, which caused labour to view courts with distrust. Therefore, a less formal tribunal staffed with labour relations experts was believed to have greater credibility with the labour community, which would then be more likely to respect its decisions.

There are different kinds of labour tribunals, each with different responsibilities, and all are creations of labour relations legislation, which sets out their powers and responsibilities. *Labour relations boards* (often called *labour boards* or *LRBs*) are responsible for interpreting and applying the majority of the collective bargaining system set out in labour statutes: certification and decertification, negotiations, and so on. *Labour arbitration boards* have a much narrower responsibility: interpreting and applying the collective agreement or, in the case of an *interest arbitration board*, setting the terms of a collective agreement where the parties can't agree. Labour arbitration boards deal with situations in which the union or employer complains that the other party has violated a term of the collective agreement, such as by improperly disciplining an employee. (These are discussed in Chapter 13.)

A unique feature of Canadian labour tribunals is that they are commonly *tripartite* in nature, meaning that decision makers are drawn from both the management and labour communities, as well as government. Often, tribunals are chaired by a person who is trusted to be neutral and unbiased. Though members of tribunals do not literally represent either management or labour in their decision making, the idea is that their contributions will result in decisions that better reflect the interests of the community as a whole and ensure that the interests of all sides are taken into account. However, it is increasingly common to have a single decision maker sitting on labour cases, as boards and parties have become more concerned about reducing the expense of hearings and having decisions issued more quickly.

Labour Board Remedies

Labour statutes give LRBs wide powers to make orders to respond to violations of the legislation. These *remedial orders* (or *remedies*) are intended to restore injured parties to the position they would have been in had the statute not been breached.[9] (The remedial powers of labour arbitration boards are discussed in Chapter 13.) Labour board remedies must meet a few requirements. They must

- be compensatory, not punitive;
- comply with the *Charter*;
- have a rational connection between the violation of the statute, its consequences, and the remedy; and
- be consistent with the objects and purposes of the labour legislation.

Remedies not meeting these requirements will likely be declared to be "patently unreasonable" by a court and struck down.[10]

Common remedies include the following:

- A *declaration* that the conduct that is being complained about violated the statute. This remedy is generally used in cases where the misconduct is not likely to continue.

- *Cease and desist orders* direct the wrongdoer to stop the conduct complained of. These orders tend to be issued in cases where the activity is ongoing or is likely to be repeated.

- *Reinstatement* with *back pay* for lost wages is commonly awarded to illegally terminated employees.

- *Communication orders* may consist of publicizing the LRB's decision among employees, giving the union an opportunity to meet with employees at the workplace during work hours, or posting the LRB decision in the workplace. These remedies seek to offset the chilling effect employer ULPs may have on employees' support for organizing and to counter misinformation from the employer.

Some LRBs can certify the union as a remedy for employer ULPs, a process called *remedial certification*. Where a representation vote has been held, some LRBs can order a new election (called a *second vote*) to remedy especially shocking employer ULPs during union organizing (the union certification process is explained in detail in the next section). *Remedial certification* is intended to compensate employer ULPs by granting employees the union representation they probably would have obtained had the employer not violated the statute; this also aims to deter illegal employer conduct.[11] A *second vote* is ordered in cases where the LRB concludes that the first representation vote was contaminated by the employer's wrongdoing and thus may not accurately reflect employees' wishes about certification. The second vote remedy is criticized as being a much less effective remedy for serious ULPs (such as in the *Baron Metal* case discussed later in this chapter in Exhibit 8.7) than is remedial certification. Neither remedial certification nor second votes are granted very often.

Organizing costs may also be awarded to the union, but only in cases where the LRB finds that the union's investment in the organizing campaign has been completely wasted, and there is no prospect of reviving employee support.[12] Finally, in some jurisdictions, such as B.C., the LRB may award *legal costs* (some proportion of the actual amount the party spent in bringing the case to the LRB) to the successful party, in exceptional cases.[13]

In addition to remedies, labour legislation specifically provides for punishment or prosecution of a party who fails to comply with an LRB order.[14] Penalties are often in the form of fines and are meant to provide reparation and protection, and are not intended to simply be a "licence fee" for law-breaking.[15] However, such penalties are seldom sought or applied. In addition, a party that does not comply with an LRB order may be found guilty of civil or criminal *contempt* by the courts, which can result in a financial penalty or prison sentence.

UNION RECOGNITION PROCEDURES: CERTIFICATION AND VOLUNTARY RECOGNITION

Collective bargaining legislation grants employees the right to freely choose to be represented by a union. These statutes provide two routes by which a group of employees can demonstrate their choice to be unionized: *certification* and *voluntary recognition* (also recall that some LRBs can order union certification as a remedy for violation of the legislation). Union certification is the process by which a labour relations board recognizes a trade union as having the exclusive right to represent a specific group of employees (the bargaining unit) in negotiating and enforcing a collective agreement with the employer.

Unfair Labour Practices: Protecting Representation Rights

To protect the right of employees to freely choose whether to be represented by a union and whether to engage in lawful union activities, and to enforce unions' and employers' obligation to bargain in good faith, labour legislation prohibits certain conduct as "unfair labour practices."

While a ULP can be committed by an employer, a union, or a person acting on behalf of an employer or union, employers most often run afoul of these prohibitions. Therefore it is important to recognize that, at certain times, the labour relations system changes the rules about what managers can and cannot do. This is especially true during the following periods:

- when a union is trying to certify a group of workers (called *union organizing*);
- the period between certification and the start of collective bargaining; and
- during collective bargaining.

During these transitional times, union–management relationships are the most vulnerable to unfair pressures, and employees feel the greatest need for protections against reprisal. Statutes prohibit activities that interfere with the establishment of collective bargaining rights, and LRBs are most likely to intervene to protect the fragile new union–management relationship from abuse.

First, employer attempts to defeat unionization may constitute a ULP. During organizing, an employer will have committed a ULP where the employer's actions interfere with the rights of employees or the union to seek union representation.[16] Common examples of such ULPs are where an employer discharges, disciplines, or otherwise discriminates against an employee because of the worker's actual or perceived support for unionization, or the employer tries to discourage the worker from joining a union. Employers are still entitled to terminate an employee for *proper cause* (that is, legitimate reasons), or discipline a worker, as long as they do so free of *anti-union animus* (meaning that the action was not motivated, even in part, by anti-union motives).[17] Employers are also limited in how and what they communicate with their employees during this period: threats, intimidation, or promises that may discourage employees from supporting a union are ULPs and hence are prohibited.[18] Some managers argue that they are entitled to free speech under the *Charter* and expressly by labour statutes, but it is important to appreciate that they may be wrong. Labour laws may greatly constrain the freedom of expression. Whether speech constitutes a ULP depends, in part, on the expected effect the communication will have on the recipient. Will the employee reasonably understand the message to be intimidating or threatening? LRBs have long recognized that the subordinate relationship of employee to employer can colour the meaning of the employer's words.[19]

In addition, a *freeze period* applies from the time a certification application is filed until it is withdrawn, dismissed, granted, or until the union notifies the employer that it is ready to begin negotiating a collective agreement.[20] This freeze limits the employer's ability to change terms or conditions of employment, such as wages, without union consent. However, it also means that routine, or previously scheduled changes, such as annual salary increases, must go ahead unless the union agrees otherwise. This freeze is meant to prevent employers from introducing changes as either an enticement or punishment to discourage employees from supporting unionization.

After certification is granted, but before negotiations begin, a second freeze period applies.[21] This is meant to prevent the employer from changing terms or conditions of employment before bargaining starts. To allow that would defeat fair negotiations by giving the employer a tremendous—and unfair—advantage by letting him or her set the starting point for negotiations.

In some cases, in considering whether an action is a ULP, labour boards will look at whether the conduct in question likely affected employees' statutory rights or obligations, and not at whether the accused party intended this negative effect. Because motive is not relevant, these are called *non-motive ULPs*. For other types of ULP prohibitions, called *illicit motive ULPs*, the LRB looks to see whether the employer's conduct was motivated by *anti-union animus*.[22] If the LRB finds that anti-union animus was even an incidental reason for the conduct (such as firing a union organizer), then the employer will be found to have committed a ULP. Recognizing that it is often difficult for unions and workers to prove that the employer had an illicit motive, the legislation does not require that such intent be proven, instead imposing a *reverse onus* on the employer.[23] This means that, instead of the union's having to prove that the employer had an illicit motive, the employer must convince the LRB that it had no illicit motive.[24]

Requirements for Union Certification

Labour relations legislation requires that a union satisfy four conditions in order to be certified:

- The union must be a "trade union" within the meaning of the legislation.
- The application must be "timely" (that is, fall within specific time limits set out in the statute).
- The bargaining unit applied for must be *appropriate for collective bargaining*.
- The union must prove that it has sufficient support for the certification application among employees in the bargaining unit.

The last two of these requirements are often contentious and are discussed below.

Appropriate Bargaining Unit

Appropriateness is a difficult question because the bargaining unit has a dual role. Not only is this group of workers the basis for determining whether there is sufficient support for certification, but this bargaining unit will be the group of workers that the union will, if certified, negotiate on behalf of, and which must later be capable of functioning under a single collective agreement. As a result, the makeup of the bargaining unit is important because it influences

- the outcome of the certification application;
- the balance of power in negotiations;
- the likelihood of breakdown of negotiations; and
- application of the collective agreement.

The question of appropriateness can also arise after certification. For instance, if a certification application is made for another group of employees at the workplace; if the business is sold and perhaps integrated into the purchaser's organization; or if another union takes over the certification (called a *raid*).

Because of the importance of the scope of the unit to negotiations, it is important that unit employees share a sufficient *community of interest*. That is, that the unit include employees with sufficiently common employment interests. Unions have difficulty representing workers with competing interests, because the more the interests conflict, the more difficulty the union has in negotiating and administering a collective agreement. A number of specific factors (set out in Exhibit 8.4) are considered in determining whether a proposed unit has a community of interest.

Also important to determining appropriateness are the competing issues of *access to collective representation* and *industrial stability*. On the one hand, labour boards want to ensure that employees have reasonable access to collective bargaining, and thus do not want the makeup of the unit to pose an additional barrier. For instance, sometimes a smaller bargaining unit (such as a single store or group of five coffee shops) is easier to organize than a larger unit (such as all 91 Starbucks stores in a province) because it may be easier to gain union support from a smaller group with a narrower range of labour interests. LRBs recognize that requiring a larger unit may result in denying employees access to collective representation—particularly in industries that are difficult to organize. However, industrial stability may favour the larger unit. One question that often arises is whether more than one worksite or group of workers should belong in a single unit because the work or operations are interdependent, such that a work stoppage at one location or by one group would halt the other. LRBs are concerned about overly *fragmented bargaining structures*. Multiple units in a single operation may increase industrial instability, hamper effective collective bargaining, and excessively burden the employer who has to deal with multiple rounds of negotiations and collective agreements. Nevertheless, on a first certification, boards tend to regard access as more important than industrial stability.

Another factor relevant to appropriateness is that bargaining units be large enough to be viable for collective bargaining. This consideration tends to favour larger units, since smaller units may lack sufficient bargaining power to be effective. Finally, boards prefer bargaining units that are stable and with clearly identifiable boundaries, as this helps to reduce problems regarding unit membership.

Sufficient Support

The level of support is determined by one of two alternative procedures: the *union membership card procedure* (also called "card-check" or "card-based" certification) and the *mandatory representation vote procedure*. Some jurisdictions use the card-check procedure; others the mandatory vote. Initially, almost all Canadian jurisdictions used card-based certification. Since the mid-1990s a number of provinces replaced it with the mandatory vote procedure; the mandatory vote is now almost as common as card-based certification.[26] See Exhibit 8.5 for a diagram setting out the steps in each system and Exhibit 8.6 for a comparison between the two certification systems.

**Exhibit 8.5
Two Models to
Test Sufficient
Support**

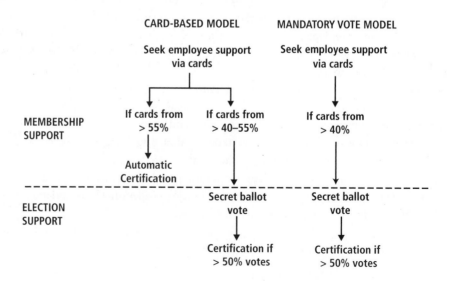

CARD-BASED MODEL

MANDATORY VOTE MODEL

Seek employee support via cards

Seek employee support via cards

MEMBERSHIP SUPPORT

If cards from > 55%

If cards from > 40–55%

If cards from > 40%

Automatic Certification

ELECTION SUPPORT

Secret ballot vote

Secret ballot vote

Certification if > 50% votes

Certification if > 50% votes

Mandatory Representation Vote

Under a mandatory vote procedure, a representation vote will be held if the union submits a certification application accompanied by signed union membership cards from a minimum percentage of employees in the unit (generally 40 percent). In representation votes, employees vote on whether or not to be represented by the union. Votes must be held within a certain number of days (generally five or ten days) following the date of the certification application or, in the case of Alberta, " . . . as soon as possible."[27] Usually certification is granted if a majority of the ballots cast are for the union, regardless of how many employees who are eligible to vote actually do so. However, to ensure that at least half of the bargaining unit supports the union, some provinces require that at least half of the eligible voters must have cast their ballots in favour of certification, in order for the union to win the election.[28]

Card-Based Certification

Under the card-check procedure, the union is entitled to a certification vote if the union shows that it has signed union membership cards from a certain percentage of employees in the bargaining unit (usually 55 percent). If the union receives cards only from a specified, lesser percentage of employees (usually 45 to 55 percent) then the union will not be automatically certified, but a representation vote will be held. The outcome of these votes is determined the same way as under the mandatory vote procedure. Few such votes are held under the card-check system; most certifications are obtained on the basis of authorization cards. If cards are signed by less than 40 percent of bargaining unit employees, the board will dismiss the application. The card-check system is largely an administrative process which, it is argued, properly reflects the fact that certification is simply a first step to bargaining and not a competition between a union and employer for the "hearts and minds" of the workers.[29]

Exhibit 8.6
Controversy Between the Card-Check and Mandatory Vote Procedure

The choice of certification procedure has been the focus of frequent legislative changes in some provinces, and ongoing debate in the United States and Canada about which is the preferred means for determining support.

Supporters of the card-check system contend that it is a more accurate test of support for unionization because it provides less opportunity for employer interference. A union may obtain sufficient signed cards and apply for certification before the employer becomes aware that a union is attempting to organize its workers and, therefore, before the employer can influence employee choice. In contrast, with an election the employer will have several days' notice of the vote in which to discourage employees (perhaps even illegally) from unionizing. Critics of the vote system argue that this not only allows, but encourages, employer anti-union responses.[30] On the other hand, allowing employers to counter union statements may also be valuable. The

---

experience of employees at Baron Metal Industries who attempted to unionize under labour legislation—including the mandatory vote system but not allowing remedial certification—is a vivid example of an employer's taking the opportunity of the pre-vote period to discourage employees from voting for the union. This case also shows how difficult it is to remedy ULPs (see Exhibit 8.7).

The card-check requirement to have signed cards from a certain proportion of the proposed unit ensures that a majority of employees in the unit (at least 55 percent) desire certification. In contrast, the calculation of support on the vote is based on the number of employees voting. To succeed on a representation vote, the union must receive more than 50 percent of the votes cast, and this may actually be an easier threshold to pass than the card-based requirement. For example, if only five employees in a ten-employee unit vote, the union is entitled to certification if three of these five employees (30 percent of the unit) vote for certification. In this respect, the card-check system requirements, which would require cards from six of the ten unit members, set a higher threshold for the union to meet than does the vote system. On the other hand, elections allow all eligible employees an opportunity to express their wishes by casting a vote, while not every employee may have an opportunity to choose whether or not to sign a card.

Critics of the card system argue that it may not accurately reflect employee wishes because union organizers and fellow employees may pressure employees to sign cards against their wishes, or may misrepresent the effect of signing a card to employees. Representation elections are perceived by some, especially employers, to provide superior evidence of employees' true wishes because of the

- secrecy of voting;[31]
- formality of the election process; and
- opportunity for employees to change their minds about unionization after choosing whether or not to sign a union membership card.

An employee may sign a card, yet later decide (perhaps legitimately and not as a result of intimidation or coercion) that he or she no longer desires union representation. Under the mandatory vote system, this employee may choose not to vote for certification.[32] The reverse may also occur: an employee may not have signed a card, yet at the time of the election may decide to support the union in the election. Proponents of the vote system argue that this leads to greater employer trust in the outcome, which promotes employer co-operation with the elected union.[33]

Exhibit 8.7
Baron Metal Industries Ltd.[34]

In 1998, the United Steelworkers union (USW) began organizing employees at Baron Metal Industries Ltd. in Woodbridge, Ontario.

Two men, known as Kuti and Kodi, began work at Baron Metal shortly after the USW began organizing. These men were known members of a Tamil gang involved in significant criminal activity. Many employees were of Sri Lankan origin, and would likely know this gang's reputation.

The Ontario Labour Relations Board (OLRB) found the men committed several serious ULPs in the few days before the representation vote. The vote resulted in a tie, with as many employees voting for certification as against.

The OLRB found that someone in management had given the men a list of names and addresses of employees believed to be union organizers, which the men showed to several employees.[35]

It also found the men had made serious threats to several employees, such as saying,

- "If the union wins you will be killed outside."
- "We won't do anything now, but if the union wins we will do it."[36]
- Kuti told at least one employee that he was a gang member and a criminal;
- he would shoot and kill that employee if he voted in the representation election;[37] and
- if employees on the list did not vote, Koti would get money for them from Baron Metal Industries.[38]

Though the OLRB found no direct evidence that Baron Metal Industries knew of the men's gang activities, it concluded they'd been recruited by, and acted with the authority of, someone in management to deter Sri Lankan employees from voting for the union.[39]

The OLRB considered these to be very serious ULPs. The threats of "violent death at the behest of management"[40] were "directly tied to the upcoming representation vote" and were "so serious and sufficiently pervasive to affect the reliability of the employees' expression of their wishes, despite the sanctity of the ballot box. . . . "[41]

In May 2001, the OLRB issued its decision. At that time the government had changed the *Ontario Labour Relations Act* to remove the OLRB's ability to order remedial certification. However, it was able to order other substantial remedies.[42]

The OLRB ordered Baron Metal to post in the workplace, and include with each employee's paystub (translated, if necessary, at the company's expense), an OLRB notice setting out the board's decision and a statement of employees' rights to unionize.

The notice also set out the remedies ordered by the OLRB, including:

- A declaration, cease and desist order, and a second vote.
- That the company:
  - allow several mandatory meetings between the union and employees in the workplace during working hours and without loss of pay;
  - give the union a list of all employees in the unit hired after the first vote;
  - meet with the union, upon its request, if any employee is suspended or fired after the OLRB decision;
  - give the union an office in the workplace for a period of time to meet with employees;
  - let the union distribute pamphlets to employees in the workplace before the second vote; and
  - pay the union organizing costs.

The second vote also resulted in a tie. However, because of voter eligibility questions, a third election was held, which the union lost. In 2006, after a new organizing campaign, the USW finally won a representation election at Baron Metal and was certified.

Voluntary recognition is an alternative to the card-check and mandatory vote systems for establishing union recognition. LRBs will treat a voluntary recognition much like a bargaining relationship established by card-check or vote, if the following requirements are met:

- The union and employer agree that
  - the union will represent a group of workers, and
  - this representation is for the purposes of negotiating and administering a collective agreement.
- There is a written collective agreement.

In the United States the use of voluntary recognition agreements (or *neutrality agreements*, as they are sometimes called) instead of statutory certification is increasing.[43] American unions see it as a way of reducing the opportunity for employer interference in employees' unionization decisions. In Canada, voluntary recognition is not commonly used, probably because we do not have the very long delay before representation votes, nor the same degree of employer interference, as in the United States.

Decertification

Once represented by a union, employees need not remain unionized. Though uncommon, employees can apply to have the union's exclusive bargaining rights terminated (called *decertification* or *deunionization*). The legislation provides that, if a sufficient proportion of employees in the unit support the decertification application, then an election will be held. If a majority of votes cast are in favour of decertification, then the LRB will terminate the union's representation rights.[44]

UNION SECURITY

Once a union is certified (or voluntarily recognized), it gains statutory authority as the exclusive representative of all employees in the bargaining unit. One implication of this is that there may no longer be individual negotiations or arrangements between any of the employees and the employer. Both negotiating and administering a collective agreement are now matters solely between the employer and union—they are the only legal parties to the collective agreement and hence have the right to oversee their relationship. This means that an employee who believes his or her employer has breached the terms of employment, such as by wrongfully terminating him or her, can no longer take this dispute to court him- or herself. It must be resolved by the union and employer. This also applies to all employees in the unit, whether or not they have joined the union as members, and whether or not they supported unionization.

The union's being responsible for representing all employees in the bargaining unit—union members or not—gives rise to the *free-rider problem*. Employees have little incentive to join the union or pay union dues if they are entitled to receive the same representation services even if they don't join or pay. This situation can be very costly to the union, draining its resources and threatening its ability to effectively represent the unit.

Some American states have what is called *right-to-work legislation*, stating that employees cannot be required to become union members or pay dues. Some argue that this legislation encourages free-ridership by discouraging union membership and paying of dues, starving unions of resources, leading to ineffective representation and lower unionization.[45]

Canadian labour laws seek to avoid this free-rider problem by permitting a variety of *union security clauses* to be negotiated into collective agreements (see Exhibit 8.8). The rationale is that employees who benefit from the services of a union should pay for these services. It also reflects the view that the representation question has already been determined, so parties' efforts should now be spent on the bargaining relationship—not on the union's status.

To avoid the difficulty of collecting dues, labour legislation in several jurisdictions requires employers to deduct union dues from all employees in the bargaining unit and to remit them to the union. This is called *compulsory dues check-off* and this system is called the *Rand formula*.[46]

Exhibit 8.8
Union Security Clauses

Several types of union security clauses exist:

- Closed shop: Employees must be union members before being hired. This is the most restrictive and least common type of provision.
- Union shop: Employees must join the union and remain a member while employed in the bargaining unit.
- Rand formula: Employees can choose whether or not to join the union. However, all employees in the bargaining unit will have union dues deducted from their salary and forwarded to the union (called a "dues check-off").
- Voluntary check-off: Employees choose whether to become a union member and to pay union dues.

The question of whether compulsory union dues check-off violated an employee's *Charter* freedoms of association and expression was considered in an early Supreme Court of Canada case: *Lavigne v. O.P.S.E.U.*[47] The employee in this case, Mervin Lavigne, objected to the dues check-off and to the fact that the Ontario Public Service Employees Union was using dues to contribute to a variety of organizations and causes which Lavigne did not want his dues to support. Lavigne argued that these donations were a forced expression of his support for these causes, and therefore a violation of his freedom of expression. The Court unanimously rejected this claim. Lavigne also argued that the *Charter* freedom of association also guarantees a right *not to associate*, and that this right was being violated. Essentially, he said, OPSEU's use of his dues was forcing him to associate himself with these groups and causes. While a majority of the Court held that the freedom of association was not violated, the Court split on whether an implied freedom to not associate exists. The upshot of this close case was that the unions could continue to collect dues and distribute them, even over some employees' objections. The Court, in a subsequent case, concluded that there is, indeed, a limited freedom not to associate.[48]

THE COLLECTIVE AGREEMENT AND COLLECTIVE BARGAINING

A collective agreement is, essentially, a contract between the employer and the union, setting out the terms and conditions of employment for all employees represented in the unit. Labour legislation regulates, to some degree, the content of collective agreements and, to a much larger degree, the resolution of disputes that arise in collective agreement negotiations.

Content of Collective Agreements

Labour legislation requires that collective agreements contain certain provisions. Generally, if the agreement fails to include these provisions, the statute will deem them to be included, anyway. For example, in Ontario, the OLRA requires that collective agreements contain provisions that[49]

- require arbitration to provide final and binding resolution for disputes arising under the agreement;
- set a one-year minimum term for the collective agreement;
- prohibit work stoppages (strikes or lockouts) during the life of the collective agreement;
- provide for compulsory dues check-off; and
- prohibit discrimination contrary to human rights legislation or the *Charter*.

Other jurisdictions have similar requirements. The rest of the contents are up to the union and employer to negotiate. Because, over the years, long-term bargaining relationships will see a series of agreements negotiated, settled, and expiring, collective agreements also commonly include *bridging clauses*. These are provisions setting out how the parties will deal with the period after an old agreement expires and before a new one comes into force. Bridging clauses minimize the disruption of an expiring collective agreement, allowing parties to focus on negotiations.

Duty to Bargain in Good Faith and Disclose Information

Labour legislation protects and encourages productive bargaining of collective agreements by imposing a duty on unions and employers to bargain in good faith and make all reasonable efforts to negotiate an agreement (called the *duty to bargain in good faith*).[50] This duty also requires employers to disclose certain information during negotiations. A breach of these duties is another type of ULP. These duties are expressed, for example in s.17 of the OLRA:

17. The parties shall meet within 15 days from the giving of the notice or within such further period as the parties agree upon and they shall bargain in good faith and make every reasonable effort to make a collective agreement.

Such regulation of negotiations is necessary because some employers are unwilling to negotiate and may even prefer that no collective agreement ever be reached. The purposes of the duty to bargain in good faith are (1) to reinforce the employer's obligation to recognize the union as the bargaining agent; (2) to foster rational, informed discussion; and (3) to minimize the potential for unnecessary conflict by trying to prevent a party from behaving in a way that is likely to frustrate negotiations.[51]

This duty focuses on the process—not the outcome—of bargaining. Actions such as failing or refusing to meet with the other party, an employer bargaining directly with workers, or a party making new demands at the last minute may be found to breach this duty. The question the LRB asks is whether the action is likely to defeat good faith negotiations. This duty is sometimes awkward to apply in practice, because it is very difficult for a board to distinguish *hard bargaining* (which is a legitimate use of bargaining strength) from *surface bargaining* (where a party is simply going through the motions of negotiating with no intention of coming to agreement).

The duty to bargain in good faith also requires employers to disclose to unions, during negotiations, information about plans that will substantially affect the bargaining unit. This is meant to ensure that parties have all relevant information to ensure bargaining efficiency. The duty lies with the employer because generally only the employer will have this information, and is a two-part duty. First, an employer must disclose *de facto decisions* (that is, final decisions) that may substantially affect the bargaining unit, such as decisions to contract out work of substantial portions of the bargaining unit, or to close a workplace.[52] Second, an employer must respond honestly to union questions during negotiations about employer plans that may substantially affect the bargaining unit.

Common remedies for a breach of these duties include a cease and desist order, and a direction that the violating party bargain in good faith. Less commonly, an LRB will order the violating party to publish retractions of false or prejudicial statements made about the negotiations, or pay the other party's negotiating costs. In extreme situations, monetary compensation for loss of the opportunity to bargain a collective agreement is available.[53] While an LRB may require a party to re-table its last offer, or order certain terms and conditions of a collective agreement, it will not impose a collective agreement on parties as a remedy.[54] To do so would be contrary to the idea of free collective bargaining and beyond an LRB's power.

Where parties succeed in negotiating a collective agreement, several provinces (B.C., Manitoba, Ontario, and Québec) require (at least in certain circumstances) that a secret ballot vote of unit members be held to ratify any collective agreement.

BREAKDOWN OF NEGOTIATIONS AND WORK STOPPAGES

In some cases, negotiations break down and the employer may *lock out* employees, or the union may call a *strike*, to try to pressure the other party to come to agreement. One distinctive feature of Canadian labour legislation is the extensive preconditions that must be met, including third-party intervention, before a work stoppage will be legal. This is intended to encourage settlements and discourage work stoppages.

Common preconditions include that any prior collective agreement has expired, that parties have sought conciliation or mediation, and that advance notice has been given of a work stoppage. British Columbia requires that at least 72 hours' notice of a work stoppage be given to the LRB, and Saskatchewan requires that a minimum of 48 hours' notice be given to the other party. Before a legal strike can commence, a majority of bargaining unit employees must also have voted to strike. Another step intended to encourage parties to settle is the *last offer vote*, whereby an employer can ask the LRB to hold a vote in which employees vote on whether or not to support the last offer the employer made in negotiations to the union.[55]

Even if these requirements are met, not all work stoppages will be a strike or lockout. Unless it meets the statutory definition of "strike" or "lockout," a work stoppage will not be within the LRB's jurisdiction and will be a matter for the courts to deal with. Collective bargaining legislation sets out the definition of lockout and strike. A typical definition of lockout is found in s.1 of the B.C. *Labour Relations Code*:

> "Lockout" includes closing a place of employment, a suspension of work or a refusal by an employer to continue to employ a number of his or her employees, *done to compel his or her employees or to aid another employer to compel his or her employees to agree to conditions of employment.* [emphasis added]

Notice that this definition requires that the employer's refusal to let its employees work must be for the purpose of pressuring workers to agree to conditions of employment.[56] A work stoppage called by an employer for any other purpose will not be a lockout.

In contrast, statutory definitions of strikes don't require that the work stoppage have a particular purpose. Generally only two conditions are necessary for a work stoppage to constitute a strike: there must be concerted employee activity, and the employer's operation must be disrupted. The *Ontario Labour Relations Act* definition of "strike" is typical:

> "Strike" includes a cessation of work, a refusal to work or to continue to work by employees in combination or in concert or in accordance with a common understanding, or a slow-down or other concerted activity on the part of employees designed to restrict or limit output.

This lack of requirement of a particular purpose of the work stoppage for strikes has important implications for the types of actions that will be found to be strikes, especially what are known as *sympathy strikes* and political protests (see Exhibit 8.9) involving work disruption. Sympathy strikes arise when workers are locked out or on strike and picketing their workplace. Other unionized workers, in a different bargaining unit at the same workplace and who are not on strike or locked out, may decide not to cross the picket line, as an expression of solidarity. Where more than one worker declines to cross, and work is disrupted, LRBs consider this a strike. Unless the sympathetic unit is otherwise in a legal strike position, it will be an illegal strike.[57]

Not only are certain work stoppages prohibited by labour legislation, but unions, employers, and others are also prohibited from calling, inducing, or doing any thing that reasonably could cause an unlawful strike or lockout.[60]

Remedies for Illegal Work Stoppages

If a work stoppage occurs before the statutory preconditions are met (including before an existing collective agreement expires) it will be illegal. Remedies for illegal strikes and lockouts may be sought through the courts, LRBs, and arbitration. Courts offer *injunctions* (a specific type of order) prohibiting illegal work stoppages, and monetary compensation (called "damages") for losses caused by illegal actions. LRBs can issue *cease and desist orders* prohibiting the illegal conduct from continuing, and employers or unions can seek consent to prosecute the party violating the legislation, which can result in fines. Illegal work stoppages will also likely violate the collective agreement, and therefore an arbitrator can award damages (such as for lost profit or lost wages) against the violating party. Finally, illegally striking employees can also be disciplined by their employer, since this conduct is contrary to the mandatory *no-strike clause* in collective agreements and is a breach of their employment obligations.[61]

Rights of Striking or Locked-Out Employees

Even though employees are not working during a legal work stoppage, the employment relationship still exists, and the law provides a number of protections to workers and their jobs during the work stoppage.[62] First, employers cannot penalize employees for engaging in legal strike activity. However, once the employee returns to work, the employer may discipline the worker for any misconduct he or she engaged in during the strike or while picketing. Employers must be careful not to discipline employees for engaging in a lawful strike, because to do so would violate the employee's right to engage in lawful union activities and, therefore, would be a ULP.[63]

Second, some jurisdictions, such as B.C. and Québec, limit the use of *replacement workers* by an employer during a work stoppage. Elsewhere, employers can hire temporary workers to replace striking or locked-out workers to maintain operations; however, employers cannot keep replacement workers in preference to striking workers after the strike, if the reason for doing so *is that the workers struck*. Punishing workers in this way for legally striking would be a ULP, but preferring replacement workers over striking workers for *other* reasons is not a ULP.[64] Whether or not to restrict the use of replacement workers during work stoppages is controversial. Those favouring restrictions argue that restricting replacement workers reduces the potential for violence and disruption, and that allowing replacement workers makes strikes ineffective. Meanwhile, opponents argue that restrictions increase the economic harm of work stoppages to employers, while employees don't suffer since they can work elsewhere and often draw strike pay from the union's funds to reduce the employees' personal costs of participating in a lawful strike.

Finally, most jurisdictions either give employees a statutory right to return to work after the strike[65] or prohibit the employer from retaining replacement workers in preference to striking workers.[66]

Interest Arbitration

Another form of third-party intervention available when negotiations run into difficulty is *interest arbitration*. Parties may agree to refer to an interest arbitration board or sole arbitrator for a binding decision on those issues on which they have not been able to agree. Many jurisdictions have made special provisions for interest arbitration where there is a new certification and the employer and union are negotiating their first collective agreement together. Called *first contract arbitration*, a neutral arbitrator (or in some cases the LRB) will produce a first collective agreement for the parties. Some jurisdictions permit first contract arbitration at the parties' request; in others it is at the discretion of the Minister of Labour, and additional preconditions (such as having tried conciliation) may apply. The purpose of first contract arbitration is to help launch management and the union into a constructive and functioning collective bargaining relationship.

Picketing

Picketing, where employees demonstrate to publicize a labour dispute, commonly occurs during a strike or lockout (though it can take place at other times, too). Often picketing involves employees' carrying picket signs and perhaps delaying people or vehicles entering or exiting the picketed location. The business being picketed may wish to limit such activity. In most jurisdictions, picketing is dealt with by the courts rather than by LRBs (B.C., Alberta, and New Brunswick are the exceptions). Courts may issue *injunctions*, and LRBs may issue *cease and desist orders* prohibiting or limiting certain picketing activities. If the activity is not picketing but *leafleting*, then the activity is much more difficult to prohibit or limit. (See Exhibit 8.10 for the test of what qualifies as leafleting.)

The question of the degree to which picketing activity can be restrained is a difficult one because picketing is recognized as an expressive activity that is protected by the *Charter*'s section 2(b) guarantee of freedom of expression.[67] So the *Charter*-protected right of picketers to communicate their message must be carefully balanced with other interests, such as that of a business to carry on as usual. *Secondary picketing* is an interesting example of how decision makers address this dilemma.

Picketing at the workplace where the labour dispute arose is called *primary picketing*. Secondary picketing describes picketing at a secondary site—that of a third party (often a vendor or key supplier) to the dispute. Secondary picketing is intended to persuade that party not to do business with the employer directly involved in the dispute.

Historically, secondary picketing was considered illegal. However, the Supreme Court of Canada's decision in the *Pepsi* case in 2002 established a new way to deal with secondary picketing, called the *wrongful action approach*.[68] The Court held that it was incorrect to treat secondary picketing as automatically illegal, and that " . . . third parties are to be protected from undue suffering, not insulated entirely from the repercussions of labour conflict."[69] Under the wrongful action approach, secondary picketing is illegal only if it involves "wrongful action." This means that the picketing activity cannot be restricted or prohibited unless it includes some other wrongful act such as a *Criminal Code* violation; breaches of provincial penal statutes such as assault, mischief, nuisance, threats of violence, and trespass; or wrongdoing such as assault, battery, trespass, defamation, or nuisance.[70] In *Pepsi*, the limitation on secondary picketing arose from the case law, not from statute. Nevertheless, this decision provides guidance about what may also be found to be the limits of statutory restrictions on secondary picketing.

Exhibit 8.10
Test for Leafleting

In its 1999 KMart decision, the Supreme Court of Canada held that leafleting (distributing informational leaflets) is distinct from picketing and that, unlike picketing, leafleting was entitled to absolute *Charter* protection, and so could not be legally restricted or prohibited.[71]

The Court set out the following conditions that must be met for conduct to qualify as protected leafleting:

1. the message conveyed by the leaflet must be accurate, not defamatory or otherwise unlawful, and must not entice people to commit unlawful or tortious acts;
2. the leaflet must clearly state that the dispute is only with the workers' employer;
3. the leafleting cannot be carried out in a coercive, intimidating, or otherwise unlawful or tortious manner;
4. the activity must not create an atmosphere of intimidation by involving a large number of people;
5. the activity must not unduly impede access to or exit from the place being leafleted; and
6. the activity must not prevent employees of the secondary sites from working, or interfere with other businesses supplying the secondary site.

DUTY OF FAIR REPRESENTATION

Unions owe a *duty of fair representation* (or DFR) to all employees in the bargaining unit, whether or not they are members of the union, therefore unions are required to represent all employees in the unit fairly (see Exhibit 8.11). Once a union is certified as the exclusive bargaining agent for a unit of employees, the trade-off is that employees are no longer able to negotiate individually with their employer. This also means that an employee who has a dispute over the terms of employment with his employer is no longer able to go to court to resolve the matter. The union is now responsible for—and controls—all such disputes, which now must be resolved through the grievance procedure and grievance or interest arbitration (see Chapter 13 for more details on arbitration). This is true for all employees in the bargaining unit, whether or not they voted for the union and whether or not they have become a union member. The question that arises from this trade-off, and that the DFR tries to resolve, is how to adequately protect individual and minority rights while still allowing the union the discretion it needs to represent the bargaining unit as a whole.

The DFR prohibits unions from acting in a manner that is arbitrary, discriminatory, or in bad faith in representing its unit members.[72] In most Canadian jurisdictions this duty is set out in the legislation; in a few, such as New Brunswick and Prince Edward Island, a DFR applies even though it's not set out in the statute.[73]

Exhibit 8.11
Ontario's Duty of Fair Representation (DFR) Provision

Section 74 of the *Ontario Labour Relations Act* is typical of many statutory DFR provisions:

> 74. A trade union or council of trade unions, so long as it continues to be entitled to represent employees in a bargaining unit, shall not act in a manner that is arbitrary, discriminatory or in bad faith in the representation of any of the employees in the unit, whether or not members of the trade union or of any constituent union of the council of trade unions, as the case may be.

DFR arises from the exclusive authority the union has to represent bargaining unit members in negotiating and enforcing the collective agreement, and is seen as necessary to balance the union's power and authority over its members' interests.[74] A union is sometimes in a position where it must decide between conflicting employee interests. Because it cannot pursue both conflicting interests, the DFR must allow the union to be able to decide which interest to pursue based on what the union believes is in the best interests of the unit as a whole.[75] If individual employees were able to take any grievance to arbitration, this would lead to a tremendous amount of litigation depleting both union and employer resources, which would be bad for the union, other employees, and the employer (see Exhibit 8.12).[76] DFR complaints are not meant to be a way for employees who are simply unhappy with their union to complain, or to appeal a union's decision.[77]

As mentioned previously, the DFR prohibits unions from acting in a manner that is arbitrary, discriminatory, or in bad faith. A union acts in an arbitrary manner where it shows blatant or reckless disregard for the interests of an employee, rather than exercising thoughtful judgment about relevant considerations.[78] It is important to recognize that simply making a mistake or "handling a matter poorly" does not constitute arbitrary conduct under the DFR.[79] LRBs recognize that unions have to deal with a great number of grievances with limited resources, and that they are not to be held to the standards of a lawyer in procedural or substantive matters,[80] though the union's conduct will be scrutinized more carefully the more important is the employee interest at stake. Situations such as termination or loss of seniority will be scrutinized most carefully.

Discriminatory treatment occurs where the union makes a decision based on what has been called "invidious distinctions without labour relations rationale."[81] This includes, but is not limited to, the type of discrimination prohibited by human rights legislation, such as gender discrimination. It can also include such things as simple personal favouritism.

Bad faith occurs where the union acts out of "personal hostility, political revenge or dishonesty."[82] Bad faith conduct can occur in two types of situations: where the union acts together with the employer against an employee's interests; or where the union is dishonest or intends to deceive an employee.[83] However, a union is entitled to decide the merits of cases, and consider the interests of other employees, even if the outcome for one employee is negative.[84]

Grievance Handling

In all jurisdictions, the DFR regulates how unions deal with grievances. Although unions are given a great deal of discretion in their decisions about grievances, and although an employee does not have an absolute right to arbitration, unions are obliged to deal fairly with grievances (see Exhibit 8.13).[85] Two distinct stages of grievance handling are recognized. In the first stage the union assesses the merits of the grievance and decides whether to take it to arbitration. It must do so reasonably. Second, if the union determines the grievance has merit, then it is obliged to represent the grievor "without serious negligence, discrimination or bad faith at all subsequent stages of the grievance procedure."[86]

Exhibit 8.12
Proportion of DFR Complaints with Merit

DFR complaints take up a great deal of LRB resources, even though the vast majority of DFR complaints have no merit. For example, in the five years from 2001 to 2005, the BCLRB dealt with 835 DFR complaints, but found the union had breached its duty in only 26 cases. The pattern across Canada is quite similar. Nevertheless, unions are quite averse to DFR complaints. As a result, unions—especially in serious situations involving job loss—will often pursue weak cases rather than deprive a worker of the opportunity for arbitration (see Chapter 13 for more details on grievance arbitration).

Exhibit 8.13
Handling Grievances

The BCLRB provides the following guidelines for unions to meet their DFR obligations in handling grievances. A union must do the following:[87]

1. Talk to the grievor and learn about the complaint.

2. Investigate, such as by:

    ■ obtaining information from those involved;
    ■ constructing a sequence of events from the information; and
    ■ offering the grievor a chance to respond.

3. Make a reasoned decision, by, for example:

    ■ considering the collective agreement language and industry or workplace practices;
    ■ considering how similar grievances have been handled in the past; and
    ■ providing the grievor with the reasons for the union's decision.

4. If the union decides to proceed with the grievance, it must do so in a manner which is not in blatant or reckless disregard of the grievor's interests.

Negotiations

In some jurisdictions (B.C., Québec, and Ontario) the DFR applies both to negotiation of collective agreements and to handling of grievances; elsewhere, it applies only to grievance handling.[88] The DFR allows the union broad discretion to make decisions about negotiating, and to agree to terms that affect members unequally. The test the union must meet is whether its decision was reasonable in the circumstances. The union must be able to point to some practical justification for its decision—it is not enough that the union's decision was based on the will of the majority of the unit.[89]

Sometimes during collective bargaining, employers and unions will agree that certain grievances will be withdrawn, and this may occur without the grievor's consent. Such *grievance swapping* is recognized as a part of industrial relations reality, since a workplace often has many more grievances than can be resolved before the expiration of the collective agreement under which they arose.[90] Though this occurs during bargaining, it is treated as a grievance handling matter for the purposes of determining the union's DFR obligations. Therefore, the union is allowed less discretion in bargaining away grievances than in negotiating other matters.

Remedying DFRs

Duty of fair representation complaints are generally handled by LRBs although, in some uncommon circumstances, a court or human rights tribunal may deal with these complaints. Common remedies include an order for the union to take the grievance to arbitration, possibly an order for the union to pay the cost of a lawyer other than the union's lawyer, or an order to compensate the employee for the union's misconduct.

DFR complaints are primarily a matter between the employee and the union representing him or her (that is, unless the employer is complicit in the union's alleged wrongdoing). However, because the employer is a party to the collective agreement, the employer is also affected by remedies awarded where a DFR has occurred. As a result, employers are generally notified of complaints and may attend hearings as interested parties.

The *Charter* and Employment-Related Statutes

Labour relations not only must be concerned with rights and obligations imposed by labour relations legislation, or agreed to by the employer and union in a collective agreement, but must also take into consideration the growing array of rights and obligations relevant to the workplace arising from other statutes. The *Canadian Charter of Rights and Freedoms*, as well as federal and provincial legislation dealing with employment standards, human rights codes, occupational health and safety, pay equity, and employment equity, all apply to relations in the workplace—whether the workplace is unionized or not. Because of Canada's remarkable decentralization, statutes differ among provinces and the federal jurisdiction.

It is now clear that the interpretation and application (and therefore the negotiation and arbitration) of collective agreements must take these other statutory rights and requirements into account. The Supreme Court of Canada, in its 2003 *Parry Sound* decision, concluded that the rights and obligations of human rights codes and other employment-related legislation are incorporated directly into every collective agreement—even if the agreement does not explicitly say so. This means that collective agreements cannot provide for less than the statutory minimum protection, and a violation of such legislation also constitutes a violation of the collective agreement. Consequently, arbitrators not only have the power, but are required, to apply and enforce these statutes as if they were collective agreement provisions.[91] Like labour legislation, employment-related statutes exist at both the federal and provincial level, and the constitutional division of powers determines which will apply to a given workplace.

Charter of Rights and Freedoms

Perhaps more than any other statute, the *Canadian Charter of Rights and Freedoms* (see Exhibit 8.14), passed as part of the Canadian Constitution in 1982, has had a profound effect on labour relations.[92] The Constitution is paramount legislation, meaning that all other statutes must comply with its requirements, and is designed to protect individuals against state action, including (but not limited to) legislation enacted by the state.[93]

Until recently, the *Charter* has been regarded as having had little effect on the collective bargaining system. However, with several recent court decisions (including some discussed earlier in this chapter), culminating in the Supreme Court of Canada's 2007 *Health Services* decision (also referred to in Chapters 1 and 6), the Court has signalled that the *Charter* is now of central importance to labour relations.[94]

The most significant change relates to section 2(d) of the *Charter* (freedom of association) which, early in the *Charter*'s history, was anticipated to be the freedom that would be most relevant to labour relations. However, in a series of cases that came to be known as the *Labour Trilogy*, the Supreme Court explicitly refused to extend the protection of freedom of association to cover collective bargaining or striking. The Labour Trilogy stated that freedom of association was a freedom held by the individual, and did not apply to activities that are purely collective in nature, such as collective bargaining. Under this reasoning, collective bargaining would not come within s.2(d) protection since it cannot be performed by an individual.

In 2007, the Supreme Court entirely reversed its interpretation of the freedom of association, explicitly and unanimously overruling the Labour Trilogy cases, in its *Health Services* decision. It held that s.2(d) does, in fact, provide protection to collective bargaining, although that protection is not unlimited: it does not guarantee a particular bargaining outcome, nor does it include a right to a particular model of labour relations or bargaining. Rather, it is a right to a general process of collective bargaining, and the type of interference that would breach s.2(d) protection would be that which substantially interferes with union members' ability to engage in meaningful negotiations.[95] The case did not decide whether strikes are protected by the freedom of association.

This decision establishes that employees have the right to unite, to present demands to government employers collectively, and to engage in discussions to try to achieve workplace-related goals. Both workers and government employers have a duty to bargain in good faith. This duty includes an obligation to meet, commit time to the process, engage in meaningful dialogue, exchange and explain positions, and to make reasonable effort to arrive at an acceptable contract. The duty does not oblige parties to reach a collective agreement or to accept any particular contractual provisions. The requirements of this duty are sensitive to urgent or emergency situations.

However, s.2(d) does not protect all aspects of collective bargaining. It protects only against "substantial interference" with associational activity. Two elements are relevant to whether action is substantial interference: (1) the importance of the matter to the collective bargaining process; and (2) whether it was imposed contrary to the duty of good faith negotiation.

The *Health Services* decision has broad public policy implications, and it will take some time before the full extent of the effect of this case on labour law is known. However it has the potential to do the following:

- limit legislated collective agreements;
- limit governments' use of back-to-work orders or to make these orders less intrusive in collective bargaining;
- lead to removing exclusions from labour legislation preventing certain workers, such as agricultural workers, from unionizing;
- revitalize the question of whether the freedom of association includes a right to strike; and
- broaden collective worker action beyond statutorily defined activities.

Human Rights and Equity Legislation

Human rights codes prohibit discrimination based on a set of proscribed grounds, generally including race, national or ethnic origin, colour, religion, age (see Exhibit 8.15), sex, marital status, disability, sexual orientation, and creed. Some, though not all, jurisdictions also prohibit discrimination based on grounds such as alcohol or drug addiction, nationality or citizenship, pregnancy and childbirth, criminal conviction, ancestry, political belief, civil status, language, source of income, social condition, or place of residence.[96]

It is not uncommon for workplace rules (either management rules or collective agreement terms) to negatively affect certain workers because of their personal characteristics, some of which may be proscribed grounds of discrimination. For instance, a rule making Saturday shifts mandatory, or a collective agreement provision preventing workers with lesser seniority from having Saturdays off, discriminates on the basis of religion against individuals whose faith observes a Saturday Sabbath.[97]

In the past, it was necessary to determine whether such a discriminatory rule constituted *direct* or *indirect discrimination* (sometimes called "adverse effect discrimination"). That is, was the rule directed at causing discrimination, or was that simply the effect of the rule. However, in 1999 the Supreme Court of Canada, in the *Meiorin* decision, set out a new approach for deciding whether a workplace rule or standard is defensible or must be struck down as discriminatory.[98] For the rule or standard to be upheld, the employer must prove that the rule or standard is a *bona fide occupational requirement* (BFOR) that

1. was adopted for a purpose that is rationally connected to performing the job;

2. was adopted in an honest and good faith belief that it was necessary to fulfill this legitimate work-related purpose; and

3. was reasonably necessary to accomplish that legitimate work-related purpose.

The SCC recently clarified that an employer need not prove that it is impossible to integrate an employee who does not meet such a rule or standard, but that to do so would subject the employer to undue hardship (called the *duty to accommodate*). This *duty to accommodate* "...ends where the employee is no longer able to fulfill the basic obligations associated with the employment for the foreseeable future" and the entire situation (not just the time of termination) must be assessed to determine whether the employer has fulfilled this duty.[99]

In the *Meiorin* case, Tawney Meiorin was a government forest firefighter who was terminated because she was unable to pass one part of a newly introduced physical fitness test. This was after Meiorin had worked in this job for three years, receiving good performance evaluations. The part of the test Meiorin failed was one that very few of even the fittest women would be able to pass. Meiorin complained that the test, which was applied the same to male and female firefighters, was discriminatory. The Supreme Court found unanimously in Meiorin's favour, holding that the test was discriminatory and could not be upheld because it did not meet the test set out above.

This duty to accommodate lies not only on the employer (to the point of undue hardship), but also on the union (to the point of "substituting discrimination against other employees for the discrimination suffered by the complainant").[100]

Exhibit 8.15
Mandatory Retirement

Treatment of mandatory retirement is an example of social and economic change causing a change in the treatment and perception of human rights in the workplace.

Though human rights codes prohibit discrimination on the basis of age, the codes in many jurisdictions contained an exception to this prohibition for workers over age 65. This exception meant that employer rules or collective agreement provisions for "mandatory retirement" at age 65 would not constitute discrimination and, therefore, would not violate the legislation.[101] A series of Supreme Court decisions upheld this exception. These cases arose during the 1980s and early 1990s, a time when there was a shortage of jobs, not workers, and there was concern about providing access to jobs for younger workers. Since then, Canada has seen a significant demographic shift with the proportion of older people rising and that of younger, working-age people shrinking. Instead of a surplus of workers, there is a shortage.

Beginning in 2006, many provinces amended their human rights legislation to remove the exception permitting mandatory retirement, so that employers can no longer require employees to retire after age 65 unless they are able to justify the mandatory retirement program as based on a BFOR.[102] This reversal began in 2001 when the Ontario Human Rights Commission released a policy document characterizing mandatory retirement as a form of workplace discrimination.[103]

One might consider whether this abrupt change in the approach to one type of discrimination was truly motivated by concerns about ending discrimination, or by economic concerns sharpened by a change in the labour market.[104]

Two other forms of equity legislation—pay equity and employment equity—can also affect negotiation, application, and interpretation of collective agreements. Pay equity is based on the principle that there should be equal pay for work of equal value, to ensure that jobs held by women are compensated equally with jobs of equal value traditionally held by males. Employment equity is meant to correct long-standing, systemic discrimination against particular groups such as women and racial minorities in hiring, retention, and promotion in the workplace. It requires that the gender and racial mix in the workplace resemble that of the outside community. Pay and employment equity can significantly affect collective agreement negotiations, especially where the unit contains little diversity, or includes occupations traditionally occupied by women.

Privacy

Privacy is another area of law regulating the workplace, and is becoming increasingly important as more Canadian jurisdictions pass privacy legislation. Labour, health and safety, human rights, and privacy law are each relevant to the workplace, with each regime reflecting different—and sometimes conflicting—values and policy objectives. Though these different rights do not "exist in compartments," when these differing regimes intersect on a particular issue, it can lead to uncertain outcomes.[105]

One situation in which this uncomfortable intersection is apparent is drug and alcohol testing in the workplace. Such testing often involves the collection and use of workers' personal information, which draws together health and safety law ensuring safe workplaces, labour law, and privacy and human rights law preserving human dignity.

While equality rights, human rights, and privacy law limit unnecessary intrusions on workers and have commonalities—"human dignity" is at the core of both equality and privacy rights[106]—they differ in terms of their scope of coverage and protection. For example, it is possible to give consent to waive privacy rights—including through employment contracts or collective agreements—but it is not possible to contract out of equality or human rights. Any such attempt will not be enforceable at law.[107]

Human rights protection may have a more limited scope than that of privacy protections, because, though it cannot be waived, it prohibits real or perceived discrimination only on certain grounds recognized in the legislation, and does not protect privacy interests.

Until recently, the strongest influence on cases of drug and alcohol testing has been human rights law, which regards drug or alcohol dependency as a physical or mental disability or handicap and, therefore, a prohibited ground of discrimination. Therefore, any discrimination based on this disability (such as refusing to hire, disciplining, or firing) must be justified as a BFOR (discussed in Exhibit 8.15). As a result of the limited scope of human rights protection, some individuals—such as casual drug or alcohol users—may not be protected from very intrusive testing because it does not constitute discrimination based on a real or perceived disability.

However, as the role of privacy law in the workplace grows, this will likely influence the limits of such testing in a different—and likely more restrictive—direction than human rights law.

CONCLUSION

Canadian labour law has developed from a relatively simple area of law, concentrated on labour relations statutes, into a complex and dynamic field informed by a large variety of statutes, legal principles, and the *Charter*. This presents an exciting challenge to industrial relations professionals and labour lawyers as they navigate the unionized workplace and its laws.

Questions

1. Is there a better alternative to card-check or mandatory vote procedures for determining whether there is sufficient support for a union to be certified?

2. Would it be more or less desirable to dispense with the preconditions to strikes and lock-outs, and with state intervention in negotiations, and simply let employers and unions use their economic power to either settle or fail to reach a collective agreement? Explain your choice.

3. Should political strikes fall within the definition of a "strike" in labour legislation?

Weblinks

Ontario Labour Relations Board:
www.olrb.gov.on.ca

The Canadian International Labour Network Site:
http://labour.ciln.mcmaster.ca/laws.html

National Labor Relations Board (U.S.):
www.nlrb.gov

National Labor Relations Act (U.S.):
www.nlrb.gov/about_us/overview/national_labor_relations_act.aspx

Canada Labour Code:
http://laws.justice.gc.ca/en/ShowDoc/cs/L-2///en?page=1

The Simsgroup (links to all federal and provincial administrative tribunals):
www.simsgroup.com/adminsearch.htm

Supreme Court of Canada:
www.scc-csc.gc.ca

Federal Labour Legislation Site:
www.hrsdc.gc.ca/en/lp/lo/fll/about-fll.shtml

Department of Justice Canada Pay Equity Review:
www.payequityreview.gc.ca

Canadian Human Rights Commission Pay Equity Submission:
www.chrc-ccdp.ca/legislation_policies/equitytaskforce-en.asp

Chapter 9

The Individual Employment Contract and Employment Legislation in Canada

Geoffrey England

Robert Dowling was a 54-year-old professional engineer who had worked for the City of Halifax for 25 years. In 1993 he was fired without notice or compensation, allegedly for fraudulently interfering with the tendering process on a waste removal contract. Dowling sued the city for wrongful dismissal. At his trial, the judge concluded that Dowling had not acted dishonestly such that summary dismissal without notice or wages was justified. But the judge found that Dowling had been seriously incompetent, warranting the imposition of a lesser penalty short of outright dismissal. The judge ruled that Dowling had been wrongfully dismissed but instead of awarding him compensation for two years' reasonable notice, as would normally have been the case, the judge reduced the notice period by six months to reflect Dowling's contributory fault, relying on the so-called "near cause" or "moderated damages" principle. The Nova Scotia Court of Appeal upheld this decision.

Mr. Dowling appealed to the Supreme Court of Canada. In 1998 the Supreme Court quashed the lower courts' decisions and directed the lower courts to award compensation without any reduction for contributory fault. The Court held that the "near cause" principle forms no part of the common law, so that a court must do one of two things: (1) award the full period of reasonable notice if it finds that the employee's misconduct falls short of the legal threshold of just cause for dismissal; or (2) reject the claim altogether if it finds that the employee's misconduct does cross the just cause threshold.[1]

The *Dowling* case shows both the strengths and weaknesses of the common law of unjust dismissal. From Dowling's point of view, he was compensated for 25 years of service to the City of Halifax and the recognition that at 54 years of age he would have some difficulty finding another job. But the case also reveals the inflexibility of the common law. There is no flexible middle ground that would allow a court to rule summary dismissal too harsh, yet recognize at the same time that Dowling bore some responsibility for his fate. Furthermore, under common law the courts refuse to reinstate wrongfully dismissed workers. This lack of flexibility contrasts with the position of unionized workers under collective agreements. Arbitrators almost always order reinstatement if there is no just cause for dismissal and have the authority to substitute a lesser penalty, such as an unpaid suspension, if the circumstances warrant. Are the different standards of industrial justice for unionized and nonunion employees justifiable?

This chapter is concerned with the laws governing job regulation between the individual employee and his or her employer in the nonunion sector. There are two cornerstones in the law governing the individual employment relationship: (1) the common law contract of employment; and (2) protective employment legislation such as labour standards acts, pension benefits acts, occupational health and safety acts, workers' compensation acts, and human rights acts.

General principles of contract law that operate in commercial relationships apply to the common-law contract of employment. These principles are designed to ensure that markets operate relatively freely according to the economic laws of supply and demand. While "freedom of contract" is eminently suitable for the purchase and sale of commodities and real estate, it ill fits the employment relationship where the subject matter is a human being. Most employers have considerably greater bargaining power than their employees, giving the principle of "freedom of contract" a hollow ring. In reality, the employer normally sets the terms and conditions of employment unilaterally, and the contract of employment becomes little more than a vehicle for confirming the employer's control over the employee. The employment relationship involves much more than an economic exchange of wages for labour, however. The psychological component of the bargain is critical for the employee, providing him or her with a sense of purpose and achievement in life, the opportunity for meaningful social interaction with others, and the chance to obtain status and satisfaction from a job well done. The risk clearly exists, therefore, that the principles of contract law will enable employers to exploit their bargaining superiority to the economic and psychological detriment of their employees.[2]

The golden thread in the historical evolution of employment contract law is the continual refashioning of the legal rules to reflect the changing standards of personnel management practice and changing societal views on how work relations should be organized. Court decisions of the 19th and earlier 20th centuries, which generally favoured the employer's interests over those of the employee, have been supplanted by ones emphasizing the importance of protecting the employee as the more vulnerable party

Photo 9.1

Robert McCall, KC (1849–1934) in his Court robes as a King's Counsel of the Bar of England and Wales. Drawing by "Spy" (Leslie Ward), published in *Vanity Fair* magazine, 1903, with the title "Ulsterman KC."

Source: Ulsterman KC (colour litho), Ward, Leslie Mathew (Spy) (1851–1922)/Private collection/ The Bridgeman Art Library

in the relationship. The shift in judicial attitudes has been gradual, spurred on by the human rights movement, the increased adoption by employers of high-performance work practices, and growing economic prosperity. Some courts, however, have cautioned that continuing to extend employee rights under the employment contract runs the risk of impairing the productive efficiency of employers, from which society as a whole benefits.[3] The future development of employment contract law will hinge on finding the appropriate balance between the sometimes (but not always) conflicting goals of enhancing employee rights and of enhancing employer productive efficiency (Arthurs, 2006: Chapters 2, 3, and 11).[4]

No matter how far the courts extend employee rights under the employment contract, the cost of civil litigation is usually beyond the pocket of all but the upper echelons of the labour market. For most nonunion workers, protective employment legislation, the second cornerstone of individual employment law, provides the only realistic means of enforcing their rights. Such legislation establishes an extensive range of irreducible rights and benefits, or a "statutory floor of rights," which the parties can improve, but not reduce, in their employment contract. Covering employment issues that range from minimum wage to discrimination and workplace safety, contractual provisions violating the legislation are void and unenforceable.[5] Accessibility is achieved by providing special administrative machinery in each statute designed to enable the employee to enforce his rights quickly, informally, and at low personal cost. Unfortunately, the processing of claims under some statutes, notably human rights acts, has proven to be extremely slow, and many employees are woefully ignorant of their legal rights.

WHO IS AN EMPLOYEE?

Not all workers enjoy the legal protections in question. Common-law contracts and protective-employment statutes apply only to those workers who meet the requirements for "employee" status. Our system assumes that business entrepreneurs will compete with each other without a social safety net for the ultimate betterment of society as a whole. Accordingly, the law distinguishes between independent contractors, who assume the risks of running their own businesses and who are excluded from employment law protections, and employees who are part and parcel of employers' businesses and who deserve protection. The test for "employee" status, therefore, boils down to asking whether, in all the circumstances of each case, the worker is running his or her own business as a going concern or is integrated into a business that his or her employer is running for the employer's profitability.[6] Some of the factors relevant in answering this question are set out in Exhibit 9.1.

The question of who is an employee is important as more Canadian companies replace their traditional permanent full-time group of employees with a contingent workforce in order to gain increased flexibility and avoid the costs imposed by employment contracts and protective legislation. So-called independent contractors account for the fastest-growing segment of the labour force and assume the risk of reporting for work only when required and can be released without any notice or severance pay. Some independent contractors unquestionably obtain benefits from such "non-employee" status—for example, they pay reduced levels of income tax, they do not have Employment Insurance and Canada Pension Plan contributions deducted from their paycheques, and they have the flexibility to work when they feel like it. Most such workers, however, do not resemble entrepreneurs running their own businesses; rather, they resemble regular employees who are especially vulnerable to those who use their services.[7]

> **Exhibit 9.1**
> **Determining Employee Status**
>
> ■ Does the worker have a significant capital investment in the tools, machinery, and equipment?
>
> ■ Who bears the risk of economic gains and losses?
>
> ■ Does the person work for one employer only?
>
> ■ Who decides when, where, and how the work is performed?
>
> ■ To the public, does the worker look like an owner or employee?
>
> ■ If there is a formal contract, does what it formally says correspond to the realities of the working relationship?

Accordingly, the traditional test for "employee" status, fashioned in an earlier era when employers undertook to provide regular, full-time work of indefinite duration, is being rethought.[8] It has been suggested that protective legislation be amended to include self-employed contractors who are substantially dependent on an employer for their livelihood, and in his 2006 report on the reform of the federal employment standards legislation, Harry Arthurs formally recommended that such "autonomous workers" be brought within the legislation.[9] Similar "dependent-contractor" provisions exist in the collective bargaining statutes of several jurisdictions that allow such workers to participate in the collective bargaining process. Common-law courts have begun to recognize a special status of "intermediate" workers who are not strictly speaking "employees" under the traditional tests, but whose position of economic subordination entitles them to many of the basic protections of the employment contract, including the right not to be dismissed without reasonable notice of termination.[10]

THE CONTRACT OF EMPLOYMENT

To form an employment contract, (1) an offer of employment must be made (usually by the employer), (2) the offer must be accepted (usually by the employee), and (3) the terms of the agreement must be sufficiently certain to enforce. An employment contract normally need not be in writing, and the vast majority are made orally. Whether oral or written, the terms of most employment contracts are implied with only the bare skeleton of the relationship expressly set out or discussed—the starting date, the wage rate, a brief description of the job, and possibly hours and vacations. The nature of the work relationship requires a high degree of imprecision in the employment contract because it is impossible to foresee all the adjustments that might have to be made as a result of economic, social, and technological changes during a possible working lifetime. To reduce some of the uncertainty, the European Economic Community introduced a directive in 1991 requiring employers to provide employees with written particulars of the main terms of employment, including notice of termination, seniority accrual, compensation, holidays and vacations, sick pay, and disciplinary procedures, and to update them as any amendments occur.[11] The *Arthurs Report* of 2006 (in its Chapter 5) recommended that this model be incorporated in the federal employment standards legislation, but so far no Canadian jurisdiction has adopted it.

The implied terms (i.e., those that are unspoken and unwritten) provide the flesh and blood of the contractual skeleton. Courts have fashioned a standardized set of rights and duties, which are implied in all employment contracts, notably in respect to reasonable notice of termination, fairness in handling dismissals and discipline, and protecting the employee's psychological status in the workplace. The contours of these implied rights and duties have been modified over time to reflect changing societal expectations of how work relations should be structured. These changes have mostly benefited employees. Even though the express terms of the contract can override these implied terms, courts usually interpret any express terms that limit an employee's implied rights strictly in favour of the employee. For example, even if express contract terms confer on the employer an absolute discretion to dismiss the employee, most courts in most provinces now imply a requirement that the discretion be exercised in good faith and fairly.

Implied Contractual Obligations of the Employee

The employee owes the employer an all-pervasive, residual obligation to further the employer's business interests, commonly referred to as the *implied duty of fidelity*. This duty originated in the employment contract of feudal England, in which the system of work relations expected the utmost loyalty of the "servant" (as the employee was then legally called) to his "master." It survived into the Industrial Revolution, providing the legal means for employers to extract total subordination of their workers to the new production techniques of the factory system.[12] Today, the duty of fidelity retains its distinctly "unitary" tone in that the employee continues to be bound to further the firm's interests, but modern courts have tempered the draconian rigour of the 19th- and early 20th-century precedents to reflect contemporary concerns with protecting the employee's personal dignity and autonomy, and economic security. The current law recognizes the legitimacy of the employee's personal interests and seeks to strike a balance between his or her interests and the interests of the employer.[13] The main elements of the duty of fidelity are set out in Exhibit 9.2.

Depending on the circumstances, failure by an employee to honour his or her duty of fidelity may be considered a breach of the employment contract, providing just cause for termination without any notice period, as well as giving rise to a damages action by the employer.

Exhibit 9.2
Employee's Duty of Fidelity to Employer

Duty of fidelity refers to the obligation to advance the employer's business interests; i.e., the employee must act in the best interests of the firm in carrying out his assigned duties, which include the following obligations:

- to obey the orders of the employer so long as they are lawful, reasonable, and within the scope of the employee's contractual duties;
- to attend the workplace at the appointed time—absenteeism and lateness are clearly in breach of the contract;
- not to act in a fraudulent, deceitful, or otherwise dishonest manner toward the employer;
- not to make a secret profit;
- not to compete with the employer's business while employed; and
- to perform work of a quality that meets the standards set by the employer.

Implied Contractual Obligations of the Employer

Changing managerial and social values have influenced the courts to rule that a relatively generous array of employee rights are implied within the employment contract. Indeed, these "residual" common-law rights under the employment contract—especially when combined with the constructive dismissal doctrine—arguably furnish the nonunion employee with greater inherent protections than the unionized employee enjoys under the "residual-rights" theory of collective agreement interpretation (see Chapter 11). Offsetting this advantage are the inferior remedies, costs, and delays of civil litigation compared with collective agreement arbitration.

The obligation to pay wages for work actually done Normally, the employer is not bound to provide actual working opportunities unless that is clearly bargained for by the employee, as is the case with stage performers, sports stars, and employees paid wholly on a commission basis. Accordingly, the employee is not entitled to layoff pay. On the other hand, the employer has no inherent right to impose a layoff in the absence of express or implied contractual provisions permitting such a measure. A layoff operates as a constructive dismissal, and the employee is entitled to quit and recover damages.[14]

The obligation to provide a reasonably safe workplace This duty exists under the tort of negligence as well as under the employment contract. The right to refuse unsafe work and to be compensated for injuries and illnesses derived from employment has largely been overtaken by health and safety and workers' compensation legislation,[15] but employees who fall outside these statutes retain their common-law rights. If an employee suffers psychological harm as a result of intimidation, harassment, or bullying by a supervisor or a fellow employee, this has been held to breach the duty to provide a reasonably safe workplace.[16] The employee may be precluded from suing the employer for damages for breach of this term, however, if the provincial workers' compensation legislation covers the psychological harm in question, since the workers' compensation acts prohibit an employee from launching a common-law action to recover compensation that is provided under the acts.

The implied obligation to provide the employee with job satisfaction In recent years, the courts have recognized that the psychological benefits derived from a job form a substantial component of the employment contract. Accordingly, some courts have ruled that an employer who deprives the employee of his or her job satisfaction by modifying his or her work duties commits a breach of contract entitling the employee to quit and sue for constructive dismissal. This development remains in its infancy. So far, it has been applied only in cases where job satisfaction clearly was of major importance to the employee in question. Also, no court as yet has awarded separate damages for loss of job satisfaction in a wrongful dismissal action.[17]

The implied obligation to treat the employee fairly   Prior to 1997, courts appeared to be on the cusp of implying an independent duty of fairness into all employment contracts that would apply to all facets of the employment relationship. However, in 1997 the Supreme Court of Canada in *Wallace v. United Grain Growers Ltd.*[18] held that there is no such independent duty, either in contract or tort law. The Court's reasoning echoes the concerns expressed by critics of an implied duty of fairness under collective-agreement arbitration, namely that the employer's flexibility would be hampered by the threat of constant litigation by aggrieved employees and that outside adjudicators would be making decisions about the pith and substance of business matters best left to professional managers. On the other hand, if the duty of fairness were given a purely procedural, rather than a substantive, meaning, the fear of second-guessing could be diminished, and the high costs of civil litigation would likely deter frivolous actions.

To date, the courts have taken a compromise approach of requiring employers to act professionally and in good faith in the limited context of dismissing workers. Exhibit 9.3 lists conduct that violates the duty placed on employers to act fairly during dismissal.[19]

**Exhibit 9.3
Violating the Duty of Fairness During Dismissal**

- Fabricating grounds for just cause and persevering with them until late in the litigation process, where the grounds seriously prejudice the employee's professional reputation or cause the employee serious financial and/or psychological harm.
- Acting in a procedurally unfair manner, e.g., failing to conduct fair and comprehensive investigations of alleged wrongdoing prior to invoking dismissal.
- Physically "turfing out" the employee from the workplace in a humiliating manner.
- Implementing dismissal at a time when the employee is psychologically vulnerable.
- Deliberately using "hardball" tactics in the litigation process to pressure the employee into dropping his lawsuit, e.g., withholding the employee's vested employment benefits.
- Deliberately seeking to harm the employee out of revenge, e.g., refusing to provide a fair reference or badmouthing the employee in the business community.

The reasonable notice period may be increased by several months on account of an unfairly handled discharge. Furthermore, several courts have held that an employee who resigns in response to unfair treatment can sue for constructive dismissal because of the employer's failure to treat the employee fairly and with dignity. This development clearly makes sense because it would be unduly harsh to expect an employee to withstand a course of unfair mistreatment until the employer resorts to dismissal before she can obtain a remedy.

Furthermore, many trial courts are making decisions that seem to be based on an independent implied duty of fairness, despite the obstacle created by the *Wallace* decision. Most of the cases involve constructive dismissal—unsurprisingly, since few workers would dare to sue their employer for damages while remaining employed. Examples of "unfair" treatment include failing to protect the employee against personal harassment, intimidation, and bullying; failing to provide the employee with sufficiently clear instructions; conducting performance appraisals in a demeaning, callous, and unprofessional manner; subjecting an employee to an impossibly over-demanding workload with inadequate resources to meet the targets; peremptorily refusing to reasonably accommodate an employee's request for work rescheduling to meet family obligations; and failing to assist an employee to learn how to operate new technology.

The obligation to give reasonable notice of termination The employer's implied duty to give reasonable notice of termination, or pay in lieu, is of pivotal importance because, in a common-law wrongful dismissal action, the amount of employee compensation is tied directly to the length of the notice period. The employee's damages are limited to the compensation and benefits he or she would have received over the notice period.[20]

The need to cushion the employee against the financial blow of unemployment The courts generally increase the notice period if the employee is likely to experience difficulty in finding replacement work due to the the state of the labour market; personal skills, qualifications, experience, or age; and the employer's conduct such as refusing to give a fair reference, or dismissing him or her in a manner that causes debilitating psychological harm. This factor, often referred to as the "cushion" theory, is normally given paramount weight. Indeed, notice periods up to, and sometimes even above, 24 months' duration are often awarded on this basis.[21] In the converse situation, where the employer is experiencing an economic downturn, the courts generally have not been prepared to reciprocate and reduce the notice period to help the employer weather the crisis. The approach, therefore, leans heavily in favour of employee rights.

The characteristics of the job Traditionally, courts have awarded a notice premium to employees in positions of high status and responsibility, presumably in order to offset some of the opportunity costs such employees incur in becoming educated.[22] The New Brunswick courts have rejected this approach as being non-egalitarian, that is, entrenching class distinctions. Nevertheless, in other provinces courts are extending the reasonable notice period even for relatively low-status workers, under the "cushion" theory.[23]

Unprofessional or bad faith conduct on the employer's part in handling the dismissal Since the landmark *Wallace* decision, the courts will award extra notice on account of such conduct, usually of between three and eight months' notice depending on the severity of the employer's actions.

The inducement factor The courts will lengthen the notice period if an employee has been induced to leave a secure, well-paid job to become employed with an employer and is shortly thereafter terminated.

Length of service Generally, the notice period increases with the employee's period of seniority with the employer. It is not always clear whether seniority is being rewarded for its intrinsic value, representing some sort of "proprietary" interest that the employee is supposed to have in his or her job, or because seniority is a proxy for age and, therefore, of re-employability.

Two other factors that many people believe to be relevant are not in fact serious considerations. The general rule of one month's notice for each year of service is an urban myth. The appeal courts in most provinces have refused to recognize any such rule. Second, the quality of the employee's prior service also is not a factor. The courts have declined to increase the notice period to reflect a good work record or, conversely, to decrease it where the employee is a poor performer; the Supreme Court of Canada has held, as we saw in the opening vignette, that it is inappropriate to reduce the notice period to reflect his contributory fault.[24] The Court reasoned that if dismissal does meet the legal threshold for "just cause," then legal theory dictates that the employee is entitled to no compensation, whereas if it does not, the employee should be entitled to full compensation.

Wrongful Dismissal at Common Law

An employer may dismiss a worker for three reasons: (1) where economic factors make it unprofitable to retain him or her; (2) where the employee commits misconduct or otherwise performs her duties unsatisfactorily; and (3) where economic and performance factors combine as the grounds for dismissal. If the employer is able to demonstrate just cause for the dismissal, no period of notice will be required and the employee receives no compensation. If the employer is unable to establish just cause, or chooses not to attempt to do so, the employee will be entitled to a period of notice based on the factors outlined in the previous section.

It is important to understand that even if there is no just cause established for dismissal, the employer still retains the common-law right of terminating the employment relationship. Virtually all wrongful dismissal lawsuits are about compensation and notice periods, not about whether the employee is entitled to keep his or her job. At common law, that question has been answered by the courts—an employee has no legal right to keep her job against the wishes of the employer.[25] The most an employee can get is money for being dismissed in a situation where the employer is unable to show just cause.

Economic Dismissals An employer can lawfully dismiss an employee for economic reasons only if the employee is given the requisite notice of termination, or pay in lieu, under the employment contract—in other words, "just cause" cannot be established for economic reasons alone. If the employment contract contains an express notice period, then this will prevail so long as it matches the statutory minimum notice period. In the absence of a valid express-notice clause, the courts will imply a reasonable notice period on the basis of the factors examined above, the most important being to cushion the employee against the blow of unemployment.

Constructive Dismissals Where the employer wishes to change the existing terms and conditions of employment for economic reasons but retain the employee on the payroll—for example by modifying the compensation structure, geographically relocating the employee, changing the employee's status from full-time to part-time, or modifying the employee's job duties or work schedule—the employer encounters the straitjacket of the constructive dismissal doctrine. The general principles of contract law dictate that a unilateral variation of any significant term in the contract by the employer constitutes a repudiatory breach entitling the employee to choose to quit and sue for damages.[26] The measure of damages is the employee's wages and other contractual entitlements over the contractual notice period. Clearly, the constructive dismissal doctrine seriously hampers the employer's flexibility to respond to changing business circumstances. In contrast, unionized employers have enormous flexibility to make such changes under most collective agreements by virtue of the management's residual-rights doctrine. Some commentators have suggested that the employer's freedom to effectively respond to changed economic circumstances is unduly hampered by excessive reasonable notice awards and a restrictive constructive dismissal doctrine, causing economic inefficiencies that prejudice society as a whole. They argue that employment standards legislation should be amended to relax the stringency of the common-law rules.[27]

Performance-Related Dismissals At common law, if an employee commits acts of misconduct or incompetence that are sufficiently serious, the employer is entitled to terminate the employment contract by dismissing the employee summarily without notice. The legal question that arises is whether the employer has "just cause" for summary dismissal. The current common-law standards of just cause are similar to those applied by collective agreement arbitrators, although some differences do exist.[28]

To meet the just-cause standard, an employer's decision to dismiss for performance deficiencies must be (1) rational, in the sense of furthering the firm's legitimate business goals; (2) made in good faith, non-arbitrarily and non-discriminatorily; and (3) proportional in the amount of harm the employee's conduct causes to the production process in the context of each case.[29] Summary dismissal is reserved for serious misconduct such as dishonesty, flagrant and deliberate insubordination, assaults on managers and other workers, sexual harassment, persistent lateness and absenteeism, abuse of the employer's trade secrets and confidential information, and gross incompetence that substantially damages production.

Even in these cases, dismissal is not automatically justified if there are mitigating circumstances or the deficiency is not seen as sufficiently serious by the court to justify termination without notice.[30] Furthermore, as under collective agreements, the employer is usually required to have first applied corrective measures prior to invoking dismissal. Typically, such measures include clear and unequivocal warnings to the employee (1) that his or her conduct is unacceptable; (2) of the exact ways in which his or her performance is unsatisfactory and what is needed to improve; and (3) that dismissal will ensue unless the employee, with assistance from the employer, meets the specified performance standards within a defined period of time. These measures can be dispensed with if the employee's attitude shows that he or she has no remedial potential or if the employee's conduct severely damages the enterprise.

Remedies The most glaring weakness of the common law of wrongful dismissal relates to remedies. Courts will not order the reinstatement of a wrongfully dismissed employee, save in exceptional circumstances. The most compelling rationale for this is the difficulty of supervising a reinstatement order in the absence of a union presence in the workplace.

Collective agreement arbitrators, in contrast, almost invariably reinstate an unjustly dismissed employee.

Nor will courts attempt to "make whole" the employee for being dismissed without just cause. Under common law the employee is compensated only for lost wages, benefits, and other expectancies during the notice period. For example, an employee who is dismissed at age 55 and will likely never again find replacement work is not entitled to compensation until normal retirement, say at 65. This means that the employee has to absorb the real-world losses caused by the dismissal—namely the lost wages, benefits, and opportunities that 10 years of work normally would be expected to bring.

As well, courts traditionally have been reluctant to compensate for psychological harm or injury to reputation. The wrongful dismissal action derives from the employer's failure to give the requisite notice of termination whereas psychological and reputational harm usually derive from the fact of being dismissed, not from technical non-compliance with the notice requirement. They are compensable only if the employer commits a separate actionable wrong, for example, a tort (civil offence) such as defamation or intentional infliction of nervous shock, or a breach of an independent term in the employment contract requiring the employer to treat the employee fairly.[31] In contrast, a "make whole" method would allow compensation for psychological and reputational harm caused by the fact and manner of dismissal.

Courts can award punitive damages to deter an employer whose mistreatment of the employee has been especially egregious. Recent decisions suggest that awards of punitive damages are becoming more frequent and larger than before. The most noteworthy example is *Keays v. Honda Canada Inc.*,[32] in which an Ontario trial judge awarded an employee $500 000 in punitive damages because of the employer's persistent, ruthless, and relentless efforts to frustrate the employee's attempts to have his disability accommodated according to his rights under the human rights act. Although the Court of Appeal reduced the amount to $100 000, the decision nonetheless sends a strong message to employers that egregious mistreatment of the employee will not be tolerated.

In sum, where the employee is dismissed for performance-related reasons, the common-law wrongful dismissal action loses "hands down" to arbitration in terms of the costs of pursuing a complaint and the remedies available. The substantive standards of just cause are roughly similar, with the notable exception of judges who apply a duty of fairness in dismissals. In cases of economic dismissals, an employee who can afford to pursue civil litigation may receive a substantial period of reasonable notice of between 12 and 24 months, especially if he or she is elderly, occupies a high-status position, or has a low chance of finding replacement work. Unionized workers rarely receive severance payments that are equally as generous under their collective agreements. As well, the nonunion worker has greater protection under the constructive dismissal doctrine than is enjoyed by his unionized counterpart. But the right to reinstatement is of such fundamental importance to most workers that any other advantages of the common-law system are overwhelmed by the absence of this remedial option.

PROTECTIVE EMPLOYMENT LEGISLATION

This section focuses on employment standards, human rights, occupational health and safety, and workers' compensation acts—core statutes that establish a "floor of rights" statute for all workers. (A plethora of other protective statutes exist to deal with specialized matters such as privacy, pensions, smoking in the workplace, and pay equity.[33]) Contracts of employment and collective agreements cannot contain less favourable terms, but are allowed to exceed the statutory minimums. Canada's statutory "floor of rights" matches and frequently exceeds the standards recommended by the International Labour Organization and North American Free Trade Agreement's Labour Side Agreement in most (but not all) areas.[34] NAFTA does not set a minimum standard that signatory states must meet; rather, it requires that each state have some domestic laws regarding each issue, that it actually enforce its domestic laws, and that it publicize them to other signatory states. The failure to establish a transnational minimum level of protections may be criticized as being too insipid, but the inescapable reality is that emerging countries regard such standards as a disguised form of protectionism for workers in the developed countries, designed to eliminate the developing countries' comparative advantage in lower wage costs. This reality will make it exceedingly difficult to negotiate transnational employment rights in free trade treaties.

Increasing competitive pressure on Canadian employers has caused governments to be cautious about further expansions to the "floor of rights" and has resulted in the repeal of some protections. In 2000, the Ontario government restructured its *Employment Standards Act* to reduce the costs to employers, and British Columbia followed in 2003. Many economists argue that the costs to employers of complying with generous employment protection legislation causes economic inefficiencies that worsen general societal conditions.[35] Others argue that legislating employee rights can result in efficiency gains for employers and improves general societal conditions.[36] Under these circumstances, one would expect governments to carefully weigh the economic costs and benefits before legislating employment rights, but in practice this often does not happen.[37] Instead, many employment rights are introduced in response to immediate political pressures.

A significant limitation on the power of governments to repeal employment rights is the *Charter of Rights and Freedoms*, especially section 15, which guarantees equal treatment under the law for disadvantaged groups such as women, visible minorities, and the disabled. If the repeal of an employment benefit would have a disproportionately harmful impact on a group protected under section 15, the government would have to discharge the burden of proving under section 1 of the *Charter* that the measure is a necessary and proportional response in a free and democratic society. In addition, any provision in a statute that disproportionately disadvantages a protected group is susceptible to challenge under section 15. For example, in the unjust dismissal scheme in Nova Scotia, the qualifying period of 10 years' continuous employment with the same employer arguably discriminates indirectly against women because the majority of short-term and casual jobs that do not qualify for protection are occupied by females. Similarly, the "domestic worker" exemption found in some employment standards acts arguably discriminates against women in breach of section 15 because most domestic servants are female.

The success of any employment protection statute depends on the efficacy of its enforcement and remedial machinery, for the most impressive body of substantive rights will be rendered meaningless if the statute cannot be enforced in practice.[38] All of the employment protection acts contain special administrative procedures that are designed to be accessible to employees in terms of cost and speed. However, these acts are notoriously difficult to enforce. Unfortunately, some violations are committed knowingly and deliberately by unethical employers who calculate that evading their legal obligations is more profitable than complying with them. Such employers frequently intimidate employees against claiming their entitlements, even though the protective legislation prohibits employers from dismissing or otherwise penalizing employees for exercising their statutory rights. In these cases, mediation by an investigation officer is normally fruitless, and complaints must be resolved by a formal tribunal hearing, a legally binding compliance order, or even a full-scale criminal prosecution. Possible suggestions for improving enforcement of the legislation include the following:

■ placing the initiative with employers proactively to establish and report defined standards of employment protection within their enterprise;

■ providing for an internal committee to monitor compliance (as is done with health and safety);

■ allowing private enforcement companies to compete with each other in acting as employee agents for a fee—this might be desirable for employees who need help in enforcing their statutory rights but do not want union representation;

■ assigning inspectors to track repeat violators;

■ substantially increasing fines; and

■ even imprisoning repeat or serious violators.

EMPLOYMENT STANDARDS ACTS

Employment standards acts attempt to draw a balance between, on the one hand, safeguarding the employee's personal dignity and autonomy in the workplace by establishing a set of irreducible substantive and procedural employment benefits and, on the other hand, ensuring that the cost of such benefits does not unduly impair the profitability of employers.[39] The role of trade unions in this process is complex. As advocates of social justice, trade unions like to champion the expansion of the statutory "floor of rights," but most unions realize that employees have a diminished incentive to unionize if the state provides them with decent protections through legislation. On the other hand, the Supreme Court of Canada has held that collective agreement arbitrators must consider employment standards and other protective legislation in their decisions.[40] Thus, the labour movement has indirectly benefited from strengthened employment standards.

Since employment standards legislation is a provincial responsibility, the specific details of employment standards acts can vary enormously from province to province, but certain rights are commonly provided in roughly similar form. These provisions are set out in Exhibit 9.4.

Not all provisions apply to all employees. The statutes contain exemptions designed to accommodate particular business circumstances or the nature of certain jobs. Maximum hours and overtime payment provisions are frequently made inapplicable to managers, taxi drivers, agricultural workers, and salespersons. In British Columbia and Ontario, the high-technology industry is exempted from certain provisions because of high start-up costs and intense work cycles.

A major advantage of Canada's constitutional devolution of power to the provinces in employment matters is that it permits experimentation. For example, part-time workers in Saskatchewan are entitled to participate in any insurance benefits such as medical, dental, and illness plans that are made available to full-time workers, on a pro-rated basis to take account of their reduced hours of work. In the federal jurisdiction, Nova Scotia, and Quebec, nonunion employees have the right to challenge their dismissal in front of a government-appointed and government-funded adjudicator who can award reinstatement and other "make whole" financial remedies.[41] Interestingly, when roughly similar unjust dismissal protection was enacted in Montana, it was found that the share prices of the companies affected by it increased in value, suggesting that investors anticipated that the result would be to increase the economic performance of the firms covered by the scheme.[42] The right not to be subjected to bullying and intimidation by the employer or by other employees was introduced into the *Quebec Labour Standards Act* in 2003, enshrining the principle that employers must exercise their power to eradicate harassment from the workplace.

Exhibit 9.4
Common Provisions in Employment Standards Acts

- Wage protection provisions including minimum wage, regularity of wage payments, wage statements and benefit records, wage deductions and assignment, and rights in the event of non-payment
- Hours of work including maximum daily or weekly work periods, overtime rate and eligibility, rest periods, and minimum call-in periods
- Annual paid vacations
- Statutory paid holidays
- Leaves of absence for specified purposes such as pregnancy, parenting, bereavement, voting, and family obligations
- Termination benefits such as minimum periods of notice (or pay in lieu) in individual terminations. When large groups of employees are terminated, additional notice periods are generally prescribed.
- Restrictions on the employment of children
- Gender-based wage discrimination prohibitions
- "No reprisal" against employees exercising their statutory rights

---

These innovations notwithstanding, it remains to be seen where the frontier of new employment standards rights will be set. While some rights may be expanding, the fierce competitive pressures of the global economy are leading to retrenchment elsewhere. The future contours of employment standards legislation are difficult to predict.

Human Rights Legislation

All Canadian provinces and the federal government have enacted comprehensive human rights legislation. Originally, the legislation outlawed only intentional discrimination where the employer penalizes an employee out of personal malice to his or her minority characteristics. This is referred to as "direct" discrimination. Modern human rights acts have extended discrimination to encompass situations where the operation of an ostensibly neutral work rule, practice, or policy has a disproportionately severe harm on certain employees (for example, disabled workers or members of certain religious groups); this is known as an "indirect" discrimination. Thus human rights legislation goes beyond applying the same rules to all people and enshrines the goal of guaranteeing all persons the right to "full participation" in the workforce.[43] There is little wonder, therefore, that this area of the law has produced intense public controversy.[44]

Discrimination is prohibited on 23 expressly protected grounds, depending on the province (listed in Exhibit 9.5). It is important to note that not all 23 grounds are listed in each of the 11 provincial and federal human rights acts, though the courts can "read in" grounds under section 15 of the *Charter* if the court concludes that the group in question has suffered a historical disadvantage. This was done in 1998 when the Supreme Court of Canada held that sexual orientation had to be "read in" to the Alberta statute.[45] In Ontario, the most frequent complaints relate to race/colour (23 percent), disability (23 percent), sex/pregnancy (16 percent), ethnic origin (13 percent), and age (7 percent).[46]

Exhibit 9.5
Prohibited Grounds of Discrimination in Federal and Provincial Human Rights Acts

- sex
- sexual orientation
- transgender
- race
- physical disability
- mental disability (interpreted to include alcoholism, drug dependency, and nicotine dependency)
- colour
- national origin
- ethnic origin
- religion

- pregnancy
- family status
- marital status
- age
- criminal convictions
- criminal charges
- ancestry
- political beliefs
- language
- place of origin
- source of income
- creed
- civil status

Human rights legislation contains broad "make whole" remedies to enable human rights tribunals to counteract the consequences of unlawful discrimination and to eliminate discriminatory practices from the workplace. Tribunals can issue orders that employees be reinstated, hired, or promoted; they can award compensation to restore any financial losses or psychological distress suffered by victims; they can award punitive damages in some jurisdictions;[47] and they can order the employer to adopt education and training programs to eliminate discriminatory attitudes. Furthermore, the tribunals are empowered to impose comprehensive affirmative action programs to eliminate systemic discrimination within an organization, which can include hiring and promotion targets for minority employees.[48]

These impressive substantive and remedial provisions have been undermined by the ponderously slow speed with which human rights complaints are processed through the often labyrinthine machinery of the human rights agencies. Delays of three years between filing the complaint and obtaining a decision by the human rights tribunal are commonplace. Typically, the complaints procedures require mediation by departmental officials and the consent of a human rights commission before they can be remitted to the tribunal. The complexity of human rights laws, the regular use of lawyers, the inadequate complement of departmental investigators, and bureaucratic procedures all combine to cause these delays.

A. Indirect Discrimination and the Duty to Accommodate The concept of indirect discrimination provides the biggest challenge in the context of the employment relationship. Its scope is enormously broad, capturing the entire spectrum of management decisions that may negatively affect a protected group in all areas of the production process.[49] Examples include alcohol and drug testing; pre-employment IQ tests, aptitude and integrity testing; physical performance testing; mandatory retirement policies; the application of seniority to employment benefits; the physical design of the tools, equipment, and workplace; assigning job duties; scheduling working hours; hiring; promotions; performance appraisal; discipline and dismissal; assigning leave of absence; and setting qualifications for entitlements under benefit schemes such as disability insurance plans. If an employer's decisions have the effect of disproportionately disadvantaging a protected employee, then indirect discrimination may be found.

In order to defend itself against a charge of direct or indirect discrimination, the employer carries the burden of proving that its decision, policy, or practice constitutes a bona fide occupational requirement (BFOR). The three elements of the BFOR defence are (1) the employer must genuinely and honestly believe that its decision, policy, or practice is reasonably necessary for the effective functioning of the enterprise; (2) the decision, policy, or practice when viewed objectively must be reasonably necessary for the effective functioning of the enterprise; and (3) the decision, policy, or practice adopted by the employer must minimally impair the employee's rights, and the employer must have attempted to accommodate within reason the employee's protected characteristics up to the point of causing an undue hardship to the production process.[50]

The duty to accommodate employees up to the point of undue hardship is of pivotal importance for it requires a balancing of the respective costs and benefits to the employee and the employer.[51] Suppose, for example, that an employee with a repetitive strain injury cannot satisfactorily perform his or her keyboarding functions. Rather than transfer the employee to a non-keyboarding position or dismiss him or her altogether, the employer might have to determine the cost of installing a voice-activated computer for the employee. Should the employer decide the cost is too high, and the employee claims discrimination, a human rights tribunal could scrutinize and possibly reverse the employer's decision. The key question would be whether the costs of accommodating the disabled employee amounted to "undue hardship" for the employer.

B. Sexual Harassment Modern human rights acts prohibit harassment of employees on a protected ground (e.g., race, religion). Sexual harassment has attracted the most attention because of the frequency of complaints, with the law distinguishing between two forms:[52]

- quid pro quo harassment, in which a superior expressly or implicitly promises to confer an employment benefit, or threatens to impose an employment-related penalty, in return for a sexual favour.

- poisoned-work atmosphere harassment, where sexual profanities, insults, and humour in the workplace cause the employee to suffer psychological distress.

Clearly, the two forms can occur simultaneously. There is a grey area between acceptable human banter and an unlawfully poisoned work environment that is difficult to define precisely.[53] If the work atmosphere has been poisoned for a long time in the past, an employee is not required to put up with it; rather, he or she can complain to the employer, who is bound to bring it to an end.[54] An employee will normally be expected to complain to the employer about harassment before the employer will be found liable.

The law places a heavy burden on the employer to eliminate harassment in the workplace.[55] Thus, the employer is expected to put a stop to any harassment of its employees committed by customers, suppliers, or other visitors to the worksite. The employer is made liable for any harassment committed by its managers, employees, or licensees at the worksite against an employee, subject only to the defence of due diligence. In order to prove due diligence, an employer must show that it has responded seriously and rapidly to eliminate any harassment as soon as it becomes aware of it, and must have introduced a sexual harassment policy into the workplace advising employees as to what conduct is not permissible and describing a procedure for making complaints to higher management.[56] If a supervisor or another employee is found to have committed sexual harassment, the employer is required to invoke discipline that may include dismissal in serious cases. The employer can even be found liable where the harassment occurs in non-working time away from the workplace, for example at a company-sponsored retreat after the day's work is over, provided that the souring effect of the perpetrator's conduct is likely to carry over into the workplace.[57] The strictness of the employer's burden is justified because it is the employer who has the power to create a harassment-free environment.[58]

The seriousness with which sexual harassment is regarded is also reflected in the unique provision in section 3(c) of the *Saskatchewan Occupational Health and Safety Act*, which expressly obliges the employer to ensure that its employees are not exposed to sexual harassment "insofar as is reasonably practicable." In other provinces, it is arguable that sexual harassment is implicitly covered by the health and safety acts. The main advantage is that the employee has a statutory right to refuse to perform unsafe or unhealthy work, and the enforcement machinery under health and safety legislation is much faster than under the human rights acts.

Health and Safety Legislation

All Canadian jurisdictions have legislation to prevent workplace accidents, illness, and disease. Defined standards for health and safety (e.g., permissible levels of asbestos, air quality, chemical labelling) are established by regulation in what has been called the "external" system for health and safety. An "internal" system, operating at the workplace level, provides joint management–labour committees and representatives to promote health and safety at the worksite. Workers' compensation legislation, which is primarily responsible for compensating injured and sick workers, also has a prevention role in that it imposes more onerous financial levies on employers with poor safety records.

A. The External System Two kinds of legal duty are established. The first compels employers to comply with detailed health and safety standards. A plethora of acts and regulations establish highly detailed safety rules, often geared to the circumstances of particular industries or occupations, relating to the work process; permissible chemicals and materials; the manufacture and use of equipment and machinery; on-site facilities such as toilets, medical care, and water; worker qualifications; and notification of hazards. These rules are normally based on the scientific recommendations of advisory agencies that have researched the relevant risks. Common criticisms of this "standards setting" approach are that the approach is slow to respond to technological advances, that general standards are difficult to apply to the unique facets of particular work processes, and that governments are too conservative in setting risk levels.

Second, the legislation imposes "performance duties" on employers and workers to promote health and safety. The employer is legally required to take every reasonable precaution to ensure the health and safety of its employees and all other workers present at the worksite. Because the employer has ultimate control over the production process, the law normally imposes specific duties on the employer to ensure

- that its employees and their supervisors have the requisite training in health and safety;
- that all equipment and machinery is properly maintained;
- that all protective equipment is being properly used; and
- that it co-operates with worker and government health and safety representatives.

Similar duties are imposed on employees and independent contractors entering the workplace. These performance duties do not create strict liability; they simply require that the parties take reasonable measures to ensure safety. In determining reasonableness, a balance is struck between the magnitude of the possible harm, the probability of the occurrence of an accident or illness, and the cost to the employer, employees, and other contractors of eradicating the potential hazard. Thus, the legislation implicitly accepts a certain risk level of accidents and injuries.

B. The Internal System All provinces have recognized that the external system must be augmented with an effective internal system through which employees and management at each workplace assume primary responsibility for dealing with their own unique health and safety issues. An effective internal system can be more cost-effective than a government-financed external system. The goals of the internal system are to identify actual and potential hazards, monitor the adequacy of existing safeguards, encourage all members of the firm to treat their health and safety responsibilities seriously, investigate accidents and injuries, and formulate proposals for improving health and safety.

Joint committees A workplace with a minimum number of employees, usually 20, must establish a joint health and safety committee consisting of equal numbers of management and employee representatives. Only Alberta and Prince Edward Island make the establishment of a committee discretionary unless ordered by the government. Arguably, the 20-employee trigger is set too high. In Nova Scotia, for example, it is estimated that only 10 percent of workplaces meet the 20-employee threshold.[60] The evidence shows that the presence of a joint committee dramatically reduces the level of workplace injuries.[61]

The committees' main tasks are processing complaints about health and safety, monitoring all facets of the production process to identify and minimize health and safety risks, educating and training employees and supervisors, and reporting health and safety violations to government inspectors. The legislation requires the employer to co-operate with the committee, and workers are entitled to receive pay for time spent on committee work. Typically, committees are empowered only to make recommendations, and the employer can decide whether or not to implement a recommendation. Nevertheless, if the employer proves to be intransigent, the committee can call a government investigator who is authorized to issue a stop work order or other directives to ensure the safety of the workplace.

Refusing unsafe work The right to refuse to perform hazardous work without fear of reprisal is clearly crucial to an effective internal responsibility system.[62] At common law, nonunion employees are implicitly entitled under their employment contracts to disobey orders that they honestly and reasonably believe to be unsafe,[63] but the absence of compulsory reinstatement and "make whole" financial remedies to counter employer retaliation render this right illusory. Unionized workers enjoy the equivalent right under the collective agreement as health and safety legislation entrenches the right to refuse in roughly equivalent form. The requirement of honesty means that the employee must be genuinely concerned with health and safety and not refuse for some ulterior purpose, such as winning a wage concession or getting back at a supervisor. The reasonableness requirement means that the average employee in similar circumstances—and these circumstances include any physical ailment such as a bad back or a heart condition—would conclude that an unacceptable degree of risk exists. It follows that if an assignment is subsequently proven to be safe, the refusal will nonetheless have been legally justifiable so long as it was "reasonable" at the time.

Hazard information The right of workers to be notified of health and safety hazards is established not only as part of the employer's general "performance duty" under the health and safety acts, but also, and more importantly, as part of the Workplace Hazardous Materials Information System (WHMIS). This is a national system for hazardous material identification and handling created as a result of extensive consultation between federal and provincial governments in the 1980s and contained in provincial WHMIS statutes based on the model established by federal legislation.[64]

The system has four main components. First, suppliers of designated "controlled products" must provide to employers "labels" and "material safety data sheets" that describe, among other things, the chemical identity of the product and the chemical composition of any ingredients reasonably believed by the supplier to be harmful. Suppliers must also describe safe handling procedures, risk descriptions, and the hazard symbol as per the designated hazard classification under the statutory regulations. This information is made available to employees. Second, employers are bound to make an assessment, according to the format required by the regulations, of whether or not any biological or chemical agent that is produced in the workplace is hazardous and to notify the workforce accordingly. Third, employers must provide workers and supervisors with a copy of the regulations. Fourth, a manufacturer can appeal to the federal Hazardous Materials Information Review Commission to exempt the disclosure of confidential business information, but even exempted information must be provided to a doctor upon request in a medical emergency, or to government officials administering safety laws.

C. Enforcement The legislation combines a blend of conciliatory and coercive enforcement techniques for, respectively, the unwitting violators and those that deliberately violate the law. Unfortunately, disobedience to health and safety laws is widespread. Enforcement is handled by government inspectors who investigate worksites either routinely or when alerted by a complaint or an accident report. Officers can issue stop work orders that require the employer to make the work safe before it can be resumed, with a right of appeal usually being provided to a higher authority within, or independent of, the department. A common criticism is that there are too few inspectors so renegade employers stand little risk of being caught, especially in nonunion organizations. As well, inspectors are sometimes reluctant to issue stop work orders with respect to sensitive managerial prerogatives or where costly capital expenditures are required.[65]

Although inspectors attempt to mediate settlements wherever possible, they can recommend that offenders be prosecuted. There are two models for prosecution in force, depending on the jurisdiction.[66] The first and most prevalent is to prosecute offenders in the regular criminal courts, and the second is to impose "administrative" penalties by a specialized health and safety tribunal. The main weakness of the first method is the difficulty of satisfying the criminal law burden of proving guilt beyond any reasonable doubt, whereas the main weaknesses of the second model are the reduced degree of social stigma and the lighter penalties of a finding of "administrative" as opposed to "criminal" guilt.

Ideally, administrative penalties should apply to run-of-the-mill violations, and criminal prosecution should apply to more serious ones. Criminal law charges such as murder or manslaughter can and have been brought against managers and directors of companies who allegedly have knowingly or recklessly caused injury to their workers.[67] This occurred, for example, following the explosion at the Westray coal mine in the early 1990s, but the charges were eventually withdrawn after a lengthy legal battle, showing how difficult it is to win such a prosecution.[68]

Workers' Compensation Legislation

The principal method for compensating victims who have been disabled by an accident or a disease "arising out of and in the course of employment" is workers' compensation legislation, which operates as an employer-funded insurance plan.[69] Under this legislation, an employee whose illness or accident arose "out of and in the course of employment" is entitled to receive a high proportion of her regular net earnings (varying by province) during the period of recovery. In return for this protection, an employee is precluded from suing the employer. The courts have held that this bar on common-law actions does not violate the *Charter*, at least so long as the statutory benefits remain reasonably similar to those available at common law. The legislation details the amount of compensation, and the system is administered by a statutory tribunal, the workers' compensation board.

The revenues for the workers' compensation system derive from a levy on employers. The amounts vary according to the accident and disease record in particular industries, so that employers in high-risk industries pay more than those in safer ones. Because this "collective" approach allows comparatively unsafe employers to take a free ride at the expense of the majority of safe employers in an industry, most provinces have complemented it with an individualized rating system wherein a single employer's premium can be reduced or increased according to that firm's own safety record. Individualized experience ratings run the risk of encouraging employers to contest more workers' compensation claims than they might otherwise do and to pressure sick employees to stay on the job instead of filing a claim.

One of the biggest challenges for workers' compensation, now and in the future, is establishing that an illness (as opposed to an injury) has arisen from employment. This can often involve difficult medical questions of causation, especially with diseases whose symptoms may not become apparent until years after contraction. As well, disentangling the work environment (exposure to small amounts of noxious fumes over many years) from the worker's personal lifestyle choices (smoking a pack of cigarettes a day) can be difficult if not impossible.

CONCLUSION

The common law of the employment contract has gradually been redesigned by the courts to provide nonunion employees with greater protections, notably in the area of wrongful dismissal, in response to growing public interest to safeguard individual rights in all walks of life. Nevertheless, the weakness of the common-law remedies and the prohibitive expense of civil litigation make these substantive rights illusory for most workers. There has also been an impressive enlargement of employee rights through legislation in human rights, employment standards, and health and safety. Again, a major weakness of the statutory "floor of rights" is enforcing the legislation.

The economic conditions that facilitated the conferral of seemingly endless employee rights in the post–World War II period began to change in the 1980s. The negotiation of trade agreements dramatically lowered trade tariffs and removed many of the protections enjoyed by Canadian companies, pressuring employers to reduce their labour costs in the face of international competition. Canadian governments, too, are under increasing pressure to reduce expenditures, which in turn threatens the role of the state in financing employment rights. Granting legal protections to employees can improve a firm's (and society's) economic efficiency and is morally and ethically proper in Canada's advanced industrial marketplace. There may come a point, however, when the pursuit of rights and efficiency will clash. Both courts and legislators will face difficult decisions in finding the right balance.

Questions

1. Has the expansion of employee rights under the contract of employment, the human rights acts, and the employment standards acts since the 1950s made it unnecessary for employees to unionize?

2. Is the test for "employee" status developed at common law and under legislation adequate in view of the proliferation of "atypical" work in the new economy?

3. Does the doctrine of constructive dismissal allow employers sufficient flexibility to adapt their employment policies to changing business circumstances?

4. What are the relative costs and benefits of notice of termination periods at common law and under employment standards acts?

5. Should the courts imply an across-the-board duty of fairness on employers under the employment contract?

6. Do the human rights acts' doctrines of indirect discrimination and the duty of reasonable accommodation unjustifiably interfere with managerial prerogatives?

7. Which protected grounds do you think should be either added to or deleted from those currently recognized in your province's human rights act?

8. Should statutory protection against unjust dismissal that includes the remedies of compulsory reinstatement and "make whole" compensation be legislated in all Canadian provinces that currently do not have it?

9. Should employees who are injured or contract a disease at work be allowed to sue their employers in a common-law action for tort instead of proceeding under the workers' compensation legislation?

10. In what ways could the current law be reformed to improve health and safety in the workplace?

11. Does the current statutory "floor of rights" strike a satisfactory balance between safeguarding employee rights and promoting economic efficiency?

Weblinks

Employment rights of Canadian employees:
http://www.workrights.ca

Canadian Charter of Rights and Freedoms:
http://laws.justice.gc.ca/en/charter

Employment standards:

For example:
Ontario—www.labour.gov.on.ca/english/es
British Columbia—www.labour.gov.bc.ca/esb
Nova Scotia—www.gov.ns.ca/lwd/employmentworkplaces

Unjust dismissal protection under the *Canada Labour Code*'s employment standards:
www1.servicecanada.gc.ca/en/labour/employment_standards/fls/research/research13/page02.shtml

Human rights commissions:

For example:
Alberta—www.albertahumanrights.ab.ca
Quebec—www.cdpdj.qc.ca/en/home.asp
Newfoundland and Labrador—www.justice.gov.nl.ca/hrc

Health and safety:

For example:
Saskatchewan (and select Occupational Health and Safety)—www.labour.gov.sk.ca/programs-services
Manitoba—www.gov.mb.ca/labour/safety
New Brunswick—www.whscc.nb.ca

Workplace Hazardous Materials Information System (WHMIS):
www.hc-sc.gc.ca/ewh-semt/occup-travail/whmis-simdut/index-eng.php

Workers' compensation:

For example:
Prince Edward Island—www.wcb.pe.ca
Yukon—www.wcb.yk.ca
Ontario—www.wsib.on.ca

Chapter 10
Collective Bargaining: Structure, Process, and Innovation

Richard Chaykowski[1]

This vignette presents examples of the bargaining process at Inco Ltd., an iconic Canadian nickel mining company.[2] In 2006, it was sold to Brazilian interests and has been renamed Vale Inco, but adversarial labour relations persist.

September 1, 1999: About 1100 unionized workers at Inco Ltd.'s Manitoba operations are livid over the company's concessionary package to settle two months of labour negotiations, a United Steelworkers of America spokesman said yesterday. With just more than two weeks before the current contract expires, the union, which represents the lion's share of the 1400 employees at Inco's operations in Thompson, MB, said no progress over pension and wage issues has been made. On September 8, union members voted 98 percent in favour of a strike mandate. But both sides are still talking. Inco's three-year deal with the union expires on September 15.

September 16, 1999: Hopes to avert a strike at Inco's Manitoba operations seemed futile yesterday as unionized workers began voting on the nickel giant's final contract offer. Results of Steelworkers Local 6166's were expected late last night, only hours before the union moved into a legal strike position at midnight. The bargaining committee unanimously recommended rejecting Inco's offer that would freeze wages for three years. "We're expecting the membership to turn down the final offer," said Steelworkers' Robert Desjarlais.

"We're still hoping membership will give [the offer] careful consideration," said Dan McSweeney, Inco spokesman. Nevertheless, the Toronto-based nickel company is prepared for the worst. "We have always required a contract to work. If the outcome of the vote is they've turned down the offer, then we will begin an orderly shutdown of operations," said McSweeney. Wages are at the centre of the dispute. Inco contends that belt-tightening is essential if the company is to remain competitive.

September 21, 1999: Inco said yesterday it had completed a shutdown of its Thompson MA operations, just days after locking out more than 1000 unionized workers in a dispute over wages. The company locked out its employees after 86 percent of Steelworkers' Local 6166 rejected the company's "final" offer.

September 28, 1999: Inco said yesterday that accepting the wage demands of more than 1000 locked-out workers would harm the future of its Thompson mining operations. "We have to make ourselves look attractive to raise this huge amount of money for capital investment. If we don't, the long-term future is not very bright for Thompson and its mining operation," said McSweeney.

October 3, 1999: As their longest labour-related shutdown since 1981 stretches to three weeks, both sides in the lockout are digging in for what could be a long fight. "We've got cabins built at all the picket lines, and they're insulated," said Desjarlais. "We're ready to take them on and our members are in for the long haul," he said. The Steelworkers are seeking a 6 percent pay hike over the next three years.

Inco originally sought wage and benefit reductions, but the company's last offer was a wage freeze with a profit-sharing plan if earnings soar. "The reality is that the union wants more money and they want it now," says McSweeney. "But we're seeking a long-term future in Thompson. We want to seize the future, not the moment." Desjarlais says massive cost-cutting has already been done in the past three years— and most of it on the backs of the workers. Nearly 400 jobs have been cut through attrition and layoffs since 1996.

October 9, 1999: Steelworkers launched an attack on Inco yesterday as a labour dispute entered a fourth week. The union accused the Toronto-based company of trying to take advantage of its workforce on the key issue of wages and pensions. The Steelworkers were particularly upset by Inco's insistence workers accept a three-year wage freeze. The demand, formally rejected by the union in September, set the stage for the company's lockout of the workers at the $1-billion operation.

October 15, 1999: Inco and the Steelworkers agreed yesterday to seek mediation to break a one-month labour dispute. They called for a Manitoba government mediator to enter the dispute after the two sides held another round of "exploratory talks" yesterday in Thompson.

December 10, 1999: More than 1000 workers were locked out in September after rejecting a three-year wage freeze and profit-sharing plan offered by the company [Inco]. But on Thursday, they voted 66 percent in favour of a return to work. The deal gives them almost everything they were asking for, a five-percent wage increase over three years and a 13-percent improvement in pensions. They had been looking for a six-percent raise. . . . A spokesperson for Inco says one of the concessions the company won is an agreement to work extended shifts at the surface plant. . . .

Inco bargains with different Steelworkers union locals, and both the union and management are very experienced at collective bargaining. Even in the most mature of bargaining relationships, however, there is the prospect that bargaining can break down and labour relations can be turbulent. For Inco and the Steelworkers, the summer of 2003 brought more difficulties:

Nickel producer Inco Ltd. and 3300 of its employees who work in its Sudbury mines and mills—and produce nine percent of the world's nickel—have walked off the job.

Sixty people were on picket lines Sunday morning at 10 of the company's 12 plants in the Sudbury area. Talks broke down late Saturday and no new negotiations are scheduled. . . .

The Steelworkers voted 94.9 percent to reject the company's offer on Friday.

"It's clear from talks today that the gulf between us is very wide and the union negotiators have failed to amend their position at all. We're miles apart at this point," [said] Scott McDonald, general manager of Inco's Ontario operations. . . .

> Local 6500 president John Fera said . . . the company should look at the union's vote and tell themselves, "Surely we made an error, let's get back to bargaining."

In October of 2006, Inco was bought by CVRD of Brazil. In early 2007, the new management quickly gained experience in Canadian labour relations when management and the staff employees of Steelworkers' Local 2020 failed to reach an agreement and went on strike. The negotiations process and outcomes had all the hallmarks of classic traditional labour relations and collective bargaining at Inco:

Local 2020 members, CVRD-Inco's office, and technical staff ratified a new, three-year collective agreement with the company, ending a two-day strike. Steelworkers' Ontario/Atlantic Director Wayne Fraser said the quick end to a strike by 330 members of Local 2020 was the result of strong solidarity among members of Local 2020 itself and Steelworkers Local 6500, production and maintenance workers at CVRD-INCO (now Vale Inco).

"The support offered by Local 6500 and their refusal to cross picket lines was key to ending this dispute quickly," said Fraser. "It is proof that preparation and solidarity work in a cynical age when employers think they can continue operating while trying to force workers to accept inferior conditions."

"It took a strike, but we look forward to a good working relationship" said Steelworkers Area Co-ordinator Dan O'Reilly. "At the same time, the company should never underestimate the power of solidarity."

Collective bargaining is a decision-making process through which union and management negotiators determine the terms and conditions of employment for a specific group of unionized workers. The results of the negotiations are set down in a contract (or collective agreement) that details what the parties have decided with respect to wages, benefits, hours of work, management rights, seniority, and the myriad other matters that may be discussed during bargaining (see Chapter 11 on the collective agreement). When major unions and employers are involved, collective bargaining can be a high-profile process that attracts a great deal of media attention. The public may be treated to the spectre of haggard negotiators putting together late-night final offers, followed by early morning "final final" offers, all amidst public posturing that may be intended to influence popular opinion and possibly garner broader support.

Negotiation processes are critical to the orderly resolution of important issues affecting people's working lives. Labour negotiations are often high-stakes situations because they pit workers' pay and working conditions against the labour cost structure of the firm and the degree of managerial authority. In a world that is increasingly globalized, the efforts of the parties to adapt the terms and conditions of employment to rapidly changing and often-adverse environmental conditions place extraordinary pressures on union and management negotiators around the bargaining table. But regardless of the initial demands of the parties, at the end of the day they must achieve an agreement if the enterprise is to continue.

The dynamics and development of negotiations are well illustrated in the opening vignette. Despite the long history of bargaining together, the negotiations between Inco and the Steelworkers remained quite challenging. The company's tabling of a tough set of demands to meet difficult economic conditions was resisted by the Steelworkers. The positions were far apart, and negotiations failed to reduce the gap sufficiently to avert strikes. In the end, the parties even tried mediation. Strikes impose costs on the parties that serve to bring them back into negotiations in order to close their deals. Globalization took on a new meaning at Inco, when in 2006 it was the object of high-stakes takeover bids by major international mining giants, including Phelps-Dodge, which were finally won by the Brazilian mining company CVRD. The new company negotiated a new collective agreement with Steelworkers in the Sudbury operations after a short strike. With new management positioning the company in a much larger, global corporate context, the future conduct of labour–management relations and collective bargaining remains uncertain.

This chapter analyzes collective bargaining to demonstrate why parties behave as they do and to reveal the less visible, but nonetheless important, processes that are carried out beneath the surface of negotiations. The first section considers the different structures of collective bargaining. The second deals with how the parties actually engage in collective bargaining and various bargaining approaches. An unsuccessful round of negotiations may be the consequence of poor union–management relations, culminating in a work stoppage. This can, and very often does, impose costs on the workers and firms involved, and sometimes on the broader public. In recognizing these *costs of disagreement*, both unions and management, as well as various governments, have sought ways in which to improve the likelihood that negotiations will be successfully concluded without a work stoppage. The use of alternative approaches to dispute resolution is increasingly prevalent, and these approaches are also considered in this chapter.

THE STRUCTURE OF COLLECTIVE BARGAINING

Bargaining structure is concerned with the number and diversity of unions and employers covered by the negotiation process. Some firms may bargain with only one union to obtain a collective agreement, whereas other firms may engage in collective bargaining with several different unions to obtain a separate collective agreement with each. There are many different bargaining configurations in Canada.

Collective bargaining is highly decentralized in Canada, with negotiations most often occurring between a single employer and a single union. Unlike the situation in Europe, a set of negotiations rarely covers employees in many companies across an entire industry or involves more than one union at a time. Six basic bargaining structures are used in ongoing practice. These structures are differentiated on the basis of (1) the number of *employers* involved (single vs. multi); (2) for single employers, the number of *establishments* involved (single vs. multi) where establishment is defined as a specific place of business; and (3) the number of unions involved (single vs. multi). Each of these six structures is set out in Table 10.1.

Structure is associated with bargaining power, the level of conflict, the types of issues that are negotiated, and the internal politics on each side of the negotiating table (Anderson, 1989). The bargaining process is difficult to evaluate without knowing to whom the collective agreement that is being negotiated will apply eventually. The 2004–2005 professional hockey lockout, an example of a multi-employer bargaining structure, is a case in point. An appreciation of this set of negotiations requires an understanding that each

Table 10.1 Bargaining Structures

STRUCTURE	DESCRIPTION	EXAMPLES	FREQUENCY
1. Single Employer—Single Establishment—Single Union	Localized negotiations at a single place of business or workplace.	Robin Hood Multi-Food and the United Food and Commercial Workers (UFCW) at its plant in Saskatoon; Carleton University and its faculty association; Dominion Textile and most Quebec plants represented by the Fédération canadienne des travailleurs du textile.	Most prevalent
2. Single Employer—Multi-Establishment—Single Union	Negotiation of a common collective agreement across several workplaces by the same employer and union. Makes a great deal of sense where the employer runs an integrated operation across many similar establishments. Efficient for both union and management negotiators.	Characteristic of public-service bargaining, e.g., between the Public Service Alliance of Canada and the federal government; telecommunications where, for example, New Brunswick Telephone negotiates a province-wide agreement with technicians represented by the Communications, Energy and Paperworkers Union; retail food industry, where the norm is a regional contract for each of the major supermarket chains and the dominant union, usually the UFCW.	Widespread
3. Single Employer—Single Establishment—Multi-Union	Negotiating partnership between two or more different unions within the same establishment. This situation might arise, for example, if production workers, represented by an industrial union, negotiated together with maintenance workers, represented by a craft union, or where a number of small craft unions join forces.	Pacific Press of Vancouver and the Joint Council of Newspaper Unions.	Rare
4. Single Employer—Multi-Establishment—Multi-Union	Most likely in industries characterized by a few very large employers and a number of small craft unions. Coalitions of different operating unions typically negotiate as a group with each major company. Negotiations take place across the entire company's operations.	Many different unions that represent workers across Canada at Canadian Pacific may bargain together (although recently the Teamsters has brought together many disparate unions under its banner).	Rare except for railways
5. Multi-Employer—Multi-Establishment—Single Union	Coalition of employers bargaining as a group with a dominant industrial or occupational union.	Found in a number of major industries, e.g., health care, construction, forestry, and garment manufacturing. In trucking, the Teamsters negotiate a series of regional contracts with associations of transportation companies. British Columbia forestry companies had a tradition of jointly negotiating regional contracts with the Woodworkers Union through an employer bargaining organization, Forest Industrial Relations (FIR).	Less frequent

STRUCTURE	DESCRIPTION	EXAMPLES	FREQUENCY
6. Multi-Employer—Multi-Establishment—Multi-Union	Most centralized form of bargaining. Involves coalitions of unions and employers at a single negotiating table. Restricted almost exclusively to construction industry negotiations where it has usually been introduced only through government pressure following difficult labour disputes.	This extremely centralized structure has been used at various times in Quebec, Alberta, and British Columbia (Rose, 1992).	Rare

team involved separate employers operating in two countries, each with different operating costs, financial resources, and philosophies. Each hockey team in Canada is subject to the labour relations laws of its own province, and American teams are answerable to U.S. national jurisdiction. Thus, the orchestration of the lockout and the conduct of the parties during the negotiations were extraordinarily complex. In contrast, bargaining with a single employer is usually simpler.

The labour laws of each province contain enough differences to make bargaining across provincial borders very difficult. Union organizing and bargaining unit determination occur worksite by worksite, and often competing unions represent workers in the same industry or occupation, creating a fragmented patchwork of certification arrangements. On a historical basis, the composition and scope of original bargaining units have reflected union attempts to separately organize craft (skilled trades) workers, production workers, and office staff at a given workplace. Labour relations boards have been reluctant to tamper with long-standing industry practices or to require that new bargaining units span more than one establishment or employer for fear of discouraging unionization. Taken together, these factors have produced one of the most decentralized bargaining systems in the world.

There are a few variations to the six basic bargaining structures in Table 10.1. The most important variation is found in situations where multi-establishment negotiations (either single or multi-employer) are combined with single-establishment negotiations. This has been a popular form of bargaining in automobile manufacturing, forestry, hospitals, and some provincial civil services. Under this arrangement, a master collective agreement is usually negotiated first at a central bargaining table. Following completion of the centralized bargaining, further negotiations then take place over local issues on an individual-establishment basis. In the automobile industry, however, local and master negotiations may have taken place simultaneously (Kumar and Meltz, 1992).

Another interesting variation occurred in the western Canada beer industry during the 1970s and 1980s. While bargaining was formally between single employers and a single union on a multi-establishment basis, the three major brewers (Molson, Labatt, and Carling) agreed among themselves to resist certain proposals made by the union. It was feared that if one of the employers conceded to the union demands, the other two employers would have little choice but to do the same. The three companies were able to time their individual negotiations such that all three collective agreements expired at the same time and had agreed that a strike against one company would produce an industry shutdown. This prevented the union from playing one company off against the others by threatening a strike that would jeopardize only the struck company's market share, a tactic that had proved very successful in the past. The employers' approach converted the bargaining structure, for practical purposes, from a single into a multi-employer one, greatly enhancing employer bargaining power. Of course, the rise of small brewers and merger activity has led to a change in this bargaining structure. This historic example illustrates why structure can be such an important ingredient in the bargaining process.

Pattern Bargaining

The outcome of negotiated settlements often exercises an indirect influence on others. Thus, any discussion of bargaining structure needs to assess not only those to whom the negotiations formally apply, but also the spillover effect. Pattern bargaining can be defined as a situation in which a key bargaining settlement sets the standard for other settlements. It was especially practised from 1950 to 1980.

Arthur Ross (1948) explained why wage gains in one set of negotiations can influence the outcomes in another. Ross referred to the range of influence of major settlements on other negotiations as an "orbit of coercive comparison."

Comparisons become coercive in the determination of wages in the following types of settings (Ross, 1948): (1) when several locals of a single international union centralize their wage policies and consolidate their strategies; (2) when separate industrial establishments are brought under common ownership; (3) when the state plays an increasingly active role in setting rates of pay; (4) when rival unions compete with one another for jurisdiction; (5) when related unions negotiate together for mutual protection, and (6) when employers organize into associations to preserve a common front.

For unions, the patterning enhances their ability to "take wages out of competition" (see Chapter 2). To varying degrees, the patterning of settlements has occurred in major industries such as steel, mining, and autos. In meat-packing, the major firms and the union actually engaged in centralized or national bargaining that led to standardized wages and contract clauses for a number of years (Forrest, 1989). Unions struggled to meet their objectives by establishing a national pattern.

By the 1980s, firms were confronted by a variety of internal and external pressures, including increased competition, the rapid diffusion of advanced technologies, and deregulation and privatization initiatives, which generated increasing diversity in business and employment conditions across establishments (Chaykowski and Verma, 1992; Verma and Chaykowski, 1999). Pattern and centralized bargaining in many industries broke down as firms pressured unions to accept wages, concessions, or various pay-for-performance systems that are more closely tied to local circumstances at the establishment level. Moreover, as economic globalization accelerates into the 21st century, and some firms may (re)locate internationally, the relevant comparison for a settlement in one country may, increasingly, be another settlement around the globe, making union enforcement of pattern bargaining more difficult. In traditionally unionized industries in Canada, such as pulp and paper, auto parts manufacturing, or automobile assembly, globalization is challenging the ability of unions to set patterns.

The negotiation of collective agreements in the Canadian auto industry has remained an important exception to the decline of pattern bargaining, although it is being challenged here, as well, by international competition and the increasingly precarious financial position of the U.S. automakers. Each of the Big Three automakers negotiates separately with the Canadian Auto Workers (CAW). But each firm negotiates a national master agreement covering major items such as wages, shift premiums, the grievance and arbitration mechanism, and hours of work, and which covers all bargaining units at that firm. Then, for each bargaining unit, the firm also negotiates a local agreement that includes establishment-specific items related to issues such as seniority, layoff and recall rules, and wage scales for various job classifications. The CAW typically targets one firm with which to bargain first; the settlement achieved is then intended to serve as a pattern for negotiations with the remaining firms (Kumar and Meltz, 1992).

In 1999, the CAW took this a step further by attempting to extend its influence into the largely nonunion auto parts manufacturing sector, which it had been trying, unsuccessfully, to organize. The CAW tried to negotiate an understanding with General Motors (GM) that would in essence have required GM to pressure its major (nonunion) parts manufacturer (Magna) to accept unionization. While unsuccessful, this would have allowed the CAW to extend patterning into the parts sector and hence to further "take wages out of competition." On October 15, 2007, Buzz Hargrove, President of the CAW, and Frank Stronach, Chairman of the Board of Magna International Inc., concluded an unprecedented "Framework of Fairness" agreement that provides a mechanism by which some Magna production employees can vote to decide upon representation by the CAW and the establishment of an employment contract, and a structure for the conduct of labour–management relations. Exhibit 10.1 provides a description of the new framework agreement that would cover about 18 000 Magna employees in Ontario (also see the vignette at the beginning of Chapter 2). Aside from skepticism about whether or not the new agreement provides for substantive worker representation, or even a first step toward the establishment of formal collective bargaining, in an increasingly globalized parts manufacturing industry the agreement may not be a step towards "taking wages out of competition."

Exhibit 10.1
News Release for CAW National Distribution

OCTOBER 15, 2007

CAW and Magna Sign Framework of Fairness, Usher in New Labour Relationship (Aurora)—Frank Stronach, Chairman of the Board of Magna International Inc., and Buzz Hargrove, President of the Canadian Auto Workers, signed a historic agreement in Toronto today that will usher in a new relationship between Canada's largest automotive employer and Canada's largest private sector union.

The agreement, called the Framework of Fairness, will allow Magna employees to participate in secret-ballot votes regarding membership in the CAW. It also establishes an innovative new structure for labour relations involving workplace elections and referenda; a multi-faceted dispute settlement process [including a no-strike pledge by the union]; and the use of final-offer arbitration instead of work stoppages to settle contract disputes.

The Framework of Fairness is not a collective agreement. It is a set of principles that will govern the process whereby Magna workers vote on union membership, negotiate and approve their contract, and resolve concerns.

Magna employees at each plant will have the chance to vote (in secret-ballot elections supervised by independent officials) on whether to approve a new contract and join the CAW. If a majority of workers in a facility support CAW membership, then that plant will be covered by a new CAW–Magna national collective agreement, and its employees will join the CAW. The national contract, CAW membership, and subsequent changes negotiated to that national contract must all be approved by Magna employees through secret-ballot votes.

Once fully implemented, the Framework would cover up to 18 000 Magna production employees working in about 45 manufacturing facilities in Ontario.

Source: "Framework of Fairness" from *News Release for CAW National Distribution* excerpted from CAW News Release accessed at: www.caw.ca/campaigns&issues/ongoingcampaigns/magna/pdf/newsrelease.pdf. Copyright © 2007 CAW. Reprinted by permission of CAW.

Further Decentralization

The pressures that led to the decline of pattern bargaining had a similar impact on bargaining structure. Though Canadian collective bargaining already is concentrated at the single-employer, single-union level, the few centralized arrangements in place came under substantial pressure beginning in the 1980s. As a result, long-standing centralized bargaining structures in meat-packing, forestry, and textiles were either abandoned or weakened, almost always at the employers' initiative. Pressures for decentralization also emerged in the public sector.

Changes in corporate and regulatory structures partially explain this trend. For example, deregulation and divestiture of rail lines, privatization of government services, and restructuring in both the private and public sectors have created a number of new, smaller firms.

These trends are not unique to Canada. Many other countries have experienced pressures toward more decentralized collective bargaining, though few started with the degree of decentralization found in this country. Katz (1993: 13) puts forward three explanations for emerging international trends toward the decentralization of bargaining:

> . . . decentralization results from shifts in bargaining power, the spread of new work organization that puts a premium on flexibility and employee participation, and a decentralization of corporate structure and diversification of worker preferences.

International evidence supports the conclusion that the first two factors have played a role in decentralization, but that the role of the third factor is probably not substantial (Katz, 1993: 16–17). At the same time as decentralization has accelerated, many unions have tried to counter this development—one that weakens their bargaining power—by merging with other unions.

MODEL OF THE COLLECTIVE BARGAINING PROCESS

Once a bargaining unit has been established and a union has been certified as the exclusive representative of the employees in the unit, collective bargaining becomes the means by which the terms and conditions of the employment contract are established (Bacharach and Lawler, 1981). Although many issues and objectives are initially brought to the negotiating table by both union and management negotiators, the negotiation process typically results in a set of agreed-upon outcomes that may differ quite substantially from the original objectives of either party. Figure 10.1 presents a conceptual framework of the determinants of the outcomes of collective bargaining that identifies the linkages between the goals and power of the union and management, the process of negotiating a contract, and the outcomes of collective bargaining. (Of course, the collective agreement is the formal outcome of the bargaining process, but there are many informal outcomes, such as the tone of the union–management relationship.)

The formal *outcomes* of the process of collective bargaining are specified in the clauses of the collective bargaining agreement (refer to Chapter 11). The specific outcomes of collective bargaining that are determined through the negotiation process in turn depend upon the *goals* of the union and management, the *power* that the parties have to achieve their desired objectives, and the statutory requirements that may constrain the bargaining process. The bargaining goals of the union and management are determined by their respective preferences for alternative bargaining outcomes (path A2 of Figure 10.1); the preferences of the parties are in turn determined by a variety of environmental, socio-demographic, and organizational characteristics (path A1 of Figure 10.1). While the relative power of the parties is also determined by various environmental, socio-

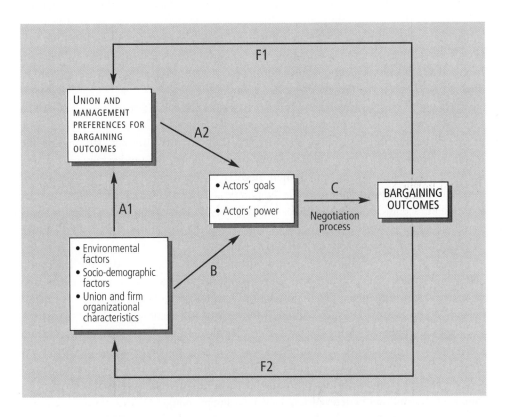

Figure 10.1 Determinants of Collective Bargaining Outcomes

Source: Chaykowski, 1990, p. 330, Figure 1. This figure is an extension of Delaney and Sockell, 1989, p. 571, Figure 1.

demographic, and organizational characteristics (path B of Figure 10.1), it is affected by the dynamics of the negotiation process as well. The *negotiation process* (relationship C of Figure 10.1) links the goals and power of both the union and management on the one hand, and the outcomes of collective bargaining on the other hand, and accounts for why the initial objectives of the union and management tend to differ from the results achieved.

Figure 10.1 depicts a rather linear, static framework in order to emphasize the basic relationships at work and to guide the following discussion of the bargaining model. However, the following examination of each of the components of the model will also reveal the complex manner in which they are interrelated and how their effects may change over time.

Union and Management Bargaining Goals

The priority that management and the union attach to each issue typically reflects the goals and objectives of the firm and the membership, respectively. In practice, both the union and management negotiating teams will determine *target* and *resistance* points for each issue they will bargain over in advance of any negotiations. For example, in negotiating over wages, the target point is essentially the most preferred outcome (typically, for the union, a larger wage increase than what management is willing to give), whereas the resistance point is generally taken to be an outcome that constitutes the lowest acceptable (wage) offer to the union and the highest acceptable (wage) offer to management. Wage offers not within the range could create an impasse in negotiations and possibly lead to a work stoppage. In the opening vignette involving the 1999 negotiations between Inco and the Steelworkers, Inco's initial demand for wage and benefit reductions seems to have been far below the union's resistance point.

When a collective agreement expires, and union and management must negotiate a new agreement, it is important to appreciate that the *whole* agreement expires. The process of establishing bargaining objectives typically involves initially determining the major issues over which each side (union and management) has unique concerns. Then, for each issue, the union and management negotiating teams must determine the range of acceptable outcomes for their membership and senior management, respectively, in order to formulate specific positions at the bargaining table. Consultation with each party's various constituent groups helps garner approval of both the bargaining issues and the range of acceptable outcomes associated with each issue.

Since unions are essentially political organizations in the sense that the leadership and policies of the union are democratically determined, the membership can be expected to have a direct influence on bargaining priorities. However, the precise degree of membership involvement varies across unions. Most unions will accumulate a list of future bargaining issues that arise during the term of an existing contract (e.g., emerging health and safety issues). In addition, as the end of the contract and beginning of negotiations approach, unions typically canvass the membership (likely through surveys or meetings) to elicit the views and priorities of the membership. Exhibit 10.2 illustrates the process that the CAW follows in determining its bargaining agenda.

On the management side, the goals and priorities of the bargaining team usually are an outgrowth of the short- and long-term business strategy and would conform to the goals identified by senior management. For example, a firm that embarks upon a strategy of becoming more competitive by improving product quality as well as productivity may decide that it wants to invest in new production technologies. However, the new technology may be expected to require increased flexibility with regard to work rules or job descriptions already stipulated in the collective agreement; therefore obtaining increased flexibility could form the basis of a management bargaining priority.

Exhibit 10.2
The Development of the Canadian Auto Workers' Bargaining Agenda

The CAW does not use a "master contract"; instead, it generally negotiates separate contracts with each company. It may, however, examine contracts in somewhat similar workplaces to see what it can learn from them.

Before collective bargaining actually begins, the union develops proposals during meetings that are open to all members of the local bargaining unit. Then a meeting is called during which each member has an opportunity to vote on the proposals that have been developed for each issue (e.g., wage demands). In addition, the membership would typically elect a bargaining committee from among the members, which would represent them during negotiations. This process allows the CAW to work with the members of the local bargaining unit to develop the set of issues and proposals that will be brought forward to the company at the bargaining table.

During negotiations with the company, other meetings are held (on an "as needed" basis) to vote on offers made by the company. The CAW stresses to each member: "*You have the final say on whether or not the proposed contract is acceptable.*"

Source: Adapted from *CAW/TCA Canada*, "Organize Canada—CAW Fact Sheet 1: Questions and Answers about CAW," www.caw.ca (December 1999).

The *goals* of management and unions may cover the full range of issues of concern to employees and managers in the workplace. Both parties are typically interested in negotiating over goals that eventually become transformed through bargaining into the contents of the collective agreement (listed in Chapter 11's Exhibit 11.3).

For a particular issue, both the union and the firm will attempt to achieve their most preferred outcomes. In some cases, the interests of management and union are likely to be directly opposed (e.g., on wages). If gains to one party in turn imply that less is available for the other, then the issue is referred to as being *distributive* in nature. For example, wage increases are a good example of a distributive issue: All else being equal, providing more of a firm's earnings to employees as wages implies that the firm then has fewer resources to distribute to the stockholders as dividends or to use for other purposes such as expansion of facilities, modernization, or managerial compensation.

In other areas, the interests of the union and management may have significant elements in common, so that providing more of the outcome will increase the well-being of both the union and management. These types of issues are referred to as *integrative*. For example, establishing joint union–management committees to examine work reorganization that is aimed at increasing productivity could benefit both parties if they agree to share any gains in productivity. Alternatively, expenditures that improve workplace health and safety could benefit both workers (directly) and the firm (by lowering accident rates and thereby lowering assessments under the workers' compensation insurance program).[3]

The goals of the union and management are shaped by a variety of influences, including environmental factors, socio-demographic factors, and organizational characteristics. Environmental factors may include the state of the economy, changes in the technology of production, or recent contract settlements in comparable workplaces. Economic factors include macroeconomic influences such as inflation, changes in economic growth, or a high Canadian dollar relative to the U.S. dollar. Inflation is an example of a macroeconomic influence that affects union goals. In periods of rapid and prolonged inflation, the union may seek a cost-of-living adjustment (COLA) clause that provides wage adjustments based upon increases in the Consumer Price Index. A high Canadian dollar would make it more difficult for Canadian firms to set product prices that remain competitive with international rivals. This might induce management to try to restrain wage increases, just as it might cause unions to fear job loss and hence negotiate hard for job protections.

The introduction of new technology may affect productivity, unit production costs, product quality, workplace safety or ergonomics, the pace of work, job skills and training requirements, or the number of workers required. For example, introducing a new technology that permits the same level of output but with higher product quality using fewer, more highly skilled workers may be viewed by management as necessary if the firm is to successfully compete in international markets; but it may also induce the union to bargain for severance packages for employees who are laid off as a result of the new technology. Alternatively, the union could seek rules governing transfer rights for displaced workers, or bargain for union involvement in worker training programs.

Socio-demographic factors may include the age or gender composition of the collective bargaining unit. These workforce socio-demographic characteristics may be systematically associated with preferences for certain types of employment outcomes. Consequently, the union leadership may attempt to formulate bargaining goals that incorporate these specific preferences. For example, if the average age of a particular workforce is high, then workers may (on average) prefer enhanced pensions or strong seniority rules governing promotions and transfers—relative to another workforce with a much lower average age. Alternatively, all else being equal, a workforce with a high proportion of females may (on average) express greater preferences for family-related benefits, such as maternity and paternity leaves, child care facilities, and workplace anti-discrimination programs. As Chapter 4 documented, recently union density among women actually exceeded that among men—recall that the numerical strength of the union movement is in the public sector, where the employment of women is particularly high.

Many private-sector unions were, at first, slow to organize women, in part because they were situated primarily in industries that tended to employ males (such as forestry, mining, rail, and many manufacturing industries such as autos). Unions began to more actively change in the 1970s and 1980s, in part because they recognized that, if they are to expand (or in some cases maintain) their membership levels, they must organize women workers; another reason for the change has been the increasing focus of major unions on organizing workers in the service industries in which many women tend to be employed. As the number of female union members has grown considerably, unions have had to work hard to transform the traditional operation of the union organization and the bargaining goals of the union to meet the needs and goals of women workers. One union that has risen to this challenge is the Canadian Auto Workers. As Exhibit 10.3 illustrates, the CAW leadership recognizes that women workers may have some priorities that go beyond traditional CAW objectives.

Finally, the characteristics of the firm or union can affect their respective bargaining objectives. Changes in business strategy and management goals are also crucially important to bargaining objectives. For example, the employee involvement movement really took off (at least, rhetorically) throughout the 1980s and 1990s. Management became especially interested in flexibility in the deployment of workers, devolution of authority from supervisors to workers, and altered production methods (and hence work organization and job content). These bargaining objectives typically involved negotiating changes to well-established workplace rules and practices (Verma and Chaykowski, 1999). Bargaining with the union may therefore involve the manner and conditions under which the union will participate in—and, indeed, support—the establishment of new workplace structures.

Importantly, as Figure 10.1 illustrates, these factors and characteristics *indirectly* influence the goals of the union leadership and management: each factor acts as a determinant of the preferences of the parties for various types of bargaining outcomes (relationship A1). But the preferences of the parties in turn shape the specific goals or objectives that are sought in the collective bargaining process (relationship A2).

Exhibit 10.3
The Extension of Union Priorities to Account for the Changing Female Composition of Membership

[W]omen's issues are union issues and . . . women's contributions are important though often undervalued. [T]here are often misconceptions about women's roles in the workplace and . . . our laws are usually inadequate. [W]omen's issues are important to the union and . . . the union is committed to women.

[F]our main areas of special interest to women in collective bargaining are the following:

1. Working conditions (including wages, benefits, and health and safety). Particularly relevant to women workers are pay and employment equity, flexible hours of work, and health issues relevant to pregnant women (such as toxic substances in the workplace).

2. Maternity and family responsibilities. Women are concerned with issues such as funding for child care and ensuring that there is no discrimination against pregnant women or women who have child care responsibilities.

3. Anti-discrimination and human rights. Developing policies against harassment and violence against women are priorities.

4. Giving women a voice by ensuring women's representation in the workplace and in the union. The representation of women on workplace committees needs to be increased, as well as within the union, on committees, in training programs, and in bargaining activities.

Source: Adapted from *CAW/TCA Canada*. CAW Women's Bargaining Agenda. Presentation by Peggy Nash, Assistant to the President, at TCA-Quebec Women's Conference, --October 16, 1998. www.caw.ca (December, 1999).

The Concept and Role of Power in Collective Bargaining

The typical observation that two parties engaged in negotiations have unequal leverage or advantage in obtaining their preferred outcome is rooted in the intuitive notion that one party has greater *power*. While power is itself not quantifiable, the concept of power can be defined, and the types of factors that give rise to power with respect to collective bargaining outcomes can be examined.

The Concept of Bargaining Power The ability of the parties to achieve their desired outcome, or objective, on a given issue will depend on their relative *bargaining power*. The classic conceptual definition of bargaining power is provided by Chamberlain and Kuhn (1986) and includes both the costs associated with a disagreement as well as the costs of agreement. Examples of the *costs of disagreement* may include the lost production (firm's loss) and wages (employees' loss) associated with a strike or lockout; the withdrawal of labour's active co-operation with management in the workplace (firm's loss); bad publicity associated with a strike (firm's loss); and threatened plant closures (employees' loss). Examples of the *costs of agreement* could include the direct costs of agreeing to increases in wages and benefits (firm's cost) or possible non-monetary costs associated with agreeing to a joint-participation program (a cost to the union leadership if the membership views union participation with management as "selling out") (Chamberlain and Kuhn, 1986: 180–196). Using the notions of costs of agreement and disagreement, power means

> . . . the ability to secure another's agreement on one's own terms. A union's bargaining power at any point of time *is*, for example, management's willingness to agree to the union's terms. Management's willingness, in turn, depends upon the costs of disagreeing with the union terms relative to the costs of agreeing to them. (Chamberlain and Kuhn, 1986: 176)

The power of a particular union (or management) in collective bargaining is clearly expected to vary over time with the specific issue being negotiated, and with the particular negotiating tactics used by the parties (Chamberlain and Kuhn, 1986: 177–178). In the following section, we examine the underlying factors that give rise to bargaining power.

The Determinants of Bargaining Power The power exerted by the union and management during collective bargaining negotiations is directly determined by a variety of environmental, socio-demographic, and organizational factors (refer to relationship B in Figure 10.1).

Environmental factors could include shifts in public support for workers who are on strike, modifications of the legislative framework governing labour relations, or changes in economic circumstances. Environmental influences can therefore affect not just the balance of power but also the goals of the parties.

The effect of public opinion on the relative power of the parties is probably more subtle than other environmental factors. For example, changes in public opinion may involve increased community support for striking workers that could induce the firm to improve its bargaining offers in order to garner public favour. Consequently, union strike strategies may include publicity efforts to encourage the public to boycott the products of the firm.

In the broader public sector, popular opinion may be an especially important factor, as is well illustrated in a number of strikes involving nurses and teachers.

The legal environment is generally believed to be a significant determinant of union power, since legislation can require that certain items be included in the contract or it can place limits on the behaviour or actions of the parties. Amendments to the labour relations legislation of British Columbia and Ontario in the early 1990s were generally viewed as providing increased support for unions (Carter, 1993). In contrast, the set of reforms subsequently undertaken by the Ontario government in the mid-1990s are generally viewed as having reversed the impact of the earlier reforms. The impact of the Supreme Court of Canada's 2007 *Health Services* decision (described in Chapters 1, 6, and 8) on bargaining is not yet known, but it might well be significant.

Economic conditions have a primary influence on the relative bargaining power of unions and management. In times of economic growth (an upswing in the business cycle), when the demand for products is increasing, employers will be reluctant to bear the losses associated with a strike, all else being equal. Alternatively, in periods of high unemployment, employment opportunities for workers tend to be fewer, so that, all else being equal, the union membership may be less willing to engage in a prolonged strike. These specific examples illustrate how economic conditions can affect the willingness of the parties to bear the costs of disagreement (in the form of a work stoppage). Another related consideration is the ease with which consumers may substitute other products for the goods that cannot be supplied during a strike. For example, during a strike by the *Calgary Herald* newspaper reporters and columnists, the owners were easily able to fill the newspaper with content by importing wire service products. Despite all the creative efforts of the union and its members (Barnett, 2003), the ability of the employer to find substitute news products meant that there was little union bargaining power. Through an analysis of the determinants of bargaining power, it would have been safe to bet that the strike was doomed to failure from the outset.

During the 1980s and 1990s, broader shifts in the Canadian economic context have had a longer-term impact on the relative bargaining power of unions and firms. An intensely competitive business environment has been fostered by numerous factors: changes in foreign and domestic public policies, such as deregulation, and the further strengthening of North–South trade links through the North American Free Trade Agreement (NAFTA); increased capital mobility and (more generally) the globalization of product markets; and the rapid diffusion of advanced production technologies (Verma and Chaykowski, 1999). These influences have created pressures on firms to reduce prices, lower the costs of production, and increase productivity. Perhaps nowhere have these factors been more apparent than in the automobile assembly and parts manufacturing industries, which are now worldwide industries with global markets.

Although Canada–U.S. trade has been growing steadily over most of the post–World War II period, the Canada–U.S. Free Trade Agreement and, subsequently, the NAFTA have created trade frameworks that have essentially accelerated the process of economic integration and increased competition. The prospect of creating a trading zone of the Americas in coming decades would serve to extend even further economic integration and increase competition. Meanwhile, increased capital mobility and new production methods have facilitated the movement of facilities "offshore" to lower-cost regions. The internationalization of production means that, in many cases, a firm's production is no longer tied to specific regions or product markets as it may have been traditionally. New production technologies continue to evolve more quickly, are much more rapidly diffused, and are often associated with fewer workers, new skill requirements, and new methods of organizing work. The acceleration of technological advances in production has pressured many firms to maintain competitiveness by acquiring and investing in the latest technologies.

Confronted with these pressures, companies have sought wage concessions or wage freezes, or engaged in downsizing their workforces in an attempt to lower costs. They have also attempted to reorganize workplaces and create more flexible work rules, and threatened to close facilities if unions do not co-operate with management demands. In turn, the power of many unions to enforce their own demands has been reduced, largely because the global expansion of markets and increased competition have reduced the ability of unions to "take wages out of competition." Recognizing the implications of bargaining in this new environment, many unions have moderated their wage demands and sought to focus their objectives on membership concerns about employment security. Unions have also carefully considered co-operating with management in its efforts to reorganize work in order to increase productivity, although most unions have developed position papers that state the conditions necessary for their involvement.

The privatization of Crown corporations (Air Canada, Petro-Canada) and the deregulation of industries (such as transportation and telecommunications) provide us with good examples of how shifts in public policies can also affect the bargaining relationship through their impact on the economic environment. The deregulation of the airline industry and various privatizations and the entry of aggressive low-cost carriers created significant competitive pressures in the industry (Bamber et al., forthcoming). Recent policy initiatives aimed at deregulating the telecommunications industry are creating similar pressures, which are most noticeable in the market for long-distance telephone services and the price war necessary to sign up cellphone customers. Unions realize that long-term growth in employee compensation can no longer be readily absorbed by rate increases once common in regulated industries and that, in the long run, increased competition may mean fewer firms and fewer jobs (therefore fewer members).

regulated industry – e.g. utilities

Diverse socio-demographic characteristics may be associated with disparate personal preferences and, therefore, bargaining preferences amongst the membership. In addition, the membership may be divided in its views on whether or not a particular issue is sufficiently important to warrant a strike if the bargaining objective is not achieved during negotiations. Consequently, union leadership must often account for diverse preferences amongst its membership when formulating bargaining objectives and when assessing the extent of membership support for engaging in a strike to achieve certain bargaining outcomes.

Organizational characteristics that affect power may be broadly defined to include the type of product produced, the technology of production, or the characteristics of the union or firm (e.g., cohesiveness of the union membership, resources available to the union during a strike). If the product is one that can be stockpiled, then management can continue to sell its product during a strike, thereby generating revenues and maintaining its contractual relationships with customers. This capability would minimize the economic impact of a work stoppage on the firm. Alternatively, if the firm produces a good that cannot be stockpiled or a service (which obviously cannot be stockpiled), then a strike would clearly have an immediate negative impact on the firm's revenues and customer base.

The nature of the technology of production has a direct impact on the ability of management to continue operations during a strike. If management employees can operate the production facilities themselves, then the impact of a work stoppage could be minimal. For example, in a refinery that requires few workers and is operated by means of control panels, supervisors and managers could maintain operations. During work stoppages in the telephone industry, supervisors have maintained a basic level of service by performing the tasks of operators. Alternatively, the technology of production may require highly specialized skills in the regular workforce; these specialized skill requirements would prevent management from performing the work of skilled workers themselves or hiring replacement workers (where allowed by labour legislation).

One of the most important organizational characteristics of the union is its status as a political organization. For example, the membership may be politically divided in its support for the elected union leadership, which could in turn undermine the solidarity of the union or the support provided to the leadership during the negotiating process. In practice, once a tentative agreement has been reached between the union and management negotiating teams, the membership will vote on the "package" offered by the firm. In some cases, the final offer, although endorsed by the leadership, may be rejected in a vote; this would likely serve to affect both the bargaining posture and authority of the leadership. Note that, while a vote that rejects a tentative package may serve to undermine confidence in the leadership and detract from its bargaining position, it may also serve to provide the leadership with a strong mandate to bargain hard for improvements—secure in the knowledge that the membership is fully supportive and possibly prepared to endure a long strike to enforce its demands—thereby increasing the power underlying the union's position.

Other characteristics of the union, such as the resources available, can affect its ability to maintain a work stoppage. The magnitude of the union strike fund could directly affect the length of time the membership is willing (or able) to maintain a strike action. Strike funds are accumulated through union dues and are used to provide small payments to workers while they are on strike. Payments are usually made weekly and are aimed at maintaining subsistence requirements. In an unusual twist, during the 2007 Edmonton Palace Casino strike, the United Food and Commercial Workers Union had to offer premium strike pay and other inducements in order to keep its members from abandoning the strike by seeking new jobs in the overheated Alberta economy.

Intra-organizational dynamics are also important within the firm. The management bargaining team typically serves a variety of interests among managers with different responsibilities. Also, while the union bargaining team must reconcile any settlement with the desires of the rank-and-file membership, so too must the management bargaining team reconcile the negotiated settlement with the goals and objectives of senior management. Centralized bargaining structures in particular may be prone to internal politics, as the objectives of several employers and unions (as the case may be) have to be melded into unified positions that inevitably reflect some compromise.

The various environmental, socio-demographic, and organizational characteristics that affect power operate simultaneously. The particular factors that determine the relative power of the union and management vary considerably over time, across industries, and across jurisdictions—which is why we expect the power of the parties to vary as well. Because the interrelationships among the factors that give rise to power are so complex, we cannot easily determine, in advance, their net effect on collective bargaining. In practice, this creates a degree of uncertainty in most negotiations; thus an important element in bargaining is the gathering of information about the other side's bargaining power through the give and take of the negotiations.

NEGOTIATING THE COLLECTIVE AGREEMENT: PROCESS AND INNOVATIONS

In the traditional system, once the term of a contract draws near, the union and management engage in negotiations with a view to agreeing upon a new collective agreement, with a specified duration, that provides the specific terms and conditions of employment and methods of administering industrial justice. While the union–management negotiations may lead directly to a settlement, the negotiations may also be punctuated by a work stoppage before a new contract is, ultimately, agreed upon. Figure 10.2 illustrates the linear process that is followed over time as successive contracts are negotiated, abided by for the term of the collective bargaining agreement (CBA), and subsequently renegotiated. The focus of the following discussion is on the negotiation process itself.

The negotiation process (refer back to relationship C of Figure 10.1) links the goals and power of the parties, on the one hand, with the outcomes of collective bargaining, on the other hand. While the union and management assert their power in order to achieve their goals, the actual process of negotiating the collective agreement can assume its own dynamic, which can itself constitute an important factor in determining the eventual

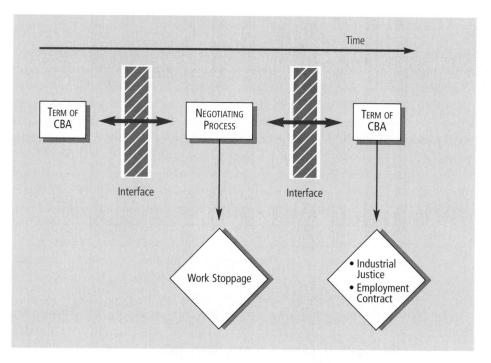

Figure 10.2 Traditional Bargaining Contract Interface

Source: Verma and Chaykowski, 1999, p. 8, Figure 3. IRC Press: Industrial Relations Centre, Queen's University.

contract outcomes. This section begins with a discussion of the concept of a "zone of agreement," which provides insight into the basis for defining a potential agreement. This discussion is followed by a brief characterization of the manner in which collective bargaining proceeds when a contract requires renegotiation, including a characterization of the process and dynamics of the negotiation process, and a discussion of why (dis)agreement, or impasses, may occur. The final section describes some of the innovations occurring in collective bargaining, largely in an attempt to avoid conflict that leads to impasse.

The Potential for Agreement in Negotiations

Most negotiations involve attempts to resolve numerous complex issues, many of which are typically interrelated. One of the most fundamental concerns is, therefore, whether a potential basis for agreement even exists. That is, do the *positions* of the parties create a common ground, or are the minimum positions of each party too far apart to permit any common ground? Further, can the parties change their positions on one issue (e.g., wages) during the negotiating process in reaction to changes in positions that occur regarding another issue (e.g., pension benefits)? In practice, it is this type of flexibility and process of trade-offs across outcomes that make an agreement possible. Defining a "potential zone of agreement" provides a theoretical basis for understanding why an agreement may, or may not, occur.

For a single issue, the notion of a potential "zone of agreement" between union and management negotiators is depicted in Figure 10.3. Consider negotiations over a single issue for which the union seeks an increased value and which management seeks to resist (e.g., wages). In Figure 10.3, the following reference points create a potential zone of agreement between the parties:

■ The left-most point (A) represents the lowest value of wages that will induce workers to offer their services, while the right-most point (B) represents the highest level of wages possible that would still permit the firm to operate;

■ UM represents the minimum wage level that the union will accept (often referred to as the union "resistance point");

■ MM represents the maximum wage level that management will offer the union (which is often referred to as the management "resistance point").

In the example of bargaining over wages, management may attempt to focus its bargaining strategy on achieving a specific wage level that it believes represents the best that it can do (that is, the lowest wage that it can offer the union). Realistically, management prefers to offer any wage level that is less than MM in Figure 10.3. Since management prefers any wage level less than MM (Area 1 and Area 3), management will certainly prefer wage levels less than UM. However, the union will never agree to any wage offers in Area 1 (i.e., wages below UM), since this area corresponds to wages that are less than the level that is minimally acceptable to the union (UM). But management may not know that wage offers below UM (Area 1) are not acceptable to the union.

From its perspective, the union may focus on a particular wage level that it believes represents the best that can be obtained from management in negotiations (that is, the highest wage it can successfully negotiate). But the union generally prefers any wage level greater than UM (Area 2 and Area 3)—so the union will certainly prefer a wage level that is greater than MM. But management will never agree to any wage demand in Area 2 (i.e., wages

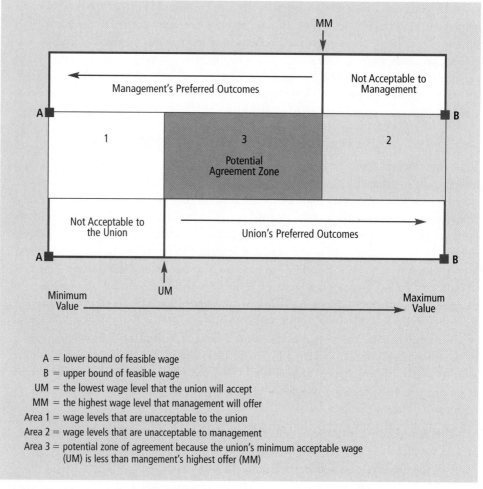

Figure 10.3 Potential Zone of Agreement for a Single Bargaining Issue

Source: Reprinted from Richard E. Walton and Robert B. McKersie: *A Behavioral Theory of Labor Negotiations: An Analysis of a Social Interaction System*, Second Edition. Copyright © 1965 by Richard E. Walton and Robert B. McKersie. Used by permission of the publisher, Cornell University Press.

above MM), since this area corresponds to wages that are greater than the maximum wage level that is acceptable to management (MM). On its part, the union may not know that wage demands that are greater than MM (Area 2) are not acceptable to the management.

Area 3 is a *potential* zone of agreement because the union's lowest acceptable demand (point UM) is less than management's highest possible offer (point MM). The *existence* of a potential agreement zone will yield a settlement as long as the parties can bargain to some point within Area 3. However, one cannot determine in advance *where* within this range the parties will settle. The process of bargaining allows an exchange of offers and information that encourages management and the union to learn more about their true "resistance" points; in general, it permits both parties to learn more about the *range* of outcomes that is acceptable to each:

> Negotiation... is back-and-forth communication designed to reach an agreement when you and the other side have some interests that are shared and others that are opposed.
> (Fisher and Ury, 1983: xi)

Obtaining a solution in Area 3 would be made easier if both sides simply revealed their true resistance points, but, in order to gain strategic advantage, the parties typically will not do so. Each will attempt to "bluff," to exaggerate their true resistance point, or to employ other tactics to obtain a solution closest to their own most preferred wage level; that is, where in Area 3 the parties ultimately settle matters very much to them.

This type of bargaining dynamic assumes that management and the union are bargaining over a single issue or, if more than one issue is being negotiated, that the parties are bargaining over each issue separately. In most cases, however, management and the union negotiate several issues at the same time and negotiations over one issue can affect the bargaining over another. This means that the process of negotiating over one issue can affect the positions that the parties take regarding the other issue. As a consequence, the union and management may seek trade-offs across these two issues because the potential gains in one issue may offset what they must offer for the other issue. For example, this trade-off may be especially appealing because one party (e.g., the union) may place a greater weight on obtaining more of Issue X (e.g., health and safety) than Issue Y (e.g., vacation)—perhaps because the membership places more value on greater health and safety than on more vacation. This type of scenario, which is typical of most negotiations, helps explain why collective bargaining is such a challenging and dynamic process and why the eventual outcomes are uncertain.

Negotiating the Collective Agreement

If a collective agreement is in effect, then near the expiration of the contract the union must give notice to the employer of its intention to bargain for a new collective agreement, after which the parties must meet within a specified period of time; the specific requirements vary across jurisdictions (refer to Table 10.2). The union and management negotiating teams prepare their positions on each issue over which they wish to negotiate.

In traditional bargaining, each team has a spokesperson. The tone of the meetings has commonly been adversarial, with each team facing the other as "opposites." The union may present its "demands," with the management team withdrawing to examine the requests and subsequently returning to respond with an "offer" (a *position* on each issue of concern). The union will usually then withdraw from the negotiating table to examine the proposal in "caucus" (in a closed meeting). Each side will caucus regularly throughout the negotiating process as each team discusses and debates the merits of the latest offer. Offers are costed and evaluated: the economic value of offers related to wages, pensions, holidays, severance packages for laid-off workers, or other issues with a monetary value are "costed"; the merits of offers related to issues with no readily quantifiable value (e.g., changes to promotion rules) are evaluated. This process of preparing and evaluating offers and counter-offers typically continues over many days or weeks either until all issues have been resolved or until an impasse is reached.

Table 10.2 Statutory Requirements for Notice to Commence and Obligation to Begin Collective Bargaining for Renegotiation of a Collective Agreement in the Private Sector

JURISDICTION	PERIOD OF NOTICE TO BARGAIN (BEFORE EXPIRY DATE OF CONTRACT)[d]	OBLIGATION TO BARGAIN (AFTER PROVIDING NOTICE)
Federal	Within 4 months[a]	Within 20 days[b]
Alberta	120 to 60 days[a]	Within 30 days
British Columbia	Within 4 months[c]	Within 10 days
Manitoba	90 to 30 days[b]	Within 10 days[a]
New Brunswick	90 to 30 days[a]	Within 20 days[a]
Newfoundland	60 to 30 days[b]	Within 20 days[a]
Nova Scotia	Within 2 months	Within 20 days[a]
Ontario	Within 90 days[b]	Within 15 days[a]
PEI	Within 2 months[b]	Within 20 days[a]
Quebec	Within 90 days[b]	"Forthwith"
Saskatchewan	60 to 30 days	"Forthwith"

Notes:

a. Union and management may agree to a longer period.

b. Union and management may agree otherwise.

c. Notice is "deemed" given at 90 days before the contract expires.

d. Changes in the notice to bargain are typically stipulated in the collective agreement.

Source: Industrial Relations Legislation in Canada. 2002 Edition. Accessed at labour.hrdc-drhc.gc.ca/psait_spila/lmric_irlc/index.cfm/doc/english. Ottawa: Minister of Supply and Services Canada (January, 2002).

While there are many factors that determine whether or not a settlement is achieved, one of the most important is the skills, abilities, and behaviours of the negotiators themselves. Experienced negotiators recognize that thorough preparation, a sense of timing and tactics during the negotiation process, and developing bargaining strategies are each important elements of not only achieving a settlement but also achieving one that meets the interests of the union or firm that they represent. Exhibit 10.4 provides a "top ten" list of key fundamentals underlying successful negotiations. While they would not guarantee a settlement of successful terms, they would increase the likelihood of success.

If the parties cannot reach an agreement, then either party may request that the government appoint a conciliation officer. (In some jurisdictions, if the conciliator cannot facilitate an agreement, then the government may—but in practice rarely does—recommend that a conciliation board be appointed.) If the impasse continues and the collective agreement has expired, the union has a legal right to engage in a work stoppage and management has a legal right to lock out. Before a strike or lockout becomes legal, certain prerequisites have to be satisfied; typically in most jurisdictions these include a strike vote and strike notice. While high-profile strikes often catch the attention of the media, and a single strike in a key sector (e.g., in rail or health care) can have a serious impact on the economy, most negotiations lead to a successful settlement without a serious impasse in the negotiations and, of those negotiations that reach an impasse at some point, not all result in an actual work stoppage. This track record of successful negotiations is illustrated by the situation in Alberta. Exhibit 10.5 reveals that over the 10-year period from 1992 to 2002, typically less than 2 percent of the collective agreements that expired in a given year were associated with an actual work stoppage. So, in the larger scheme, collective negotiations prove to be a very successful way of dealing with the need of workers and management to revisit their contracts.

Exhibit 10.5
Expiring Collective Agreements Resulting in Work Stoppages in Alberta

While many of the major strikes that occur catch the public attention, and strikes are generally in the news, the vast majority of collective agreements are settled before they expire. Of those contracts that are not renegotiated before they expire, very few result in a strike or lockout.

A good example of this may be drawn from the Alberta experience with strikes. Overall, roughly one quarter of employees are covered by a collective agreement. In 2002, there were approximately 886 collective agreements in effect in Alberta; by year-end of 2002, roughly 47 percent were in effect, while around 53 percent (or 467) of contracts required settlement. Of these, roughly 6.0 percent resulted in a work stoppage.

The line graph in Figure 10.4 indicates the number of contracts that expired in each year over the 1992–2002 period, while the bar graph indicates the proportion of these that ended in a work stoppage (% at impasse). Notice that the proportion of expired contracts that end in a work stoppage varies somewhat in relation to the busi-

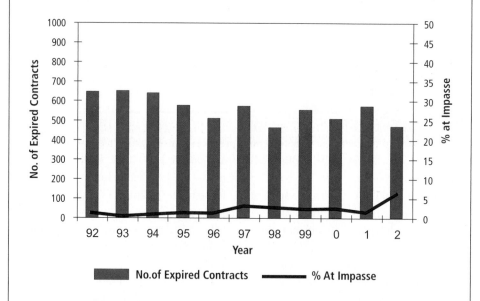

Figure 10.4 Number of Expired Contracts vs. Percentage at Impasse in Alberta, 1992–2002

ness cycle, that the proportion of expired contracts is typically less than 2 percent, and that the total number of contracts involving a work stoppage is typically around a dozen or fewer.

Since the number of strikes alone does not convey the impact of strike activity, we usually also consider the number of person-days lost in a work stoppage as well as the effect that a strike may have on other industries. For example, the 28 impasses that occurred in 2002 resulted in roughly 212 000 person-days lost, whereas in 1997 the 16 impasses that occurred resulted in just over 473 000 person-days lost! The situation was similar in Ontario, where the 117 strikes that occurred in 2002 resulted in 1 510 580 person-days lost, while in 1997 the 113 stoppages resulted in a significant 1 904 210 person-days lost.[5]

Source: Data provided by Alberta Employment and Immigration (AE&I) upon request. (Data available in Settlements for Collective Bargaining Agreements and Legal Work-Stoppages Report Alberta, published by AE&I and online at www.employment.alberta.ca/cps/rde/xchg/hre/hs.xsl/3240.html).

Even after a work stoppage occurs, the parties will continue their negotiations, often with the help of a government-appointed mediator. While a mediator may assist in achieving an agreement, the process of collective bargaining is affected by a diverse set of factors including the power of the parties (including the costs associated with a strike or lockout), the skill and personalities of the negotiators, and union and management access to information regarding the true positions of the other side.

Innovations in the Process of Bargaining

Since the issues that are subject to collective bargaining are of consequence to both parties, the process of bargaining is typically pursued strenuously and often results in strained relationships—whether or not a strike or lockout occurs. Achieving a new contract is important in itself, but the union and management also attempt to resolve their differences in a way that each considers workable during the term of the collective agreement. The traditional approach to improving the negotiating process, thereby increasing the likelihood of obtaining a collective agreement without an impasse, is to engage in some form of conciliation or mediation. Recognizing that the process of negotiating itself can help the parties to exchange information and to better appreciate their true target and resistance points, many unions and firms have also tended to lengthen the bargaining process, essentially by beginning to exchange information and even to negotiate well in advance of the expiration date of the contract.

Another development has been to increase the number of joint union–management committees as well as to extend the areas of concern that these committees deal with. For example, there are joint committees on such diverse areas as health and safety, work reorganization, job content, technological change, environmental issues, and contracting-out. These committees are often established either by letter of agreement or in the collective agreement and operate during the term of the collective agreement. The benefit from a negotiations standpoint is that the union and management can address problems on an ongoing basis, instead of simply identifying an issue during the term of a contract and "saving" it until the next round of negotiations. This can reduce the number of issues at the bargaining table, allow the parties to address issues before they "become big problems," and allow the parties to discuss issues in a less adversarial setting.

However, these types of developments, including third-party interventions or variations in the length of bargaining, occur in the context of traditional bargaining, and therefore tend not to alter the actual *negotiation process*. The effectiveness of these approaches and developments are therefore constrained by the limitations associated with traditional adversarial bargaining itself.

In recent years, several approaches to improving the process of collective bargaining have been developed in order to avoid costly strikes and lockouts and to improve the quality of the relationship after the negotiations are concluded. The core of these approaches is an attempt to alter the focus of the bargaining and the behavioural approach to negotiating. One of the more successful and widely attempted of these approaches is "interest-based" negotiations (IBN) or "mutual gains" bargaining (MGB).

These techniques are rooted in the generic approach to bargaining referred to as *principled bargaining* (Fisher and Ury, 1983). This approach was developed as an alternative to traditional confrontational bargaining, which is characterized by situations involving low levels of trust, high conflict, the use of tactics for advantage, a focus on the positions that the parties bring to the negotiations, and an emphasis on win–lose outcomes. Instead of focusing on the *positions* that the parties may assume in a negotiating situation, this approach centres on the underlying *interests* of the parties. Recognizing that the interests of the parties may conflict, Fisher and Ury suggest moving away from traditional adversarial bargaining through four procedures:

- separating the personalities of the people from the problem under discussion;
- focusing on the underlying interests of the parties, and not on their bargaining positions;
- inventing options that give rise to mutual gain, instead of win–lose, solutions; and
- in negotiating outcomes, developing objective criteria that involve fairness in both standards and procedures.

The bargaining concepts advanced by Fisher and Ury (1983) are general in nature, so that aspects of principled bargaining have been successfully adopted by negotiators in the process of collective bargaining. Recent analyses of mutual gains bargaining have raised concerns about the inherent limitations to its effectiveness: because the process is based primarily on behavioural principles, it may give insufficient weight to either the importance of the relative power of the parties or the institutional context in which the parties function and conduct negotiations (Friedman, 1994; Heckscher and Hall, 1994).

However, Friedman has provided suggestions to increase the effectiveness of current practices. These suggestions focus on minimizing barriers to increased trust, altering the roles of the parties in negotiations, and modifying power imbalances between the union and management (Friedman, 1994).

What happens when one party is more powerful than the other? Fisher, Ury, and Patton (1991) acknowledge that mutual gains bargaining cannot guarantee success when the leverage is all on one side. The question of power remains a permanent threat to establishing and sustaining MGB. MGB will be successful if the parties are willing to focus on their common interests and on their will to use tactics based on principles and objective arguments, and not on the manipulation of the other party's constraints through coercion.

While there appears to be continued interest in these "principled" types of bargaining innovations, traditional "hard bargaining" probably remains the predominant approach. Even so, anecdotal evidence indicates that some major unions and employers are partaking in principled bargaining.

There is little systematic evidence currently available regarding the extent of usage of these principled approaches, their success, or whether their use tends to be sustained over time. However, Exhibit 10.6 presents a summary of the experiences of a number of prominent firms and unions with MGB in the 1990s that provides insight into some of these issues. The experiences of the parties reveal many of the factors that led the parties to attempt mutual gains approaches; the factors that, in their view, had an impact on the likelihood of the approach succeeding; and a range of considerations for using a principled approach as an alternative to traditional bargaining.

Exhibit 10.6
From Traditional to Mutual Gains Bargaining in Canada

In October of 1994, the Federal Mediation and Conciliation Service (of what is now Human Resources and Social Development Canada) invited representatives of 13 major companies and unions from all sectors of the federal jurisdiction to Ottawa to share their experiences with mutual gains bargaining.

THREE BEHAVIOURS THAT INCREASE THE LIKELIHOOD OF SUCCESS WITH MGB

1. Openness and honesty: Full disclosure of information throughout collective bargaining and, in some cases, during the normal business operations of the company.

2. Trust: Viewed as perhaps the most critical dimension, but also one of the most difficult to attain, since deeper trust typically evolves slowly over time and often must survive setbacks.

3. Respect: At all times.

PROCESS CONDITIONS TO INCREASE THE LIKELIHOOD OF SUCCESS WITH MGB

Joint Organizational Conditions

Training

- Establish joint union and management training in the interest-based approach to bargaining.
- Train at all levels of the organization.
- Recognize that there is a role for a facilitator (i.e., consultant) in training.

Consultancy

- Use an outside facilitator.
- Allow the choice of facilitator to be made jointly between the union and management.

Devote Resources

- Training may require sizeable amounts of financial resources that should be committed on an ongoing basis.
- Time required to develop the process can be substantial.
- Communications regarding the process should be established throughout the management and union.

Management Intra-Organizational Factors

Commitment

- Obtain commitment to change from the highest levels.
- Develop commitment that outlasts changes in particular players or champions.

Authority

- Support the authority of the negotiating team to create solutions that the firm will stand by (e.g., ensure no mismatch with top management).

Line Supervision

- Address the needs of first-line supervisors—especially in cases where mutual gains bargaining leads to significant change in the broader, ongoing relationship.

Union Intra-Organizational Factors

Education

■ Explain the nature of the mutual gains bargaining process and the benefits to the membership.

■ Continually educate and inform the membership of any broader change process.

Membership Support

■ Cultivate ongoing membership support for the process; some results take time to develop.

Joint Process Conditions

Interests

■ Focus on interests and not on positions.

■ Stay away from agendas.

■ Coordinate communications; explore the use of joint releases to avoid unwanted positioning.

Comprehensive Change

■ Approach mutual gains bargaining as part of a broader change in the relationship; it often cannot survive in isolation.

■ Use face-to-face, ongoing problem-solving approaches in bargaining.

■ Emphasize ongoing problem solving during the term of the contract as well as during negotiations.

Innovate

■ Craft your own approach to change.

■ In changing your approach to bargaining, create your own procedural rules for engagement.

■ Tailor the collective agreement to your particular needs and circumstances.

Source: Excerpted from Chaykowski and Grant, 1995. Reproduced with the permission of the Minister of Public Works and Government Services, 2000.

One serious issue that confounded many attempts to move away from adversarial bargaining was the ability of the firm to meet union concerns over job security, an issue that often arose in connection with the negotiation over issues related to increasing productivity or reducing costs (e.g., increasing workplace flexibility, downsizing). The parties felt that some issues (notably wages) ought to be handled through traditional collective bargaining, whereas others would more readily lend themselves to being channelled through mutual gains bargaining. In deciding which areas are best handled through mutual gains principles, many participants felt that starting with less contentious areas would build confidence and success.

The outcomes of MGB were mixed. Many of the participants suggested that the adversarial approach to collective bargaining may continue to be the best strategy. In some cases, the attempt to adopt MGB had actually harmed the relationship. But other participants experienced improved industrial relations outcomes and measurably better outcomes in organizational performance, including productivity, flexibility, and co-operative relations (Chaykowski and Grant, 1995).

Governments have also recognized that two of the primary "costs" associated with ineffective and conflictual negotiations include the possible damage to the union–management relationship itself and the potential costs associated with a work stoppage due to a strike or lockout. In the case of soured union–management relations, the effects may show up during the term of the collective agreement through lower trust and morale, an unwillingness to work together, or a reluctance to facilitate workplace change and innovation—each of which could have negative consequences for productivity. In the case of a work stoppage, there is a loss of output to an individual firm that is undesirable; moreover, losses to the economy as a whole can be substantial if strike activity becomes widespread. Even a single strike in a crucial sector—such as auto manufacturing, health care, rail transport, or ports—can have a major and often immediate impact on many other firms connected to these activities; indeed, whole sectors can be affected by a single strike. If, for example, a shipping port or an airport has a work stoppage, there can be widespread disruption.

Some forms of government intervention are well established (e.g., conciliation) and continue to be mandated in some jurisdictions (i.e., before a strike is allowed); other forms of intervention are more recent and are purely voluntary. In some jurisdictions, the role of government has gradually shifted over time, so that the variety and scope of the voluntary services available to labour and management to support more effective negotiations and improve the overall labour–management relationship have gradually increased. These services tend to be focused on preventing a breakdown in negotiations or preventing the escalation of problems, typically by focusing on improving communication and, importantly, on substantively improving the tenor of the labour–management relationship. The acceptability of these types of government services depends upon whether union and management perceive that the service providers are truly neutral, and are there to help the process rather than interfere in the outcomes. Figure 10.5 presents the range of services offered by the government of Newfoundland and Labrador and by the federal government to unions and employers in their jurisdictions. These two examples illustrate how governments in several Canadian jurisdictions have recognized that they can play a more supportive role in the provision of "preventive services" and in the diffusion of constructive new approaches to negotiating.

Most of these types of dispute resolution focus directly on the process of collective bargaining, and the system is designed with a view to a heavy reliance upon governments to provide dispute resolution services. But private-sector independent neutrals also play a

NEWFOUNDLAND CONCILIATION SERVICES
Conciliators provided by the province "assist the parties to reach a collective agreement and avoid a work stoppage."

NEWFOUNDLAND INTEREST-BASED NEGOTIATIONS PROGRAM
"The IBN process represents a shift from the traditional, adversarial approach to dealing with issues. Instead of presenting positions, the parties jointly decide which issues need to be addressed and then discuss their interests on each issue. Once all the interests have been explored, the parties jointly generate a number of options to resolve the issue."

Seminars in IBN for management and union staff and members of the collective bargaining team facilitated by mediators provided by the Department of Environment and Labour.

NEWFOUNDLAND PREVENTIVE MEDIATION PROGRAM
This program, which has six components, "encourages a shift to a more positive labour relations environment and promotes more responsible collective bargaining in the Province." The elements of the program include:

Consultation with a neutral mediator

First-agreement orientation to the parties about legislative requirements and conducting successful negotiations

Mediator assistance with joint committees

Seminars in communications and joint decision making aimed at supervisors and shop stewards

Mediation of grievances (to avoid arbitration)

Seminars on "relationship by objectives" (to achieve better conflict resolution)

GOVERNMENT OF CANADA MEDIATION SERVICES
Mediators are appointed at any time by the minister, but usually following the conciliation process, and with the goal of resolving an impasse and avoiding conflicts.

GOVERNMENT OF CANADA CONCILIATION SERVICES
Conciliators are appointed before a strike or lockout can legally occur and are appointed "to assist them [the parties] in resolving the impasse and reaching a collective agreement."

GOVERNMENT OF CANADA PREVENTIVE MEDIATION PROGRAM
Offered during the term of the collective agreement "to help improve ongoing relationships and keep the lines of communication open between employers and unions … [and] designed to help parties build and maintain a constructive working relationship, while providing them with a forum for improving their joint problem-solving skills."

NEGOTIATION SKILLS WORKSHOP
Workshops focusing on "interest-based negotiation" techniques

COMMITTEE EFFECTIVENESS WORKSHOP
Designed to assist the parties in creating and operating joint labour–management committees more effectively

JOINT PROBLEM-SOLVING WORKSHOP
Designed to apply interest-based approaches to ongoing workplace issues

GENERAL FACILITATION
A neutral facilitator is provided at the request of the parties to assist in resolving issues arising in the context of joint activities

"RELATIONSHIP BY OBJECTIVES" WORKSHOPS
Designed to improve the working relationship of the parties through joint seminars designed to uncover problems and provide solutions

Figure 10.5 Bargaining-Related Services Offered by the Government of Canada and Newfoundland and Labrador

Sources: www.hrle.gov.nl.ca/lra/programs/unionized.htm and www.hrsdc.gc.ca/en/labour/labour_relations/mediation/resolution/index.shtml.

variety of roles in dispute resolution. As the interface between labour and management during the process of collective bargaining and their relationship during the term of the contract has become more interrelated, the roles of neutrals in dispute resolution and relationship building have been extended to assist the parties in more varied and complex ways. As Exhibit 10.7 shows, professionals in the field of dispute resolution are increasingly focused on ensuring that, as their roles evolve and expand, they develop principled approaches to facilitating dispute resolution.

Exhibit 10.7
Advancing Dispute Resolution to the Next Level: Guiding Principles for Dispute Resolution Professionals Working in Unionized Operations

The *Society of Professionals in Dispute Resolution* (SPIDR) initiated a Task Force on Alternative Dispute Resolution in the Organized Workforce as part of a larger project developed in order to " . . . describe the processes, practices, and outcomes of existing and emerging dispute resolution activities in the workplace." In their report, they concluded:

> We focus here on three critical roles neutrals play in contemporary collective bargaining: mediating negotiations, training for and facilitating interest-based negotiations (IBN), and designing and facilitating labour–management committees that sometimes precede and help prepare for negotiations and sometimes follow and help implement negotiated settlements.
>
> Labour mediators need to hold themselves and the process accountable for achieving outcomes that address the parties' underlying interests and enhance their relationship.
>
> Facilitators of interest-based negotiations processes should ensure that both parties are adequately trained in appropriate skills and methods.
>
> Interest-based negotiation facilitators need to address the roles of constituents in the process.
>
> Facilitators need to ensure that interest-based processes are adequate to handle issues on which there are deep conflicts of interest and in which the exercise of power is central.
>
> Third parties have to strike an appropriate balance between abandonment and dependency.
>
> Labour–management committees, like workplace participation processes, should be linked to the collective bargaining agreement and other labour–management forums so as to support (and not undermine) the bargaining relationship and negotiations process.
>
> Neutrals need to ensure that labour–management committees have clear goals, adequate resources, and shared commitment in order to achieve their assigned mandate.

Source: *Facilitating Conflict Resolution in Union-Management Relations: A Guide for Neutrals* by Chaykowski, Cutcher-Gershenfeld, Kochan & Merchage. Copyright © 2000 Institute on Conflict Resolution, Cornell University. Reprinted by permission of Cornell University.

THE OUTCOMES OF COLLECTIVE BARGAINING

The final component of the conceptual framework presented in Figure 10.1 is the bargaining outcomes. Generally, the outcomes of collective bargaining include both the contractual agreement as well as impacts at the organizational (i.e., micro) level. At the contractual and organizational level, the outcomes of collective bargaining include several basic elements:

1. The immediate contractual results of the collective bargaining process include the terms and conditions of employment specified in the collective bargaining agreement (see Chapter 11 on the collective agreement).

2. Many aspects of the contract can affect the operating efficiency and functioning of the firm. In particular, changes in the collective agreement can have important consequences for compensation systems, productivity levels, and management practices (see Chapter 14).

3. The tone and dynamics of the negotiation process itself can have a substantial "spillover" impact on the ongoing relationship between employees and managers during the term of the collective agreement. Specifically, whether the negotiations can be characterized as adversarial, bitter, and highly conflictual on the one hand, or more co-operative and positive on the other hand, can affect the conduct of management and employees during the day-to-day operations of the company, and foreshadow the degree of adversarialism at the bargaining table when the contract is due for renegotiation.

Considered across firms and unions, the results of collective bargaining can also have a range of impacts on broader, socio-economic (i.e., macro-level) outcomes including aggregate economic output (through strike activity and productivity) or inflation (through wage increases).

Taken together, the interrelationships presented in the framework in Figure 10.1 describe the set of factors and processes that determine collective bargaining outcomes. But the model depicted in Figure 10.1 conveys only a *static* sense of the processes. The feedback loops in Figure 10.1 (loops F1 and F2) indicate that there is a *dynamic* element to the process over time because, as noted above, the outcomes achieved in one round of collective bargaining can in turn affect the objectives of the management and union in a subsequent round. This concept of feedback loops highlights the fact that the union–management relationship is a long-term one. The way in which collective bargaining has functioned in previous stages of the relationship affects the way collective bargaining will function in the future.

CONCLUSION

The bargaining goals and priorities of unions and firms are being continuously shaped by a variety of environmental factors. In particular, increasingly competitive economic conditions brought on by the internationalization of markets, social pressures for workplace change, and shifts in composition of the workforce over the past 25 years have translated into new concerns and priorities. Both employers and unions have reacted to these pressures at the bargaining table, while governments have engaged in changes to the public-policy environment.

Employers have undergone significant changes in attempting to increase productivity and reduce costs. In many cases, firms have changed organizational structures, reorganized the workplace, introduced new technologies, and altered the nature of their workforces. Organizational changes have included reductions in the levels of hierarchies and the size of the workforce to lower the costs of production. Efforts to reorganize work and introduce new technologies have often been accompanied by changes in the number of tasks performed by employees and in employee skill levels. In addition, many firms have attempted to introduce new types of employee compensation systems (e.g., profit-sharing or lump-sum payments). Over the past decade, these changes have transformed the bargaining agenda of many employers across industries; for unions, they have highlighted the importance of issues related to job security, the scope of work, job descriptions and work rules, and the basis of pay. The ongoing changes have also affected bargaining structure, weakening traditional pattern bargaining arrangements and placing even more emphasis on decentralized negotiations.

Several emerging trends in the labour movement may be expected to have an important, yet somewhat complex, impact on both the structure and the process of collective bargaining. First, partly as a result of the changes in employment patterns arising from industrial restructuring—including shifts away from traditional areas of union strength in heavy industry—and partly as a result of the ongoing downsizing of workforces across organizations, there has been an erosion of union membership, which has served to weaken union power. Many major unions have therefore begun to organize workers outside of their traditional industries. As examples, the United Steelworkers have organized taxi drivers, fishery workers, and university support staff. The United Food and Commercial Workers Union has organized nursing home workers. The Canadian Auto Workers has organized rail workers, and the Canadian Union of Public Employees has organized workers in both the airline and longshoring industries. These cross-jurisdictional initiatives often incite bitter rivalries within the union movement.

Second, merger activity among unions in both the private and public sectors has been considerable—often among unions that might otherwise, based on their traditional composition and coverage, appear unlikely to join. Although most mergers involve a small and a large union, a significant merger among major unions occurred with the integration of the Communications and Electrical Workers of Canada (which is primarily in telecommunications), the Energy and Chemical Workers (organized in the energy sector), and the Paperworkers Union (traditionally in the forest products manufacturing industry) into the Communications, Energy and Paperworkers Union. Many of these types of changes have altered the membership composition of unions and are expected to have major long-term implications for their priorities and bargaining objectives, their power, and the breadth of their activity. To renew their strength at the bargaining table, unions have realized they need to revitalize their organizing efforts and seek advantageous merger possibilities.

Third, during the formative years of the growth of contemporary unionism, the bargaining priorities of many private-sector unions were traditionally determined by a membership base that was fairly uniform in terms of demographic characteristics (i.e., primarily white and male). While the demographic makeup of the labour force generally, and of the labour movement specifically, has become progressively more diverse over the past several decades, the single most important change in the labour force has been the significant and ongoing increase in the labour market participation of women (see Chapter 4). Not surprisingly, a number of top bargaining priorities arise from the fact that women now have a strong presence in the labour market and that they want to make women's issues a priority in collective bargaining.

For many firms and unions, the difficult socio-economic challenges of the past decade have translated into increasingly adversarial negotiations as firms have often sought wage concessions, engaged in layoffs, or changed work organization in order to reduce costs and increase productivity, while unions have struggled to protect pay levels and preserve job security. For other organizations, a major challenge has been to achieve better solutions through collective bargaining. This has in turn encouraged the parties to experiment with innovative approaches such as mutual gains bargaining. However, despite the range of pressures confronting and shaping the system, in this first decade of the new millennium the traditional approach to collective bargaining remained the centrepiece of Canadian industrial relations.

Questions

1. Identify the major factors that can have an influence on
   a) the process of collective bargaining;
   b) the outcomes of collective bargaining.

2. Define each of the different types of collective bargaining structures.

3. What types of bargaining structures tend to be most prevalent in Canada? Explain why these types of structures predominate.

4. Why might pattern bargaining be breaking down in Canada? How would you document such a trend? Would you expect differences between the public and private sectors?

5. Using the concepts of bargaining target and resistance points, explain how a management and union bargaining session could lead to
   a) a zone of potential agreement;
   b) a range of potential disagreement.

6. Explain the difference between *positions* and *interests* in collective bargaining.

7. Analyze a recently completed labour–management contract negotiation using the model in Figure 10.1.

8. Identify an alternative method or approach to collective bargaining that management and unions may use—often in an attempt to avoid strikes and to achieve a settlement. Why might management and the union prefer one method over another?

9. Consider the pros and cons of expanding the role of government in providing voluntary services that help to improve the conduct of negotiations and reduce conflict.

10. Identify the major environmental pressures affecting the collective bargaining system and consider why and how they are influential.

Weblinks

Bargaining-related services:
Newfoundland and Labrador:
www.hrle.gov.nl.ca/lra/programs/unionized.htm
Canada:
www.hrsdc.gc.ca/en/labour/labour_relations/mediation/resolution/index.shtml
www.hrsdc.gc.ca/en/labour/labour_relations/mediation/prevention/index.shtml

Information and research about conflict resolution in industrial relations:
www.acrnet.org/ and www.ilr.cornell.edu/conflictRes/

Chapter 11

The Collective Agreement

Anthony Giles and Akivah Starkman

In 2003, facing enormous debt, declining revenues, and mounting pressure from its creditors, Air Canada filed for legal protection from bankruptcy. This move provided the company with a period of time in which to attempt to restructure its debt and develop a long-term survival plan. The Court overseeing this process urged the company's management and its unions, who had blamed each other for the airline's problems, to work together toward this end.

After two months of intense negotiations, Air Canada and the Canadian Auto Workers (CAW) reached an agreement to change the working conditions of nearly 7000 employees. In this agreement, the union agreed to forgo a previously negotiated pay increase, and to reduce all wages by 10 percent for a 60-day period. Following those 60 days, wages would return to their previous levels, but new productivity gains would be achieved through major changes in work rules, greater flexibility in scheduling, and a reduction in shift premiums and vacations. The collective agreement was extended for six years, to 2009.

For its part, the union maintained its permanent wage scales and health care benefits, and protected the pension plan. It also reduced potential layoffs by agreeing to a number of one-time retirement incentives, including a severance payment of up to 52 weeks' salary, and lifetime travel privileges on the airline for the retiring employee, his or her spouse, and dependants. A program was introduced to permit employees to move from full-time to part-time status and to pursue educational or retraining opportunities. The union also maintained the right to reopen the collective agreement after three years only for the purpose of renegotiating wages.

Overall, the deal provided the company with approximately $150 million in annual labour-cost savings, and the stability of a long-term collective agreement. At the same time, it protected existing wages, benefits, and pensions for union members who were under the shadow of bankruptcy and massive job losses. In a similar context, Air Canada also reached new agreements with other unions representing nearly 20 000 additional workers.

In 2006, the collective agreement was in fact reopened and wages were renegotiated for several employee groups (pilots, flight attendants, mechanics, passenger-ticket agents, and clerical employees). Any unresolved wage issues were referred to binding arbitration since, for the purpose of maintaining labour stability, the parties had previously agreed not to exercise their right to strike and lock out during the reopener period.[1]

Although the exact circumstances surrounding this case were exceptional—notably the renegotiation of the terms of an existing agreement under such pressures—the company's desire to revamp the collective agreement to provide more flexibility in work organization and the union's determination to protect its members' jobs, wages, and benefits are not unique in contemporary Canadian industrial relations.

The mass media usually focus attention on the most dramatic activities of unions and employers—midnight negotiations, nationwide strikes, picket-line incidents, and other highly visible events. Less well understood is the tangible result of all the sound and fury that accompanies negotiations—the collective agreement. For unionized workers, "the agreement" (or "the contract") is an important factor shaping their work lives: stewards, elected union officers, and paid union officials spend much of their time ensuring that management lives up to its side of the agreement; supervisors and human resource managers closely monitor the application of the agreement; and labour arbitrators settle grievances over the interpretation of provisions in the agreement. In short, for those involved in industrial relations on a day-to-day basis, the collective agreement is a matter of critical concern.

THE EVOLUTION OF THE COLLECTIVE AGREEMENT

Before the Second World War, most collective agreements in Canada were very brief and simple (see Exhibit 11.1). Although the issues covered by these early agreements still figure prominently in union–management relations, most modern collective agreements are much longer, more complex, and cover a wider range of issues. In fact, collective agreements in this country (and in the United States) are also longer, broader, and more detailed than are contracts in most other advanced industrial societies. These distinctive characteristics of Canadian collective agreements emerged as one part of a broader restructuring of industrial relations in the 1940s (MacDowell, 1978).

Exhibit 11.1
Collective Agreements 100 Years Ago

In 1901, when Local 713 of the Carpenters' Union reached an agreement with contractors in Niagara Falls, Ontario, the contract contained only eight brief clauses:

1. The rate of wages for journeymen carpenters and joiners shall be 25 cents per hour.

2. The hours of work shall be nine (9) hours per day.

3. The rate of pay for legal holidays and overtime shall be time and one-half, except for mill hands.

4. No union man shall take any kind of lump work or sub-contract from a carpenter-contractor.

5. If a contractor applies to the union for men and the union cannot supply them, the contractor can hire any men he likes at any rate of wages, but these men must be discharged before any union man is laid off.

---

6. Planing mill proprietors shall be bound by these promises only as far as they apply to carpenters and bench hands.

7. Pay days shall be on Saturdays, and the contractor shall pay the men their wages on the job where they are working.

8. The agreement shall go into effect on May 1, 1901, and shall continue for one year.

Source: "Collective Agreements 100 Years Ago" (p. 3) from *The Development and Enforcement of the Collective Agreement* by C. H. Curtis. Copyright © 1966 Kingston: Industrial Relations Centre, Queen's University. Reprinted by permission of Industrial Relations Centre, Queen's University.

Early craft unions, like the Carpenters, were often able to defend their interests by exercising control over the supply of skilled labour and instituting a variety of work rules. However, the unskilled and semi-skilled workers who flocked into industrial unions in the 1930s and 1940s were in a different position. Lacking scarce skills, workers in industrial unions concentrated on obtaining their goals through negotiations with individual employers. In addition, the relative political weakness of the Canadian labour movement meant that they had to look to the negotiating process as the principal means of advancing their members' interests. They could not act like unions in many European countries, where government legislation played a more important role in regulating the employment relationship.

Even more important than the nature of unionism, however, were the strategies and policies pursued by employers and the government, particularly those adopted in response to the industrial and political unrest of the 1940s. Paradoxically, the fierce resistance of Canadian employers to their employees' attempts to unionize was (and, to a degree, still is) a major cause of the growth of detailed collective agreements. Because employers chose to resist unionization, "unions were generally forced to seek recognition on a plant-by-plant basis, and the process of recognition took on the characteristic of a battle for the hearts and minds of the workers involved. Where the union won, it was typically powerful enough to require management to sign a collective agreement that, over time, became increasingly elaborate" (Adams, 1995: 502). Furthermore, once required to negotiate with a union, most employers tend to seek ways to restrict the workplace activities of unions, to reduce the number of issues subject to union influence, and to adhere to collective agreements in a narrowly legalistic manner, all of which adds to the formality of agreements.

This strategy of limiting the impact of industrial conflict has been abetted by state policy and by the way collective agreements have come to be interpreted by arbitrators. Since 1944, most jurisdictions in Canada have required collective agreements to be binding for periods of no less than one year, and have banned most work stoppages during the life of the agreement. Thus, unlike countries where agreements can be renegotiated whenever one side or the other feels some change is warranted, Canadian management and union negotiators must strive for collective agreements that are comprehensive and detailed. Moreover, because most arbitrators hold that management retains authority over any matter not explicitly mentioned in the collective agreement, unions are compelled to channel their concerns into the negotiating process, rather than deal with management more informally. Last, because grievance arbitration (the approved method of resolving disputes during the term of the agreement) has become so legalistic, contract language has to be drafted with great care.

Collective agreements have also been influenced by legal developments in another way. General labour statutes, human rights legislation, occupational health and safety acts, and employment standards laws all set out a number of requirements to which the collective agreement must conform. For example, it is illegal to discriminate against employees on a number of specific grounds, including age, sex, religion, and disability; in most provinces, joint safety committees must be established; and employees must be provided with a paid day off on certain statutory holidays.

The parties have often attempted to incorporate such legal requirements explicitly into the collective agreement, even though this is not strictly necessary (e.g., even if a contract has no anti-discrimination clause, it is still illegal to discriminate). There are several reasons for including these kinds of legal requirements in the agreement. First, the contract provisions are a good way of educating those bound by the contract, employees and management alike, about their legal obligations. Second, through negotiation the parties are able to specify the manner in which the legal requirements might best be made to fit their specific needs (e.g., the composition of a safety committee or what happens when some employees must work on a statutory holiday). Third, by including certain legal requirements in the collective agreement, the issue becomes subject to the grievance procedure, which is usually a speedier and less expensive way to settle problems than through a human rights tribunal or the courts. For all these reasons, the collective agreement plays a central role in Canadian labour–management relations.

Still, it must not be forgotten that relationships in the workplace are not fully regulated by formal agreements. In nonunion settings, of course, employment relations are governed by the individual contract of employment and employment legislation. Although some nonunion employers follow employment policies that are closely modelled on collective agreements (often in an attempt to dissuade their employees from unionizing), individual employees in such workplaces are usually powerless to win improvements in their terms and conditions of employment in the face of employer recalcitrance. Indeed, at their heart, collective agreements reflect a transformation of this relationship into one of collective regulation of employment (see Exhibit 11.2).

Exhibit 11.2
What Makes Canada Unique?

North American collective agreements differ from collective agreements in many other countries in a number of ways:

- Most are negotiated at the level of the establishment and not the industry or regional level.
- They are generally longer and more complex.
- They cover a wider range of issues.
- They are legally binding for a fixed period of time; in many other countries, agreements are not legally enforceable and may be reopened at any time at the request of one of the parties.
- Disputes between the parties about the interpretation, application, or administra-

tion of collective agreements are usually settled by binding arbitration, not through labour courts or other government bodies.

Even though Canadian agreements are often very similar to American agreements, there are some differences:

- Canadian collective agreements commonly contain union security clauses, which are illegal in many U.S. states.
- By law, work stoppages are banned during the term of Canadian collective agreements, and grievance arbitration must be used instead; in the United States, the parties must determine these issues for themselves.

THE COLLECTIVE AGREEMENT: AN OVERVIEW

Anyone who leafs through a collective agreement for the first time finds a bewildering array of articles, clauses, subclauses, appendices, schedules, letters of intent, and other sections, many with mysteriously phrased names (see Exhibit 11.3). Collective agreements are sometimes so complex and legalistic that workers and supervisors barely understand their contents and need to rely on experienced shop stewards, union business agents, and specialized managers to explain them. For the student of collective agreements, matters are made worse by the fact that the thousands of collective agreements in effect in Canada at any one time differ from each other quite substantially. After all, each agreement is the product of a unique negotiating relationship, and each is amended many times as the two sides renegotiate the terms and conditions of employment.

Nevertheless, most collective agreements have some basic similarities, as well as a common structure that underlies their many complexities and surface variations. Like most legal contracts, collective agreements are divided into articles (also called sections or clauses), which are usually further divided into subclauses. Almost all collective agreements begin with an article (or a "preamble") explaining the purpose of the agreement.

If the agreement is complex, a list of definitions may also appear near the beginning of the document. Most agreements then include a number of clauses that define and regulate the relationship between the union and the employer—clauses setting out the definition of the bargaining unit, outlining management rights and union security, establishing a grievance arbitration procedure, and so on.

The second major group of articles in the agreement specifies hours of work and details of compensation. Here one finds articles that define the normal length of the work day, rules about overtime, rights to time off with and without pay, wage schedules covering different classifications of employees, various wage premiums (such as shift bonuses), and other matters that together constitute what is called the wage–effort bargain.

Exhibit 11.3
Table of Contents of a Typical Collective Agreement

1. Definitions
2. Management Rights
3. Union Recognition
4. Union Security and Check-Off
5. No Strikes or Lockouts
6. No Other Agreement/Representation
7. No Discrimination
8. New Employees
9. Correspondence
10. Municipal Council Minutes
11. Grievance Procedure
12. Arbitration
13. Seniority
14. Posting and Filling Vacancies
15. Lay Off, Recall and Bumping
16. Hours of Work
17. Overtime
18. Wages and Allowances
19. Vacation
20. Statutory Holidays
21. Sick Leave
22. Effect of Absence on Sick Leave, Vacations and Statutory Holidays
23. Job Evaluation Program
24. New or Revised Classifications
25. Bereavement Leave
26. Jury and Court Witness Duty
27. Leave of Absence of Union Officials
28. Maternity and Adoption Leave
29. Leave of Absence
30. Benefit Plans
31. Technological Change
32. Occupational Health and Safety
33. Sexual and Personal Harassment
34. Contracting Out
35. Employee Records
36. Discipline
37. Rehabilitation and Retraining Program
38. Multi-Employer Agreement
39. Volunteers
40. Bulletin Boards
41. Term of Agreement
42. Letters of Understanding
43. Wage Schedules

Source: Extract from agreement between the Corporation of the District of Saanich and the Police Board of the Corporation of the District of Saanich and the Canadian Union of Public Employees, Local 374 (January 1, 2005, to December 31, 2006). Reprinted with permission of the Canadian Union of Public Employees & the Corporation of the District of Saanich.

A third group of clauses in collective agreements deals with how the organization's internal labour market and work system will be operated. For example, agreements often include rules governing how promotions are to be made, how technological changes are to be instituted, how layoffs are to be handled, and so on. Although articles dealing with these matters are not necessarily grouped together in the agreement, they have in common the function of controlling individual and group rights with respect to the allocation of tasks and job opportunities.

The fourth group of clauses typically found in agreements (again not necessarily all in one place) sets out conditions with respect to the physical work environment (such as safety rules), behaviour in the workplace (for example, rules on discipline), and the broader "human rights" of employees that must be respected by all of the parties to the agreement.

The collective agreement usually concludes with a clause that specifies the duration of the agreement, followed by the signatures of the employer and union representatives. Many agreements also include appendices containing details of particular arrangements considered too lengthy or complex to include in the body of the agreement (such as wage schedules). Lastly, attached to some agreements are letters of understanding, memoranda of agreement, or other supplementary documents; depending on the wording, these may be considered part of the agreement, or they may be unenforceable promises made by one side or the other. Exhibit 11.4 contains suggestions on how to draft a collective agreement.

Exhibit 11.4
Tips on Drafting the Collective Agreement

- Use plain language so that workers and supervisors can understand and work with the provisions in the agreement.
- Avoid ambiguous language that may create difficulties of interpretation later.
- Use terms consistently throughout the agreement.
- Use non-sexist language.
- Pay attention to the relationship between the different clauses, especially when renegotiating part of an agreement that may have implications for other provisions.
- Remember that the agreement must respect legislation regarding employment standards and human rights. Collectively negotiated clauses that do not conform to such legislation are unenforceable.
- When an agreement is reached after the previous agreement has expired, be careful to specify which provisions of the new agreement are retroactive.
- Structure the agreement in a logical way by putting all related clauses together, and use headings, subheadings, a table of contents, and an index to allow workers and supervisors to find their way around the document.
- Put lengthy details in appendices, but remember to refer to them in the body of the agreement as being considered part of the agreement.

Source: Sack and Poskanzer, 1996.

The remainder of this chapter discusses the four main groups of articles just outlined. Because it would be impossible to discuss every conceivable type of clause in each of the four categories, the emphasis is on types of clauses that are common, generally significant, or of special contemporary relevance.[2]

THE UNION–MANAGEMENT RELATIONSHIP AND THE CONTROL OF CONFLICT

Inherent in the very idea of a collective agreement is the existence of a relationship between an employer and a group of employees acting collectively through a union. Thus, an agreement does more than define the terms and conditions of employment; it establishes and regulates a relationship between two organizations, a process that normally entails conflict over the division of authority and the definition of rights and responsibilities. In practice, the contours of the union–management relationship are defined by three central features of collective agreements: the extent to which joint decision-making replaces unilateral managerial authority, the status and role accorded to the union, and the manner in which disagreements and disputes that arise during the life of the agreement are handled.

Management Rights

Most collective agreements contain a *management rights* clause, which acknowledges the employer's right to manage the establishment, subject to other provisions in the collective agreement (see Exhibit 11.5). To understand the function and significance of the management rights clause, we first need to consider the wider issue of authority in the unionized workplace.

In a nonunion workplace, employers enjoy wide discretion in managing the organization and in determining the terms and conditions of employment, working conditions, and the organization of work. Legislated employment standards must be observed, of course, and some individual employees or small groups, particularly those who possess a special skill, may have the leverage to win improvements in their employment conditions. But, on the whole, managers are entitled to run their organizations pretty much as they see fit.

However, when employees unionize, unilateral management control is replaced, to some extent at least, by bilateral control. Indeed, a collective agreement embodies a set of compromises and joint decisions over a range of issues affecting the employees. But although it is clear that the issues spelled out in a collective agreement are no longer the sole prerogative of management, what about issues not dealt with explicitly in the agreement? This question has given rise to considerable controversy over the years.

The traditional view—called the *residual-rights* (or *reserved-rights*) *theory*—is that the employer retains complete control over any issue not spelled out in the collective agreement. This interpretation has been challenged, not only by labour leaders but also by some industrial relations scholars and arbitrators. For instance, it has been argued that the advent of collective bargaining fundamentally alters the relationship between labour and management by making them equal partners. On this view, it is therefore unfair to give one of the parties all of the rights at the outset and to require the other to whittle away at them. Instead, where a collective agreement is silent on a particular disputed issue, consideration should be given to the whole agreement and to the wider relationship between the parties, or there should even be an obligation to negotiate a joint solution.

Critics of the residual-rights theory have not prevailed, however, and managerial authority over issues and decisions not specifically governed by the collective agreement remains largely unimpaired. The major exceptions are cases where it can be shown that, in exercising its rights under the collective agreement, management acted in bad faith, in an arbitrary or discriminatory manner, or for the primary purpose of subverting the collective bargaining relationship (Fisher and Sherwood, 1984).

Exhibit 11.5
Management Rights Clauses

A "GENERAL" MANAGEMENT RIGHTS CLAUSE:

Management Rights

28.1 The Union recognizes that the Company has the exclusive right to operate and manage the business, to maintain order and efficiency and to hire, promote, and with just cause to demote, discipline or discharge employees.

The rights reserved to Management herein are subject to the other provisions of this Agreement and should be exercised in a manner consistent with them. Management shall exercise its rights in a manner that is fair, reasonable and consistent with the terms of this Agreement.

Source: Agreement between Legacy Hotel Corporation (The Fairmont Hotel Vancouver) and the National Automobile, Aerospace, Transportation and General Workers Union of Canada (CAW-Canada), Local 4275 (August 1, 2005 to July 31, 2008). Copyright © CAW Canada. Reprinted with permission of CAW-Canada.

A "DETAILED" MANAGEMENT RIGHTS CLAUSE:

Management Rights

4.01 The Union acknowledges that it is the exclusive function of the Company to:
- (i)   Maintain order, discipline, and efficiency;
- (ii) Hire, classify, direct, and lay off;
- (iii) Discharge, transfer, promote, demote, suspend or otherwise discipline employees subject to the right of the employee concerned to lodge a grievance as herein provided;
- (iv) Make and alter from time to time, rules and regulations to be observed by the employees provided that they are not inconsistent with the provisions of this Agreement;
- (v)   Generally to manage the industrial enterprise in which the Company is engaged and without restricting the generality of the foregoing, the right to plan operations, to determine services to be performed and the methods, procedures and equipment in connection therewith, the engineering and designing of its products, the control of materials and parts to be incorporated in the products produced, and the extension, limitations, curtailment or cessation of operations.

4.04 The Company agrees that these functions will be exercised in a manner consistent with the provisions of this Agreement.

Source: Extracted from collective agreement between H. J. Heinz Company of Canada Ltd. and United Food and Commercial Workers Union, Local 459 (May 1, 2007 to April 30, 2011). Reprinted with permission of UFCW Canada.

But this leaves us with something of a puzzle: If the residual-rights approach is so deeply entrenched, why bother to include a management rights clause at all? Even if there is no management rights clause, arbitrators still apply the rule that any issue not dealt with in the collective agreement remains within the prerogative of the employer. Furthermore, most experts admit that the exact wording of the management rights clause only rarely has any importance in determining the outcome of grievances or arbitration cases.

One reason why so many agreements include a management rights clause is that the practice was established in the years during which there still was debate and uncertainty over the issue, a tradition that simply continued long after the debate was settled. Second, since arbitral principles are not cast in stone, the continued inclusion of such clauses may simply reflect management's reluctance to leave itself vulnerable should arbitrators' thinking change. Third, it has been suggested that management rights clauses are included as a sort of psychological concession to employers, who do not otherwise gain very much in a collective agreement, or as a means of reminding employees that the employer continues to possess a wide range of unilateral rights (Hébert et al., 2003: 78).

No matter what the reason for their inclusion in agreements, management rights clauses typically come in two different types (see Exhibit 11.5). Some employers prefer a "general" clause that simply affirms the principle of residual rights. Other employers prefer a clause that spells out their rights in some detail, though they are usually careful to include a phrase making clear that the list is not exhaustive. For unions, the following is crucial: (1) that the clause make clear that the provisions of the collective agreement take precedence over any general management rights; (2) that any reference to management's right to discipline employees be limited to cases where there is "just cause"; and (3) that, if possible, the clause should include a more general statement that the exercise of management rights must be consistent with the spirit of the collective agreement and be applied in a reasonable manner.

Although the management rights clause is sometimes considered to be a mere formality, its significance rests in the underlying issues. According to two labour lawyers, the clause is "a battleground for the competing interests of the parties: management wants to assure maximum flexibility by including a clause giving it wide powers as well as specific authority; the union wishes to limit management's discretion by resisting a management-rights clause altogether or by narrowing it as much as possible" (Sack and Poskanzer, 1996: 8-5).

Union Rights and Security

When a union becomes the certified bargaining agent for a group of employees, it is said to have been "recognized" by the employer. Most collective agreements contain a clause (often simply repeating the certifying agency's definition of the bargaining unit) making this recognition explicit and defining which employees are members of the unit.

Certain categories of employees are commonly excluded from the bargaining unit, for example, supervisors, security personnel, and employees who have access to confidential information regarding labour relations. More significant is the exclusion of part-time, casual, and temporary employees. From the employer's point of view, excluding such employees from the coverage of the collective agreement is often advantageous because it is thereby possible to pay them at lower rates than unionized full-time workers, to avoid providing them with certain employee benefits, and more generally to treat them as a flexible, reserve labour force with few job rights. In the past, unions often tacitly or overtly approved of this strategy, not least because it provided full-time, male workers with greater employment security and higher wages, leaving the predominantly female and young peripheral labour force as an inexpensive cushion against risk.

The dramatic growth in recent years of part-time and other "atypical" forms of employment, as well as the expansion of the services sector in which such jobs are concentrated, has led unions to pay more attention to improving collective agreement provisions for these workers. As Figure 11.1 shows, the number of major collective agreements that contain provisions regarding part-time workers has increased substantially over the last two decades. Of the various part-time issues that might be dealt with in a collective agreement, seniority appears to be a central preoccupation; other important issues include the hours of work of part-time employees and various types of leave provisions.

In any event, the struggle for real recognition and stability does not end with the recognition clause. First, a union is by nature external to the employing organization. Although the union's members are employees of the organization, the union itself has a separate existence and therefore enjoys no automatic status as a part of the organization. Second, many Canadian employers are hostile to unionism, which means that union members and officials must work continuously to ensure that management respects the role of the union. Third, like any other organization, unions need a degree of institutional stability. Fourth, under existing Canadian labour laws, the collective agreement covers all

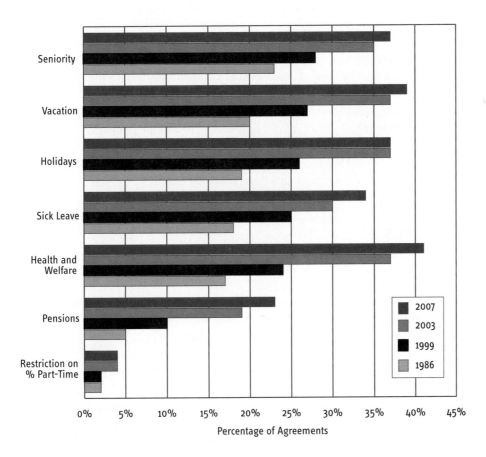

Figure 11.1 Clauses Affecting Part-Time Workers in Major Collective Agreements, Various Years

members of the bargaining unit, not just union members, which means that the union works on behalf of nonunion employees as well as its own members.

For these reasons, unionized employees normally attempt to negotiate a variety of provisions that allow their union to make its presence felt in the workplace and give it a degree of security. For example, the right of the union to appoint shop stewards (whose duties include helping workers prepare and present grievances) stems from the collective agreement. Sometimes the agreement specifies how many stewards are to be appointed, and it usually spells out the circumstances under which they and other union officials may leave their workstations to attend to union business.

The most controversial aspect of a union's attempts to establish a degree of stability centres on the interrelated issues of union security and the payment of union dues. A variety of types of union security clauses are found in collective agreements (see Exhibit 11.6). The *closed shop* is a system under which an employer agrees to hire and retain only those workers who are members of the union. A *union shop* clause requires that all employees join the union within a specified period of time after having been hired. A *modified* union shop means that, at the time the collective agreement is signed (or, in some cases, the initial certification), the current employees are not obliged to join the union, but all employees hired subsequently must join. *Maintenance of membership* clauses require that employees who have joined the union (and those who join in the future) must remain in the union. *Rand formula* clauses do not impose any requirements regarding union membership, but they do require all members of the bargaining unit, whether or not they are union members, to pay union dues (a process called dues check-off). Some Rand formula clauses exempt certain workers from this requirement (for example, if they have religious objections to paying union dues) or permit nonunion members to stipulate that their dues be donated to a charity instead of going to the union. Almost all major collective agreements in Canada have a Rand formula clause. If unions are unable to convince their employer to agree to any form of union security, this is known as the *open shop*.

Most collective agreements in Canada provide for some degree of union security (Figure 11.2). Almost half (48.9 percent) provide for either a full or modified union shop, and a further 7.5 percent impose a closed shop. Slightly more than 40 percent of agreements, covering almost 45 percent of employees, contain no union membership requirement, although most of these contain a Rand formula clause.

Exhibit 11.6
Union Security Clauses

A *closed shop* clause:

2.01 (a) The employers shall employ as employees members of the Union in good standing in the performance of all work coming within the scope of this Agreement and shall continue in their employ only employees who are in good standing with the Union.

2.01 (b) (i) All such employees shall be hired through the Union office, except as thereinafter provided . . .

Source: Extract from Agreement between the Master Insulators' Association of Ontario Inc. and the International Association of Heat and Frost Insulators and Asbestos Workers, Local 95 (June 7, 2004 to April 30, 2007).

A *union shop* clause:

(IV, 2) All employees in the employment of the Company shall, as a condition of continued employment, maintain membership in good standing in the Union. New employees shall, as a condition of continued employment, become members of the Union thirty (30) days after becoming employed by the Company.

Source: Extract from Labour Agreement between Norske Canada, Powell River Division, and the Communications, Energy and Paperworkers Union of Canada, Local 76 (April 30, 2003 to April 30, 2008). Reprinted with permission of CEP of Canada.

A *Rand formula* clause:

(10.01) The Employer will as a condition of employment deduct an amount equal to the amount of the membership dues from the monthly pay of an employee.

(10.04) An employee who satisfies the Employer . . . that he or she is a member of a religious organization whose doctrine prevents an employee as a matter of conscience from making financial contributions to an employee organization and that the employee will make contributions to a charitable organization . . . equal to dues, shall not be subject to this Article . . .

Source: Extract from Agreement between the Treasury Board of Canada and the Canadian Association of Professional Employees, Economics and Social Sciences Services Group (Expiry June 21, 2007).

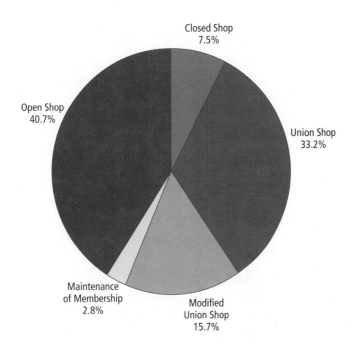

Figure 11.2 Union Membership Provisions in Major Collective Agreements, 2007 (percentage of agreements)

The predominance of the Rand formula is related to the wider controversies that swirl around the issues of union security and the deduction of union dues. On one side, many employers claim that union security clauses infringe upon the rights and freedoms of individual workers who may not wish to join a union. On the other side, unions argue that the absence of such clauses can easily undermine their effectiveness by allowing nonunion workers to remain on the job while union workers are out on strike. They also contend that such clauses are needed to discourage "free riders"—those workers who, as members of the bargaining unit, are legally entitled to the benefits and protections negotiated by the union, but who might be tempted to avoid their share of the costs and sacrifices by not joining. The Rand formula was devised as a compromise between these two positions; it prevents nonunion workers from taking a "free ride" but does not entail compulsory unionism.

In 22 American states, legislation prohibits unions and employers from negotiating various types of union security provisions, including the closed shop, the union shop, and dues check-off. These acts are called "right-to-work" legislation and reflect the view that the right of an individual employee to refuse to join a union or pay union dues outweighs the collective rights of the majority of workers in a bargaining unit to ensure institutional security and a fair sharing of the costs entailed in negotiating and administering the collective agreement.

In Canada, despite occasional calls to import right-to-work legislation, such restrictions have not been adopted. In fact, most jurisdictions in Canada require that, at a minimum, the Rand formula be included in collective agreements. Employers and unions are therefore free to negotiate any provision regarding union membership that they wish.

Workplace Conflict and the Contract

Although collective agreements establish the terms and conditions of employment for a set period, numerous sources of tension remain that can spark disputes at any time. Unanticipated changes in economic conditions may lead to calls for adjustments, such as wage increases if inflation suddenly surges, or wage reductions or other concessions if profitability drops. Similarly, issues not covered by the agreement may suddenly emerge; an example is technological change in the workplace that threatens jobs or disturbs established patterns of pay. More generally, the day-to-day management of work is a permanent source of potential conflict, since employees and their managers do not necessarily see eye to eye on such issues as the pace of work, the style of supervision, and adequate working conditions. Finally, the collective agreement itself may give rise to disputes, since its meaning may not always be clear and its application in particular circumstances may be disputed. For all these reasons, collective agreements usually contain provisions for dealing with conflict.

No-Strike Clause One of the chief mechanisms for regulating conflict is the *no-strike clause*, in which the parties agree that there shall be no strikes or lockouts during the life of the collective agreement, and instead, that they will use the dispute resolution procedures available under the agreement, e.g., grievance procedures and third-party arbitration.

That a majority of collective agreements in Canada contain such a clause is hardly surprising since Canadian labour law generally prohibits the use of strikes or lockouts while the contract is in effect. The legal and contractual prohibitions on the use of work stoppages are not always effective, however, and mid-contract work stoppages do occur in Canada (see Chapter 12). Because arbitrators, labour boards, and the courts tend to disapprove of such strikes and have proved willing to assess damages against unions that encourage or condone them, these clauses play an important role in forcing union leaders to restrain their own members, to bring an end to mid-contract strikes, or at least to remain uninvolved, thus depriving the strikers of legitimacy and organizational support. In addition, employers can use the threat of applying these clauses as leverage to end the strike on terms that are unfavourable to the strikers (Wells, 1986). Thus, even if no-strike clauses do not actually prevent conflict from breaking out into the open during the life of an agreement, they play an important role in reducing the incidence and effectiveness of this open conflict.

Grievance Arbitration A second conflict regulation mechanism, found in virtually every collective agreement in Canada, is the *grievance arbitration procedure*. Grievance arbitration procedures provide a means of settling any differences between the parties arising from the application, interpretation, administration, or alleged violation of the collective agreement. Collective agreements usually require that a grievance be taken first to the immediate supervisor. If the grievance is not resolved there, it may be appealed to one or more higher levels of management. If it still cannot be resolved, collective agreements almost always provide for binding settlement by an outside arbitrator or arbitration board (see Chapter 13 for a full treatment of this subject).

For our purposes, it is important to stress that such procedures became required by law at the same time that industrial conflict during the collective agreement was banned; indeed, the requirement that grievance arbitration procedures be included in collective agreements was an attempt to provide workers and unions with a method of dealing with problems while they were legally prevented from exerting pressure through a strike. Grievance arbitration is not a full substitute, since the disputes that are technically arbitrable include only those covered by the collective agreement; moreover, the rule that workers must usually "obey now, grieve later" means that management's decisions must be followed when they are issued, while the aggrieved employee can only complain through the sometimes cumbersome and lengthy grievance procedure. In practice, of course, workers and unions can bring their concerns to the attention of management by using a range of informal tactics, including slowdowns, work-to-rule campaigns, and even sabotage. It is also common for stewards and supervisors to reach informal agreements in response to grievances that are not likely to receive an arbitrator's ruling.

Labour–Management Committees Collective agreements sometimes create a special mechanism for raising and discussing non-contractual issues related to labour–management relations—the *labour–management committee*. Plant-level or firm-level labour–management committees, made up of representatives from both union and management, can serve as a forum to discuss matters of mutual interest. These committees, which can be permanent or ad hoc, might deal with health and safety, alcohol and drug abuse, the introduction of changes into the workplace (like telework or job sharing), work schedules, training and retraining, technological changes, quality and efficiency, reduction of waste, or any other issue that the parties want to handle away from the negotiating table.

The growth of labour–management committees in recent years has been significant. In the mid-1980s, 38 percent of major collective agreements provided for such a committee; by 2007, the frequency had soared to 90 percent. The effectiveness of labour–management committees varies considerably, often reflecting the nature of the relationship between the parties. Decisions or recommendations normally require mutual agreement. Participation on such committees does allow workers and their unions an opportunity to influence management decisions, but in the absence of mutual agreement, management's decisions prevail.

Joint-Governance Agreements   Another mechanism designed to regulate the relationship between labour and management is the *joint-governance agreement* (Verma and Cutcher-Gershenfeld, 1993). These agreements, which tend to last between four and six years (instead of the more common two or three), typically involve a trade-off whereby employers secure the stability and predictability that comes with a long-term agreement, as well as concessions designed to reduce labour costs and increase productivity; in return, unions usually gain greater job security and more involvement in organizational decision making. For example, an agreement signed in 2000 between Zehrs Markets and the United Food and Commercial Workers contained an employer pledge not to lay off any full-time employees and to hire 300 new full-time clerks over the life of the agreement, which extended to 2006.

In some of these agreements, mechanisms are established (such as joint committees) that allow what is in effect "continuous bargaining" on issues related to the organization of work. In addition, because of their lengthy duration, joint-governance agreements often contain provisions for mid-term or periodic revisions of wage rates subject to binding arbitration if an agreement is not reached by the parties.

To a certain extent, these agreements can be seen as an attempt to put the union–management relationship on a new, more stable and co-operative footing; however, the fact that they have often been negotiated against the background of threatened layoffs or plant closures raises the question of their long-term durability. Nevertheless, if the average duration of collective agreements is taken as a rough indicator of the frequency of joint-governance agreements, it would appear that they have grown strongly in popularity since the early 1990s. The average duration of major agreements ratified in the year grew (with some fluctuations) from less than 20 months in 1991 to more than 40 months in 2006. Long-term collective agreements are especially prevalent in smaller bargaining units, in the private sector, and in three industries—wholesale and retail trade, primary industries, and manufacturing (especially pulp and paper). In Quebec, where such agreements (known there as "social contract agreements") are especially popular, by 2002 the average duration of agreements was 46.8 months and almost three-quarters of agreements then in force had an average duration of three years or more. Conversely, the average duration of agreements in Alberta and Ontario in 2006 was shorter than the national average.

THE WAGE–EFFORT BARGAIN

The essence of the employment relationship is the exchange of work time for remuneration. Employers agree to pay wages and other benefits, and in return, they become entitled to direct the work activities of employees during the time for which they have paid. Naturally, employers and workers often have different opinions as to what constitutes a "fair wage" or a "fair day's work." Thus, from the exchange of remuneration for work time and effort springs a wide range of issues that are commonly negotiated and set out in collective agreements. Taken together, the provisions in collective agreements that regulate hours of work, compensation, and incentives constitute what is called the wage–effort bargain.

Hours of Work and Scheduling

Most collective agreements specify the number of daily and weekly hours that workers are normally expected to work, the starting and ending times of the workday, the length of meal breaks, rest breaks, wash-up time, and so on (see Exhibit 11.7). However, for a variety of reasons, the "normal" workday or workweek is not always possible: "only three-quarters of full-time, permanent employees—and fewer than sixty percent of part-time or temporary employees—work a regular, daytime schedule" (Kapsalis and Tourigny, 2004). As a result, many collective agreements contain special rules regarding work time. In cases of shift work, for example, a system may be negotiated for rotating shifts among employees, or shift scheduling may be handled by seniority. Where necessary, the collective agreement will contain provisions for workers who are called in to work for short periods, asked to be on standby (i.e., to remain available during non-working hours), or required to work on weekends.

Exhibit 11.7
Hours of Work Clause

The following clause is typical of an industrial setting where there is shift work.

Article 16: Hours of Work

16.1 Except as otherwise provided in this agreement, the normal working week shall be one of forty (40) hours consisting of five (5) consecutive days from Monday to Friday.

16.1.1 The work week for third (3rd) shift employees is one of thirty-two and one-half ($32\frac{1}{2}$) hours consisting of five (5) consecutive days of six and one-half ($6\frac{1}{2}$) hours, paid for eight (8) hours.

16.2 Regular Shifts

16.2.1 Working hours shall be as follows:

First shift: 06:45 to 15:25
Second shift: 15:20 to 00:00
Third shift: 23:50 to 06:50

16.2.2 Lunch periods: Employees on the regular first and second shifts and all special shifts will be entitled to a 40-minute unpaid lunch period. Third (3rd) shift employees will be entitled to a 30-minute unpaid lunch period.

16.2.3 Rest periods: Each shift shall include one (1) paid ten (10)-minute rest period.

Source: Collective Agreement between Bombardier Aerospace, Canadian Division, Dorval, Mirabel, and St. Laurent, Quebec, and the International Association of Machinists and Aerospace Workers, Montreal Aircraft, Local 712 (December 1, 2005, to November 30, 2008).

Because the regular hours of work specified in the collective agreement may sometimes be insufficient due to work volume, collective agreements commonly deal with the issue of overtime. Apart from the question of the premium to be paid, overtime is contentious because of the differing objectives of management and labour. Employers generally want to be able to require that overtime be worked and to choose the employees who will work the overtime. On the other hand, employees and their unions typically prefer that overtime hours be worked on a voluntary basis and that such hours be distributed fairly. Most agreements do not give workers the right to refuse overtime, and, as of the mid-1980s (the last time statistics were gathered on this question), fewer than half provided for equal sharing of overtime hours. Those agreements that do provide for equal sharing use a number of different systems, since overtime can be shared on a plant- or department-wide basis, within an occupational bracket, by seniority, or some combination of these.

Collective agreements regulate not only daily and weekly hours, but also the amount of working time over the year. Most agreements include clauses specifying the length of annual vacations. Usually the length of vacations is tied to length of service: the longer employees remain with an employer, the longer their vacation periods become. The paid holidays that are provided for in collective agreements (usually between 10 and 13 per year) are generally not tied to length of service. Collective agreements may also specify paid or unpaid leaves of absence of various kinds; among the most common are unpaid personal leave, paid sick leave, and leave for political activity, jury duty, and medical appointments. Recent collective agreements signed by the federal government provide employees with one day per year of paid "volunteer leave" to allow them to work for a charitable or community organization.

The growing number of women in the paid labour force and in the labour movement, as well as changes in family structure, has given rise to a number of changes in collective agreement provisions regarding working time. For example, unions have sought to provide more generous maternity benefits than those required by legislation or available through Employment Insurance (EI). These may include longer periods of leave, payment during the two-week EI waiting period, a higher level of income replacement, stronger protection of seniority during maternity leave, and other enhancements over legislated minimums. In addition to maternity leave, some collective agreements now provide long-term leave for fathers and for parents who adopt children. However, coverage has been less than complete, and many workers still have no access to extended parental leave or enhanced income support.

These trends have also had implications for approaches to work time and work scheduling, as families struggle to balance the demands of work and home (Rochon, 2000). A number of collective agreements now contain flexible work-time provisions that offer employees some leeway in choosing their start and finish times or compressed workweeks (longer hours over fewer days per week). In addition, provisions that permit leaves for the care of a family member, for bereavement, or for responsibilities such as parent–teacher interviews or professional appointments are intended to build a more "family-responsive" workplace. Coverage has been steadily growing: in 2007, around 40 percent of employees covered by collective agreements—predominantly white-collar employees in large bargaining units—benefited from flex-time provisions, and 45 percent were entitled to leave (sometimes paid, sometimes not) to attend to family responsibilities. Only a handful of agreements, however, contained provisions regarding daycare facilities.

A second labour market trend is the growing importance of education and skills in an economy increasingly based on knowledge, information, and advanced technology. Unions have therefore attempted to expand education leave provisions, primarily to enable their members to attend job-related or union-sponsored educational programs. Provisions allowing paid or unpaid job-related education leave are now contained in more than half of agreements, covering more than 60 percent of employees. Provisions for education leave not specifically related to the job are not as common, although 40 percent of agreements contain provisions related to reimbursement for tuition fees and books, and around one-quarter of agreements, covering nearly one-third of employees, provide for employer contributions to a training fund.

A third labour market trend is an increased degree of variability in patterns of working time and income. The continuing shift in employment from manufacturing to the services sector, along with the proliferation of part-time, temporary, and casual work, has increased the number of people who work fewer hours than the traditional 40-hour workweek. This trend can be seen in Table 11.1, which reveals a steady decline in the number of major collective agreements setting the workweek at 40 hours, accompanied by an increase in the number of agreements specifying a shorter workweek. At the same time, however, there is a growing number of workers who regularly put in overtime after their "normal" workweek: for the labour force as a whole, in 1998 "just under a million Canadians put in an average of 8.7 paid overtime hours per week, and another one million worked an average 9.5 unpaid overtime hours" (Hall, 1999: 34).

Compensation

Wages are at the heart of the collective agreement. For most employees, their pay is the chief determinant of their standard of living and one of the main reasons they are in paid employment. For the employer, compensation costs have a significant impact on

Table 11.1 Standard Weekly Working Hours in Collective Agreements,[a] Various Years (percentage of agreements)

	MAJOR AGREEMENTS		
Hours	1990	1999	2007
Less than 35	2.4	2.3	2.7
35 to 39	40.2	43.2	48.0
40	53.4	50.5	45.8
More than 40	4.0	4.0	3.5
Totals	100.0	100.0	100.0
Number of agreements	946	733	971

[a] These figures are based on those collective agreements in which hours of work are specified on a weekly basis.

competitiveness and financial performance. Thus, an important aspect of the collective agreement is the wage level; but just as important is the way the agreement affects the wage structure, wage premiums, and whether wages are linked to performance. In addition, the compensation received by employees includes not only their wages, but a range of other monetary benefits as well.

Wage Structures Sometimes all of the employees covered by a collective agreement receive the same wage rate or salary, but it is more usual for agreements to set out a number of different wage rates (generally hourly rates for production employees and weekly, monthly, or annual rates for office workers and professionals). The pattern of differentials between these rates is known as the *wage structure*. Two types of such structures are common. First, different jobs may be paid different rates. For example, in a pattern common to collective agreements in the steel industry, jobs at Prudential Steel Ltd. are grouped into 27 classes with a differential of 36 cents per hour between adjacent classes. Thus, a Material Handler (Job Class 4) is entitled to a $1.08 per hour premium over the base rate of $22.78, giving a total of $23.86 per hour; a millwright in Class 20 receives an hourly premium of $6.84; a shift leader (Class 27) benefits from a premium of $9.36; and so on.

The second common type of wage structure links wages to length of service. Such systems are common where there are few opportunities to progress upwards through various job classifications. For instance, agreements covering white-collar and professional employees often set out a number of pay steps within each job category, with employees moving up one step at fixed intervals of time. In some cases, progression through these increment levels is also tied to satisfactory job performance. It is also common for the two types of structures to be combined, resulting in a wage or salary "grid" in which the wage rate of an individual employee is determined by both his or her specific job and length of service (see Exhibit 11.8 for an example).

Recently there has been some interest in a third type of wage structure—*pay-for-knowledge*—in which wages are determined by the skills and knowledge that employees possess rather than the particular job that they perform (Celani and Weber, 1998). In some professions this has been a long-standing practice, e.g., where teachers' salaries are tied, in part, to their level of education. Recent attempts to develop pay-for-knowledge systems for other workers reflect the desire of employers to encourage multi-skilling of employees (becoming proficient in multiple areas of expertise within the organization or profession) and to increase their flexibility and discretion in the deployment of workers. Although growing in popularity, pay-for-knowledge pay structures remain less common than other, more traditional wage structures, especially in unionized establishments (Betcherman et al., 1994: 40–42). Almost 30 percent of collective agreements (covering around 35 percent of employees) contain pay-for-knowledge provisions.

Setting rates for particular jobs can give rise to much controversy, since subjective judgments about the relative worth of particular tasks and skills cannot be avoided. Jobs done predominantly by women workers have frequently been placed low on the wage hierarchy because the classification process has been dominated by male assumptions about the nature of skill and ability (Warskett, 1993; Lamson, 1986). In order to redress this, some collective agreements specify that equal pay be accorded to men and women for performing similar work, or work deemed to be of comparable worth; by 1999, around 15 percent of major agreements contained such a provision, compared to fewer than

Exhibit 11.8
A Wage Grid

The grid below illustrates a wage structure that is linked to both the type of job (classified into salary groups) and the length of service (the five "steps"). Note that employees in Salary Group 2 have only two steps instead of five.

For purposes of illustration, the rates are shown for only five of the thirteen groups, and, although the actual agreement sets out the rates for each group on an hourly, biweekly, monthly, and annual basis, only the biweekly rates are shown in this extract.

SALARY STRUCTURE—JULY 1, 2002 (BIWEEKLY RATES)

Salary Group	Entry Level	Step 1	Step 2	Step 3	Step 4	Step 5
Salary Group 2 (e.g., Clerk II)	—	—	—	$1070.12	—	$1150.90
Salary Group 5 (e.g., Cheque Control Clerk)	$1254.70	$1320.74	$1370.23	$1421.55	$1478.88	$1530.32
Salary Group 8 (e.g., Technical Writer)	—	$1671.91	$1735.08	$1801.57	$1871.92	$1945.89
Salary Group 11 (e.g., Webmaster)	—	$2130.20	$2215.78	$2302.67	$2395.97	$2491.91
Salary Group 13 (e.g., Senior Database Administrator)	—	$2491.91	$2592.99	$2699.24	$2808.04	$2920.72

Source: Extract from Collective Agreement between Insurance Corporation of British Columbia and the Canadian Office and Professional Employees' Union, Local 378 (July 1, 2006, to June 30, 2010). Reprinted with permission of ICBC.

6 percent in 1986. In addition, many Canadian jurisdictions have some kind of pay equity legislation. Because of such legislation, the federal government agreed to provide several classifications of workers represented by the Public Service Alliance of Canada a total of $3.6 billion in pay equity payments covering the period 1985 to 1998. However, winning pay equity payments from employers has not always been easy. For example, unions representing Bell Canada employees launched a pay equity claim in the early 1990s that, when it was finally resolved in 2006, resulted in a settlement totalling $104 million.

Performance-Based Wage Systems In all of the wage structures discussed above, an individual's wage or salary rate is *fixed*, either in relation to his or her specific job, length of service, or level of education or skill (or some combination of these factors). However, some collective agreements provide for *performance-based pay*, usually as a supplement to the basic rates.

One traditional method of linking pay to performance is known as *piecework*, in which workers' pay is determined, at least in part, by their rate of output (the number of "pieces" they produce). These systems can be quite complex, since circumstances such as machine breakdown and other necessary interruptions in work have to be taken into account. Because each task must have a piecework rate set for it, the administrative costs can be high, and the setting of rates may give rise to considerable conflict. For these reasons, only a handful of contracts (mostly in the clothing and forestry industries) incorporate a piecework system.

Another method of linking pay to performance is through the use of bonuses, which can be paid to individuals, groups, or all employees based on some measure of performance. When paid to individuals, bonuses are generally based on supervisors' evaluations and are known as merit bonuses. For groups of employees, bonuses are commonly based on some measure of productivity or cost savings achieved in their work area or department. Finally, profit-sharing and stock-ownership plans link employees' pay to the broader performance of the firm.

Performance-based pay is often favoured by employers, who argue that it stimulates work effort and rewards above-average performance. Unions have been more skeptical, believing that such schemes introduce an element of subjectivity and uncertainty into the compensation package, and may create competition between workers that will undercut collective solidarity. Less than 10 percent of collective agreements currently include any form of individual or group wage-incentive plan.

Wage Levels, Adjustments, and Premiums The wage *level* is the amount of pay for each classification of employee. For much of the 1980s and 1990s, Canadian employers attempted to improve their competitiveness by reducing labour costs. During the 1993 recession, for example, a record number of major agreements contained wage freezes or cuts: 44.8 percent of agreements negotiated that year, covering nearly two-thirds of unionized workers, provided for either no increase or a reduction in wages. Since then, as the economy has improved, the number of major collective agreements containing wage freezes or cuts has declined dramatically. Similarly, real negotiated wage rates (that is, wage rates adjusted to account for inflation) actually declined through much of the 1980s and early 1990s; but in most of the last 10 years, negotiated wage adjustments have matched or been slightly above the rate of inflation.

Another innovation proposed by some employers as a means of reducing total compensation costs is the use of *two-tiered* wage structures, in which new employees are paid lower rates than are incumbent employees. In some cases these differences disappear as the new employee progresses, but in others the differential is permanent. Most unions have fiercely resisted this strategy because it creates two classes of employees, thus threatening the principle of equality of treatment. Currently, less than 10 percent of collective agreements contain a two-tiered pay scale (though around one-quarter provide for two-tiered employment conditions of some sort).

Another method of lowering labour costs has been to use lump-sum payments (sometimes called "signing bonuses") in place of all or part of an increase in actual wage rates. Such payments reduce increases in wage-related benefits and premiums and, because they are not included in wage rates, allow subsequent contract renegotiations to begin from a lower base. Lump-sum payments have received only limited acceptance in Canada.

In one-year agreements, wage and salary rates are generally fixed, but in multi-year agreements there is often a provision for *wage adjustments*. For example, the agreement might provide for an increase in the wage rates or salary levels at one or more points in time during the life of the agreement. Another method of adjusting the wage level is the inclusion of a "reopener clause," in which the parties agree to renegotiate the wage level at a particular point in time.

Collective agreements can also provide for wage adjustments through cost-of-living allowance (COLA) clauses. COLAs are a special form of premium that began to grow in popularity in the 1950s and became especially common during the inflationary 1970s. The basic idea is that wages should be adjusted to the rate of inflation so that the purchasing power of workers' wages is maintained during the life of the agreement. Therefore the parties can agree to multi-year contracts without risking the erosion of negotiated wages by unanticipated inflation. Actually, very few COLA clauses provide full protection against inflation: some COLAs are triggered only above a certain level of inflation; some are capped (limited to a certain amount of increase); some do not cover the whole contract period; and some do not provide for a full adjustment to the rate of inflation (Wilton, 1980). The decline in the rate of inflation since the early 1980s has meant that many of the remaining COLAs have not been triggered, thus aiding the efforts of employers to remove such protection from collective agreements. Whereas 38 percent of major agreements in 1981 contained COLA clauses, only around 18 percent of those in force in 2007 contained such clauses.

Finally, the wages received by employees can be augmented by a variety of *wage premiums*, which are supplements to basic pay that arise from certain circumstances, such as shift work, overtime, or work on holidays and weekends. The most usual rate for overtime hours is time-and-one-half, though a small number of agreements simply prescribe straight time for excess hours, and some agreements require more than time-and-one-half. Some collective agreements also have special overtime rates for days worked in excess of the normal workweek. Besides specifying wage premiums, agreements often include special payments for certain circumstances, such as travel allowances for remote worksites, clothing and tool allowances, meal allowances for employees working overtime, "call-in" pay, standby pay, and so forth.

Employee Benefits Compensation includes much more than the actual pay received by employees. In fact, more than 30 percent of total compensation costs in Canada are represented by *employee benefits*. The most common types of benefits found in collective agreements are pensions, long-term and short-term disability plans, sick leave plans, drug plans, vision plans, extended health care, life insurance, and dental insurance (see Figure 11.3). The collective agreement usually spells out the details of the various plans, the eligibility rules (often linked to length of service), and the respective contributions of employer and employees toward the costs of the plans. Such plans used to be considered "fringe" benefits, but they are now so widespread that they are central features of the overall compensation package.

Of the various types of benefits found in collective agreements, pension plans have probably given rise to the most controversy. For example, employers have recently been moving to abandon traditional "defined-benefit" plans (in which pension benefits are fixed) to "defined-contribution" plans (in which the level of the contribution is fixed, but the actual benefit received can vary depending on the performance of the pension fund), since the latter type limits the employer's liability and reduces uncertainty. Defined-contribution and hybrid plans grew from 4.3 percent of major collective agreements in 2003 to 9.2 percent in 2007. (A hybrid plan has features of both: e.g., a base fixed benefit that could be augmented or superceded by an amount determined by the contribution to or performance of the fund.)

More generally, unions regard pension contributions, whether paid by the employer or the employee, as deferred wages. On this basis, they argue that the administration of pension funds should be the joint responsibility of unions and employers. Employers have taken a different view. Since most pension plans in the unionized sector are defined-benefit plans that set out the specific pension benefits, employers argue that, so long as they ensure that these benefits are paid, they should retain control over the funds accumulated and the disposition of any "surplus assets" from pension funds. Currently, about one-third of collective agreements provide for union participation in the administration of the fund, which represents a significant increase since the mid-1980s when less than 10 percent contained such a provision.

The recent economic and political climate has not been conducive to the introduction of new benefits. Indeed, as with wages, many employers have attempted to reduce benefits or to shift a higher proportion of the costs of benefit packages to employees. Nonetheless, recent years have seen a number of innovations that may become more common in the future.

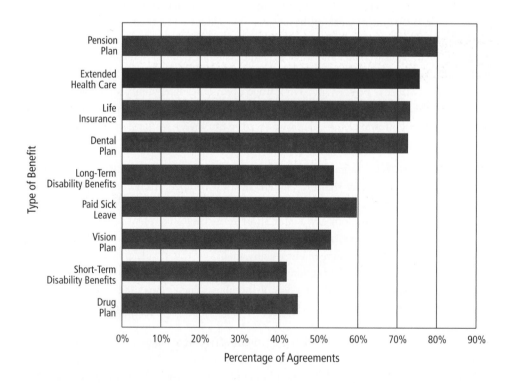

Figure 11.3 Employee Benefits in Collective Agreements Partially or Wholly Paid by Employer, 2007

One recent trend is the increasing use of "flexible benefits" packages (sometimes called "cafeteria-style benefits"). In these benefits systems, employees are allowed more choice in the benefits to which they are entitled (and toward which they contribute part of the costs). This development is meant to make employee benefits packages more responsive to the varying needs and preferences of individual employees. For example, married and single employees may have very different needs for insurance.

In addition, some agreements have begun to incorporate benefits provisions that are more sensitive to the needs of particular groups. For example, some agreements (e.g., between the federal government and its employees, and between the CAW and the major auto manufacturers) now treat same-sex couples on the same footing as other common-law couples. In addition, some recent CAW agreements have also provided for employer-sponsored child care programs and the availability of workplace advocates to provide assistance to women facing harassment on the job or abuse at home.

In conclusion, the wage–effort bargain, encompassing provisions on working time, wages, and employee benefits, is a prominent feature of the collective agreement. Indeed, unionization is often seen solely as an attempt by employees to offset the power of the employer to determine the wage–effort trade-off. However, the employment relationship is much more than a simple exchange of time for money: even after wages and working hours have been agreed on, the organization and control of the workforce and the workplace naturally give rise to a host of issues, many of which centre on disputes between employers and employees over the control of jobs.

THE CONTROL OF JOBS AND WORK

In the absence of unions, management normally controls decisions that affect the internal labour market and the organization of work: how many workers to employ, whom to hire, the types of jobs to be established, the assignment of individual employees to particular tasks, how tasks are to be performed, the pace or quantity of work, whom to promote, how layoffs are to be handled, and so on. For management, decisions about such matters revolve around its desire to minimize labour costs and to maximize productivity. In practice, this means that managers want the rules regulating the internal labour market and the work process to be as efficient and flexible as possible.

These issues look very different from the workers' standpoint. In particular, workers and their unions are concerned that too much managerial flexibility can result in a sense of permanent insecurity for employees, a lack of autonomy for workers and work groups, and the abuse of discretion by managers. Unions have therefore traditionally sought some input into the management of the internal labour market, especially on matters that affect job security. The efforts to secure job rights inevitably conflict with management's desire for flexibility and control, so collective agreements often contain negotiated provisions arising from the struggle for the control of jobs.

Entering the Internal Labour Market

The struggle for control over jobs begins with the processes of hiring and job assignment, which collective agreements regulate in a variety of ways. For example, collective agreements may address hiring and job-assignment decisions by

- stipulating the minimum qualifications or training for new or reassigned employees,
- establishing union–management apprenticeship programs,
- requiring that vacancies be filled from within the organization when possible, or
- restricting supervisors and other non–bargaining unit personnel from performing tasks normally done by union members.

Newly hired employees are usually put on probationary status. Most agreements specify probationary periods for new employees, usually of less than five months, but occasionally longer. The significance of probationary status is that such employees are often not entitled to a number of the protective features of the collective agreement, particularly protection against dismissal if their performance is judged not acceptable. Thus, the use of a probationary period permits management to retain a considerable amount of control over hiring.

Another method by which collective agreements can affect the hiring process is through closed shop arrangements or hiring halls. As discussed earlier, closed shop agreements are a form of union security—the only one that regulates the hiring decisions of the employer. A hiring hall is a union-operated placement office that furnishes registered recruits for employers who have a collective bargaining agreement with the union. The longshoring industry offers a good example of the way union hiring halls function. On the Vancouver waterfront, the composition of work gangs and the allocation of gangs and individual workers to particular tasks are controlled by the workers themselves through a union hiring hall and a joint union–management dispatch system. In this way, longshore workers have been able to exercise a considerable amount of control over hiring, job assignment, and production (Jamieson and Greyell, 1995).

Work Rules

Once employees have been hired and trained, another issue arises: how is the actual work to be performed? Management has traditionally regarded decisions about the speed and quantity of production, the way tasks are defined, the number of employees assigned to particular operations, and so on, to be within its domain. On the other hand, workers and their unions have sometimes sought to win influence over these matters. The speed of an assembly line, or the number of employees allocated to a particular task, for example, are issues of efficiency from management's point of view. From the employees' point of view, however, they affect the quality of working life and the level of employment. The result of this divergence of interests is a struggle over the "frontier of control" (Gilson, 1985). Although such disputes often involve informal tactics and result in unwritten arrangements, such rules are sometimes formalized through the collective agreement.

One type of work rule that is occasionally negotiated is workload. For example, school teachers in a number of provinces have negotiated average and maximum class sizes. Another type of work rule arises in cases where a job classification system is in place. In such circumstances, collective agreements may restrict the assignment of individual workers to jobs within their classification or prohibit supervisors and other employees not in the bargaining unit from performing tasks for which there is a classification. The construction trades in particular attempt to maintain strict control over which workers are permitted to do certain tasks.

Systems of collectively negotiated job classifications have been criticized in recent years by employers on the grounds that they prevent the most efficient allocation of labour. As a result, two types of modifications to existing structures of job classifications have become more common. First, research indicates that job classification systems are being simplified through the reduction of the number and type of job classes (Beaucage and Lafleur, 1994). Second, some employers and unions have introduced measures in collective agreements designed to promote new ways of organizing work. For example, 6.6 percent of major collective agreements now contain multi-skilling provisions, and 17.4 percent include provisions on flexibility in work assignments. However, several unions have resisted the introduction of multi-skilling, expressing concerns about its effect on job protection for traditional tradespersons, or increased stress levels for employees. In this context, the Canadian Auto Workers Skilled Trades Council identified the resistance to multi-skilling as an explicit bargaining strategy at its 2005 Collective Bargaining Convention.

In addition to encouraging multi-skilling, employers have also sought to reorganize work through the introduction of techniques such as teamwork and quality circles (a volunteer group of employees that meet to discuss workplace improvement and present their ideas to management). Because such innovations may affect salary differentials, job classifications, and patterns of authority in the workplace, they are often introduced through the collective agreement (see Exhibit 11.9, and Chapter 6). Such arrangements have often proved to be fragile, however, especially when they have been introduced in the context of negotiations focused on solving a short-term financial crisis.

Exhibit 11.9
Work Organization Clauses

TRADES AND OPERATOR FLEXIBILITY

Flexibility Concept

The company and the union, realizing that the long-term security of our employees will be enhanced by improved productivity, agree to implement flexible work practices.

A committee consisting of company and union executives will meet to establish methods of implementing flexibility and resolve problems or concerns which may arise as a result of flexibility implementation.

It is not the intent of the company to make tradesmen out of operating employees and operating employees out of tradesmen.

Maintenance—Flexibility

1. Flexibility will not result in the elimination of any trade currently in existence in the Dryden operation.
2. Trades employees working alone or on a team will perform all required maintenance, repair, and related work for which they have the ability, regardless of trade.
3. Upon full implementation of flexibility, day tradesmen will receive the additional $.50 premium. . . .

Operating—Flexibility

1. An employee's basic work assignment will be tasks associated with their classification and department.
2. [. . .] Operating employees in a bottom position may be assigned to another department . . . as necessary.
3. When a department is not operating, in whole or in part, any assignments that may be required to another department . . . will first be made to junior employees.
4. Employees will be paid at the rate of their regular occupation . . . or at the rate of the job to which they are assigned, whichever is greater.

General

1. Any task or work which does not require a specialized competency or extensive training can be performed by any unionized employee. [. . .]

Source: Extract from Collective Agreement between Weyerhaeuser (Dryden Operations) and Communications, Energy and Paperworkers Union of Canada, Locals 105 and 1323 (September 1, 2004, to September 1, 2009) Used with permission of the CEPU.

JOB ROTATION GROUPS

27.01 The Company will identify the positions within each category and employees will be allowed to rotate jobs within their job categories in order to promote greater productivity, safety on the job, and job satisfaction. The Company agrees to consult with the affected employees to determine job rotation based on the principle that there is no job ownership. The length of time or duration shall be determined by the Company, consistent with the objectives of the rotation system.

The Company agrees to form a job rotation committee composed of two (2) employees designated by the Union, one of whom may be a full-time union representative, and two (2) company representatives designated by management, one of whom shall be the Operations Manager.

In identifying the position(s) within each category for rotation, the committee shall take into consideration the safety and ergonomic needs of the employee(s), their ability to do other job(s), and the length of time that employee(s) have been working on a similar job. The company agrees that not necessarily all jobs will rotate.

Source: Extract from Collective Agreement between Maple Leaf Pork (Marion Street plant, Winnipeg) and the United Food and Commercial Workers Union, Local 832, July 1, 2005, to June 30, 2009. Reprinted with permission of UFCW Canada.

Movements Within the Internal Labour Market

After they are hired, employees might change jobs within the bargaining unit for a variety of reasons—replacing another employee who is absent or on leave, winning a promotion to a better job, being laterally transferred to a different department that suddenly needs extra help, and so forth. The management of these movements within the internal labour market is a central feature of the collective agreement.

Unions generally favour the principle of seniority—that is, that long-serving employees, because they have invested a considerable portion of their working lives in the organization, are entitled to preferential treatment in job opportunities and security against layoffs. In addition, seniority rights "provide an element of due process by limiting nepotism and unfairness in personnel decisions" and serve "to buttress the bargaining power of unions by curbing competitive and aggressive behaviour that pits one worker against another" (Gersuny, 1982: 519). Although some managers favour a limited use of seniority as a means of reducing tensions over promotion and other decisions, most prefer to retain control over such decisions because they believe that they are in the best position to judge which employees are the most deserving.

In around two-thirds of collective agreements, promotion decisions must take some account of seniority. A small number of these specify that seniority is the only factor to be taken into account, but the great majority specify that seniority will be one criterion (along with skill and qualifications), or that it will be the deciding factor only if all others are equal (see Exhibit 11.10). Even when seniority is not the sole determining factor, it may still be the most important criterion because skill and ability can be difficult to assess, and because management sometimes finds it simpler to use seniority in cases where there is not a great difference in ability (Chaykowski and Slotsve, 1986).

Exhibit 11.10
Sample Seniority Clause

The weight given to seniority vis-à-vis other criteria depends on the exact wording of the clause. The following clause illustrates two common formulas. For some positions (section 12.4.a), the employee with the most seniority will be given the promotion provided that he or she meets the minimum level of "ability, qualifications, and merit." This is known as the "sufficient ability" formula. For other, higher-level positions (12.4.b), seniority comes into play only when these other factors are "relatively equal," a formula known as "relative ability." In another common formula (not illustrated here), seniority is given equal weighting with the other criteria.

ARTICLE 12—SENIORITY

12.1. a) Where the Company determines it necessary to fill a vacant position, other than entry level, within the scope of this Agreement, the position shall be posted. Vacancies will be open to applicants for ten (10) days. It will be the policy of the Company that in filling posted positions, present members of the staff will be given first consideration.

12.4. a) When filling a posted position ranked below that of Manager Customer Service II or below the level of Maintenance Supervisor, Scale Technician or Electrical Supervisor, seniority shall prevail subject to ability, qualifications and merit.

b) When filling a posted position at the level of Manager Customer Service II and above or at the level of Maintenance Supervisor, Scale Technician or Electrical Supervisor and above, or a position of Electrical Technician or Automation Technician, the Company shall select the candidate who, based on ability, qualifications, and merit is determined by the Company to be best suited for the position, and in the event two or more candidates are relatively equal, the Company shall appoint the more senior.

Source: Excerpt from Collective Agreement covering County Operations & Maintenance between Saskatchewan Wheat Pool and Grain Services Union (ILWU–Canada) (February 1, 2000 to January 31, 2003).

It is important to remember that seniority is used in many other decisions besides the regulation of internal movements. Seniority is often used in determining who is offered overtime, who is given first choice of vacation periods, who is given preference in the choice of particular shifts, and who is to be laid off in the case of workforce reductions. In addition to these cases of "competitive seniority" (so called because it is used to settle competing claims among employees), seniority also commonly determines the level of benefits of individual employees (e.g., the length of vacations, eligibility for pensions, etc.).

The pervasive use of seniority as a criterion in decisions about the allocation of jobs and benefits means that agreements frequently contain considerable detail about how seniority is calculated, and it is not unusual for them to require the posting of seniority lists at regular intervals. In fact, although the basic idea of seniority is easy to grasp, its measurement and application are often extraordinarily complex (Hébert et al., 2003: 167–171). For example, seniority can be calculated organization-wide, at the level of the establishment or department, or within an occupational group. A single agreement may use each of these methods for a different purpose, which means that each employee might have several different levels of seniority at the same time.

Aside from the complexity of its calculation, the use of seniority has become contentious in recent years for two other reasons. First, because it favours employees with more years of continuous service, seniority has been challenged on the grounds that it serves as a mechanism of systemic discrimination against women and other comparatively recent entrants to the labour force (Forrest, 1993). Second, as part of the wider pattern of detailed job regulation in North American collective agreements, seniority and other provisions that hamper employers' ability to increase flexibility in the organization and management of work have been criticized. Despite these pressures, the use of seniority as one of the principles used to govern movements within the internal labour market continues to be common.

Exiting the Internal Labour Market

Employers want to be free to reduce the labour force as they see fit, whereas workers and their unions want to avoid job losses, especially during periods of high unemployment. In theory, a clause could be negotiated to guarantee employees employment security, but only a very few collective agreements contain such clauses, and those are predominantly in the public sector. Furthermore, few employment guarantees are absolute; most are limited either to a particular group of employees (e.g., the most senior) or to certain circumstances. Finally, a collectively negotiated employment guarantee is effective only for the duration of the collective agreement, and only for so long as the firm stays in business. In practice, therefore, the main role of the collective agreement is to determine *how* workforce reductions are effected.

Seniority plays an important role in determining which employees are to be laid off. In slightly more than 70 percent of agreements, seniority has to be taken into account in selecting employees for layoffs and in establishing the order in which employees are recalled from layoffs. Collective agreements may also contain "bumping rights." "Bumping" is the practice of allowing senior employees who have been laid off to take the jobs of more junior employees, who may, in turn, take the jobs of even more junior employees. For example, an employee laid off because his or her shift has been eliminated might be permitted to take the job of an employee with less seniority from a different shift, a different job classification, or a different department; the employee who is "bumped" in this way might be able to bump someone else, and so on. More than half of collective agreements contain bumping provisions, though the great majority restrict a worker's ability to bump, for example, by limiting it to certain locations, or requiring a certain level of ability.

In addition to the method of effecting layoffs, collective agreements can offer other forms of protection for employees. One basic type of protection is the requirement that employers notify employees and the union of impending layoffs in order to give them time to make adjustment plans. Although one might think that such provisions would be common, in the late 1990s (the last time statistics were collected on this issue) only a little more than half of major agreements made any mention of layoff notification. Of these, the vast majority provided for less than 45 days' notice. It is possible that the existence of legislation requiring advance notice of layoffs in most Canadian provinces, and at the federal level, makes the achievement of parallel collective agreement provisions less pressing.

Almost one-half of major collective agreements have severance pay plans, and a small number (particularly in the primary metal and transportation equipment sectors) provide for supplementary unemployment benefits. Other examples of workforce reduction protection in agreements include provisions regarding the distribution of work among employees during slack periods, rights to new job openings in other establishments run by the employer, early retirement provisions, and the continuation of benefits in the case of layoffs. But layoff notices, severance pay, supplementary unemployment benefits, and the like only cushion the impact of job loss. Although such provisions may help prevent hasty or unnecessarily drastic reductions, employers still retain the power to reduce the workforce at their discretion. Indeed, despite the emphasis that unions put on improving job security in recent decades, and despite substantial gains in a few cases—including agreements between the federal government and the Public Service Alliance of Canada and between Canada Post and the Canadian Union of Postal Workers—there has been no widespread improvement in any of these types of security.

One particularly contentious area related to workforce reductions is the practice of contracting out, where an employer hires another firm to do work for it rather than using existing employees or hiring new employees. For example, many large institutions, such as universities, subcontract their cleaning operations to independent firms. Because contracting out threatens the jobs of existing employees or prevents growth of the unionized workforce, it is bitterly opposed by workers and their unions. Management, on the other hand, typically wants to be able to contract out, primarily to reduce labour costs (since smaller, specialized firms are not likely to be unionized and often pay lower wages), but also to exercise leverage over its existing employees by raising the possibility of contracting out at the negotiating table.

Unions have had some success in introducing collective agreement provisions restricting the use of contracting out. Between 1986 and 2007, the incidence of such provisions in major collective agreements grew from 36.4 percent to 62.3 percent. The most frequent restriction is the ban on contracting out if it leads to layoffs. Also common are clauses that require the union to be notified if management is planning to contract out. Only a small minority of agreements provide a complete ban on contracting out (see Exhibit 11.11).

> # Exhibit 11.11
>
> ## Contracting-Out Clauses
>
> ### A COMPLETE BAN ON CONTRACTING OUT:
>
> 10.04 The Employer agrees that there will be no new contracting out for the period of this agreement.
>
> 10.05 The Employer will not contract out any work that is performed by employees in the bargaining unit.
>
> Source: Extract from Collective Agreement between Transit Windsor and the Amalgamated Transit Union, Local 616 (October 1, 2005 to September 30, 2009).
>
> ### RESTRICTIONS ON CONTRACTING OUT:
>
> 2.03 Persons not included in the bargaining unit will not perform work which is normally performed by the bargaining unit. . . .
>
> 2.04 The Employer understands the concern of the Union regarding contracting out. When the Employer believes that it may be necessary to contract out work, it will advise the Union in writing seven (7) days in advance, except in cases of emergency. Such written notice shall inform the Union as to the nature of the work to be performed, the name of the contracting Company and the expected duration of the project. If the Union so requests, the Employer will meet with the Union prior to the commencement of the project to discuss alternatives to contracting out. In the case of unforeseen work required to be done during regular hours, before contracting out of any work, the Employer will make every reasonable effort to have the work performed by available bargaining unit employees who would normally perform the work.
>
> The Company agrees that contracting out of any work will not result in the lay-off of any of its employees.
>
> Source: Extracted from Agreement between St. Mary's Cement and United Steelworkers of America, Local 9235 (August 1, 2005 to July 31, 2008).

Technological Change

Differences between workers and employers over the handling of technological change have been occurring since the Industrial Revolution, but these disputes become particularly sharp in times of heightened competitive pressures. Management seeks ways to cut labour costs and increase productivity through technology, while workers are increasingly concerned about job security and the integrity of their skills. Over the last two decades, there has been a slow increase in the proportion of collective agreements that included provisions regarding technological change; currently, almost 60 percent of collective agreements deal specifically with technological change. One out of every two agreements requires the employer to notify and/or consult with the union in advance of technological changes; and around 10 percent require that special layoff notices be provided to employees affected by technological change.

Some form of training or retraining of employees affected by technological change is mandated in about two-fifths of agreements, and a smaller number provide workers with some form of income or employment security in the case of technological change. In a few jurisdictions, legislation exists that allows for the reopening of collective agreements. In general, employers in Canada have been steadfast in their determination to preserve their control over the process of technological change.

THE CONTROL OF WORK BEHAVIOUR AND THE WORK ENVIRONMENT

To this point, we have looked at how collective agreements affect the union–management relationship, the contours of the wage–effort bargain, and the regulation of the internal labour market and the organization of work. To complete the discussion, we now turn to a fourth set of issues—those arising from the social and physical environment in which work is performed. Collective agreements cannot possibly regulate even a small proportion of the issues, tensions, and relationships that spring from the social and physical setting of work. However, negotiated rules frequently do come into play in three general areas: human rights, workplace behaviour, and occupational health and safety.

Human Rights and the Collective Agreement

We have seen throughout this chapter that the collective agreement codifies a wide range of employee and employer rights. For employees, the agreement establishes their right to be paid a certain wage rate and receive certain benefits, to have their seniority taken into account in numerous decisions, and so on. For employers, the management rights clause and prevailing arbitral opinion work together to preserve a considerable degree of authority over the workplace. But the issue of "rights" also crops up in collective agreements in a broader way, through various types of clauses that protect employees from certain types of actions by management, by other employees, or, indeed, by their own union (Scott, 1996).

One common way in which the human rights of employees are protected through the collective agreement is the non-discrimination clause (see Exhibit 11.12). Such clauses typically prohibit discrimination on the basis of sex, race, religion, union activity, and other objectionable grounds; this protection is usually expressed in a general way so that it covers hiring, promotion, job assignment, compensation, and other areas where discrimination may occur. By the late 1990s (the last time statistics were collected on these clauses), around half of major collective agreements in Canada included such a clause, usually written by the parties themselves, but sometimes merely incorporating the human rights code of the relevant government.

Other rights clauses are aimed at protecting specific groups. For example, around 40 percent of collective agreements contain special protections for disabled workers, especially in terms of opportunities to transfer to suitable jobs; and a small number also contain special protection for older workers. Clauses specifically targeted at the problem of sexual harassment have also become more common and are now found in 40 percent of agreements.

Finally, some collective agreements contain clauses with respect to the right to privacy where employers use various means of surveillance. The collective agreement between Canada Post and its employees, for example, limits the use of the "watch and observation system" to the purposes of "protecting the mail and the property of the State against criminal acts" and expressly prohibits its use "as a means to evaluate the performance of employees and to gather evidence in support of disciplinary measures unless such disciplinary measures result from the commission of a criminal act" (CUPW, 2007: s.41.02). The growing use of technology as a means of controlling employees has increased union efforts to protect their members' right to privacy through the collective agreement. Although still not widespread, clauses regulating testing for AIDS and drug use (see Exhibit 11.13), electronic surveillance in the workplace, and the monitoring of electronic mail are likely to grow in coming years.

Exhibit 11.13
Substance Abuse Testing

(24.01) The parties agree that it is in the best interest of all concerned to promote a safe working environment. Accordingly, the Union has no objection to pre-employment and post incident substance abuse testing. The cost of such testing is to be paid for by the employer. Should an individual test positive, such is cause for immediate dismissal. The employer is responsible to notify the Union of an employee testing positive.

Source: Bricklayers Provincial Collective Construction and Maintenance Agreement between Masonry Contractors Association of Alberta and the International Union of Bricklayers and Allied Craftworkers, Local Unions #1 and 2 (May 1, 2005 to April 30, 2007).

Behaviour and Discipline at Work

The modern workplace is pervaded by rules established by management to regulate the behaviour of employees. The purposes of such rules include safety concerns (e.g., procedures in nuclear plants), hygiene considerations (e.g., cleanliness in a food-processing factory), attempts to maximize work time (e.g., limitations on break periods), customer relations (e.g., the attempt by one airline to ban the wearing of earrings by its male flight attendants), general standards of decorum (e.g., "no fighting"), and efforts to reinforce the structure of authority (e.g., respecting the decisions of supervisors). These examples may be rooted in very different circumstances, but they have an important feature in common: they are rules established by management, the enforcement of which entails an array of disciplinary sanctions.

Collective agreements usually grant management the power to institute rules of behaviour and to mete out punishment, subject to the employees' right to grieve. Unions usually prefer not to incorporate specific rules in the collective agreement, since this preserves their right to dispute disciplinary action. Most collective agreements allow management to suspend or discharge employees provided that there is "just cause"—a criterion that is almost always arguable. Some contracts, however, include specific rules and/or penalties (see Exhibit 11.14).

Exhibit 11.14
Specific Discipline Clauses—Example

ABSENTEEISM CONTROL PROGRAM

Unauthorized absences [including late arrivals and early departures] are recorded within a moving 12-month period. According to the number of absences accumulated by the employee during the 12 months immediately preceding the last unauthorized absence, the following disciplinary measures will be applied:

Number of absences during the 12 months preceding the last unauthorized absence	Disciplinary measures to be applied
2nd absence	Verbal reprimand
3rd absence	Written reprimand
4th absence	5-day suspension
5th absence	7-day suspension
6th absence	10-day suspension
7th absence	Discharge

Source: Extract from Convention collective entre Bridgestone/Firestone Canada Inc., usine de Joliette, et Le Syndicat des travailleurs(euses) de Bridgestone/Firestone (CSN) (September 1, 2005 to August 31, 2011). [Translated by authors.]

The imposition of discipline is subject to a number of procedural limitations in some collective agreements, such as the right of an employee to be represented by the union at disciplinary meetings with management, or the requirement that an employee's disciplinary record be "cleared" after a specified period of time (usually one to three years).

Health and Safety

Work kills, maims, and sickens at a horrifying rate. The Canadian Centre for Occupational Health and Safety (2007) reports that more than 850 employees—more than two every day—die from work accidents each year: "From 1993 to 2005, more than 11 203 people lost their lives due to workplace incidents. Another 900 000 per year are injured or become ill."

Occupational health and safety issues are not solely technical questions. As one authority in the field points out, "In all technical questions pertaining to workplace health and safety there is the social element. That is, for example, the power relations in production: who tells whom to do what and how fast. After all, the machine does not go faster by itself; someone designed the machinery, organized the work, designed the job" (Sass, 1982: 52). At times the core issue is money. From the point of view of a small number of employers, improved occupational health and safety may involve short-term losses in efficiency, as well as the extra costs of administration and protective equipment. The report of the public inquiry into the 1992 Westray Mine explosion that killed 26 workers observed that, among the factors that contributed to the tragedy, "Management, through its actions and attitudes, sent a . . . message [that] Westray was to produce coal at the expense of worker safety" (Richard, 1997: 21). Occasionally, workers themselves resist efforts to increase safety. Shortcuts are enticing when pay and performance are judged on speed of production (as in some coal mines). Sometimes workers take risks out of bravado or a supposedly macho approach to the job. Nonetheless, at many job sites, health and safety is a matter not of dollars and cents but of life and death, and both employers and unions place great emphasis on accident prevention.

Some of the clauses in collective agreements already discussed (such as rules affecting the pace of work) have an indirect effect on health and safety. More directly, collective agreements typically address health and safety by establishing special safety programs or joint committees. Some agreements make specific provisions obliging the employer to furnish and pay for safety equipment, allowing employees the right to refuse to perform unsafe work, or dealing with particular issues like work with video display terminals.

In most Canadian jurisdictions, occupational health and safety committees are required by law, even in nonunion workplaces. Such legislation usually gives workers the right to refuse to perform tasks that they believe are hazardous or potentially injurious. Recent legislation also requires that information be provided on hazardous materials used in the workplace. Such requirements are typically referred to as the Workplace Hazardous Materials Information System (WHMIS). In addition to these legislative requirements, however, the inclusion of provisions in collective agreements—such as those that allow employees to obtain information about and/or to refuse unsafe work—enables unions to deal with specific problems through grievance and arbitration procedures rather than having to rely solely on the enforcement of health and safety laws or the policies agreed on by joint committees.

CONCLUSION

Given the largely unfettered power of management to rule over a nonunion workforce, collective agreements represent a step toward industrial democracy (see Exhibit 11.15). Yet when judged against the democratic standards that govern political life in our society, collective agreements represent only a partial step toward full economic democracy. Collective agreements *do* make a difference, but employers have been successful in retaining many of their traditional prerogatives. Indeed, the manner in which collective agreements are administered, particularly with respect to management residual rights, serves to legitimize and bolster managerial powers.

The collective agreement reflects these basic authority relationships and also the ebb and flow of economic and political power in society. For example, the 1980s and 1990s were marked by recession, high rates of unemployment, and a resurgent conservatism. The bargaining power of unions deteriorated, and Canadian employers took advantage of this situation to launch an offensive against many of the provisions in collective agreements. Unions and workers were confronted with employer demands to reduce or freeze wages and benefits, to tie compensation more closely to productivity, and to make work rules and job classifications more flexible. Even management proposals for greater employee participation in decision making, quality circles, and autonomous work groups were at times coloured by anti-union motivation, since these techniques often seek to strengthen employees' identification with the firm's goals, which can weaken union solidarity.

In more recent years, a stronger economy has dampened management's bargaining advantage. Even so, the current context is marked by continued pressures on firms operating in a highly competitive global economy and parallel pressures on governments to contain spending and reduce taxes. In that context, workers and their unions, although successful in protecting most acquired rights and benefits, have been unable to make significant gains or innovations in collective agreements.

Despite these swings in relative bargaining power, the collective agreement remains at the centre of the Canadian industrial relations system. It provides both a detailed set of rules to govern the workplace and a benchmark of union ability (or inability) to win for its members a voice in the management of the workplace. For the union, the negotiation and administration of the collective agreement is the cornerstone of its activity, and to union members it represents the tangible results of union membership. Whatever changes take place in Canadian industrial relations will undoubtedly be reflected in the content and substance of the collective agreement.

Questions

1. Obtain a collective agreement and categorize its contents according to the four general types of clauses outlined in this chapter.
2. Describe the distinctive characteristics of Canadian collective agreements. Discuss the reasons for these characteristics.
3. Outline the arguments for and against the residual-rights theory of managerial prerogatives. In your view, does this doctrine promote or retard organizational effectiveness?
4. Discuss the different types of union security clauses found in collective agreements. In your opinion, does the Rand formula establish a balance between individual and collective rights?

5. Describe the ways in which collective agreements might be used to remove the barriers to equality faced by women workers and by workers with disabilities.

6. What are the various wage incentive systems? Why are they not commonly found in collective agreements?

7. Discuss how the conflict between management's concern with efficiency and workers' concerns with job security and working conditions is manifested in collective agreements.

8. Discuss the recent moves by Canadian employers to alter many of the traditional features of collective agreements in their favour. What long-run effects are likely?

9. Why do collective agreements sometimes include provisions that are already required by legislation, such as employment standards legislation, human rights codes, or occupational health and safety legislation? Give examples.

10. What do you think the typical Canadian collective agreement will look like 10 years from now, and why?

Weblinks

Annual country reviews of industrial relations developments in Europe (including information on collective agreements):
www.eurofound.europa.eu/eiro/annualreports.html

Work–life balance in Canadian workplaces:
www.hrsdc.gc.ca/en/lp/spila/wlb/rtm/15other_format.shtml
www.hrsdc.gc.ca/en/lp/spila/wlb/01home.shtml

Ontario collective bargaining highlights:
www.labour.gov.on.ca/english/lr/pdf/cbh2007-11.pdf

British Columbia Labour Relations Board (access to 500 B.C. collective agreements):
www.lrb.bc.ca/cas

Negotech (searchable database containing a sample of collective agreements from across Canada):
http://206.191.16.137/gol/main_e.shtml

Treasury Board of Canada (access to collective agreements between federal government and its unionized employees):
www.tbs-sct.gc.ca/pubs_pol/hrpubs/coll_agre/siglist_e.asp

Chapter 12
Strikes and Dispute Resolution

Morley Gunderson, Bob Hebdon, and Douglas Hyatt[1]

Strikes by the United Food and Commercial Workers (UFCW) and employers in the hog-slaughter industry illustrate various principles in the strike literature.

In November 1997, the United Food and Commercial Workers Union (UFCW) went on strike against Maple Leaf Foods in Edmonton. The plant, formerly Gainers owned by Peter Pocklington, had gone through a violent strike in 1986 when replacement workers were brought in. The 1997 strike was to call the company's bluff when it threatened to close the plant if concessions were not made. The strategy backfired, however, and the plant was closed. While this appeared to be a miscalculation on the part of the union, many workers had also "grown tired of the increasing uncertainty about their future" and others "were angry over what they believed was the lack of respect they received."

Subsequently, in March 1998, perhaps believing that the company's threats were credible, striking workers in Burlington, Ontario, voted to accept the company's offer under the threat of a plant closure. Wage cuts of around $9 per hour were involved, which the company argued were necessary to bring its costs in line with major U.S. competitors. In return for the wage cuts, the company agreed to give each worker a one-time cash payment of between $10 000 and $33 000, regardless of whether they stayed with the company. Presumably, the unusual settlement was part of a strategy to ensure that the remaining workers would be content with their pay: those who wouldn't be content would leave and those who stayed at the lower wage would have the lump-sum payment. New workers would be willing to sign on for the lower pay and, importantly, would be paid the same as incumbent workers (rather than there being a two-tiered wage structure).

The settlement soon led to domino effects and a strike at Quality Meat plants in Toronto and Brampton in December of 1998. That company also demanded wage concessions, citing "competition at home, especially from Maple Leaf Foods as well as from U.S. processors . . . we're dictated by international supply and demand conditions."[2]

This chapter provides an overview of the causes and consequences of strike activity in Canada. First, the functions and causes of strikes are discussed, focusing on both economic and non-economic causes. Next, we describe the frequency, size, and duration of strikes and their distribution by industry and province. Also, we outline the role of dispute resolution procedures in reducing strike activity. Finally, the chapter concludes with a brief discussion of the potential consequences of strikes.

Strikes are one of the most visible outcomes of union–management relations in Canada, and they are often used as a barometer to gauge the health of the industrial relations system. (Hereafter, *strikes* will be used to refer to both strikes and lockouts unless otherwise noted.) As the opening vignette shows, strikes can play a variety of functions both in the union–management relationship and in society:

- supporting bargaining demands;
- revealing information on the parties' true settlement points;
- establishing reputations;
- placing pressure on both sides to make negotiating concessions;
- solving intra-organizational bargaining problems;
- providing a safety valve to release pent-up frustrations;
- supporting or protesting government policy;
- enhancing political consciousness; and
- showing solidarity with workers' causes elsewhere.

Just as strikes have different purposes, the set of conditions that can combine to cause a strike is complex. In any given union–management relationship, the prevailing economic conditions, community characteristics, internal dynamics of the union and management organizations, the nature of the relationship, and the history of collective bargaining may contribute to producing a settlement or a strike.

Strikes also have costs. For workers, a strike almost always means a substantial loss of income while the strike lasts. The union may provide strike pay, but the amount is usually sufficient only for basic subsistence. If the strike shuts down operations, the employer may be faced with loss of profit, loss of customers, and a permanent decline in market share. The same may happen to other employers who rely on the services of an organization shut down because of a strike. The public may also be affected if, for example, the major employer in a small town is shut down or a service on which people rely, such as mass transit, is no longer available. These issues are of particular importance given our high strike rate by international standards (see Exhibit 12.1).

**Exhibit 12.1
We're Number 1!**

On an international basis, Canada has always had a high volume of strike activity, usually second only to Italy. This has occurred in part because strikes in Canada tend to be of long duration. From 1986 to 1995, however, Canada has achieved the dubious distinction of having the highest strike rate (days lost per worker) of *all* G-7 Industrial Nations (the United States, Germany, France, the United Kingdom, Italy, and Japan). Over that period, Canada's strike rate was about 2.5 times the average of the G-7 Industrial Nations, and also about 2.5 times that of the average of the 24 nations of the Organisation for Economic Co-operation and Development.

Source: Calculations from data given in Sweeney and Davies, 1997.

ANATOMY OF A STRIKE

What constitutes a strike and a lockout? When is a lockout used? It may help to start with some definitions. The *Canada Labour Code* defines a strike as "a cessation of work or a refusal to work or to continue to work by employees, in combination, in concert, or in accordance with a common understanding, and a slowdown of work or other concerted activity on the part of employees in relation to their work that is designed to restrict or limit output."

A lockout is similar but is initiated by an employer. Typically a management lockout is a response to a strike. Unions that take selective rotating strikes, for example, may find themselves locked out when they try to return to work.

Prior to a strike, both management and the union must make contingent plans. The union might prepare for a strike by building a substantial strike fund; ensuring that production will be disrupted; seeking allies; forming local committees; and coordinating public relations. Management, on the other hand, will attempt to maintain production through such strategies as shifting to alternative sources and using managers to perform tasks of unionized employees. Management might attempt to maintain sales by building up inventories.

For their part, individual workers may postpone major purchases in the buildup to conflict. The fundamental paradox of this conflict is that unions and employers that are fully prepared for a strike may have a better chance of avoiding one—the greater preparedness of both sides may elicit improved offers in collective bargaining.

In making a democratic decision to strike, workers must calculate intuitively the costs and benefits of striking. Today, more than 90 percent of the time, workers decide not to strike. On those increasingly infrequent occasions when a strike cannot be avoided, the conflict becomes one of competing pressures and ever-depleting resources. The impact of income loss on the individual will be set against the impact of lost production on the company. The length of the strike may well depend on the intensity of these dual pressures. For example, the strike outlined in Exhibit 12.2 illustrates the stresses that a strike can generate on both sides. These powerful forces on management and employees in this example ultimately led to the mutual concessions in bargaining that produced a settlement and a relatively short three-day strike.

Exhibit 12.2
A Strike Over Weekend Work—A Positive Outcome

AS DESCRIBED BY A SENIOR MANAGEMENT OFFICIAL

INTRODUCTION

This strike took place in Montreal in a plant that makes plastic containers mostly for export to the United States. The plant was unionized in 1984 and has 80 employees. The process is highly capital intensive with huge start-up costs. Since it was essential to operate at full capacity, management needed to maintain production on weekends. The plant gradually became cost ineffective as lower-skilled workers selected weekend work. Weekend scheduling eventually became a strike issue in the 2002 negotiations.

THE PARKING LOT MEETING

After six months of negotiations, employees rejected the seven-day schedule offered by management. By taking a strike vote the union hoped to force management back to the negotiating table. The local union was plagued by internal problems including a lack of direction and dissension between rival ethnic factions. The national union representative wanted the members to stop arguing and take action. The morning the strike began, everyone showed up in the parking lot (all the employees, the management, and the union bargaining team). Out of fear, many employees apologetically approached management. According to a management official, the employees were reassured that they were exercising their democratic rights and their bargaining position would be respected. As she put it: "the fear was palpable." Management further assured the strikers that it would not take reprisals against them after the strike was settled because so many expressed a fear of punishment. It was a bizarre scene.

THE STRIKE

The strike lasted three days during the hottest days of the summer. Management worked hard to keep the plant going and the customers happy. Their lawyers and consultant advised them that they would have to keep this up for at least two or three weeks before they could meet again at the negotiating table. But, by the end of the third day, management was already exhausted. The employees also set up a picket line during the day. It was a quiet one, subdued, and without a lot of spirit. The workers too were suffering from the heat and occasionally, someone would come out of the office and give them water and Gatorade.

On the fourth morning, the union rep called a meeting and the two sides met on the front lawn of the plant. "There we were, all of us, at the picnic table." The union agreed to the new seven-day schedule. In the long run, the seven-day continuous production schedule proved successful.

OUTCOMES

The employees accepted the changes and felt comfortable. With the new schedule, employees found that they had more time for family matters and personal business. A few went back to school. A few were unhappy and tried to look for other jobs, but they found that the rate of pay and benefits at the plant were the best available, so they never left. Management was able to hire the new staff required to fill the fourth shift. They were people who liked the continuous production schedule. Management quickly met the production and quality requirements that were desperately needed and the financial benefits became quickly obvious. It was a success.

The strike served another important purpose: it forced the union bargaining unit (which was fractured by diverse interests and a lack of trust) to produce a coherent response to the management weekend-work proposal.

Source: From an unpublished student term paper. Used with permission.

FUNCTIONS AND CAUSES OF STRIKES

Strikes can serve a variety of functions (and dysfunctions) that are intricately related to the causes and determinants of strikes.

Functions of Strikes

Since strikes can serve a variety of purposes and can occur for a variety of reasons, it is not really feasible to talk about a unique cause of strike activity. Strikes may occur to win recognition for a particular union or to win concessions from the other side. They may serve an important information-generating function by shedding light on the true settlement points of both parties and on the internal trade-offs being made within both the union and the firm. In that vein, strikes may serve an important role in adjusting the expectations of the parties. A strike may also be a mistake or accident made by the parties, like the UFCW's miscalculation at Maple Leaf Foods' Edmonton plant (see the opening vignette) or the newsroom employees' strike against Hollinger Inc. (see Exhibit 12.3), given the complexities and uncertainties of the bargaining process. Strikes may reflect pent-up, unresolved grievances over working conditions or be spontaneous acts in response to a particular working condition. (The latter often results in a strike during the term of an existing collective agreement—when not sanctioned by the union this is termed a "wildcat strike.") A strike may be a cathartic event, providing a safety valve for employee frustration, or it may be a political act of worker solidarity or even a way of getting a vacation. Strikes may also be used by union leaders to solidify the rank and file, to find out what they really want and are prepared to give up, or to lower their expectations as the strike runs its course (Exhibit 12.2 provides an example of the last purpose). The parties may also use strikes to establish or enhance reputations for subsequent rounds of bargaining (Exhibit 12.3). This factor can complicate the analysis of strike activity, since the ultimate purpose of the strike may appear unrelated to the events at hand.

Strikes can also occur over a range of issues. Conventionally, strikes occur over wages. However, in recent years job security and working time have emerged as prominent strike issues. These issues have become more prominent because downsizing and restructuring have increasingly threatened the jobs of the typical union member, and those who remain employed have often seen the pace of their workload intensify. These issues have been prominent in a number of recent high-profile strikes. Strikes can be extremely difficult phenomena to analyze, in part because they involve bluffs and posturing, as well as the "calling" of bluffs (Exhibit 12.4).

Exhibit 12.3
Cyber Striking and the Use of Technology in Strikes

As part of a newspaper-buying spree in the 1990s, the *Calgary Herald* was bought out by Conrad Black's Hollinger Inc. That company appeared to be emphasizing a higher return on investment and announced the intent of restructuring so that only one-third of the staff would be permanent, with one-third freelance, and the remaining one-third contract workers. Management also forbade meetings of a newsroom group that

---

often met informally to deal in part with employee grievances. As a result "attention throughout the newsroom quietly turned to the possibility of more formal representation for employees"—an unusual act in a fervently free-enterprise province. The newsroom employees unionized and on November 1999 announced their intention to strike in their dispute over establishing a first contract.

The newsroom employees were completely inexperienced in collective bargaining and had misread the resolve of the employer to establish a precedence for its other papers. Two days before their strike notice was to apply, they were locked out by their employer. The company's elaborate computer-based surveillance system was re-programmed to deny entry to all but those who informed the company that they would cross the picket line.

Both sides made extensive use of cyberspace and information technology. The union set up an email system and a strike website. The website was to serve numerous functions:

- to appeal to public opinion;
- to offset what the strikers perceived as negative coverage by other newspapers owned by Hollinger Inc.;
- to provide pictures of stacks of undelivered newspapers in the hope that such images would deter advertisers;
- to show photos of replacement workers and those who crossed the picket line in the hope that such "internet outing" would deter such activity; and
- to boost morale by publicizing statements of support from other groups.

The email system served many similar functions, especially to boost morale and to provide strikers with information on alternative jobs and sources of income support. As well it was used to provide information on companies that advertised with the paper in the hope that those companies would be boycotted. The company also used email to boost morale among replacement workers, whom they labelled as fighting for "job freedom." Cellphones were also crucial to the union, especially to foster communication on the picket line. Both sides used video cameras to record alleged misbehaviours on the part of the other side.

The company used electronic surveillance that picked up conversations on the picket line (used later in a hearing before the Labour Relations Board). The union countered by disseminating false information and playing loud rock music, especially by Jimi Hendrix.

Perhaps the most unusual technology was the use by the union of Globo stage lights that enabled them to block out the name of the newspaper on the building on the top of a hill visible from two of the busiest thoroughfares in the city.

In spite of this extensive use of technology, after about a year of being on strike, the union essentially caved in and strikers were given the choice of returning to work without a union or accepting a severance package. About two-thirds took the severance package and many who returned to work subsequently left.

Whether technology favoured the union or the employer is an open and interesting question. Clearly in the new information economy, technology is permeating all aspects of life—including strikes.

Source: Barnett (2003).

Exhibit 12.4
The Strike That Almost Was

On October 5, 1999, the CAW negotiated a settlement with DaimlerChrysler that followed the pattern established with Ford earlier in the year. In that earlier Ford negotiation, the CAW had taken the unprecedented step of releasing the first offer by the company to the rank and file in the plants. This had the predictable effect of solidifying the rank and file to take strike action if necessary.

In the subsequent Chrysler negotiations, the CAW took another unusual step—threatening to strike if DaimlerChrysler did not compel one of its major parts suppliers, Magna, to voluntarily recognize the union at one of its plants in Windsor where an organizing drive was underway. The CAW had been trying to organize the parts suppliers because around 80 percent of the jobs in the auto industry are in the parts industry. As Sam Gindin (assistant to the CAW president in 1999) indicated, "you can't be this little island of unionized workers surrounded by deunionization" (*The Globe and Mail*, October 23, 1999, p. B14).

While the objective was important for the union, it is unlikely that the rank and file at DaimlerChrysler could have been mobilized for a sympathy strike to facilitate unionization in parts suppliers where there is little history of unionism and worker solidarity. As CAW president Buzz Hargrove indicated, "bargaining is about posturing and getting yourself in certain positions. . . . Sometimes you stick your neck out. In this case, I got clipped a bit. . . . I put myself in a box and I know that. . . . It was a gamble I took to make Magna a separate strike issue. But in the end, I could not justify a strike on the Magna issue alone" (*Toronto Star*, October 7, 1999).

While Hargrove describes himself as "getting clipped a bit," the facts are that the Magna demand was dropped in part for company concessions to invest more in the Windsor assembly plant and to avoid job losses in the Ajax trim operation. If he was "clipped a bit," he clearly did not pay for the clipping! He was able to negotiate terms that were of clear benefit to his existing membership.

Causes or Theoretical Determinants of Strikes

Theories about the causes of strikes attempt to relate measures of strike activity to various observable characteristics that are believed to affect strike activity. Such characteristics, or strike determinants, can be related to the social, economic, political, and legal environment in which the parties operate and can be characteristics of their respective organizations as well as of the negotiators and the bargaining process itself.

Any theory that tries to explain how these observable characteristics affect strike activity must confront a basic dilemma: such variables do not have a direct impact on the level of strike activity so long as the variable's effect on each party's bargaining power is understood by both. For example, strike incidence is often high at the peak of a business cycle because labour has more bargaining power at that time (since workers have job opportunities elsewhere, and employers are reluctant to lose business). If this is also known by employers, however, they have an incentive to increase their offer to avoid the strike. The factor giving labour more bargaining power, therefore, has implications for the magnitude of the settlement but not necessarily for striking or not striking. Differential bargaining power is a theory of wages, not of strikes. In a world of perfect information, strikes would serve no useful function; each party would realize each other's position and settle accordingly, dividing up the savings from the avoidance of a costly strike. Hence, a statement by Hicks (1963: 146–147) is often cited: "The majority of actual strikes are doubtless the result of faulty negotiation. . . . Any means which enables either side to appreciate better the position of the other will always make a settlement easier; adequate knowledge will always make a settlement possible."

At the theoretical level, attempts have been made to identify a causal connection between strikes and a variety of observable variables that appear to be determinants of strikes. One procedure is to assume that the parties base their offers and demands on different factors. Rees (1952), for example, argued that unions base their demands on current or lagging indicators such as employment and the cost of living, while management bases its offers on leading indicators such as business failures, security prices, and new contracts. Mauro (1982) theorizes that firms make their offers on the basis of product prices, while employees base their demands on the consumer price index. Kaufman (1993) argues that both parties base their positions on inflation, but they have divergent views about its expected level. In all these circumstances, the parties' offers and demands may not offset each other, and strikes may ensue. Ashenfelter and Johnson (1969) emphasize the importance of the strike in adjusting the expectations of the parties. Godard (1992) emphasizes the importance of strikes in mobilizing workers who are driven by concepts of fairness and solidarity. Although these theories do provide an explanation for strikes, they do not explain why such divergences in expectations or in the determinants of offers and demands should persist.

An alternative theory,[3] the asymmetric-information perspective, views strikes as serving the purpose of eliciting information from employers, who tend to have more information on the true state of their product market and financial position. Given this situation of asymmetric or private information on the part of employers, unions try to prevent them from bluffing about the true state of their financial position. They do this by compelling the firm to endure a strike if it argues that wage concessions are necessary because of its bad financial position. In such circumstances, the firm can endure the strike only if its particular situation is so adverse that the loss of output from the strike is not as costly as a high wage settlement would be. In essence, a firm that insists its particular situation is adverse is compelled to accept the lower employment that results from a costly strike; this, in turn, deters a firm from bluffing about its true position. It is the firm's particular situation relative to the general state of the economy that is at issue, not the general state of the economy itself. The former is private information; the latter (that is, the business cycle) is public information.

This asymmetric-information perspective is appealing since it provides a theoretical rationale for the existence of strikes. It is not clear, however, that such private information—held only by the firm—is so important in today's world of sophisticated information processing. In addition, it is not clear why the parties would not agree to contractual arrangements whereby compensation depends upon the true state of the firm, as that information is revealed over time.

A third theory, the joint-cost perspective, emphasizes that strikes will depend on the joint or total cost to both parties of using the strike as opposed to other mechanisms for sorting out differences between the parties.[4] As discussed previously, strikes serve a variety of functions—eliciting information, establishing reputations, solving intra-organizational problems, venting frustrations, adjusting expectations, mobilizing workers, protesting government policy, supporting workers' causes elsewhere—or they may just be mistakes or accidents. In other words, strikes help the parties sort out their differences over the division of the wealth of the enterprise and over everyday employment practices. These purposes can also be served by other mechanisms, including continuous bargaining, joint committees, grievance arbitration, voluntary arbitration, and absenteeism and turnover. All of these mechanisms are costly in terms of uncertainty and their use of real resources.

Simply put, the argument for this joint-cost perspective is that whatever the function or benefits of strikes—and there are many—they are used less often and less intensely when they are more costly than the other mechanisms that can serve the same purposes. Similarly, strikes that are mistakes or accidents will occur less often when the costs of such mistakes are high. It is the joint cost to *both* parties that is important. If a certain factor or variable increases the cost of a strike to only one of the parties, that party will have to "bribe" the other with more favourable settlement terms to reduce the likelihood or duration of a costly strike. The fact that a variable has a differential effect on the parties means that it has implications for settlement terms as well as strike incidence. However, this perspective holds that incidence and duration are reduced even though the cost of strikes is higher for one party, since the cost to that party is a component of the total cost to both parties. For example, if unemployment insurance became available to workers on strike, the joint-cost theory predicts that the use of strikes would increase because, in effect, the state would be subsidizing the joint cost of this method of dispute resolution. It also predicts that settlement terms would be more favourable to the union because, in effect, the bargaining power of the union would be enhanced.

It is interesting that both of the most recent theoretical developments in the strike literature—the asymmetric-information perspective and the joint-cost perspective—predict that strike activity will be reduced when strikes are costly. The asymmetric-information models predict this on the basis that the firm will opt for the strike as a means of getting wage concessions when the cost of the strike to the firm is lower than the cost of conceding to the wage demands. The joint-cost model predicts that strikes will be used more often when the costs are lower for a strike than for the other procedures for solving basic differences at the workplace.

The recent theoretical developments in the strike literature emphasize the importance of strikes as an information-generating mechanism, compelling the parties to articulate their preferences and trade-offs (including those within the organization) and to reveal what otherwise might be private information. They also emphasize focusing on the costs and benefits of strikes relative to other mechanisms for solving basic differences at the workplace. Although often formidable in their mathematical procedures, these models essentially formalize ideas that have long been recognized in institutional industrial relations. More important, they provide a convenient way of incorporating a wide array of institutional industrial relations variables, including policy variables, as strike determinants. In essence, they suggest the *causal* mechanism for the effect on strike activity by the institutional industrial relations variables. That is, strike activity is likely to be higher if the variable increases the need for the strike to elicit information from the parties (if, for example, the variable increases uncertainty, misinformation, divergent expectations, or intra-organizational differences) or if the variable reduces the cost of using the strike as opposed to other mechanisms for solving basic differences at the workplace.

Categorizing Strike Determinants

There are almost as many ways of categorizing the causes of strikes as there are ways of classifying strikes themselves. To a certain degree, the categorization reflects the perspectives of the different disciplines that have contributed to our understanding of strike activity. Economists have focused on the economic environment (notably the business cycle, market characteristics, and inflationary expectations); sociologists have focused at the macro level on class conflict, class solidarity, and dramatic changes in the social system and in the relations of production, and at the micro level on the process of bargaining and on interpersonal relations and concepts of fairness; political scientists and historians have emphasized the political environment and the importance of the strike in achieving political ends; and industrial relations analysts have emphasized dispute resolution procedures and characteristics of the bargaining structure and relationship.

For our purposes here, we have categorized the determinants of strikes as either economic or non-economic factors, the latter including legal and procedural factors, political and historical factors, characteristics of the various actors and of the bargaining structure, and personal and interpersonal relationships. Many of these categories are obviously interdependent and overlapping; they are used simply as a convenient way to summarize the current theoretical and empirical literature and to illustrate its interrelatedness—as well as, at times, the isolation of particular disciplinary perspectives.

ECONOMIC DETERMINANTS OF STRIKES

The economic determinants of strikes can be categorized according to the ways in which strikes have been analyzed empirically: the early studies of strikes and the business cycle; the more recent studies of the changes over time in the pattern of aggregate strike activity; recent cross-sectional studies that seek to explain variation in strikes across industries, unions, regions, cities, or collective agreements; and recent studies that use hazard function procedures to analyze determinants of strike duration.

Business Cycles and Strike Cycles

The earliest economic studies of the time pattern of aggregate strike activity focused on the relationship of strikes to the business cycle. The expectation was for a positive relationship, with strikes being highest at the peak of a business cycle. The reasoning for this theory (usually derived in an ad hoc fashion) was that at the peak of a business cycle—when unemployment is low and profits are high—workers are willing to incur the cost of a strike, largely because they are more likely to be able to find jobs elsewhere and because they feel employers can pay more since profits are high and inventories low. This line of reasoning, however, begs the question of why the parties should not settle for large wage increases in such circumstances. More bargaining power in the hands of labour should lead to larger wage settlements, not necessarily more strikes. In spite of their inadequate theoretical explanation, the earliest studies of aggregate strike activity tended, with some notable exceptions, to find a positive relationship between strikes and the business cycle.[5]

Recent Studies of the Time Pattern of Aggregate Strike Activity

The more recent studies of the time pattern of aggregate strike activity differ from the earlier studies because they endeavour to establish a more rigorous theoretical relationship between strikes and various measures of business cycle activity, and also because they use more sophisticated statistical techniques to try to disentangle the complex relationship between strikes and various measures of economic activity.

Many of the recent studies take as their departure the model developed by Ashenfelter and Johnson (1969). Theirs was the first attempt to develop a formal model whereby strikes resulted from optimizing behaviour. The essence of their model is that a firm decides on the "optimal" profit-maximizing duration of the strike by trading off strike costs with expected future wage costs, adjusting its expectations as the strike progresses. Subsequent theoretical work has analyzed the analogous decision with respect to unions, both parties, and when union leaders' and management's objectives differ not only from each other's, but also from their constituents' (Eaton, 1973).

Although the recent studies differ considerably in the precise specification of the variables, most relate various measures of aggregate strike activity to a variety of explanatory variables reflecting measures of aggregate business conditions (economic conditions such as inflation and unemployment).[6] Even though particular studies always have some exceptions, the empirical results generally find economic factors to be important determinants of the time pattern of aggregate strike activity. In particular, strike activity diminishes in periods of high unemployment and increases in periods of inflation or when real wages are eroded. In Canada, economic factors have been more successful in explaining the frequency of strikes than their size or duration, and they have been less successful in explaining strikes before the Second World War when strikes over the initial establishment of unions were prominent. The ability of economic factors to explain strikes is highest for contract-renewal strikes, second-highest for first-agreement strikes, and lowest for strikes during the term of the contract.

The relationship between economic factors and strike activity is weaker in Canada than in the United Kingdom or, especially, the United States. This weaker relationship between strikes and economic factors in Canada may occur for a variety of reasons:

1. Because Canada has a smaller population than either the United Kingdom or the United States, its strike activity may be more dominated by "unusual" events.

2. To the extent that long-duration strikes are more prominent in Canada and strike duration cannot be explained by economic factors as easily as strike incidence can, Canadian strike activity (at least for measures involving duration) will appear to be less dependent on economic activity.

3. Strikes during the life of the contract are more often illegal in Canada than in the United States, where the right to strike during the contract is often negotiable. Since there is more pressure in Canada to wait until the contract expires before striking, strike activity is less likely to reflect economic conditions than to reflect the timing of the end of the contract. In essence, in Canada there is less flexibility to strike in response to current economic conditions, although illegal mid-contract strikes occur frequently, and they appear to be responsive to economic factors.

4. Differences in the political and sociological environments of Canada and the United States may make Canadian strike activity less dependent on economic activity (Vanderkamp, 1970).

Cross-Sectional Studies and Economic Variables

The importance of economic factors in explaining strike activity has also been tested in cross-sectional studies (sometimes pooling time-series data also), which try to explain differences in strike activity across unions, cities, regions, or industries.[7] Empirical studies at the micro level, using the collective agreement as the unit of observation, are particularly informative since their analysis is at the level of the bargaining unit, where bargaining actually occurs, and they often incorporate numerous explanatory variables describing the negotiation environment.[8]

Unfortunately the cross-sectional studies of strike activity are exceedingly difficult to compare because of the different units of observation (for example, industry, union, region, collective agreement) and the different variables used to explain strike variation or to control for the other relevant factors. In general, however, it appears that characteristics of the economic environment are not as consistently or quantitatively important in explaining strike activity in the cross-sectional studies as they are in the aggregate time-series studies. Presumably, the effect is dominated by non-economic factors that do not change much over time (and hence that do not "explain" much of the variation in the time pattern of aggregate strike activity).

Hazard Estimates of Strike Duration

A number of recent econometric studies[9] have focused on analyzing strike duration by examining the strike settlement probabilities as the strike progresses (termed the "hazard rate"). Generally, as the strike progresses, the probability of settling the next day (the conditional strike probability) declines, implying that the remaining life expectancy of the strike actually increases as the strike progresses. Much of this simply reflects the fact that the composition of the strikes remaining in the sample increasingly consists of strikes that are hard to settle, the easy ones having been settled earlier and dropped out of the sample. When these factors are controlled for, however, the conditional settlement probabilities increase substantially as the strike progresses, although there is no consensus on the exact configuration of those settlement rates. The evidence appears to indicate, however, that the expected duration of strikes is counter-cyclical (that is, decreases at the peak of the business cycle) while strike incidence is pro-cyclical (increases at the peak of the business cycle).

NON-ECONOMIC DETERMINANTS OF STRIKES

It is somewhat of a misnomer to categorize some determinants of strikes as non-economic since many of these factors (such as a legislative change) may alter the costs and benefits of strikes to the parties. Conversely, many of the economic or market variables may operate through intervening variables categorized as non-economic.

Numerous studies have emphasized the non-economic determinants of strikes, focusing on behavioural, organizational, and political aspects.[10] Many of the studies attempt to relate strike activity to one or more of the following aspects: characteristics of the community, union and management organizations, the negotiation process and the bargaining parties, as well as the legal and historical context in which bargaining occurs, issues related to solidarity and mobilization, concepts of fairness, personality factors, and the broader socio-political environment.

Worker and Community Characteristics in Mobilizing Workers

Sociological investigations of the determinants of strike activity have viewed strikes as an example of collective behaviour. As a result, sociologists especially have attempted to identify characteristics of the community and the union that may increase the mobilization and threat potential of the bargaining unit.

Resource mobilization theories emphasize that strikes are more likely when unions have the strength and resources to mobilize individual workers into collective action.[11] This ability to mobilize resources can be associated with a wide range of factors such as male dominance of the industry and other personal characteristics (e.g., the age or immigrant status of the workforce), as well as with characteristics of the community (e.g., its working class orientation),[12] large plant sizes (Enderwick and Buckley, 1982), and the "explosion of class consciousness" that often accompanies major strikes, strike waves (Kelly, 1988; Langford, 1996), and labour regulation (Turnbull and Sapsford, 2001).

Frustrated Expectations and Collective Action

Wheeler (1985) emphasizes that strikes are not so much the result of rational calculations on the part of parties; rather, they tend to occur when individuals are frustrated over the gap between their expectations and their economic and social circumstances. This individual frustration gets translated into collective action when certain preconditions are present, including group solidarity. Wheeler suggests that this perspective is able to explain considerable strike behaviour.

Godard (1992) also emphasizes the importance of strikes as a behavioural manifestation of worker discontent through a "collective voice." Based on Canadian data, his research provides evidence that strikes are more likely in workplaces where there is a lack of autonomy or progressive managerial practices, where union leaders are under pressure to appear militant, and where large operations create a sense of alienation.

Political Environment

A general political environment that is favourable to labour may encourage workers to mobilize into forms of collective action such as strikes, and it may raise expectations about gains they can achieve by striking. It may also, however, facilitate gains by labour unions at the political level through social policies that can benefit labour, and this may move the forum for collective action from strikes at the workplace to action at the political level. Overall, therefore, it is not clear whether a general political environment that is favourable to labour will increase or decrease strikes at the workplace. It is also difficult to separate the independent effect of the general political environment from other factors that are at work simultaneously.

Within Canada, Quebec has tended to have a political and legislative environment that favours labour, and yet it has a high level of strike activity (see Chapter 16). In the United States, strikes increased in the 1930s within the pro-labour environment of the New Deal, and they decreased in the anti-labour environment of the Reagan era. Labour was also more likely to "lose" strikes in an anti-labour political environment such as the 1980s and to "win" them in a pro-labour environment such as the New Deal era.[13] Similarly, in Britain, strikes decreased substantially in the 1980s in a political and legal environment that was not supportive of labour (Ingram, Metcalf, and Wadsworth, 1993).

These examples illustrate the idea that strike activity is likely to increase within a pro-labour political environment and to decrease within an anti-labour political environment, perhaps reflecting changing expectations. There is, however, also considerable international evidence indicating that strikes appear to be less likely in corporatist, social-democratic political environments where organized labour and other social interest groups have considerable influence over the negotiation of social programs that can benefit labour.[14] Clearly, more research in this area would be welcome to sort out the underlying relationship between the general political environment and strike activity.

A number of studies have emphasized strikes as the manifestation of a political struggle between labour and management for power and control at the shop-floor workplace level.[15] From this perspective, strike activity can be altered by various institutional and organizational factors; nevertheless, it is an inevitable by-product of the struggle between labour and capital for control at the workplace.

Union and Management Organization Characteristics

Intra-Organizational Conflict A major component of the bargaining process is the negotiations that occur within the union and management sides (Ghilarducci, 1988; Kramer and Hyclak, 2002). Often a great diversity of interests results in potentially conflicting goals and priorities for the collective bargaining process. Factions and different degrees of militancy often exist within the union on the basis of age, sex, occupation, seniority, or political affiliation, as well as between union leaders and the rank and file. Unless mechanisms exist within the union to resolve these conflicts, the potential for a strike may increase because of the inability of union members to agree on management's offers. For example, studies (Gramm and Schnell, 1994; LeRoy, 1992) indicate how the decision to cross the picket line and return to work (a decision that signals internal conflict within the union and that can cause an end to the strike) is related to the individual characteristics of strikers, such as seniority, income, and racial identification with union leadership. The lack of consensus on the union side was a major contributing factor to the strike described in Exhibit 12.2.

Inadequate Decision-Making Authority Inadequate decision-making authority, particularly on the management side, increases the probability of a strike. For example, in the 1960s and early 1970s, the final decision on management's position often resided in the U.S. headquarters of Canadian subsidiaries, leading union negotiators to believe that the Canadian management negotiators were little more than messengers who ran back and forth between the table and top management. In such situations, the likelihood of a strike can increase for two reasons. First, union leaders may feel that the only way to bring the real decision makers to the bargaining table is to apply pressure through a strike. Second, not having the real decision makers involved in the day-to-day negotiating process increases the likelihood that they have either unrealistic expectations about the point of settlement or inaccurate perceptions of the expectations of the union.

Foreign Ownership and Multinationals Based on the notion of inadequate decision-making authority within foreign-owned firms, a number of studies have examined the extent to which such firms may be more strike-prone than domestically owned firms. The issue is complicated, however, by the fact that foreign-owned firms tend to be large multinationals that have considerable bargaining power because they can diversify their production to other plants (Rose, 1991). The issue is especially important in the Canadian context, given the significant role of foreign ownership and multinationals. Canadian studies that have used statistical techniques to control for the influence of other determinants of strikes have produced mixed results.[16] Studies of multinational management practices, discussed in Chapter 5, show that companies tend to adapt their industrial relations practices to conform to the country in which they are operating.

Size and Number of the Bargaining Units Knowing the impact of the size of the bargaining unit on strike activity is important because labour relations boards can influence bargaining unit size in their certification decisions. There is also the perception that some of Canada's poor strike record is attributable to the proliferation of small bargaining units, which characterize its decentralized bargaining structure. The limited empirical evidence that is available on this topic, however, suggests that, other things being equal, strikes are less likely in single-plant bargaining units[17] and in smaller bargaining units.[18] This also suggests that strikes may decline even more in the future if the trend to smaller bargaining units continues (see Exhibit 12.5).

Exhibit 12.5
Fewer Strikes, More Conflict?

Hebdon, Hyatt, and Mazerolle (1999) provide empirical evidence for Ontario indicating that strikes are less likely in smaller bargaining units and with independent local

---

unions that are representative of non-traditional forms of employee representation. Over time, smaller bargaining units are becoming more prominent, reflecting the growth of small firms, decentralized bargaining, and the fact that most large bargaining units are already organized in the public sector. Non-traditional forms of employee representation that tend to be more co-operative and non-adversarial are also growing in importance in such forms as enterprise unions, joint health and safety committees, plant-level work councils, and independent local unions that are not affiliated with national or international unions.

The fact that strikes are less likely in smaller bargaining units and under non-traditional forms of employee representation suggests that strikes are likely to decline even more in importance if these forms of employee representation become more prominent. The authors also find, however, that these alternative forms of representation are associated with greater individual expressions of conflict such as grievance arbitrations and health and safety complaints. In essence, smaller bargaining units may lead to less *collective* conflict like strikes, but more *individual* conflict like grievances and health and safety complaints. As such, future dispute resolution should emphasize internal conflict resolution procedures such as peer review panels, mediation, labour–management committees and joint forums, as well as internal problem solving and process consultation among union and management decision makers.

Negotiator and Bargaining Process Characteristics

Union and Management Trust or Hostility Interpersonal sources of conflict may make it extremely difficult for union and management representatives to accept the position of the other side, to back down from an extreme position taken early in bargaining, or to compromise. As a result, hostility and a lack of trust may increase the probability of a strike.[19]

Negotiator Skills and Experience As previously noted, Hicks (1963) states that most strikes are the result of faulty negotiations. Inexperienced negotiators are more likely to provide incorrect cues to their opponents, generating unrealistic expectations about the terms of settlement. Moreover, inexperience may lead a negotiator to become overcommitted to a position that may be unacceptable. Movement from that position may then be impossible without a loss of face, both for the other side and for the negotiator's own constituency. Thus, a lack of skill and experience on the part of either or both negotiators is likely to increase the probability of a strike.[20]

Bargaining History

Whether or not a strike is going to occur in a given round of negotiations may be affected as much by the historical context of the relationship as by current economic and non-economic conditions. Past struggles and hostilities may well exacerbate subsequent conflict; the parties may develop a habit or pattern of conflict. Alternatively, strikes may serve as a safety valve and learning experience, thereby decreasing subsequent conflict. The negative experience of a strike may also discourage subsequent conflict through what is known as a "teetotaller" effect (see Exhibit 12.6). The empirical studies[21] generally yield conflicting results on these effects, although the Canadian evidence tends to suggest that long strikes in previous contracts have a sobering teetotaller effect, reducing subsequent conflict, while short strikes leave unresolved issues that lead to more strikes in subsequent rounds.

Exhibit 12.6
From Sit-In to Love-In

A bitter three-week strike occurred between the Canadian Auto Workers and General Motors in October 1996, including the occupation of a parts plant in Oshawa that the company wanted to sell. GM was also hit by strikes in the United States in Dayton, Ohio, in 1995 and in Flint, Michigan, in 1998. These disputes and the accompanying poor labour relations likely contributed to GM's loss of market share and the associated fall in its stock price.

These events may have served as a catalyst for both sides to improve labour relations to facilitate their joint survival. GM, for example, appointed labour relations managers who were prepared to work and share information with the union. As GM's chief negotiator, Al Green, indicated, "I spent a lot of time getting to know Buzz [Buzz Hargrove, CAW president]. . . . The union and the company have spent much time exchanging information about the business challenges. There are very real challenges that threaten the existence of both of us" (*The Globe and Mail*, October 23, 1999, p. B14).

The spirit of co-operation led to a settlement at 5:00 p.m. on October 19, 1999, well before the usual 11th-hour settlement (or later) that typifies negotiations. More surprisingly, and "absolutely unheard of" in the words of CAW president Buzz Hargrove, the CAW bargaining team gave the GM negotiating team a standing ovation that was returned by the GM team for about eight minutes.

Whether the mutual lovefest will last and survive a possible downturn in the auto industry will likely depend on the extent to which both parties can translate the new-found spirit of co-operation in the collective bargaining arena into everyday actions at the workplace level.

MEASURING STRIKE ACTIVITY

As with most seemingly simple statistics, the measures of strike activities are replete with problems—problems that are accentuated when comparisons are made over long periods of time or across diverse countries. These problems[22] include what to count as a strike (in Canada, strikes involving a total loss of fewer than 10 working days are excluded), how to treat political strikes or protests, how to classify people who may not officially be on strike but are not working because of the strike, and how to determine when some protracted strikes have ended. Quantitative studies of strike activity are also difficult to compare because of differences in the measures used (Stern, 1978). As well, the format for publishing strike statistics can change. For example, prior to 1982 the United States classified work stoppages involving six or more workers as a strike. After 1982, only stoppages involving 1000 or more workers were included in the series. This has led some researchers to question the appropriateness of generalizations based on large strikes, although others find that small and large strikes both have similar underlying determinants (Garen and Krislov, 1988; Skeels, McGrath, and Arshanapalli, 1988).

Most developed nations, Canada included, publish strike statistics in three series: (1) the frequency or number of strikes per year; (2) the total number of workers involved in strikes; and (3) the volume or total days lost through strikes, often expressed as a percentage of working time. These raw measures do not, however, directly indicate the average size of each strike (the average number of workers involved) or the average duration (the average length of time each worker remains on strike). Hence, the raw measures by themselves do not indicate if a high volume of strike activity, as measured by days lost, resulted from a large number of strikes (frequency), a large number of workers involved in each strike (size), a series of long strikes (duration), or some combination of these three components.

As illustrated in Table 12.1, however, some basic manipulations of the raw numbers enable the calculation of the three components of the total volume of strike activity—frequency, size, and duration. These three components, when multiplied together, give the overall volume of strike activity, or total days lost (Forchheimer, 1948). Expressed as a percentage of time worked, this is a measure of the relative degree of overall strike activity in the economy.

To put this latter measure in perspective, a figure of 1 percent of working time lost due to strikes would imply that approximately 1 out of every 100 working days would be wiped out. A figure of 0.40 percent implies roughly 1 day per year lost (based on 250 working days in a year). The average time lost in the period since 1976 is slightly under half of that (i.e., 0.18 percent), which implies slightly under a half-day per year per worker lost due to strikes.

Canadian Strike Activity

Strike activity in Canada has been historically volatile. The percentage of working time lost due to strikes has ranged from a low of 0.01 in the Depression of 1930, to a high of 0.60 in 1919 after the First World War and 0.59 in 1976. Even in these years of peak strike activity, considerably less than 1 percent of total working time is lost to strike activity. Table 12.1 reveals that there have been distinct phases: moderate levels of strike activity in the prosperous years of the early 1920s, low levels in the depression years of the late 1920s and early 1930s, low levels in the war years 1939–1945, a spurt in 1946 followed by moderate levels until the mid-1960s, extremely high levels from 1970 to 1981, moderate and declining levels throughout the 1980s, and a sharp drop in the 1990s that continued into the 2000s.

Strike activity generally drops in periods of recession and stagnant economic activity. Since the recession of the early 1980s, and especially during the 1990s, strike activity has declined markedly, perhaps heralding an end to the wave of strike activity that began in the mid-1960s. While strike activity in Canada has been declining markedly in recent years, there have also been notable deviations in that trend. There was a noticeable increase in strike activity in 1996 and 1997, attributable to a number of large and long-lasting strikes in the public sector (i.e., the Canada Post and Ontario Teachers' Federation strikes in 1997 as well as the CAW strike against General Motors in Ontario in 1996). Furthermore, in 1996, there was a large number of short "days-of-protest" strikes in Ontario, especially in the public sector, to protest against the policies of the newly elected

Table 12.1 Various Measures of Strike Activity, Canada, 1901–2006

Year	Frequency[a]	Size[b]	Duration[c]	Person-Days Lost[d]	Volume As Percentage of Working Time[e]
	(1)	(2)	(3)	(4)	(5)
1901	99	243	30.6	737 808	——
1902	125	102	16.0	203 301	——
1903	175	219	22.4	858 959	——
1904	103	111	16.9	192 890	——
1905	96	130	19.7	246 138	——
1906	150	156	16.2	378 276	——
1907	188	181	15.3	520 142	——
1908	76	343	27.0	703 571	——
1909	90	201	48.6	880 663	——
1910	101	220	32.9	731 324	——
1911	100	292	62.4	1 821 084	——
1912	181	237	26.5	1 135 787	——
1913	152	267	25.6	1 036 254	——
1914	63	154	50.5	490 850	——
1915	63	181	8.3	95 042	——
1916	120	221	8.9	236 814	——
1917	160	314	22.4	1 123 515	——
1918	230	347	8.1	647 942	——
1919	336	443	22.8	3 400 942	0.60
1920	322	187	13.3	799 524	0.14
1921	168	168	37.1	1 048 914	0.22
1922	104	421	34.9	1 528 661	0.32
1923	86	398	19.6	671 750	0.13
1924	70	490	37.7	1 295 054	0.26
1925	87	333	41.2	1 193 281	0.23
1926	77	310	11.2	266 601	0.05
1927	74	301	6.8	152 570	0.03
1928	98	179	12.8	224 212	0.04
1929	90	144	11.7	152 080	0.02
1930	67	205	6.7	91 797	0.01
1931	88	122	19.0	204 238	0.04
1932	116	202	10.9	255 000	0.05
1933	125	212	12.0	317 547	0.07
1934	191	240	12.5	574 519	0.11
1935	120	277	8.7	288 703	0.05
1936	156	223	8.0	276 997	0.05
1937	278	259	12.3	886 393	0.15
1938	147	139	7.3	148 678	0.02
1939	122	336	5.5	224 588	0.04
1940	168	361	4.4	266 318	0.04
1941	231	377	5.0	433 914	0.06
1942	354	322	4.0	450 202	0.05

Table 12.1 (continued) Various Measures of Strike Activity, Canada, 1901–2006

Year	Frequency[a]	Size[b]	Duration[c]	Volume	
				Person-Days Lost[d]	As Percentage of Working Time[e]
	(1)	(2)	(3)	(4)	(5)
1943	402	543	4.8	1 041 198	0.12
1944	199	378	6.5	490 139	0.06
1945	197	488	15.2	1 457 420	0.19
1946	226	614	32.4	4 494 833	0.54
1947	234	442	22.9	2 366 339	0.27
1948	154	278	20.7	885 793	0.10
1949	135	347	22.1	1 036 818	0.11
1950	161	1200	7.2	1 388 110	0.15
1951	258	392	8.9	901 625	0.09
1952	219	513	24.6	2 765 506	0.29
1953	173	315	24.1	1 312 715	0.15
1954	173	327	25.3	1 430 300	0.15
1955	159	378	31.2	1 875 400	0.19
1956	229	387	14.1	1 245 824	0.11
1957	245	329	18.3	1 477 105	0.13
1958	258	425	24.4	2 673 481	0.24
1959	216	440	23.4	2 226 891	0.19
1960	274	180	15.0	738 701	0.06
1961	287	341	13.6	1 335 081	0.11
1962	311	239	19.1	1 417 361	0.11
1963	332	251	11.0	916 991	0.07
1964	343	293	15.7	1 580 421	0.11
1965	502	342	13.4	2 301 088	0.17
1966	617	667	12.6	5 179 993	0.34
1967	522	483	15.8	3 975 792	0.25
1968	581	385	22.7	5 077 609	0.32
1969	597	514	25.2	7 733 287	0.46
1970	544	481	25.0	6 539 500	0.39
1971	569	421	11.9	2 854 480	0.16
1972	598	1180	10.9	7 716 287	0.43
1973	724	484	16.4	5 761 150	0.30
1974	1217	487	15.6	9 222 256	0.46
1975	1170	431	21.6	10 877 291	0.56
1976	1040	1524	7.3	11 544 170	0.53
1977	806	270	15.3	3 320 050	0.15
1978	1057	379	18.4	7 357 180	0.32
1979	1049	441	16.9	7 819 350	0.33
1980	1028	427	20.2	9 129 880	0.37
1981	1049	326	25.9	8 850 040	0.35
1982	679	684	12.3	5 702 370	0.23

Table 12.1 (continued) Various Measures of Strike Activity, Canada, 1901–2006

Year	Frequency[a]	Size[b]	Duration[c]	Person-Days Lost[d]	Volume As Percentage of Working Time[e]
	(1)	(2)	(3)	(4)	(5)
1983	645	512	13.4	4 440 890	0.18
1984	716	261	20.8	3 883 390	0.15
1985	829	198	19.0	3 125 560	0.12
1986	748	650	14.7	7 151 470	0.27
1987	668	872	6.5	3 810 170	0.14
1988	548	378	23.7	4 901 260	0.17
1989	627	710	8.3	3 701 360	0.13
1990	579	468	18.7	5 079 190	0.17
1991	463	548	9.9	2 516 090	0.09
1992	404	377	13.8	2 110 180	0.07
1993	381	268	14.9	1 516 640	0.05
1994	374	216	19.8	1 606 580	0.06
1995	328	455	10.6	1 583 070	0.05
1996	330	836	11.9	3 269 060	0.12
1997	284	908	14.0	3 607 710	0.12
1998	381	641	10.0	2 433 870	0.08
1999	413	388	15.3	2 442 580	0.08
2000	379	379	11.5	1 656 790	0.05
2001	381	580	9.9	2 198 850	0.07
2002	294	571	18.1	3 033 430	0.09
2003	266	305	21.4	1 736 312	0.05
2004	298	873	12.4	3 224 528	0.09
2005	260	766	20.8	4 149 130	0.12
2006	155	281	18.6	808 046	0.02

[a] Number of strikes in existence during the year, whether they began in that year or earlier.

[b] Average number of workers involved per strike, calculated as the number of workers involved (from the basic data source, not shown on the table) divided by the number of strikes.

[c] Average days lost per worker on strike, calculated as total person-days lost (column 4) divided by the number of workers involved. This is a measure of the average length of time that each worker who is on strike remains on strike. An alternative measure of duration is the average length of each strike, which can be calculated as the days lost divided by the number of strikes (i.e., frequency of column 1).

[d] Product of frequency (strikes) times size (strikers/strikes) and duration (days lost/striker). Numbers are approximate because of rounding.

[e] Beginning in 1975, potential working time is based on employed workers. Prior to 1975, working time is based on paid, non-agricultural workers.

Sources: 1901–1945—Labour Canada, *Strikes and Lockouts in Canada*, various issues.

1946–1975—Calculations by the authors based on the Bureau of Labour Information, Work Stoppage File.

1976–2006—Figures for columns 1, 4, and 5 are from Human Resources Development Canada, Workplace Information Directorate, adapted with the permission of the Minister of Public Works and Government Services Canada 2000, www.110.hrdc-drhc.gc.ca/millieudetravail_workplace/chrono/index.cfm/doc/english. Figures for columns 2 and 3 are calculated by the authors as discussed, respectively, in notes b and c above. Both calculations required data on the total number of workers involved from the Web address above.

Conservative government. Briskin (2007) highlights the importance of key strikes in affecting aggregate strike statistics.

A breakdown of the time pattern of strike activity for the public and private sectors respectively (Gunderson and Hyatt, 1996; Gunderson and Reid, 1995) indicates that strike activity has declined since the mid-1970s in both sectors; however, the decline has been more rapid in the private sector compared to the public sector. As such, the public-sector share of total strike days lost has increased since the mid-1970s. In fact, in 1991, a record high of 57 percent of all strike days lost was accounted for by public-sector strikes, although in more typical years they account for roughly 20 to 30 percent of all strike activity—approximately their same percentage of total employment.

The recent decline in strikes is an international phenomenon, also having occurred in the United States and Western Europe (Aligisakis, 1997). Whether this reflects a "withering away" of the strike or a temporary phenomenon is an interesting and important question (see Exhibit 12.7).

Components of Strike Activity

The first three columns of Table 12.1 indicate the contribution of each of the components of strike activity—frequency, size, and duration—to the overall volume of strike activity. With the exceptions of both world wars, Canada has almost always had strikes of fairly long duration compared to most other countries. Over the full period 1901 to 1998, the average strike lasted 18.8 days, though it dropped to 16.6 days in the 1980s, and 13.8 days in the 1990s. This recent drop in duration, which has been accompanied by a decline in strike frequency, has resulted in a substantial reduction in the percentage of working time lost due to strikes. The 1970s were a particularly volatile period in Canadian industrial relations, and this is reflected in strike activity. Two very large strikes occurred in 1972 and 1976—the Common Front general strike of public employees in Quebec, and a Day of Protest throughout Canada in opposition to wage controls introduced by the federal government the previous year. The average size of strikes in these two years increased dramatically as a result. The frequency of strikes also increased because the average length of contracts shortened during the inflationary cycle of the 1970s. This meant that more contracts were being negotiated each year and hence the potential for strikes rose.

Exhibit 12.7
A "Withering Away" of the Strike?

The decline of strike activity in the 1980s and 1990s is not confined to Canada and the United States. It has also occurred in Western Europe, and especially in otherwise strike-prone countries like Italy and the United Kingdom. Interrelated reasons for the decline include (Aligisakis, 1997):

- The high unemployment of the last 20 years
- Industrial restructuring and new technology, which are not conducive to worker mobilization
- A political decision on the part of the Italian trade unions, especially in the public sector, to pursue more peaceful labour relations

---

- Restrictive legislation under Thatcher in Britain
- Increased worker participation in the joint management of the organization

Undoubtedly, globalization has also played an important part since both labour and management run a greater risk of permanently losing market share to other countries if the organization is shut down due to a strike. As well, business investment and the jobs associated with that investment may shift away from countries where strikes are prominent.

While the recent decline of strike activity may have occurred across many countries, it may be premature to conclude that the strike has "withered away."

Strike Duration—An Alternative Interpretation

The macroeconomic measurement of strikes as lost work time necessitates a view of strikes from an employer perspective. That is, the emphasis is on production losses due to strikes as measured by lost time. In the following section we will depart from this approach and look at a strike from the perspectives of individual workers and managers.

Previously we measured strike duration as average days lost per worker on strike (see Table 12.1). Such a measure is influenced by the size of strikes (i.e., the number of workers involved in strikes). An alternative measure would be the average length of a strike in calendar days (not weighted by the number of workers involved in each strike). This is the number most likely reported in the news or reported by management or union as the actual length of the strike. If we then average calendar days over each decade from 1950 to 1999, a clear pattern emerges (see Table 12.2). Strikes have been getting longer in Canada, increasing from about 3.5 weeks to 8.5 weeks over this 50-year period. Strike duration seems to have peaked at an average of 60 calendar days. Canada's problem with strike duration continues unabated.

Table 12.2 Average Strike Duration by Decade in Calendar Days

Period	Strike Duration (average calendar days)
1946–49	21.3
1950–59	24.7
1960–69	27.4
1970–79	35.7
1980–89	49.9
1990–99	60.6
2000–06	60.1

Source: Computed using Work Stoppage data, Workplace Information Directorate, Human Resources and Social Development Canada.

Contract Status at Time of Strike

It is useful to distinguish strikes by the status of the contract at the time of the strike because different kinds of strikes may well have different underlying causes. First-contract or recognition strikes occur over the establishment of the first collective agreement following the certification of the union; contract-renewal strikes occur over the renegotiation of an existing collective agreement; mid-contract strikes occur during the term of an existing collective agreement.[23]

Table 12.3 provides information on the status of the contract at the time of the strike. From 1986 to 2002, the vast majority of strike activity according to all measures was accounted for by regular end-of-contract disputes that occur during the renegotiation of an existing collective agreement. This result is not unexpected, since the overwhelming majority of contract negotiations occur in this category and since strikes during the term of the collective agreement are illegal. Recognition or first-agreement strikes accounted for 14.2 percent of strikes and lockouts, but because they tended to occur mainly in small establishments, they involved only 1.9 percent of workers on strike. In spite of their illegality in all jurisdictions (except Saskatchewan), mid-contract strikes during the term of an existing collective agreement accounted for 6.2 percent of all work stoppages and 20.3 percent of workers involved in strikes. Because they are illegal, these strikes tended to be of short duration, hence explaining why they accounted for a mere 3.8 percent of person-days lost because of strikes.

Although the earlier periods are not shown in the table, mid-contract strikes as a proportion of all strikes have declined substantially since the 1970s—from 25.2 percent in the period 1970–1979, to 11.8 percent in the period 1980–1985, to 6.2 percent in the period 1986–2002. Research would be needed to establish the reasons for this decline. Some of the change may be due to the emergence of new grievance arbitration procedures (for example, expedited arbitration and grievance mediation) and employment standards innovations (for example, health and safety committees and advance layoff notice) to

Table 12.3 Strikes and Lockouts by Contract Status for Various Measures of Strike, 1986–2002

Contract Status	Strikes and Lockouts (%)	Workers Involved (%)	Person-Days Lost (%)
First agreement	14.2	1.9	4.6
Renegotiation of agreement	77.5	64.8	86.2
During term of agreement	6.2	20.3	3.8
Other[a]	2.1	13.0	5.4
Total	100.0	100.0	100.0

[a] Includes instances where there was no collective agreement before the work stoppage and where the conclusion of a final agreement was not a basic issue.

Source: Calculations by the authors based on data from the Human Resources Development Canada, Work Stoppage File.

deal with problems that arise during the term of the collective agreement. As well, with the increased use of just-in-time delivery, mid-contract strikes could be particularly disruptive, leading management to take defensive moves against them (e.g., increasing the use of supervisory personnel who would not go on strike) so as to reduce the likelihood of their being used.

Clearly, the underlying causes of these different types of strikes may differ. First-contract strikes may reflect the inexperience of the parties, an especially important factor because this inexperience is likely to lead to misperceptions and a lack of knowledge about the other's position. They may also arise as a continuation of bitter and difficult union organizing campaigns. Mid-contract strikes, on the other hand, usually occur in response to a particular work situation or working condition and may reflect pent-up frustration and lack of confidence in the grievance procedure. Such strikes may also be a way for union members to show discontent over the contract negotiated by their leadership. All too often, the discussion and analysis of strikes assumes that they are a relatively homogeneous phenomenon, and therefore all strikes are analyzed as regular end-of-contract disputes. Most certainly, the determinants of strikes may differ depending on the type of strike.

Industry and Regional Variation

As indicated in Table 12.4, there is considerable industrial and some regional variation in strikes in Canada and also considerable variation within an industry or province over brief periods of time. Between the 1980s and 2000s, the average strike time lost per worker fell by more than half, from 0.41 days to 0.12 days. In the 1980s, the three most strike-prone industries were manufacturing, construction, and information and culture, while the least strike-prone industries were finance, real estate, and management services, wholesale and retail trade, and entertainment and hospitality. During the 2000s, public administration has become the most strike-prone industry, while the category of finance, real estate, and management services remains the least affected by strikes. The most noticeable changes that have occurred over the period are the continued drop in overall strike activity; the drop in most industries; the pronounced drop in both manufacturing and construction; and the slow drop in public administration between the 1980s and 1990s and the rise in the 2000s. As such, public administration moved from being a sector that was slightly below average in strike activity in the 1980s to one that was twice the average in the 1990s, to being almost five times the national average by the 2000s—currently by far the most strike-prone industry in Canada.

The provincial figures do not exhibit the same degree of variation. In the 1980s, Newfoundland, British Columbia, and Quebec had the highest volume of strike activity. To a large degree, this reflects the concentration of strike-prone industries in those provinces. This is borne out in econometric studies that indicate strike probabilities in the private sector in Canada are fairly similar across regions when other factors, including industrial distribution, are held constant.[24] In the 1990s and 2000s, there was greater convergence in strike activity across the provinces, with the conventionally strike-prone provinces of Newfoundland and Labrador, British Columbia, and Quebec reducing their strike activity the most, the latter two provinces moving very close to the national average. For each of these provinces, strike activity dropped to roughly one-quarter of its 1980 level, while the average across all provinces dropped by 70 percent.

Table 12.4 Person-Days Lost per Employed Worker by Industry and Province, Canada, 1980–2006

	1980–89	1990–99	2000–06
Industry			
Primary	0.74	0.31	0.24
Utilities	0.74	0.42	0.11
Construction	0.96	0.28	0.03
Manufacturing	1.00	0.41	0.22
Trade	0.13	0.09	0.06
Transportation	0.55	0.30	0.14
Information and culture	0.79	0.17	0.56
Finance, real estate and management services	0.07	0.03	0.02
Education, health and social services	0.37	0.19	0.14
Entertainment and hospitality	0.13	0.09	0.09
Public administration	0.47	0.34	0.58
Province			
Newfoundland	1.07	0.25	0.47
Prince Edward Island	0.06	0.00	0.02
Nova Scotia	0.24	0.06	0.07
New Brunswick	0.25	0.28	0.12
Quebec	0.59	0.15	0.16
Ontario	0.30	0.21	0.11
Manitoba	0.11	0.12	0.05
Saskatchewan	0.20	0.12	0.08
Alberta	0.17	0.07	0.04
British Columbia	0.78	0.19	0.14
Average	0.41	0.17	0.12

Note: Calculated as person-days lost due to strikes and lockouts divided by the number of employed workers in each industry and province.

Source: The number of person days lost to strikes by industry and province are from Work Stoppage Data, Workplace Information Directorate, Human Resources and Skills Development Canada, and include work stoppages involving one or more workers. The number of people employed by industry and province are from Canada. Statistics Canada / Labour force historical review CD-ROM, 2006: Labour force estimates by detailed industry, sex, age group, Canada, province, annual average [computer file]. Ottawa, Ont: Statistics Canada [producer]; Communications Canada. Depository Services Program [distributor], Feb. 20, 2006. (STC cat. 71F0004XCB).

Strike Rates and Settlement Stages

Another measure of strike activity is the strike rate or proportion of collective agreements that are signed after a strike has occurred. This information is provided in Table 12.5, which shows the stage at which each collective agreement was settled (hence the term "settlement stage"). The last column of Table 12.5 indicates that from 1980 to 1998,

Table 12.5 Settlement Stages, Major Collective Agreements—Public and Private Sectors, 1980–1998

	PROPORTION OF AGREEMENTS SIGNED AT EACH STAGE[a]					
Settlement Stage	Early Period 1980–1989		Later Period 1990–1998		Full Period 1980–1998	
	Public	*Private*	*Public*	*Private*	*Public*	*Private*
Direct bargaining	46.3	45.1	50.5	59.1	48.2	50.7
Conciliation	11.9	17.8	6.3	13.5	9.4	16.1
Post-conciliation	3.1	7.1	2.7	5.3	2.9	6.4
Mediation	9.9	12.8	9.5	9.0	9.7	11.3
Post-mediation	2.7	0.7	1.1	0.6	2.0	0.7
Arbitration	8.6	0.9	4.2	1.6	6.6	1.2
Strike	4.2	15.1	3.0	9.5	3.7	12.9
Legislated[b]	12.7	0.2	22.4	0.9	17.0	0.4
Other, Unknown	0.6	0.3	0.3	0.5	0.5	0.3
Total	100.0	100.0	100.0	100.0	100.0	100.0

[a] In order for the data to be defined consistently across time periods, contracts covering 200 or more workers in the federal jurisdiction were excluded after the 1986 settlement year and construction contracts after the 1983 settlement year. Thus, the table includes non-construction contracts covering 500 or more employees.

[b] Includes contracts reopened under the Ontario Social Contract of 1993. These amounted to 12.5 percent of the 22.4 percent in the period 1990–1998 and 5.6 percent of the 17 percent over the full period 1980–1998.

Source: Calculations by the authors based on data from the Bureau of Labour Information's Major Wage Settlements database, for major collective agreements of 500 or more employees. Reproduced with permission of the Minister of Human Resources Development Canada. Data to update the figures to 2007 is not available.

12.9 percent of private-sector agreements were signed after a strike. The strike rate in the private sector was lower (9.5 percent) in the more recent 1990–1998 period than in the earlier 1980–1989 period (15.1 percent).

During the period 1990–1998, 59 percent of private-sector agreements were settled at the stage of direct bargaining, with an additional 28.4 percent settled with the assistance of conciliation or mediation. The use of third-party arbitration is extremely rare in the private sector (1.6 percent), the parties being loath to hand this decision over to a third-party arbitrator.

In the public sector, strike rates initially appear considerably lower, at 3 percent in the period 1990–1998. This apparently low rate may be misleading because the public sector had a substantial proportion of contracts settled through direct legislative intervention (22.4 percent in the period 1990–1998). In some cases, legislation takes place *after* a strike has occurred; in others, legislation suspends collective bargaining and imposes collective agreements. Furthermore, arbitrated settlements are much more common in the public sector. Combining arbitrated collective agreements with agreements achieved after a strike or through legislation would show that between 1990 and 1998, public-sector collective agreements were achieved by the parties themselves (or through the assistance of a mediator or conciliator) only about 70 percent of the time. By comparison, private-sector negotiations successfully produced collective agreements 88 percent of the time. The special circumstances of the public sector are discussed in Chapter 15.

Summary of the Basic Picture

Historically, there have been wide fluctuations in the various components of strike activity in Canada. From the mid-1960s to the early 1980s, strike activity was particularly high, but it dropped markedly during the 1980s and especially the 1990s and 2000s. Whether this is simply a short-run phase or the beginning of a long-run trend reflecting greater competitive pressures is an important but unanswered question.

Although most strikes occur during the renegotiation of a collective agreement, a substantial number of illegal strikes occur during the term of the collective agreement. Recognition or first-agreement strikes occur quite often; however, they do not involve many workers and hence do not contribute much to the total person-days lost because of strikes.

There is substantial industry and regional variation. In the 1980s, Newfoundland and Labrador, British Columbia, and Quebec experienced the highest volume of strike activity, in part because they have a concentration of strike-prone industries, including fishing, mining, construction, lumber, and pulp and paper. In the 1990s, strike activity dropped markedly across almost all industries, and the largest drop occurred in the otherwise strike-prone provinces, thus bringing a considerable convergence of strike activity across the provinces. It is worth noting that strike activity in public administration did not drop by much. As such, its strike activity was twice the national average in the 1990s and almost five times the national average in the 2000s.

In the 1990s, almost 90 percent of private-sector agreements were settled by direct bargaining or with the aid of conciliation or mediation. Slightly less than 10 percent required a strike, and very few required legislation or arbitration. Conversely, in the public sector, about 70 percent were settled by direct bargaining or with the aid of conciliation. Almost 30 percent were settled by other means: legislation (22 percent), arbitration (4 percent), or a strike (3 percent).

DISPUTE RESOLUTION PROCEDURES

All Canadian jurisdictions have established a number of procedures, usually involving the intervention of a neutral third party, to help the parties resolve their disputes (Ponak and Falkenberg, 1989). Some purposes of third-party intervention are

- to provide information and help the parties articulate their preferences and trade-offs;
- to provide a period for emotions to ebb and hostilities to cool off;
- to solve interpersonal and political problems through enabling the parties to save face by yielding to the suggestions of a third party;

- to bring public awareness to, and perhaps put pressure on, the parties; and
- in the most extreme form of intervention, to provide a substitute for the strike by means of compulsory interest arbitration.

These objectives are facilitated to varying degrees by a variety of forms of third-party intervention, including conciliation, mediation, fact-finding, and arbitration.[25]

Types of Dispute Resolution Procedures

Compulsory Conciliation Canada was one of the few countries to adopt a system of compulsory conciliation during the early 1900s. In the current context, however, most jurisdictions do not require conciliation/mediation as a precondition to a work stoppage. Conciliation/mediation is not required before a legal strike may take place in the federal jurisdiction, British Columbia, Manitoba, Ontario, Quebec, and Saskatchewan, but is mandatory in the remaining provinces of Alberta, New Brunswick, Nova Scotia, Prince Edward Island, and Newfoundland and Labrador.

At the request of either party or on an order of the minister, a government conciliator may be appointed by the provincial ministry of labour. The conciliator meets with the parties and reports the possibilities of a settlement to the minister of labour. After the report has been filed and a specified period of time has elapsed (usually 7 or 14 days), the union obtains the right to strike and management the right to lock out.

In some jurisdictions, if conciliation is unsuccessful, the dispute is forwarded to a conciliation board (usually tripartite), also charged with investigating the dispute and reporting to the minister.

Mediation Although the terms "mediation" and "conciliation" are sometimes used interchangeably, mediation is often reserved for the voluntary use of a neutral third party, often a non-government professional, who gets involved after the conciliation process is exhausted and possibly when the strike is in progress. Mediation usually is more interventionist than conciliation, with the mediator not just providing information at the early stages, but also suggesting compromises at subsequent stages, and ultimately even suggesting proposals and possibly settlement terms. The mediator's views can be used or ignored by the parties (hence the importance of trust and confidence in the mediator); they need not involve a recommendation, and they are usually not made public, except possibly in public-sector disputes.

Fact-Finding Fact-finding, a task often performed by conciliation boards, is a more formal process than mediation. The fact-finder (or fact-finding board) is charged with the responsibility of investigating the issues in dispute and making formal recommendations to the labour relations board and possibly to the public. As in mediation, however, the recommendations of the fact-finder do not have to be adopted by the parties.

Typically, the fact-finding process includes formal briefs from both union and management as well as a formal hearing where both parties are allowed to present their views. In some situations, however, the term "fact-finding" is used (as the word implies) to refer to a stage in which a third party simply helps the parties compile the relevant facts before any intervention by a conciliator or mediator.

Arbitration Arbitration is the strongest form of third-party intervention, since it involves the establishment of terms and conditions of the collective agreement by a third-party arbitrator. Such arbitration is termed "interest arbitration" to distinguish it from "rights or grievance arbitration," the latter involving a neutral third party to interpret the existing collective agreement. Interest arbitration is a substitute for the strike in situations in which strikes are banned, as is often the case for various elements of the public sector, such as police, firefighters, hospital workers, teachers, and the civil service—hence it is often referred to as "compulsory arbitration." Canadian jurisdictions vary considerably in requirements for interest arbitration for the different elements of the public sector (see Chapter 15). Although the arbitration decision itself is binding on both union and management, the decision to engage in arbitration may be voluntary. Such voluntary arbitration is rare, however, compared to compulsory arbitration.

Two main forms of interest arbitration exist. Under the most common or traditional format, arbitrators are free either to accept the position that one of the parties has submitted or to fashion their own solution usually somewhere in between. A second format is final-offer selection (FOS). Under FOS, the arbitrator must choose, without alteration, either the position submitted by management or that submitted by the union. Arbitrators cannot, as they can under the traditional format, fashion a solution they believe most beneficial to the parties; rather, they are obliged to accept one party's position or the other's. The idea behind FOS is that the two parties would rather make the concessions needed to achieve settlement during negotiations than face the risk of an arbitration award in which the other side's position, in its entirety, could be incorporated into the new collective agreement. Final-offer selection is often used in the United States, especially for police and firefighters, but it tends to be rarely used in Canada. The recent new framework agreement between Magna and the CAW is a noteworthy exception (see Exhibit 12.8; also see the vignette at the beginning of Chapter 2). The CAW has given up the right to strike in favour of final-offer arbitration. Although the U.S. experience generally shows that FOS is capable of producing a higher rate of negotiated settlements than traditional arbitration, it tends to be rejected in Canada by all parties, arbitrators included. FOS can lead to poor collective agreements if neither side submits reasonable proposals and it can produce a damaging win–lose mentality in the labour–management relationship.

Exhibit 12.8
Union Agrees to a No-Strike Policy

In an unprecedented framework agreement, the CAW has agreed to give up the right to strike in all contract negotiations with its bargaining units in Magna International Inc. In exchange for a non-adversarial organizing process, in which Magna has agreed to be neutral, the CAW has agreed to submit all contract disputes to final-offer arbitration. If some 18 000 Magna employees choose to join the CAW in 45 plants across Canada, then this may be the start of a new collective bargaining model. The new paradigm reflects a reality of globalization that management and labour have a common stake in competing with foreign competition and keeping jobs in Canada. The paradigm departs from the *Wagner Act* model in three key ways:

- A non-adversarial organizing procedure
- A co-operative method of resolving conflict at work
- All contract disputes to be settled by final-offer arbitration and not work stoppages

Arbitration, especially in its traditional form, has been criticized as an unacceptable strike substitute since it does not provide the same inducements to the parties to settle as would a strike. Canadian industrial relations places a high value on the ability of labour and management to resolve differences themselves through the give and take of the bargaining process. Specifically, arbitration has often been found to chill genuine collective bargaining. This "chilling effect" is said to occur because the parties may hold back concessions during bargaining, believing that the arbitrator is likely to split the difference between their final positions. Arbitration has also been criticized because it may create a "narcotic effect," making the parties dependent on the arbitrator to determine their terms and conditions of employment. The existing empirical evidence (reviewed in Ponak and Falkenberg, 1989, and Hebdon, 1996) in general does not yield conclusive results on the existence of chilling and narcotic effects, but almost all available evidence indicates that compulsory arbitration systems lead to a lower rate of negotiated settlements than do systems in which strikes are permitted. One study by Hebdon, Hyatt, and Mazerolle (1999) did find evidence of a chilling effect in Ontario in the 1980s and 1990s, particularly in the health care arbitration sector.

Other Forms of Dispute Resolution In the Canadian public sector, the government has often taken an alternative approach to resolving disputes, especially strikes by public employees. More and more frequently, both the federal and provincial governments have been willing to pass special back-to-work legislation requiring the termination of a strike and forcing the parties back to the bargaining table (see Chapter 15). Thus, strikes may be reduced through mediation and fact-finding, prohibited and replaced by arbitration, or ended through special legislation.

Social Contracts Especially in the 1990s in the private sector in Quebec, a number of long-term contracts have been signed in traditionally strike-prone industries like pulp and paper and steel (see Chapter 16). The agreements have generally been for longer than the conventional maximum of three years—a maximum that is usually required by law, but that the government has extended in these cases in the hope of fostering labour relations peace. Conventionally, wage arbitration is required after three years. In return for forgoing the right to strike that is implied by such long-term contracts (since strikes during the term of a collective agreement are not allowed), labour has generally been guaranteed job security as well as a promise of continued investment in plant and equipment (often facilitated by government). The Quebec government has been involved not only in supporting the investment in plant and equipment, but also in facilitating the negotiation of these social contracts. The term "social contracts" is often used to describe these contracts since they involve all of the social partners (labour, management, and governments) in negotiating private collective agreements with a view toward enhancing private outcomes such as industrial peace, job security, and investment that also serve broader social purposes.

The term social contracts is also used to describe the programs imposed by various provincial governments in the early 1990s whereby mandatory unpaid days of leave were imposed on public-sector workers as an alternative to layoffs (Gunderson and Hyatt, 1996: 256). For example, Hebdon and Warrian (1999) examined the impact of the Ontario social contract at the local level of bargaining. A conclusion of their study was that, despite the severe political backlash, collective bargaining could be creatively transformed to effect fundamental changes in the method of service delivery and to facilitate co-operative relations and negotiated restructuring in a widely centralized environment.

Effect of Dispute Resolution and Other Policy Variables

There is little empirical evidence on the effect of various dispute resolution procedures or other labour relations policy variables on the level of strike activity. This is particularly unfortunate since, by definition, such variables could be manipulated to reduce the level of strike activity, if this outcome was considered desirable. In contrast, other possible strike determinants, such as the economic variables and the season, region, and industry, are subject to little or no policy manipulation.

Specific Laws The few empirical studies that have included policy variables have generally simply added a variable to reflect the impact of a particular law. Laws include the *Landrum–Griffin Act* (Ashenfelter and Johnson, 1969), right-to-work laws (Gramm, 1986), state penalties for public-sector workers who go on strike or prohibitions on school districts to qualify for state aid if they reschedule teacher strike days (Montgomery and Benedict, 1989; Olson, 1984, 1986), the availability of unemployment insurance for workers on strike (Hutchens, Lipsky, and Stern, 1992; Ondrich and Schnell, 1993), or an index of labour law changes that affect collective bargaining and union power (Ingram, Metcalf, and Wadsworth, 1993). These studies generally find that laws and policies designed to discourage strikes or make them more costly or difficult do tend to reduce strike activity.

Prohibitions on the Right to Strike in the Public Sector Empirical studies have also examined the extent to which legislative prohibitions on union activity and the right to strike in the public sector have deterred strikes.[26] Most find public-sector strike activity is deterred, but by no means eliminated, by prohibitions and penalties on the right to strike (see Exhibit 12.9).

Exhibit 12.9
Does Prohibiting the Right to Strike Reduce Dispute Costs?

Currie and McConnell (1991) find that granting public-sector workers the right to strike does lead to significantly higher strike frequencies, compared to when the right is prohibited and arbitration is required. Furthermore, the cost per dispute is much higher when the dispute takes the form of a strike rather than arbitration. For these reasons, dispute costs (strikes plus arbitrations) increase because the cost increase due to increased strikes is greater than the cost saving due to reduced arbitrations. They argue that this must be traded off against higher wage costs, which tend to occur under arbitration. These general conclusions tend to hold up when their data is reanalyzed to account for discrepancies in their legislative coding and the content of the relevant statutes, as well as the actual practice (Gunderson, Hebdon, and Hyatt, 1996).

The analysis becomes even more complicated, however, since prohibiting the right to strike among public-sector workers leads to more grievances, job actions (e.g., slowdowns, working-to-rule, sick-outs), and political activities. In essence, restricting the right to strike simply redirects conflict into other costly forms such as grievances, job actions, and political activities (Hebdon and Stern, 1998, 2003). Thus any cost–benefit analysis of arbitration versus strike ought to take into account these other potentially costly expressions of conflict.

Labour Relations Policy Variables A comprehensive analysis of the impact that a wide range of Canadian labour relations policy variables have on strike activity is summarized in Table 12.6, based on the econometric studies cited in the source. The first column gives the effect of each policy variable on strike incidence—that is, the probability that the contract will require a strike before it is settled. These changes should be interpreted relative to the average strike incidence of 15.9 percent; that is, over the period 1967–1985 almost 16 percent of contracts involved a strike. The second column gives the effect of each policy variable on strike duration—that is, the length of the strikes that occurred (which averaged 35 days over that period). The discussion here will focus on those variables that had a statistically significant (as denoted by an asterisk) and quantitatively large impact on strike activity, since they are of most relevance to policy.

The existence of a conciliation officer and board is associated with a substantial 12.8 percent reduction in the likelihood that a strike will occur. A mandatory strike vote (a majority of bargaining unit members must vote in favour of the strike before it can occur) is associated with an 11.1 percent reduction in strike incidence as well as a reduction of seven days in the duration of strikes. Dues check-off is associated with a substantial 9.1 percent reduction in the likelihood of a strike but a 6.4-day increase in the duration of strikes. The existence of automatic reopener provisions (whereby the collective agreement can be reopened in the event of technological change that was unanticipated at the time the contract was signed) is associated with a 3.4-day reduction in the length of strikes.

Table 12.6 Effect of Labour Relations Policy Variables on Strike Activity

Labour Relations Policy Variable	Effect on Incidence (percent)	Effect on Duration (days)
Average Incidence and Duration	15.9	35.0
Conciliation officer	−7.9	1.2
Conciliation officer and board	−12.8*	−1.1
Cooling-off period (days)	0.2	0.5
Mandatory strike vote	−11.1*	−7.4*
Employer-initiated vote option	18.9*	−1.5
Dues check-off	−9.1*	6.4*
Prohibition on replacement workers	24.4*	6.9*
Negotiated reopeners	−5.4	1.5
Automatic reopeners	6.6	−3.4*

*Statistically significant at $p < .05$ level.

Source: Strike incidence effects are from Gunderson, Kervin, and Reid (1989) based on Labour Canada's Major Collective Agreements (500 or more employees) database for the years 1971–1985. Strike duration effects are from Gunderson and Melino (1990) based on Labour Canada's Work Stoppage File for strikes of any size for the years 1967–1985. A non-technical summary of these studies, and the qualifications that are appropriate given the nature of the data, are given in Gunderson, Melino, and Reid (1990).

The most controversial, and perhaps unexpected, result is that legislation prohibiting the use of replacement workers (so called "anti-scab" legislation) is associated with a 24.4 percent increase in strike incidence and a 6.9-day increase in the length of strikes.

While these magnitudes are large, they should be regarded with caution since they are based exclusively on the anti-strikebreaking provisions that were introduced in Quebec in 1977; other pro-labour legislative changes were also introduced in Quebec at the same time (see Chapter 16). But consistent with these results, Lacroix and Lesperance (1988) also found for the period 1961–1981 that bans on replacement workers and laws permitting secondary picketing have led to increased strike incidence in Quebec, Ontario, and British Columbia.

A number of theoretical explanations have been offered for why the restrictions on the use of replacement workers can lead to increased strike activity. In their review of the game theory analysis of strikes, Kennan and Wilson (1989) indicate that banning replacement workers actually increases the union's uncertainty about the firm's willingness to pay to end the strike since that willingness is no longer constrained by the firm's option of using replacement workers. When the firm could use replacement workers, the union knew that this would place an upper limit on the firm's willingness to pay to end the strike—that upper limit is removed if replacement workers are not an option. As well, a ban on replacement workers makes the strike a more attractive weapon to the union compared to other mechanisms such as continuing to work without a contract (Cramton and Tracy, 1992). Whatever the reason, the limited evidence from Canada suggests that legislative bans on replacement workers are associated with an increase in both the incidence and duration of strikes. These results continue to hold based on an updated and more extensive analysis that also includes the effect that the ban on replacement workers has on wages (see Exhibit 12.10).

Exhibit 12.10
What Effects Do Legislative Bans on Replacement Workers Have on Wages and Strikes?

Cramton, Gunderson, and Tracy (1999a, 1999b) analyzed the effect on wages and strike incidence and duration in large bargaining units in Canada over the period of January 1967 to March 1993. Bans on replacement workers existed in British Columbia from January 1993 and Ontario from January 1993 to November 1995, as well as in Quebec since February 1978. Their results suggest that the bans on replacement workers were associated with the following effects:

■ An increase in the probability of a strike occurring of 0.12, a substantial magnitude relative to the average probability of 0.16.

■ An increase in the length of the strike of 32 days, a substantial magnitude relative to the average of 59 days for strikes that occurred.

■ An increase in real wages of 4.4 percent over the life of a contract or almost 2 percent per year.

- A net gain to the union of almost $3 million (wage gain of almost $4 million less strike cost of $1 million) and a net loss of almost $5 million to the firm (wage loss of almost $4 million plus strike cost of $1 million) in a typical contract renegotiation under a ban on replacement workers.

With such large gains and losses to the parties, it is not surprising that the legislative ban on replacement workers generates such intense controversy.

The authors emphasize that their analysis deals only with the effect that a legislative ban on replacement workers has on wages and strike incidence and duration. Other important dimensions beyond the scope of the analysis include: picket line violence; the post-strike relationship between strikers, employers, and replacement workers; the balance of power and the viability of the collective bargaining system itself; workplace injuries (Exhibit 12.11) and product quality (Exhibit 12.12). For a review of the law and some of the empirical research on replacement workers see Singh and Jain (2001).

CONSEQUENCES OF STRIKE ACTIVITY

Strikes are of policy interest in large part because of their perceived effects on the parties themselves, on third parties, and on the economy as a whole. Canada's poor strike record by international standards has been cited as a possible contributor to its poor productivity performance and as a possible concern to foreign investors and importers. Although conjecture abounds, there is very little rigorous statistical analysis of the effects of strikes, certainly much less than that of the factors that influence strike activity. Nevertheless, a few empirical studies estimate the diverse consequences of strikes.

With respect to the effect of strikes on wages, Canadian studies show mixed results.[27] Based on U.S. data, McConnell (1989) finds that strikes lead to lower wage settlements. Some Canadian evidence indicates that the costs of a strike for workers are outweighed by the wage gains for shorter strikes but not for longer ones (Ng, 1993; Reid and Oman, 1991). This tends to confirm the industrial relations stereotype that unions "win" short strikes, but "lose" long ones.

The empirical evidence also indicates that strikes have the following effects:

- Negative effects on the stock-market value of struck firms.[28]

- Postive effects on the stock-market value of the competitors of struck firms (DeFusco and Fuess, 1991; Kramer and Hyclak, 2002; and Kramer and Vasconcellos, 1996) but negative effects on suppliers (Persons, 1995).

- Negative feelings toward the government as well as replacement workers, police, and management in the case of public-sector disputes (Langford, 1996).

- Increasing workplace injuries (see Exhibit 12.11).

- Negative psychological consequences for the workers involved in the strike (Stoner and Arora, 1987).

- Galvanizing community support for strikers (Gilson, Spencer, and Granville, 1989; MacDowell, 1993).

- Cathartic and constructive effects on labour–management relations (Beatty and Ganz, 1989).
- Mixed effects on productivity.[29]
- No dramatic effects in general, in part because the parties adjust before, during, and after the strike.[30]

Certainly, the consequences are not as substantial as is often portrayed in the media at the time of a strike. Gunderson and Melino (1987), for example, indicate that in the North American auto industry the typical pattern has been for inventories to be built up prior to a strike through increased production and increased prices, with the latter having deterred consumption. After a strike, inventories were again restored in the same fashion. The authors indicate that "both consumers and producers rationally respond to the expected and the actual event of the strike through a variety of inter-temporal adjustments; and, while the initial effects are in some instances quite pronounced, the long-run effects are usually minimal" (p. 1). But, as the survey evidence of Tang and Ponak (1986) indicates, the perceived costs of strikes differ dramatically across different organizations.

Exhibit 12.11
Strikes, Replacement Workers, and Workplace Injuries

The conventional argument for banning the use of replacement workers during a strike is to reduce the picket line violence that often occurs when replacement workers are used. Empirical evidence based on data for New York in the 1970s (Allen, 1994) indicates that strikes can lead to increased workplace injuries as firms hire replacement workers who are unfamiliar with the jobs and the associated dangers. The injuries could also occur if there is a "speed-up" after the strike to replace lost output.

Exhibit 12.12
Strikes, Replacement Workers, and Product Quality: Don't Drive and Strike

In analyzing strikes and the use of replacement workers, we conventionally focus on the impact on such factors as strike duration and wages. The impacts, however, can be much broader. Krueger and Mas (2004) find that the demand for wage concessions and the use of replacement workers were associated with significantly higher rates of tire defects in a large tire manufacturing company. Clearly such impacts should be considered in any decision to demand wage concessions or use replacement workers. For a qualitative, case-study overview of the strikes see Franklin (2001).

Further, it must be emphasized that the empirical literature on strike effects tends to focus on private-sector strikes, where customers usually have options in terms of other suppliers or of postponing purchases. In the public sector, the situation is quite different because of the essential nature of many of the services and the lack of alternatives. Here, the third-party effects on the general public can be quite substantial; this is, of course, the rationale for binding interest arbitration as an alternative to a strike. In the quasi-public sector and for regulated utilities (for example, telephone, transportation), the situation is likely to fall in between those of the private and public sectors; third parties (that is, customers) usually have some alternatives, although these alternatives are not as readily available as in the private sector. This threat of a loss of customers puts some pressure on the parties to settle—more so than in the public sector, but less so than in the purely private sector.

CONCLUSION

Although there is a voluminous literature on strike determinants, most of it simply relates measures of strike activity to a variety of variables for which data are available. Little effort is made to understand the causal mechanisms through which these observable factors affect strike activity. Recent theoretical work has somewhat improved on this lack of analysis by emphasizing that strikes have benefits, especially in terms of the information they generate. The work also emphasizes that, whatever the function of strikes, they will be used less when the joint costs to both parties are great relative to the costs of other mechanisms for achieving the same end.

On the empirical side, the most important recent advances involve the use of large-scale data sets with the individual contract (that is, the collective agreement) as the unit of observation. This is important, not only because this is the level at which bargaining actually occurs, but also because it allows a number of characteristics of the bargaining unit to be incorporated into the study. Longitudinal data sets can also be constructed that involve bargaining rounds for the same bargaining pair. Such longitudinal data, in turn, are important because they facilitate controlling for the effect of otherwise unobserved factors that may give rise to persistent strike-proneness. In addition, the effect of labour relations policy variables are beginning to be analyzed, an important consideration since these are the levers that can be manipulated to alter strike activity. The recent theoretical and empirical advances may help explain a variety of phenomena associated with Canadian strike activity: the high level by international standards; the increase, especially from the mid-1960s to the mid-1970s; and the decline since the mid-1970s.

Since the mid-1960s, the Canadian economy has been subject to considerable growth involving new entrants into the market and new unionization. New bargaining relationships carry with them little mutual information about each party's "resistance points" and involve a desire on the part of each to establish a reputation. In addition, in the 1970s the economy was subject to numerous shocks, including oil price changes, unanticipated inflation, and trade shocks. These increased uncertainty, especially about the firm's ability to pay. A premium was put on the strike as a mechanism to elicit information and re-establish the appropriate division of the firm's rents (or above-normal profits). The greater uncertainly also led to shorter contracts, increasing the number of times the parties were exposed to the risk of an end-of-contract dispute. This, in turn, may have led to an increased use of renegotiation strikes as opposed to mid-contract dispute resolution procedures such as grievances, joint committees, and continuous bargaining (although the extent to which these serve as substitute dispute resolution procedures remains empirically unknown and an interesting subject for research).

Canada's high strike record reflects not only these information problems, but also a concentration of strike-prone, resource-based industries, which tend to be strike-prone in other countries as well. Information problems are exacerbated by the open nature of the Canadian economy and the extent of foreign trade and possibly even foreign control. In addition, Canadian unions negotiate a wide range of items. In contrast, in many European countries, many of these issues (for example, hours of work) are addressed at the political level, where the unions are involved as partners in establishing a broad social contract.

With respect to the decline in strike activity that has occurred since the mid-1970s, the joint-cost and asymmetric-information perspectives also provide some insights. That period has been characterized by intense international competition and dramatic restructuring and downsizing. Information is no longer asymmetric, with firms knowing more about the true state of demand and ability to pay than do workers; rather, both parties know that economic difficulties prevail, a fact that has been revealed through the trend toward downsizing and restructuring. There is less uncertainty about the "economic rents" or excess profits to bargain over, since such rents have been dissipated by international competition. In essence, there is less need to fight over the "spoils" when there are no spoils to divide! The joint cost to both parties of engaging in strikes is also higher because competitors from abroad may permanently replace the lost output and the jobs associated with that output. Furthermore, multinationals may locate their new plants and investment in countries where there is less risk of strikes. This is especially the case since just-in-time delivery systems put a premium on being able to deliver products and services with a high degree of certainty and reliability.

In essence, in recent years the cost of using the strike mechanism has increased and the benefits have declined—the latter especially in terms of eliciting information from the parties. This may explain some of the decline in strike activity that has occurred in Canada, at least since the 1970s. Since these economic pressures are stronger in the private sector than in the public sector, this may also explain why strike activity has declined more steeply in the private sector than in the public sector. The increase in the cost and the decline in the benefits of using the strike mechanism may also explain some of the increased use of alternative dispute resolution procedures and co-operative as opposed to adversarial bargaining that has occurred. These may be necessary for the joint survival of both business and jobs in times of intense international competition, when business investment and plant location decisions are increasingly made on an international basis. Just as "necessity is the mother of invention," it may also be the mother of innovation in alternative dispute resolution procedures.

Although these explanations of our changing pattern of strike activity are plausible, it must be admitted that neither the state of theory nor evidence in the strike literature gives us a very complete—some would say even adequate—explanation of the various dimensions of strike activity over time or across various industries, regions, countries, and bargaining units. For every generalization and empirical regularity there is an exception; often no generalizations are possible. Strikes remain somewhat of a mystery, an area where we should be modest about our ability to predict behaviour and consequences. This uncertainty reflects the variety of institutional, economic, and process factors that impinge on the parties, as well as the fact that if strikes and their outcomes were completely predictable, they would serve little purpose.

Questions

1. What measures of strike activity are typical? What information does each provide about strikes?

2. Describe the main function that strikes serve.

3. Describe four main dispute resolution mechanisms.

4. How does mediation work to reduce the likelihood of a strike?

5. In your opinion, what impact do strikes have on the Canadian economy? Why might this impact differ among sectors (private, regulated, public)?

6. "Unequal bargaining power on the part of one of the parties in the negotiation process has implications for wage determination, not for strikes." Discuss.

7. Why may one expect the relationship of strike cycles to business cycles to differ in Canada and the United States?

8. Discuss how strikes may arise because of an asymmetry of information between employers and employees. What does this imply about the effect of changing economic conditions?

9. Discuss the joint-cost perspective as a theory of strikes. Given this perspective, how would you expect strike activity to be affected by each of the following:

    a) compulsory conciliation?

    b) the availability of unemployment insurance for workers on strike?

    c) an increase in unemployment?

10. What impact would you expect free trade between Canada and the United States, and globalization in general, to have on strike activity in Canada?

11. Use the joint-cost perspective and the asymmetric-information theories of strike activity to explain the following empirical "facts" about strike activity in Canada:

    a) its high level relative to other countries.

    b) its increase between the mid-1960s and mid-1970s.

    c) its decline since the mid-1970s.

    d) the greater decline in the private sector compared to the public sector.

Weblinks

Canada Labour Code:
http://laws.justice.gc.ca/en/l-2/16087.html

CBC interactive site (provides a brief history of strike activity in Canada):
www.cbc.ca/news/background/strike/

Cyber Picket Line (British list of strikes around the world):
www.cardiff.ac.uk/socsi/union/

Industrial relations legislation in Canada:
www.hrsdc.gc.ca/en/lp/spila/clli/irlc/01industrial_relations_legislation_canada.shtml

Strike Page North American listings:
www.cardiff.ac.uk/socsi/union/namer/canada.htm

Chapter 13

The Grievance Arbitration Process and Workplace Conflict Resolution

Kenneth Wm. Thornicroft[1]

Arbitration—the process of having a neutral party adjudicate a dispute—is only one of many ways to manage conflict. A variety of techniques replace or complement arbitration. Since the first edition of this book was published, Canada's military has become a fighting force abroad. It is instructive to examine how the large, complex, and hierarchical organizations that support Canada's peace and security initiatives abroad have developed internal competency in solving interpersonal conflicts.

The Canadian Forces (CF) and the Department of National Defence (DND) employ approximately 80 000 military and 20 000 civilian employees. Most civilians belong to the Union of National Defence Employees (UNDE), a division of the Public Service Alliance of Canada. The CF/DND launched the "Conflict Management Program" (CMP) in 2001 following a successful three-year pilot project.

From the outset, CMP was presented by both senior management and the union as complementary to the conventional grievance procedures. Under the parties' collective agreement, a grievance may be processed through three internal steps and, if not resolved, it may then be referred to an external arbitrator for a final and binding decision. Peter Cormier, former Executive Vice-President of UNDE, observes, "The grievance system works well [when the issue] has to do with management's or union's interpretation of the rules at the workplace [however] the problem is that grievances having to do with interpersonal relationships don't work." Lucie Allaire, former CMP Director-General, emphasizes that the traditional grievance process "is not at all amenable to interpersonal conflicts because when there is a winner and there is a loser, even the winner loses in the relationship. It doesn't get to the bottom of the issue. It doesn't resolve anything. It renders a decision but it doesn't actually help the parties to move on and turn the page."

As CMP challenged the status quo, it required a considerable educational effort and the involvement of all stakeholders in the program's design. The union believed that CMP could help its members who never file grievances but who experience legitimate work-related concerns. The union was especially interested in addressing harassment and interpersonal issues that were proving extremely slow, expensive, and difficult to satisfactorily resolve.

CMP mediation is voluntary and absolutely confidential. Mediation must be initiated by the individual seeking to resolve his or her issue with a peer, superior, or subordinate. A mediation occurs only if *both* parties agree to participate. Both parties are free to offer creative solutions, but the resolution must be mutually acceptable. Either party can walk away from mediation at any time before signing an agreement (and, if they wish, pursue the matter through the traditional grievance process).

The CMP mediation is a multi-step process: (i) a pre-mediation meeting sets expectations and helps prepare the parties; (ii) an introductory phase takes place to review ground rules and establish a respectful tone; (iii) each party outlines his or her understanding of the issues and the mediator helps identify underlying concerns and interests; (iv) the parties and the mediator brainstorm settlement options; and finally (v) the mediation ends and, if the dispute is resolved, both parties sign an agreement.

Unlike formal grievances, which can take several years to resolve especially if interpersonal issues are at stake, mediations typically take only a few weeks. Therefore, in addition to avoiding a zero-sum "winner/loser" result, mediation allows the parties to quickly return to an acceptable working relationship without imposing the high costs and tensions created by years of grievance proceedings.

The cornerstone of the program is the group of 40 highly trained mediators. Demand for CMP services, which include (besides mediation) dispute resolution consultation, conflict coaching, facilitation, and group intervention, has grown since the program's inception. Mediation is automatically offered to the grievor when a formal grievance is filed and remains open even at later stages in the grievance process. During 2004–2005, 70 employees took up mediation at the first step of the civilian grievance process, and 39 employees chose mediation at the second level.

CMP's 2003–2004 Annual Report noted that 251 mediations were concluded in the reporting year with 78 percent fully resolved, 11 percent partially resolved, and only 13 percent unable to reach resolution. The disputes fell into the following categories: work relationships (49 percent), harassment (21 percent), grievance (15 percent), performance evaluation (6 percent), discipline (5 percent), and other (4 percent). The next year, the program's success rate remained 78 percent. A total of 3305 persons sought assistance through CMP during its first three years of operation.

The role of the union is crucial. Lucie Allaire acknowledges that "the union plays a very strong role. I would say the union has been actively proposing alternative dispute resolution as a means to settle problems, as opposed to the grievance process." Harassment grievances have been substantially reduced, from 33 percent of all grievances in 2001 to 8 percent in 2004. In addition to the positive human relations impacts of mediation, "it's much more economical and efficient to run a mediation process than to run a grievance process."

One-to-one conflict coaching was added to CMP in 2003, and has been growing rapidly. It empowers employees to take actions they deem appropriate based on what they discovered through coaching. As Lucie Allaire states, "The main goal of the program is to create competency in the organization in resolving conflict. . . . We don't want 'repeat' business. We don't want to create dependency." Ideally, competence in handling interpersonal conflict "is not something separate, it's actually part of who you are when you are in this organization." Former union executive Peter Cormier is confident that "over time, CMP is going to take hold within the department and become one of the major tools that a [union shop] steward will use."[2]

Canadian labour laws generally prohibit strikes and lockouts during the term of a collective agreement. For example, section 58 of the B.C. *Labour Relations Code* requires that collective agreements contain the following provision (or the equivalent): "there must be no strikes or lockouts so long as this agreement continues to operate."[3]

It is sometimes assumed that legislators, by way of such provisions, have mandated a particular bargain—the union's "no-strike" pledge is exchanged for the employer's undertaking not to lock out the bargaining unit employees during the term of the agreement. However, it is more accurate to characterize both the no-strike and no-lockout provisions as one side of the coin and the *grievance arbitration process* as the other. Rather than resorting to the use of economic pressure tactics such as strikes, lockouts, and picketing, disputes about the parties' respective rights and obligations under their collective agreement can be resolved through the grievance arbitration process without a work stoppage and without the need for time-consuming and expensive court proceedings.

The grievance process is very important to union–management relations. In many ways, grievances are a barometer of the underlying labour climate. There is evidence that unresolved grievances can have a "spillover effect" leading to lower organizational efficiency and productivity and increased workplace conflict (Lewin, 1999).

A *grievance* is simply a dispute regarding the parties' rights or obligations under a collective agreement or the scope of that agreement. Usually grievances are filed by the union, although management has an equal right to do so.[4] Historically, grievances could be filed only if there was an allegation of a breach of the collective agreement. Today, grievances may be filed where the dispute arises from employment and concerns a common-law principle (for example, privacy rights), a statute (such as human rights legislation), or even a constitutional principle (for example, a person's rights under the *Canadian Charter of Rights and Freedoms*). Nevertheless, most grievances concern alleged breaches of specific provisions of the collective agreement—in essence, an allegation of breach of contract.

The grievance arbitration process typically involves two separate dispute resolution procedures. First, most collective agreements contain an *internal grievance process* pursuant to which grievances may be filed. Both the union and the employer have an obligation to meet and attempt to consensually resolve the grievance. An *internal grievance process*, although commonly found in collective agreements, is not mandated by law. The second process, *grievance arbitration*, is mandated by law and may be invoked if a grievance cannot be consensually resolved between the parties. The grievance arbitrator is a neutral third party who is charged with the responsibility of rendering a final and binding decision regarding the grievance.

The success of alternative dispute resolution methods developed in the labour relations context, and in particular mediation and the grievance arbitration process, has spurred the adoption of these procedures in many other settings. Today, arbitration clauses can be found in nonunion employment contracts (McCabe, 2002; Wheeler et al., 2004), franchise agreements, and commercial leases. Further, many nonunion firms have instituted grievance systems (Feuille and Hildebrand, 1995), although third-party arbitration is infrequently a component of such systems. Approximately 35 percent of nonunion employees have access to some sort of grievance process at their workplace (Akyeampong, 2003). Nonunion firms, both in Canada and the United States, are increasingly including mandatory arbitration of certain types of employment disputes, especially dismissals, in their employment policies and employees' employment contracts (Akyeampong, 2003;

Wheeler et al., 2004). Some have questioned the procedural fairness of many nonunion grievance and arbitration procedures, especially where there is no recourse to an independent third-party adjudicator (Peterson and McCabe, 1994; Wheeler et al., 2004; Zack, 1999).

Quite apart from the use of arbitration in other settings, the range of disputes now addressed by grievance arbitrators in union settings has dramatically expanded over the past few decades. The courts have ruled that a wide variety of disputes that arise in unionized workplaces—disputes that traditionally were adjudicated by the courts or other administrative tribunals—can now *only* be adjudicated through grievance arbitration.[5]

The grievance arbitration process was originally conceived as an equitable, inexpensive, and expeditious mechanism to resolve contract disputes between union and management. The grievance process has been lauded as an effective mechanism for improving workplace democracy and for providing employees with a meaningful "voice" in matters affecting their employment (Freeman and Medoff, 1984). Despite such favourable comments, however, others have argued—with some justification—that the contemporary process needs repair: the process is too slow, too expensive, and overly "legalistic." A 2002 Ontario study found that, although 75 percent of respondents felt that the arbitration process was fair, a significant majority believed that the process was too slow, and about one-half of the respondents felt the process was too costly.[6]

In light of these criticisms, both policy-makers and labour relations practitioners have modified existing grievance arbitration processes and have formulated alternative systems for resolving workplace disputes. This chapter's opening vignette, describing the CF/DND "Conflict Management Program," is an excellent example of one organization's attempt to resolve workplace conflicts outside the traditional grievance arbitration process.

In this chapter, we describe the modern grievance arbitration process, outline some of the criticisms of the process, and examine some of the more innovative approaches to resolving workplace disputes.

GRIEVANCE PROCEDURES IN CANADA

It is important to distinguish grievance or *rights arbitration* from *interest arbitration* and, in turn, to distinguish *arbitration* from *mediation*. Mediation, a consensual process described in the opening vignette, involves a neutral third party assisting the parties in resolving their dispute. A mediator does not, however, have the legal authority to adjudicate the dispute. An arbitrator, on the other hand, is very much like a judge; the arbitrator, after hearing the parties' respective evidence and argument, renders a final and binding decision.

In interest arbitration, a neutral third party, after hearing the submissions from both union and management, determines the terms and conditions of the parties' collective agreement. Parties occasionally voluntarily agree to settle their dispute by interest arbitration; more usually, it is mandated by legislation as a substitute for the right to strike or lock out in the event of a bargaining impasse. Interest arbitration is rarely used in the private sector. Interest arbitration is most commonly used in the public sector to settle impasses involving police and firefighters. When striking employees are ordered back to work by ad hoc legislation, the "back-to-work order" often directs that the dispute be resolved by interest arbitration (see Chapters 12 and 15 for a discussion of interest arbitration).

Rights or grievance arbitration, on the other hand, is exclusively concerned with the enforcement of rights and obligations arising from the parties' collective bargaining relationship. In essence, interest arbitration is a process that determines the terms and conditions of a collective agreement (especially wages and benefits), while grievance arbitration focuses on the parties' rights and obligations that arise (either expressly or by reasonable inference) from their existing collective bargaining agreement. This chapter addresses the grievance arbitration process.

Who Files Grievances and Why?

The *grievance rate* refers to the number of grievances filed per bargaining unit employee. Grievances are one mechanism that bargaining unit employees can use to voice their dissatisfaction with the status quo (Lewin, 1999). Certain employees—especially those who are comparatively well paid or whose alternative job prospects are bleak—may prefer to file a grievance (i.e., a "voice" response) than to quit (i.e., an "exit" response) (Cappelli and Chauvin, 1991). Employees are apparently less likely to quit when they have access to a grievance process (Olson-Buchanan, 1996), and, in general, unionized firms have lower turnover than similarly situated nonunion firms (Freeman and Medoff, 1984). Grievances can be a useful diagnostic tool. A careful examination of grievances may reveal problems that must be addressed. For example, a large number of harassment grievances may speak to the need for an organization-wide educational initiative and revamped human resources practices.

Research on individual grievor characteristics indicates that grievors are younger, less well educated, more highly skilled, and more likely to be members of minority groups than are employees who have not filed grievances (Allen and Keaveny, 1985; Bacharach and Bamberger, 2004). As well, highly loyal employees may be more prepared to "suffer in silence" than to file a grievance (Lewin, 1999). On the other hand, some employees may be reluctant to grieve management decisions for fear of retaliation (Boroff and Lewin, 1997). Research suggests that "whistleblowers" often experience retribution (Ewing, 1989) and several studies suggest that grievors are also systematically subjected to various forms of employer retaliation. For example, grievors, relative to non-grievors, have lower performance ratings, lower promotion rates, and higher termination rates in the post-grievance period (Lewin and Peterson, 1988, 1999; Klaas and DeNisi, 1989; Lewin, 1999; Olson-Buchanan, 1996). While it is quite possible that grievors are less competent (which would explain the levying of employer sanctions that, in turn, lead to grievances being filed), Lewin and Peterson's (1999) study does not support this theory—in the "pre-grievance" period, there was no significant difference between grievors and non-grievors in terms of performance ratings. In fact, grievors had higher promotion and attendance rates than non-grievors.

Employees' perceptions about their supervisors' styles and perceived competence, as well as their perceptions about their own relative market power, also appear to affect grievance rates (Allen and Keaveny, 1985; Bacharach and Bamberger, 2004; Bemmels, 1994; Bemmels, Reshef, and Stratton-Devine, 1991). Unionized firms that have implemented various "employee-involvement" programs (such as problem-solving groups and work teams) tend to have lower grievance rates (Colvin, 2004). This finding suggests that grievances are not necessarily the only "voice" mechanism open to employees, and that employees may view the grievance process as a "last resort" option. Interestingly, high employee-involvement programs remain relatively uncommon, with less than 50 percent of Canadian collective agreements containing such provisions (Akyeampong, 2005).

Although nonunion firms frequently have internal dispute resolution processes, they very rarely allow final and binding resolution by an outside third party (Akyeampong, 2003). Further, the employee does not have the institutional support of a union that may serve as a deterrent to any sort of retaliatory behaviour by the employer toward the complainant. In light of these concerns, many would-be grievances are simply not filed in nonunion firms. For example, victims of sexual harassment are significantly more likely to complain about the harassment if they work in a unionized firm with a formal grievance procedure (Perry, Kulik, and Schmidtke, 1997; O'Hare and O'Donohue, 1998). Recall that 70 percent of the issues addressed in the CF/DND "Conflict Management Program" concerned either work relationship or harassment issues.

Grievances, Conflict, and Organizational Performance

Although lower grievance rates often indicate a better union–management relationship (Gandz and Whitehead, 1982), a low rate does not necessarily imply an absence of workplace dissatisfaction. A comparatively low grievance rate may be attributed to managerial domination of the bargaining unit employees or to the employees' fear of retaliation if they file grievances. Alternatively, a low grievance rate might suggest managerial timidity. Workplace disputes may be informally resolved by the mere threat of a grievance if supervisors are unwilling to test their managerial prerogatives via the grievance process. Lewin and Peterson (1999) found that grievors' supervisors tended to have lower performance evaluation and promotion rates and higher involuntary turnover rates compared to supervisors of units with low grievance rates, which might explain why some supervisors would quietly acquiesce to union demands.

High grievance rates may result from several conditions: union domination of the workplace (Lewin and Peterson, 1988), the fact that the union's internal constitution obliges it to file and even arbitrate certain types of grievances (e.g., terminations), the length of the current agreement (some "collective bargaining issues" may be expressed as grievances if the next round of bargaining is not imminent), or the fact that the employees do not have the right to strike (Hebdon and Stern, 1998). Other factors that affect grievance rates include supervisors' behaviour, the extent to which shop stewards and supervisors prefer to resolve matters informally rather than through the formal grievance process, the industry, the rate of technological change, the state of the local labour market, and the general organizational climate (summarized in Lewin, 1999).

Early resolution of grievances (e.g., at the first or second step) is usually believed to be in the best interests of all parties. The following factors are associated with early settlement of grievances: co-operative bargaining relationships (Turner and Robinson, 1972), experienced first-line supervisors (Knight, 1986a), a willingness to learn from past grievances (Knight, 1986b), and the exclusion of lawyers from the settlement process (Deitsch and Dilts, 1986), although it should be noted that in Canada lawyers are rarely involved in the early stages of the grievance process.

Though grievances are an imperfect measure of the relative degree of conflict present in any given workplace, the grievance rate is nonetheless suggestive of the underlying "labour climate"—that is, the relative degree of trust, co-operation, and goodwill that exists between the employer and the union (Gandz and Whitehead, 1982; Dastmalchian and Ng, 1990). Further, high grievance rates have been consistently linked to lower organizational productivity and profitability (Gandz, 1979; Katz et al., 1983, 1985; Norsworthy and Zabala, 1985; and Ichniowski, 1986).

Types of Grievances

Although employers can file grievances against the union, in almost all cases, the union is the initiating party. An employer can apply the collective agreement in a manner consistent with its own view of its rights and obligations (though it may subsequently be found to have acted in error). If the union disagrees with the employer's view, its remedy is to file a grievance. Until such time as an arbitrator rules otherwise, employees are bound to respect the employer's view concerning the proper interpretation of the collective agreement—this is known as the "obey now, grieve later" principle.[7] Employees who dispute their employer's directions or orders must nonetheless comply or else risk being disciplined for insubordination (as one arbitrator famously described the situation, the workplace is not a "debating society"); the appropriateness of the direction or order is a matter for the arbitrator to decide.

Most union-initiated grievances are filed on behalf of individual employees and are referred to as *individual grievances*, for example, where an employee claims that he or she was wrongfully denied a job promotion or that a certain disciplinary action was inappropriate. Other times, the dispute affects a number of employees or even the bargaining unit as a whole, for example, whether or not the "night shift" employees are entitled to a shift premium under the collective agreement or whether a profit-sharing bonus has been correctly calculated. Such grievances are referred to as *group* or *policy* (or *union*) *grievances*.

Grievances may be filed regarding any term or condition of the collective agreement, including seniority rights, pay and benefits, promotions, and layoffs. Quite frequently, grievances are filed regarding employee discipline or discharge. In discipline and discharge grievances, the onus of proof (and the corresponding obligation to proceed first at the hearing) rests with the employer to show that it had *just cause* either to discipline or terminate the grievor. In all other cases, the party filing the grievance (invariably the union) bears the burden of proof. If the arbitrator concluded that some disciplinary action was appropriate, he or she would address the five factors set out in Table 13.1.

In discipline and discharge grievances, the burden of proving just cause is appropriately placed on the employer because it is the employer who is best able to explain why the employee was disciplined or terminated. If the employer is unable to prove that it had just cause for the particular disciplinary action meted out, the arbitrator will cancel the disciplinary action. If some lesser disciplinary action was appropriate given the conduct in question (say, a suspension but not termination), the arbitrator can substitute a lesser penalty, including giving the grievor "one last chance" to salvage his or her job (for a further discussion regarding the use and efficacy of "last chance agreements," see Bamberger and Donahue, 1999).

The Internal Grievance Process

Most collective agreements include an internal two- or three-step process in which the grievance is reviewed at successively higher levels of the organization. A typical grievance

Table 13.1 "Just Cause" and Employee Misconduct[8]

THE "THREE QUESTIONS": DISCHARGE CASES

1. Has the employee given just and reasonable cause for some form of discipline by the employer?

2. If so, was the employer's decision to dismiss the employee an excessive response in all of the circumstances of the case?

3. If dismissal was excessive, what alternative measure should be substituted as just and equitable?

THE PROPER PENALTY: THE "FIVE FACTORS"

1. How serious is the immediate offence of the employee (e.g., theft versus absenteeism)?

2. Was the employee's conduct premeditated or repetitive, or was it a momentary and emotional aberration, perhaps provoked by someone else (e.g., a fight between two employees)?

3. Does the employee have a record of long service with the employer in which he or she proved an able worker and enjoyed a relatively free disciplinary history?

4. Has the employer attempted earlier and more moderate forms of corrective discipline of this employee that did not prove successful in solving the problem (e.g., in cases of persistent lateness or absenteeism)?

5. Was the penalty imposed by the employer in accord with its workplace policies or does it appear to single out the grievor for arbitrary and harsh treatment?

procedure is set out in Figure 13.1. The process usually begins with the local union representative (usually the *shop steward*) filing a grievance, usually in writing, alleging a violation of the collective agreement. The union and the employer often meet prior to a grievance being filed in order to informally resolve the dispute, and many workplace disputes are resolved either prior to, or shortly after, a formal grievance is filed. The CF/DND "Conflict Management Program" is an example of a formal system designed to resolve grievances (as well as other disputes that might not constitute "grievances" under the collective agreement) separate from the normal grievance adjustment machinery. Further, in several provinces, the governing labour relations statute provides for a formal grievance mediation process; however, these statutory schemes are not available unless a formal grievance has been filed.

The local shop steward (who usually is a bargaining unit employee) will typically draft the grievance on behalf of the *grievor* (the party on whose behalf the grievance is filed; referred to as the *grievant* in the United States). A formal written grievance is usually a brief document that sets out the relevant facts and the provisions of the collective agreement that have allegedly been contravened. Most unions and employers (especially large firms and governmental organizations) have detailed policies regarding how grievances should be addressed.

A bargaining unit employee rarely has the authority to file a grievance on his or her own behalf—the decision to grieve rests with the union ("the union owns the

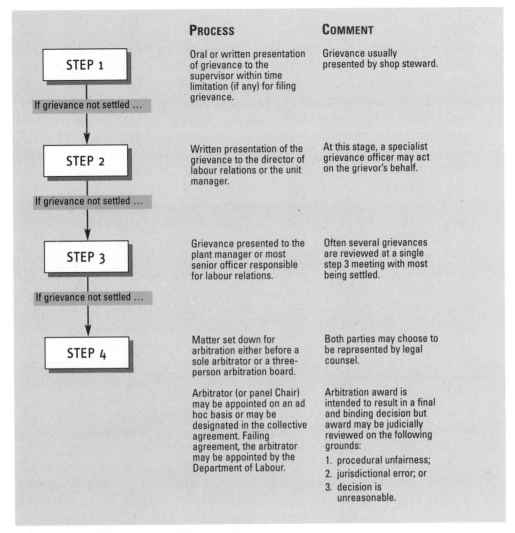

	PROCESS	COMMENT
STEP 1	Oral or written presentation of grievance to the supervisor within time limitation (if any) for filing grievance.	Grievance usually presented by shop steward.
If grievance not settled …		
STEP 2	Written presentation of the grievance to the director of labour relations or the unit manager.	At this stage, a specialist grievance officer may act on the grievor's behalf.
If grievance not settled …		
STEP 3	Grievance presented to the plant manager or most senior officer responsible for labour relations.	Often several grievances are reviewed at a single step 3 meeting with most being settled.
If grievance not settled …		
STEP 4	Matter set down for arbitration either before a sole arbitrator or a three-person arbitration board. Arbitrator (or panel Chair) may be appointed on an ad hoc basis or may be designated in the collective agreement. Failing agreement, the arbitrator may be appointed by the Department of Labour.	Both parties may choose to be represented by legal counsel. Arbitration award is intended to result in a final and binding decision but award may be judicially reviewed on the following grounds: 1. procedural unfairness; 2. jurisdictional error; or 3. decision is unreasonable.

Figure 13.1 Typical Grievance Procedure

grievance"), and thus not all workplace disputes are formalized into a grievance.[9] Even so, many disputes—whether or not they are grievable—are resolved between the union and the employer on an informal basis. As the grievance moves through the internal dispute-resolution process, it may be settled or withdrawn. Failing resolution or withdrawal, the final step is a hearing before a neutral arbitrator or three-person arbitration board. Not all grievances that proceed through the final step of the internal grievance process end up in arbitration. For a variety of reasons—the fundamental importance of the dispute, costs, union bargaining strategy, or internal union politics—the union may decide not to refer the dispute to arbitration. In the vast majority of cases, grievances are settled internally, thereby avoiding the expense, delay, and conflict inherent in the arbitration process. For example, a Quebec study found that 97 percent of grievances were settled short of arbitration (Foisy, 1998); similar results have been reported elsewhere (Graham and Heshizer,

1978; Gandz, 1979). Recall that the CF/DND "Conflict Management Program" resulted in 89 percent of all disputes being either fully (78 percent) or partially (11 percent) resolved.

Very often, the collective agreement will provide for a "limitation period"—if the grievance is not filed within the time limited by the agreement, the employer is not obliged to consider the matter at all (i.e., the grievance is not *arbitrable*). The vast majority of collective agreements contain time limits within which grievances must be filed; most often, agreements require that grievances be filed within a few weeks of the dispute. However, in several jurisdictions, arbitrators have been given the statutory authority to override time limits or other procedural irregularities relating to the grievance and, in addition, arbitrators have sometimes found that contractual time limits may be set aside if they are "directory" rather than "mandatory."[10]

Of course, there are always strategic considerations involved in refusing to deal with a grievance that is "out of time." Will the same issue merely arise once again in another grievance? Will the unresolved conflict "spill over" into the workplace? Will the unresolved dispute simply appear as an agenda item in the next round of collective bargaining? There may be other strategic considerations. Although unions are generally very keen to have dismissal cases heard as quickly as possible, the union may wish to delay the case if, for example, there is an underlying drug or alcohol problem and the union wishes to place before the arbitrator evidence of the grievor's post-termination treatment.[11]

Once referred to arbitration, the grievance may be decided by a single arbitrator or by a three-person arbitration board. In the latter case, the union and management each name one person (referred to as a "nominee") to the board, and a neutral chair is selected by the parties or appointed by some third party—for example, the minister of labour or the labour relations board. The chair effectively is the decision maker, however, since the panel need only reach a majority, not a unanimous, decision. If both nominees disagree with the chair's decision, it nonetheless stands as the final award.

Although there are regional variations, most arbitration awards are issued by sole arbitrators; nevertheless, arbitration boards continue to be used in about one-quarter to one-third of all cases despite the additional costs, scheduling delays, and lengthier deliberations. Some parties believe that the presence of their nominee on the board ensures that their particular position will be, if not accepted, at least fully aired.

The Union's Role in the Grievance Process

Unions fulfill a "gatekeeper" function for employee access to the grievance process. As previously noted, unions are not required to take each and every unresolved grievance to arbitration, but in deciding to file and then proceed with a grievance, the union must not be motivated by some improper or discriminatory purpose. Under both Canadian and U.S. labour laws, unions have a statutory duty of fair representation ("DFR"; see Exhibit 13.1 and Chapter 8). If a bargaining unit employee believes that their union has treated them unfairly, a complaint may be filed with the labour relations board. If the board finds that the union breached its DFR, it has wide-ranging remedial powers including the right to refer the matter to arbitration.

Exhibit 13.1
The Union's Duty of Fair Representation

Certification gives the union an exclusive right of representation. The union thus becomes the only party authorized to represent all present and future employees in the bargaining unit for an indeterminate period. The exclusivity of union representation is also the basis for the union's other rights, including the right to receive the union dues the employer must collect.

In return, the union assumes a duty of fair representation, that is, it "shall not act in bad faith or in an arbitrary or discriminatory manner or show serious negligence in respect of employees comprised in a bargaining unit represented by it, whether or not they are members." This duty must be discharged in all the union's collective representation activities, whether during bargaining or in applying a collective agreement.

Source: *Isidore Garon Ltée v. Tremblay*, [2006] 1 S.C.R. 27 (Supreme Court of Canada).

While DFR complaints are not uncommon, very few succeed. For example, in British Columbia during the period 2001 to 2007, the labour relations board received 970 DFR complaints. However, 479 were dismissed outright (49%), 151 were settled before hearing (15%), and in only 27 cases (3%) was the union ultimately determined to have breached its DFR obligation (the balance of the complaints were not dealt with by the board, most likely because they were formally withdrawn or otherwise abandoned).

Criticisms of the Grievance Arbitration Process

Excessive Cost Relative to the costs of litigating civil claims in the courts, arbitration appears to be a comparative bargain, but arbitration costs can hardly be characterized as modest. Although there are no grievance "filing fees" (unlike the courts) and no direct out-of-pocket expenses for the grievor (unlike the civil claimant who must retain legal counsel at her own expense), grievance arbitration nonetheless involves significant expense. Recall that the union's participation in the CF/DND "Conflict Management Program" was motivated, in part, by a desire to reduce the costs of processing certain types of grievances. Each party is responsible for paying the fees of their own legal counsel or representative, and without a specific "costs" provision in the parties' collective agreement, the arbitrator's fees and expenses are shared equally between the parties regardless of the outcome.

Arbitrators' fees reflect the time spent on pre-hearing matters (pre-hearing conferences, advance rulings on procedural matters, scheduling the hearing, issuing hearing notices, etc.), presiding at the hearing, and preparing a written decision with reasons. An arbitrator's fee for sitting and writing an award can range from $1000 to over $2500 per day plus related expenses (such as transportation costs and hearing-room rental). These fees appear to vary more by region than by individual arbitrator. The total charged by an arbitrator for a one-day hearing and award can be over $5000. If the parties have opted for an arbitration board, the fees and expenses payable to the nominees will increase the total costs payable.

The parties (employers more often than unions) may choose to be represented by legal counsel whose fees typically range from $200 to $500 per hour, adding up to somewhere between $2500 and more than $10 000 for a one-day case. Many unions, and increasingly, large employers, do not use the services of independent lawyers, preferring instead to rely on in-house "grievance officers" (union) or "labour relations officers" (employer) whose duties include appearing before arbitrators. In such cases, a fair assessment of the costs of arbitration must include some allocation of the officer's wages and benefits and related overhead expenses.

To put the costs of arbitration into perspective, consider a small employer, say 10 to 20 bargaining unit employees, and its associated union local. With an annual dues base of between $5000 and $10 000, how many arbitrations could the union afford to take on in a given year, taking into account all of the other activities that it wishes to undertake on behalf of its members (such as collective bargaining)? Increasingly, arbitration has become the preserve of large unions and employers that have the institutional resources to arbitrate contentious disputes—small employers and unions must find some other way to resolve their disputes. The high costs associated with collective agreement administration, including grievance arbitration, may explain, at least in part, the recent trend of smaller unions merging with larger unions (Chaisson, 1996).

Excessive Delay: "Justice Delayed Is Justice Denied" Originally conceived as a relatively quick way to resolve collective agreement disputes, there is mounting evidence that the grievance arbitration process is not achieving this goal. It is not uncommon for a grievance that ultimately proceeds to arbitration to take a year or more to be resolved, that is, from the date the grievance was filed to the date the arbitrator's decision is issued (Ponak et al., 1996; Thornicroft, 1993).

There are two main components of delay in the grievance arbitration process: pre-hearing and post-hearing delay (the former being the larger component by far) (Ponak et al., 1996).[12] Pre-hearing delay may be attributed to a variety of factors, including the congested schedules of prominent arbitrators and the parties' legal counsel or other representatives, unavailability of witnesses, and time spent addressing the grievance in the internal (often two- or three-step) grievance process. This latter source of delay might be eradicated if the parties agreed to streamline their internal grievance process by eliminating one or more of the internal steps.

Once the parties finally get to an arbitration hearing, matters tend to proceed quickly. Although cases may drag on because an insufficient number of days was set aside to hear the evidence (thus necessitating an adjournment to another date convenient to all participants), arbitrators typically render a decision within six to eight weeks after the hearing is completed. Decisions in discipline and (particularly) discharge cases are usually rendered more quickly compared to other cases. One study suggests that grievances arising in the public sector take longer to conclude than similar private-sector cases, perhaps because of the bureaucratic nature of many public-sector organizations or their tendency to use three-person boards rather than sole arbitrators (Ponak and Olson, 1992; Foisy, 1998). It is not clear from the evidence whether the participation of lawyers affects time delay.

Delay is a particular problem in discharge grievances because the grievor cannot return to work until the grievance is resolved in his favour. Even if the grievor is returned to work, say, one year after discharge, the remedy can prove unsatisfactory because the grievor may have found a new job and might be reluctant to return to her former position or, indeed, may have relocated to another city or province in search of new employment. The employers' liability for back pay increases with the passage of time. If a grievor is reinstated, the employer also may face the delicate situation of dealing with not only the grievor but also another employee who may have been hired (or reassigned) as the grievor's replacement.

"LEGALISM" IN GRIEVANCE ARBITRATION: BANE OR BENEFIT?

It has become fashionable to decry the creeping "legalism" of the grievance arbitration process. Lawyers are well entrenched in the grievance arbitration process, in most cases at the initiative of the parties themselves. However, this criticism goes beyond the mere involvement of lawyers. The arbitration process has taken on the "look and feel" of a courtroom trial—arbitrators seem to be overly concerned with applying "arbitral principles" derived from the large body of arbitration case law, dealing with evidence on the basis of court-derived rules, and focusing on the parties' respective legal rights rather than the underlying equities of the actual dispute. The temptation for advocates, whether lawyers or non-lawyers, to provide arbitrators with a litany of prior cases is irresistible in Canada, where arbitrators' decisions are filed with labour boards and are easily accessible in full-text retrieval databases. Most arbitrators or arbitration board chairs are lawyers, and parties often choose to retain legal counsel to appear on their behalf at the arbitration hearing because they do not have the expertise, time, or organizational skills to prepare and present a case on their own.

The available empirical evidence suggests that lawyers have little, if any, impact on grievance arbitration outcomes when each or neither party is represented, but may favourably shift the odds (in favour of the represented party) when only one party is legally represented (Block and Steiber, 1987; Thornicroft, 1994; Wagar, 1994). These findings imply that unions and employers could reduce their arbitration costs if they would mutually agree not to retain legal counsel to appear on their behalf at the arbitration hearing—a policy that has been embodied in some collective agreements.

Who Are the Arbitrators?

The arbitrator profession is largely unregulated. Although there is no legal impediment to anyone "hanging out a shingle" and announcing their availability to arbitrate unresolved grievances, in fact, a small number of individuals conduct the majority of arbitrations within any given province. The parties are usually unwilling to allow inexperienced arbitrators to adjudicate their disputes. Many collective agreements contain a roster of experienced arbitrators who are called on, in rotation, to arbitrate unresolved grievances. If the minister of labour or labour board is requested to appoint an arbitrator, they will invariably draw a name from their own panel of experienced arbitrators, each of whom has been deemed acceptable by the labour relations community (Ponak and Benjamin, 2007).[13]

As a result, in almost every province there are a few arbitrators who are extremely busy, and many others who are underused. One study found that 13 arbitrators issued 76 percent of the arbitration awards in Ontario (Gandz and Warrian, 1977), and similar levels of arbitrator concentration have been reported elsewhere (Thornicroft, 1993). The growing use of expedited arbitration (discussed in more detail later) may reduce the reliance on a small corps of arbitrators (Rose, 1991).

Most labour relations practitioners have well-defined views about what makes a good arbitrator, and experience and good judgment are two characteristics that are likely to appear on any list of desired attributes. In a survey of nearly 300 members of the American Arbitration Association (Allen and Jennings, 1988), the following attributes were listed as being the most important (in descending order): personal integrity; experience, both as an arbitrator and within labour relations generally; and perceived neutrality. The respondents did not believe that a legal education was particularly necessary to succeed as an arbitrator, although a majority of arbitrators are lawyers.

The typical arbitrator is a relatively older male, university trained in law or labour relations, and experienced in labour relations as a union or management advocate, labour relations board member, or university professor (Lewin, 1999). Most arbitrators do not work full-time, although in each province, especially Ontario, Quebec, and British Columbia, there is a small corps of full-time arbitrators.

Unlike professions such as law, medicine, and engineering, no self-governing regulatory body exists for arbitrators. However, many arbitrators are members of one or more of the following organizations (all of which hold annual conventions or workshops): the National Academy of Arbitrators (which has an extensive code of ethics), the American Arbitration Association, the Association for Conflict Resolution (formerly the Society of Professionals in Dispute Resolution), the Industrial Relations Research Association, and the Canadian Industrial Relations Association. In addition, in some provinces the arbitrator community has established a local organization—for example, the Ontario Labour–Management Arbitrators Association.

Little formal training is provided to prospective arbitrators although different organizations in several provinces have initiated structured training programs for new arbitrators. Such programs typically involve a rigorous selection process for trainees, seminars on the law of evidence and arbitration procedure, and decision-writing workshops. Often the trainees are asked to attend a series of actual arbitration hearings conducted by experienced arbitrators and are then required to draft decisions for review and critique. Although relatively inexperienced labour arbitrators have a difficult time establishing a professional foothold, many are finding that their adjudicative expertise can be applied in a number of other settings such as nonunion employment disputes; disputes regarding franchise, partnership, and shareholder agreements; and insurance claims.

RESOLVING GRIEVANCES: REMEDIES

The vast majority of grievances are resolved consensually between the parties and thus very few grievances proceed to an arbitrated outcome. Nevertheless, arbitrators' decisions are very important because they provide guidelines that the parties rely on when attempting to resolve workplace disputes. Several books are devoted to analyzing arbitration trends, serving as important resources for labour relations managers and union officials (Brown and Beatty, 2006; Mitchnick and Etherington, 2002, 2006; Palmer and Palmer, 1991).

A bargaining unit employee who is discharged without just cause is usually entitled to reinstatement to his former position, a remedy that is generally unavailable in a nonunion wrongful dismissal lawsuit (see Chapter 9). *Reinstatement orders* are generally accompanied by an order for monetary compensation (referred to as a *back-pay order*) reflecting the grievor's lost wages during the period between discharge and reinstatement. In all cases where a grievance is upheld, the arbitrator has a great deal of discretion to fashion an appropriate compensatory remedy, which may involve the payment of money, directions regarding the employer's records or policies, or declaratory orders (for example, the arbitrator might declare that a particular employer policy violates human rights legislation).

Arbitrators have substantial flexibility in fashioning appropriate remedies and the range of disputes for which any sort of remedy may be granted has dramatically expanded over the last several decades. As grievance arbitration was originally envisioned, the arbitrator's authority or *jurisdiction* was limited to interpreting and applying the express terms of the collective agreement. Since 1974, the Supreme Court of Canada has steadily expanded the scope of an arbitrator's jurisdiction and remedial authority (see Table 13.2).

As the law currently stands, any dispute that "arises from the collective agreement" must be adjudicated through the grievance arbitration process—access to any other forum is now presumptively foreclosed. Thus, claims for invasion of privacy,[14] defamation,[15] monetary claims for reimbursement for property damage,[16] disability benefit claims against a third-party insurer,[17] and possibly even human rights claims[18]—to list but a few examples—may all fall within the exclusive domain of the arbitrator, depending on the language of the collective agreement. This trend is all the more remarkable because once an arbitrator has rendered a decision, that decision is considerably more difficult to overturn than if the same decision had been issued by a court.

Table 13.2 The Arbitrator's Growing Power

YEAR	DECISION	COMMENT
1974	*McLeod v. Egan*[19]	Arbitrators must take into account relevant legislation when interpreting collective agreements and must override the express language of a collective agreement when it conflicts with external legislation, for example, human rights or employment standards legislation.
1986	*St. Anne Nackawic Pulp & Paper Co. v. C.P.U., Local 219*[20]	Legislatively mandated grievance arbitration procedures effectively oust the courts' general jurisdiction to deal with disputes that could otherwise be the subject of a court action. In this case, an employer's civil suit against its union for damages suffered as a result of an illegal strike was dismissed on the ground that the employer was obliged to proceed with its claim through the grievance arbitration process.
1990	*Douglas/Kwantlen Faculty Assn. v. Douglas College*[21]	Arbitrators may apply the *Canadian Charter of Rights and Freedoms* to declare a collective bargaining provision null and void because it conflicts with a *Charter* right.
1995	*Weber v. Ontario Hydro; O'Leary v. New Brunswick*[22]	Any dispute that "arises from the collective agreement" falls within the exclusive jurisdiction of an arbitrator. An arbitrator (or arbitration board) is a "court of competent jurisdiction" for purposes of granting constitutional remedies under section 24 of the *Charter* (for example, awarding compensation) for a breach of a *Charter*, as opposed to a collective agreement, right.
2000	*Regina Police Assn. v. Regina (City) Board of Police Commissioners*[23]	The Weber "deferral doctrine" equally applies in the case of competing statutory regimes.
2006	*Bisaillon v. Concordia University*[24]	Arbitration may be the exclusive forum even though the dispute concerns several separate bargaining units and collective agreements.

Enforcement and Review of Arbitration Awards

Arbitrators do not have the formal authority to enforce their awards. If a party ignores an arbitrator's order, that order can be filed in a registry of the provincial superior court and thereafter enforced as an ordinary court order. A party who continues to ignore an arbitrator's order after it has been filed with the court risks a fine or even imprisonment for contempt of court. In light of these potential sanctions, few parties flout an arbitrator's order. Rather, the losing (or only partially victorious) party might seek to have a court overturn the arbitrator's decision through a process known as *judicial review*.

A "review" is not an "appeal," and the courts have generally taken a "hands-off" approach to arbitrators' decisions—the courts refer to this as *judicial deference*. A court will not overturn an arbitrator's decision simply because the court disagrees with the arbitrator's analysis and conclusions. So long as the arbitrator is acting within her jurisdiction, the decision will not be overturned unless it is unreasonable—in other words, conclusions reached by the arbitrator were not supported by evidence or the decision wholly lacks any tenable analysis.[25] The courts have shown a greater willingness to intervene when the arbitrator, in the court's view, obviously misstated a general legal principle; is, or appears to be, biased[26]; or failed to ensure that the hearing was conducted in a procedurally fair manner. One empirical study found that 7 percent of Alberta decisions were subject to judicial review between 1996 and 2001, and of these, only one-third were overturned by the courts (Ringseis and Ponak, 2007). This study suggests that the vast majority of arbitration awards are "final and binding," as intended.

Predicting Grievance Outcomes

There is substantial interest in who wins and who loses in arbitration and the factors that affect these results. Arbitrators are not usually bound by other arbitrators' decisions (the one recognized exception being where another arbitrator has previously ruled on the identical provision in the same collective agreement) or by the technical rules of evidence; each case must be decided on its own merits. Although arbitrators have considerable flexibility in fashioning their awards, some believe that arbitrators tailor their awards so that neither party is unduly offended. Since arbitrators are, for the most part, selected by mutual agreement of the parties, arbitrators may have an incentive to "keep the scales in balance." Such behaviour may be motivated by the "decision statistics" or "box scores" that are compiled by some unions and employers. Arbitrators, not surprisingly, often declare that they have no idea what their decision ratios might be and contend that they base their decisions only on the merits of the case before them.

Some research suggests that arbitral outcomes are influenced by arbitrators' background characteristics such as age, education, and experience, but other studies have concluded that arbitrators' background characteristics have little, if any, impact on arbitrators' decision making (Bemmels, 1990; Lewin, 1999). Legal training has little effect on outcome (Thornicroft, 1994). Labour relations researchers have also examined whether or not grievors' personal characteristics, or the characteristics of the grievance itself, are systematically related to grievance outcomes. For example, one study found that arbitrators treated grievors whose misconduct involved alcohol rather more leniently than grievors whose misconduct involved narcotics (Thornicroft, 1989). Consistent with the theory of "progressive discipline" (namely, that repeated acts of misconduct will be met with increasingly more severe penalties), grievors with poor work records are less likely to succeed in arbitration compared to grievors with unblemished work histories (Thornicroft, 1989, 1994).

Perhaps the most commonly examined personal characteristic is gender (Bemmels, 1988, 1991). There are two competing "gender hypotheses": the "chivalry" hypothesis (which operates in favour of women, particularly given that most arbitrators are male) and the "evil woman" hypothesis (which operates to the detriment of female grievors). The findings have been mixed. Of 17 published studies, 10 found a pro-female bias, 1 found an anti-female bias, and 6 found gender to be irrelevant (Thornicroft, 1995). These results are all based on an analysis of arbitration awards; gender-based differences that may exist in grievance-filing behaviour or arbitration-referral behaviour have yet to be systematically investigated.

ALTERNATIVES TO CONVENTIONAL GRIEVANCE ARBITRATION

Mounting criticisms of traditional grievance arbitration have led many parties to explore alternatives such as *expedited arbitration* and *grievance mediation*.

While there are many variants, expedited arbitration generally involves procedures designed to reduce the delay and expense associated with traditional grievance arbitration. For example, in an expedited arbitration system the parties may agree that

- the matter will be heard by a sole arbitrator rather than a tripartite panel;
- the arbitrator will issue (either immediately upon the conclusion of the hearing or within one or two days thereafter) an oral decision to be followed by a brief written award;
- all evidence will be submitted in the form of written witness statements with no oral testimony whatsoever, or the number of witnesses may be limited (say, one witness for each party);
- neither party will retain legal counsel; and
- the hearing is subject to some time limit, say one or two hours, which may allow the arbitrator to hear several cases in a single hearing day.

An expedited arbitration process may be established by mutual agreement of the parties or may be imposed by statute, as is the case in Ontario and British Columbia. The former are voluntary systems, whereas the latter are established by legislation and may be invoked without joint agreement. Expedited arbitration systems typically provide for an early hearing date before an arbitrator selected (usually without the parties' formal consent) from an existing roster and a time limit within which the arbitrator must deliver her reasons. There is some evidence that these statutory systems are more expeditious than conventional arbitration (Thornicroft, 1996) and can produce significant cost savings for the parties (Rose, 1991). Private expedited arbitration systems (usually, but not always, set out in the parties' collective agreement) are also becoming more common.

Grievance mediation is another effective alternative to the grievance arbitration system. It is sometimes incorporated as a voluntary step in either an expedited or conventional grievance arbitration process. The labour relations statutes of several provinces provide for the appointment of a settlement officer, i.e., a grievance mediator, with mutual consent of the parties. As discussed in this chapter's opening vignette, grievance mediation involves a third-party neutral (the mediator) assisting the employer and the union representatives in reaching a voluntary settlement of the grievance. Mediators usually endeavour to clarify the issues in dispute, seek out the parties' respective "bottom lines," and may even offer proposals for settlement. Unlike an arbitrator, a mediator has no formal authority to resolve the dispute. If the grievance cannot be resolved through mediation, the only remaining option—other than withdrawal of the grievance—is arbitration. During mediation, information may be disclosed to the mediator that would not otherwise be disclosed to the other party—all such disclosures remain confidential even after the mediation process has ended and usually cannot be used during any subsequent arbitration hearing.

Some of the benefits of grievance mediation include the following (Feuille, 1999):

- *Faster resolution of cases.* There is no waiting for a written decision.

- *Cost savings.* Mediation is usually less expensive than arbitration (e.g., settlement officers are usually provided at little or no cost to the parties).

- *Less adversarialism.* The focus of mediation is reaching a mutually acceptable agreement rather than winning a rights dispute. To put the matter another way, in a dispute settled by arbitration, only one party wins; in a mediated dispute, both parties win.

- *Improved labour–management relations.* The positive experience of settling disputes through mediation may enhance the probability that future disputes will be resolved amicably and without resorting to some form of adjudicative process.

In addition to formal grievance mediation, many arbitrators, either at the invitation of the parties or on their own initiative, attempt to mediate a settlement prior to or during the arbitration hearing. Indeed, some arbitrators are specifically appointed because of their skills as a mediator and, as has been the experience in the CF/DND "Conflict Management Program," mediation is a powerful tool for resolving grievances, with some 8 or 9 out of every 10 cases being resolved (Fraser and Shime, 1989; Goldberg, 1989; Whitehead, Aim, and Whitehead, 1988). Such mediation success rates may reflect, at least in part, the fact that parties who agree to mediate a particular grievance are often predisposed to settlement.

Overall, the evidence indicates that expedited arbitration and grievance mediation are effective mechanisms for resolving disputes more efficiently than traditional arbitration procedures. The time and cost savings clearly are compelling; in addition, grievance mediation may also improve the parties' problem-solving ability and their overall bargaining relationship. Both grievance mediation and expedited arbitration offer sufficient promise to warrant their expanded use and further empirical evaluation.

FORMAL DISPUTE RESOLUTION PROCEDURES IN NONUNION FIRMS

Quite apart from nonunion arbitration requirements that may arise under certain statutes like the *Canada Labour Code* (Eden, 1994), a recent development has been the voluntary adoption of arbitration to settle employment disputes in nonunion organizations (Wheeler et al., 2004). Because employees lack union representation, arbitration and dispute resolution procedures in nonunion firms are usually introduced at the behest of the employer—typically, as a term of all job offers made by the firm. These systems may include a variety of dispute resolution procedures including "peer review panels" and, in some cases, third-party arbitration. They are often introduced in an effort to forestall employee-initiated litigation (which in the United States can be very costly for employers) and as a union-substitution strategy (see Chapter 5). Recent evidence suggests that nonunion arbitration coverage has now outstripped union coverage (Colvin, 2003). Although most nonunion arbitration systems are found in the United States, many Canadian firms are now including arbitration provisions in employment contracts—especially those involving middle and senior managers. In such cases, employees give up their right to sue their employer in court over termination of employment.

Unionized employees also relinquish their right to go to court but they have access to a negotiated grievance arbitration procedure that is backed by the union's institutional power and resources. While fairness in the grievance arbitration process is not absolutely guaranteed, it is at least safeguarded. The main criticism of employer-initiated dispute resolution systems is that they may lack basic fairness, tilting the outcome in favour of the employer. For example, the employee, who typically lacks any expertise in arbitration, may be precluded from having legal representation or from having any say in the selection of the arbitrator.

In light of these concerns, several organizations with stakes in employer-promulgated arbitration systems, including the National Academy of Arbitrators, the American Bar Association, the labour movement, and the American Civil Liberties Union, negotiated a set of rules designed to satisfy concerns about fairness. This set of rules, known as the "Due Process Protocol," establishes a voluntary framework for employer-promulgated arbitration schemes (Exhibit 13.2). Among other things, the protocol provides representation rights to employees, access to information prior to the hearing, participation in the selection of the arbitrator, and the creation of a roster of experienced, neutral arbitrators (Wheeler et al. 2004). As nonunion arbitration systems continue to flourish, and with the Protocol in place, nonunion arbitration may satisfy the "same goals of employee fairness that spawned the labor–management model of dispute resolution" (Zack, 1999: 89). At present, there is no such protocol in place governing employment-related arbitrations in Canada other than the general procedural rules set out in provincial commercial arbitration statutes.

Exhibit 13.2
Due Process in Nonunion Arbitrations

EXCERPTS FROM DUE PROCESS PROTOCOL FOR MEDIATION AND ARBITRATION:

. . . The focus of this Protocol is on standards of exemplary due process.

RIGHT OF REPRESENTATION

Choice of Representative Employees considering the use of or, in fact, utilizing mediation and/or arbitration procedures should have the right to be represented by a spokesperson of their own choosing.

Fees for Representation The amount and method of payment for representation should be determined between the claimant and the representative. The arbitrator should have the authority to provide for fee reimbursement, in whole or in part, as part of the remedy in accordance with applicable law or in the interests of justice.

Access to Information Adequate but limited pre-trial discovery is to be encouraged and employees should have access to all information reasonably relevant. . . .

MEDIATOR AND ARBITRATOR QUALIFICATION

Roster Membership Mediators and arbitrators selected for such cases should have skill in the conduct of hearings, knowledge of the statutory issues at stake in the dispute, and familiarity with the workplace and employment environment. Regardless of their prior experience, mediators and arbitrators on the roster must be independent of bias toward either party. They should reject cases if they believe the procedure lacks requisite due process.

Conflicts of Interest The mediator and arbitrator has a duty to disclose . . . conflicts of interest.

Authority of the Arbitrator The arbitrator should be bound by applicable agreements, statutes, regulations, and rules of procedure . . . [and] should be empowered to award whatever relief would be available in court under the law.

Compensation of the Mediator and Arbitrator Impartiality is best assured by the parties sharing the fees and expenses of the mediator and arbitrator. In cases where the economic condition of a party does not permit equal sharing, the parties should make mutually acceptable arrangements to achieve that goal if at all possible. In the absence of such agreement, the arbitrator should determine the allocation of fees.

Source: Excerpted from Zack, 1999, pp. 90–94.

CONCLUSION

The grievance arbitration process plays a central role in the union–management relationship. It was originally conceived as an equitable, inexpensive, and expeditious mechanism for resolving unionized workplace disputes. This still remains true in a comparative sense. For example, arbitration is a much less expensive and more accessible procedure for remedying a wrongful dismissal than is a lawsuit in the civil courts. The grievor need not incur expenses for pursuing his or her grievance—that cost is absorbed through the payment of union dues. Unlike civil litigation, the grievance arbitration process is largely within the exclusive control of the parties themselves; the parties are free to select their own decision maker; and the parties can jointly determine the most appropriate procedure. The grievance arbitration process has also been lauded as an effective mechanism for improving workplace democracy and for providing employees with a meaningful voice in matters affecting their employment.

Notwithstanding these benefits, it has been suggested that the process, as presently constituted, is too slow, too expensive, and overly legalistic. In light of these criticisms—all of which have at least some merit—both policy-makers and labour relations practitioners have attempted to formulate alternative systems for resolving workplace disputes, such as expedited arbitration, grievance mediation, and coaching in conflict resolution. The available evidence indicates that these initiatives have led to the settlement of disputes and produced substantial savings in both time and money. We can expect continued experimentation with these and similar processes in the hope of restoring the grievance arbitration process to its original purpose: to serve the needs of the participants in the labour relations system.

Questions

1. To what extent can the grievance process be used as a mechanism for employees to "voice" their concerns about workplace issues?

2. The grievance process has been said to be the quid pro quo for a no-strike/no-lockout clause in the collective agreement. Is this a fair trade-off?

3. Some parties choose sole arbitrators while others prefer to use three-person panels. What are the pros and cons of each format?

4. What remedy does a bargaining unit employee have when the union does not take his or her unresolved grievance to arbitration?

5. What changes, if any, would you propose to the contemporary grievance arbitration process to ensure that it is a relatively quick, inexpensive, and just process?

6. How does "expedited arbitration" differ from "conventional arbitration"?

7. Do you feel that lawyers should be banned from the grievance arbitration process? Why or why not?

8. Can measures be introduced into nonunion (employer-promulgated) arbitrations that will make them as fair as those in the unionized setting?

Weblinks

BC Public Service Agency (guidelines for documenting the grievance/arbitration process):
www.bcpublicservice.ca/FOI/LR/GAGlines.htm

Government of Canada—Federal Mediation and Conciliation Service (dispute prevention):
www.hrsdc.gc.ca/en/labour/labour_relations/mediation/prevention/index.shtml

Saskatchewan Public Service Commission (HR manual):
www.publications.gov.sk.ca/details.cfm?p=10842

CUPE Local 1816 (Grievance Fact Sheet):
www.cupe1816.bc.ca/grievance.htm

B.C. Labour Relations Board Collective Agreement Arbitration Bureau:
www.lrb.bc.ca/caab

B.C. Labour Relations Board ("Towards Better Labour Management Relations"):
www.lrb.bc.ca/mediation

Saskatchewan Labour (search under Labour, Programs & Services, Grievance Mediation):
www.labour.gov.sk.ca/

Newfoundland and Labrador Labour (Grievance Mediation):
www.hrle.gov.nl.ca/lra/labourrelations/grievancemediation.htm

National Academy of Arbitrators:
www.naarb.org

Chapter 14

Union Impact on Compensation, Productivity, and Management of the Organization

Morley Gunderson and Douglas Hyatt

The CAW recently negotiated contracts with the Big Three automakers that included substantial wage increases for all of its members. As well, the union negotiated fringe benefits that would appeal to its membership for all different age groups. Generous pensions were negotiated for the older workers, tuition allowances for older members with children in university, and child care allowances for younger employees with preschool children.

The union also negotiated substantial retroactive pension increases for its membership that was already retired. At first glance, this may seem odd because these retirees are not voting members. The incumbent older workers, however, are voting members, and they realize that what is now done for retirees will soon be done for them when they retire.

The union even tried to get DaimlerChrysler to pressure one of its parts suppliers, a Magna corporation plant in Windsor where an organization drive was underway, to voluntarily recognize the union. Although this demand was subsequently dropped, it does illustrate the attempts of the union to influence the way in which the organization is run, since subcontracting to parts suppliers is increasingly important in that industry.

This chapter begins with a discussion of union power and moves to the methods used by unions for attaining their objectives, to the actual impact of unions[1] on wages, wage structures, fringe benefits, productivity, and the management of the organization itself.

UNION POWER AND METHODS FOR AFFECTING COMPENSATION

Union power and various market conditions affect the ability of unions to garner pay increases for their members.

Internal Power

The power of a union to fulfill its goals depends, in part, on a consensus within the union about those goals. This agreement must come from the various groups within the union, from the leadership and the rank-and-file members, and from other unions and affiliated bodies. Jurisdictional disputes, rank-and-file discontent with union leadership, and rivalry within the membership can all dissipate the energies of the union and prevent it from marshalling its power.

External Power and Elasticity of Demand for Labour

A union's power to realize its wage demands depends not only on its internal strength but also on the particular objective circumstances it faces. Many of these factors can be summarized under the determinants of the elasticity of demand related to substitute products, substitute inputs, and labour costs as a proportion of total costs.

Substitute Products If few good substitutes exist for the products or services produced by unionized labour, union wage cost increases may be passed on to the consumer in the form of price increases without a substantial reduction in the demand for those products and, therefore, without a fall in the derived demand for union labour. This may occur under the following circumstances, for example:

- if a tariff or import quota protects the product from foreign competition;

- if the product is advertised through the union label or a "social label" (see Exhibit 14.1);

- if sufficient time has not passed (i.e., the short run) so that substitute products are not yet available;

- if the industry is in decline so that new nonunion firms are not entering (see Exhibit 14.2); and

- if the whole industry is organized so as to prevent the substitution of nonunion-made products for union-made products.

Exhibit 14.1
Is the Social Label Replacing the Union Label?

In earlier days of union organizing, the union label indicating that the product was "union made" was an important strategy to inhibit the substitution of nonunion products for union products. Good trade unionists would not purchase products without the union label.

In recent years, the "social label" has been proposed whereby the product would be labelled as being produced under satisfactory working conditions and without the use of child labour. The hope is that good, socially minded citizens would not purchase products without the social label.

Multinationals have also been under pressure to adopt voluntary corporate codes of conduct, especially under the threat of consumer boycotts. Advocacy groups have exposed the working conditions involved in multinational production, and especially in subcontractors that produce for multinationals.

For more information about these practices, see: www.corpwatch.org.

Exhibit 14.2
Milking a Dead Cow: An "End-Game" Strategy

In declining industries, there may be very little threat of new entry from nonunion firms. In such circumstances, unions may engage in an "end-game" strategy whereby they demand high wage increases in spite of the declining demand because they know that the lower-paying nonunion firms are not likely to enter the industry, given that it is in decline. In such circumstances, unions may be able to garner a larger *share* of profits, even though overall profits are declining (Lawrence and Lawrence, 1985).

Difficulty in Using Substitute Inputs If there are few good and cheap substitute inputs for union labour, or if it is technologically or institutionally difficult to substitute other factors of production for union labour, unions can obtain wage increases with less worry about substitutes being used for unionized labour. Hence, unions are very concerned about technological change and alternative processes that represent a substitution of capital for union labour. Craft unions can protect the jobs of their members through such mechanisms as the hiring hall, apprenticeship ratios, and restrictions on who can practise in the trades. Restrictive work practices ("featherbedding" rules—an expression meaning that unions establish a requirement for the use of excess amounts of union labour) are designed, in part to prevent the substitution of other inputs for union labour. Professional associations try to control the substitution of less highly trained workers for professionals, and can restrict the use of non-professionals through occupational licensing or certifications. Unions try to control the use of subcontracting to nonunion labour or the extensive use of probationary workers or supervisors who are not in the bargaining unit. Unions try to control the use of nonunion labour, in part through union security provisions whereby unions do the hiring (hiring halls) or whereby all persons in the bargaining unit are required to join the union as a condition of employment (union shop) or to pay union dues (agency shop or use of the Rand formula).

To the extent that a reserve of low-wage labour in the economy is also a threat to union labour, unions may try to reduce that reserve by supporting policies like full employment, income maintenance, and restrictive immigration, and resisting programs such as "workfare," which require recipients of welfare or social assistance to work. If the size of the low-wage labour pool cannot itself be controlled, unions at least want to make that pool of labour more expensive. To do this they may support wage-fixing policies (minimum wages, equal pay, "fair" wages in government contracts, and wage-extension decrees) as well as labour standards programs that make the use of such nonunion labour more expensive (see Exhibit 14.3). This is not the only reason for union support of these policies, but it may be one reason.

Exhibit 14.3
Humanitarianism or Protectionism?

Organized labour generally supports the requirement that trade agreements incorporate labour standards, especially in such areas as the use of child labour. The rationale may be humanitarian, but the poorer, developing countries have also accused the developed countries of "thinly disguised protectionism" since the humanitarian objective seemed to surface only when low-cost imports from developing countries were threatening high-wage jobs in the developed countries.

Labour Cost Portion In general, if the costs of unionized labour are a small proportion of the total costs for a firm, the firm can more easily absorb union wage increases; the resultant cost increases simply do not matter much relative to the total cost picture of the firm. This may be the case, for example, for certain skilled craft workers and small professional groups, and for capital-intensive industries. It may, in part, explain the reluctance of these groups to merge with larger groups within whose wage demands their own demands would be subsumed.

Non-Competitive Markets

The degree of competition prevailing in the environment affects the power of unions and hence their ability to win gains for their members. Non-competitive situations can prevail in the product market and in the labour market, with both situations affecting the power of unions.

Monopoly in the Product Market A firm that has a monopoly in the product market has a greater ability to pay out of monopoly profits (see Exhibit 14.4), and unions can garner high wage increases in such circumstances. In addition, if the firm is a regulated monopoly, it may be concerned about its public image and hence willing to "buy" good labour relations by paying high wages; it may also feel that it can obtain permission from regulatory agencies to pass any wage increase on to the public in the form of rate increases. Working in the other direction, monopolies may have a greater ability to pay, but they may also have a greater ability to resist union wage demands. They may use their monopoly profits to resist unionization or to set up structures (for example, using capital equipment or extensive nonunion supervision) that weaken the power of unions or that enable employers to withstand a lengthy and costly strike.

**Exhibit 14.4
Strange Bedfellows**

The attempted takeover of Air Canada by Onex would have led to the merger of Air Canada and Canadian Airlines, a merger that subsequently occurred without Onex. Many were concerned that this would create a monopoly, especially because foreign airlines are restricted from competing.

There was also general surprise when CAW president Buzz Hargrove supported the Onex-led merger—union leaders do not generally support business takeovers because the restructuring generally leads to job losses and demands for concessions on wages and work rules. In this particular case, however, guarantees were provided that any job reductions would occur through attrition and retirements. As well, any resulting monopoly situation could benefit both the employer and the union.

Public-Sector Employees There is a presumption that unions in the public sector can become quite powerful because their employers are not subject to a competitive profit constraint. In essence, says the theory, the political constraint in the public sector is not as binding as the profit constraint in the private sector. Union wage increases can be passed on to taxpayers, who must have the essential services and cannot buy them elsewhere, who are often ill-informed about the "tax price" of public services, and who exercise their democratic prerogatives only occasionally by voting on a package of issues of which the wage costs of services may be only a small part. Of real concern is the possibility that public-sector employers may try to save on current wage costs by granting liberal compensation to be paid by future taxpayers, possibly when another political party is in power. Such deferred wages can come in the form of regular seniority-based wage increases, liberal retirement pensions, or job security.

Although these arguments do suggest that public-sector unions should be quite powerful, there are also forces—usually more subtle ones—working in the opposite direction. Taxpayers are scrutinizing government with increasing severity, and they may sympathize more with employers, forgetting that it takes two sides to create a dispute. Politicians may seek to curb inflation and private-sector settlements by moderating public-sector wage settlements, and they may even prolong or foster strikes to gain the media exposure that is crucial to their prominence. Employers in the public sector, unlike those in the private sector, do not usually lose their (tax) revenues during a strike. Some U.S. jurisdictions have also experimented with having citizen observers present in collective bargaining.

Monopsony Non-competitive conditions also prevail in labour markets that are dominated by a single employer—termed a *monopsonist* to indicate that the firm is a monopolistic buyer of labour. Such a firm is so large relative to the size of the local labour market that it might have to raise wages to attract additional workers; conversely, it would not lose all of its workforce if it lowered wages. A monopsonist is extremely sensitive about raising wages to attract additional workers because it knows it will have to pay these higher rates to its existing workforce in order to maintain internal equity of the wage structure. This fact serves to depress wages paid by the monopsonist relative to what it would pay if it were a competitive buyer of labour.

Monopsonists are ripe for union organizing because union wage increases, at least within a certain range, can actually lead to their hiring more labour. This paradoxical result occurs because when faced with a fixed union wage that they must pay to all their workers, monopsonists are no longer constrained in their hiring decisions by the fact that they have to raise wages to attract additional workers; all workers are paid the union rate for each job. Thus, the wage demands of unions, at least for a range of wage increases, are not constrained by the possibility of reduced employment opportunities. Clearly, these circumstances afford room for considerable bargaining in that there is a range of wage increases that the monopsonist can absorb. With so much to gain and lose, one would expect a high degree of conflict in organizing and in bargaining—an observation that seems borne out in the isolated one-industry towns that characterize monopsony.

MEASURING THE UNION IMPACT

Attempts to quantify the impact of unions have met with numerous estimation problems. The most important are those of separating cause and effect and of controlling for quality differences.

Separating Cause and Effect

Conventional wisdom suggests that unions may tend to cause higher wages in the union sector. Causality, however, may also operate in the other direction. That is, unions may be more likely to be formed in situations in which high wages already exist because they are easier to organize and because the higher wages may enable workers in such sectors to afford to buy more of everything, including union services. Furthermore, workers in high-wage firms are reluctant to leave or "exit" because of the high wages—hence they turn to "voice" (e.g., through unions) as the mechanism to improve the non-wage aspects of their situation (Freeman and Medoff, 1984). The causality in such a situation runs from high wages (and hence reduced exit) to unionization (as the form of voice).

An appealing element of this perspective is that it reconciles the views of industrial relations analysts, who emphasize the importance of the union in achieving due process and job security at the workplace, with the views of economists, who emphasize the wage impact of unions. Unions are associated both with higher wages for their members and with job security and due process at the workplace.

Quality Differences

Firms that pay the higher union wage rate are likely to have a queue of applicants, which should afford them the luxury of being more selective than nonunion firms in their hiring and recruiting procedures. Such firms can obtain higher-quality workers with more education, training, and experience, as well as more of such typically unobserved characteristics as motivation. Working in the opposite direction, it may be more difficult for employers to dismiss poorer-quality workers in the union sector or poorer-quality workers may try to obtain secure union jobs, knowing that it will be difficult for them to be dismissed. For these reasons, it is important to control for the reverse causality and the quality differences in estimating a pure union wage impact.

Measurement Techniques and Data

The impact of various factors that can affect wages is usually controlled through the use of multiple-regression analysis, which indicates the effect on wages of each explanatory variable, including a measure of unionization, while holding the other wage-determining factors constant. The regression equation is estimated on various types of data: cross-sections of aggregate or macro data relating wages in an industry, city, or state to the proportion of the industry, city, or state that is unionized[2]; micro data sets[3] that have the individual worker as the unit of observation[4]; and panel or longitudinal data produced from following the same individuals over time.[5]

UNION IMPACT ON COMPENSATION

In varying degrees, the numerous empirical studies of the impact of unions attempt to account for the measurement problems just discussed. Unions can affect various aspects of compensation, including wages and wage structures, nonunion wages, and fringe benefits.[6]

Impact on Wages and Wage Structures

In a review of the evidence based on the different methodologies, Kuhn (1998: 1037) concludes "there is abundant and robust evidence that identical workers in North America earn about 15 percent more in unionized than in nonunion jobs." This is in the mid-range of the 10 to 25 percent noted in other Canadian reviews (Benjamin et al., 2007; Renaud, 1997).

The union impact on wages tends to be larger in recessions and smaller at the peak of the business cycle, reflecting the fact that union wages are less sensitive to economic fluctuations than are nonunion wages (in part because union workers have long-term wage contracts). Real wages in collective agreements do decline as nominal wage increases do not keep up with inflation, but nominal wage reductions (wage concessions) are rare, leading to a degree of wage rigidity, especially in periods of low inflation.[7]

The union impact is higher for blue-collar and less-skilled workers than for those who are white collar and more skilled.[8] Generally, union workers tend to get a flat union premium, but that amount declines with productivity-related characteristics such as experience, education, and skill. This phenomenon gives rise to union wage profiles that are higher but flatter (i.e., start higher but rise less steeply) than do nonunion wage profiles with respect to factors such as age, experience, and education. This finding is consistent with the view of unions as institutions that blunt the impact of market forces by gaining a constant increase for members, but having their wages increase less than the wages of nonunion workers for increments in productivity-related characteristics.

Thus, with respect to the overall dispersion of wages, unions exert two opposing effects. They narrow wage differentials that reflect such factors as skill, education, and experience; however, they widen the overall dispersion by creating a new source of dispersion—the union–nonunion wage differential. There is some evidence that the equalizing effect dominates, so that unions tend to reduce the overall dispersion of wages.[9]

The union–nonunion wage gap tends to be similar for men and women, based on U.S. data.[10] However, based on Canadian data[11] researchers find the union wage impact tends to be larger for females than for males, but females benefit less from unions because they are less likely to be covered by a collective agreement. These opposing effects offset each other, so that, overall, unions neither increase nor decrease the male–female wage gap.

Although the limited empirical evidence that exists is not always in agreement, many studies suggest that the union impact on wages is greater in decentralized than in centralized bargaining structures.[12] The union wage premium also tends to be smaller when product markets are more competitive, such as when there is deregulation[13] or greater import competition under freer trade.[14] Earlier empirical evidence suggested that the union impact on wages tends to be smaller in the public sector (around 5 percent) than in the private sector, although there was considerable diversity in this result.[15] Importantly, more recent U.S. evidence suggests that the union impacts have increased in the public sector and decreased in the private sector so that they are currently fairly similar in the two sectors (Belman, Heywood, and Lund, 1997; Blanchflower and Bryson, 2007: 88; Gunderson, 2007).

The evidence on the union wage premium for workers who are covered by a collective agreement but are not union members tends to be mixed. Budd and Na (2000) review the evidence and provide U.S. data suggesting that the union wage premium for members is substantially larger than for non-members.

Importantly, over time the union wage impact appears to have increased in the 1970s and declined since that time, reaching a level of around 10 percent in the 1990s and beyond (see Exhibit 14.5).

Impact on Nonunion Wages

Unions can affect the wages of nonunion workers through a variety of mechanisms. To the extent that unionized wage increases reduce employment opportunities in the unionized sector, the excess supply of labour from that sector should serve to depress wages in the nonunion sector. This effect may, however, be mitigated if unions are able to "featherbed."

On the demand side, the demand for nonunion labour—and hence the nonunion wage—is affected in an indeterminate manner by an increase in the wages of union workers. The demand for nonunion labour may increase to the extent that nonunion labour is substituted for the now more expensive union labour. In addition, output demand may shift from the products produced by the more expensive union sector to those produced by the cheaper nonunion sector. (This effect may be minimized if the whole sector can be organized.) On the other hand, the demand for some nonunion labour may decrease to the extent that it is complementary to (i.e., works in tandem with) union labour or to such an extent that firms reduce their scale of output (in the extreme, perhaps even closing down) in response to the higher union labour cost; in such circumstances firms may employ less of both union and nonunion labour.

Exhibit 14.5
The Declining Union Wage Impact

In his comprehensive review of the Canadian evidence, and based on his own analysis, Renaud (1997) indicates that the union–nonunion wage differential in Canada

- was approximately 15 percent at the beginning of the 1970s;
- rose throughout the 1970s to a peak of around 25 percent by the end of the decade; and
- fell throughout the 1980s to around 10 percent by the end of the decade.

He also concludes (p. 223): "In the coming years, the size of the union–nonunion differential might keep shrinking. Forces like freer-trade and the deindustrialization of the Canadian economy will make it more difficult for unions to do what industrial relations specialists were first noting that they were doing, that is taking wages out of competition."

Some recent evidence suggests that this prediction is correct. Gunderson, Hyatt, and Riddell (1999) found that by 1997, Canadian workers covered by a collective agreement earned 8 percent more than persons not covered, with similar results found in Fang and Verma (2002).

Whether this decline in the union impact reflects a decline of union power or a strategic reorientation to other objectives such as employment and job security or less costly forms of employee "voice" remains an interesting and important question.

Other studies that generally confirm the declining union wage premium, especially since the 1980s, include Addison and Belfield (2004), Blanchflower and Bryson (2007), Bratsberg and Ragan (2002), Forth and Millward (2002), Hildreth (1999), Hirsch and Macpherson (2002), Hirsch, Macpherson, and Schumacher (2004), Hirsch and Schumacher (1998, 2002), and Stewart (1995).

Other forces are at work institutionally whereby nonunion wages are affected by unionization. As discussed previously, unions can affect nonunion wages by supporting wage-fixing legislation, which applies mainly to the nonunion sector. In addition, nonunion firms may raise their wages to avoid the threat of becoming unionized. In the extreme, they may pay wages in excess of the going union wage rate to avoid what they regard as other costs associated with becoming unionized, notably interference with managerial prerogatives (Taras, 2000; Verma, 2007). Nonunion firms may also be compelled to raise their wages so as to compete with unionized firms for a given workforce or to restore traditional wage relativities that existed before unionization. The last argument, however, ignores the fact that nonunion firms should not have to worry about recruiting problems or restoring traditional wage patterns because they will have a supply influx of workers who cannot get jobs in the high-wage union sector.

Clearly, unions affect the wages of nonunion workers through a variety of institutional, market, and legislative forces. Since these forces do not all work in the same direction, it is not possible to state theoretically the expected impact of unions on the wages of nonunion workers; one must appeal to the empirical evidence. Earlier studies tended to find that unionism lowered the wages of nonunion workers but by a small amount—less than 3 or 4 percent (Kahn, 1980; Lewis, 1963). Other studies, however, including more recent ones, have found small positive effects of unions on the wages of nonunion workers.[16] One Canadian study found that unions were associated with higher executive compensation, but that this effect disappeared after controlling for the effect of other variables such as firm size (Singh and Agarwal, 2002).

Impact on Employee Fringe Benefits

Empirical evidence[17] indicates that unions increase the employee fringe benefits of their members even more than they increase their wages. This may occur for a variety of reasons.

To the extent that unionization makes workers better off, they can afford to buy more of everything, including employee benefits; this will be especially important if they enter the higher tax brackets and if employee benefits are not taxed. In addition, unions, being a political institution of "voice," can be expected to represent the wishes of the average worker (more specifically, the median voting member) as opposed to the marginal worker whose interest is most likely to be represented by the mechanism of exit or mobility. Since the average worker is more likely than the marginal worker to be older, with seniority, and with a family, the collective preferences are more likely to favour employee benefits, especially pensions and life, accident, and health insurance.

Employee benefits, as a form of deferred compensation, may also be more prevalent in unionized establishments than in nonunion ones.[18] Employers may prefer deferred compensation because it provides a threat that can be used to ensure effort from their employees. The threat is the possibility of dismissal and therefore the loss of deferred wages. Deferred wages can also provide employees with an interest in the financial solvency of the firm. In addition, deferred compensation reduces turnover, since employees who quit would lose some or all of their deferred wages (for example, pension and vacation rights). Employees may willingly accept a deferred wage if they are given a sufficiently high wage to compensate for some of its being deferred (and hence its receipt being uncertain), or if they are provided with sufficient guarantees that the employer will ultimately pay. Such guarantees have more credence when they are provided in a collective agreement, which, for example, prevents arbitrary dismissal and reinforces the legal obligation to provide the promised payments. In essence, unionization makes the payment of fringe benefits in the form of deferred wages a feasible compensation scheme. Hence, one can expect such employee benefits to be associated with unionization.

UNION IMPACT ON PRODUCTIVITY, PROFITABILITY, EMPLOYMENT, AND INVESTMENT

While the impact of unions on various dimensions of compensation tends to receive the most attention, increasing attention is being given to the impact of unions on other dimensions, including productivity, profitability, employment, and investment. In the global economy, these other dimensions can have crucial implications for the joint survival of both unions and their organizations.

Impact on Productivity

Although recognized for a long time by industrial relations analysts (Slichter, Healy, and Livernash, 1960), the potential positive impact of unions on various aspects of productivity has only recently been analyzed and quantified by labour economists.[19] As Freeman and Medoff (1984) indicate, there are two dominant views of trade unions. The monopoly view regards unions as creating economic inefficiency by raising wages above the competitive norm, by inducing strikes, and by requiring featherbedding work rules that compel the employer to use inefficient amounts of union labour. An alternative view is that unions have positive effects on productivity by reducing turnover, "shocking" management into more efficient practices, improving morale and co-operation among workers, providing information about the collective preferences of workers, and improving communications between labour and management.

The literature on the impact of unions on various aspects of productivity examines the *direct* effects on productivity after controlling for the fact that the union wage premium results in an *indirect* productivity increase by inducing firms to substitute capital for labour and by enabling them to hire workers that are more productive. This indirect effect on productivity leads to inefficiencies,[20] since management will use excessive amounts of capital and nonunion labour relative to higher-priced union labour. Management will also use union labour that is of excessively high quality.

With respect to the direct effect on various aspects related to productivity, unions have been found to lower quit rates,[21] to increase tenure with the firm (Addison and Castro, 1987), and to enhance product quality (see Exhibit 14.6). Overall their net effect on productivity or output per worker is mixed but averaging close to zero or possibly slightly positive.[22] In their meta-analysis of 73 studies, Doucouliagos and Laroche (2003b) summarize the effect as slightly negative for the U.K. and slightly positive for the United States in general and in manufacturing. The results are often sensitive to the type of data used and the specification of the output equation.[23] There is also conflicting evidence on the effects of unions on productivity in the public sector, although most studies show unions there to have had no net effect, either positive or negative.[24]

Evidence indicates that unionized environments have more strenuous working conditions than nonunion ones, with, for example, a structured work setting, inflexible hours, and a faster work pace,[25] often leading to greater employee dissatisfaction in union environments. Canadian evidence on this is provided in Meng (1990b) and Renaud (2002), with review of that literature in Addison and Belfield (2004, 2007) and Hammer and Avgar (2007). This may reflect the fact that unionism is more likely to occur in response to such working conditions, or that some employers are able to respond to the union wage advantage by changing the pace and conditions of work, partly to take advantage of a higher-quality workforce. As well, unions may raise awareness of adverse working conditions and raise expectations of dealing with them so that the greater extent of employee dissatisfaction in union workplaces reflects frustrated expectations. Whatever the reasons, there may be concern given that meta-analysis indicates that employee dissatisfaction leads to poorer job performance (Judge et al., 2001).

Exhibit 14.6
The Importance of Union Support for Quality Improvements and Organizational Performance

Quality improvement is generally regarded as a key ingredient of firm performance in a world of global competition. As such, it is crucial to know if unions enhance or impede quality improvements.

Empirical evidence based on U.S. data indicates that quality circles are more likely to survive in unionized environments (Drago, 1988). Quality circles are a form of employee participation in the management of the organization. They involve a work group that meets voluntarily, typically once per week, to discuss, analyze, and solve problems common to the work group.

Cooke (1992) also finds quality improvements to be higher in workplaces with employee participation than in the more traditional workplaces with no participation. Of particular note, the greatest quality improvements occurred in firms with joint union–management administration of the program. If management unilaterally ran the program, there was no quality improvement, as was also the case when there was traditional adversarial bargaining with no employee involvement. Additional U.S.

The labour relations climate in the workplace can also influence the productivity of union workers. A good union–management relationship can amplify the productivity-enhancing effects of unions, especially through information sharing and a focus in bargaining on mutual gains rather than on rules that control the behaviours of the parties (see Exhibit 14.7). Conversely, a poor industrial relations climate can exacerbate the negative impacts on productivity. A number of studies have found negative productivity effects where labour relations are generally bad, as evidenced, for example, by a large number of grievances or strikes.[26]

Impact on Profitability

Although these productivity-inducing effects probably offset some of the wage cost increases resulting from unionism, they are unlikely to offset all of them. If they did, one would expect to see managers, or at least shareholders, welcoming unions—a phenomenon rarely observed (except in cases of "company unions" that management controls). At least some union wage gains must represent real gains to union workers and real costs to employers, otherwise one would not see workers organizing or employers resisting unionization. The empirical evidence also generally confirms that unionization reduces profitability and the stock market value of firms[27] (see Exhibit 14.8) but not to the point of inducing bankruptcy (see Exhibit 14.9).

compared to nonunion establishments. However, this was because the positive effect of gain-sharing in union establishments *when unions were involved* with the program was offset by the negative effect in union establishments when unions were *not* involved. In essence, if gain-sharing is to be successful in unionized establishments, it is crucial that unions be involved in its design and implementation. If they are not involved, the program can be counterproductive. Based on Canadian data, Wagar (1997) also found productivity, quality, and organizational performance to be positively related to a positive co-operative labour–management climate.

Kaufman (1992) found profit-sharing plans to be more successful in unionized compared to nonunion establishments. Interestingly, Cooke (1994) found gain-sharing to enhance productivity more in unionized compared to nonunion establishments, but because unions were able to appropriate more of the gains through higher wages, gain-sharing contributed less to profits in unionized firms than in nonunion firms.

Exhibit 14.8
Does the Stock Market Adjust to Reflect the Cost of Unions?

Based on U.S. evidence, Ruback and Zimmerman (1984) find that the stock market value of a firm falls by about 1.4 percent when a petition to hold a union election is put forward, by a further 1 percent if the petition succeeds, and by a further 1.4 percent if the election succeeds and a union is certified. The cumulative drop in the share value turns out to be very close to the cost of a 15 percent wage increase associated with unionization, which is the typical wage impact. This suggests that the stock market perfectly adjusts to reflect the cost increase associated with unions, at least as reflected in expected wage increases. To the extent that the stock market should adjust to reflect the *cost* increase, this suggests that the wage impact of 15 percent may be a good reflection of the net cost increase that would also include other factors such as fringe benefits and productivity.

Exhibit 14.9
Are Unions Likely to Kill the Goose That Lays the Golden Egg?

If unions reduce profitability, it is possible that they could cause firms to go into bankruptcy. Based on U.S. evidence, Freeman and Kleiner (1999) find that this does not occur. Unionized firms are no more likely to declare bankruptcy than nonunion firms. As such, they conclude: "unions reduce profits but they do not 'destroy the goose that lays the golden egg.' They would be foolish to do so, and while they may make mistakes in collective bargaining (just as management may), they are not so foolish as to force organized firms out of business."

As such, they indicate (p. 510) that unions do not contribute to Samuel Gompers' "worst crime" when he stated, "the worst crime against working people is the company which fails to operate at a profit."

Impact on Employment

If unions raise wages and costs, it would appear that this should lead to reduced employment as firms substitute capital for the more expensive labour and as some reduce their output (perhaps even going out of business) because of the higher costs. Unions, however, also bargain over employment levels, both directly and indirectly, in such forms as no-layoff provisions, restrictions on subcontracting and overtime, featherbedding work rules, restrictions on plant closings, and requirements for additional plant investments. Thus, powerful unions could increase *both* wages and employment.[28] The extent to which a union would opt for one or both of these elements that it values depends, in part, on the collective preferences of the membership. If the jobs of the voting members are reasonably secure, they may opt for wage increases knowing that their own jobs are not at risk. However, if their own jobs are at risk (as is increasingly the case with downsizing and plant closings), they may opt for employment guarantees. Certainly unions have been able to prevent employers from reducing the employment of union labour by as much as they would probably like to, given the union wage increase. Of course, unionized plants may have had still higher employment had they not also received higher wages, and the empirical evidence generally suggests that unions have reduced employment.[29]

Impact on Investment

Unions can have an indirect impact on the investment decisions of firms through various mechanisms. They may encourage investment by inducing firms to substitute capital for the more expensive union labour. They may also bargain directly for more investment in specific plants to sustain employment. Unions may indirectly discourage investment, however, to the extent that investors are reluctant to invest in unionized sites. In the extreme, if a plant goes out of business because of higher union costs, then there is no investment. Firms may be especially reluctant to invest in situations where unions are likely to appropriate the benefits of successful investments (termed the "hold-up" problem) since it is difficult to move capital once it is in place. The empirical literature generally finds a negative effect of unions on investment.[30]

UNION IMPACT ON MANAGEMENT OF THE ORGANIZATION

Unions can have a substantial impact on the way management runs the organization—restricting the otherwise unfettered rights of management (within the law) to run the firm in what could be an arbitrary or even impulsive manner with respect to employees. Unions may do so by regulating specific provisions (e.g., seniority) in the collective agreement as well as in the grievance procedure. Unions have also been instrumental in encouraging—and at times helping to enforce—legislative employment standards, which regulate such factors as minimum wages, pay and employment equity, hours of work and overtime, paid vacations and holidays, maternity leave, and employee termination. They can also be involved in joint union–management committees (most noticeably on health and safety), and union representatives may even be on the board of directors of the company.

Legislative Assistance

Legislative initiatives have often helped unions achieve due process and circumscribe the otherwise unfettered rights of management in the employment relationship. This aid has taken a variety of forms: the legal obligation to recognize a certified union as the workers' exclusive bargaining agent and to bargain in good faith; the legal recognition of collective agreements and of the grievance procedure with its own jurisprudence; and the establishment of employment standards and health and safety legislation that effectively give government backing and enforcement to a number of issues over which unions might otherwise have to negotiate. On many issues, legislative initiatives have used the existing machinery of collective bargaining and the union's communications network to provide effective enforcement. Such is the case, for example, in the health and safety area (with the use of joint committees as part of the "internal responsibility" system) and in pay equity (with unions to be involved in job-evaluation procedures and in the allocation of awards pertaining to equal pay for work of equal value).

Examples of Impact on Management of the Organization

Given their emphasis on the rights and well-being of workers, unions' effects on the management of the organization have been mainly on those dimensions of managerial decision-making that impinge most directly on the workforce. Many of these are discussed in Kaufman and Kaufman (1987: 342), who conclude that "union firms in our sample are significantly more likely to have grievance procedures, job-posting systems, and other restrictions that limit management's prerogative in promotion, classification, and job assignment" (see Exhibit 14.10). Other recent reviews of the effect of unions on managerial prerogatives include Addison and Belfield (2007) and Verma (2007).

Exhibit 14.10
The Impact of Unions on Human Resource Practices

Human resource practices can be used strategically by organizations to enhance productivity and hence firm competitiveness and performance. Ng and Maki (1994) examine the impact of unions on 37 human resource practices in Canadian manufacturing firms. They find that unionization leads to more formal managerial practices such as job posting, formal probationary periods for new hires, and explicit criteria governing promotion, all of which tend to reduce managerial discretion. Unions, however, tend to reduce the use of formal appraisal systems that are often associated with individual incentive pay systems involving merit pay and piece rates. Canadian evidence from Betcherman et al. (1994, 1997) also indicates that unions foster seniority-based pay increases rather than flexible individual performance-based compensation schemes, and they foster training perhaps by reducing turnover.

Similar results are generally found in other studies including Balkin (1989), Bemmels (1987), Freeman and Kleiner (1990), and Kaufman and Kaufman (1987).

At the hiring stage, the union impact is usually negligible except for requiring that the jobs be formally posted and that layoffs be recalled before hiring from the outside. This lack of intervention normally extends for a brief probationary period, when managerial discretion is largely unfettered. The exception is the situation in which unions have negotiated union security clauses involving a "closed shop" (only union members can be hired). This is often coupled with the union's running of a "hiring hall" (the union acts as the employment agency, having the exclusive right to refer employees to the firm). These forms of union security provisions are rare, however, existing mainly in some areas of construction and longshoring.

Unions, however, can have a more indirect effect at the hiring stage. They tend to reduce the use of formal selection tests (Cohen and Pfeffer, 1986) as well as the resources firms devote to recruitment sources that would otherwise expand the applicant pool (Koch and Hundley, 1998), the latter already having been expanded by the union wage premium.

After the hiring and probationary period, the union impact becomes more prominent. Almost invariably, collective agreements contain clauses requiring "just cause" for discipline and discharge, and situations involving these clauses are the most common source of grievance arbitration cases. Seniority provisions regulating managerial discretion in matters such as promotion, transfer, layoff, and recall are also very common in collective agreements as well as a common source of grievance arbitration cases.

Restrictions on contracting out are also prevalent in collective agreements, in part because employers can undercut the power of a union by contracting out certain jobs to the nonunion sector. This issue is currently highly contentious: management wants the right to contract out as part of its increased drive for flexibility, and unions fear the loss of union jobs, especially in the current climate of downsizing. Policy-makers also have some concern that contracting out may be used as a way of getting around legislative intervention in such areas as employment standards and equal-pay legislation. Often the subcontracting goes to self-employed individuals or to small firms, where the legislation is more difficult to enforce. In part to enhance their own job security, unions have also bargained for investment guarantees in their own plants, and they have even bargained for organizations to put pressure on their parts suppliers to voluntarily recognize the union (see the opening vignette).

Regulations on job assignment (who can do what work) can also restrict managerial discretion. The extreme form of these rules often involves featherbedding practices such as requiring that containers be unloaded and reloaded at ports. Other restrictions on managerial discretion include the right to refuse overtime and requirements for advance notice or transfer rights in the case of plant closings or technological change. In most circumstances, however, these restrictions are not prominent features of collective agreements; they are more often introduced by legislation.

Just as unions have a threat effect that can enhance the wages of *nonunion* workers, they can also have a threat effect on nonunion human resource and workplace practices, especially in ways that provide forms of "voice" at the workplace as a possible alternative to union forms of voice that are likely to be more restrictive on managerial prerogatives. As summarized in Taras (2000) and Verma (2007) these can take various forms including nonunion grievance procedures, joint labour–management committees, and employee surveys and suggestion schemes. Luchak (2003) provides Canadian evidence indicating that loyal employees who are more likely to put forth discretionary effort to foster organizational goals are more likely to use nonunion forms of voice compared to union forms of voice such as grievance filing.

Some empirical evidence suggests that the large increases in shareholder wealth that occurred as a result of the takeover boom of the 1980s, and that were larger in unionized firms subject to takeover, were a result of the increased managerial discretion in running the firms after the takeover (see Exhibit 14.11).

Exhibit 14.11
Do the Substantial Gains to Shareholders in Takeover Firms Come from Unionized Workers?

The 1980s witnessed a remarkable takeover boom involving mergers and acquisitions, often of unionized firms that paid substantial union wage premiums and fringe benefits. That boom placed considerable constraints on managerial authority in running the organization. Based on U.S. evidence, Becker (1995) found that the average returns to shareholders from the takeover activity were higher in unionized firms that were taken over (41 percent) compared to nonunion firms (35 percent). He calculates that these effects are *equivalent* to a loss of 8 percent of annual earnings of unionized workers, which is approximately half of the union wage premium. This larger gain to shareholders in unionized establishments that are taken over suggests that these additional gains come from more restrictions placed on the wages and fringe benefits of workers in unionized establishments, and from fewer restrictions placed on managerial authority.

Becker reviews a small number of other studies, most of which find negligible negative effects on wages and benefits from takeover activity. This suggests that the larger gains to shareholders in unionized establishments that are taken over come mainly from reduced restriction on managerial authority after the takeover.

Perhaps this is why, in the proposed Onex takeover of Air Canada and merger with Canadian Airlines, guarantees were made to the union that there would be no wage or involuntary employment reductions. Perhaps the gains were to come from increased managerial discretion in the operation of the companies. Of course, the gains to shareholders could also come from other factors such as economies of scale and monopoly pricing.

Some Unintended Side Effects

In some instances, union practices that restrict managerial discretion can have unintended side effects. For example, seniority provisions can be an obstacle to attempts to achieve pay and employment opportunities that are equal for men and women since women tend to accumulate less seniority (especially if they leave the labour market for child rearing). Seniority provisions can also be an obstacle in accommodating the needs of disabled persons at the workplace. Requirements for specific ratios of apprentices to journeypersons can inhibit firms from expanding their training to meet certain shortages. Prohibitions on the use of part-time labour can inhibit employers from reducing overtime and sharing the available work. Requirements for severance pay and advance notice and concern over unfair or unjust dismissal cases can make employers reluctant to hire new workers who might eventually have to be laid off.

Restrictions in the Public Sector

In many parts of the public sector, unions try to bargain over broader issues that may encroach on managerial authority. Such is especially the case with professional employees who invariably want more say in the management of the organization, and who often possess the expertise to make such decisions.

The limited empirical evidence available in this area tends to suggest that public-sector unions do have a considerable impact on the management of the organization. Teachers, for example, often bargain over pupil–teacher ratios, curriculum content, class sizes, placement of suspended students, and the selection and transfer of students (Hall and Carroll, 1973; Woodbury, 1985). Goldschmidt and Stuart (1986) conclude that these items usually put severe constraints on the ability of school districts to adapt to changing circumstances. On the other hand, in a study of the U.S. federal civil service, Beyer, Trice, and Hunt (1980) found that when a union is present and articulates its position, supervisors tend to be more aware of, and use, policies to deal with equal employment opportunities and alcoholism problems related to the workplace.

CONCLUSION

Unions tend to increase the compensation of their members (usually by 15 percent albeit declining) and slightly reduce the compensation of nonunion workers. The union impact is largest for blue-collar and less-skilled workers. In fact, union workers tend to get a flat wage premium, but then receive relatively low returns for increases in such factors as skill, education, and experience. Overall, unions have likely reduced wage disparities and had a larger impact on employee benefits than on wages. The union premium is similar for men and women, although some Canadian evidence suggests it is larger for females. Women, however, tend to be less unionized and receive fewer benefits of unionism for that reason. The union wage is generally lower when the economy is more subject to competitive pressures such as from deregulation and imports from foreign competitors. The union premium has generally declined, especially since the 1970s. This likely reflects the effect of greater competitive pressures including free trade, deregulation, privatization, and the shift to the more competitive service sectors, as well as the residual lessening of union bargaining power associated with the general decline in unionization.

Unionism may be a result of, as well as a cause of, high wages, and union workers may differ from nonunion workers in terms of unobserved, as well as observed, characteristics. Also, unionized establishments may adjust to costly union wage increases by raising their hiring standards and altering their work conditions. Unions may also have a beneficial impact on productivity, which may offset some of the wage cost increase associated with unionization, albeit unionization does reduce profitability.

Unions reduce managerial discretion through provisions in collective agreements, through the grievance procedure, and through support of legislative regulation of the work environment. At the workplace, unions limit managerial discretion through such mechanisms as seniority provisions, requirements for just cause in cases of discipline and discharge, restrictions on contracting out, job assignments, and, to a lesser degree, safety, work-time practices, plant closings, and technological change (those last four issues are more often the subject matter of legislation than of collective bargaining).

Public-sector employees, mainly professionals, have done more direct bargaining than private-sector workers over what might be perceived as managerial issues. This likely reflects a combination of professional concern over these issues and a realization that influence over managerial decisions can be an important way of affecting working conditions and job security.

Unions are generally found to reduce quits, increase tenure, and enhance product quality, but they also reduce investment as well as research and development. Their effects on productivity are mixed, with the average effect being close to zero or perhaps slightly positive. Overall, they tend to reduce firm profits and the stock market value of the firm.

The future will be interesting for analyzing the impact of unions on a variety of outcomes—wages, job security, fringe benefits, productivity, and managerial discretion. Unions are clearly on the defensive in the United States, and this situation is likely to affect Canadian unions, especially given the spread of foreign competition, deregulation, and freer trade. In these circumstances, employers are likely to want more managerial discretion and flexibility, and unions are likely to seek more job security and better fringe benefits, such as generous retirement pensions (in part as a work-sharing device). However, this conflict also provides the opportunity for the parties to deal creatively with challenges stemming from the dramatic changes in the Canadian industrial relations system and its environment.

Global competition, trade liberalization, and the greater international flow of capital are likely to have a profound impact on union goals and strategies, and ultimately on wage and other outcomes. Unions may simply not be able to continue to obtain wage premiums of 15 percent because this higher labour cost will lead to more imports of lower-priced, foreign-produced goods. As well, employers may locate their plants in countries where labour costs are not as high.

In essence, it is difficult for unions to "take wages out of competition" now that the labour market is international. Labour will be under pressure to adopt more international strategies. It will also have to focus less on wages and other outcomes that impose costs on employers and more on ensuring due process and "voice" mechanisms that may be less costly to employers. There will also be more emphasis on labour–management co-operation and on reducing adversarial bargaining. Unions will also likely have to direct more of their efforts toward the political level to influence governments into increasing the "social wage." It is clear that the next few years pose some interesting and important challenges and opportunities for unions.

Questions

1. "The power of unions depends on the economic environment in which unions operate." Discuss.

2. Discuss the determinants of the elasticity of demand for union labour in both the construction industry and the public sector, indicating what this implies about the ability of unions to achieve wage gains in those sectors.

3. "Unions can have no long-run impact on wages, because if they did then unionized firms would go out of business." Discuss.

4. Discuss the impact of unions on the wages of nonunion workers.

5. Discuss how unionized firms may adjust their hiring standards and working conditions when faced with unions. What does this imply about the measured union–nonunion wage differential?

6. Discuss the mechanisms whereby unionism may be a response to high wages as well as a cause of high wages. What does this imply about the measured union–nonunion wage differential?

7. Why may fringe benefits be a preferred form of compensation for union members even more than for nonunion members?

8. Discuss the mechanisms whereby unions can affect productivity. What does this imply about the costs to the firm that result from unionization?

9. Discuss the various ways in which unions may affect managerial discretion in running the organization. Is such union impact greater in the public or the private sector?

10. What effects would you expect global competition and trade liberalization to have on the impact of unions?

11. Why may union members express more dissatisfaction with their working conditions than do nonunion workers, given the gains that unions get for their members? And why do they quit less if they are more dissatisfied?

Weblinks

CorpWatch—Multinational codes of conduct:
www.corpwatch.org

Canadian Association of Labour Media:
www.calm.ca

Chapter 15

Public-Sector Collective Bargaining[1]

Mark Thompson and Patrice Jalette

The public sector in Canada has experienced some of the greatest challenges facing labour relations in the past two decades compared to any other time. Many relationships unravelled, and examples of hostile situations are plentiful. This vignette takes a different approach. The history of Calgary Laboratory Services (CLS) demonstrates that, even in daunting conditions, it is possible to build excellent labour relations.

A funding crisis in 1996 resulted in the creation of CLS to support health care in Southern Alberta. The laboratory services budget in Alberta was reduced by 31 percent. In order to accommodate the deep cut, laboratory medicine changed from "fee for service" to global funding, and approximately 100 private and public lab service facilities were dramatically reconfigured into one new medical laboratory services provider. The birth of CLS consolidated the previously fragmented medical laboratory industry by merging a number of public and private organizations of varying size and union status into one new entity. The creation of CLS was dogged by controversy over the alleged privatization of part of the health care system and the loss of hundreds of jobs.

This complex, diverse, for-profit company with a highly educated workforce began by selecting top management. After hiring the President, the next person chosen was the Vice-President of Human Resources (HR), Susan Cassidy. The decision to focus on HR as a core concern reflected the need to effectively manage the changes necessitated by the funding crisis and the resulting merger. The impact on employees, 90 percent of whom were female, would be felt with the decisions to downsize from seven hospital labs to four, from 124 patient sample collection sites to 24, and from three community testing labs to one central lab.

CLS management and the Health Sciences Association of Alberta (HSAA) union avoided a potential labour–management disaster by providing strong leadership and focusing on working together to deal with the merger. The new company was announced in a press release on July 15, 1996. Two days later, Susan and the CLS President delivered a number of presentations in large auditoriums to announce the merger plans to the staff of the various organizations. Susan recalls that day:

> We actually stood up and told employees that hundreds of them would lose their jobs. It was very stressful for people. There was a lot of anxiety and concern around it. . . . How am I going to be impacted? What is my job going to be? Who is going to be my boss? Those are the big issues for staff.

Susan decided from the beginning how CLS would handle employees' concerns and fears:

At the town hall sessions we were just brutally honest . . . yet treated the employees with respect and integrity. . . . We gave them as much information as we could give them about work. . . . I am a firm believer that people become empowered the more information you give them. . . . Put them in the driver's seat as much as possible. . . . Then they can decide for themselves what is going to work best for them and their families.

While the seeds of the partnership were planted in 1996 during the difficult merger, the first round of collective bargaining created its own issues. Eighty percent of the CLS workforce was composed of medical laboratory technologists and assistants. Seventy-five percent of the workers were unionized, as many of the private-sector employees had become union members in previous mergers. The unionized employees were represented by three different unions: Health Sciences Association of Alberta (HSAA), Canadian Union of Public Employees (CUPE), and Alberta Union of Provincial Employees (AUPE). As CUPE and AUPE had fewer members among the staff, HSAA and CLS made a successful case at Alberta Labour Relations Board hearings to have all bargaining unit members transferred to HSAA. That meant that Susan would be sitting down with John Vanderkaay, Director of Labour Relations for HSAA.

John and the HSAA had vigorously opposed the enormous cuts made by the Alberta Government in funding and the majority ownership of the private sector, but knew they had to work with the new situation. Given the stated need for CLS to reduce the workforce from 1000 to 700, the five disparate collective agreements currently in force, and the merging of unionized with nonunion workers, all the ingredients for an acrimonious battle between union and management were in place.

Surprisingly, from the beginning, it wasn't a battle. John recalls that CLS "never opposed us or tried to get rid of the union in any shape or fashion." CLS and HSAA began bargaining in the fall of 1996 with the common goal of merging the existing five contracts into one contract. Susan had a very transparent approach to the first round of collective bargaining: "I am a firm believer in getting the union involved from the start. I never want to be in a situation where we are 10 steps ahead of them and we are trying to sell them on an idea or program or concept. I want us to be working together from the start of an issue." Susan's open, direct, and focused communication was a good fit for John's personality: "I don't beat around the bush and I don't have any hidden agendas. I knew what the employer wanted. So we had a very good, open communication. . . . So we were able to agree and disagree. We had some pretty darn good arguments."

Management of CLS was working within "tight, tight budgets" and wanted to eliminate all pension plans. John and the union's number-one objective was keeping the pension plan and preserving as much of the more generous public-sector conditions as possible. In fact, negotiations were stalled by HSAA until CLS agreed there would be a pension plan. The two sides finally agreed to a defined-contribution plan to replace the local authorities pension plan (LAPP) defined-benefit plan. Although this was a gain for private-sector employees, it was a big loss for the public-sector employees. The loss was exemplified by lab technologist Diane Emshey's comments: "Losing the local authorities pension plan with my 20 years of experience, I lost a lot of money."

Susan, John, and their respective teams of negotiators made similar compromises to solve problems on each issue on the table. They did this by ignoring the text of the existing agreements and focusing on a set of principles for each of the major issues. Once the principles were decided, the employer agreed to have the union negotiators write up the clauses for the collective agreement. Despite the complexity, the speed of this process allowed negotiations to be completed in two to three months.

The next challenge was to convince the union members to accept the new agreement that was, by John's admission, "not a perfect agreement, not as good as the previous one in the public sector." John had the difficult task of convincing an educated membership that the first contract was acceptable and that the union could improve the agreement in future negotiations. In the end, 75 percent of members voted for the new CBA.

Many years later, the relationship between HSAA and CLS has grown into a successful partnership, despite tremendous challenges. CLS ran a deficit for each of its first three years. Then a population explosion in Calgary meant that CLS would have to grow by approximately 10 percent annually to keep up with Calgary's booming growth. Ironically, the new problems at CLS were cramped lab space and staffing shortages. These problems hit a critical point in 2000, when lab technologist Diane Emshey led a walkout due to crowded, unclean, and generally unprofessional working conditions in the labs. Diane recalls, "I persuaded everyone to picket for an hour to make our point to the media and show management we had the power to strike if we wanted." The union and management agreed to create a joint committee to solve the problem. In the following months, management re-committed to erecting a new building for laboratory services. Diane and her fellow workers were not disciplined by CLS for their actions, but instead were eventually rewarded with a new building that is "nice, clean, very professional" and has "lots of room."

Through all these developments, CLS and HSAA practised high-integrity labour relations, consisting of mutual respect, clear communications, and a common-sense approach to problem solving on a daily basis. This relationship is about doing the little things right.[2]

The opening vignette illustrates the tensions of public-sector industrial relations: disputes are highly visible; they touch on services that affect the public at large; and politics are central to many decisions. They also illustrate the significant features of Canadian public-sector collective bargaining: a highly unionized work force, extensive legal regulation, and frequent shifts in government policy conflicting with a workplace culture that values job security.

This chapter reviews the evolution, distinguishing features, and special problems of collective bargaining in the Canadian public sector. Collective bargaining functions differently in the public sector than in the private sector, in particular because of pronounced differences in public- and private-sector employers. These differences, as well as other factors, have given rise to persistent problems in dispute resolution and wage determination. The changing role of government itself has created further challenges. Since the 1970s, the public sector has become the most heavily unionized part of the Canadian economy. The collective bargaining process in which these new union members engaged affects how public services are provided, disrupts those services from time to time, exerts pressure on public-sector salaries and budgets, and brings new challenges to public managers.

Government's response to these developments has been intertwined with attitudes about the role of government itself. Historically, the public sector has been important to Canada. Public agencies and branches of government built much of the country, thanks to a legacy of colonialism, a weak private sector, and the fear of U.S. domination. Public institutions promoted public interests in transportation, communications, cultural spheres, and social services. These bodies once provided most of the infrastructure of a modern society (Thompson, 2000). The state operated the overwhelming majority of all educational services, transportation systems, and a public broadcasting system. After the Second World War, Canadians generally welcomed government intervention to reduce major fluctuations in the business cycle and encourage high levels of employment (Haiven, McBride, and Shields, 1991). During the same period the modern welfare state emerged, including universal health care, public pensions, and social assistance of various kinds. By 2006, Canada ranked slightly below the average of developed countries in terms of gross domestic product consumed by government, higher than the United States or Japan, but well below Northern Europe. This level is consistent with other mid-sized developed nations with relatively open economies. Canada's low population density also contributes to the cost of public services (OECD, 2006).

Beginning in the late 1980s, the traditional government role underwent critical scrutiny in Canada and elsewhere. Governments of all political stripes, from conservative to social-democratic, reduced the role and size of government to decrease deficits and stimulate the economy (Beaumont, 1995; Swimmer and Thompson, 1995). In many countries, Canada included, massive public deficits caused governments to change their financial priorities (Bordogna, 2003).

New policies emphasized the primacy of free-market forces. Virtually all levels of government restricted spending, and per capita spending by government declined throughout the 1990s (Thompson, 2000). Governments privatized many enterprises, from airlines and telephone companies to liquor stores. Services performed by government employees, including snow removal, highway maintenance, safety inspections, and licensing, were contracted out. Service levels were reduced in health and education, and public–private partnerships were sought in order to renew aging infrastructures and develop new ones. Not surprisingly, these and other changes placed great stress on the public-sector collective bargaining system.

SIZE AND SCOPE OF THE PUBLIC SECTOR

For purposes of this discussion, the public sector includes federal and provincial civil services, municipalities, health care, education, and government-owned enterprises (for example, the Canadian Broadcasting Corporation and Hydro-Québec). Table 15.1 provides data on public-sector employment in selected years from 1994 to 2006, excluding government enterprises. Total public-sector employment was estimated at 3.1 million in 2006, comprising 22.5 percent of all employees in Canada.

Health care and education are by far the largest components of the public sector, accounting for three-quarters of all public employees. The federal government employs relatively few people, contrary to popular perceptions. Internationally, Canada ranks slightly above the average for developed nations in terms of the ratio of public to overall employment, showing a ratio similar to Australia, France, Ireland, and the United States (Bordogna, 2003).

Table 15.1 Public-Sector Employment, 1994–2006

	1994 (THOUSANDS)	1998 (THOUSANDS)	2002 (THOUSANDS)	2006 (THOUSANDS)	ANNUAL PERCENTAGE CHANGE 1994–2006
EDUCATION	819.2	816.8	913.3	976.1	1.6%
HEALTH AND WELFARE	739.3	695.1	723.9	780.4	0.5%
LOCAL GOVERNMENT	366.1	341.1	359.3	385.6	0.4%
PROVINCIAL GOVERNMENT	360.4	334.2	333.2	350.8	−0.2%
FEDERAL GOVERNMENT	394.1	331.0	359.5	393.1	0.0%
TOTAL PUBLIC SECTOR	3002.7	2779.0	2953.0	3148.7	0.4%
ECONOMY-WIDE EMPLOYEES	11030.3	11640.5	12996.0	13986.3	2.2%
% PUBLIC SECTOR[a]	27.2%	23.9%	22.7%	22.5%	−1.4%
TOTAL ECONOMY[b]	13058.7	14046.3	15310.4	16484.3	2.2%
% PUBLIC SECTOR[c]	23.0%	19.8%	19.3%	19.1%	−1.4%

[a] PUBLIC-SECTOR EMPLOYEES AS A PERCENTAGE OF ECONOMY-WIDE EMPLOYEES
[b] TOTAL ECONOMY INCLUDES SELF-EMPLOYED
[c] PUBLIC-SECTOR EMPLOYEES AS A PERCENTAGE OF TOTAL ECONOMY

Source: Adapted from CANSIM Tables 183-0002—Public Sector Employment, Wages and Salaries, Monthly; and 282-0011—Labour force survey estimates (LFS).

Data in Table 15.1 confirm the impact of government policies introduced in the last half of the 1990s aimed at reducing the role of government. Between 1994 and 2002, total employment fell in health and welfare, in local governments and in the provincial and federal civil services (although not in education). Overall, public-sector employment as a proportion of economy-wide employment decreased from 27 percent to 23 percent. Put another way, while employment in the rest of the economy expanded, public-sector employment hardly grew at all, thus accounting for a significantly smaller part of the economy as a whole. Canadian trends are not unique: the proportion of public employees has declined in most industrialized countries since the early 1990s (Bordogna, 2003). After 2002, employment grew slightly in all segments of the public sector.

In Canada, the reversal in public-sector growth rates, driven by the desire to reduce labour cost, was achieved in three principal ways: the sale of government assets and enterprises (privatization), the turning over of work previously performed by public employees to private contractors (contracting out), and the reduction in the level of public services (Thompson, 1995; Swimmer and Bartkiw, 2003). In the 21st century, governments turned to "public–private partnerships" to remove some functions from the public sector, at least formally. Governments contracted with private firms to build and operate capital projects to repay the cost of capital over long terms without these obligations appearing as public debt.

Privatization has taken several forms, but has most often involved the sale of Crown corporations to private-sector firms engaged in the same or related industry. For example, the federal government sold two aircraft manufacturing firms to Boeing and Bombardier, and the British Columbia government sold its gas distribution system to companies already active in the province (Thompson, 1995). In other cases—for example, Alberta Government Telephones (now Telus), Petro-Canada, and Air Canada—the government owners issued public shares, which were widely distributed. Social services, such as group homes for the disabled, have also been shifted to the private sector, often to non-profit organizations.

The contracting-out of services previously performed by public employees to the private sector has also been extensive, particularly at the municipal level, in hospitals, and in educational institutions (for municipal level see Hebdon and Jalette, 2008). The most common candidates for contracting-out are solid waste disposal (i.e., garbage collection), building maintenance and security, laundries, food services, snow removal, and road and highway maintenance (Thompson, 1995). Privatization has not been universally successful. Reverse privatization, or contracting back in, also occurred when a previously privatized service is brought back to be performed in-house by a local government (Warner and Hebdon, 2001; Cyr-Racine and Jalette, 2007). The municipalities of Hamilton, Ontario, and Westmount, Quebec, returned the management and maintenance of water and sewer systems to government.

A third strategy to reduce government is simply to decrease or eliminate specific public services, reducing employment at the same time. This approach has been noticeable in health care with the closure of acute-care hospitals, the elimination of certain departments (e.g., emergency departments), or the reduction in the number of beds (Swimmer, 2000). In Saskatchewan, for example, rural hospitals were closed, and in Calgary two large acute-care hospitals were shut down (the largest of the two, the Calgary General Hospital, was physically demolished in 1998). In education, schools have been closed, class sizes increased, and special programs eliminated. Other examples of reduced services include cutting maintenance of infrastructure, closing foreign embassies and consular offices, shortening library operating hours, or simply reducing by attrition the number of staff in various government departments (see Exhibit 15.1). Taken together, privatization, contracting out, and service reductions in the 1990s reversed four decades of public employment growth.

Exhibit 15.1
How to Reduce Public Employment

- Privatize: Sell government-owned companies to the private sector (e.g., Air Canada).
- Contract Out: Have services previously performed by government employees done by private-sector contractors (e.g., garbage collection, hospital laundry).
- Reduce Services: Reduce the amount of services, shrinking employment levels (e.g., shorter operating hours, fewer government offices, close hospitals and schools).
- Public–Private Partnerships: Contract with private firms to build and operate public facilities.

DEVELOPMENT OF PUBLIC-SECTOR COLLECTIVE BARGAINING

Public-sector collective bargaining became common in Canada in the mid-1960s. Previously, few public employees engaged in formal collective bargaining, except for blue-collar municipal workers. Today the situation is very different: most public employees are covered by collective agreements; Canada's two largest unions (Canadian Union of Public Employees and National Union of Public and General Employees, NUPGE) operate almost exclusively in the public sector; and the level of collective bargaining in the public sector far exceeds that found in the private sector. More than half of all union members in Canada work in the public sector (Akyeampong, 2002).

Table 15.2 provides the latest available information on public-sector union density (Statistics Canada, 2007). The level of unionism in 2006 ranges from 60 percent in local government to 76 percent in health and social services. The union density rate in the public sector at 71 percent is obviously much higher than the rate of 29 percent for the economy as a whole and the rate of 18 percent for the private sector (Statistics Canada, 2007).

Local, provincial, and federal employees (plus firefighters) are mainly represented by national or international unions; but teachers, registered nurses, and police thus far have remained in provincial or local independent labour organizations. Almost all unionized public employees, except firefighters, belong to Canadian-based national unions. Table 15.3 sets out membership patterns of the various public-sector labour organizations.

Association–Consultation

The current extent of public-sector unionism belies its recent origin. Associations of public employees existed before 1900, and then, as now, these workers shared at least some of the many concerns of their private-sector counterparts in terms of salaries and employment conditions (Logan, 1948). Early in the 20th century, Canadian public employees spurned

---

Table 15.2 Public-Sector Union Density (percentage)

PUBLIC SECTOR	UNION DENSITY (PERCENTAGE)			
	1993	1998	2002	2006
Local Government	55.7	60.6	62.5	60.5
Provincial	60.7	70.2	69.5	71.7
Federal	60.9	65.7	70.0	69.0
Education	77.7	74.8	74.9	72.4
Health and Social Services*	69.9	71.3	75.9	75.5
Public Sector	67.9	69.9	71.7	71.0
Total Economy	31.8	30.0	30.1	29.4

*Labour Canada's union density statistics exclude private medical offices from other parts of health and social services in calculating density rates.

Sources: Adapted from the Statistics Canada Data: Survey of Labour and Income Dynamics, Person File 1993; and Labour Force Survey, 1998, 2002, & 2006. Accessed from the SDA System at the University of Toronto Data Library Service. *The sources changed after the repeal of a statute that required collection of union density data leading to new data collection procedures.*

Table 15.3 Membership of Public-Sector Unions (thousands)

Unions	1980	1994	1998	2002	2006
PSAC[a]	155.7	167.8	142.3	148.7	162.3
NUPGE	195.8	307.6	309.0	325.0	340.0
CUPE	257.2	409.8	389.3	521.6	548.9
Teachers'	276.8	404.6	404.6	390.1	417.6
Nurses'	78.1	166.5	166.2	172.8	185.9
Police	34.5[b]	43.5	42.2	52.3	53.6
Firefighters'	19.4[b]	27.2	30.8	22.3	25.9

[a] Public Service Alliance of Canada

[b] Membership is for 1986.

Source: Labour Canada, Directory of Labour Organizations, 1980, 1994, 1998, 2002, and 2006; and Rose, 1995, Table 1. Figures for teachers', nurses', police and firefighters' unions gathered by summing membership in individual union and association listings in the Directory.

unionism and collective bargaining. Instead, they formed public employee associations. These organizations avoided union tactics, especially strikes, were independent of any labour body, and preferred consultation to bargaining (Chaykowski, 2000).

This approach to employer–employee relations is referred to here as "association–consultation" (see Exhibit 15.2). It was the prevalent form of public-sector labour relations until the mid-1960s, when it yielded to the more familiar unionism and collective bargaining approach. The transition from association–consultation to union collective bargaining began in the 1950s, and was virtually complete by the mid-1970s.

Exhibit 15.2
Association–Consultation Model of Employment Relations

- non-certified employee organizations
- minimal dues, minimal budget; few, if any, permanent staff
- unaffiliated with labour movement
- membership included senior levels of management
- rejected collective bargaining, grievance arbitration, strikes
- periodic consultation with government over wages and conditions of employment
- employer makes final decision on all employment matters

The major catalyst in the movement to full collective bargaining was the removal of legal obstacles. Saskatchewan had set a precedent in 1944 by including civil servants under the coverage of the provincial *Trade Union Act*, undermining the proposition that government sovereignty prevented public-sector bargaining. Other governments slowly accepted that certain limitations in their own discretion might be necessary if collective bargaining rights—to which public employees felt strongly entitled—were to be provided. In many jurisdictions, the substitution of arbitration for the right to strike overcame misgivings about work stoppages. Gradually, the legislative environment began to change from one that was hostile to the collective bargaining model to one that was supportive.

The most important breakthrough for employee associations seeking collective bargaining occurred in 1963. Astute political lobbying by employee organizations persuaded the newly elected federal government of Prime Minister Lester Pearson to promise collective bargaining rights for the federal civil service (Edwards, 1968). The *Public Service Staff Relations Act* (PSSRA) was enacted several years later, and more than 100 000 federal employees were soon covered by collective agreements. In 1965, the *Quebec Labour Code* extended bargaining rights to all public employees in that province, and 40 000 workers started their first round of bargaining. Political pressure mounted for other governments to emulate these examples. One by one, the remaining provinces enacted collective bargaining legislation for various groups of public employees.

By 1975, the rights of virtually all public employees to engage in collective bargaining were established and protected by law. Access to certification procedures, conciliation machinery, and labour boards, together with public employers' acceptance of unionism and collective bargaining, stimulated a period of substantial union growth. Once committed to collective bargaining, public-sector employee organizations quickly exercised their newly acquired rights. Existing associations converted themselves into unions, eliminating the need for extensive membership campaigns, and unionization spread rapidly. By the late 1970s, most eligible public employees in the country belonged to unions.

DISTINGUISHING FEATURES OF PUBLIC-SECTOR COLLECTIVE BARGAINING

As public-employee unionism spread rapidly, it became obvious that bargaining is different in the public sector compared to the private sector. Important differences between public- and private-sector employers, employees, legislation, and public pressures produce distinctive bargaining dynamics.

Employer Differences

The most important special features of public-sector labour relations stem from differences between public employers and private employers. Most public employers (a small number of government enterprises excepted) do not have a profit motive. They are evaluated on the services they provide or on political as well as financial considerations. Federal and provincial government employers also enjoy the ability to legislate on industrial relations, including the outcome of disputes—an advantage unmatched by their private-sector counterparts. All public-sector employers operate in a more transparent environment than do their private-sector counterparts. Each of these features can have substantial implications for bargaining dynamics in the public sector.

Political considerations dominate management's view of work stoppages. While strikes impose financial losses on private-sector employers, public employers normally save money during a strike since revenues continue. On the other hand, public-sector strikes frequently disrupt services that are not easily substituted for (e.g., schools) and that affect many citizens. In the private sector the presence of competitors gives customers alternatives and lessens the pressures of a given work stoppage on third parties. Ultimately, the decision about a public-sector work stoppage involves an employer's political and financial assessment of the consequences of a settlement or stoppage. It should be noted that public-sector employers generally do not have the right to lock out as do their private-sector counterparts. It would be inconsistent for some employers to allege that their employees give essential services while at the same time having the right to lock them out, but for others the industrial relations system is inconsistent by not giving the equivalent right to both parties to launch a work stoppage. Thus it creates an imbalance toward public-sector employers, especially in the municipal sector.

The political element in public-sector bargaining translates into substantial efforts by the parties to make their case to the public, particularly with respect to work stoppages. Thus, negotiations may take place not only at the bargaining table but also in the media, as each side attempts to win public support. Teachers and hospital workers, for example, usually frame their bargaining demands not in terms of better wages and working conditions but in terms of improvement in the quality of education or health care.[3] Public employers take great pains to justify back-to-work legislation in the name of public interest, not on the grounds that such tactics enable them to achieve a particular bargaining objective.

Canadian public-sector employers use several organizational forms for labour relations. Provincial and federal governments, led by Quebec, developed highly centralized bargaining structures. The City of Vancouver and a dozen surrounding suburban communities have given bargaining authority to an employers' association. Several provinces created a small number of health care regions with budget authority, effectively eliminating individual hospitals from bargaining (Haiven and Haiven, 2002). In education, provincial bargaining has become widespread as governments seek to control costs (Thomason, 1995). In Quebec and New Brunswick, provincial government officials have represented management at the bargaining table in health care and social services negotiations, while a government observer has been part of the employer bargaining team in Saskatchewan hospital negotiations (Haiven, 1995). The British Columbia government established a "Public Sector Employers' Council" in 1993 to coordinate bargaining for the entire public sector in the province. The Council issues wage and benefits guidelines, which effectively bind the various public-sector employers (Thompson, 2000).

The most fundamental difference is the fact that federal and provincial governments play a dual role in labour relations. They are both large employers and holders of sovereign authority over their territories, with the power to legislate the rules under which they and their employees must function. The power to legislate tempts governments to adjust labour relations rules in their own self-interest as employers. In the 1990s, the federal government and most provincial governments rolled back or froze wages for public employees through legislation (Rose 2004; Swimmer, 2000).

Employee and Union Differences

Public–private sector differences that exist on the employer side are not matched on the employee and union side. Pressures on public-sector union leaders to achieve collective bargaining objectives resemble the pressures experienced by their private-sector counterparts. While the subject matter of negotiations might vary between the two sectors, bargaining is still focused on the traditional issues of "wages, hours, and conditions of employment" in both sectors. The major cost of strike action—immediate loss of income—also is the same for public- and private-sector employees, except that most public-sector workers have little reason to fear that their employer will close permanently, even if, to some degree, the threat of contracting out or privatization achieves the same end in public-sector collective bargaining (Warrian, 1996). Public-sector workers typically expect greater job security than their private-sector counterparts.

Demographic differences also exist between public- and private-sector employees and, by extension, their unions. The public sector employs a higher proportion of women than does the private sector; overall, 60 percent of the public-sector workforce is female. Union density among men and women is very similar; thus 61 percent of public-sector union members are female. In comparison, only 30 percent of private-sector union members are women (Akyeampong, 2002). Furthermore, the public sector contains a higher proportion of white-collar workers and professionals than does the private sector. These differences mean that whereas most private-sector unions are essentially blue-collar and male-dominated, public-sector unionism is heavily white-collar and female-dominated. Virtually all professionals who engage in collective bargaining are employed in the public sector. By 2007, most of the largest public-sector unions had been led by women, including the current president of the Canadian Union of Postal Workers.

A feature of public-sector labour forces that has emerged in recent years is a "demographic bulge." Other industries face the same factor, but demography is especially significant in the public sector. The growth period in most elements of the public sector took place in the 1960s and 1970s. Workers hired during that period have begun to reach retirement age in the 2000s. Limited hiring in the 1980s and 1990s, plus the reluctance of public-sector employers to offer permanent jobs in some occupations, has created a gap in the age distribution of many workforces. Since most public-sector workers are covered by pension plans, they retire earlier than do other Canadians. Across the country, a large number of vacancies will soon occur—if they haven't already—in occupations such as nurse, teacher, police officer, and firefighter. The federal public service is in a similar situation. The impact of this factor on labour relations has only just begun, most conspicuously for nurses, who have received wage increases far above other public-sector groups.

The high proportion of females in the public sector requires that special attention be paid to pay equity and anti-discrimination issues. Public-sector unions have been among the strongest advocates of workplace equity. In 1999, the Public Service Alliance of Canada (PSAC) settled a long-standing pay equity case against the federal government, which resulted in a multibillion-dollar payout to many female employees, paid less than male counterparts with similar qualifications. In 2006, a similar settlement was concluded in Quebec's civil service, health, and education sectors where pay equity adjustments benefited more than 360 000 workers, the majority of them women. These wage payments amounted to, on average, between 5 and 6 percent and were retroactive to 2001.

Unions of professional employees also negotiate over issues relating to professional concerns, possibly creating clashes about managerial prerogatives and policy (Ponak, 1981).

Policy and Legislative Distinctions

The right of public employees to unionize and engage in collective bargaining is enshrined in law, much as it is in the private sector. In addition, the right of public employees to form unions freely is protected by the *Charter of Rights and Freedoms*. Public employers are obliged to recognize and bargain in good faith with labour organizations that enjoy majority support. Public-sector collective bargaining legislation is extremely diverse, however, compared to the private sector. Whereas private-sector legislation in each of the provinces and at the federal level generally follows principles derived from PC 1003 (enacted in 1944) as well as earlier conciliation legislation (see Chapter 8), there is no similarly accepted framework in the public sector. Hence, considerable differences exist in legislation between the public and private sectors and in the treatment of different groups of public employees (see Exhibit 15.3).

Exhibit 15.3
Private- vs. Public-Sector Legislation

BARGAINING

- Private—almost everything is negotiable
- Public—variety of restrictions on what can be bargained and arbitrated

CERTIFICATION

- Private—any bona fide labour organization can represent employees; labour board determines bargaining unit
- Public—labour organization may be specified in legislation; employee choice restricted; bargaining units established in legislation

STRIKES

- Private—almost all employees have the right to strike and employers have the right to lock out
- Public—many employees prohibited from striking or must carry out certain designated services during a strike; lockouts are often forbidden

WAGES

- Private—unions and employers bargain over wage rates
- Public—wages often set unilaterally by special legislation in the 1970s, 1980s, and 1990s

---

Over 40 different pieces of legislation regulate industrial relations in the federal government and provinces of Canada, including general industrial relations statutes.[4] Except for municipal employees, most public employees do not fall under general private-sector labour codes. For example, in eight provinces, collective bargaining for teachers is governed either by a special statute established for that purpose (e.g., the *Teachers' Collective Bargaining Act* in Nova Scotia), the basic legislation governing education (e.g., the *Public Schools Act* in Manitoba), or some combination of these statutes and the general labour code (e.g., in Ontario).

Even where superficially it may appear that labour relations are governed by the general private-sector statute, as in the case of hospital workers in several provinces, special provisions often exist, within the general labour code or in other legislation, that create distinctive regulatory procedures. In British Columbia and Newfoundland and Labrador, for example, hospital unions must negotiate coverage of essential services with their employer prior to striking. In Alberta, provisions of the labour relations code prohibit strikes by hospital workers and set out an arbitration system. In Quebec, other statutes replace the labour code for bargaining structure while the labour code addresses the maintenance of essential services (Adell, Grant, and Ponak, 2001).

The multiplicity of statutes and diversity of approaches governing the public sector reflect both the absence of a generally accepted labour-law model for public employees and the dual role of government as employer. As various groups of public employees sought enabling legislation for collective bargaining, legislators experimented freely (Goldenberg, 1988) while protecting their own and the public interest. As well, the early experience with bargaining differed widely across the country, again giving rise to distinct regulatory approaches.

While generalizations are difficult to make, public-sector statutes differ most from the private-sector model in three areas. First, labour relations boards have less discretion with respect to certification and recognition. A number of statutes—for example, the federal *Public Service Staff Relations Act* (Finkleman and Goldenberg, 1983)—have established occupational bargaining units, an approach very different from the discretion given labour boards in the private sector. British Columbia established three bargaining units under its provincial civil service law (the *Public Service Labour Relations Act*, PSLRA), as did the Northwest Territories under its *Public Service Act*, and more recently Quebec with its controversial Bill 30 in the social affairs sector. Also in contrast to private-sector practice, a number of organizations were granted statutory representation rights, particularly teachers' unions, faculty associations, and, to a lesser degree, civil service unions.

A second area of difference has been the tendency to restrict the scope of bargaining in many parts of the public sector. Private-sector negotiators are almost universally free to bargain over any issue they choose. General private-sector labour codes that permit bargaining to proceed over "wages, hours, and working conditions" are interpreted very liberally. Less negotiating latitude is permitted under a variety of public-sector statutes. The PSSRA removes from the scope of bargaining such issues as classifications; criteria for promotion, transfers, and layoffs; technological change; and pensions. Similar constraints on bargaining scope are found in a majority of provincial civil service statutes. Local government employees, teachers, and hospital employees are frequently covered by non-negotiable pension plans. The negotiating scope for police and firefighters may be limited, particularly with respect to disciplinary arrangements and superior–subordinate relations, owing to the paramilitary nature of these services. Since the early 1980s, many governments have legislated wage controls, effectively removing wages from the negotiations during subsequent rounds of bargaining.

Dispute resolution procedures provide a third, and the most controversial, major area of legislative difference between the public and the private sectors. Almost all private-sector employees enjoy a right to strike over the renegotiation of a collective agreement once certain preconditions (e.g., a strike vote) have been satisfied. Public-sector employees, by comparison, are much more fettered. Frequently their right to strike is removed and replaced by arbitration, even in situations—as for New Brunswick firefighters and Alberta nurses—in which a general labour code provides basic statutory coverage. If strikes are permitted, the preconditions are normally more severe than in the private sector. Quebec and British Columbia public employees cannot withdraw their services until agreement is reached on maintaining essential services; federal civil servants must participate in a two-stage conciliation process before their right to strike becomes operative; and fact-finding is a precondition to work stoppages for Ontario teachers.

Since the mid-1980s, the *Charter of Rights and Freedoms* has regulated government action. Section 2(d) protects "freedom of association." Early Supreme Court of Canada decisions ruled that freedom of association did not include any fundamental right to strike, right to bargain collectively, or right to choose a bargaining agent.[5] In a far-reaching decision issued in 2007, the Court declared that freedom of association *did* include the right to collective bargaining, reversing the earlier line of cases. The decision overturned legislation passed in 2002 by the government of British Columbia that unilaterally removed major protections contained in collective agreements covering health care workers.[6] Similar laws also altered the agreements for teachers and government employees, and unions affected challenged these actions too. By the fall of 2007, the B.C. government had not responded formally to the decision of the Court, which gave it one year to implement the ruling. Public-sector unions hailed the Court decision as a great victory. Certainly, governments will have less freedom to intervene in collective bargaining than previously. More specific implications will become clear through litigation and legislation.

STRIKES AND DISPUTE PROCEDURES

Strikes have caused the most difficult problems in public-sector collective bargaining. Policy-makers are clearly divided, as demonstrated by the diversity of dispute resolution procedures in use. For example, half the provinces allow their civil service to strike, the other half do not. Teachers have the right to strike in most provinces, but not in Manitoba or Prince Edward Island. Both advocates and opponents of a right to strike can offer strong arguments in support of their position (see Exhibit 15.4).

Opponents of strike rights for public employees make their case mainly on the grounds that public-sector work stoppages impose too much inconvenience on the public. Private-sector disputes often do not affect third parties seriously, since substitutes are usually available for products cut off by strikes. This is in sharp contrast with the public sector. The effects of strikes by teachers, postal workers, air traffic controllers, and transit workers, among others, inevitably go beyond the parties at the bargaining table, disrupting heavily used and irreplaceable services. In stoppages involving employees such as hospital workers, police, and firefighters, service interruptions may pose immediate danger to the health and safety of those who must rely on the struck services. The monopoly status of most public services can lead to higher settlements than a market-based employer would concede. For these reasons alone, it is argued, public employees should be prohibited from striking. These arguments have not gone unchallenged. Analysis of public-employee strikes suggests that damage to the public is much less than commonly claimed (Adell, Grant, and Ponak, 2001; Gunderson, 1995). Many public-sector employees perform services that are not essential, at least in the short run. For truly essential services, requirements exist to protect the public during work stoppages, for example, that certain essential employees remain at work. Research has shown that managers and employees can be remarkably innovative at providing essential services even in the face of a complete withdrawal of services (Adell, Grant, and Ponak, 2001; Haiven and Haiven, 2002).

Exhibit 15.4
Arguments for and Against Public-Sector Strikes

RESTRICT PUBLIC-SECTOR STRIKES

- Strikes create inconvenience and possibly endanger the public.
- They give unions too much power, leading to over-generous wages and working conditions.
- They create destabilizing and tumultuous political confrontations.

PERMIT PUBLIC-SECTOR STRIKES

- Strike impact is exaggerated; most public employees are not essential, and service levels during strikes are often higher than on holidays, vacations, or weekends.
- Techniques are available to ensure truly essential services are maintained, reducing public risk.
- Strike substitutes, such as arbitration, are inefficient and produce poor contracts.

But the strongest argument in favour of the right to strike in the public sector lies in the lack of acceptable substitutes for strikes. Removing the right to strike from the collective bargaining process necessarily implies replacing it with some other mechanism capable of resolving disputes. Many of those who defend the right to strike contend that they are not so much enamoured of the strike weapon as they are disillusioned with the alternatives, such as arbitration and final-offer selection (Weiler, 1980). As already discussed in Chapter 12, strike substitutes are criticized on the grounds that they weaken the collective bargaining process, lead to excessive third-party intervention, and generally produce inferior collective agreements (Ponak and Falkenberg, 1989; Haiven and Haiven, 2002; Hebdon and Mazerolle, 2003).

Public-Sector Strike Record

To assess the debate about the right to strike, the first step is to examine the strike record. Table 15.4 presents public-sector strike frequency and volume (person-days lost) from

1975 to 2007, inclusive, and also shows public-sector strike frequency and volume as a proportion of the economy-wide strike frequency and volume (public and private sectors combined). There are wide fluctuations from year to year both in terms of absolute public-sector strike volume and frequency and the public sector's share of overall strike activity. These yearly fluctuations notwithstanding, annual public-sector strike activity has declined discernibly since 1984. From 1975 to 1984, the average annual public-sector strike volume was relatively constant at approximately 1.8 million days lost per year. From that peak, annual public-sector strike volume has declined by more than half. The number of public-sector strikes also has declined, from an average of more than 200 strikes per year in the late 1970s to about one-third of that number by the mid-2000s.

The decline in public-sector frequency and volume is similar to the general decline in work stoppages in Canada and most other industrial countries since the late 1980s (see Chapter 12). However, as public-sector strike volume has fallen, its share of total strike activity has increased. The latest data show that public employees now account for almost 40 percent of all person-days lost in Canada, Thus, while public-sector strike activity is declining, it is equally true that public-sector strikes comprise a larger share of industrial disputes than their proportion of the economy. Concern about public-sector work stoppages, therefore, is not misplaced.

Compulsory Arbitration

Because public-sector work stoppages cause inconvenience and in some cases could endanger the public, compulsory arbitration is the traditional substitute for strikes, either as part of a general strike ban (e.g., the Toronto police) or to end specific disputes, such as the 2002 Alberta teachers' strike. Publicly, public-sector unions oppose bans on strikes. Privately, many prefer arbitration. Employers realize that the outcome of a labour dispute can have huge implications for their budgets, especially where working conditions are involved. Consequently, they prefer bargaining to arbitration when that system is feasible.

The practice of arbitration is well established. The union and employer normally select an arbitrator acceptable to both sides. If they are unable to agree on an arbitrator, an accepted neutral agency, such as the labour relations board, mediation services, or even the chief justice selects the arbitrator. The courts expect arbitrators to be acceptable to the parties.

In the 1990s, the Ontario government restricted arbitrator appointments to retired judges in a health care dispute, excluding experienced arbitrators. The Supreme Court ultimately ruled that "the appointment of an inexpert and inexperienced chairperson who is not seen as broadly acceptable in the labour relations community is a defect in approach that is both immediate and obvious" (Re *CUPE v. Ontario (Minister of Labour)*, 2003 S.C.C. 29). This landmark decision should help ensure that where compulsory arbitration is invoked, an experienced, independent, and generally acceptable arbitrator will decide disputes.

Designation Model

Efforts to devise better methods of public-sector dispute resolution have resulted in an approach that permits strikes and protects the public at the same time. First introduced in

Table 15.4 Public-Sector Work Stoppages by Year

Year	Number of Work Stoppages	As a Percentage of Total Work Stoppages in Canada	Person-Days Lost (in thousands)	As a Percentage of Total Person-Days Lost in Canada
1975–79 *(mean)*	214	20.9	1724	21.1
1980–84 *(mean)*	168	20.4	1800	28.1
1985	158	19.1	628	20.1
1986	128	17.1	796	11.1
1987	105	15.7	885	23.2
1988	76	13.9	2167	44.2
1989	139	22.2	1658	44.8
1985–89 *(mean)*	121	17.7	1267	27.0
1990	119	20.6	786	15.5
1991	115	24.8	1429	56.5
1992	80	19.8	496	23.4
1993	85	22.3	362	22.6
1994	55	14.7	414	25.8
1990–94 *(mean)*	91	20.7	696	27.1
1995	54	16.5	215	13.6
1996	73	22.1	1451	43.3
1997	50	17.6	1489	41.3
1998	135	35.4	618	25.9
1999	118	28.4	882	45.9
1995–99 *(mean)*	86	24	931	34
2000	92	24.3	512	30.9
2001	98	25.7	822	37.4
2002	54	18.4	1576	52.0
2003	67	25.2	311	17.9
2004	71	23.8	1895	58.8
2000–04 *(mean)*	76	23.5	1023	39.4
2005	92	35.4	2048	49.4
2006	32	20.6	195	24.1
2007*	34	26.6	169	24.1
2005–2006 *(mean)*	62	28.0	1122	36.8
2005–2007 *(mean)**	53	27.5	804	32.5

* Current as of August 2007

Source: Calculations based on data provided by Workplace Information Directorate, Human Resources and Social Development Canada.

Photo 15.1

Firefighters use alternatives to strikes. Here is a firefighter in Moose Jaw, Saskatchewan.

Source: © 2008 Mark Duffy and World of Stock. Unlicensed use prohibited.

the federal sector (PSSRA), the designation model is now used for at least part of the public sectors in six provinces (Adell, Grant, and Ponak, 2001). This approach permits work stoppages but requires that certain employees be "designated" to remain on the job to provide essential services. The number and role of such employees are generally subject to negotiation between the parties. If they cannot agree, a labour relations tribunal makes the final determination. Under the PSSRA, the proportion of employees designated within a given bargaining unit has varied from 2 percent or less among librarians and social science support services to 100 percent of air traffic controllers, firefighters, and veterinary scientists (Swimmer, 1995).[7] In Montreal, transit workers may strike but must provide service during rush hour. In British Columbia, up to 65 percent of striking nurses were required to remain at work, depending on the services they were providing.

In theory, the designation model could satisfy the needs of policy-makers, unions, and employers. The union exercises its right to strike. It is under pressure to settle because the majority of its members are forgoing their paycheques while the employer is in partial operation. The employer is under pressure because it is unable to provide normal levels of service and may be forced to mount a strenuous effort to maintain even its limited operations. The public interest is protected because the designated employees maintain essential services.

In practice, it becomes obvious that designating the "correct" proportion of bargaining unit personnel is crucial to the success of this dispute procedure. If too many employees are designated, the pressure on the employer may be inconsequential; if too few employees are at work, even minimum service requirements may not be met and the union may enjoy a bargaining advantage. Thus, negotiations between the union and employer to determine the proportion of employees who will not strike are often difficult and protracted. For example, in the face of an impending strike of non-professional employees at the Vancouver General Hospital, management took the position that all 2000 employees were essential, while the union claimed that none of its members should have to "scab on their own union's strike" (Weiler, 1980). Eventually the labour board designated 100 employees as essential. In an excellent review of essential service procedures during nurses' strikes in five provinces between 1988 and 1991, Haiven (1995) found that labour tribunals tend to set designation levels too high, preferring to err on the side of caution. In one Quebec hospital, 110 percent of the usual nurse complement was required during a tight labour market for nurses. Even with high levels of coverage, Haiven and Haiven (2002) found that many hospitals failed to prepare adequately for strikes, resulting in chaotic conditions.

Recent research concludes that, despite the practical difficulties of implementation, the designation model has great potential to satisfy the conflicting interests of all participants (see Haiven and Haiven, 2002, for a dissenting view). Moreover, there is good evidence that the parties gain confidence over several rounds of bargaining and that, after some frustrating early experience (see Exhibit 15.5), subsequent negotiations over which services to maintain prove easier (Adell, Grant, and Ponak, 2001). For these reasons, the designation model is likely to continue to spread within the public sector.

Exhibit 15.5
Negotiating the Level of Essential Services

In an interview, a British Columbia management negotiator summed up his frustration with the difficulty of negotiating the level of essential services as follows:

> It's . . . massive, time consuming, incredibly wasteful . . . the essential services process. I would say without exaggeration in the fifteen years I've been a labour negotiator, of all the things I've done, however cooperative or uncooperative they've been in the union–management process, it is the single most wasteful exercise.

Source: Adell, Grant, and Ponak, 2001.

Emergency Legislation

Legislation to end particular strikes has long been a feature of the public sector. Between 1965 and 2007, Parliament and provincial legislatures have enacted 101 laws ending public-sector strikes (Table 15.5), the great majority of which were legal (a detailed list of this legislation can be found on the Industrial Relations Legislation section of the Human Resources and Social Development Canada website, www.hrsdc.gc.ca/en/labour/labour_law/index.shtml). In most cases, arbitration was also invoked to resolve the issues in dispute once the strike was terminated. More recently, as was the case in the 2002 B.C. teachers' and health care disputes, legislation imposed the wages and terms and conditions of employment (usually the employer's final offer). Thus, in these disputes the final contours of the collective agreement were not left to the determination of an arbitrator, but were established unilaterally through legislation, an action the Supreme Court eventually declared unconstitutional.

The use of special legislation has not been evenly distributed across the country. More than one-quarter of the back-to-work laws were enacted in Quebec, a province marked by particularly tumultuous public-sector disputes as well as a tradition of legislative

Table 15.5 Emergency Legislation in the Public Sector

Year	Federal	Quebec	Ontario	B.C.	Sask.	Others	Total
1950–64	0	0	0	0	0	0	0
1965–69	0	4	1	0	1	1	7
1970–74	0	2	2	1	0	0	5
1975–79	2	5	6	4	1	0	18
1980–84	0	8	3	1	2	3	17
1985–89	2	3	2	1	3	0	11
1990–94	2	1	3	2	0	0	8
1995–99	2	1	2	2	2	1	10
2000–04	0	1	3	9	0	6	21
2005–07	1	1	0	2	0	0	4
Total	9	26	24	22	9	11	101

Source: Updated from Thompson and Ponak (1995, Table 15-9), and Human Resources and Social Development Canada, Highlights of Major Developments in Labour Legislation, 1993–94 to 2005–07 (HRSDC Website).

intervention in industrial relations (see Chapter 16). Ontario and British Columbia each accounted for more than 20 percent. Given the relatively small size of its workforce, Saskatchewan has also seen a high utilization of legislation to end strikes (approximately 10 percent). Conversely, the federal government has resorted infrequently to legislation.

The incidence of back-to-work legislation peaked in the 1975 to 1984 period, declined in the next decade, but increased dramatically after 2000 (see Table 15.5). Some observers believe that the use of special legislation to end otherwise legal strikes, and the unilateral imposition of contract terms, is part of a fundamental retreat by governments from endorsing any kind of free collective bargaining system for public employees (Rose, 2004; Haiven and Haiven, 2002; Panitch and Swartz, 1993). Others are less ready to accept that frequent use of back-to-work legislation marks the end of free collective bargaining in the public sector (Thompson and Swimmer, 1995; Swimmer, 2000; Adell, Grant, and Ponak, 2001; Swimmer and Bartkiw, 2003).

Whatever one's view of the long-term implications of the trend to greater use of legislation to end strikes, this history has had an impact on collective bargaining in the public sector. Unions enter bargaining knowing that if they fail to reach agreement on terms acceptable to the employer/government, a settlement is likely to be imposed, which may be the inevitable fate of those who negotiate with the state.

COMPENSATION ISSUES

Questions surrounding public employee compensation, though less visible than disputes, have proven almost as troublesome. Soon after the inception of collective bargaining, a public perception arose that government employees were overpaid and too successful at winning generous wage increases. Private employers complained that government wage settlements established patterns that the private sector, limited by profit–loss considerations, could not match. Union officials responded that such allegations were untrue and that seemingly high wage increases reflected the need of some groups of low-paid public employees to catch up to the private sector. Furthermore, union officials argued, even if a few government employees were paid more than their private-sector counterparts, there was nothing inherently wrong with government being a wage leader. Public employers should be model employers, setting standards for the rest of the community.

Public–Private Wage Differentials

Philosophies and perceptions aside, the following factors suggest that compensation in the public sector usually will exceed the private sector (Gunderson, 1995):

1. Political pressures are less stringent than the profit constraint.

2. There is pressure on government to be a model employer.

3. The public sector is more highly unionized.

4. Wage surveys on which public-sector wage increases are based tend to focus on large, higher-paying private employers.

5. Public employers have the ability to defer costs to future taxpayers.

There are also reasons for public-sector compensation to lag behind private-sector pay. First, the public sector has traditionally provided more job security than the private sector, which should lead to a private-sector wage premium. Second, public-sector wages are subject to more outside scrutiny (from taxpayers) than the private sector, which guards compensation information closely. Third, the public sector is much more likely to be singled out for special wage restraints, depressing wages. Fourth, government is much more likely to intervene in public-sector strikes, depriving more powerful public-sector unions of the opportunity to win large wage increases. For a number of occupations like university professors or nurses, the public sector is effectively the only employer (monopsony power), giving the employer bargaining leverage that few private-sector employers enjoy (Gunderson, 1995; Mueller, 2000).

Empirical studies from the 1990s confirmed that the upward bias outweighs the downward pressures, although the difference is not large and varies across the public sector. Data show that public employees enjoy a wage premium of between 5 and 10 percent more than their private-sector counterparts, and that public-sector fringe benefits are slightly more generous than in the private sector. The public-sector advantage is greatest at the provincial and local level, is much larger for women than for men, is greater at the lower ranges of the pay scales, is negative at senior levels, and has been diminishing for a number of years. The research also shows that there is no significant spillover effect from the public to the private sector; i.e., public-sector wage levels do not drive up wages in the private sector (Gunderson, 1995). The studies upon which these conclusions are based predate the wage controls introduced in the early 1990s and the reversal in public-sector employment growth. Taking these factors into account may well demonstrate that the public-sector wage premium has disappeared. Indeed, the federal government has had to offer special bonuses to hire and retain staff in certain high-demand occupations. Wage surveys comparing jobs similar in terms of qualifications, tasks, and responsibilities also conclude that public-sector wages more often lag behind those paid in the private sector (see for example the annual report of the Institut de la statistique du Québec: www.stat. gouv.qc.ca).

Further insight into public- and private-sector wage differentials can be gained by examining time-series data on wage changes in the two sectors. Table 15.6 reports annual wage increases between 1979 and 2007, based on collective agreements involving 500 or more employees. It shows the wage changes for the private and public sectors as a whole and also disaggregates the public-sector data by major group. Data in the table indicate that, since 1979, unionized private-sector employees have received substantially higher cumulative wage increases than unionized public employees. Between 1979 and 2006, private-sector employees won cumulative wage increases of 278 percent; public-employee wages increased by 261.5 percent. In only 12 of 28 years did public employees negotiate higher wage settlements than their private-sector counterparts. Looking at the various components of the public sector shown in Table 15.6, we can see that local government employees received the largest overall wage increases and that federal government employees received the lowest increases. Taking the data in this table as a whole, there is no support for the contention that unionized public-sector wage settlements have outstripped those in the private sector since 1979; indeed the reverse appears true.

Public-Sector Wage Controls

The imposition of wage controls during the 1980s and 1990s targeted exclusively at public employees caused public-sector wage increases to lag behind those in the private sector. The federal Anti-Inflation Program of 1975 allegedly covered both sectors, but really applied only to the public sector. The first round of public-sector wage restraint programs occurred in the early 1980s when the Canadian economy fell into a severe recession, causing government revenues to fall sharply. With the encouragement of Prime Minister Pierre Trudeau, every province in the country restricted public-sector compensation in 1982 and 1983, either through a formal system of wage controls or through spending limits. A review of the impact of the restraint programs in British Columbia, Manitoba, Ontario, and New Brunswick found that (1) there was no direct relationship between provincial economic growth and the degree of restraint; (2) wage increases varied considerably among different groups within the public sector of each province; and (3) the number of provincial civil servants rose during the restraint period (Thompson, 1988).

Since the 1980s, public-sector wage restraint programs have been the norm for federal and provincial governments. Initially, controls were based on legislation. By the 1990s through the early 2000s, governments simply announced acceptable increases (not infrequently zero) and bargained over other issues. Knowing that legislation was a likely outcome if they resisted too strenuously, unions had little choice but to accept the standard offers and attempt to achieve gains by restructuring wage scales and improving fringe benefits, job security, and the like. The main political rationale for the new wage restraint programs was pressure on government to reduce spending in recessionary times to tackle public debt. In periods of prosperity, wage control programs also fit well with sentiment in favour of a smaller role for government and were part of broader campaigns that included privatization, contracting out, layoffs, and reductions in services.

Table 15.6 Average Annual Percentage Wage Changes, Major Collective Agreements, 1979–2007

Year	Overall Private	Overall Public	Federal	Provincial	Local	Education/ Health/ Welfare	Crown	Utilities
1979	10.8	9.2	8.4	9.1	9.4	8.2	12.4	9.1
1980	11.6	10.9	11.3	11.3	10.8	10.8	11.1	10.2
1981	12.7	13.2	12.7	13.5	12.7	13.5	12.7	13.3
1982	9.7	10.6	8.3	11.8	12.1	11.4	10.6	12.3
1983	5.4	4.6	5.5	5.0	5.7	3.6	5.6	6.6
1984	3.2	3.9	5.0	5.2	3.3	3.1	4.6	2.6
1985	3.4	3.8	3.2	4.4	4.7	3.4	4.0	3.4
1986	3.0	3.8	3.6	3.9	4.9	3.6	3.7	2.8
1987	3.8	4.2	3.4	4.5	4.2	4.2	2.6	2.0
1988	4.9	3.9	3.5	4.3	4.6	3.8	3.1	3.0
1989	5.3	5.3	4.2	5.7	6.1	5.9	4.0	5.0
1990	5.9	5.6	5.3	5.8	4.9	5.4	4.5	5.3
1991	4.3	3.5	1.7	3.9	5.1	3.8	4.4	2.3
1992	2.3	1.5	1.7	1.0	4.6	1.4	3.0	3.1
1993	0.9	0.5	0.0	0.3	0.7	0.7	2.3	1.5
1994	1.2	0.0	0.0	0.1	0.8	0.3	2.0	0.3
1995	1.4	0.6	0.0	0.9	0.6	0.5	0.8	0.4
1996	1.7	0.5	0.0	0.2	1.1	0.5	0.4	0.9
1997	1.8	1.2	3.2	1.2	1.2	1.0	1.4	1.6
1998	2.0	1.7	2.1	1.7	1.6	1.5	2.2	1.5
1999	2.7	2.0	2.5	1.6	2.3	1.9	2.0	2.0
2000	2.4	2.6	2.2	2.6	2.6	3.0	2.8	3.2
2001	2.8	3.3	3.7	3.4	2.7	3.4	3.6	2.7
2002	2.6	3.1	3.2	2.3	3.1	3.2	2.6	2.9
2003	1.6	2.8	3.1	2.5	2.8	3.5	3.1	2.7
2004	2.2	1.6	2.6	2.2	2.6	1.6	2.8	3.2
2005	2.4	2.4	2.5	2.2	3.1	2.4	2.2	2.0
2006	2.2	2.6	2.6	2.6	3.4	2.6	2.6	2.5
2007*	2.6	3.3	0.0	4.0	3.9	3.1	0.0	3.3
Cumulative (%)	278.5	261.5	250.2	272	286.6	257.9	279.9	257.8

*Data from the first quarter.

Source: Data until 1992 based on Appendix A and Appendix B in Gunderson (1995), both of which were compiled from Labour Canada, Bureau of Labour Information, Major Wage Settlements; data from 1992–1997 from Statistics Canada, Wage Increases in Collective Agreements, CANSIM matrix 4049; data for 1998–2007 from Statistics Canada, Wage Increases in Collective Agreements, CANSIM II, Table 278-0007.

The most tumultuous wage restraint exercise took place in Ontario (Reshef and Rastin, 2003). In the first part of the 1990s, the NDP government, faced with a ballooning deficit, attempted to negotiate a combination of cost savings and public-sector restructuring with close to one million public employees represented by several different unions. In doing so, it asked that existing collective agreements be reopened and scheduled wage increases rescinded. Public-sector unions bitterly opposed the Ontario government's approach. The government and most of the various unions did negotiate agreements; they included a combination of wage reductions and unpaid days. But bargaining took place under a government deadline, after which the *Social Contract Act*—which contained the government's contract objectives—was to go into effect. The labour organizations that had helped elect the NDP government felt betrayed (Fryer, 1995), and this disenchantment was a major factor in the government's defeat and replacement by Mike Harris's Conservatives in 1995. The new government enacted legislation that removed important job protections (such as successor rights in the event of privatization) and then negotiated a four-year contract with no wage increases. This contract was signed after a five-week strike and union-orchestrated "days of protest" amidst calls for a province-wide general strike (Swimmer, 2000).

The most enduring significance of the NDP "Social Contract" was the legitimacy it gave to direct government intervention in public-sector collective bargaining in other jurisdictions. When an NDP government, elected with labour support, took such drastic measures, other governments less dependent on (or hostile to) organized labour concluded that they could act in similar fashion with relative political impunity.

Ironically, in a review of the wage-control experience in the 1990s, Swimmer (2000) concluded that the governments that achieved reductions through negotiations were just as successful at meeting their fiscal goals as governments that relied on legislated solutions. In particular, the province that engaged in the most co-operative bargaining approach, Saskatchewan, also managed to achieve the highest relative budgetary surplus (as measured against provincial GDP) in 1997. Ontario and Quebec, which relied on a combination of legislation and adversarial bargaining, lingered in the worst relative deficit positions.

CONCLUSION

Public-sector collective bargaining has gone through three distinct phases. The first phase, which lasted from the 1960s until the early 1980s, was marked by rapid unionization, the liberalization of labour laws, strong public-sector employment growth, and high wage settlements as unions sought to "catch up" to the private sector. This phase, then, can be thought of as an expansionary one, both in terms of public-sector collective bargaining and of the role of government in general.

The second phase, which lasted through most of the 1980s and through the 1990s, was retrenchment. It was characterized by wage controls aimed exclusively at public employees and by low wage settlements even in the absence of formal controls. Employment growth began to slow, unions reached a saturation point in terms of public-sector organizing opportunities, and strike volume began to decline, although at a slower rate than in the private sector. Public-sector labour laws remained largely intact, but it was obvious that governments could and would suspend such laws to impose wage controls, issue back-to-work orders, or deem entire groups of employees as essential and hence unable to strike. Federal and provincial governments, though proclaiming the virtues of the emerging philosophies favouring less government, had not as yet abandoned Canada's traditional commitment to an active public sector.

The third phase in public-sector collective bargaining, a period of consolidation, began in about 1998. This phase initially included government policies to reduce the size of the public sector through privatization and contracting out and through outright decreases in government services. Layoffs became a common feature of public employment, reversing a long tradition of job security as an important ingredient of government employment. The 1990s also saw the widespread renewal of public-sector wage restraints, with significant wage decreases for many employees. Time lost due to public-sector strikes continued to decline (Rose, 2004).

The events in this latest phase of public-sector collective bargaining have been driven by two developments. One has been a change in the way governments view their own role, resulting in reductions in the part governments play in many spheres of economic, social, and cultural activities. The rethinking of the philosophical limits of government coincided with a period of recession and high public debt, which placed practical limits on the scope of government undertakings. As a result, severe pressures were placed on the public-sector collective bargaining system, as unions, employees, and public-sector managers all attempted to cope with a very different environment than the one that shaped the original contours of the system.

As government finances improved and populations increased, the pressure to cut government waned. However, public-sector employers resorted to hard bargaining, imposing wage settlements that often barely equalled increases in the cost of living, continuing to privatize some services, and accepting strikes when necessary. Senior managers rejected a proposal for far-reaching reforms in the federal system of collective bargaining (designed to make the process less adversarial).

The Canadian system (or systems) of public-sector collective bargaining has become well established. Even in their most hostile periods, governments have not sought to remove the basic rights of public-sector employees to collective representation indefinitely. In the past, they were comfortable in removing bargaining rights temporarily to reduce deficits or to contain inflation or tax increases. The *Health Services and Support—Facilities Subsector Bargaining Association* decision of the Supreme Court presumably will restrain government action somewhat. It is clear that governments will continue to restrain public spending and employee compensation to levels they regard as appropriate. Unions will continue to resist policies such as contracting out and other measures to undermine job security (Jalette, 2005; Jalette and Warrian, 2002). Their success or failure is likely to depend on local political and economic conditions. Clearly the ability of even the largest public-sector unions to alter established government policies remains limited.

The courts probably will continue to influence the development of public-sector collective bargaining. It is now clear that the *Charter of Rights and Freedoms* protects the right to unionize and bargain collectively. It is too early to state how those protections will expand in the future, but it is unlikely that governments will be able to impose collective agreements as freely as they have in the past. The Court decision will protect public-sector workers more effectively than Canada's commitment to the International Labour Organization declaration on freedom of association and right to bargain collectively.

Indeed, ILO investigators have ruled that the federal and provincial governments have not met ILO obligations several times (Swimmer and Bartkiw, 2003).

A new factor is the impact of demography and the related increases for public services, especially health care. Shortages are predicted for a number of public-sector occupations. In 2001–2002, nurses in most provinces obtained substantial wage increases to attract and retain members of the profession. Other groups have tried without success to emulate their gains. However, for the first time in more than 30 years, some public-sector unions may have substantial power in negotiations based on labour market conditions. By 2007, only a handful of unions had been able to capitalize on these circumstances. This suggests conversely that bargaining will be tougher for other public employees in occupations less in demand.

Finally, a former public-sector union leader suggests that unions must be much more willing to abandon their traditional adversarial mentality if they are to have any hope of achieving tangible gains for their members (Fryer, 1995). It is argued that the economic realities of the 1990s gave governments very little choice but to reduce the level and scope of the public sector. While recognizing that problem solving is a two-way street, Fryer argues that public-sector unions can be most effective by attempting to work together with governments to bring about necessary changes while protecting the interests of their members. A report to the federal government suggested policies to reduce the adversarial nature of bargaining (Fryer, 2001). In the summer of 2003, a bill adopting some of those suggestions had passed the House of Commons. The Public Service Alliance of Canada opposed these changes, largely because of possible effects on bargaining structures, signalling limited interest in more co-operative labour relations (for U.S. trends in public-sector co-operation, see Thomason and Burton, 2003). When asked to contribute to this debate, neither labour nor management was interested in fundamental change.

Collective bargaining can still flourish, even in the face of public-sector decline. It has proven resilient in private-sector industries, like textiles and clothing, which have been in a state of decline and restructuring for decades. Indeed, meaningful collective bargaining can assist the process of change to the benefit of all participants. Such a scenario is possible in the public sector if both parties are prepared to abandon old habits. This happened in the situation described in the opening vignette. For employers this means refraining from legislative intervention that eliminates wage negotiations, ends legal strikes, and otherwise manipulates the rules in a way guaranteed to sow mistrust and anger. For unions it means accepting that the expansion years of the 1960s and 1970s are over and adjusting to the economic and political realities of the new century.

Questions

1. Explain the role consultation played in the development of public-sector collective bargaining.

2. Describe the key differences between private- and public-sector employers, and discuss the implications of these differences for collective bargaining in the public sector.

3. Why is the question of dispute resolution procedures such an important issue in the public sector?

4. "Public employees should have the right to strike." Discuss.

5. "Public-sector wage controls are justified by the necessity of keeping public-sector wage increases behind private-sector wage increases." Discuss.

6. Describe the changes in the role of government during the past 15 years, and indicate the implications of these changes for public-sector collective bargaining.

7. If you were a public-sector union leader, how would you respond to the changing role of government in order to best advance the interests of union members?

Weblinks

Canadian Union of Public Employees:
www.cupe.ca

Canadian Union of Postal Workers:
www.cupw-sttp.org

Human Resources and Social Development Canada:
www.hrsdc.gc.ca

British Columbia Public Sector Employers' Council:
www.fin.gov.bc.ca/psec

Public Service Alliance of Canada:
www.psac.com

Public Service Labour Relations Board:
www.pslrb-crtfp.gc.ca

Québec secrétariat du Conseil du trésor:
www.tresor.gouv.qc.ca/en/index.asp

Chapter 16

Union–Management Relations in Québec

Esther Déom and Jean-Noël Grenier in collaboration with Marie-Pierre Beaumont

The evolution of labour–management relations in Québec can be understood only with reference to the specific social and historical contexts within which Québec society has developed from the time of the British conquest to the contemporary period. As is well known, Québec forms the only predominantly French-speaking society in North America. As such, Québec has built its institutional framework for work and employment by borrowing from the American model for the purpose of collective bargaining and labour–management relations (the *Wagner Act* model) and from Northern Europe in the field of labour market policy-making. Indeed, while labour–management relations are arms-length at the level of the workplace, Québec has built institutions for co-operation and consensus related to economic growth, training, and economic adjustment.

A second historical feature has been the strong role played by the state in promoting control of key industries by French-speaking entrepreneurs, and state involvement in the development of strategic economic sectors. The two features can be thought of today as part of a legacy of nationalism and corporatism that was strongly influenced by the Catholic Church until the 1960s. This legacy was challenged during the Quiet Revolution of the 1960s, but corporatism and consensus-building remain profoundly embedded in the Québec industrial relations system.

Since the Quiet Revolution and the election of the first PQ government in 1976, nationalism has been shaped by economic and social issues rather than by the conservative agenda of the Catholic Church. As will be seen in the following section of this chapter, the industrial relations institutions are challenged today by the deregulation of trade and profound changes in the labour market.

This chapter is divided into three sections. The first provides the reader with the evolution of the socio-political and economic contexts that have shaped labour–management relations in Québec. The second deals with employer and employee associations. The third presents some particular features of Québec's public policies on work, such as pay equity legislation.

THE SOCIAL, POLITICAL, AND ECONOMIC CONTEXT

Three key factors have to be kept in mind when trying to understand the functioning of labour–management relations in Québec: nationalism, state interventionism, and the political strength of the labour movement.

The first factor stems from the fact that, in 2007, 82 percent of Québec's 7.7 million people were French-speaking and surrounded by more than 300 million English-speaking neighbours. Nationalism has been a permanent feature of Québec's society since the British conquest of Canada in 1759, and Québec's political, religious, and intellectual leaders have always nurtured the instinct of survival among the population. Such strong nationalistic sentiment exists even among citizens who want to remain part of Canada.

The second factor—the very active role played by the provincial government in all aspects of Québec's economic and social activities—is a phenomenon that started in the early 1960s during a period that historians have called Québec's Quiet Revolution. It later gained considerable momentum under the leadership of a ruling provincial party (the Parti Québécois, or PQ) that seeks to achieve full sovereignty for Québec. A good indicator of this reality is the fact that the share of Gross Domestic Product related to government activities was 54.6 percent in Québec in 1995 while the Canadian figure was 47.9 percent and the U.S. figure was 33.2 percent (Treff and Perry, 1998).[1]

The third factor—the political strength of the labour movement—is a by-product of the previous one. That strength still exists in 2007, even in the face of a hostile economic environment in the manufacturing sector (Labrosse, 2007). The labour movement's political power is not the result of formal relationships with a specific party, as is the case in the rest of Canada with the labour ties to the NDP, nor is it caused by the ability of labour organizations to mobilize voters during elections, although this can happen sporadically. Instead it comes from two sources. First, the neo-corporatist ideology that prevails in Québec enhances the capacity of labour organizations to influence governments. For example, after the failure of the Meech Lake Accord, leaders of central labour organizations were part of the constitutional commission that was set up by the Québec government to examine various scenarios for the place of Québec within Canada. Second, the centralized nature of collective dealings between employers and unions under the Decree System (see Exhibit 16.1) or in key sectors of the economy such as construction and the public sector yields considerable influence to labour organizations in Québec.

Exhibit 16.1
Basic Functioning of the Decree System

Step one: Either a very large firm or a group of small firms of the same economic sector gathered into an association bargain a collective agreement with the local union that represents their employees. This is done under the general rules of the *Labour Code*.

Step two: If the employers and the local union are interested in having the basic terms of their collective agreement (wages, hours of work, working days, vacations with pay, social security benefits, classification of operations, and classes of employees and employers) extended to the whole economic sector, they petition the minister of

---

labour to this effect. The parties involved must also determine the scope of the decree by defining the type of activity that will be covered as well as the geographical area, whether the whole province or just a region.

Step three: The text of the agreement is sent to the minister of labour, who publishes it in the *Gazette officielle du Québec* and in one French and one English newspaper. Third parties have 30 days to file any objections.

Step four: The minister, "if he deems the provisions of the agreement have acquired a preponderant significance and importance for establishing conditions of labour, without serious inconvenience resulting from the competition of outside countries or the other provinces, may recommend the approval of the petition... with such changes as are deemed expedient, and the passing of a decree for such purpose" (section 6 of the legislation). The minister has the discretionary power to change some provisions of the agreement.

Step five: If the minister approves the petition, a joint committee is formed with equal numbers of representatives from both the employers and the unions who signed the agreement. The minister may add an equal number recommended by employers and employees who are not parties to the agreement. The committee appoints a general manager, secretary, and inspectors, and it acts on behalf of employees in the enforcement in the courts. The committee's operating costs are mainly covered by a levy of one-half of 1 percent of the employers' payroll and of the employees' salaries. The joint committee negotiates the renewal of the decree, making the extension system a type of multi-employer, and sometimes multi-union, collective bargaining.

Conservative Nationalism (1900–1960)

Until the early 1960s, Québec's nationalism was based on the preservation of two fundamental values: the French language and the Catholic religion. The Catholic Church had a strong hand in almost every aspect of Québec's socio-economic life, and it played a major role in shaping the population's attitudes and behaviours toward work, business activities, and labour unions.

In the first half of the 20th century, although rural values still predominated, industrialization was progressing rapidly and the number of factory workers was rising accordingly. On the business side, people who were interested in setting up their own private commercial enterprises were often discouraged from doing so because the accumulation of wealth was considered sinful by the Catholic Church. The few students who attended post-secondary institutions were mainly oriented toward theology, medicine, and law. As a result, very few French-speaking Québecers worked as supervisors or were found on companies' executive boards. Rather, the bulk of the population was working as cheap labour for businesses that were run by English-speaking Canadians and Americans.

The Catholic Church had finally accepted the idea that workers could form labour unions, although Catholic leaders did not want workers to join locals of international unions for two major reasons: "These organizations did not share the language, nor the values nor the culture of French Canadian Catholic workers" (Babcock, 1973), and "they were socialistic since they were advocating measures like free and mandatory public

schools, free universal Medicare, old age pensions, and employers' liability for occupational injuries" (Rouillard, 1989). For this reason, the Catholic Church took it upon itself
to set up independent "confessional" (religious) labour unions run by French-speaking
leaders. At the same time, similar confessional unions were also being established in countries like France, Belgium, and the Netherlands. The fear of Marxism explains why the
Catholic Church became involved in labour relations throughout the world. But in
Québec, the attack on international unions was dictated more by the Catholic Church's
fear of losing its influence and control over vital institutions such as schools, hospitals,
and the welfare system than by the fact that existing international unions were leaning
toward Marxism.

As one might expect, confessional unions were not militant. They very seldom
engaged in strikes, and when they intended to do so, their action had to receive prior
authorization from the local union's chaplain. These organizations accounted for 20 to
40 percent of total union membership in Québec between 1930 and 1960 (Rouillard,
1989).

Despite the conservatism that prevailed in Québec society, the provincial government introduced two pieces of legislation that favoured the development of union activities. In 1924, the *Professional Syndicates Act* gave individuals engaged in the same
profession or trade the right to set up associations and register them as civil entities. The
Act recognized that an important function of these associations was the enhancement of
the economic interests of their members, and it gave them the right to sign legal contracts
and enforce them in courts.

In 1934, the *Act Respecting Collective Agreement Decrees* gave the minister of labour
the power to extend some provisions of collective agreements (namely monetary clauses)
to nonunion employers of the same economic sector. The main goals of the legislation
were, first, to give nonunion workers the benefits of better working conditions found in
collective agreements, and second, to eliminate competition over wages and working conditions in low-wage sectors characterized by a large number of small and medium-sized
firms operating in highly competitive markets.

The Decree System described in Exhibit 16.1 is still in force, but its importance has
been substantially reduced since the enactment of the Free Trade Agreement with the
United States and the slackening of interprovincial trade regulations within Canada. This
situation has led Québec employers' associations to successfully lobby the Québec government to remove from the jurisdiction of the Decree System those industrial sectors in
which Québec firms compete with those located outside the province. As a consequence,
only 18 decrees were in force at the end of 2006, most of them in the service sector of the
economy (i.e., security guards, maintenance of public buildings, hairdressers, automobile
mechanics, solid waste disposal, and local road hauling). These decrees covered 9034
employers and 79 922 employees, a substantial decrease from 1990 when the then-existing
34 decrees covered 16 094 employers and 142 704 employees.

Despite the adoption in 1943 by the Liberal Party of legislation proclaiming the right
of workers to unionize and the obligation of employers to collectively bargain with the
certified representative of their employees (*Labour Relations Act*), the persistence of conservative values among the population and the overt opposition of the Union Nationale
government, which stayed in power between 1944 and 1960, made it very difficult for the
labour movement to make any significant progress until the mid-1960s.

State Interventionism and Labour's New Legitimacy and Militancy (1960–1976)

The Quiet Revolution: A Modernized Form of Nationalism The return of the provincial Liberal Party to power in 1960 signalled the beginning of Québec's Quiet Revolution. From 1960, a strong impetus was given to the modernization of Québec's institutions through the development of state-owned enterprises and the creation of a professional civil service that replaced the old spoils system. It also provided a more favourable environment for the labour movement, whose leaders were intellectually very close to some influential ministers of the party in power. One of the key pieces of legislation adopted by the Liberal government was the replacement of the *Labour Relations Act* by a modernized *Labour Code*, which included many provisions facilitating the expansion of collective bargaining rights. Among other things, civil servants and professional workers were granted the right to join a union, all public-sector employees except police and firefighters were granted the right to strike, and conciliation procedures were simplified so as to make it less cumbersome for unions to declare a legal strike. As a result, the number of unionized workers increased by 42.8 percent between 1963 and 1966, and the unionization rate went from 30.5 percent in 1960 to 35.7 percent in 1966 (Rouillard, 1989: 289).

The modernization of Québec would not mean an abandonment of nationalism, as was demonstrated by the slogan adopted by the Liberals in the 1960 electoral campaign, "Maîtres chez nous" (Masters of Our Own Destiny). A new form of nationalism emerged based on social and economic development rather than on the preservation of religious and conservative values. This new form of nationalism placed at its centre the role of the State in economic and social development and promoted the emergence of institutions to further these goals. The nationalization of private hydroelectric companies, which were integrated into Hydro-Québec in 1962, was the first expression of this "economic liberation" of French-speaking Québecers. The immediate effect of this decision was to allow many French-speaking engineers (and other professionals) to make a career in a company that would soon be identified as the leader of Québec's economic development and recognized as a world-class organization.

Two important economic institutions were also created during that period. The General Investment Corporation (Société générale de financement du Québec) was to accelerate industrial development by promoting and financing Québec's companies. The Québec Deposit and Investment Fund (Caisse de dépôt et placement du Québec) was to manage the assets of the Québec Pension Plan, which had been established as a separate entity from the Canada Pension Plan. Over time, these institutions have become very powerful financial instruments in the hands of the Québec government.

The role of the Québec government as a leading agent of change in socio-economic development was put on the back burner in 1966 when, surprisingly, the Union Nationale party regained power for a final four-year stint. The loss of the election led to a split within the Liberal Party: the more nationalistic elements left to form the Parti Québécois. The Union Nationale government did not abolish any of the institutions that had been put in place during the Quiet Revolution. It just slowed down the rate of involvement of the State in the economy. Unions, for their part, continued to gain new members in both the private and public sectors, and the unionization rate climbed to 37.6 percent in 1971 (Rouillard, 1989: 289).

The Liberal Party returned to power between 1970 and 1976 and, although it did not create new financial or economic institutions, it did actively stimulate Québec's socio-economic development through massive public investments in education, health, road construction, hydroelectricity, and social programs. Working conditions of public-sector employees were also improved considerably as a result of the militancy of workers, many of whose jobs were taking on increased importance in the day-to-day life of Québec citizens.

Radicalization of the Labour Movement At the end of the 1960s and throughout most of the 1970s, many labour organizations in Québec adopted radical ideological positions. Some of them—notably the former confessional federation, which had become a lay organization in 1960 as the Confederation of National Trade Unions (Confédération des syndicats nationaux, or CNTU), and the Centrale des syndicats du Québec (CSQ)—went so far as to suggest that Québec become a truly socialistic, independent country. Such radicalization led to a schism within the CNTU in 1972 as some 35 000 members left to set up a new federation.

Even the more pragmatic Québec Federation of Labour (Fédération des travailleurs et travailleuses du Québec, or QFL) flirted with radicalism. At its 1973 general meeting, the QFL president exhorted its troops to "the inescapable battle against the existing economic and political regime" (Fournier, 1994: 91). However, time and events would show that the QFL was seeking the electoral defeat of the ruling Liberal Party rather than the destruction of the capitalist system.

The ideological radicalization of labour organizations combined with the inflationary period that followed the oil-price shock of 1973 and the political agitation created by the Front de libération du Québec (FLQ)—a small group of individuals who were seeking Québec's political independence by violent means—helped to create a very chaotic social situation in the 1970s. That situation was exacerbated by the numerous conflicts that took place during the renewal of collective agreements in the construction and public sectors.

In the 1972 negotiations of the public sector, labour organizations representing all categories of personnel (civil servants, teachers, hospital workers, and government agency workers) formed a Common Front to back their monetary demands. They staged an 11-day general work stoppage that was finally ended by special legislative intervention. A few weeks later, the leaders of the three main labour federations were sentenced to jail for six months because they had recommended that their members not respect court injunctions. In the next round of negotiations, public-sector unions changed their strategy and opted for sector-based strikes. Once again, injunctions were issued, labour unions defied them, and special legislative intervention was used.

The Quiet Revolution Rekindled: The First PQ Mandate (1976–1985)

The 1976 election of the Parti Québécois led to a resurgence of Québec's economic nationalism. Reaffirming the ideal of the Quiet Revolution, the PQ government put forward an economic development strategy based on self-sufficiency, i.e., the extension of ownership and control of enterprises by Québec interests. One of the pillars of this strategy was the nationalization of the U.S.-owned Asbestos Corporation. Also part of that strategy was the creation of a financial institution that would provide venture capital to private enterprises—the Société de développement industriel du Québec (Québec development corporation), renamed Invest Quebec (Investissement Québec) in 1998.

These and other government initiatives such as the workers' Solidarity Fund QFL (see Exhibit 16.2) provided considerable help to firms controlled by French-speaking executives (such as Bombardier, Quebecor, Cascades, Canam Manac, and Culinar). By the mid-1980s, the expression "Québec Inc." became part of the financial vocabulary in Québec (Fraser, 1987).

Exhibit 16.2
The Québec Federation of Labour's Solidarity Fund

In 1982, the president of the QFL brought forward the idea of setting up a labour-sponsored investment fund that would help preserve and create jobs. At first received coolly by the government, business leaders, and even some trade unionists within the QFL, the idea became feasible when the Québec government adopted enabling legislation on June 23, 1983. The Québec Federation of Labour's Solidarity Fund officially began its operations on February 3, 1984, after the government had injected $10 million.

KEY CHARACTERISTICS OF THE FUND

- Sixty percent of the Fund must be invested as venture capital in small and medium-sized firms based in Québec. The rest is invested in bonds and equities.
- The Fund participates in many local, regional, and sectoral venture capital funds with other financial institutions and community or co-operative groups.
- Value of Fund's assets: $7.24 billion; investments in Québec firms: $3.7 billion in 1680 Québec firms; number of shareholders: 574 794 (May 2007).
- Permanent and temporary staff of 400 employees.

INVESTMENT POLICY

Before making an investment, the Fund does an analysis that includes social, economic, and financial considerations. Once a decision to invest has been made, it carries specific conditions:

- The company must reveal financial situation to employees.
- The company must allow employees to attend two- or three-day courses on subjects such as understanding financial statements and analysis of the employer's market situation.
- Courses are offered through an education and economic development foundation, largely funded by employer contributions from firms in which the Fund has invested.
- Present on a company's board of directors, but never as a majority partner except under exceptional circumstances, the Fund ensures employees keep receiving financial information.
- The Fund plays a key role in promoting labour training and a good climate of industrial relations.

The government also initiated a series of socio-economic summits between 1977 and 1984, aimed at establishing a permanent dialogue among employers' organizations, unions, the co-op movement, and community groups. The 17 sector-based summits were aimed at solving industry problems such as the lack of competitiveness of exports, while the two general summits were exercises in consensus-building to reflect this party's corporate ideology. One of the positive benefits of the general summits was an easing of the social climate at the end of the 1970s. The "friendliness" of the PQ toward organized labour was also demonstrated when the charges laid against labour organizations in the aftermath of public-sector negotiations were dropped by the newly elected government.

The government also introduced a series of amendments to the *Labour Code*, most of which were requested by the QFL and welcomed by all labour unions, even those that were ideologically opposed to the government. Among the most important amendments were anti-strikebreaking provisions (see Exhibit 16.3); an automatic deduction of union dues from the paycheques of all employees included in the bargaining unit (whether or not they were union members); provisions for first collective agreement arbitration; voluntary conciliation; and certain obligations imposed on labour unions such as secret ballots to be held for the election of officers, the approval of a collective agreement, and strike authorization.

Despite ideological criticisms by two of the four major labour federations (the CNTU and the Teachers' Federation) most private-sector union activists believed that the PQ's amendments would help the development of union activities in Québec. The relationships between the PQ and public-sector unions, however, were not so friendly, and they had negative political consequences for the government.

Exhibit 16.3
Anti-Strikebreaking Provisions

Article 109.1 of the *Labour Code* reads in part as follows:

For the duration of a strike declared in accordance with this Code or a lockout, every employer is prohibited from:

a) Utilizing the services of a person to discharge the duties of an employee who is a member of the bargaining unit then on strike or locked out when such person was hired between the day the negotiation stage begins and the end of the strike or lockout;

b) Utilizing, in the establishment where the strike or lockout has been declared, the services of a person employed by another employer or the services of another contractor to discharge the duties of an employee who is a member of the bargaining unit on strike or lockout;

c) Utilizing, in an establishment where a strike or lockout has been declared, the services of an employee who is a member of the bargaining unit then on strike or locked out unless certain specified conditions have been met;

d) Utilizing, in another of his establishments, the services of an employee who is a member of the bargaining unit then on strike or lockout;

e) Utilizing, in an establishment where a strike or lockout has been declared, the services of an employee he employs in another establishment;

> f) Utilizing, in an establishment where a strike or lockout has been declared, the services of a person other than an employee he employs in another establishment, except where the employees of the latter establishment are members of the bargaining unit on strike or locked out;
>
> g) Utilizing, in an establishment where a strike or lockout has been declared, the services of an employee he employs in the establishment to discharge the duties of an employee who is a member of the bargaining unit on strike or lockout.

The first encounter between the PQ and public-sector unions came in 1979–1980, a few months prior to the referendum on Québec's political future. Despite very generous offers made by the government early in negotiations to prevent the usual social crisis accompanying the renewal of public-sector collective agreements, public-sector unions maintained their traditional strategy and engaged in a series of militant actions. Special legislation was used and, once again, the settlements were reached in a context of social chaos. Some PQ political strategists affirmed that the loss of the referendum (by a 60 percent to 40 percent margin) was in part caused by the militant action of labour organizations in the public sector, which antagonized both the natural clientele of the PQ (public-sector employees) and the population in general.

Despite this political defeat, the PQ easily won the 1981 election. However, it returned to power in the midst of a severe economic recession that would once again put the PQ on a collision course with the public-sector unions. In 1981, the president of the Treasury Board asked the unions to forfeit the wage increase that was scheduled for the last year of the collective agreement (1982). After the unions declined the government's proposal, the latter enacted special legislation that suspended the collective bargaining process and unilaterally imposed working conditions for the next three years. Even worse, in the first three months of 1983, the salaries of most public-sector employees were reduced in such a way as to allow the government to recoup the monetary increments it had given the previous year.

An Era of Restraint (1985–1994): Economic Nationalism, Social Contracts, and the Recession

Labour–Management Collaboration in the Private Sector The Liberal Party returned to power during the economic recovery that followed the 1980–1982 recession. They would be re-elected in 1989 before once again becoming the Opposition in 1994. Although the Liberals had been very critical of the increased size of government as a result of too much state intervention in the economy under the PQ administration, their actual behaviour did not match their words once they were elected. They made the same political decisions that they were decrying while in opposition, such as bailing out a shipyard or a ski resort (Gélinas, 2002).

In regard to union–management policy, the Liberals took a slightly different approach but the objective was the same: the pursuit of union–management dialogue to enhance the economic competitiveness of Québec firms. The strategy of industrial clustering developed by the ministers of industry, commerce, science, and technology, inspired by the work of Michael E. Porter of the Harvard Business School (1990), pursued the same objectives as the sector-based economic summits of the PQ; it even took them one step further.

The minister was an ardent believer in union involvement in the operation of firms, and he promoted the practice of "social contracts" between unions and management. These contracts took the form of memorandums of agreement, which complemented collective agreements (Gouvernement du Québec, 1993b). To favour the diffusion of social contracts, the government amended the *Labour Code* to allow collective agreements to last for longer than three years (except for first agreements). Although government financial participation was not a necessary condition for a social contract, it was common practice for the Québec Development Corporation to require that most of the elements of the social contract be present before investing in a particular company.

The minister also established a program favouring the development of worker–shareholder co-ops, which enabled workers to collectively own up to 30 percent of the shares of a company and have representation on its board of directors. The acquisition of shares was facilitated by the Québec Development Corporation's guaranteeing loans to workers. Some 30 such enterprises existed in 1997 (Grant and Lévesque, 1997: 247). Work co-ops in general are more numerous in Québec than anywhere else in Canada (Quarter and Melnyk, 1989).

The Québec government also used its fiscal policy to promote greater employer–employee partnership in small and medium-sized firms. The plan, translated as "workers' participation scheme in a total quality management context," provided tax deductions for both employees and employers who became involved in a profit-sharing plan.

If it is true that the Liberal government was instrumental in fostering a renewed dialogue between management and unions in the private sector, many unions were also aware of the necessity of committing themselves to workplace transformation in order to save and create jobs. The CNTU, for instance, concluded that unions should even propose changes to achieve better productivity rather than remain reactive and wait for employers' proposals for adjusting to the new economic reality.

The Public Sector's Financial Crisis One of the first tasks awaiting the newly elected Liberal government in 1985 was the renewal of the collective agreements in the public sector. Even if the level of militancy was not as high as in previous rounds of negotiations, hospital unions were nonetheless in the process of threatening to resort to some job actions when the government adopted legislation preventing them from doing so. The legislation also stipulated some very harsh penalties against union members, union officers, and the union itself in case of an illegal strike in the health sector. As a result, the government was able to reach a deal with the unions without having to face a series of job actions or strike threats as is usually the case in such circumstances.

In 1989, the government used the provisions of the above-mentioned legislation against nurses and other hospital employees who struck illegally during the collective-agreement negotiations that took place during the electoral campaign. The Liberal government easily won that election.

When the most severe economic recession since the Great Depression hit Canada in 1990, it had very negative consequences for the government's financial situation. As was the case in other Canadian provinces and with the federal government, Québec's public-sector employees would be the preferred target of the restrictive measures since their compensation represented approximately 50 percent of the provincial budget.[2]

First, the Québec government asked all public-sector unions to postpone, until June 1993, the renewal of collective agreements that expired in December 1991. In exchange, it granted wage increases of 4 percent over that period. The unions reluctantly accepted, but not without publicly demonstrating against the government's original proposals, which were even more drastic.

Second, in January 1993 the government enacted legislation that froze public-sector salaries for two years and gave public employers the authorization to reduce their wage bill by 1 percent annually. The law also allowed municipalities to be covered by the legislation if they so chose. Additional legislation required all government departments and public agencies to reduce their supervisory personnel by 20 percent in the next three years (1993–1996) and to reduce the rest of their workforce by 12 percent over the next five years (1993–1998).

Public-sector unions felt betrayed by these measures because they had already accepted an extension of their collective agreements. The unions recognized that Québec had serious financial problems, but they claimed that the government could solve its problems by modifying taxation so as to eliminate many tax evasion schemes and increase taxes on higher revenues and corporate profits, rather than by realizing short-term economies on the backs of public employees. They tried to mobilize their members and the population against the government, but to no avail. One year later, with an election looming, the austerity plan was abandoned and the Liberals ran a record-high $6-billion deficit in 1994. The government was defeated in the September 1994 election.

An Era of Retrenchment (1994–2003): The Carrot and Stick Approach and the PQ's Political Agenda

The Zero-Deficit Target and the Labour-Cost Reduction Strategy The electoral victory stirred up the PQ's interest in a new referendum, which the new government scheduled for October 30, 1995. However, a major stumbling block stood on the road to this fateful encounter with the population: the renewal of the 450 000 public employees' collective agreements, a task that had always been very difficult for any government, be it Liberal or Parti Québécois. On the positive side for the new government, all but one of the central trade union organizations in Québec had officially endorsed the objective of an independent status for Québec. On the negative side was the financial situation of the government. The ratio of Québec's debt to its GDP had risen from 28.3 percent in 1990 to 44.7 percent in 1995, the second highest among Canadian provinces.

One month prior to the referendum, and without any demonstration of strength on either side, the government and the various public-sector and broader public-sector (health and education) unions reached an accord whose major features were the following: repeal of the legislation ordering the yearly reductions of 1 percent in total compensation; lump-sum payments representing 0.5 percent of employees' salaries for 1996; salary increases of 1 percent to be awarded on January 1 in 1997 and 1998; reduction of actuarial penalties on pension plans to encourage early retirements; no change in clauses that would give public employers additional managerial flexibility; and collective agreements to be valid until June 30, 1998. The total cost of these measures was estimated at $930 million ($770 million for salary increases and $160 million for early retirement provisions).

A few weeks after the referendum was lost by the narrowest of margins (50.4 to 49.6 percent), the premier resigned. Under a new leader, the government's utmost priority became the fight against budgetary deficits. The provincial government had to restore the province's public finances if it wanted to convince the Québec population and key monetary institutions that an independent Québec could be economically viable. Therefore, it set out a strategy to achieve a zero-deficit budget for the fiscal year 1999–2000. Accordingly, the government prepared a budget that drastically cut various programs and set the goal of a recurrent reduction of $800 million in unionized public employees' labour costs starting in the fiscal year 1997–1998. It also requested an additional reduction of $100 million in global compensation for the year 1996–1997.

How was the new premier going to sell such an idea to labour organizations? After a first proposal suggesting that public employees' gross salaries be reduced by 6 percent was massively rejected by the unions, an agreement was reached in which the government's objectives of labour-cost reduction could be achieved through a program of voluntary retirements. It was expected that some 15 000 employees would be permanently removed from the public sector before July 1, 1997.

There was a serious misunderstanding, however, over how to reduce the personnel in the health and education sectors because of the constraints imposed by existing collective agreements. Hence, the government came forward with specific proposals to remove these constraints. The unions systematically refused to have their collective agreements altered and threatened to resort to work stoppages. The government counterattacked by introducing special legislation, which stipulated that if its proposals were not accepted, an automatic 6 percent reduction of salaries would ensue. In the end, although legislation had to be adopted in order to cover certain categories of nonunion personnel and some recalcitrant unions in colleges, an agreement was reached with most groups. During the final talks, though, the government dropped most of its demands about modifications to the collective agreements.

This approach to labour-cost reduction in the public sector led to very important organizational problems. First, because the program was voluntary, many more individuals left their jobs than was necessary (37 000 instead of 15 000). Second, the voluntary nature of the early retirement program led to the loss of many experienced employees, including many in services that were vital to the population, such as nursing. Despite the unpopularity of many reforms that were introduced, the PQ was re-elected in November 1998.

Regarding the renewal of collective agreements that had expired in June 1998, for the first time since 1989 the collective bargaining process was going to unfold according to the normal "rules of the game"—there was no economic recession justifying the extension of existing agreements or the enactment of special legislation suspending the collective bargaining process, nor was a political referendum looming. Moreover, the zero-deficit budget had been reached one year ahead of schedule, and Québec's economy was in much better shape than in the preceding rounds of negotiations.

At the start of negotiations, the expectations of public-sector unions were very high, as they anticipated that their members could share in the new prosperity and recoup some of the purchasing power that had been lost in the last decade. For its part, the government affirmed that one of its priorities was to lower income taxes so that all citizens could benefit from recent economic growth. As a result, public employees had to accept wage increases that were in line with what was being offered in the economy in general and forget about any "catching up" effort. Using the Compensation Research and Information Institute's 1998 Annual Report, the government claimed that public-sector employees' pay was on par with that of their private-sector counterparts and that its actual offers maintained this parity.

The first test of the government's wage policy came in the summer of 1999 when nurses belonging to the Québec Federation of Nurses engaged in 23 days of illegal strikes despite the threat of stiff penalties. The Federation was seeking three main objectives: a reduction of the nurses' workloads, since the latter had increased considerably as a result of both the drastic health care reform and the massive early retirement; better job security; and better pay (Malo and Grenier, forthcoming). They were successful on the first two counts, but, despite the great show of sympathy by the population for the nurses' cause, the government did not make any concession on salaries and enacted special legislation ordering the nurses back to work.

In the fall of that year, negotiations with the rest of public-sector unions resumed (including the nurses), and an agreement was reached just prior to Christmas without any overt conflict. The government agreed to increase its salary offer slightly to 9 percent covering the four-year period 1999–2002.

The PQ government, having dropped drastically in public opinion polls in 2001 and early 2002, decided to wait until the spring of 2003 before calling an election. It also convinced public-sector unions to extend their collective agreements one more year during which an extensive pay-equity operation would be completed throughout the whole public sector. Nonetheless, the Liberal Party won the April 14, 2003, election despite gathering almost the same percentage of votes as in 1998. The fact that a third party—the Québec Democratic Alliance (Alliance démocratique du Québec) that was set up in 1993 in the aftermath of the doomed Meech Lake Accord—collected 18 percent of the popular vote contributed to the defeat of the PQ.

Consolidation and Restructuring (2003–2007): The Liberal Party's Political Agenda

During the campaign, the Liberals loudly proclaimed that, if they were elected, they would substantially reduce the role played by the government in the economy and proceed to a review and rationalization of the public sector (including education and health care). In fact the Liberals proposed nothing less than a radical transformation to a more liberal state in which the public sector would play a secondary role to private-sector initiatives, even in areas normally left to public-sector organizations. The new premier went so far as to propose that the model of state governance inherited from the Quiet Revolution be set aside in favour of a leaner and non-interventionist approach to social and economic management. Clearly, the first budget adopted in June 2003 demonstrated this intent since grants and subsidies to enterprises were reduced by 25 percent. In terms of labour–management relations in the private and public sectors, the same message was delivered through a series of other budgetary and political decisions.

Convinced that the *Labour Code* provisions (article 45) regarding subcontracting presented an impediment to labour market flexibility, the Liberal government proceeded to modify article 45 so as to allow employers to subcontract work more freely. The new provisions stipulate that in cases of subcontracting parts of an operation, the union certification as well as the existing collective agreement would become redundant for the targeted jobs. Needless to say, the government antagonized the entire labour movement, which reached levels of mobilization rarely seen since the high point of militancy in the 1970s.

This was, however, only the opening round of a wider program of restructuring that would target the public sector more directly. Here the Liberal government's approach was no different from that seen elsewhere in Canada and other Western democracies. Its action took form at two interrelated levels: legislative change and the restructuring of work (Grenier and Malo, forthcoming). Simply put, the Liberal government had in mind legislative changes aimed at consolidating and deepening gains made by previous governments and especially those of the previous PQ zero-deficit agenda.

Most prominent on the legislative front were the modifications brought to the health care sector. The Liberal government imposed the merger of bargaining units without the consent of unions and forced the partial decentralization of negotiations over matters related to the organization of work and human resource management. Under the new rules, local bargaining over 26 items such as shift scheduling, job descriptions, temporary assignments, and workloads must be achieved without the right to strike, and any agreement must meet a zero-cost test. Failure to reach such an agreement within two years leads to final-offer compulsory arbitration, and awards must be based on a zero-cost approach.

While these two changes attracted media attention, other legislative initiatives also signalled the Liberal government's intent to weaken public-sector unions and to maintain a tight lid on cost increases. For example, Bills 7 and 8 made it illegal for home-based day-care workers and for those providing at-home health and social services to join a union.[3] These laws applied retroactively so as to destroy the emerging unionization movement for these mostly female workers who were in the process of joining either the CNTU or the CSQ. Other legislative changes directed at the public sector were defined more narrowly. The government legislated the creation of an agency for public–private partnerships and decreed that all projects had to be submitted to review under closely defined criteria of efficiency and short-term cost savings.

Other legislative initiatives included the government's Modernization Plan, which called for a 20 percent reduction in the size of the public service (through non-replacement of 50 percent of departures from the civil service), the merger of many government services, and the centralization of decisions regarding service delivery and staffing arrangements into the hands of a new agency (Centre de services partagés du Québec, or CSPQ). A new human resources strategy was developed in support of the Modernization Plan. Strategy set the framework for the reorganization of work, requiring labour-cost reductions, job mergers, and greater numerical and functional flexibility from civil service staff. Taken together, these changes have set a framework within which subcontracting becomes the preferred alternative for the delivery of public services.

Needless to say, the labour movement reacted strongly to these initiatives. Its response, however, took two traditional forms. The first response was political and preceded the public-sector bargaining round of 2005. In a show of unity not seen since the late 1970s and early 1980s, all labour federations joined together and with other social organizations in a movement of protest that culminated with a siege of the Québec National Assembly in the hope of forestalling the government's legislative agenda. While this mobilization did not bring about immediate results, it did lead to the formation of a Secretariat for the protection of public services (Secrétariat intersyndical des services publics, or SISP) and the Réseau de vigilance.[4]

The second response of labour was in line with the sectoral and fragmented approach to public-sector collective bargaining adopted since 1985. Public-sector unions were unable to come to an agreement about a common bargaining strategy and response to the government proposals of a 6-year-term collective agreement that included wage freezes for the first two years and incorporation of the pay equity settlement in future wage hikes. Sensing the government's inclination toward legislation of a settlement, the public-sector unions avoided a general strike and based their mobilization efforts on temporary (half-day or one-day) strikes. While the unions can claim some success in slowing down the pace of reform, the Liberal government remained firm and opted for special legislation imposing the terms of a settlement that did not depart significantly from the parameters established at the outset of negotiations. Bill 142 (now known as Bill 43) also made it illegal for public-sector unions and individual workers to publicly protest against the Liberal government policies and to undertake any actions that would disrupt the "normal operations" of any public-sector establishment.[5]

In the private sector, the impetus for collaboration may grow or at least remain strong in the near future as the manufacturing sector faces the challenges of economic restructuring. This is especially true in the traditional soft industries (clothing, textiles, furniture, and shoemaking), and in the more important forestry industries. Recent plant closings and offshoring of work have resulted in the loss of more than 10 000 jobs in each subsector, and many believe these jobs will not return in the event of an eventual, but unlikely, return to prosperity. Finally, it should be noted that collaboration has not suppressed conflict in the private sector, as is demonstrated by the strikes and lockouts at Vidéotron (a cable giant in Québec), Olymel (meat packing), Station de la Petite-Rivière-Saint-François (ski resort), and Le Journal de Québec (local newspaper). In all four, the issue was restructuring of work and concessions in working conditions in exchange for short-term job security.

EMPLOYER AND EMPLOYEE ORGANIZATIONS

The next section of this chapter is devoted to describing the major labour organizations in Québec as well as the major employer organization (the Conseil du patronat du Québec). But first of all, major changes in labour market and workforce characteristics affecting union membership are briefly described.

Labour Market and Workforce Characteristics

In 2006, 65.5 percent of the Québec population over 15 years old participated in the labour force, and 8.0 percent were unemployed. In comparison, those rates for Canada are respectively 67.2 percent and 6.3 percent (Statistics Canada, 2007b). According to the Institut de la statistique du Québec (2007), the gap between the employment rate of women and men continues to decline, and the presence of women in the labour market continues to increase, irrespective of marital status or the presence of infants at home. On the other hand, the employment rate of men is stable, confirming the ongoing but now slightly slowing feminization of the Québec workforce that started decades ago. Nevertheless, as we shall see more acutely in a later section, this process occurs unevenly among industry sectors and employment statuses.

The aging of the Québec workforce continues. Workers over 55 years old have the highest employment rate increase amongst all workers—the rate was 68.8 percent between 1998 and 2006, compared to a decrease of 0.1 percent for workers 25 to 44 years old. Between 1998 and 2006, unlike in other Canadian provinces, part-time job offers increased more rapidly than full-time job offers in Québec (1.8 percent compared to 1.2 percent). During this same period, part-time job offers decreased at a rate of 0.8 percent in the rest of Canada. Indeed, part-time jobs represented 18.2 percent of all jobs in 2006 in Québec, mostly in the tertiary sector of industry, representing an increase of 20.2 percent since 1998. Temporary jobs have increased by 26 percent between 1998 and 2006, while permanent jobs have grown by only 17 percent. Finally, 13.3 percent of workers were self-employed in 2006, representing a 2 percent decrease since 1998, and 68.2 percent of the Québec workforce has completed post-secondary studies—the highest rate in Canada.

We can safely conclude that the labour market in Québec is generally characterized by the presence of educated workers, almost equally men and women, and by the ever-growing presence of older workers. In addition, more part-time and temporary jobs are created than full-time and permanent jobs, partly due to the growth of the service sector and an increased demand for flexibility from employers. In spite of these changes, union membership in Québec is stable at about 40 percent. Interestingly, the union membership rate is now higher for women than for men (Institut de la statistique du Québec, 2007).

Trade Union Structure and Membership

The Québec Federation of Labour (QFL) The Québec Federation of Labour (QFL) (Fédération des travailleurs et travailleuses du Québec) is by far the largest central organization in Québec. In 1997, it represented 37 percent of all employees covered by collective agreements falling under the jurisdiction of the provincial *Labour Code* (that is, all employees except construction workers and workers under federal jurisdiction). In 2007, the QFL website reported over 500 000 members representing 43 percent of all unionized workers in Québec. The bulk of its membership comes from the private sector, but it also has considerable strength in the municipal sector and significant representation in the parapublic sectors. The QFL's affiliates in the construction industry have always obtained the largest share in the representation elections held periodically under the *Construction Industry Labour Relations Act*. The same goes for those that come under the jurisdiction of either the *Canada Labour Code* or the *Public Service Labour Relations Act*.

Although affiliation of local unions to provincial federations such as the QFL is not mandatory under the Canadian Labour Congress's constitution, the QFL has been able to increase its percentage of CLC union affiliates substantially, from a mere 37 percent one year after the historic 1956 merger of the Trades and Labour Congress of Canada (TLC) and the Canadian Congress of Labour (CCL) to almost 100 percent today. See Table 16.1 for distribution of workers in Canada according to union affiliation.

Table 16.1 Union Membership by Congress Affiliation in Canada, 2006

Union	Workers	%
CLC[a]	3 197 600	72.0
AFL[b]–CIO[c] / CLC[a]	818 770	18.4
CLC[a] only	2 376 990	53.5
CSN[d]	284 280	6.4
CSQ[e]	123 510	2.8
CSD[f]	59 160	1.3
CCU[g]	9390	0.2
AFL–CIO only[h]	74 650	1.7
National Unions (non affiliated)	531 720	12.0
International Unions (non affiliated)	2150	0
Independent Local Organizations	158 085	3.6
Total[i]	4 441 000	100.0

[a] CLC = Canadian Labour Congress
[b] AFL = American Federation of Labour
[c] CIO = Congress of Industrial Organizations
[d] CSN = Confédération des syndicats nationaux
[e] CSQ = Centrale des syndicats du Québec
[f] CSD = Centrale des syndicats démocratiques
[g] CCU = Canadian Confederation of Unions
[h] Unions affiliated to AFL–CIO only (not affiliated to CLC)
[i] Due to rounding, sums may not always equal totals.

Source: Labour Policy and Workplace Information. 2006. Union Membership in Canada. HRSDC. www.hrsdc.gc.ca/en/lp/wid/pdf/Union_Membership.pdf (accessed April 20, 2007).

Special Status within the CLC The Québec situation of trade-union pluralism and cultural specificity has led the QFL to behave like an independent labour body. Unlike other provincial federations, the QFL must compete with three other major labour organizations to obtain union members' allegiance. This unique situation has gradually led QFL leaders to ask for additional powers and more autonomy from their parent body, the CLC.

The process of gaining more autonomy has led to an agreement in 1994 that the QFL labelled a "sovereignty-association" agreement. This agreement became a necessity because of the deterioration in relations between the QFL and CLC after the electoral failure of the QFL candidate at the CLC national convention in June 1992.

Confédération des syndicats nationaux (CSN) The Confédération des syndicats nationaux (CSN) was originally a confederation of Catholic trade unions created in 1921. At the time, it represented approximately 26 000 workers and was known as the Confédération des travailleurs catholiques du Canada (CTCC). By 2006, it included approximately 285 000 workers (see Table 16.1). In contrast to the QFL, the majority of whose members come largely from the private sector, more than 50 percent of the membership of the CSN is in the broader public sector, particularly in health care, and 60 percent of its affiliated unions have fewer than 50 members. Since its creation in 1921, the CSN has undergone profound changes in the composition of its membership, its structure, and its ideology.

At its 1960 convention, the CTCC dropped the last vestiges of its identification with the Catholic Church and renamed itself the Confédération des syndicats nationaux

(CSN). The CSN grew rapidly in size and in influence during the Quiet Revolution of the 1960s. It benefited most from the organization of professional and other salaried employees in the public service, but it also won certification campaigns over the CLC–QFL on many occasions.

The early 1970s were favourable for union radicalism within both the CSN and the QFL. One important consequence of this growing radicalism was serious splits within the CSN: the first led to the creation of the Centrale des syndicats démocratiques (CSD) in May 1972. Then, in September 1972, 30 000 civil servants also pulled out of the CSN; they decided to create an independent labour organization. One year later, some 5000 workers in the aluminum industry also left the CSN and formed another independent organization.

The loss in membership suffered by the CSN during the 1970s, as well as the severe economic crisis of the early 1980s, contributed to a reduction in the influence of the radical elements within the CSN. Once strongly opposed to co-operation with management, the CSN, as well as other labour organizations such as the QFL, are now actively involved in labour–management co-operation experiments. For example, the president of the CSN played a decisive role in the establishment of the social contract at Sammi Atlas Inc. This move from a quasi-Marxist orientation in the mid-1970s to a more pragmatic one in the mid-1980s is reflected in the themes debated by the delegates at the 1991 convention (CSN, 1992) and by the creation, in 1996, of a worker solidarity fund—Fondaction.

Centrale des syndicats démocratiques (CSD) Created in 1972, the CSD is structured on the same model as the CSN except that affiliation with professional federations and labour councils is not mandatory for local unions. Since its creation in 1972, the CSD has not significantly increased its membership. In 2006, it represented nearly 60 000 workers (see Table 16.1). As a matter of philosophy, the CSD wants to remain absolutely neutral vis-à-vis political parties. It does not profess any particular social doctrine; an article in its constitution even states that the adoption of a particular ideological orientation would require a referendum of the whole membership.

Centrale des syndicats du Québec (CSQ) The unionization of teachers in Québec dates from 1936; the first provincial federation was formed 10 years later. Like most other union organizations, the Corporation des instituteurs et institutrices catholiques du Canada had a rough time during the Duplessis regime. It dropped its confessional name in 1967 and became the Corporation des enseignants du Québec (CEQ). That year also saw the first confrontation between teachers and the provincial government, which led to the first special legislation to end a wave of teachers' strikes. Like the CSN at the beginning of the 1970s, the CEQ went through a substantial ideological reorientation. One aspect of this reorientation was the transformation of the organization from a "corporation"—in which membership was mandatory according to a government charter and restricted to elementary and secondary school teachers—to a genuine labour organization, the Centrale de l'enseignement du Québec, representing all categories of workers in the field of education, from caretakers to classroom teachers at the elementary, secondary, and post-secondary levels. As a consequence, the CEQ became involved alongside CSN, CSD, and QFL affiliates in representation elections for certain categories of employees. In 2000, the CEQ changed its name to become the Centrale des syndicats du Québec (CSQ). In 2006, the CSQ lost 20 000 members because of a profound disagreement about its position on education reform and pay equity. The dissatisfied members quit the CSQ to form the Fédération autonome de l'enseignement (FAE). In 2006, the CSQ represented approximately 124 000 workers (see Table 16.1).

Independent Labour Unions Despite the presence of four major labour federations in Québec, almost one-quarter of the province's union members are not affiliated with any of these organizations. The most important independent unions are the Syndicat de la fonction publique du Québec (the Civil Service Union) and the Fédération interprofessionnelle de la santé du Québec (nurses' and cardio-respiratory care professionals' associations). This situation has been an area of major concern for central labour organizations because independent labour organizations grew from 15.5 percent of unionized workers in 1975 (Delorme and Veilleux, 1980: 17) to 27 percent by 1987, plateauing at 25 percent by 1997 (Shawl, 1998: 8).[6]

Employer Organizations

There are many types of employer organizations in Québec, including sectorial groups directed toward economic and social interests, economic promotion groups, business groups, professional associations, and even employer associations responsible for negotiating with trade unions, usually in sectors where decrees exist (Delorme, Fortin, and Gosselin, 1994: 169).

More importantly, Québec is characterized by the existence of a prominent confederation of employer associations, the Conseil du patronat du Québec (CPQ). This organization was created in 1969 to attain three specific goals: (1) to have a single spokesperson for employers in dealing with the Québec government, which wanted to deal with only a single organization during consultation with employers; (2) to integrate English-speaking businesses; and (3) to highlight the employers' perspective on labour legislation (Boivin, 1989). The CPQ is mainly a group of associations, not individual companies. Contributions from individual firms, or corporate members, represent a considerable part of its revenue; however, corporate members are not part of the CPQ decision-making structure. These members form the Bureau des gouverneurs, which acts only as a consultative body. It is estimated that employers directly or indirectly represented by the CPQ employ 70 percent of the Québec labour force (Conseil du patronat du Québec, 2007: 1).

Over the years, the CPQ has managed to become the main voice of the employers' community in Québec. It represents management in the majority of existing tripartite structures such as the Advisory Council on Labour and Manpower, the superior education council (Conseil supérieur de l'éducation, Commission de la santé et de la sécurité), and the Health and Safety Commission. The CPQ presents briefs on all questions that are likely to be of interest to its members, takes part in conventions and press conferences, publishes studies, states opinions, and organizes colloquiums and conferences. In fact, the CPQ performs most activities that are usually expected from a representative organization in labour relations, with the exception of collective bargaining.

There is also a Québec branch of both the Canadian Manufacturers and Exporters (Manufacturiers et exportateurs du Québec) and the Canadian Federation of Independent Business (Fédération canadienne de l'entreprise indépendante). In addition, employers are represented by branches of Chambers of Commerce, as in any other province.

PUBLIC POLICY ON WORK

The *Québec Labour Code* is, as in other jurisdictions in Canada, the major piece of legislation dealing with labour–management relations. In this regard, its major characteristics are quite like those of other provinces and of the *Canada Labour Code*, except for the provisions regarding strikebreakers (see Exhibit 16.3). Between 1969 and 2001, Québec experimented with a Labour Tribunal for the adjudication of matters that are usually dealt with by labour relations commissions (LRC) in the rest of Canada and in the United States. However, in 2001, Québec abolished the Labour Tribunal and reinstated the LRC.

Québec, like other provinces, also has established a number of important policies on work, which deal with labour standards, pay and employment equity, and occupational health and safety.

Labour Standards

The regulation of minimum working conditions is one of the oldest forms of government intervention in the area of paid work (Trudeau, 2004). In Québec, the first government interventions date back to the end of the 19th century and were aimed at protecting women and child labour. In 1937, minimum wages were to be applied universally. In 1940, the *Fair Wage Act* was amended and became the *Minimum Wage Act*, with numerous modifications from 1940 to 1979. From 1979 to the present, minimum working conditions have been governed by the *Labour Standards Act*, which replaced the *Minimum Wage Act* and codified numerous rulings previously adopted.

The *Québec Labour Standards Act* is similar to other labour standards legislation in Canada, both in regard to its content and in that it is applied by a Labour Standards Commission operating on a complaint procedure. However, the Québec legislation also includes stipulations for the protection of workers against unjust dismissal. It is the Labour Relations Commission that makes final decisions in these matters. Only two other jurisdictions (Manitoba and the federal *Labour Code*) provide similar protection.

Amendments introduced in 1990, 1999, and 2003 provided additional protections dealing with various types of maternity, parental, and family leaves; prohibition of grandfather clauses in collective agreements[7]; protection against psychological harassment; and a reduction of the eligibility period from five to three years (1990) and then to two years (2001) in cases of wrongful dismissal.

Particular amendments introduced in 2003 concern work–family balance. Since 2003, the *Québec Labour Standards Act* has provided all workers with short and long absences for family matters (including senior management personnel and employees governed by the construction decree, and unless self-employed). In a complementary fashion, since 2006, the *Québec Parental Insurance Plan* has stipulated that financial benefits be paid to all eligible workers, salaried or self-employed, who take maternity leave, paternity leave, parental leave, or adoption leave. This program is innovative in North America because it includes paternity benefits for the father exclusively, which are not transferable to the mother. Only a few North European countries, such as Sweden, have set up such incentive measures to promote gender equality within families. This incentive measure facilitates an active role for men in the family and could be seen as an important milestone in the pursuit of gender equality in Québec.

The amendments to the *Québec Labour Standards Act* combine with the *Québec Parental Insurance Plan* to constitute the actual response from public policy-makers to the ever-growing conflict between family and work. Work–family balance is broadly recognized as a major preoccupation shared by many and will challenge unions and employers' representatives as well as public policy-makers and academics for years to come, particularly in terms of work organization and work benefits.

Pay and Employment Equity

In all spheres of social and economic activity, the last three decades of the 20th century were characterized by an organized and systematic fight against discrimination toward certain groups, especially women. Even though current laws are meant to tackle discrimination against several groups, called "target groups," it is women who are at the forefront of the anti-discrimination movement. Thus reference will be made most often to their situation.

Discrimination at Work and Policy Responses Although women workers have made some breakthroughs in areas of training and employment previously occupied almost exclusively by men, the majority are still concentrated in a limited number of sectors of activity and employment categories, while at the same time they are largely—even totally—absent from certain fields (Commission de l'équité salariale, 2006: 41–43). Although there has been some narrowing of the wage gap between men and women since the end of the 1960s, the gap between men's and women's average income has barely narrowed at all during the last 10 years.[8]

The two major problems are the existence of wage differentials between men and women within the salary structures of firms, and the prevalence of occupational segregation. The latter involves the *concentration* of women in a limited number of jobs in the labour market and the *feminization* of these jobs (the fact that women occupy the majority of these jobs). Although the wage gap and occupational segregation are two aspects of discrimination against women in the labour market, they are different in nature and therefore require different policy responses.

Equal access aims first to eliminate discrimination in all human resource management practices in order to guarantee equal opportunity: this is the dimension of equality of opportunity. A further objective of equal access is equal representation of members of groups that have been discriminated against in jobs offered by a firm: this is the dimension of equality of outcome. *Pay equity* is specifically aimed at obtaining equal pay for work of equal value, which would help narrow the wage gap between men and women. These two aspects of anti-discrimination policy are dealt with in the *Québec Charter of Human Rights and Freedoms* as well as in the two following laws: the *Act Respecting Equal Access to Employment in Public Bodies* (2001) and the *Pay Equity Act* (1996).[9]

Charter of Human Rights and Freedoms In Québec, legislators chose to address employment discrimination in a charter, which also guarantees fundamental freedoms. The *Québec Charter of Human Rights and Freedoms*, ratified in 1975, is intended to be the preferred tool in the fight against discrimination in the workplace. Québec is alone among Canadian legislators in having adopted a definition of the concept of discrimination (outlined in Exhibit 16.4).

Thus the objective of Québec's *Charter* in the area of employment is to "neutralize" work environments by eliminating all manifestations of discrimination. Two distinct and complementary series of measures have been utilized: provisions prohibiting discrimination and provisions aimed at promoting the rights of groups that have been discriminated against.

Québec's Human Rights Commission is responsible for overseeing, in the first instance, the application of the *Charter*. Created in 1975, the Commission was for 15 years the only organization overseeing the *Charter*. Although it may carry out investigations on its own initiative, its limited resources and the fact that it must oversee the application of all *Charter* provisions essentially means that the Commission functions on the basis of complaints filed by people, groups, or organizations. This has limited the *Charter*'s impact. Until 1990, the Commission restricted its role to conciliation and was empowered to make recommendations only. The Commission had to go to court if it wished to have its recommendations enforced.

The establishment of a human rights tribunal in 1990 did not alter this fundamental operating characteristic. The tribunal hears appeals against the Commission's recommendations; however, the Commission is still the starting point for all *Charter*-related complaints.

When compared to the proactive laws adopted by Ontario and some other provinces to require pay equity, this method of functioning can be described as passive because it relies on complaints being filed. Even if organizations are required to respect the *Charter*, in reality, the law of "nothing seen, nothing done" applies. This complaints-based method of functioning is based on the idea that discrimination in the labour market is an exception rather than the rule.

Equal Access When it was adopted in 1975, the *Charter* recognized only the principle of *equality of opportunity* in employment between men and women; it addressed problems of access only by prohibiting discrimination in human resource management practices. At the time, it was believed that giving everyone equal opportunities would be sufficient to allow the employment systems of organizations to improve the diversity of the labour force. In the light of experiences with these measures and the relative failure of programs that addressed only equal opportunity, the objective of equal access was reinforced in 1982 by the introduction of the concept of equality of outcome. The *Charter* was then amended to include a section related to equal access programs. However, it was not until 1985 that this section came into effect.

Regulations related to equal access programs hold that they must include equality of opportunity measures whose goal is to eliminate discriminatory practices permanently, as well as corrective measures aimed at correcting the under-representation of groups discriminated against. Nevertheless, for private-sector firms, equal access programs are still voluntary, and participation in such programs remains largely dependent on a favourable economic context and an awareness of the situation by the management of these firms. Equal access includes dual objectives: (1) to detect and eliminate all sexist and discriminatory aspects of employment policies and practices, and (2) to eliminate occupational segregation by increasing the representation of women (and members of other target groups) in jobs where they are under-represented.

In April 2001, the *Act Respecting Equal Access to Employment in Public Bodies* was implemented. This Act covers public organizations with over 100 employees, hence including many municipalities, hospitals, and universities. The groups covered by the Act are women, visible minorities, natives, and ethnic minorities not speaking either French or English. The Québec Human Rights Commission is responsible for its application. However, the Commission can be more proactive under this Act than it can under the *Charter*.

Pay Equity Since it came into effect in 1976, the *Charter* has recognized the principle of "equal pay for work of equal value" by stipulating that "every employer *must*, without discrimination, grant equal salary or wages to the members of his personnel who perform work of equal value at the same place" (emphasis added). The term "work of equal value" refers to a reality that is quite different from that referred to by the term "equal work." The early anti-discrimination laws included the notion of equal pay for equal work in order to end *obvious* sources of wage discrimination such as different wage scales for men and women doing the same jobs (e.g., male cashier and female cashier). Given occupational segregation, this principle could affect only a small part of the wage gap because men and women generally do not have the same jobs. According to the principle of equal pay for work of equal value, an employer must pay a secretary the same wage as that of a playground maintenance worker if the two jobs are of *equal value* as determined by job evaluation.

The Québec *Charter* may have been very progressive in its early recognition of the principle of pay equity in 1976, but since its introduction the situation in Canada has changed considerably. For example, in Ontario, all public-sector employers and all private firms with 10 or more employees must achieve pay equity according to implementation deadlines established in 1988. Numerous other provinces have also adopted a proactive approach. The passive approach of the *Charter*, the cumbersome complaint process with its burden of proof on the complainant, and the reproaches often made about the Commission's weak and ineffective process for dealing with complaints (Côté and Lemonde, 1988) help explain why few real gains have been made with regard to pay equity, and why most successes have been achieved in unionized sectors.

In 1994, the Parti Québécois won the election and emphasized its willingness to adopt proactive legislation on pay equity. After two governmental commissions, many public hearings, and a strong show of disagreement by employers' organizations, the bill was finally adopted unanimously by the National Assembly on November 21, 1996 (see Exhibit 16.5). Employers' obligations came into force in November 1997. A Pay Equity Commission (Commission de l'équité salariale, CÉS), responsible for the law's administration, was created in March 1997. The law does not require notifying the Pay Equity Commission about the process, but programs must be posted in the workplace. The Minister of Labour is accountable for enforcement, and appeals from the Commission's decisions are directed to the Labour Relations Commission instead of the existing tribunal for human rights.

Exhibit 16.5
Basic Features of the *Pay Equity Act*

- It covers all public and private employers over 10 employees.
- There is extensive definition of salaried employees (including part-time and contract employees but excluding executive managers and police and firefighters).

  Employers with 50 employees or more must implement a pay equity program that includes these four steps:

  Step One: identification of predominantly male and female job categories;
  Step Two: description of the job evaluation method and tool;
  Step Three: evaluation of the job categories, comparison, wage-gaps estimation, and wage adjustments calculation;
  Step Four: methods of wage adjustments payments.

- Predominantly male and female job categories are defined as those having 60 percent or more persons of one sex.
- The job evaluation tool must include the four legally required criteria: skill, effort, responsibility, and working conditions.
- The job evaluation tool must avoid gender bias.
- Employers must achieve the pay equity program (or ascertain the wage adjustments) before November 2001.
- Pay equity adjustments must take place within a four-year period between November 2001 and November 2005.
- There are special provisions of the law for programs having been completed or being in progress before the adoption of the law.[10]

The law allows for employee (nonunion and union) participation through a pay equity committee that is mandatory for employers with more than 100 employees. Employers must pay for the committee members' training. The general principle is "one employer–one program." However, the law allows many exceptions to this principle so that it is possible, for example, to have as many separate programs as there are bargaining units in one organization. However, the actual trend followed by the Pay Equity Commission is to allow implementation of a separate program only when the bargaining unit represents at least one predominantly female job category.

Review of the Current Situation on Pay Equity and Equal Access Up to 1997, Québec's experience with pay equity had been mostly through negotiation, occasionally through the filing of complaints, and sometimes through both channels.

Negotiations were mostly undertaken in the Québec public and parapublic sectors under pressure from unions. Just before the adoption of the *Pay Equity Act* of 1996, there were no significant settlements involving pay equity, especially in nonunion environments in the private sector where the wage gap attributable to discrimination is likely to be the most pronounced.

Although the legislation was enacted in 1996, significant change has yet to occur. This is so for a variety of reasons. The law itself keeps employee participation at a minimum level, especially for women in nonunion workplaces. During the first year of its mandate, the Pay Equity Commission did not fully play the role that was expected. The actors have not rallied behind the Commission since its formation. Indeed, the choice of the commissioners has not been unanimous; the government created the Commission when the context was one of budget cuts, and the assigned budget for the first year was insufficient to launch a wide information campaign. In March 1999, two years after its creation, the Commission launched a very discreet publicity campaign in the press, which did not seem to rectify the situation. As well, the material published by the Commission and the diffusion channels it favours—largely the internet—are less accessible to women workers, unionized or not. The Commission's annual report highlights that its own body has not been very active on the pay equity stage. The nomination in February 2002 of a second president, however, moved the Commission's orientation toward a more proactive approach. A third president was nominated in June 2007 against the recommendation of both unions and feminist organizations.

The implementation of the *Pay Equity Act* got mixed results. By November 2001, employers were to have had their pay equity programs completed. According to the Québec Minister of Labour Report on the *Pay Equity Act* published in November 2006 by the Commission de l'équité salariale (CÉS), only 47 percent of private enterprises and 50 percent of those in the public and parapublic sectors have fulfilled their obligations regarding the *Pay Equity Act*. Furthermore, almost 4 out of 10 private enterprises have not yet started any plan or work concerning pay equity (CÉS, 2006: 57). On the other hand, wage gaps were found in 32 percent of completed equity plans (CÉS, 2006: 61) and were or will be eliminated by compensation adjustments paid to employees who were discriminated against. Also, confronting economic arguments expressed largely by employers against the implementation of the *Pay Equity Act*, one-third of the enterprises surveyed admitted to having spent nothing or less than $1000 to fulfill their obligations and 70 percent spent less than $5000. Overall, the results in Québec show—and the same was observed in Ontario—that the smaller the organization, the lower the probability that the pay equity program would be completed; and the bigger the organization, the greater are the resources used to fulfill its obligations regarding pay equity. The next challenge facing enterprises, beyond starting and completing their programs, is to maintain pay equity. Not much research has yet focused on this challenge, and we consider that it is too soon to address this issue effectively. Perhaps the expertise and apparatus, well developed by the Commission over the years, will help employers and unions to reach this goal and will adequately sustain them throughout the process.

With respect to equal access, the Québec *Charter* is the main source of impetus, as discussed previously. However, these programs are voluntary (with the exception of those in the public service), which explains why they have not been adopted more widely. Since 1986, equal access programs have been introduced in government departments and organizations. In addition, pilot projects allowing for the establishment of such programs have been set up in 76 organizations in the parapublic, private, and municipal sectors. At that time, this has had an effect on nearly 900 establishments and 150 000 people (Gouvernement du Québec, 1993a: 19). Québec's council on the status of women, however, determined that the equal access programs had a limited effect due to their short duration and the weakness of measures adopted. The council indicated that "instead of being genuine equal access programs with established numerical goals and corrective measures, projects put into place more often resemble equal opportunity programs" (CSF, 1993: 21).

In 1989, the government established a contract compliance program modelled on the Federal Contractors Program. The Québec program requires all firms with more than 100 employees, and with a Québec government grant or contract for goods or services in the amount of $100 000 or more, to introduce an equal access program. According to the minister responsible for the status of women, these initiatives have not produced the expected results, as only a little over 5 percent of firms with more than 100 employees are establishing an equal access program. A report issued in 1998 by the Québec Human Rights Commission indicates that even if some significant progress for women has occurred over the past few years, there still remains a significant gap between their abilities and their share of non-traditional jobs. The same problem has been diagnosed for visible minorities and natives (Commission des droits de la personne et des droits de la jeunesse, 1998).

The implementation of the *Act Respecting Equal Access to Employment in Public Bodies* had the same results. According to the *Equal Access to Employment in Public Bodies Triennial Report 2001–2004* (Commission des droits de la personne et des droits de la jeunesse, 2005), despite their presence in almost every sector studied, women are still under-represented in executive positions and non-traditional jobs. The presence of visible and ethnic minorities must be enhanced, particularly in multi-ethnic areas such as Montreal, where they are mostly concentrated in the educational sector. Also, handicapped people are under-represented in all sectors, and accommodating measures should be put in place to increase workplace accessibility for them. Native people are by far the most under-represented group in public bodies, and the report points out the huge work still ahead in terms of promotion and education to fight stereotypes and prejudices against them.

Occupational Health and Safety[11]

There are two laws in Québec that provide the framework for the main aspects usually considered in an occupational health and safety program: prevention and compensation. The *Occupational Health and Safety Act*, which was passed in 1979, encompasses the entire area of prevention, while the *Workers Compensation Act*, which was first passed in 1931 and drastically upgraded in 1985, regulates compensation. The Occupational Health and Safety Commission (Commission de la santé et de la sécurité du travail du Québec, or CSST) was primarily created to oversee the application of these two laws. In fact, the Commission oversees the application of several laws, policies, and regulations spread through different ministries and agencies. Although Québec was one of the last provinces to adopt health and safety laws, in doing so it has benefited from experiences elsewhere and thus has included some innovative provisions in the law, especially in the field of prevention.

With respect to workers' compensation, the situation in Québec is similar to that of the other provinces and the federal government. Compensation is governed by the no-fault principle, which entails collective responsibility of employers, and mandatory insurance guaranteed by a state fund. However, in the area of prevention, Québec, Ontario, Manitoba, and Alberta are at the forefront. Provisions such as the precautionary cessation of work by pregnant workers and the recognition of the right of an injured worker or victim of an occupational disease to return to work are seen as innovative. The main distinctive feature of the legislation in Québec, however, is in the way it is applied. Three mechanisms are used to ensure parity for and participation of both parties:

1. The board of directors of the Occupational Health and Safety Commission, which has jurisdiction over all aspects of occupational health and safety (prevention, inspection, compensation, and funding), is a joint labour–management body.

2. Occupational health and safety committees in firms are also joint committees. Most provinces also provide for the establishment of such committees.

3. Joint consultation at the sectoral level is also established through sectoral occupational health and safety associations, which are *voluntary* groupings of union and management associations.

Appeals can be made through an appeals tribunal, which is external to the CSST and is under the authority of the minister of justice. This body can intervene in all appeals of CSST rulings. Another peculiarity of this mechanism is that the appeals tribunal can play a conciliatory role between the parties. This has led to the unblocking of the system through out-of-court settlements of outstanding compensation claims.

Currently, the main interrelated preoccupations of the occupational health and safety system are controlling the costs of administering the system, reducing the length of time taken to settle cases, and reducing the emphasis on legal aspects in the processing of files by the CSST. Despite a decrease in the number of accidents at work in the past few years, the costs of operating the system have continued to increase, due mainly to an increase in the average period of compensation and to an increase in the duration of relapses. However, there have been ups and downs in the average rate of employer contributions since 1995.

In January 1999, the CSST introduced a new insurance concept—mutual insurance—for small employers paying less than $18 000 in annual contributions to the CSST. In the past, these employers had to pay their sector's rate. Now, by joining the mutual insurance program, the rates paid by employers will reflect their individual performance with respect to health and safety. This should lead to an improvement of workers' health and safety because one of the major conditions for joining the mutual insurance group is to develop a prevention program.

However, a new type of occupational hazard has recently emerged in Québec, as well as in the rest of Canada. It relates to burnout, stress, and overwork. The CSST has now recognized these hazards in some specific cases.

CONCLUSION

We have used three key concepts in discussing the evolution of union–management relations in Québec: nationalism, state interventionism, and the political strength of the labour movement. What lessons can be drawn from our overview?

First, Québec's cultural identity explains why the provincial government has historically intervened in the economic and industrial relations spheres to a greater extent than has any other government in North America. Québec has developed into a neo-corporatist society where interest groups are regularly consulted over major economic and political issues (e.g., the numerous economic, financial, and even constitutional summits organized by the Québec government). Such a situation also explains the presence of an organization that acts as the "official voice" of all employers in Québec (the Conseil du patronat du Québec), something that is unique in North America. It also explains why labour unions, although divided into four separate central organizations, nevertheless have tremendous lobbying power within all provincial governments. However, the Liberal government, which is still in power after being elected on April 14, 2003, modified the rules of union–government negotiations by decreeing work conditions for thousands of public and parapublic sector employees. Now in minority after being re-elected on March 26, 2007, will the Liberal government be forced to adopt a less autocratic approach in public-sector labour relations, or is it the end of the unions' lobbying power as we know it?

Second, an important division has developed over the years between private-sector and public-sector labour relations. The main factor explaining this dual evolution is the state of the economy: the two recessions of the early 1980s and the early 1990s transformed private-sector labour unions from ideologically oriented and very militant organizations into more pragmatic ones. On the other hand, a confrontational approach to labour relations has always prevailed in the public sector (including municipalities) except for a brief period in the 1990s.

This confrontational mood contrasts with the more collaborative labour–management relationships that have been developing in the private sector recently, in which unions and employers are driven toward "mutual gains" or "interest-based" negotiations (IBN) sometimes more by necessity than by choice. Signs of the changes can be seen in a number of areas: conciliation officers at the department of labour have all been trained to develop the skills required to act as "facilitators" when requested by the parties; private consultants and some university professors run training sessions and aid in the IBN process; "Saturn-type" collective agreements have also been signed alongside the "social contracts" described above.

In 1997, a document on work reorganization (*Document de réflexion sur une nouvelle organisation du travail*) was published by the Joint Consultative Committee on Labour (Gouvernement du Québec, 1997) to stimulate more collaborative labour–management relations in the private sector. This document, which received the unanimous approval of all interested parties, states that work reorganization is no longer an exclusive "management rights" domain, that unions have a legitimate stake in it, and that they will increasingly have a say in the matter. Both union and employer representatives acknowledge that, to achieve profitability, a firm must be able to adapt rapidly and use its personnel efficiently. Job protection and training must also be shared goals (Gouvernement du Québec, 1997: 9). Paradoxically, despite the active role played by unions, employers, and government representatives in emphasizing the need for a collaborative approach, confrontation still characterizes labour–management relations. In fact, strategies recently used by employers to pressure unions or unions-to-be include close-down or relocalization threats (as in the Olymel case); lockouts (as in *Le Journal de Québec* case); and actual close-downs (as in the Wal-Mart case in Saguenay, unofficially to avoid unionization). On the other hand, strikes are still part of union strategies.

As explained by Boivin and Sexton (2007), the actual labour relations model prevailing in Québec is ironically characterized by its heterogeneity. Labour–management relations are changing under environmental pressures, namely increased competitiveness and capital volatility, and new tendencies are emerging. As a result, there is cohabitation of collaborative and traditional approaches to collective bargaining depending on the parties' evaluation of their ability to achieve their goals. Generally speaking, employers ask for more flexibility while unions ask for more job security. Employers and unions, depending largely on the economic health of their industry sector, will react differently and choose a particular path toward the conclusion of a collective agreement.

Consequently, the future direction of labour relations in Québec is uncertain. We could see a proliferation of labour conflict due to rigidity amongst the parties, as well as innovative collective agreements allying flexibility and job security.

Questions

1. What factors must be considered in order to understand labour–management relations in Québec?

2. What is the official platform adopted by most central labour organizations in Québec with regard to the province's future political status?

3. Describe the functioning of the Québec Federation of Labour's Solidarity Fund.

4. Explain the major consequences of Bill 142 (now known as Bill 43) for unions.

5. Explain the relationship that exists between the CLC and QFL.

6. Describe the anti-strikebreaking provisions of the *Québec Labour Code*.

7. Explain the dilemma of labour organizations when faced with a government formed by the Parti Québécois.

8. What lessons can be drawn from the experience of collective bargaining in Québec public and quasi-public sectors between 1972 and 2007?

9. Describe the functioning of the Decree System.

10. Overall, would you say that Québec public policy on work is substantially different from that in the rest of Canada?

Weblinks

Canadian Labour Congress:
www.clc-ctc.ca

Centrale des syndicats démocratiques du Québec (CSD):
www.csd.qc.ca

Commission de l'équité salariale:
www.ces.gouv.qc.ca

Commission des droits de la personne et des droits de la jeunesse du Québec:
www.cdpdj.qc.ca

Confédération des syndicats nationaux (CSN):
www.csn.qc.ca

Conseil du patronat du Québec (CPQ):
www.cpq.qc.ca

Ministère du travail du Québec:
www.travail.gouv.qc.ca

Secrétariat du Conseil du trésor:
www.tresor.gouv.qc.ca

Chapter 17

Trade Unions and Labour Relations Regimes: International Perspectives in a Globalizing World

Carla Lipsig-Mummé

"Outsourcing is Climbing [the] Skills Ladder. The globalization of work tends to start from the bottom up. The first jobs to be moved abroad are typically simple assembly tasks, followed by manufacturing, and later, skilled work. At the end of this progression is the work done by scientists and engineers in research and development laboratories. A new study . . . suggests that more and more research work at corporations will be sent to fast-growing economies with strong education systems, like China and India. In a survey of more than 200 multinational corporations . . . 38% said they planned to 'change substantially' the worldwide distribution of their research and development work over the next three years, with . . . China and India . . . attracting the greatest increase in projects."[1]

New York City. "Herding freelancers is a bit like herding cats. . . . Nonetheless, Sara Horowitz has figured out a way to bring together tens of thousands of freelancers: Web designers, video editors, writers, dancers and graphic artists, into a thriving organization. . . . [T]he Freelancers Union offer[s] members lower-cost health coverage and other benefits freelancers often have a hard time getting. . . . "This really is about a new unionism," she said. . . . "More and more people are not going to get their benefits from an employer. . . . Our ultimate goal is to update the New Deal. It is to create a new safety net that's connected to the individual as they move from job to job." . . . Membership in the Freelancers Union is free. To finance itself, the group uses an entrepreneurial model: it earns modest commissions on the benefits that its members buy."[2]

Lusaka, Zambia. "The boulders here are hard enough that the scavengers . . . prefer not to strike them directly with their hammers. They heat the rocks first with flaming tires, scrap plastic, even old rubber boots so that the stones will fracture more easily. . . . A boy named Alone Banda works in this purgatory six days a week. Nine years old, nearly lost in a hooded sweatshirt with a skateboarder on the chest, he takes football-size chunks of fractured rock and beats them into powder. . . . In a good week, he says, he can make enough powder to fill half a bag. His grandmother . . . sells each bag . . . for less than $3. Often, she said, it is the difference between eating and going hungry. . . . Across the globe, the number of children forced to work is in sharp decline. But in sub-Saharan Africa . . . more than one in four children below age 14 works . . . nearly the same percentage as the worldwide average in 1960. . . . They are prostitutes, miners, construction workers, pesticide sprayers, haulers, street vendors, full-time servants, and they are not necessarily even paid for their labor."[3]

Modern labour relations regimes in the advanced industrial countries of the Global North took shape in the years between World War II and the 1960s, with the nation-state as the basic unit of regulation. Today, however, these "post-war settlements" are eroding, under significant pressure because welfare states (in which the states assume broad responsibility for the welfare of their citizens) are scaling back their regulation of employment conditions and protection of unions' traditional rights to represent workers. In addition, the profound transformation of the world economy in the past 20 years under the impetus of globalization and neoliberalism has made the economies of high-wage and low-wage countries increasingly interdependent. But the spread of precarious employment throughout the high-wage countries of the Global North has also contributed to the weakening of trade unions' workplace and political power (Munck, 2002). While traditionally each country has developed its own unique national labour relations regime, contemporary globalization is stimulating the new development of transnational labour and commercial regulation, regional unionism, global sectoral unionism, global agreements, and a growing array of union–community alliances.

In this chapter we look at the four post-war patterns of labour regulations, and move to examine the emergence of regional labour regimes and the differential response of trade unions to the volatile international work order created by globalization in the 1980s, linking advanced economies to industrializing countries. Why do some countries' labour movements continue to play an important role while others do not? The chapter then turns to look at the most important issue of the 21st century: global warming, or global climate change, and the opportunity it provides for labour worldwide.

LABOUR RELATIONS IN ADVANCED INDUSTRIAL COUNTRIES: POST-WAR PATTERNS

National Labour Relations Systems

A national labour relations system, or regime, is the web of social institutions, including legislation and administrative practice, that structures the relationships among the three major actors regulating the world of employment and work. These actors are: workers and their unions; employers and their associations; and the state. Each actor operates at several levels, both within its own group and in interaction with the others. While most labour relations systems have as their formal goal co-operation among the actors (or social partners), conflict of interest is recognized as unavoidable, and conflict-resolving mechanisms are usually built into the regulatory framework.

In all countries, labour relations systems take shape historically and continue to reflect the particular national or regional culture and class relations that have developed over time (Hyman, 2001; Martin and Ross, 1999). During the Keynesian era, national labour relations systems made a formal place for trade unions, and most considered them to be the workforce's most important spokesgroup. Today, some labour relations systems also make space for other workplace organizations that represent workers, or for the individual voice of unorganized workers in the workplace. Only a few labour relations systems make a place for input by citizens, consumers, and other members of civil society who are not directly involved in work relations but may be affected by its outcomes.

The end of World War II in 1945 is usually deemed the beginning of the era of modern welfare states and labour relations. This is true for Canada, but some countries (Sweden, the United States, and Great Britain) developed their welfare states earlier, during the Depression. Still others (Germany and New Zealand) date the origins of their welfare states from the last decade of the 19th century. Countries defeated in World War II (Germany, Japan, Austria, and Italy) began the reconstruction of their economies, governing systems, trade unions, and industrial relations under the aegis of U.S. authorities after 1945. Although modern labour relations systems have been shaped by the welfare states, their unions and employers' associations sometimes draw on older traditions, stretching back to the 19th century.

Four Patterns

Labour relations systems are nationally specific. Does this mean that every one is so different from the rest that we cannot identify patterns and types? Jacoby (1995) proposes a categorization of labour relations regimes. This typology is constructed on the basis of the experience of the developed countries, and is based on two questions:

- Is collective bargaining centralized or decentralized?
- Does the state play an interventionist or minimalist role in regulating the economy and labour relations?

Four "types" of national labour relations systems can then be identified: corporatism, decentralized marketism, statist micro-corporatism, and regional concertation.

Corporatism *Corporatism* describes a system of regulating labour–capital relations in which the state plays an interventionist role in organizing employer associations and trade unions in order to maintain centralized wage fixing, eliminate industrial conflict, and ensure support for its economic and social goals. Corporatist systems may operate at the national or sectoral level. They may be bipartite or tripartite. Tripartite corporatism refers to the state's integration of *both* capital *and* labour together. Bipartite corporatism refers to the state's integration of *either* labour *or* capital into its regulatory framework.

Macro-corporatism refers to a corporatist regulatory framework operating at the level of central government (Munck, 2002: 28). Macro-corporatist labour relations systems have traditionally been associated with strong economies, low unemployment, and rapid recovery from international dislocations such as the 1970s oil crisis. They typically have had high union density, strong unions, and comprehensive welfare, training, and education systems. Wage dispersion is less likely in macro-corporatist systems, and citizens in general, not just union members, have benefited directly and indirectly from the results of macro-corporatist labour relations. In addition, when macro-corporatist labour relations continue for a considerable period of time, as they did in Sweden, they provoke centralization of power within each corporatist partner, unions, and employer groups. Union power tends to be drawn up to the central, or peak labour body, and rank-and-file militancy tends to shrivel. Among private-sector employers, strategic decisions are often displaced to the level of the employer association.

While Sweden has been the example par excellence of tripartite macro-corporatism and a strong national economy (Mahon, 1999), Australia also introduced a macro-corporatist system under a labour government, from 1983 to 1996 (Peetz, 2006). Its unique labour relations system, dating from the early 1900s, combined centralized arbitration with tariff protection, a white-Australia policy for immigration, long-established trade unionism, and an accepted tradition of workplace militancy that was legally prohibited and informally accepted. After the election of the Australian Labor Party (ALP) in 1983, efforts were made to create a macro-corporatist social and economic framework—to "Swedify" Australia. This included maintaining the historic arbitration system and developing a new Accord (a bipartite wages agreement between the government and the Australian Council of Trade Unions), and creating a network of consultative institutions around economic development, skills training, and macroeconomic policy. But the ALP had come to office at a time when international pressures to replace protectionism with trade liberalization were particularly strong. By the early 1990s, the ALP itself was dismantling the tariff barriers, weakening the arbitration system, and decentralizing wage bargaining to the workplace. By the time the ALP was voted out of office in 1996, the Australian labour movement had declined from 56 percent of the labour force to less than 30 percent. Today, it is 19 percent. The ALP experiment with macro-corporatism was terminated by the Liberal government that succeeded the ALP and remained in office through 2007. The Liberal government's controversial overhaul of the labour relations system since 1996 severely limited the ability of trade unions to represent workers.

Corporatist labour relations systems also operate at the sectoral level. In contrast to macro-corporatism, *meso-corporatism* refers to coordinated decision making by employers and unions at the level of industrial sectors, with the state facilitating and setting parameters for sectoral bargaining. In other words, this is sectoral corporatism combined with state-level economic planning. Despite the impact of the merger of East and West Germany, Germany's "dual system" of industry-wide sectoral bargaining remains a successful example of meso-corporatism. Meso-corporatism encourages centralization of power (at the industry-wide level) and consultative relationships, while discouraging union militancy and industrial conflict. Like macro-corporatism, meso-corporatism is associated with high wages, generous welfare provisions, the sectoral commitment to take wages out of competition, and national economic prosperity.

The German model developed additional components (Jacobi, Keller, and Muller-Jentsch, 1992). First, co-determination, or the "dual structure" of representation, separated worker organizations in the workplace from collective bargaining at the sectoral level. Collective bargaining was the precinct of unions and employers' associations at the sectoral level: this effectively took wages out of competition. At the workplace, works councils and local management dealt with the daily issues that arose. Union members, and sometimes union officials, sat on the works councils. Second, German labour relations are comprehensively regulated by law. Labour law sets the terms for collective bargaining and regulates industrial conflict and workplace labour relations. While strikes might result from collective bargaining at the sectoral level, they were illegal in the exercise of co-determination at the workplace. Therefore, "structural conflicts between labour and capital could be broken down and dealt with in two arenas" (Jacobi, Keller, and Muller-Jentsch, 1992: 218). Third, unions and employers' associations were designated by law to represent their entire constituencies, whether members or not. Fourth, as in other meso-corporatist systems, collective bargaining in Germany was centralized at the sectoral level. The tradition of industrial rather than craft unions went back to before World War II, and the union commitment to centralized decision making rather than local autonomy dates from the 19th century. Although unions in the inter-war period were ideologically divided and competitive (Radosh, 1969), the post-war decision for unitary, rather than pluralist and competitive, unions contributed to the effectiveness both of the unions and of the collective bargaining system, until reunification at the beginning of the 1990s.

Reunification between West and East Germany caused "severe gyrations to the economy" (Silvia, 1999: 83), but the meso-corporatist industrial-relations system was simply extended without change from the West to the East. By the end of the 1990s, however, Germany's meso-corporatism was under attack from breakaway employers quitting unified sectoral bargaining in the metalworking sector, and from the emergence of plural unionism in the East. Under these pressures, the impact of tenaciously high unemployment in the East contributed to the rolling back of Germany's training and benefits systems, a hardening of employer attitudes toward social partnership, and the return to industrial militancy.

While Germany's post-war trajectory is unique, Germany is not alone in the change in employer attitudes towards meso-corporatist partnership. In recent years, employer pressures to decentralize and deregulate have put real pressure on all meso-corporatist systems, opening gaps between the healthy and threatened industrial sectors and between large and small industry.

Decentralized Marketism *Decentralized marketism* is the second major pattern of labour relations systems in high-wage countries. In this, the state plays only a minimal role in labour-market regulation and economic policy-making, leaving the market to make decisions and individual firms and unions to battle it out within a minimalist legislative framework. Unions have little or no formal (institutional) role in economic and labour-market policy-making. Consultation is sporadic and at the will of particular governments. Significantly, the union movement's links to a political party capable of gaining office are often but not always weak. Typically, decentralized market systems are characterized by low union density with considerable sectoral and sometimes geographic variation. The United States and Canada are examples of decentralized marketism (Drache and Glasbeek, 1992; Clawson, 2003; Lichtenstein, 2002; Milkman and Voss, 2004; Yates, 1998).

Great Britain is now another variant of decentralized marketism. In Great Britain, where the trade union movement founded the Labour Party at the beginning of the 20th century, the state was traditionally a moderate economic planner but also intervened very little in legislative regulation of labour relations. This system was known as voluntarism. Voluntarism is characterized by decentralized collective bargaining and minimal labour law. Exceptional periods have occurred when the Labour Party was in office, particularly during the period 1945–1979 when bipartite corporatism took shape, and the state intervened vigorously in economic and social planning (Edwards et al., 1992; Hyman, 2001). More recently, the 18 years of Conservative rule beginning in 1979 undid the Labour years. The Thatcher government crafted or presided over five major changes that weakened and then transformed the world's oldest labour movement (Hyman, 2001): (1) the extensive legal formalization of union activity and industrial relations made strikes and union recognition more difficult, interposing the state between unions and their members; (2) the deterioration of the post-war labour market, characterized by rising unemployment, de-industrialization, and casualization, hollowed out the labour movement's core membership; (3) the decline of trade union membership from 45 percent in 1970 to 29 percent in 2003 led to several waves of union mergers (Visser, 2006); (4) the emergence of managerial militancy ended the social partnership that had characterized the post-war years; and (5) strike activity almost disappeared.

Most recently, during the Blair government's mandates, the trade union movement saw its historic influence in the Labour Party weakened and its role in economic and social policy-making marginalized. In the face of Blairism following Thatcherism, the British labour movement crafted five responses (Hyman, 2001). First was a search for new forms of solidarity in order to recruit new professions and casual employees. Second was a turn toward the state and its ability to enshrine union rights in law. Third was a "pessimistic" turn toward social partnership, as the capacity to mobilize members dwindled. Fourth was an attempt to regain social authority and public profile for the labour movement. Fifth was a systematic attempt to implant an organizing culture.

Decentralized marketism exacerbates the variation in wages between strong and weak industrial sectors, as well as between secure and precarious workers, and union and nonunion workers. It impedes the flow of collective bargaining gains from the more powerful to the weaker or excluded.

Statist Micro-Corporatism *Statist micro-corporatism* is Jacoby's memorable characterization of the third major pattern of national industrial relations, the Japanese system. The Japanese system combines interventionist activity by the state with workplace-based regulation of working conditions. At the macro level, the state works closely with industry to obtain markets, reduce competition among Japanese companies abroad, and regulate the currency. This might be called statist entrepreneurism. Companies are organized sectorally into industry associations that work with the government. Labour, however, is absent at the level of state policy-making. This model of statist industrial entrepreneurism has been reproduced elsewhere in East Asia.

In Japan, ongoing, or core, workers are organized into company unions whose real life is at the level of the workplace (Inoue, 1999). Unlike German unions, Japanese unions are weak at the sectoral level. Company-based unionism and seniority-based wages have made the local level most important. Unlike Swedish and Austrian unions, Japanese unions are absent at the level of national economic policy-making and wage bargaining. At the workplace, however, Japanese workers and their unions are incorporated into an elaborate web of consultative and participative structures, tying the worker to the company through socialization into corporate culture and reducing the union's ability to articulate and defend workers' interests autonomously. This has been called "private-welfare corporatism" (Jacoby, 1995). Between "corporatism without labour" at the national policy-making level and corporatist workplace relations, Japanese unions have rightly been considered weak, docile, and ineffective.

In recent years, however, economic crises and Japan's economic ups and downs have placed a profound strain on the two-level system of bipartite corporate–government macroeconomic policy-making and micro-corporatism in the workplace. Although large Japanese companies had long employed a core of permanent workers and a cushion of precarious employees—the former could assume employment security until late in their working life, and the latter would be laid off or hired according to the ebbs and flows of the market—recent economic strains have led to layoffs in unprecedented numbers. This in turn has provoked questioning about the effectiveness of the unions and the fairness of the core/precarious tradition of employment. While it has also contributed to a real decline in union density, it has triggered the merger of the union federations, so that the peak body, Rengo, now has eight million members. In turning to mergers to offset membership loss and decline of authority, the Japanese unions join a trend that has become increasingly common in high-wage developed countries.

Regional Concertation *Regional concertation*, the fourth major type of labour relations system, would not come into importance in Italy and France until the late 1980s, when it emerged as an innovative way for local communities to take their own economic development in hand outside the firm and outside national governments. In regional concertation, municipal or regional governments attract and encourage the growth of small and medium-sized businesses, often in new manufacturing sectors (Ferner and Hyman, 1992; Hyman, 2001; Martin and Ross, 1999). Collaborative efforts by local unions, local government, large and small corporations, and local employers' associations "incubate" training facilities, research and development services for small businesses, and the social services of the region, such as co-ops and credit unions. Of particular note is the fact that regional concertation in Italy attracted the involvement of socialist and communist unions and municipal governments.

Taking the long view, the half-century since World War II divides into two distinct periods: from 1945 to the late 1970s, and from the early 1980s to the present. The earlier period was characterized by widespread economic growth and prosperity in the developed countries, the pre-eminence of the welfare state and Keynesian economic strategies, low unemployment, and nationally autonomous labour relations systems (Trubek and Rothstein, 1998).

THE EMERGENCE OF A NEW INTERNATIONAL WORK ORDER

The past 30 years, however, have seen a veritable revolution in world economic and political organization, the role of nation-states in regulating labour relations, and the profile of employment. The industrial and political authority of unions has declined, and nongovernmental organizations (NGOs) and social advocacy groups play a new role in working with trade unions and organizing vulnerable workers who fall outside the traditional structures of protection. In the next section, we look at the "structural" transformations that are associated with this new wave of globalization, leading to an end to the post–World War II patterns of national labour relations systems.

Worldwide, both vertical and horizontal corporate mergers have tightened economic integration between developed and developing countries. This increased international economic integration has shifted manufacturing production out of North America, Australia, and Northern Europe into the poorer countries of Asia, Latin America, and Eastern and Southern Europe. The decline of agricultural employment is even more striking. It represents one in ten jobs in the high-wage countries (Lipsig-Mummé, 1997).

A new international division of labour is emerging (Munck, 2002). Countries and regions within countries seeking to attract or retain manufacturing employment choose to reduce government regulation of standards of work and employment (Klein, 2000). Across the developed world and since the mid-1980s, a pattern of reduced government regulation of employment and labour relations can be seen (Hyman, 1999). This has gone hand-in-hand with decentralization of collective bargaining, particularly important in Great Britain, the United States, Canada, and Australia. It also has contributed to increasing the difficulty for trade unions in organizing new members.

In contrast to the decline of manufacturing and agricultural employment in high-wage countries, the service sector continues to grow. In Canada, three out of four jobs are in the services, one of the highest proportions in the world. But the service sector has two faces: the public and the private, and working conditions are very different in each. The public sector, which includes direct and indirect public services, has traditionally provided "good jobs," particularly for women, with secure employment, defined career paths, decent wages, and retirement provisions—although gender-based wage inequalities have persisted. The public sector is usually the most highly unionized in a country. But most developed countries have been reducing employment in their public sector in the context of post-Keynesian neoliberal politics. Privatization has contributed to the mushroom growth of private services at the expense of public employment. The wave of public-sector strikes in Europe over the past decade testify both to the continued dynamism of public-sector unionism, and to the anxiety of public-sector workers.

The private-services sector, in most high-wage countries, is the "bad jobs" face of service employment. It is usually weakly unionized, under-regulated, and characterized by precarious employment, uneven safety standards, and extremes of employer size and solvency. Private services also account for approximately 50 percent of the jobs in all the high-wage countries.

As large-corporation reorganization shakes up the viability of private-sector employers, labour market "flexibility" has been widely advanced as a competitive solution. Following 20 years of the highest unemployment rates since World War II (1970s to the late 1990s), the proliferation of "non-standard" and precarious employment has contributed to the seemingly permanent shrinkage of secure employment in developed countries, and the spread of informal employment in developing countries. We call this "eroding the core." In some countries like Australia, casual employment represents more than 25 percent of all jobs, and is the fastest-growing form of employment tenure. In the context of weakened government regulation of employment standards and trade union rights, casualization has become an important factor in the decline of union membership. The two recessions that bracketed the 1980s weakened unionism in the traditional bastions of union strength: heavy industry, mining, and the public sector.

The spread of non-standard forms of employment tenure may be thought of as contributing to a "feminization of employment" (Jenson et al., 1988; Vosko, 2000). Since the mid-1970s, male labour-force participation has declined while female participation has grown, leading to a gendered convergence in labour-force participation rates. The shrinking of manufacturing, agriculture, and forestry work is a major factor in the decline in male participation. But as fragmented employment spreads at the expense of ongoing full-time employment, men and women are both taking up precarious jobs. The feminization of employment patterns has affected men as well as women, young workers, and mid-career and older workers. The growth of precarious employment also contributes to the polarization of wages and working time (Lipsig-Mummé and Laxer, 1998; ACIRRT, 1999).

The feminization of employment also produces unexpected results. In Canada, women's union membership has grown more rapidly than men's since 1976, contributing to the relative stability of union density (Lipsig-Mummé and Laxer, 1998). In Australia, a country in which union density has been halved since 1985, women's membership has declined less rapidly than men's, buffering what is nevertheless a dramatic decline (Lipsig-Mummé, Curtin, and Nielsen, 2003).

Over the past 30 years, the high-wage economies have shared the decline of traditional male manufacturing and primary-sector jobs, shrinkage of the public sector and the spread of private-service jobs, an increase in women's labour-force participation and a decrease in men's, and the deregulation of employment in ways that pose a threat to conventional trade unionism and the post-war culture of government protection of labour standards as well as the right to trade union representation.

The Political Climate

Compared with 1945–1975, 1975–2007 is characterized by a chilly climate for unions. Indeed, widespread adoption of neoliberal policies, privatization of welfare state services, and rejection of policies for social expenditure and of the philosophy of social responsibility for all citizens have combined with the embracing of both trade liberalization and intensified international competition. Together, these have contributed not only to the deregulation of the labour market in the quest for flexibility, but to decentralization of collective bargaining, an increasing number of citizens who drop out of the safety net, and increasing difficulties for trade unions in attracting and organizing members of the next working class.

While the political climate has made it more difficult for trade unions to organize new members and defend working conditions, wages, and benefits for core membership, countries have varied considerably in the depths of changes they have made to their labour relations systems in this era of the welfare state. Why, in the face of common changes to the structure of their national economies, have some countries turned radically away from their post-war systems, while others have not? The growing but uneven impact of globalization may be one reason.

The End of an Era: Globalization, Regionalities, and National Labour Relations Regimes

Globalization refers, first, to the increasing integration of national economies into international economic organizations and structures. This integration may be geographic—regional trading zones like the European Union, NAFTA, or MERCOSUR—or global—such as the World Trade Organization (WTO). These supra-national bodies may directly and indirectly influence national labour relations systems, in terms of labour standards, workers' rights, and trade liberalization (Gunderson and Verma, 2003). Second, globalization refers to the growing role that transnational corporations (TNCs) play in national and regional economics and politics, as evidenced by their growing share of economic output, the increasing number of workers who are directly or indirectly employed by them, and their growing influence on national and regional governments and on the regulation of labour relations (Monbiot, 2000, 2003; Klein, 2000; Burawoy et al., 2000; Cohen and Kennedy, 2000). Third, globalization refers to the space that non-governmental and non-corporate actors in civil society are newly occupying in defining and advocating social justice. In the field of labour relations, new or newly important cross-national alliances link local trade unions and international labour bodies like the newly founded International Trade Union Congress and the newly merging Global Unions with international tripartite bodies like the International Labour Organization (ILO), NGOs, religious organizations, and social advocacy groups. They work together on campaigns and movements rather than on organizational and structural action concerning the impact of globalization on work, standards of living, and democracy (Monbiot, 2000, 2003; Klein, 2000).

But prior to 1970, national labour relations systems in developed countries had operated autonomously, because their national economies were considered to be sovereign. These labour relations systems had been protected in their *national* autonomy by an *international* consensus. As stated by Trubek and Rothstein (1998: 6), "Firms tended to operate within national borders [as opposed to internationally], tariffs were still a significant barrier to trade, industry was largely located within the richer countries of the north, trade was heavily weighted to intra-industry exchanges, and capital markets were weak and not well integrated across national boundaries."

International support for national autonomy in labour relations came in the form of the Bretton Woods monetary system and the International Labour Organization (Trubek and Rothstein, 1998). But Bretton Woods, with its system of fixed exchange rates, ended in 1973, the oil crisis began, inflation and unemployment rose simultaneously, and the whole cocktail contributed to the first wave of corporate mergers and the internationalization of production and distribution.

Patterns of Economic Regionalism

Out of the breakdown of the post-war system of "national autonomy internationally reinforced," a number of arrangements have emerged, all responding to globalization through some form of transnational economic rapprochement. None, however, has yet created regional or international labour relations systems. We highlight three: the European Union, the evolving free trade arrangements in the Americas, and trade and bilateral accords.

The European Union (EU) The European Union (EU) is both the oldest and the most ambitious system of regional integration. Beginning in 1950 with the United Europe project, it moved slowly to reduce the barriers to the free movement of people, products, and services. At its inception a customs union, it has established free internal trade, common external tariffs, labour mobility among member countries, and a common currency (Gunderson and Verma, 2003). While the EU is the most developed and successful of regional unions, it has favoured economic integration over harmonizing social issues. In the domain of labour relations, the Social Charter outlines labour standards, and important steps have been taken to set Europe-wide protections for workers and the free movement of labour, but "transnational markets [have been created] in the context of national industrial relations systems" (Ross and Martin, 1998).

Martin and Ross (1999) see more progress than they expected. The "market-building" emphasis in European integration pressed for trade liberalization and deregulation, rather than the creation of Europe-wide social and labour standards. Unions needed, then, to "transnationalize" their strategies and organizational structures. But the national nature of their structures, organizational patterns, and cultures created considerable obstacles. Yet, against the odds, the "Europeanization" of labour relations and trade union action is occurring. The possibility of Europe-wide collective bargaining is becoming a reality, with over 90 "cross-border agreements" signed in 2006. The European Trades Union Confederation (ETUC) plays a respected role in labour and economic policy formation in EU countries. However Martin and Ross conclude that Europe has a long way to go before a regional industrial-relations system can be said to exist. In other words, the development of transnational markets does "hollow out" national labour relations systems and does weaken unions, but it does not necessarily lead to the transnationalization of labour relations.

The North American Free Trade Agreement (NAFTA)

NAFTA was signed by Canada, the United States, and Mexico and came into effect in 1994, following the Free Trade Agreement of 1989 between the United States and Canada. Both were opposed by the Canadian and American labour movements. While NAFTA liberalizes trade among the three countries, it contains no provisions for monetary integration or for the harmonization of economic and social policies as the EU is beginning to do.

In the face of labour opposition to NAFTA, labour and environmental "side accords" to the core agreement were negotiated. The side agreement for labour—the North American Agreement on Labor Cooperation (NAALC)—includes formal protection for the right to bargain collectively, occupational health and safety, freedom of association, freedom from discrimination, minimum wages, and a ban on child labour. However, each country has considerable leeway to observe the regulation as it sees fit. Says one observer, "The NAALC provides for no regional level norms or law making, and specifically renounces the idea of harmonizing labour standards in North America. . . . There are no sanctions for failure to do so except in certain very limited areas" (Trubek and Rothstein, 1998: 34). NAFTA is, in other words, a narrow form of regional economic integration, lacking a social dimension or effective transnational political regulatory bodies (Bacon, 2004).

While each of the three NAFTA countries has held tenaciously to its national labour laws and institutions, NAFTA has made uneven modifications to the three national labour relations systems. NAFTA's impact has first been felt in the redistribution of manufacturing jobs from Canada and the United States to Mexico, a transfer that has impacted on the organizing ability and the collective bargaining strategies of manufacturing unions in both Canada and the United States. Since many of these Canadian and American manufacturing unions have reinvented themselves as general unions, the impact is felt beyond manufacturing as well.

Second, NAFTA intensified the upheaval within the Mexican labour movement, where forces inside and outside the official unions continue to struggle to reinstate democratic processes in union practices. In addition, the *maquiladora* border regions (where assembly and shipping plants are located on either side of the border to take advantage of low Mexican wages and lax enforcement of workers' rights) are contested terrain between transnational corporations (TNCs), several levels of Mexican government, and sometimes the official unions on one side, and workers seeking to unionize—working with the independent unions and some Canadian and U.S. unions—on the other (LaBotz, 1992; Bacon, 2004). Within the Canadian labour movement, NAFTA divided Quebec unions from their English-Canadian counterparts, since Quebec labour remains cautiously enthusiastic about regional globalization. NAFTA also stimulated the highly competitive Canadian unions in heavy industry and mining to seek partners in Mexico and elsewhere in Latin America, as they squared off against each other in an essentially internal-to-Canada competition for membership. Within the United States, opposition to NAFTA pitted the AFL–CIO (American Federation of Labor–Congress of Industrial Organizations) against the Clinton administration, underscoring the weakness of the union movement in influencing policies of the Democratic Party. The Bush administration has, instead, attracted the support of some large national unions like the Teamsters, widening the gap between them and the AFL–CIO.

NAFTA, like the EU, highlights the fact that trade liberalization and the regionalization of markets do not lead easily or quickly to the creation of a regional labour relations system or regionally coordinated unions. As in the EU, the creation of transnational markets may well weaken the national labour relations system and national unions, but it does not create a regionalized, international alternative.

Elsewhere in the Americas, MERCOSUR, the Andean Pact, and CARICOM are free trade agreements for South America, the Andes, and the Caribbean respectively. MERCOSUR in particular sees itself as a potential common market and a regional bulwark against the United States' aspirations for a pan-American free trade zone, and has reached out to the European Union in the areas of co-operation, trade, and investment. In none of the American accords is the regionalization of labour unions or labour relations on the horizon.

Trade and Bilateral Accords But what of the rest of the world? Trade agreements and bilateral accords in the absence of institutional integration is the third pattern of economic transnationalism. Global trade and tariff agreements have been the subject of intense and growing social debate in Europe, North America, and Australia as well as in low-wage countries. Linking the General Agreement on Tariffs and Trade (GATT) with the World Bank and the International Monetary Fund (IMF), the debates began taking popular-protest form at the end of the 1990s, most spectacularly in large street demonstrations in Seattle in 1999 that linked Canadian, Mexican, and American trade unions with a range of international environmental, child labour, and human rights advocacy groups. These demonstrations, which were reproduced in Quebec City, Genoa, Sydney, and elsewhere, triggered intense organizational self-questioning among participating unions and signalled the public entry into the question of workers' rights by civil society actors who had previously not been recognized as participants in labour relations regimes. The anti-globalization movements are, in turn, linked to a range of from-the-bottom-up, locally and internationally based workers' rights groups. They act, diversely, to monitor workers' rights in China; organize women workers in India; boycott products produced by child labour; create effective monitoring of corporate codes of ethical production in the Caribbean, Asia, and Latin America; and protect trade unionists from jail and death in countries across the globe.

Whether one welcomes globalization as heralding an era of free trade, rejects it in the name of national economic sovereignty, or sees in it an irreversible movement of capital that also creates a democratic space for reconstructing workers' organizations, the current confrontations and upheavals have, unexpectedly, renewed a wide public debate about workers' rights, the power of capital, and societal democracy. This debate links traditional and new social actors in dialogue about the future shape of global labour relations.

GLOBALIZATION AND LABOUR

How well have trade unions adapted to the new, chilly climate that began in the 1980s? There is a great deal of variation. We can answer the question by looking first at union presence and then at union reach: how well the unions reach new groups coming into the labour market.

Union Presence

In the high-wage countries, the post-war pattern for union membership divides into two periods, as does the development of national labour relations systems. From 1950 to the mid-1970s, most advanced countries experienced growth in union density. Since 1985, national union movements have declined in the proportion of workers they represent, although the date of the beginning of the decline, its speed, and the magnitude of loss vary greatly. Certainly the United States, Japan, Australia, and France have been the hardest hit. All have more than halved their union density rates (i.e., union members as a percentage of the non-agricultural paid workforce). In 1950, the French labour movement represented almost one in three workers. Most recent comparative data places France's union density at 8 percent. In 1950, Japanese unions represented 46 percent of the working class. In 2003 they represented less than 20 percent. U.S. union density is 13 percent, up slightly from 1995. In Australia, union density has declined from 50 percent in 1970 and the early 1980s to 23 percent in 2003 and 19 percent in 2007. Austria, whose membership remained above 50 percent until the mid-1990s, was 35 percent unionized in 2003. In Germany, where almost two in five workers were unionized for decades, one in five now remains a union member.

Some union movements withstood these complex changes. The Danish movement grew from 60 percent in 1970 to 70 percent in 2003, and the Swedish movement from 68 percent in 1970 to 78 percent currently. Norway remains around 55 percent in density (Table 17.1). Over all, union density in the European Union has declined 11.5 percent since 1970. In Canada the decline is 6.5 percent; in the United States, 11.1 percent; and in Australia, 27.3 percent.

Canada is a special case. Union membership hovered around 30 to 33 percent for most of the past 30 years. In fact, it had been the strong growth of the public-sector and women's trade union membership that had supported the Canadian labour movement during the years of decline in other countries. When the growth in the public-sector and women's union membership faltered (the former in the 1980s and the latter after 1992), Canadian union density began to decline. Today it is 28 percent.

Union Reach

The emerging map of employment and the contemporary map of trade union presence do not fit each other. The map of union presence charts the industrial and public-sector

Table 17.1 Union Density in Selected Countries and the European Union, 1970–2003 (percentages)

Country	1970	2003	Absolute change 1970–2003
Australia	50.2	22.9	–27.3
Austria	62.8	35.4	–27.3
Canada	31.6	28.4	–6.5
Denmark	60.3	70.4	+10.1
France	21.7	8.3	–13.4
Germany	32.0	22.6	–9.5
Italy	37.0	33.7	–3.3
Japan	35.0*	20.2 **	N/A
Korea, Republic of	12.6	11.2	–1.5
Norway	56.8	53.3	–3.5
Sweden	67.7	78.0	+10.3
United Kingdom	44.8	29.3	–15.5
United States	23.5	13.2	–11.1
European Union	37.8	26.3	–11.5

*   Figures from 1980
** Figures from 2002

Sources: Visser, J. (2006). "Union Membership Statistics in 24 Countries," *Monthly Labor Review*, v. 129, January, pp. 38–49. For Japan: Japanese Ministry of Health, Labour & Welfare (2002). *Basic Survey on Labour Unions*.

points of strength of the post-war working class. The map of the emerging labour market, in contrast, charts job growth and concentration in casual and non-standard employment, those sectors where unions are weak or weakened by governmental anti-unionism and managerial militancy, and in the under-unionized occupations and employment statuses within traditionally strong union sectors. We can take this further.

A *double polarization* is occurring; it is characterized by the hollowing out of the traditional core of the securely employed, unionized workforce. There is a growth of non-standard precarious employment on the one hand, and increasing competition between workers in high- and low-wage countries on the other. Within high-wage countries, the secure/precarious divide is also a generational divide: age matters. The working young, increasingly, believe employment security belongs to their parents' generation, and respond through alienation, individualism, and cynicism (Lipsig-Mummé and Nielsen, 2003). They are not uninterested, however, in street-level environmental, anti-globalization, or peace campaigns. The prematurely elderly, on the other hand—the group of mid-career workers squeezed out of the labour force during the 1980s and 1990s to allow for "flexibility" to casualize national labour forces and strip the public sector—returned to take part-time, less-skilled jobs than they had held, often at a fraction of their original wages. Because the labour market is suffering shortages, the early retirement set is now courted by the governments that previously turned a blind eye to their extrusion.

What does this tell us about the ability of unions in advanced countries to withstand the dislocations of globalization in the 1980s and 1990s? First, what accounts for a strong union presence in the first place? Jacoby (1995) suggests that the small countries with concentrated economies—in which labour has control of social resources such as the unemployment or social welfare system and in which employers seek to co-opt socialist unions rather than confront them—have historically developed a strong union presence.

Second, what allows national union movements to withstand or respond effectively to political and economic developments that weaken the power they have gained historically? Jacoby (1995) identifies the factors. Surprisingly, these are located in the *structure* of national labour regimes, rather than in the ideology or strategies of the unions themselves. These structures have long histories. Countries with centralized wage bargaining, national- or sectoral-level negotiating, long-standing corporatist arrangements, and a centralized labour movement suffered the fewest losses during the 1980s and 1990s. Scandinavia in particular falls into this category, even when social-democratic governments were replaced by conservatives, perhaps because the culture of social-democratic corporatism was solidly entrenched in the national value system. On the other hand, Jacoby (1995) argues, countries that had decentralized bargaining, little state intervention in wage setting, the exclusion of labour from politics, and multiple or weak central labour bodies fared poorly. The United States, France, and Japan fall into this category.

Since the mid-1990s, a number of national labour movements have dropped out of their logical place in the Jacoby pattern. In particular, Germany, the U.K., Australia, and Canada stand out. The integration of East Germany and West Germany has created so many dislocations in terms of unemployment, training, and the breakdown of the former West Germany's meso-corporatism that union membership has declined sharply and is undergoing a painful reconsideration of its commitment to "the German model."

In the post-war era, the United Kingdom constructed so compelling a labourist welfare state that the Labour Party was seen as the natural party of government. Following the election of Margaret Thatcher in 1979, the government oversaw the dismantling of the welfare state through privatization of state-owned industries and deregulation. During the Thatcher years, union density in the U.K. dropped from 55 to 29 percent. On the defensive, the labour movement undertook deep-seated strategic and structural changes, including mergers, centralizing union organizing, and partnering with employers in a wide number of industries at the workplace level. With the election of Labour under Tony Blair, the government applied its "third way" ideology to strengthen protection for workers and employment standards in the private sector, but not necessarily for unions or public-sector workers. As the union movement watches its role in the Labour Party shrink, its membership is not rising either. Does the United Kingdom defy the Jacoby categorization? It may be argued that in the two decades of radical dismantling of the welfare state, politics has remade the national labour relations regime.

The British experience has something in common with the Australian. In both, the transition from a social-democratic to a free-market government and from Keynesianism to neoliberalism led to a paradigm shift: from a large role for the state in economic planning and centralized wages bargaining, to radically decentralized collective bargaining and debilitating new legal limits placed on trade union functioning. In both cases, the national union movements flourished under social-democratic governments, but found themselves in decline when successor governments transformed the national labour regimes.

The story of union decline has two dimensions, and these expose an immediate dilemma. First, despite the uneven emergence of *regional* labour-relations regimes, the structure of *national* labour regimes continues to play a pivotal role in a labour movement's ability to adapt and survive, although there are variations among industries and regions. Second, the emergence of regionalities in Europe and North America tends to weaken national labour regimes, although Canada's has proven unexpectedly durable. But globalization has also intensified new *global* issues for those regimes, catalyzing transnational, nontraditional activists to confront the issues it throws up. How do trade unions—the largest continuing organized public interest group in any country—engage with these newly urgent issues, and the nontraditional mobilizers? Will involvement with the big issues slow or reverse union decline? The dilemma for labour is nowhere clearer than around the issue of global climate change.

GLOBAL CLIMATE CHANGE: DILEMMAS AND OPPORTUNITIES FOR UNIONS

Adapting Richard Hyman's analysis of European unions (2001), while globalization is affecting every labour regime, it is not affecting them in the same way. Socially oriented climate scientists are mapping the impact of global warming on economic growth, health, food and water security, and the survival of the poorest regions. But meanwhile, there has been little mapping of the impact of global warming on work, employment transitions, and training within the Global North, or the changed links it will create between the Global North and the Global South. Research reported by the International Trade Union Confederation (ITUC, 2006) indicates that worldwide there will be a slight gain in jobs, offset by massive losses in some industries and uneven impact on geographic regions. The poorest and lowest-lying regions of the world are the most threatened, but the threats come first from flood and disease.

This differentiates the strategic reality for unions. Yet the issue of global warming can transcend differences. It also offers trade unions the opportunity to emerge as social citizens in two new ways: as the organizations most able to chart and audit the contribution of public and private enterprise to global warming; and as the largest public interest group in any country, capable of engaging very large numbers of citizens in implementing a transformative climate agenda that links employment transition to other social priorities.

Labour is beginning to work through the issues, as the November 2006 meeting of the ITUC showed. There is a spectrum of labour responses that, interestingly, has echoes of Jacoby.

In the EU, the trade union thrust is to use the omnipresent social partnership paradigm to place climate change strategies within a sustainable development framework, with British, Spanish, and Belgian projects taking the lead. Recognizing that jobs will be lost and jobs created at unprecedented levels, employment transition (and training) is pivotal. Elements of the strategy focus on retraining and redeployment, green job creation, and concentration on key industrial sectors that are particularly affected by, or contribute to, climate change.

In Canada, because it is a decentralized labour relations regime, unions are not included in federal public-policy formation, and the federal government is following the United States on Kyoto. Trade union response to global warming is decentralized, and therefore privileges rank-and-file workplace intervention. New strategies include mobilizing around nationwide workplace audits by members (CUPE, 2007), or nationwide training of workplace trainers in climate change: a train-the-trainer strategy (ITUC, 2006). For Canadian unions, rank-and-file climate change activism offers the opportunity to mobilize internally and make links externally, beyond their membership.

In Australia, a climate-extreme country, the unions have historic ties of mutual dependence with the Australian Labor Party (ALP). In the wake of its recent federal election victory, the ALP has signed Kyoto. The union movement may well use the government as its agent to develop and implement climate strategy, reproducing an environment accord similar to the bilateral labour market accords that were the signature of the ALP in office in the 1980s and 1990s.

Yet, as the climate scientists say, understanding the impact of global warming on work and employment worldwide has not really begun. Can trade unions take up this challenge, craft a broader role for themselves in civil society, and in so doing redefine union reach and union presence?

CONCLUSION: CANADIAN LABOUR AND INTERNATIONAL PATTERNS

Setting Canadian labour relations in an international context, these conclusions emerge:

First, the decentralized structure of Canadian collective bargaining, the minimalist involvement of the federal state with economic planning, and the increasing competition among unions are also characteristic of those industrial relations systems in Europe that have been most gravely weakened by globalization. European experience indicates that centralization of collective bargaining and rationalization of union structure buttress the shocks of internationalization better than do decentralization and internal competition.

Second, the structure of Canadian unions has been changing rapidly since the 1980s, but in a direction likely to weaken them. The creation of a mosaic of large general unions causes them to compete with each other for members in every sector.

Third, the comparative study of labour relations under the impact of globalization indicates that whether national systems and labour movements survive intact or emerge weakened seems to be strongly influenced by the structure of the labour relations regime itself. But the Canadian experience seems to add a wrinkle to the story: the impact of strategic choice by unions and consistent attention to involvement of membership contributes to lessening the impact of neoliberalism and globalization on union reach and presence.

Finally, truly global issues like global climate change, by their very scale and urgency, offer a challenge and an opportunity to unions, the largest public interest group in any developed country. The challenge is to engage communities and citizens more broadly than other interests can, in developing and realizing socially equitable climate change strategy. Labour movements have an opportunity to reach beyond their borders, redefining their role as collective citizens in an anxious world.

Questions

1. Define and contrast macro-corporatism and meso-corporatism.

2. How does Canadian trade union density compare to density in the United States, the U.K., Australia, and Sweden over the past 20 years?

3. What are the principal differences between the European Union and the North American Free Trade Agreement in terms of standardizing trade union rights?

4. What role are social advocacy groups identifying for themselves in international labour relations?

5. Define "the Europeanization of labour relations."

6. Define "the feminization of employment patterns."

7. How has the Canadian trade union experience in the past 20 years differed from the American?

8. Global warming poses both a challenge and an opportunity to unions in developed countries. Discuss.

Weblinks

UNITE-HERE, the merger of UNITE and HERE:
www.unitehere.org

World Trade Organization:
www.wto.org

European Trade Union Confederation (ETUC):
www.etuc.org

Canadian Centre for Policy Alternatives:
www.policyalternatives.ca

Canadian Labour Congress:
www.clc-ctc.ca

International Trade Union Confederation:
www.ituc-csi.org

European Industrial Relations Observatory Online:
www.eurofound.europa.eu/eiro

Endnotes

Chapter 1

[1] *Alberta Labour: A Heritage Untold* by Warren Caragata. (Toronto: James Lorimer & Company, 1979), pp. 83–85. Reprinted with the permission of the publisher.

[2] The ILO Conventions present a confusing picture because they contain many pieces of precursor conventions. For example, in 1972 Canada ratified the Freedom of Association and the Right to Collective Bargaining Convention, originally developed in 1948 (known as Convention No. 87).

[3] These terms are taken from titles of William Lyon Mackenzie King's 1899 talks at the Passmore Edwards Settlement House in Bloomsbury, England, while he was a PhD student at Harvard. See Ferns and Ostry, 1955, p. 42. The "labor problem" was first described as such in North American scholarship by Wisconsin professors Adams and Summer in 1905.

[4] This definition became quite widespread in the late 1980s, and appeared on page 1 in a widely used text by Kochan and Katz, 1988.

[5] On similarities, see Lawler, 1990, page 67. On differences, see Horwitz, 1990 and 1991. The most-cited mainstream North American IR journals are listed in Exhibit 1.2. Mainstream HRM research appears in *Human Resource Management* and various Academy of Management publications.

[6] Kochan and Katz, 1988. Paul Weiler, a former British Columbia Labour Relations Board chair, who was instrumental in drafting and applying that province's labour code, and is now a chaired professor at Harvard University, wrote an important (1980) book on Canadian labour policy that focused on bridging the conflict of interests.

[7] There currently are as many jurisdictions in Canada that cover NHL hockey as there are Canadian hockey teams. In addition, the NHL teams in the United States are protected by the U.S. federal *National Labor Relations Act*. Coordinating a League-wide strike or lockout is a complicated affair!

[8] *Toronto Electrical Commissioners* v. *Snider*, in the Privy Council [1925] A.C. 396.

[9] Adams (2002: 126) criticizes the Canadian focus on achieving a balance. He argues that it should be more appropriately placed on the rights of workers to influence their conditions of work. See his extensive body of scholarship on this point. For a discussion by many Canadian scholars of various features of Canadian public policy, see a special issue of *Canadian Public Policy*, Volume 28, Number 1 (March 2002).

[10] Under Canada's parliamentary system, so-called "third parties" have the potential to wield far more influence than do U.S. third parties. Thus, while the formation of a labour party may have made little sense in the United States, chances for success in furthering union objectives were far greater in Canada.

[11] Chapter 4 contains much of the data on which this graph is based, but there may be small discrepancies due to sources from which the data are drawn. For explanations of Canadian–U.S. density differences see J. Godard, 2003, "Do Labor Laws Matter: The Density Decline and Convergence Thesis Revisited," *Industrial Relations* 42, No. 3, pp. 458–492; G. Chaison and J. Rose, 1991, "Continental Divide: The Direction and Fate of North American Unions," in *Advances in Industrial and Labor Relations*, D. Sockell, D. Lewin, and D. B. Lipsky, eds. (Greenwich, CT: JAI Press), pp. 169–205; W. C. Riddell, 1993, "Unionization in Canada and the United States: A Tale of Two Countries," in *Small Differences That Matter*, D. Card and R. Freeman, eds. (Chicago: University of Chicago Press), pp. 109–147; and Taras, 1997.

[12] The poor coverage of industrial relations within organizational behaviour texts is detailed in Barling, Fullagar, and Kelloway, 1992, Appendix (pp. 202–205). They provide a list which states that 21 of 77 current textbooks do not mention unions at all. Our experience is that even Canadian or Canadianized HRM texts often devote only one or two chapters to unions. Business strategy texts rarely mention unions, and when they do, the connotation is usually negative: that unions are a threat, limit flexibility, and must be avoided.

Chapter 2

[1] *Canadian HR Reporter*, Toronto: Nov 5, 2007. Vol. 20, No. 19, p. 30. Copyright © 2007 Carswell Publishing. Reprinted with permission of the publisher.

[2] This is a simplified version of Gompers' response. Gompers actually responded with the much more thoughtful and nuanced statement: "What does labor want? We want more school houses and less jails, more books and less arsenals, more constant work and less greed, more justice and less revenge; in fact, more opportunities to cultivate our better natures." (August 28, 1893. Chicago).

[3] The concept of the "wage–effort bargain" was developed by W. Baldamus in his 1961 book.

[4] *Labour of Love.* Copyright © 1998 by Buzz Hargrove and Wayne Skene. Reprinted by permission of Buzz Hargrove.

[5] For additional information about collective bargaining in sports, see Paul D. Standohar, *Playing for Dollars: Labor Relations and the Sports Industry* (Ithaca NE: ILR Press, 1996), and his article "Labor Relations in Basketball: The Lockout of 1998–99," *Monthly Labor Review*, 4 (April 1999), pp. 3–9. See also Kenneth A. Kovach, Nancy Greer Hamilton, and Meg Meserole, "Leveling the Playing Field," *Business and Economic Review*, 44, no. 1 (Oct.–Dec. 1997), pp. 12–18. To understand similar labour–management pressures in the entertainment industry, see Lois S. Gray and Ronald L. Seeber, eds., *Under the Stars: Essays on Labor Relations in Arts and Entertainment* (Ithaca, NY: ILR Press, 1996).

[6] Frederick Winslow Taylor criticized this tendency to cut labour rates, arguing instead that the focus should be on productivity. See his treatise "The Principles of Scientific Management," *Bulletin of the Taylor Society* (December 1916). Jeffrey Pfeffer begged managers to cease confusing labour costs (a measure that considers productivity per worker) with labour rates (hourly wages) in "Six Dangerous Myths About Pay," *Harvard Business Review* (May–June 1998), pp. 109–19.

[7] John R. Commons' 1909 classic article remains one of the industrial relations field's pre-eminent examples of developing theory from institutional research and case study methods.

[8] Many former international unions in Canada broke away from their American parents in the 1970s and 1980s to become independent national unions. This trend is examined in Gregor Murray's chapter on unions in this volume (Chapter 4).

[9] Today part of the giant Communications, Energy and Paperworkers Union.

[10] See Slichter, Healy, and Livernash, 1960, for the classic account of this process.

[11] *Westfair Foods Ltd. v. United Food and Commercial Workers Union*, Local 401 (Mohamed Grievance), 2005 A.G.A.A. 64 (arbitrator Ponak). Upheld at Alberta Court of Queen's Bench [2006] A.J. No. 130, 2006 ABQB 103, Docket No. 0503 13778 (Sanderman, J.).

[12] This of course may be because union workers feel more able to complain about perceived dissatisfactions at work than do their nonunion counterparts.

[13] Personal interview with Buzz Hargrove, CAW president (March 17, 1999).

[14] Of course, just because workers in the United States want to be unionized does not mean they will become unionized. Most American employers are strongly anti-union, and U.S. labour laws make unionization difficult for employees in the face of strong employer opposition. See T. A. Kochan, H. Katz, and R. B. McKersie, *The Transformation of American Industrial Relations* (New York: Basic Books, 1986); and J. J. Lawler, *Unionization and Deunionization* (Columbia, South Carolina: University of South Carolina Press, 1990).

[15] Task Force on Reconstructing America's Labor Market Institutions, 1999, "Reframing Institutions of Representation," *Blueprint* (Research and Policy Newsletter of the Task Force, Sloan School of Management, M.I.T.), 2, No. 5 (October), p. 9.

[16] For a discussion on supplements to traditional collective bargaining such as ownership campaigns by unions, employee ownership, and "social investing," see various chapters in Estreicher (1998).

Chapter 5

[1] Research cited in this chapter was funded by a Social Sciences and Humanities Research Council grant. Michael Piczak and Louise Verschelden provided valuable assistance in completing interviews. The author is solely responsible for the views expressed.

[2] Shenfield and Ponak. "From Acrimony to Respect," *Canadian HR Reporter*. Toronto: Feb 26, 2007. Vol. 20, Iss. 4; pp. 10–11. Updated for 2007 from the Catalyst Paper Corporation website: http://catalystpaper.com. This vignette can be viewed in the film *Beyond Collision: High Integrity Labour Relations*.

[3] British Columbia Labour Relations Board, *Re P. T. Savage Enterprises Ltd. and National Automobile Aerospace, Transportation and General Workers Union of Canada (CAW-Canada)*, BCLRB No. B508/98.

Chapter 6

[1] A greenfield site is usually a new workplace built at a site where none existed before. Since all the employees would be new, they are likely nonunion.

[2] Excerpts from Darcy Shenfield, Allen Ponak, and Bert Painter,

"Beyond Collision: High Integrity Labour Relations, CPR Short-line Railway Case Study" Retrieved from www.hrsdc.gc.ca/en/lp/ wid/articles/article6.shtml#_ftn2. Reprinted with permission of the authors. This vignette can be seen in the film *Beyond Collision: High Integrity Labour Relations*.

[3] This term originated with the study of the American auto industry, although it has also been extensively practised in Sweden and Canada. See Berggren, 1992; Askin and Goldberg, 2002. The CAW studies are Robertson et al. (1993), "The CAMI Report: Lean Production in a Unionized Auto Plant," and CAW (1993), "Work Reorganization: Responding to Lean Production."

[4] Mayo (1933) and Roethlisberger and Dickson, 1939. Revisionist studies have argued that workers continued to improve their productivity because they were concerned with job loss during the Depression and knew they were being scrutinized by the research team. For a critique of the Hawthorne studies, see Baritz, 1960, and Gillespie, 1991.

[5] There is a debate among scholars and practitioners over whether it also is necessary to change incentive compensation systems so that there is a linkage between pay and demonstrable performance. Some firms do this and others do not. It is quite possible to have performance-based pay systems that are not designed to produce a high-involvement workplace. No one would claim that a home worker who is paid on a piece-rate system based on the number of zippers she can sew into a garment is part of a high-involvement system. A company can be considered to practise high-involvement techniques if it can demonstrate the adoption of a cluster of practices to foster employee involvement.

[6] Establishment surveys of training, in general, do not ask about the extent of coverage (the proportion of employees covered by the workplace practices): i.e., two establishments, one with 100 percent of its employees covered and another with only 10 percent of its employees under training, would be counted similarly. Thus, such data needs to be interpreted cautiously.

[7] Reviews of many of these studies can be found in Locke and Schweiger (1979); Miller and Monge (1986); Cotton et al., (1988); Cotton (1993); and Wagner (1994).

[8] Measurement of outcomes such as costs and productivity should not be confused with general assessment and evaluation of the EI program. In fact, many of the firms that do not collect data on costs and output relating to EI do conduct employee surveys and focus groups to get subjective feedback from the employees on the EI program.

[9] These include NCR, Stelco's Lake Erie Works, Canada Post, BPCO, Kruger, Abitibi-Price, NBTel, NorSask, and other studies compiled by Human Resources and Social Development Canada's *Innovative Workplace Practices in 2007—Annual Overview*, at www.hrsdc.gc.ca/en/lp/wid/win/pdf/Innovations. Overview_2007.pdf.

[10] Policy-makers have established various institutions and initiatives since the 1980s to support workplace innovations. Examples include the Canadian Labour Market and Productivity Centre (CLMPC), the Canadian Labour Force Development Board (CLFDB), and the Ontario Training and Adjustment Board (OTAB). A minister of the government may convene a meeting of the leading unions and employers in an industry or may engage in trilateral negotiations with a company and its

union (Verma and Meltz, 1994). This approach produced a number of agreements in Quebec. The Canadian Workplace Research Network (formed in 1994) offers another forum for information dissemination. In addition, sector-specific labour–management councils have been created by the federal government. The Canadian Steel Trade and Employment Council (CSTEC) in the steel industry and the Sectoral Skills Council for the electrical and electronics industry are two examples (Gunderson and Sharpe, 1998).

[11] Canada Labour Relations Board in *C.U.P.E. v. C.B.C.* 1994, pp. 121–122. On the other hand, the Canada Labour Relations Board commented in this case that employee-involvement initiatives were commendable, and that on their own they would not violate labour laws provided that management first attempted to deal with employees through the union.

[12] In truth, conventional measures were always harder to interpret than they seemed. For example, absenteeism merely measures absence from work, but tells us very little about the causes or consequences. In 2002, the average full-time employee in Canada missed 9 days per year, adding to a total of 92 million workdays. Even if we were to dramatically reduce the level of absenteeism through a variety of interventions, we might inadvertently create a "presenteeism" problem. Presenteeism describes two unhealthy phenomena: first, workers feel an overwhelming need to put in long hours to cope with their feelings of job insecurity. Second, presenteeism describes the tendency of employees to go to work even when they are sick or injured, and incapable of being fully engaged and productive. Presenteeism may have a worse impact on productivity than does absenteeism. See Lowe (2002).

Chapter 7

[*] This chapter was originally co-authored with the late Noah Meltz. This chapter is dedicated to his memory and his impact in the field of Industrial Relations.

[1] Adapted from information provided in the article by T. Van Alpen, "No sex, please, it's GM night shift." *Toronto Star* (February 24, 1994), pp. A1 and A7.

[2] Card (1992); Card and Krueger (1995). See also the Review Symposium on the topic in the July 1995 issue of the *Industrial and Labor Relations Review*.

[3] Statistics Canada, 2006, "Canada's Changing Labour Force, 2006 Census: Findings," www12.statcan.ca/english /census06/analysis/labour/index.cfm.

[4] The part-time employment rate was 18.7 percent in 2002 (Statistics Canada. catalogue 89F01331F).

[5] In the 1950s part-time work was, as defined by Statistics Canada, considered to be any job that required less than 35 hours of toil per week—the increase in part-time work would have been even greater if the definition had remained consistent.

[6] "Tax cuts for middle class Martin's priority," *National Post* (September 27, 1999).

[7] HRDC, *Workplace Gazette,* vol. 5, no. 4 (Winter 2002), p. 20.

[8] Statistics Canada, www.hrsdc.gc.ca/en/gateways/topics/axe-rsr.shtml.

[9] Data for the year 1999 cited in Benjamin, Gunderson, and Riddell (2002), p. 160.

Chapter 8

[1] *Re Starbucks Corp*, BCLRB Decision No. B323/96. For a similar decision in the following year see: *Re Starbucks Corp*, BCLRB Decision No. B231/97.

[2] *Re Starbucks Corp*,BCLRB Decision No. B183/97.

[3] *Industrial Disputes Investigation Act*, 1907 (6 & 7 Edw. 7, e. 20, Can.).

[4] *National Labor Relations Act*, 29 U.S.C. Sec. 151–169.

[5] *Wartime Labour Relations Regulations*, P.C. 1003 (1944).

[6] *Toronto Electric Power Commissioners v. Snider*, (1925) 2 D.L.R. 5 (P.C.).

[7] *Constitution Act*, 1867, s.92(13).

[8] These territorial governments have delegated power over labour relations, but have not yet passed their own labour relations legislation.

[9] See: B.C. *Labour Relations Code*, R.S.B.C. 1996, c. 244, ss.14(4)(b), 133(1)(c)-(f); *Re Tandy Electronics Ltd. and United Steelworkers of America* (1980), 115 D.L.R. (3d) 197 (Ont. S.C.J.), at p. 215; *Re P.R. Foods Ltd.*,[2005] B.C.L.R.B.D. No. 223, at para. 47.

[10] *Royal Oak Mines Inc. v. Canada (Labour Relations Board)*, [1996] 1 S.C.R. 369 [*Royal Oak Mines*].

[11] Remedial certification is provided for by the B.C. *Labour Relations Code,* ss.14(4)(f) and (5); authority to order a second representation vote is found in B.C. *Labour Relations Code*, s.133(1)(d).

[12] *Kidd Brothers*, [1976] 2 Can LRBR 304 (BCLRB), and cited in Baron Metal Industries Inc., [2001] O.L.R.D. No. 2732 [*Baron Metal*], at para. 30.

[13] This is similar to the practice in civil court proceedings where, in virtually every case, parties request and courts award legal costs to the successful party. Note that LRBs in other jurisdictions, such as Ontario, refuse to order legal costs (see, for instance, *National Grocers Co. Ltd.*,[2003] O.L.R.D. no. 1447, at paras. 18-20).

[14] For example, B.C. *Labour Relations Code* s.158 makes it an offence for a person to refuse or neglect to comply with an order made under the statute. Individuals are subject to a maximum fine of $1000; corporations, unions, and employers' organizations to a fine of up to $10 000. Other jurisdictions provide greater opportunities for penalties, such as providing that any contravention or failure to comply with the legislation is an offence subject to monetary penalty (see Alberta *Labour Relations Code*, R.S.A. 2000, c.L-1, s.161; Manitoba *Labour Relations Act*, R.S.M. 1987, c.L-10, s.149; Ontario *Labour Relations Act*, S.O. 1995, c.1, s.104(1); *Canada Labour Code*, R.S.C. 1985, c.L-2, s.104), or that each day of non-compliance constitutes a separate offence (Ontario *Labour Relations Act*, s. 104(2)) or the penalty is calculated according to the number of days in breach (Manitoba *Labour Relations Act*, s.145).

[15] George W. Adams, *Canadian Labour Law*, 2nd ed. (Aurora: Canada Law Book, 1993), at para. 10.2280.

[16] See B.C. *Labour Relations Code*, ss.6, 9, 14.

[17] B.C. *Labour Relations Code*, ss.6, 9.

[18] B.C. *Labour Relations Code*, ss.6(3)(d) and 9 restrict employer communication with employees, while s.8 explicitly recognizes a limited employer right to communicate with employees.

[19] *NLRB v. Federbush*, 121 F.2d. 954 (1941).

[20] See, for example, Ontario *Labour Relations Act*, s.86(2).

[21] See, for example, Ontario *Labour Relations Act*, s.86(1).

[22] See, for example, Ontario *Labour Relations Act*, s.72, *Canada Labour Code*, s.94(3).

23 See, for example Ontario *Labour Relations Act*, s.96(5) or *Canada Labour Code*, s.98(4).

24 B.C. *Labour Relations Code*, s.14(7).

25 George W. Adams, "Canadian Labour Law," *supra*, note 15. Factors differ slightly among jurisdictions. For the B.C. Board's list of factors, see: *Island Medical Laboratories* (1993) 19 C.L.B.R. (2d)161, and for the Canada Industrial Relations Boards factors, see: *Canadian Broadcasting Corporation* [1979] 2 Can. L.R.B.R. 41.

26 A card-check procedure is now used in the Federal jurisdiction (*Canada Labour Code*, s.28), Manitoba (*Labour Relations Act*, s.40), Quebec (*Labour Code*, R.S.Q., c.C-27, s.28), New Brunswick (*Industrial Relations Act*, R.S.N.B. 1973, c.I-4, s.14), and Prince Edward Island (*Labour Act*, R.S.P.E.I. 1988, c.L-1, s.13(5)). A mandatory representation vote procedure is now used in British Columbia (*Labour Relations Code*, s.24), Alberta (*Labour Relations Code*, s.34), Ontario (*Labour Relations Act*, s.8), Saskatchewan (*Trade Union Act*, R.S.S. 1978, c.T-17, s.6), Nova Scotia (*Trade Union Act*, R.S.N.S. 1989, c.475, s.25), and Newfoundland (*Labour Relations Act*, R.S.N. 1990, c.L-1, s.38).

27 In contrast, the *National Labor Relations Act* provides no time limit for elections to be held, and there the median time between certification application and vote is 50 days ("Fact Finding Report Issued by the Commission on the Future of Worker–Management Relations" [U.S.: Commission on the Future of Worker-Management Relations, 1994], p. 82). Alberta simply requires that the vote occur "as soon as possible" (*Labour Relations Code*, s.34(3)).

28 This reflects the union certification legislation in Quebec and New Brunswick. Some jurisdictions, such as British Columbia (*Labour Relations Code*, s.24.3) and Newfoundland (*Labour Relations Act*, s.38(2)), have provisions effectively requiring that a minimum proportion of eligible voters cast ballots in order for a representation election to be valid.

29 Paul C. Weiler, *Reconcilable Differences: New Directions in Canadian Labour Law* (Toronto: Carswell, 1980), p. 1809.

30 S. Slinn, "An Analysis of the Effects on Parties' Unionization Decisions of the Choice of Union Representation Procedure: The Strategic Dynamic Certification Model," *Osgoode Hall Law Journal* 43 (2005): 407.

31 Keep in mind that voting does not occur in conditions where employees are free from scrutiny by their employer, other employees, or the union. Both union and employer representatives are present at the election and, particularly in the case of small units, it is apparent not only which employees voted, but once the outcome is known, it may be possible to draw conclusions about how particular employees voted. Therefore, the secrecy of a "secret ballot" should not be overstated.

32 It is important to note that some Canadian labour legislation allows employees to revoke their cards.

33 Interestingly, given the seemingly compelling arguments suggesting that employees would favour elections over card-based certification, a committee charged by the British Columbia government to review its labour laws found that it is not employees who want certification elections, but employers. This committee chose to respect the wishes of employees and recommend that the card-check system then in place not be replaced by mandatory votes. (Minister of Labour, Government of British Columbia, British Columbia Labour Relations Review Committee, 1998).

34 Baron Metal, *supra*, note 12.

35 *Ibid*, at para. 129.

36 *Ibid*, at para. 39.

37 *Ibid*, at para. 129.

38 *Ibid*, at para. 129.

39 *Ibid*, at paras. 108, 104 and 117.

40 *Ibid*, at para. 130.

41 *Ibid*, at para. 130.

42 Note that, in June 2005, the Ontario *Labour Relations Act* was amended to reinstate the OLRB's power to order remedial certification.

43 For a good discussion of this phenomenon, see J. J. Brudney, "Contractual Approaches to Labor Organizing: Supplanting the Election Paradigm?" (2005), *Labor and Employment Relations Association Series*, Proceedings of the 57th Annual Meeting, p. 106.

44 See, for example, *Canada Labour Code*, s.38, Ontario *Labour Relations Act*, s.63.

45 For a good review of studies examining the effects of right-to-work laws see F. G. Mixon Jr. and R. W. Ressler, "Union influence and right-to-work law passage: evidence from hazard model estimates" (1993), *Am. J. Economics & Sociology* 52, p. 183.

46 The "Rand formula" is named after Justice Ivan Rand of the Supreme Court of Canada who arbitrated a lengthy and bitter strike over union recognition that took place in 1945 at the Ford Motor Company plant in Windsor. Among Justice Rand's orders was that there was to be compulsory check-off of union dues for all employees in the bargaining unit, whether or not the employee had joined the union.

47 *Lavigne v. O.P.S.E.U.*, [1991] 2 S.C.R. 211.

48 *R. v. Advance Cutting and Coring Ltd.*, [2001] 3 S.C.R. 209.

49 Ontario *Labour Relations Act*, ss.48(1), 58(1), 46, 47(1), 54.

50 See, for example, Ontario *Labour Relations Act*, s.17.

51 *DeVilbiss Canada Ltd.*, [1976] OLRB Rep. March 49.

52 *Westinghouse Canada Ltd.*, [1980] 2 Can LRBR 469 (OLRB). The de facto decision standard is criticized as being too favourable to employers, but so far LRBs have refused to alter it. See *IWA, Local 2-69 v. Consolidated Bathurst Packaging Ltd.*, [1983] O.L.R.B. Rep. 1411 for an excellent summary of the pros and cons of alternative tests for triggering the duty to disclose.

53 Damages for loss of opportunity: United Steelworkers of America and Radio Shack, [1980] 1 Can LRBR 99 (Ont); Consolidated Bathurst, *ibid*.

54 *Royal Oak Mines*, *supra* note 10.

55 The federal jurisdiction, B.C., Alberta, Manitoba, Saskatchewan, Ontario, Quebec, and New Brunswick have last offer vote provisions.

56 See *Re Trail Regional Hospital and British Columbia Nurses' Union* (2003), 119 L.A.C. (4th) 54 (Gordon).

57 See for instance, *Toronto Transit Commission*, [1984] OLRB Rep. Dec. 1781, application for judicial review dismissed June 23, 1986 (Div. Ct.).

58 See *British Columbia Hydro and Power Authority*, [1976] 2 Can. L.R.B.R. 410.

59 See *Domglas Ltd.*, [1976] OLRB Rep. Oct. 569; affirmed by the Divisional Court (1978) 19 O.R. (2d) 353.

60 See for e.g. s.81 of the Ontario *Labour Relations Act*.

61 In *Re Oshawa Group Ltd.-and-Teamsters Union Local 419* (1988), 33 L.A.C. (3d) 97, the arbitrator upheld a 14-day suspension

without pay for an employee who was engaging in an illegal strike.

62 See Ontario *Labour Relations Act*, s.1(2); *R v Canadian Pacific Railway Co.* 1962, 31 D.L.R. (2d) 209 (Ont. H.C.) [The Royal York Case].

63 Ontario *Labour Relations Act*, s.72; Royal York, *ibid*; International Wall Coverings Ltd., [1983] O.L.R.B.R. 1316; *CEETSWC v Graham Cable TV/FM* (1986), 12 Can LRBR (N.S.) 1 (CLRB).

64 Ontario *Labour Relations Act*, s.72, also see *Ottawa Citizen*, [1999] O.L.R.D. No. 1445 (Q.L.) and *Mini-Skool Ltd.* (1983), 5 Can LRBR (N.S.) 211 (OLRB).

65 See for example: Ontario *Labour Relations Act* s.80 for up to six months; *Canada Labour Code* indefinitely.

66 Manitoba and Alberta.

67 Constitution Act, 1982, s.2(b); *U.F.C.W., Local 1518 v. KMart Canada*, [1999] 2 S.C.R. 1083 [Kmart]; *R.W.D.S.U. Local 558 v. Pepsi-Cola Canada Beverages (West) Ltd.*, [2002] 1 S.C.R. 156.

68 *Pepsi, ibid*; see B. Adell, "Secondary Picketing after *Pepsi-Cola*: What's Clear, and What Isn't?" (2003) 10 C.L.E.L.J. 135 for an excellent analysis of this decision.

69 *Pepsi, ibid*, at para. 44.

70 Adell, *supra*, note 68 at 140.

71 Kmart, *supra*, note 67.

72 Closely related to the DFR is the duty of fair referral of union members where, for instance, the union is responsible for running a hiring hall (for example Ontario *Labour Relations Act*, s.75).

73 In *Gendron v. Supply and Services Union of the Public Service Alliance of Canada, Local 50057*, [1990] 1 S.C.R. 1298 [*Gendron*], the Supreme Court of Canada held that that the DFR applies, even if the collective bargaining legislation does not specifically include this duty.

74 *Steele v. Louisville & Nashville Railroad Co*, 323 U.S. 192 (1944).

75 *Re Judd*, [2003] B.C.L.R.B.D. No. 63 at para. 38.

76 *Ibid* at para. 37.

77 *Ibid* at para. 71.

78 *Rayonier Canada (B.C.) Ltd. and International Woodworkers of America, Local 1-217*, [1975] 2 Can. LRBR 196 (BCLRB) [*Rayonier Canada*] at pp. 201–202.

79 *Judd, supra*, note 75 at para. 68.

80 *Ibid* at para. 70.

81 *Lissety Soriano*, [1996] O.L.R.D. No. 452 at 21; *ibid* at para. 55; *Rayonier Canada, supra*, note 78 at p. 201.

82 *Rayonier Canada, ibid*, at p. 201.

83 *Judd, supra*, note 75 at paras. 50–54.

84 *Ibid* at para. 51.

85 *Gendron, supra*, note 73 at 527.

86 *Centre Hospitalier Régina Ltée v. Quebec (Labour Court)*, [1990] 1 S.C.R. 1330, at para. 37.

87 *Judd, supra*, note 75 at para 110.

88 Note that, where the legislation is silent or inapplicable, then the common law duty may still apply (e.g., where the statutory duty applies only to administration and not negotiation then there may be some room for the common law duty to apply).

89 *Radenko Bukvich*, [1982] 1 Can L.R.B.R. 422 (OLRB).

90 *Bachiu and United Steelworkers of America, Local 1005*, [1976] 1 Can. L.R.B.R. 431 (OLRB), at p. 439.

91 *Parry Sound (District) Social Services Administration Board v. O.P.S.E.U.*, [2003] 2 S.C.R. 157.

92 *Constitution Act, 1982*.

93 *Ibid.*, s.32.

94 *Health Services and Support—Facilities Subsector Bargaining Assn. v. British Columbia*, [2007] SCC 27.

95 *Ibid*, at para 91.

96 This passage draws substantially from a previous version of this chapter (Jackson, 2005).

97 See *Renaud v. Central Okanagan School District No. 23*, [1992] 2 S.C.R. 970 [Renaud]; *Ontario Human Rights Commission v. O'Malley v. Simpson-Sears Inc.*, [1985] 2 S.C.R. 536.

98 *British Columbia (Public Service Employee Relations Commission) v. BCGSEU*, [1999] 3 S.C.R. 3 [Meiorin].

99 *Hydro-Québec v. Syndicat des employé-e-s de techniques professionnelles et de bureau d'Hydro-Québec, section locale 2000 (SCFP-FTQ)*, 2008 SCC 43 at paras. 12, 19, 21.

100 *Renaud, supra*, note 97 at para 45.

101 Human rights legislation in B.C., Saskatchewan, Ontario, New Brunswick, Newfoundland and Labrador, and Nova Scotia permitted mandatory retirement, with some exceptions. The other provinces and territories did not permit mandatory retirement.

102 Human rights legislation has been amended such that mandatory retirement is no longer an exception to age discrimination in B.C. (effective January 1, 2008), Saskatchewan (effective November 17, 2007), Ontario (effective December 12, 2006), Newfoundland and Labrador (effective May 26, 2007), and Nova Scotia (effective July 1, 2009). However, in some of these jurisdictions, mandatory retirement is still exempted if certain other requirements are met regarding a retirement plan provided by the employer.

103 "Policy on Discrimination Against Older Persons Because of Age" (2002), available online: Ontario Human Rights Commission http://ohrc.on.ca/english/publications/age-policy.shtml.

104 For a discussion of this phenomenon, see Morley Gunderson, 2003, "Age Discrimination in Employment in Canada," *Contemporary Economic Policy*, 21, No. 3, 318–328.

105 *Alberta (Human Rights and Citizenship Commission) v. Kellogg Brown & Root (Canada) Co.*, [2006] ABQB 302 at para. 99.

106 *Ibid* at para. 99.

107 *Ibid* at para. 99.

Chapter 9

1 *Dowling v. Halifax (City)*, [1998] 1 S.C.R. 22. For a detailed critique of this decision, see G. England, "Dowling v. Halifax (City): the Shortest Hard Case Ever?" (1998) 6 C.L.E.L.J. 455.

2 Recent decisions of the Supreme Court of Canada have ruled that courts will seek to protect employees against this risk. E.g., *Re Rizzo and Rizzo Shoes Ltd.*, [1998] 1 S.C.R. 27; *Wallace v. United Grain Growers Ltd.*, [1997] 3 S.C.R. 701.

3 E.g., *Bartlam v. Saskatchewan Crop Insurance Corp.* (1993), 49 C.C.E.L. 141 (Sask. Q.B.).

4 G. England, "Recent Developments in the Law of the Employment Contract: Continuing Tension Between the Rights Paradigm and the Efficiency Paradigm," (1995) 20 Queen's L.J. 557.

5 *Machtiner v. H.O.J. Industries Ltd.*, [1992] 1 S.C.R. 986.

6 The authorities are comprehensively reviewed in *Sagaz Industries Canada Inc. and Kavana v. 67122 Ontario Ltd.* (2002), C.L.L.C. 210013, at paras 141148–141150 (SCC).

[7] H. Arthurs, 2006, *Fairness at Work*, at pp. 61–66; 230–241.

[8] J. Fudge, E. Tucker, and L. Vosko, "Employee or Independent Contractor? Charting the Legal Distinction and Significance in Canada" (2002), 10 C.L.E.L.J. 193. Compare G. Davidov, "The Reports of My Death are Greatly Exaggerated: 'Employee' as a Viable (Though Overused) Concept" in G. Davidov and B. Langille (eds.) *Boundaries and Frontiers of Labour Law* (Oxford and Portland: Hart Publishing, 2006), at p. 133, who argues that the traditional approach remains useful.

[9] H. Arthurs, 2006, *Fairness at Work*, at pp. 64–66.

[10] E.g., *Aqwa v. Centennial Homes Renovations Ltd.* (2002), C.L.L.C. 210016 (Ont. S.C.J.).

[11] See generally J. Clark and M. Hall, "The Cinderella Directive? Employee Rights to Information About Conditions Applicable to their Contract of Employment" (1992), 21 I.L.J. 106.

[12] A. Fox, *Beyond Contract: Work, Power and Trust Relations* (London: Faber, 1974), esp. pp. 184–86.

[13] Usually this is achieved under the legal rubric of the "just cause" doctrine. Most cases arise where an employee has been dismissed for violating the duty of fidelity and the question is whether or not there is "just cause" for dismissal.

[14] E.g., *Martellacci v. CFC/INX Ltd.* (1997), 28 C.C.E.L. (2d) 75, at p. 83 (Ont. Gen. Div.).

[15] This legislation is examined *infra*, at pp. 25–31.

[16] *Haggarty v. McCullogh*, [2002] A. J. No. 7 (Prov.Ct.).

[17] *Tanton v. Crane Canada Inc.*(2000), C.L.L.C. 210–023 (B.C.S.C.).

[18] [1997] 3 S.C.R. 701.

[19] It is interesting to note that most collective agreement arbitrators have refused to imply a duty of fairness onto the employer during the dismissal process, reasoning that the presence of a grievance and arbitration procedure renders unnecessary the imposition of procedural safeguards prior to dismissal.

[20] The seminal authority is *Bardal v. Globe and Mail Ltd.* (1960), 24 D.L.R. (2d) 140 (Ont. H.C.).

[21] E.g., *Dey v. Valley Forest Products Ltd.* (1995), 11 C.C.E.L. (2d) 1, at p. 9 (N.B.C.A.).

[22] *Cronk v. Canadian General Insurance Co.* (1995), 14 C.C.E.L. (2d) 1 (Ont. C.A.), quashing a ruling of MacPherson J. that job status does not automatically warrant a larger notice period, (1994), 94 C.L.L.C. 14032 (Ont. C.J.).

[23] For rejecting the approach, see *Bramble v. Medis Health and Pharmaceutical Services Inc.*(1999), 99 C.L.L.C. 210-045 (N.B.C.A.). For extending the approach, see *Tanton v. Crane Canada Inc.*(2000), C.L.L.C. 210-023 (B.C.S.C.), where a low-skilled warehouseman with 25 years' seniority was given 24 months' reasonable notice.

[24] The leading authority is *McKinley v. B. C. Tel* (2001), C.L.L.C. 210027. See *Dowling, supra* note 1.

[25] The important exception is where an employee is dismissed for illegal reasons, for example, because of religious discrimination or for forming a union. In such limited circumstances, reinstatement to employment is a legal option.

[26] *Farber v. Royal Trust*, [1997] 1 S.C.R. 846.

[27] G. England, "Recent Developments in Employment Law: Tell Me the Old, Old Story" (2002), 9 C.L.E.L.J. 37, who argues for relaxing the laws on economic dismissals while simultaneously strengthening the legal safeguards for employees in performance-related dismissals.

[28] H. Collins, *Justice in Dismissal* (Oxford: Clarendon Press, 1992).

[29] *McKinley, supra* note 24, esp. para 141206, and *supra* note 27 for a discussion.

[30] *Vorvis v. Insurance Co. of British Columbia*, [1989] 1 S.C.R. 1085.

[31] L. Batton, "International Labour Law: Selected Issues" (Deventer: Kluwer, 1993).

[32] *Keays v. Honda Canada Inc.*,[2005] O.J. No. 1145 (S.C.J.), varied [2006] Can. L11 33191 (Ont. C.A.).

[33] For a detailed review of these and other specialized protective employment statutes, see England, Wood, and Christie, *Employment Law in Canada*, ch. 8.

[34] Detailed examination of the enforcement mechanisms in the Labour Side Agreement are provided in L. Compa, "NAFTA's Labour Side Agreement Five Years On: Progress and Prospects for the NAALC" (1999), 7 C.L.E.L.J. 1; J. Stensland, "Internationalising the North American Agreement on Labour Cooperation" (1995), 4 *Minn. Jo. of Global Trade* 162.

[35] See, for example, R. Di Tella and R. MacCulloch, "The Consequences of Labour Market Flexibility: Panel Evidence Based on Survey Data," at pp. 1–4, currently unpublished, available from Professor Di Tella at rditella@hbs.edu; A. Lindbeck and D. Snower, *The Insider–Outsider Theory of Employment and Unemployment* (M.I.T. Press, 1991); R. Posner, "Some Economics of Labor Law" (1984), 51 *U. of Chicago L. Rev.* 988; M. Gunderson, "Social and Economic Impact of Labour Standards," Research Report for the Federal Labour Standards Review Commission, 2006, available at website: www1.servicecanada.gc.ca/en/labour/employment _standards/fls/research/research01/page00.shtml.

[36] See, for example, S. Deakin and F. Wilkinson, "Labour Law, Social Security and Economic Inequality" (1991), 15 *Camb. Jo. of Economics* 125; S. Deakin and F. Wilkinson, "Equality, Efficiency and Economic Progress: The Case for Universally Applied Equitable Standards for Wages and Conditions of Work" in W. Sengenberger and D. Campbell (eds) *Creating Economic Opportunities: the Role of Labour Standards in Economic Restructuring* (Geneva: I.L.O. Institute for Labour Studies, 1994) p. 422; H. Collins, "Regulating the Employment Relationship for Competitiveness" (2001), 30 I.L.J. 17.

[37] A noteworthy exception is the careful analysis of the recommendations to reform Part 111 of the Canada Labour Code in Arthurs, 2006, *Fairness at Work*, chapters 2, 3, and 11.

[38] In the context of the employment standards acts, see Arthurs, 2006, *Fairness at Work*, chapter 9. In the context of human rights acts, see "Promoting Equality: A New Visions," Report of the Canadian Human Rights Act Review Panel, Chair Laforest (Ottawa: Department of Justice, 2000), Part 2. A comprehensive historical account is provided by P. Malles, *Canadian Labour Standards in Law, Agreement and Practice* (Ottawa: Economic Council of Canada, 1976).

[39] See generally Arthurs, 2006, *Fairness at Work*.

[40] *Parry Sound (District) Social Services Administration Board v. Ontario Public Service Employees Union, Local 324*, [2003] SCC 42.

[41] G. England, "Section 240 of the Canada Labour Code: Some Current Pitfalls" (1999), 27 *Man. L. J.* 17.

[42] S. Abraham, "Can a Wrongful Dismissal Statute Really Benefit Employers?" (1998), 37 *Rel. Ind.* 499.

[43] For an excellent review of the problems common to all human rights acts across Canada, but written in the context of the federal act, see "Promoting Equality," *supra* note 37.

44 For a critical analysis of the assumptions behind the legislation, see R. Knopff, *Human Rights and Social Technology: The New War on Discrimination* (Ottawa: Carleton University Press, 1989).

45 *Vriend v. Alberta*, [1998] 1 S.C.R. 493.

46 "Ontario Human Rights Commission Annual Report, 1999–2000" (Toronto: Ontario Human Rights Commission, 2000) Table 1.

47 E.g., *Canadian Human Rights Act* R.S.C. 1985, c.H-6, s.53(3) which allows the tribunal to award up to $20 000 punitive damages if the employer has acted "wilfully or recklessly."

48 *National Capital Alliance on Race Relations v. The Queen* (1997), 28 C.H.R.R. D/179 (Can. H.R.T.).

49 M. Gunderson, "Implications of the Duty to Accommodate for Industrial Relations Practice" (1992), 2 C.E.L.J. 294.

50 *British Columbia (Public Service Employee Relations Commission) v. B.C.G.S.E.U.*, [1999] 3 S.C.R. 3.

51 Gunderson, *supra* note 49.

52 *Janzen v. Platy Enterprises Ltd.* (1989), 25 C.C.E.L. 1 (SCC).

53 The cases are examined in detail in A. Aggarwal and M. Gupte, *Sexual Harassment in the Workplace*, 3rd ed. (Toronto: Butterworths, 2000) ch. 3.

54 *Bannister v. General Motors of Canada Ltd.* (1998), 98 C.L.L.C. 210031 (Ont. C.A.).

55 K. Schucher, "Achieving a Workplace Free of Sexual Harassment: The Employer's Obligations" (1995), 3 C.L.E.L.J. 171.

56 A useful template is provided in the *Canada Labour Code* R.S.C. 1985, c.L-2, s.247.4(2).

57 E.g., *Cluff v. Canada (Department of Agriculture)* (1992), 20 C.H.R.R. D/61 (Can. H.R.T.), affm'd (1993), 94 C.L.L.C. 17018 (F.T.D.).

58 *Robichaud v. Canada (Treasury Board)*, [1987] 2 S.C.R. 84.

59 K. Swinton, "Enforcement of Occupational Health and Safety: Role of the Internal Responsibility System" in K. Swan and K. Swinton (eds.) *Studies in Labour Law* (Toronto: Butterworths, 1983) p. 143.

60 *Nova Scotia Occupational Health and Safety Advisory Council Discussion Paper*, Oct. 20, 1993, p. 10.

61 Relevant Canadian studies are K. I. George, "Les comites de sante, et de securite du travail" (1985), *Rel. Ind.* 512; G. Bryce and P. Manga, "The Effectiveness of Health and Safety Committees" (1985), 40 *Rel. Ind.* 257. In the United States, the presence of a union strengthens compliance with health and safety laws: D. Weil, "Are Mandated Health and Safety Committees Substitutes for or Supplements to Labour Unions?" (1998/99), 52 *Rel. Ind.* 339.

62 M. Harcourt and S. Harcourt, "When Can an Employee Refuse Unsafe Work and Expect to Be Protected from Discipline? Evidence from Canada" (1999–2000), 53 *Ind. and Lab. Rel.* Rev. 684; R. Brown, "The Right to Refuse Unsafe Work" (1983), 17 *U.B.C. L. Rev.* 1.

63 *Ottoman Bank v. Chakarian*, [1930] A.C. 277 (H.L.).

64 C. Moser and P. Simon, *Hazardous Products: Canada's WHMIS Laws*, 2nd ed. (Don Mills: C.C.H. Canadian Ltd., 1989).

65 On this topic generally, see E. Tucker, *Administering Danger in the Workplace: The Law and Politics of Occupational Health and Safety Regulation in Ontario, 1850–1914* (Toronto: University of Toronto Press, 1990), and Tucker, ed., *Working Disasters: The Politics of Recognition and Response* (New York: Baywood Publishing Company, Inc., 2006).

66 R. Brown, "Administrative and Criminal Penalties in the Enforcement of Occupational Health and Safety Legislation" (1992), 30 *Osgoode Hall L.J.* 691.

67 H. Glasbeek and S. Rowland, "Are Injuring and Killing at Work Crimes?" (1979), 17 *Osgoode Hall L.J.* 506.

68 The sorry saga is recounted by E. Tucker, "The Westray Mine Disaster and its Aftermath: the Politics of Causation" (1995), 10 *Can. J. L. and Soc.* 91.

69 The best critical analysis remains P. Weiler, "Reshaping Workers Compensation for Ontario: A Report Submitted to Robert G. Elgie, MD, Minister of Labour" (Toronto: Ministry of Government Services, 1980). See also T. G. Ison, *Workers Compensation in Canada* (Toronto: Butterworths, 2nd ed., 1989); and T. Ison, *Compensation Systems for Injury and Disease: the Policy Choices* (Toronto: Butterworths, 1994).

Chapter 10

1 The author acknowledges the input of Bill Murnighan, Morley Gunderson, Allen Ponak, Daphne Taras, and Caroline Weber on earlier or current versions of this chapter.

2 Slightly rewritten excerpts are from the *National Post*, September 1, 1999 (C6); September 16, 1999 (C6); September 21, 1999 (C2); September 28, 1999 (C2); October 9, 1999 (D8); October 15, 1999 (C2); Canadian Press Newswire, October 3, 1999; CBC News, "Inco Employees Ink Deal," December 10, 1999, available at www.cbc.ca/news/story/1999/12/10/mb_101299inco.html; CBC News, "Inco Workers Strike in Sudbury," June 1, 2003, available at www.cbc.ca/canada/story/2003/06/01/inco030601.html; and United Steelworkers, "Solidarity Won the Day: Steelworkers Ratify Agreement with CVRD-INCO," April 3, 2007, Steelworkers' News Release, available at www.usw.ca/program/content/3995.php.

3 This simple example assumes that the gains from lower assessments are greater than the cost of the expenditures undertaken to improve health and safety. For more details on distributive and integrative outcomes, see Walton and McKersie, 1991.

4 Professor Robert Hickey of the Queen's University School of Policy Studies is a faculty member in the Masters of Industrial Relations program. He teaches unions and collective bargaining, as well as negotiations and dispute resolution and, in addition, participates in continuing education programs for union officers and staff. Prior to becoming a professor he spent 10 years as a union representative and organizer in the Teamsters Union.

5 Ontario Ministry of Labour. 2006, *Collective Bargaining Highlights* (December), Collective Bargaining Information Services, p. 12, Table 8.

Chapter 11

1 We are grateful to Heather Calder, Federal Mediation and Conciliation Service, Labour Program, Human Resources and Social Development Canada, for her assistance in updating this vignette.

2 Unless otherwise noted, the statistics cited in this chapter were provided by the Workplace Information Directorate, Labour Program, Human Resources and Social Development Canada. These statistics cover all bargaining units in Canada with 500 or more employees. We are grateful to Frédéric Mercier and Janson LaBond of the Workplace Information Directorate for their generous assistance in providing us with, and helping us to interpret, these statistics.

Chapter 12

1 The authors acknowledge material in this chapter that appeared in previous editions of this textbook, formerly titled *Union–Management Relations in Canada*. See Gunderson, Hebdon, Hyatt, and Ponak (2005), Gunderson, Hyatt, and Ponak (1995), and Anderson, Gunderson, and Ponak (1989), and references to earlier versions cited therein. Readers should consult those versions, especially for references to the earlier literature, since such references have often been removed from this current version.

2 Based on articles from *The Globe and Mail* (December 5, 1997), p. A2; (March 7, 1998), p. 83; and (December 8, 1998), p. B3. Reproduced with permission from *The Globe and Mail*.

3 Abowd and Tracy (1989); Cramton, Gunderson, and Tracy (1999b); Cramton and Tracy (1992, 1994); Hayes (1984); Kennan and Wilson (1989); McConnell (1989); Tracy (1987).

4 Cousineau and Lacroix (1986); Gunderson, Kervin, and Reid (1986); Gunderson and Melino (1990); Kennan (1980); Maki (1986); Reder and Neumann (1980); Siebert and Addison (1981).

5 Reviewed in Kennan (1986).

6 References to the large number of specific studies that relate strikes to these different measures of aggregate business conditions are contained in the chapter on strikes in the earlier editions of this textbook. Other contributions include McConnell (1989) and Kramer and Hyclak (2002).

7 References to the particular studies are given in the strike chapter in earlier editions of this book.

8 Abowd and Tracy (1989); Budd (1994, 1996); Card (1990); Cramton, Gunderson, and Tracy (1999a, 1999b); Cramton and Tracy (1992, 1994); Cousineau and Lacroix (1986); Dussault and Lacroix (1980); Gramm (1986, 1987); Gramm, Hendricks, and Kahn (1988); Gunderson, Kervin, and Reid (1986, 1989); Gunderson and Melino (1990); McConnell (1989, 1990); Schnell and Gramm (1987); Swidinsky and Vanderkamp (1982); Tracy (1986, 1987); Vrooman (1989).

9 Campolieti, Hebdon, and Hyatt (2005), Card (1990); Gunderson and Melino (1990); Harrison and Stewart (1989); McConnell (1990); Ondrich and Schnell (1993); Tracy (1986, 1987); Vrooman (1989); and earlier references cited in Kennan (1986).

10 Excellent reviews and discussions of many of these studies are given in Edwards (1992), Godard (1992) and Kaufman (1993).

11 Cohn and Eaton (1989); Franzosi (1989).

12 Martin (2001); McClendon and Klaas (1993); Ng (1991, 1993); Schutt (1982); Tomkiewicz, Tomkiewicz, and Brenner (1985).

13 Cohen (1990); Kaufman (1993).

14 See Chapter 17 in this volume as well as Edwards (1992) and references cited therein.

15 Many of these studies are discussed in Edwards (1986).

16 Cousineau, Lacroix, and Vachon (1991) find strike activity to be less in foreign-owned firms. Ng and Maki (1988) find that it is the same, but that members of national unions are more likely to strike than are members of international unions. Budd (1994) finds no difference in strike activity between foreign-owned firms and Canadian-owned firms, nor between members of national or international unions. He argues that the differences disappear when adequate control variables are included to control for the effect of other determinants of strike activity, especially industry and firm size. Budd also reviewed the results from a number of similar studies in the United Kingdom and Ireland, and found that there is no consensus regarding the effect of foreign ownership.

17 Cousineau and Lacroix (1986); Ingram, Metcalf and Wadsworth (1993); Schwarz and Koziara (1992); Swidinsky and Vanderkamp (1982).

18 Currie and McConnell (1991); Cramton, Gunderson, and Tracy (1999b); Godard (1992); Gramm (1986, 1987); Gunderson, Kervin, and Reid (1986, 1989); Hebdon, Hyatt, and Mazerolle (1999); Swidinsky and Vanderkamp (1982). Based on Ontario data, Campolieti, Hebdon and Hyatt (2005) found that smaller bargaining units were less likely to strike but had longer strikes when they occurred. The authors attributed the longer strikes to greater worker solidarity and commitment in smaller bargaining units.

19 Horn, McGuire and Tomkiewicz (1982) find mistrust and lack of communication between union and management to be important predictors of teacher strikes.

20 For teachers, Montgomery and Benedict (1989) found that bargaining experience led to fewer and shorter strikes.

21 See the previous editions of this book for a discussion of the earlier evidence. Also, see Campolieti, Hebdon, and Hyatt (2005) for recent evidence of the "teetotaller" effect in Ontario.

22 Discussions of measurement problems are given in Aligisakis (1997), Briskin (2007), Cameron (1983), Franzosi (1989), Garen and Krislov (1988), ILO (1990), Lacroix (1986b), Segella (1995), Shalev (1978), Stern (1978), and Sweeney and Davies (1997). Briskin (2007) provides a particularly detailed account of how strike statistics are compiled in Canada.

23 In Canada, mid-contract and other illegal strikes have been described and analyzed in Jones and Walsh (1984) and Ng (1987).

24 Dussault and Lacroix (1980); Gunderson, Kervin, and Reid (1986); Swidinsky and Vanderkamp (1982).

25 The terms "conciliation," "mediation," and "fact-finding" are sometimes used interchangeably and are often used differently in different jurisdictions as well as in different labour relations laws. Hence, the terminology used here should be regarded as a common, but not exclusive, way of defining these concepts.

26 Currie and McConnell, 1991; Gunderson, Hebdon, and Hyatt, 1996; Ichniowski (1988); Olson (1986, 1988); Partridge (1988).

27 Lacroix (1986a) cites numerous studies that find that strikes lead to higher subsequent wage settlements; however, his own results suggest that this is sensitive to the specifications of the estimation equation. Card (1990) finds no relationship between strikes and subsequent wage settlements, except for very long strikes which lead to lower wage settlements.

28 Becker and Olson (1986); Davidson, Worrell and Garrison (1988); DeFusco and Fuess, 1991; DiNardo and Hallock (2002); Kramer and Hyclak (2002); Neumann (1980).

29 Strike effects on productivity have been found to be both negative (Flaherty, 1987) and positive (Knight, 1989). Other studies have found that negative productivity effects in linked industries that supplied or depended upon the struck industries were stronger than in the struck industries themselves (McHugh, 1991).

30 Gunderson and Melino (1987); Hameed and Lomas (1975); Knight (1989); Maki (1983); Neumann and Reder (1984); Paarsch (1990).

Chapter 13

[1] This chapter is a further revision of a chapter that first appeared in the third edition (entitled *Union-Management Relations in Canada*), co-authored by K. Wm. Thornicroft and G. Eden.

[2] Ponak, Painter, and Shenfield, "Beyond Collision: High Integrity Labour Relations. National Defence/Canadian Forces—U.N.D.E Case Study." This case study is based on interviews and employer and union documents. The DND/CF–UNDE case study is featured in the award-winning documentary film *Beyond Collision: High Integrity Labour Relations* produced by Bert Painter and Allen Ponak. For film information, visit: www.moderntimesworkplace.com.

[3] BC *Labour Relations Code*, RSBC 1996, c.244 as amended, s.58.

[4] In *St. Anne Nackawic Pulp & Paper v. C.P.U.*, [1986] 1 S.C.R. 704, the employer sued a union for damages sustained as a result of the union's unlawful "sympathy" strike; the Supreme Court of Canada held that the civil courts did not have any jurisdiction to adjudicate the dispute and that the employer should, if it wished to pursue the claim, file a grievance under its collective agreement.

[5] See *Weber v. Ontario Hydro*, [1995] 2 S.C.R. 929 (SCC), and *New Brunswick v. O'Leary*, [1995] 2 S.C.R. 967 (SCC), where the Supreme Court of Canada ruled that arbitrators have the "exclusive jurisdiction" to resolve all disputes that "arise from the collective agreement."

[6] The results of this on-line survey are summarized at: www.nupge.ca/news_2002/news_de02/n16de02b.htm.

[7] See *Kelso v. The Queen*, [1981] 1 S.C.R. 199. Employees are not required to "obey" if the employer's order places their health or safety in jeopardy or is otherwise unlawful. It has been suggested, however, that employees' right to refuse "unsafe" work is more theoretical than real (Harcourt and Harcourt, 2000).

[8] See *Wm. Scott & Company Ltd. and Canadian Food and Allied Workers Union*, [1977] 1 C.L.R.B.R. 1 (Weiler).

[9] This is to be contrasted with the situation in the United States where, by virtue of section 9(a) of the *National Labour Relations Act*, bargaining-unit employees "shall have the right at any time to present grievances to their employer and have such grievances adjusted. . . . "

[10] *C.U.P.E., Local 3373 v. Queen's County Residential Services Inc.* (2004), 236 D.L.R. (4th) 133 (P.E.I.C.A.), leave to appeal to the Supreme Court of Canada refused: September 2, 2004.

[11] However, the extent to which the union may rely on such "post-discharge" evidence has been limited by the Supreme Court of Canada's decision in *Cie Minière Québec Cartier v. Québec*, [1995] 2 S.C.R. 1095.

[12] In turn, pre-hearing and post-hearing delay may be more finely subcategorized. For example, pre-hearing delay includes delay associated with selecting an arbitrator as well as delay in fixing a hearing date once an arbitrator has been selected. Different factors come into play at each stage. Thus, lawyers are associated more with delay in fixing a hearing date than with delay in selecting an arbitrator; see Ponak et al. (1996).

[13] Arbitrator "acceptability" within the larger labour relations community has been elevated to something approaching a legal requirement: see *C.U.P.E. v. Ontario (Minister of Labour)*, [2003] 1 S.C.R. 539.

[14] *Weber v. Ontario Hydro, supra*.

[15] *Rucetta v. Graham*, [1998] O.J. No. 1198 (Ont. C.A.); leave to appeal to Supreme Court of Canada refused; *Giorno v. Pappas* (1990), 170 D.L.R. (4th) 160 (Ont. C.A.); but *cf. Fording Coal Ltd. v. U.S.W.A., Local 7884* (1999), 169 D.L.R. 4th 468 (B.C.A.A.).

[16] *New Brunswick v. O'Leary, supra.*

[17] *Pilon v. International Minerals Chemical Corp. Canada Ltd.* (1996), 31 O.R. (3d) 210 (Ont. C.A.).

[18] *U.S.W.A. Local 7884 v. Fording Coal Ltd.*, [1999] B.C.J. No. 2109 (B.C.C.A.) but *cf. Saskatchewan Human Rights Commission v. Cadillac Fairview Corporation* (1999), 173 D.L.R. (4th) 609 (Sask. C.A.). It is interesting to note that the leading Supreme Court of Canada authority regarding the scope of the bona fide occupational requirement (BFOR) defence under human legislation—*B.C.(P.S.E.R.C.) v. B.C.G.S.E.U.*,[1999] 3 S.C.R. 3—was originally filed as a grievance rather than a complaint to the provincial human rights commission.

[19] *McLeod v. Egan*, [1975] 1 S.C.R. 517 (SCC).

[20] *St. Anne Nackawic Pulp & Paper Co. v. C.P.U., Local 219*, [1986] 1 S.C.R 704 (SCC).

[21] *Douglas/Kwantlen Faculty Assn.v. Douglas College*, [1990] 3 S.C.R. 570 (SCC).

[22] *Weber v. Ontario Hydro*, [1995] 2 S.C.R. 929 (SCC) and *New Brunswick v. O'Leary*, [1995] 2 S.C.R. 967 (SCC).

[23] *Regina Police Assn. v. Regina (City) Board of Police Commissioners*, [2000] 1 S.C.R. 360 (SCC).

[34] *Bisaillon v. Concordia University*, [2006] 1 S.C.R. 666 (SCC).

[25] *Voice Construction Ltd. v. Construction & General Workers' Union, Local 92*, [2004] 1 S.C.R. 609 (SCC).

[26] *C.U.P.E. v. Ontario (Minister of Labour)*, [2003] 1 S.C.R. 539.

Chapter 14

[1] The goals of unions are discussed in Chapter 2 in this text. No attempt is made here to review the empirical literature exhaustively. Lewis (1986a) reviews approximately 200 U.S. studies and Jarrell and Stanley (1990) review 114 U.S. studies of the union impact on wages alone. International evidence is reviewed in Andrews et al. (1998), Blanchflower (1999), and Kaufman (2002). Benjamin et al. (2007) review 15 Canadian studies, and Renaud (1997) reviews 20 Canadian studies of the wage impact.

[2] Comprehensive reviews of these earlier macro studies are contained in Lewis (1963) for U.S. studies prior to 1963 and in Lewis (1983) for studies after 1962.

[3] Reviewed in Lewis (1986a, 1986b), with methodological problems also discussed in Andrews et al. (1998).

[4] Such studies often control for the selection bias that may occur if union workers are sorted into the union sector on the basis of unobserved characteristics that also affect wages. Canadian studies that deal with the selection bias include Kumar and Stengos (1985), Renaud (1998), Robinson and Tomes (1984), and Simpson (1985).

[5] In the panel studies, the analyst makes the reasonable assumption that the conventional unobserved factors (for example, motivation) remain constant for each individual. The union impact is identified when these individuals change their union status over time. Unfortunately, this methodology gives rise to problems of its own since only a small sample of individuals change their union status. When they do so, it is often under unusual circumstances and other factors are also often changing, thereby making a pure union impact difficult to disentangle. Generally, estimates of the union impact obtained from

longitudinal panel data have been slightly smaller than those obtained from cross-sectional data. An example of a U.S. study using longitudinal data is Jakubson (1991). Canadian studies include Grant, Swidinsky, and Vanderkamp (1987), Robinson (1989), and Swidinsky and Kupferschmidt (1991). Freeman (1984) reviews the methodological problems with such studies.

[6] Reviews of this evidence are contained in Hirsch and Schumacher (1998), Kuhn (1998), and Lewis (1963, 1986a, 1986b). Reviews of the Canadian evidence are given in Benjamin et al. (2007) and Renaud (1998).

[7] See Christofides and Stengos (2003) for Canadian evidence and a discussion of the literature, and Bratsberg and Ragan (2002) and Grant (2001) for the United States.

[8] Based on Canadian data; however, White (1994) indicates that professionals benefit from unionization. Klaff and Ehrenberg (2003) review U.S. evidence indicating that university faculty salaries are slightly higher in unionized universities compared to comparable nonunion ones. For non-professional staff they find a union wage premium of 9–11 percent, close to the average union wage premium. For low-wage child care services in Canada, Cleveland, Gunderson, and Hyatt (2003) also find a substantial union wage premium of 15 percent.

[9] Belman, Heywood, and Lund (1997); Card (2001); DiNardo, Fortin, and Lemieux, 1996; Freeman, 1980; and Meng (1990a). Freeman (1993) finds that about one-fifth of the increase in wage inequality for males over the period 1970 to 1987 in the United States can be attributed to the decline of unionization over this period. Based on Canadian data, Lemieux (1993, 1998) finds that unions reduce overall wage inequality for men but not for women, because higher-wage women tend to be unionized. Fairris (2003) finds that unions reduced wage inequity in Mexico in the 1980s, but this effect diminished in the 1990s as union density fell and as unions were less able to offset competitive market pressures.

[10] Almost 50 studies reviewed in Lewis (1986a, 1986b).

[11] Christofides and Swidinsky (1994), Doiron and Riddell (1994), Kumar and Stengos (1985), Lemieux (1993), and Renaud (1998).

[12] Reviewed in Davies (1986: 242–45).

[13] Hirsch (1988, 1992) and Rose (1987), although there is considerable variation by industry depending upon the extent to which deregulation fostered competition (Bratsberg and Ragan, 2002; Hendricks, 1994; and Hirsch and Macpherson, 1998, 2000).

[14] See Brown and Sessions (2004), Freeman and Katz (1991), Gaston and Trefler (1995), Macpherson and Stewart (1990), Shippen and Lynch (2002), but not in Bratsberg and Ragan (2002).

[15] Reviews are contained in Ehrenberg and Schwarz (1986), Freeman (1986), and Mitchell (1983), all based on U.S. data, and Renaud (1997, 1998), Riddell (1993), Robinson and Tomes (1984), and Simpson (1985), based on Canadian data.

[16] See Corneo and Lucifora (1997), Ichniowski, Freeman, and Lauer (1989), and Zwerling and Thomason (1995). Neumark and Wachter (1995) find positive effects at the city levels and negative effects at the industry level.

[17] See Freeman (1981), Freeman and Medoff (1984), Ichniowski (1980), and Renaud (1998).

[18] For Canadian evidence, see Swidinsky and Kupferschmidt (1991).

[19] Brown and Medoff (1978), Clark (1980), Freeman and Medoff (1979, 1984), and others comprehensively reviewed in Belman (1992).

[20] Estimates of the output loss due to these inefficiencies are 0.14 percent of gross national product (GNP) in the United States according to Rees (1963) and 0.10 percent of GNP according to DeFina (1983). Larger negative effects are estimated in Vedder and Gallaway (2002).

[21] See Blau and Kahn (1983) and Rees (1994) based on U.S. data; Addison and Belfield (2001) and Fernie and Metcalf (2005) based on British data; and Swidinsky (1992) using Canadian data.

[22] Studies reviewed in Belman (1992), Benjamin et al. (2007), Freeman and Medoff (1984), and Wilson (1995), with a particularly comprehensive review in the meta-analysis of 73 studies in Doucouliagos and Laroche (2003b).

[23] See, for example, Maki (1983) and Mitchell and Stone (1992), which are based on Canadian data.

[24] Earlier studies are reviewed in Freeman (1986). In a more recent study, Hoxby (1996) finds unions to have had a negative effect on the productivity of U.S. public school teachers.

[25] Duncan and Stafford (1980) estimate that about two-fifths of the union–nonunion wage differential reflects a compensating wage for these more demanding working conditions. Kalachek and Raines (1980) find that employers are able to offset some of the union wage cost increase by more stringent hiring standards, notably with respect to the education qualifications of their workers.

[26] See Belman (1992), Bemmels (1987), Flaherty (1987), Ichniowski (1986), and Maki (1983).

[27] See Laporta and Jenkins (1996) and Maki and Meredith (1986) based on Canadian data; Abowd (1989), Becker and Olson (1989, 1992), Belman (1992), Bronars and Deere (1990, 1994), Brunello (1993), Hirsch (1991a, 1991b), Ruback and Zimmerman (1984), and Voos and Mishel (1986) based on U.S. data; and Addison and Belfield (2001), Machin (1991), and Menezes-Filho (1997) based U.K. data. Reviews are given in Addison and Hirsch (1989), Becker and Olson (1989), and Hirsch (1999). Based on U.S. data, Allen (1987) found that unions reduced costs in the construction of large office buildings because union hiring halls were able to co-ordinate the casual market in skilled labour. Unions, however, increased costs in other areas of construction. Based on Canadian data, Laporta and Jenkins (1996) also found that unions actually increased profitability in industries with large numbers of competitive firms but they reduced profits in industries that were dominated by a few firms (i.e., unions could appropriate monopoly profits). Interestingly, Pearce, Groff, and Wingender (1995) found that shareholder wealth does not appear to increase when unions are decertified, perhaps because of the costs involved in implementing the new managerial policies designed to deal with the change from a union to a nonunion environment.

[28] Formal models of what are termed "efficient wage and employment contracts" are set out in Benjamin et al. (2007: Chapter 15), Kuhn (1998), and Pencavel (1991). These studies also review the limited empirical literature on the topic.

[29] The empirical evidence, reviewed in Hirsch (1999), indicates employment growth to be lower in union compared to nonunion plants, although much of this simply reflects the

predominance of unions in large firms and sectors where growth is slow. Even after accounting for this, however, Long (1993) finds employment growth in Canadian manufacturing to be lower in unionized compared to nonunion plants. Similar evidence for the United States is provided in Freeman and Kleiner (1990).

30 See Allen (1988), Becker and Olson (1992), Bronars, Deere, and Tracy (1994), Connolly, Hirsch, and Hirschey (1986), Cooke (1997), Hirsch (1991a, 1991b, 1992) for the United States; Addison and Wagner (1994) and Denny and Nickell (1991) for the U.K.; Odgers and Betts (1997) and Betts, Odgers, and Wilson (2001) for Canada; with reviews in Kuhn (1998) and Hirsch (1999). An important exception is Menezes-Filho, Ulph, and Van Reenen (1998) who find that the negative effect of unions on investment disappears when one controls for the fact that unions are less prominent in the high-tech industries that invest considerably in R & D. They argue that the greater emphasis on jobs compared to wages by British unions could also explain the reluctance of British unions to deter investment. As well, at a more aggregate level, Karier (1995) does not find any evidence indicating that firms in heavily unionized industries in the United States are more likely to transfer their investments out of those industries and into foreign countries. Doucouliagos and Laroch (2003a) found that French unions in general did not have a negative effect on investment, although such an effect was found for militant unions.

Chapter 15

1 The authors would like to acknowledge the contributions to the chapter made by Allen Ponak, who authored and co-authored this chapter in previous editions of the book. They also thank Cameron Bean, a student at the Haskayne School of Business, University of Calgary, for his research assistance in updating the tables in this chapter.

2 Ponak and Shenfield, "Beyond Collision: High Integrity Labour Relations: Calgary Laboratory Services—HSAA Case Study." This vignette can be seen in the film *Beyond Collision: High Integrity Labour Relations*, Calgary Laboratory Services website: www.calgarylabservices.com, and Health Sciences Association of Alberta website: www.hsaa.ca.

3 For a good illustration of how parties attempt to publicly frame bargaining issues for strategic advantage, see the discussion of the 1987 Toronto teachers' strike in Thomason (1995).

4 A complete and current compilation of these industrial relations laws can be found at the HRSDC website: www.hrsdc.gc.ca/en/lp/spila/clli/irlc/01industrial_relations_legislation_canada.shtml.

5 These cases are: (1) Re *Public Service Employee Relations Act, Labour Relations Act,* and *Police Officers Collective Bargaining Act* (1987) 38 DLR (4th) 161 (SCC); (2) *Public Service Alliance of Canada v. The Queen in Right of Canada* (1987) 38 DLR (4th) 249 (SCC); and (3) *Government of Saskatchewan v. Retail, Wholesale, and Department Store Union* (1987) 38 DLR (4th) 277 (SCC).

6 *Health Services and Support–Facilities Subsector Bargaining Association,* [2007] SCC 27.

7 A 1982 court decision significantly altered the designation process under the PSSRA. The federal government can now declare that full service must be maintained, virtually guaranteeing that almost all employees providing the service will be deemed essential. For example, prior to the ruling, approximately 10 percent of air traffic controllers were deemed essential because most commercial aviation would be suspended during a strike. Following the ruling, 100 percent of air traffic controllers must remain on the job because the government has decreed that commercial aviation must continue normally (Swimmer, 1995). This has removed in practice the ability of a number of groups to engage in even a limited strike.

Chapter 16

1 We were unable to find more recent statistics for this situation. However, as far as we know, this situation still prevails.

2 In 2007–2008, the Québec government's expenditure budget amounted to $61 046.2 million, of which $30 007.1 million were allocated to remuneration (Conseil du trésor, 2007).

3 You can access the full text of Bill 7 at www2.publicationsduquebec.gouv.qc.ca/dynamicSearch/telecharge.php?type=5&file=2003C12A.PDF and of Bill 8 at www2.publicationsduquebec.gouv.qc.ca/dynamicSearch/telecharge.php?type=5&file=2003C13A.PDF.

4 The Réseau vigilance is an umbrella organization that brings together the major labour organizations in Québec and approximately 60 community groups in defence of public services and against the policies of the current provincial government. It was created in the aftermath of the 2003 election and gained more momentum in 2004 when the ruling party made public a plan to restructure public services.

5 For the purpose and scope of Bill 142 go to www2.publicationsduquebec.gouv.qc.ca/dynamicSearch/telecharge.php?type=5&file=2005C43A.PDF.

6 In 1998, the Québec Ministry of Labour ceased to produce data from the collective agreements database. Reliable data no longer exist on the distribution of workers according to union affiliation and economic sectors since the annual survey of HRSDC provides information only on total union membership.

7 This prohibition applies to various working conditions including salary, work duration, and annual holidays.

8 The ratio for full-year, full-time workers was at 58.4 percent in 1969, 67.7 percent in 1990, 72.2 percent in 1993, 72.5 percent in 1997 (Statistics Canada, 1999), 70.2 percent in 2002 and 70.5 percent in 2005 (Statistics Canada, 2007a). Until 1997 data were drawn from Survey of Consumer Finances (SCF) and data since 1998 are taken from the Survey of Labour and Income Dynamics (SLID).

9 Except for employers with fewer than 10 employees, who still remained covered only by the *Charter*.

10 Some employers had already completed an exercise of pay equity or salary relativity in their organizations before the

adoption of the law in 1996. Chapter 9 of the law acknowledged this situation by allowing employers to submit an implementation report so the Pay Equity Commission could determine whether their program conformed with the law or not. Given that the obligations of the employers contemplated in this section of the law appeared more flexible than those applicable to other employers, some groups challenged the constitutionality of this section. On January 9, 2003, a judge of the Québec Superior Court struck down Chapter 9 of the *Pay Equity Act*. Consequently, employers who were first exempted according to Chapter 9 were obligated to complete an exercise of pay equity in respect of the law.

[11] This revised section benefited from input from Manon Truchon, to whom we are thankful.

Chapter 17

[1] Lohr, S. 2006. "Outsourcing Is Climbing Skills Ladder," *New York Times*, February 16. © The New York Times. All rights reserved. Used by permission and protected by the Copyright Laws of the United States. The printing, copying, redistribution, or retransmission of the Material without express written permission is prohibited. www.nytimes.com

[2] Greenhouse, S. 2006. "Labor Union, Redefined, for Freelance Workers," *New York Times*, January 27. © The New York Times. All rights reserved. Used by permission and protected by the Copyright Laws of the United States. The printing, copying, redistribution, or retransmission of the Material without express written permission is prohibited. www.nytimes.com

[3] Wines, M. 2006. "Africa Adds to the Miserable Ranks of Child Workers," *New York Times*, August 24. © The New York Times. All rights reserved. Used by permission and protected by the Copyright Laws of the United States. The printing, copying, redistribution, or retransmission of the Material without express written permission is prohibited. www.nytimes.com

References

Chapter 1

ADAMS, R. 2002. "Implications of the International Human Rights Consensus for Canadian Labour and Management." *Canadian Labour and Employment Law Journal*, 9, no. 1, pp. 119–39.

ADAMS, T. S. and H. L. SUMMER. 1905. *Labor Problems*. New York: Macmillan.

ARTHURS, H. W. 1988. "'The Right to Golf': Reflections on the Future of Workers, Unions and the Rest of Us Under the Charter," *Queen's Law Journal*, 13, pp. 17–31.

———. 2006. *Fairness at Work: Federal Labour Standards for the 21st Century (The Arthurs Report)*. Federal Labour Standards Review. Ottawa: Human Resources and Social Development Canada. Available at www.hrsdc.gc.ca/en/labour/employment_standards/fls/final/page00.shtml.

BARBASH, J. 1984. *The Elements of Industrial Relations*. Madison, Wisconsin: University of Wisconsin Press.

———. 1997. "Industrial Relations as Problem-Solving," in *Theorizing in Industrial Relations*, edited by J. Barbash and N. M. Meltz. Australian Centre for Industrial Relations Research and Training (April).

BARLING, J., C. FULLAGAR, and E. K. KELLOWAY. 1992. *The Union and Its Members*. New York: Oxford University Press.

BUDD, J. 2004. *Employment with a Human Face: Balancing Efficiency, Equity, and Voice*. Ithaca, NY: Cornell University Press.

CHAYKOWSKI, R. P. and C. WEBER. 1993. "Alternative Models of Industrial Relations Graduate Programs in Canada and US Universities." Kingston, ON: Queen's University Industrial Relations Centre.

CRAVEN, P. 1980. *'An Impartial Umpire': Industrial Relations and the Canadian State 1900–1911*. Toronto: University of Toronto Press.

DRUCKER, P. F. 1954. *The Practice of Management*. New York: Harper and Row.

DUNLOP, J. T. 1958/1993. *Industrial Relations Systems*, Revised Edition. Harvard Business School Press.

DUXBURY, L., C. HIGGINS, and D. COGHILL. 2003. *Voices of Canadians: Seeking Work–Life Balance*. Human Resources Development Canada.

FERNS, H. S. and B. OSTRY. 1955. *The Age of Mackenzie King*. London: William Heinemann, Ltd.

FUDGE, J. 1988. "Labour, The New Constitution and Old Style Liberalism," *Queen's Law Journal*, 13, No. 2, pp. 61–87.

———. 1999. "The Commercialization of Canada Post: Postal Policy, Business Strategy and Labour Relations," in *Contract and Commitment: Employment Relations in the New Economy*, edited by Anil Verma and Rick Chaykowski. Kingston, ON: Queen's University Press, pp. 293–337.

HENEMAN, H. G., D. P. SCHWAB, J. A. FOSSUM, and L. D. DYER. 1989. *Personnel/Human Resource Management*, 4th Edition. Homewood.

HORWITZ, F. 1990. "HRM: An Ideological Perspective." *Personnel Review*, 19, no. 2, pp. 10–15.

———. 1991. *Managing Resourceful People*. South Africa: Juta and Co.

HUMAN RESOURCES DEVELOPMENT CANADA (HRDC). 2001. *Briefing Document for the Minister of Labour's Roundtable*. Meech Lake, October.

KAUFMAN, B. E. 1993. *The Origins and Evolution of the Field of Industrial Relations in the United States*. Cornell: ILR Press.

———. 2004. *The Global Evolution of Industrial Relations*. Geneva: International Labor Organization.

KAUFMAN, B. E. and D. G. TARAS, eds. 2000. *Nonunion Employee Representation*. Armonk, NY: M. E. Sharpe.

KING, W. L. M. 1918/1973. *Industry and Humanity*. Toronto: University of Toronto Press.

KOCHAN, T. A. 2008. "Conclusion: The Future of Industrial Relations, A.K.A. Work and Employment Relations," in *New Directions in the Study of Work and Employment: Revitalizing Industrial Relations as an Academic Enterprise*, edited by C. Whalen. Edward Elgar Pubs.

KOCHAN, T. A. and H. KATZ. 1988. *Collective Bargaining and Industrial Relations*, 2nd Edition. Richard D. Irwin, Inc.

LAWLER, J. J. 1990. *Unionization and Deunionization: Strategy, Tactics, and Outcomes*. Columbia, SC: University of South Carolina Press.

LEWIN, D. 1991. "The Contemporary Human Resource Management Challenge to Industrial Relations," in *The Future of Industrial Relations*, edited by H. Katz. Ithaca: Institute of Collective Bargaining, Cornell University, pp. 82–99.

LIPSET, S. M. 1995. "Trade Union Exceptionalism: The United States and Canada."*Annals of the American Academy*, AAPSS, 538 (March), pp. 115–30.

LIPSET, S. M. and N. M. MELTZ. 2000. "Estimates of Nonunion Employee Representation in the United States and Canada: How Different Are the Two Countries?" in *Nonunion Employee Representation*, edited by B. E. Kaufman and D. G. Taras. Armonk, NY: M. E. Sharpe.

LIPSET, S. M., N. M. MELTZ with R. GOMEZ and I. KATCHANOVSKI. 2004. *The Paradox of American Unionism: Why Americans Like Unions More than Canadians Do But Join Much Less.* Ithaca, NY: Cornell University ILR Press.

LOWE, G. and G. SCHELLENBERG. 2001. *What's a Good Job? The Importance of Employment Relationships.* Ottawa: Changing Employment Relationships Projects, Canadian Policy Research Networks.

———. 2002. "Employment Relationships as the Centrepiece of a New Labour Paradigm." *Canadian Public Policy*, 28, no. 1, pp. 93–104.

———. 2007. *21st Century Job Quality: Achieving What Canadians Want.* Ottawa: Canadian Policy Research Network.

MARCIANO, V. M. 1995. "The Origins and Development of Human Resource Management," *Academy of Management (Best Papers Proceedings)*.

SIMS, A. C. L. 1994. "Wagnerism in Canada: A Fifty-Year Check-Up." H. D. Woods Memorial Lecture. *Proceedings of the 31st Conference.* Calgary, Alberta: Canadian Industrial Relations Association.

———. 1995. *Seeking a Balance: Canada Labour Code, Part 1, Review.* Ottawa, ON: Government of Canada.

TARAS, D. G. 1997. "Collective Bargaining Regulation in Canada and the United States: Divergent Cultures, Divergent Outcomes," in *Government Regulation of the Employment Relationship*, edited by B. E. Kaufman. Industrial Relations Research Association 50th Anniversary Research Volume, pp. 295–342.

———. 2002. "Alternative Forms of Employee Representation and Labour Policy." *Canadian Public Policy*, 28, no. 1, pp. 105–16.

———. 2008. "How Industrial Relations is Marginalized in Business Schools: Using Institutional Theory to Examine Our Own Home Base," in *New Directions in the Study of Work and Employment: Revitalizing Industrial Relations as an Academic Enterprise*, edited by C. Whalen. Edward Elgar Pubs.

THOMPSON, M., J. B. ROSE, and A. E. SMITH, eds. 2004. *Beyond the Continental Divide: Regional Dimensions of Industrial Relations.* McGill-Queen's University Press.

TIMUR, A. T. and A. PONAK. 2002. "Labor Relations and Technological Change at Canadian Pacific Railway." *Journal of Labor Research*, 24, no. 4, pp. 535–58.

VERMA, A. and R. P. CHAYKOWSKI, eds. 1999. *Contract and Commitment: Employment Relations in the New Economy.* Kingston, ON: IRC Press, Queen's University.

WEILER, P. 1980. *Reconcilable Differences: New Directions in Canadian Labour Law.* Toronto: Carswell.

WHALEN, C., ed. 2008. *New Directions in the Study of Work and Employment: Revitalizing Industrial Relations as an Academic Enterprise.* Edward Elgar.

Chapter 2

ADAMS, J. S. 1965. "Inequity in Social Exchange," in *Advances in Experimental Social Psychology*, Vol. 2, edited by L. Berkowitz. New York: Academic Press, pp. 267–300.

ADAMS, R. J. 1999. "Why Statutory Union Recognition Is Bad Labour Policy: The North American Experience." *Industrial Relations Journal*, 30 (2), pp. 96–100.

———. 2003. "Voice for All: Why the Right to Refrain from Collective Bargaining Is No Right at All." In *Workers Rights as Human Rights*, edited by J. A. Gross. Ithaca, NY: Cornell University Press, pp. 142–59.

AKYEAMPONG, E. B. 2002. "Unionization and Fringe Benefits." *Perspectives on Labour and Income*, 14, no. 3, pp. 42–46.

BALDAMUS, W. 1961. *Efficiency and Effort: An Analysis of Industrial Administration.* London: Tavistock Publications.

BARLING, J., C. FULLAGAR, and E. K. KELLOWAY. 1992. *The Union & Its Members.* Oxford University Press.

BERNARD, E. 1998. "Creating Democratic Communities in the Workplace," in *A New Labor Movement for the New Century*, edited by G. Mantsios. New York: Garland Publishers, pp. 7–19.

BIBBY, R. 1997. "Canadians and Unions: A National Survey of Current Attitudes." Mississauga, Ontario: Work Research Foundation.

BRUCE, P. G. 1989. "Political Parties and Labor Legislation in Canada and the US." *Industrial Relations*, 28, pp. 115–41.

BUTTIGIEG, D. M., S. J. DEERY, and R. D. IVERSON. 2007. "An Event History Analysis of Union Joining and Leaving." *Journal of Applied Psychology*, 92, no. 3, pp. 829–39.

CLEVELAND, G., M. GUNDERSON, and D. HYATT. 2003. "Union Effects in Low-Wage Services: Evidence from Canadian Childcare." *Industrial and Labor Relations Review*, 56, no. 2, 295–305.

COMMONS, J. R. 1909. "American Shoemakers, 1648–1895." *The Quarterly Journal of Economics*, 24 (November).

ESTREICHER, S., ed. 1998. *Employee Representation in the Emerging Workplace: Alternatives/Supplements to Collective Bargaining.* Kluwer Law International.

FANG, T. and A. VERMA. 2002. "Union Wage Premium." *Perspectives on Labour and Income*, 14, no. 4, pp. 17–23.

FREEMAN, R. 1980. "The Exit-Voice Tradeoff in the Labor Market: Unionism, Job Tenure, Quits, and Separations." *Quarterly Journal of Economics*, 94, pp. 643–74.

———. 1984. *Fixed Effects Models of the Exit-Voice Trade-off.* National Bureau of Economic Research Working Paper.

FREEMAN, R. and J. MEDOFF. 1984. *What Do Unions Do?* New York: Basic Books.

FREEMAN, R. and J. ROGERS. 1995. "Worker Representation and Participation Survey: First Report of Findings," in *Proceedings of the Forty-Seventh Annual Meeting of the Industrial Relations Research Association* (January 6–8), Washington, D.C.

———. 1998. "What Do Workers Want? Voice, Representation and Power in the American Workplace," in *Employee Representation in the Emerging Workplace: Alternatives/Supplements to Collective Bargaining*, edited by S. Estreicher. Boston: Kluwer Law International, pp. 3–38.

———. 1999. *What Workers Want*. Ithaca, NY: Cornell University ILR Press.

GINDIN, S. 1995. *The Canadian Auto Workers: The Birth and Transformation of a Union*. Toronto: James Lorimer and Company.

GODARD, J. 1997. "Beliefs About Unions and What They Should Do: A Survey of Employed Canadians."*Journal of Labor Research*, 18, pp. 619–40.

GOMEZ, R., M. GUNDERSON and N. MELTZ. 2002. "Comparing Youth and Adult Desire for Unionization in Canada."*British Journal of Industrial Relations*, 40, no. 3, pp. 521–42.

HARGROVE, B. and W. SKENE. 1998. *Labour of Love: The Fight to Create a More Humane Canada*. Toronto: Macfarlane Walter & Ross.

HIRSCHMAN, A. O. 1971. *Exit, Voice, and Loyalty*. Cambridge, MA: Harvard University Press.

HURD, R. 1996. "Contesting the Dinosaur Image—The Labour Movement's Search for a Future," in *A Half Century of Challenge and Change in Employment Relations*, edited by M. Neufeld and J. McElvey. Ithaca, NY: Cornell University ILR Press.

KUMAR, P. and G. MURRAY. 2002. "Union Bargaining Priorities in the New Economy: Results from the 2000 HRDC Survey on Innovation and Change in Labour Organizations in Canada." *Workplace Gazette* 4, no. 4, pp. 43–67.

LIPPERT, J. 1999. "Magna Hits Campaign Trail Before CAW Vote: Could Bring in Union."*National Post* (October 14).

LIPSET, S. M. and N. M. MELTZ. 1997. "Canadian and American Attitudes Toward Work and Institutions."*Perspectives on Work*, 1, no. 3, Industrial Relations Research Association.

LOWE, G. S. and S. RASTIN. 2000. "Organizing the Next Generation: Influences on Young Workers' Willingness to Join Unions in Canada."*British Journal of Industrial Relations*, 38, no. 2, pp. 203–22.

MILTON, L. P. 2003. "An Identity Perspective on the Propensity of High-Tech Talent to Unionize."*Journal of Labor Research*, 24, no. 1, pp. 31–53.

MURRAY, G. 1995. "Unions: Membership, Structures, and Actions," in *Union–Management Relations in Canada*, 3rd

Edition, edited by M. Gunderson and A. Ponak. Toronto: Addison-Wesley, pp. 159–94.

PIORE, M. 1995. *Beyond Individualism*. Cambridge, Mass.: Harvard University Press.

SAYLES, L. R. and G. STRAUSS. 1967. *The Local Union*. New York: Harcourt, Brace and World, Inc.

SIMS, A. 2000. "A Canadian Policy-Maker's Perspective on Nonunion Representation," in *Nonunion Employee Representation*, edited by B. Kaufman and D. G. Taras. New York: M. E. Sharpe.

SLICHTER, S., J. J. HEALY, and E. R. LIVERNASH. 1960. *The Impact of Collective Bargaining on Management*. Washington, D.C.: The Brookings Institution.

TARAS, D. 2007. "Reconciling Differences Differently: Employee Voice in Public Policymaking and Workplace Governance,"*Comparative Labor Law and Policy Journal*, 28, 167–91.

TARAS, D. G. and J. COPPING. 1998. "The Transition from Formal Nonunion Representation to Unionization: A Contemporary Case."*Industrial and Labor Relations Review*, 52, no. 1, pp. 22–44.

WADDINGTON, J. and A. KERR. 2002. "Unions Fit for Young Workers?"*Industrial Relations Journal*, 33, no. 4, pp. 298–315.

WHEELER, H. and J. A. McCLENDON. 1991. "The Individual Decision to Unionize," in *The State of the Unions*, edited by G. Strauss, D. G. Gallagher and J. Fiorito. Industrial Relations Research Association series, pp. 47–84.

WILLIAMS, K. and D. G. TARAS. 2000. "Reinstatement at Arbitration: The Grievors' Perspective."*Relations industrielles/Industrial Relations*, 55, no. 2, pp. 227–48.

WILLIAMS, L. 1997. "Facing Tomorrow: A Union Perspective."*Perspectives on Work*, 1, no. 1, Industrial Relations Research Association.

Chapter 3

ARTHURS, H. W., D. D. CARTER, and J. H. GLASBEEK. 1981. *Labour Law and Industrial Relations in Canada*. Toronto: Butterworths.

BAUMAN, Z. 1989. *Modernity and the Holocaust*. Cornell UP.

BERCUSON, D. 1990. *Confrontation at Winnipeg*. Montreal: McGill-Queen's University Press.

BHASKAR, R. 1986. *Scientific Realism and Human Emancipation*. Verso.

CLAWSON, D. 1980. *Bureaucracy and the Labor Process: The Transformation of U.S. Industry, 1800–1920*. New York and London: Monthly Review Press.

FORSEY, E. 1982. *Trade Unions in Canada 1812–1902*. Toronto: University of Toronto Press.

GARTMAN, D. 1979. "Origins of the Assembly Line and

Capitalist Control of Work at Ford," in *Case Studies on the Labor Process*, edited by A. Zimbalist. New York and London: Monthly Review Press.

GIDDENS. A. 1992. *The Transformation of Intimacy*. Polity.

GILLIGAN, C. 1982. *In a Different Voice*. Harvard UP.

HARVEY, D. 1989. *The Condition of Postmodernity*. Blackwell.

HERON, C. and R. STOREY, eds. 1986. *On the Job: Confronting the Labour Process in Canada*. Montreal: McGill-Queen's University Press.

HOCHSCHILD, A. 1983. *The Managed Heart*. Berkeley, CA: University of California Press.

HYMAN, R. 1975. *Industrial Relations*. London: Macmillan.

JARDINE, L. 1996. *Worldly Goods: A New History of the Renaissance*. Macmillan.

KEALEY, G., ed. 1973. *Canada Investigates Industrialism: The Royal Commission on the Relations of Labor and Capital 1889*. Toronto: University of Toronto Press.

KLEIN, N. 2000. *No Logo*. Toronto: Vintage Canada.

LITTLER, C. R. 1982. *The Development of the Labour Process in Capitalist Societies*. London: Heinemann Educational Books.

MARSDEN, R. 1999. *The Nature of Capital: Marx After Foucault*. London and New York: Routledge.

MENZIES, H. 1996. *Whose Brave New World? The Information Highway and the New Economy*. Toronto: Between the Lines.

MORTON, D. 1982. "The History of Canadian Labour," in *Union–Management Relations in Canada*, 1st Edition, edited by J. Anderson and M. Gunderson. Don Mills, ON: Addison-Wesley.

NELSON, D. 1975. *Managers and Workers: Origins of the New Factory System in the United States 1880–1920*. Madison: University of Wisconsin Press.

PALMER, B. D. 1982. "The Culture of Control," in *Canada's Age of Industry, 1849–1896: Readings in Canadian Social History*, Volume 3, edited by M. S. Cross and G. S. Kealey. Toronto: McClelland & Stewart.

———. 1983. *Working Class Experience: The Rise and Reconstitution of Canadian Labour, 1960–1980*. Toronto: Butterworths.

———. 1992. *Working Class Experience*, 2nd Edition. Toronto: McClelland & Stewart.

RAY, A. J. and D. FREEMAN. 1978. *"Give Us Good Measure": An Economic Analysis of Relations Between the Indians and the Hudson's Bay Company before 1763*. Toronto: University of Toronto Press.

RITZER, G. 1996. *The McDonaldization of Society*. Thousand Oaks, California: Pine Forge.

STANFORD, J. 1999. *Paper Boom: Why Real Prosperity Requires a New Approach to Canada's Economy*. The Canadian Centre for Policy Alternatives/James Lorimer.

TAYLOR, F. W. 1911. *The Principles of Scientific Management*. New York: Harper and Brothers.

THOMPSON, E. P. 1968. *The Making of the English Working Class*. Harmondsworth: Penguin.

WHITAKER, R. 1979. "Scientific Management Theory as Political Ideology."*Studies in Political Economy*, no. 2 (Autumn).

WILLIAMS, J. 1975. *The Story of Unions in Canada*. J. M. Dent and Sons.

Chapter 4

ADAMS, R. 2005. "Organizing Wal-Mart: The Canadian Campaign."*Just Labour*, 6–7, Autumn, pp. 1–11.

AKYEAMPONG, E. B. 1997. "A Statistical Portrait of the Trade Union Movement."*Perspectives on Labour and Income*, Statistics Canada, Catalogue no. 75-001-XPE, 9, no. 4, pp. 45–54.

———. 1999. "Unionization—An Update."*Perspectives on Labour and Income*, Statistics Canada, Catalogue no. 75-001-XPE, 11, no. 3, pp. 45–65.

ARTHURS, H. W. 2006. *Fairness at Work: Federal Labour Standards for the 21st Century (The Arthurs Report)*. Federal Labour Standards Review. Ottawa: Human Resources and Social Development Canada. Available at www.hrsdc.gc.ca/en/labour/employment_standards/fls/final/page00.shtml.

BAIN, G. S. and R. PRICE. 1983. "Union Growth: Dimensions, Determinants, and Destiny," in *Industrial Relations in Great Britain*, edited by G. S. Bain. Oxford: Basil Blackwell, pp. 3–34.

BLOCK, R. 1993. "Unionization, Collective Bargaining and Legal Institutions in the United States and Canada." *Queen's Papers in Industrial Relations* (1993–4). Kingston, ON Queen's University Industrial Relations Centre.

BLS (Bureau of Labor Statistics). Annual. "Union Members in 2006." *Labor Force Statistics from the Current Population Survey—BLS*, January 2007. Available at http://stats.bls.gov/news.release/pdf.

BRISKIN, L. and P. McDERMOTT, eds. 1993. *Women Challenging Unions: Feminism, Democracy and Militancy*. Toronto: University of Toronto Press.

BRONFENBRENNER, K., S. FRIEDMAN, R. W. HURD, R. A. OSWALD, and R. L. SEEBER, eds. 1998. *Organizing to Win: New Research on Union Strategies*. Ithaca: ILR Press.

BRUCE, P. G. 1989. "Political Parties and Labor Legislation in Canada and the US."*Industrial Relations*, 28, pp. 115–41.

CALURA. various years. *Annual Report of the Minister of Industry, Science and Technology Under the Corporations and Labour Unions Returns Act, Part II—Labour Unions*. Statistics Canada. Cat 71-202. Ottawa: Minister of Industry, Science and Technology. For 1999, see Mainville and Olineck.

CAW–MAGNA. 2007. "Framework of Fairness Agreement Between Magna International Inc. and National

Automobile, Aerospace, Transportation and General Workers of Canada (CAW-Canada)," October 15. Available at **www.caw.ca/campaigns&issues/ongoingcampaigns/ magna/pdf/FF_Agreement.pdf**.

CHAREST, J. 1999. "Articulation institutionnelle et orientations du système de formation professionnelle."*Relations industrielles/Industrial Relations*, 54, pp. 439–71.

CLEGG, H. A. 1976. *Trade Unionism Under Collective Bargaining*. Oxford: Basil Blackwell.

CLMPC (Canadian Labour Market and Productivity Centre). 1992. "The Role of Business–Labour Sectoral Initiatives in Economic Restructuring."*Quarterly Labour Market Productivity Review*, no. 1–2, pp. 26–38.

DION, G. 1986. *Dictionnaire canadien des relations du travail*, 2nd Edition. Québec: Presses de l'Université Laval.

FOURNIER, L. 1991. *Solidarité Inc.: Un nouveau syndicalisme créateur d'emplois*. Montréal: Éditions Québec/Amérique.

FREEMAN, R. B. 1990. "Canada and the World Labour Market to the Year 2000," in *Perspective 2000*, edited by K. Newton, T. Schweitzer, and J. Voyer. Ottawa: Supply and Services Canada, pp. 187–98.

FROST, A. 2000. "Explaining Variation in Workplace Restructuring: The Role of Local Union Capabilities." *Industrial and Labor Relations Review*, 53, no. 4, pp. 559–78.

GODARD, J. 2003. "Do Labor Laws Matter: The Density Decline and Convergence Thesis Revisited."*Industrial Relations*, 42, no. 3, pp. 458–92.

GREENHOUSE, S. 2007. "Steelworkers and British Unions Seek Merger." *The New York Times*, 19 April.

GUNDERSON, M. and A. SHARPE, eds. 1998. *Forging Business–Labour Partnerships*. Toronto: University of Toronto Press.

HAIVEN, L. 1995. "Industrial Relations in Health Care: Regulation, Conflict and Transition to the *Wellness* Model," in *Public Sector Collective Bargaining in Canada: Beginning of the End or End of the Beginning?* edited by G. Swimmer and M. Thompson. Kingston, ON: IRC Press, pp. 236–71.

HAMMER, N. 2005. "International Framework Agreements: Global Industrial Relations Between Rights and Bargaining."*Transfer: European Review of Labour and Resarch*, 11, no. 4, pp. 511–30.

HEMMINGWAY, J. 1978. *Conflict and Democracy*. Oxford: Clarendon Press.

HRSDC (Human Resources and Social Development Canada—Labour Policy and Workplace Information). Annual until 1999. *Directory of Labour Organizations in Canada*. Ottawa: Canadian Government Publishing. Available at www110.hrdc-drhc.gc.ca/millieudetravail_workplace/ot_lo/index.cfm/doc/english.

———. 2007. "Union Membership in Canada—2007." Available at **www.hrsdc.gc.ca/en/lp/wid/pdf/Union _Membership.pdf**.

HUNT, G. and J. HAIVEN. 2006. "Building Democracy for Women and Sexual Minorities: Union Embrace of Diversity."*Relations industrielles/Industrial Relations*, 61, no. 4, pp. 666–83.

HYMAN, R. 1975. *Industrial Relations*. London: Macmillan.

KAPLAN, W. 1987. *Everything That Floats*. Toronto: University of Toronto Press.

KRAHN, H. and G. S. LOWE. 1984. "Community Influences on Attitudes Towards Unions."*Relations industrielles/ Industrial Relations*, 39, pp. 93–113.

KUMAR, P. 1995. *Unions and Workplace Change in Canada*. Kingston, ON: IRC Press.

KUMAR, P. and G. MURRAY. 2002. "Canadian Union Strategies in the Context of Change."*Labor Studies Journal*, 26, no. 4, pp. 1–28.

———. 2006. "Innovation in Canadian Unions: Patterns, Causes and Consequences," in *Paths to Union Renewal: Canadian Experiences*, edited by P. Kumar and C. Schenk. Peterborough: Broadview Press, pp. 79–102.

KUMAR, P., G. MURRAY, and S. SCHETAGNE. 1998. "Workplace Change in Canada: Union Perception of Impacts, Responses and Support Systems."*Workplace Gazette*, 1, no. 4, pp. 75–87.

KUMAR, P. and C. SCHENK, eds. 2006. *Paths to Union Renewal: Canadian Experiences*. Peterborough, ON: Broadview Press.

LABOUR CANADA, BUREAU OF LABOUR INFORMATION. Various years. *Directory of Labour Organizations in Canada*. Ottawa: Minister of Supply and Services Canada.

LÉVESQUE, C. and G. MURRAY. 2002. "Local Versus Global: Rethinking and Reactivating Local Union Power in the Global Economy."*Labor Studies Journal*, 27, no. 3, pp. 39–65.

LEWCHUK, W. and D. WELLS. 2006. "When Corporations Substitute for Adversarial Unions: Labour Markets and Human Resource Management at Magna."*Relations industrielles/Industrial Relations*, 61, no. 4, pp. 639–65.

LFS. Annual. *Labour Force Survey*. Ottawa: Statistics Canada. Catalogue 71–201.

LIPSET, S. M. and N. M. MELTZ. 1997. "Canadian and American Attitudes Toward Work and Institutions." *Perspectives on Work*, 1, no. 3, pp. 14–19.

MAINVILLE, D. and C. OLINECK. 1999. *Unionization: A Retrospective*. Statistics Canada. Supplement. Catalogue no. 75-001-XPE (Summer).

MARTIN, D. 1995. *Thinking Union: Activism and Education in Canada's Labour Movement*. Toronto: Between the Lines.

MASTERS, M. F., R. GIBNEY, and T. ZAGENCZYK. 2006. "The AFO-CIO v. CTW: The Competing Visions, Strategies, and Structures."*Journal of Labor Research*, 27, no. 4, pp. 473–504.

MICHELS, R. 1962. *Political Parties*. New York: Collier Books, first published 1911.

MURRAY, G. 1998. "Steeling for Change: Organization and Organizing in Two USWA Districts in Canada," in *Organizing to Win: New Research on Union Strategies*, edited by K. Bronfenbrenner, S. Friedman, R. W. Hurd, R. A. Oswald and R. L. Seeber. Ithaca: ILR Press, pp. 320–38.

MURRAY, G., J. BELANGER, A. GILES, and P-A. LAPOINTE. 2002. *Work and Employment Relations in the High Performance Workplace*. Florence, KY: Routledge.

MURRAY, G. and P. VERGE. 1999. *La représentation syndicale: Visage juridique actuel et futur*. Quebec: Les Presses de l'Université Laval.

NISSEN, B., ed. 1999. *Which Direction for Organized Labor? Essays on Organizing, Outreach and Internal Transformations*. Detroit: Wayne State University Press.

PANITCH, L. and D. SWARTZ. 2003. *From Consent to Coercion: The Assault on Trade Union Freedoms*, 3rd edition. Toronto: Garamond Press.

PIORE, M. 1983. "Can the American Labor Movement Survive Re-Gomperization?" in *Proceedings of the Thirty-Fifth Annual Meeting*, edited by B. D. Dennis. Madison: Industrial Relations Research Association, pp. 30–39.

PONAK, A. and D. G. TARAS. 1997. "Right to Work Study: Submission to the Alberta Economic Development Authority Joint Review Committee," mimeo. Alberta Economic Development Authority.

RIDDELL, W. C. 1993. "Unionization in Canada and the United States: A Tale of Two Countries," in *Small Differences That Matter: Labor Markets and Income Maintenance in Canada and the United States*, edited by D. Card and R. B. Freeman. Chicago: The University of Chicago Press, pp. 109–48.

RINEHART, J., C. HUXLEY, and D. ROBERTSON. 1997. *Just Another Car Factory: Lean Production and Its Discontents*. Ithaca: ILR Press.

ROBINSON, I. 1994. "NAFTA, Social Unionism, and Labour Movement Power in Canada and the United States."*Relations industrielles*, 49, pp. 657–95.

———. 1998. "Réactions des centrales syndicales nord-améri-caines à la restructuration néolibérale," in *L'intégration économique en Amérique du Nord et les relations industrielles*, edited by R. Blouin and A. Giles. Sainte-Foy: Les Presses de l'Université Laval, pp. 119–48.

ROSE, J. B. and G. N. CHAISON. 1990. "New Measures of Union Organizing in the United States and Canada."*Industrial Relations*, 29, pp. 457–68.

STATISTICS CANADA. 2007. "Unionization."*Perspectives on Labour and Income*, August. Statistics Canada, Catalogue no. 75-001-XIE. Available at www.statcan.ca/english/freepub/75-001-XIE/comm/fact-2.pdf.

THOMPSON, M. and A. A. BLUM. 1983. "International Unionism in Canada: The Move to Local Control."*Industrial Relations*, 22, pp. 71–86.

TROY, L. 2000. "U.S. and Canadian Industrial Relations: Convergent or Divergent?"*Industrial Relations*, 39, no. 4, pp. 695–713.

VERGE, P. and G. MURRAY. 1991. *Le droit et les syndicats*. Sainte-Foy: Presses de l'Université Laval.

VISSER, J. 2006. "Union Membership Statistics in 24 Countries."*Monthly Labor Review*, 129, pp. 38–49.

WEILER, P. 1984. "Striking a New Balance: Freedom of Contract and the Prospects for Union Representation." *Harvard Law Review*, 98, pp. 351–420.

WHITE, J. 1993. *Sisters and Solidarity: Women and Unions in Canada*. Toronto: Thompson Educational Publishing, Inc.

WORKPLACE INFORMATION DIRECTORATE (Human Resources Development Canada). 1999. "Union Membership in Canada—1999."*Workplace Gazette*, 2, no. 3, pp. 61–62.

YATES, C. 1998. "Unity and Diversity: Challenges to an Expanding Canadian Autoworkers Union."*Canadian Review of Sociology and Anthropology*, 35, pp. 93–118.

———. 2000. "Staying the Decline in Union Membership: Union Organizing in Ontario, 1985–99." *Relations industrielles*, 55, no. 2, pp. 640–74.

———. 2005. "Segmented Labour, United Unions? How Unions in Canada Cope with Increased Diversity." *Transfer*, 4, pp. 617–28.

Chapter 5

BCLRB (British Columbia Labour Relations Board). 2003. *Starbucks Corporation [Certain Employees of] and Starbucks Corporation and National Automobile, Aerospace, Transportation and General Workers' Union of Canada (CAW—Canada)*, Local 3000. B123/2003.

BÉLANGER, J., ed. 1999. *Being Local and Worldwide: ABB and the Challenge of Global Management*. Ithaca: Cornell University Press.

BENTHAM, K. J. 2002. "Employer Resistance to Union Certification: A Study of Eight Canadian Jurisdictions." *Relations Industrielles*, 57, no. 1, pp. 159–87.

BETCHERMAN, G., N. LECKIE, and A. VERMA. 1994. "HRM Innovations in Canada: Evidence from Establishment Surveys." School of Industrial Relations/Industrial Relations Centre, Queen's University, Kingston, Ont.

BOONE, D. J. 2000. "Operation of the Production District Joint Industrial Council, Imperial Oil," in *Nonunion*

Employee Representation: History, Contemporary Practice and Policy, edited by B. E. Kaufman and D. G. Taras. New York: M. E. Sharpe.

BRAY, M. and R. LANSBURY. 1998. "Local versus Global: Employment Relations in a Global Corporation," delivered to the World Congress of the International Industrial Relations Research Association, Bologna, Italy.

BRODY, B., K. SEAVER, and T. TREMBLAY. 1993. "The Deunionization of Canadian Banks," in *Proceedings of the Canadian Industrial Relations Association*, edited by T. S. Kuttner. Fredericton, NB: CIRA, 1, pp. 381–96.

CHAYKOWSKI, R. P. 1999. "Adaptation Within the Traditional Industrial Relations System: The Development of Labour Relations at Inco Limited," in *Contract & Commitment: Employment Relations in the New Economy*, edited by A. Verma and R. P. Chaykowski. Kingston, ON: Queen's University IRC Press, pp. 41–81.

COATES, M. L. and B. DOWNIE. 1999. "The Changing World of Industrial Relations at CPR," in *Contract & Commitment: Employment Relations in the New Economy*, edited by A. Verma and R. P. Chaykowski. Kingston, ON: Queen's University IRC Press, pp. 241–92.

FROST, A. C. and A. VERMA. 1999. "Restructuring in Canadian Steel: The Case of Stelco Inc.," in *Contract & Commitment: Employment Relations in the New Economy*, edited by A. Verma and R. P. Chaykowski. Kingston, ON: Queen's University IRC Press, pp. 82–112.

GODARD, J. 1997. "Managerial Strategies, Labour and Employment Relations and the State: The Canadian Case and Beyond."*British Journal of Industrial Relations*, 35, no. 3, pp. 399–426.

———. 1998. "Workplace Reforms, Managerial Objectives and Managerial Outcomes: The Perceptions of Canadian IR/HRM Managers."*International Journal of Human Resource Management*, 9, no. 1, pp. 18–40.

———. 2004. "A Critical Assessment of the High Performance Paradigm."*British Journal of Industrial Relations*, 42, no. 2, pp. 349–78.

HARSHAW, M. 2000. "Nonunion Employee Representation at Dofasco," in *Nonunion Employee Representation: History, Contemporary Practice and Policy*, edited by B. E. Kaufman and D. G. Taras. New York: M. E. Sharpe.

JACOBY, S. M. 1997. *Modern Manors: Welfare Capitalism Since the New Deal*. Princeton, NJ: Princeton University Press.

KAINER, J. 1998. "Gender, Corporate Restructuring and Concession Bargaining in Ontario's Food Retail Sector."*Relations industrielles*, 53, no. 1, pp. 183–205.

KOCHAN, T. A., R. McKERSIE, and P. CAPELLI. 1984. "Strategic Choice and Industrial Relations Theory." *Industrial Relations*, 23, pp. 16–39.

KUMAR, P. 1999. "In Search of Competitive Efficiency: The General Motors of Canada Experience with Restructuring,"

in *Contract & Commitment: Employment Relations in the New Economy*, edited by A. Verma and R. P. Chaykowski. Kingston, ON: Queen's University IRC Press, pp. 137–81.

McQUEEN, R. 1998. *The Eatons: The Rise and Fall of Canada's Royal Family*. Toronto: Stoddart.

PALMER, B. D. 1992. *Working Class Experience: Rethinking the History of Canadian Labour, 1800–1991*. Toronto: McClelland & Stewart.

PURCELL, J. 1987. "Mapping Management Styles in Employee Relations."*Journal of Management Studies*, 24, pp. 533–48.

SKOGAN, J. 1999. "Once Upon a Tim."*Saturday Night*, September, pp. 69–73.

SMITH, A. E. 1993. "Canadian Industrial Relations in Transition."*Relations industrielles*, 48, no. 4, pp. 641–60.

STOREY, R. 1983. "Unionization Versus Corporate Welfare: The Dofasco Way."*Labour/Le Travailleur* (Fall), pp. 7–42.

TARAS, D. G. 1994. "Impact of Industrial Relations Strategies on Selected Human Resource Practices in a Partially Unionized Industry: The Canadian Petroleum Sector." Unpublished Ph.D. dissertation, University of Calgary.

———. 1997. "Managerial Intentions and Wage Determination in the Canadian Petroleum Industry." *Industrial Relations*, 36, no. 2, pp. 178–205.

———. 2000. "Contemporary Experience with the Rockefeller Plan: Imperial Oil's Joint Industrial Council," in *Nonunion Employee Representation: History, Contemporary Practice and Policy*, edited by B. E. Kaufman and D. G. Taras. New York: M. E. Sharpe.

TARAS, D. G. and J. COPPING. 1998. "The Transition from Formal Nonunion Representation to Unionization: A Contemporary Case."*Industrial and Labor Relations Review*, 52, no. 1, pp. 22–44.

TARAS, D. G. and A. PONAK. 1999. "Petro-Canada: A Model of a Union Acceptance Strategy within the Canadian Petroleum Industry," in *Contract & Commitment: Employment Relations in the New Economy*, edited by A. Verma and R. P. Chaykowski. Kingston, ON: Queen's University IRC Press, pp. 211–40.

THOMPSON, M. 1995. "The Management of Industrial Relations," in *Union–Management Relations in Canada*, 3rd Edition, edited by M. Gunderson and A. Ponak. Don Mills: Addison-Wesley, pp. 105–30.

TIMUR, A. T. 2005. "The Impact of Nonunion Employee Representation Plans on Union–Management Relations: A Comparative Study of Three Industries." Unpublished Ph.D. dissertation, University of Calgary.

TIMUR, A. T. and A. PONAK. 2002. "Labor Relations and Technological Change at Canadian Pacific Railway."*Journal of Labor Research*, 33, no. 4, pp. 535–57.

VERMA, A. 1999. "From POTS to PANS: The Evolution of Employment Relations in Bell Canada Under Deregulation," in *Contract & Commitment: Employment Relations in the*

New Economy, edited by A. Verma and R. P. Chaykowski. Kingston, ON: Queen's University IRC Press, pp. 182–210.

WAGAR, T. H. 1994. *Human Resource Management Practices and Organizational Performance: Evidence from Atlantic Canada*. Kingston, ON: Queen's University IRC Press.

Chapter 6

APPELBAUM, E., T. BAILEY, P. BERG, and A. L. KALLE-BERG. 2000. *Manufacturing Advantage: Why High-Performance Work Systems Pay Off*. Ithaca, NY: Economic Policy Institute and Cornell University ILR Press.

ASKIN, R. G. and J. B. GOLDBERG. 2002. *Design and Analysis of Lean Production Systems*. New York: Wiley.

BARITZ, L. 1960. *The Servants of Power: A History of the Use of Social Science in American Industry*. Westport, Conn.: Wesleyan University Press.

BECKER, B. E. and M. A. HUSELID. 1998. "High Performance Work Systems and Firm Performance: A Synthesis of Research and Managerial Implications."*Research in Personnel and Human Resources Journal*, 16, no. 1, 53–101.

BÉLANGER, J. 2001. "The Influence of Employee Involvement on Productivity: A Review of Research." *Workplace Gazette*, 4, no. 4, pp. 65–79.

BENDIX, R. 1956. *Work and Authority in Industry*. New York: Harper & Row.

BERG, P. 1999. "The Effects of High Performance Work Practices on Job Satisfaction in the United States Steel Industry."*Relations industrielles*, 54, no.1, pp. 111–35.

BERGGREN, C. 1992. *Alternatives to Lean Production: Work Organization in the Swedish Auto Industry*. Ithaca, NY: Cornell University ILR Press.

BETCHERMAN, G. and K. McMULLEN. 1986. *Working With Technology: A Survey of Automation in Canada*. Ottawa: Ministry of Supply and Services.

BETCHERMAN, G., K. McMULLEN, N. LECKIE, and C. CARON. 1994. *The Canadian Workplace in Transition*. Kingston, ON: IRC Press.

CAW. 1993. "Work Reorganization: Responding to Lean Production." Available at **www.caw.ca/whatwedo/health&safety/cawlean.asp**.

CEP. 1994. *New Directions: CEP Policy on Workplace Reorganization*. Toronto: Communications, Energy and Paperworkers Union of Canada. Available at **www.cep.ca/policies/policy_906_e.pdf**.

CHAMBERLAND, R. 1997. "High-Performance Work Practices at Abitibi-Price," in Innovative Workplace Practices: Case Studies, *Collective Bargaining Review*. Workplace Information Directorate, Labour Branch, Human Resources Development Canada (March), pp. 115–19.

COMMUNICATIONS WORKERS OF CANADA (CWC). 1992. *Prosperity and Progress: CWC's Vision for Shaping the Future*, 9th Annual Convention (June 15–19).

CONGER, J. A. and R. N. KANUNGO. 1988. "Behavioral Dimensions of Charismatic Leadership," in *Charismatic Leadership*, edited by J. A. Conger and R. N. Kanungo. San Francisco: Jossey-Bass, pp. 78–97.

COTTON, J. L. 1993. *Employee Involvement*. Newbury Park, CA: SAGE.

COTTON, J. L., D. A. VOLLRATH, K. L. FROGGATT, M. L. LENGNICK-HALL, and K. R. JENNINGS. 1988. "Employee Participation: Diverse Forms and Different Outcomes."*Academy of Management Review*, 13, no.1, pp. 8–22.

CUTCHER-GERSHENFELD, J. 1988. *Tracing a Transformation in Industrial Relations: The Case of Xerox Corporation and the Amalgamated Clothing and Textile Workers Union*. Washington, D.C.: Bureau of Labor–Management Relations and Cooperative Programs, U.S. Department of Labor (BLMR 123).

CUTCHER-GERSHENFELD, J., T. A. KOCHAN, and A. VERMA. 1991. "Recent Developments in U.S. Employee Involvement Initiatives: Erosion or Transformation," in *Advances in Industrial & Labor Relations*, Vol. 5, edited by D. Sockell, D. Lewin and D. Lipsky. JAI Press, pp. 1–31.

DiGIACOMO, G. 1997. "High Involvement Work Reorganization at NB Tel," in Innovative Workplace Practices: Case Studies, *Collective Bargaining Review*. Workplace Information Directorate, Labour Branch, Human Resources Development Canada (January), pp. 91–99.

DOMPIERRE, G., N. LANGIS, S. MASSÉ, and S. ST-ONGE. 2003. "Managing by Work Teams at Aluminerie Lauralco Inc." *Workplace Gazette*, 6, no. 1, pp. 42–49.

DRUCKER, P. F. 1954. *The Practice of Management*. New York: Harper & Row.

EDWARDS, P., M. COLLINSON, and C. REES. 1998. "The Determinants of Employee Responses to Total Quality Management: Six Case Studies."*Organization Studies*, 19, no. 3, pp. 449–75.

GALLIE, D., M. WHITE, Y. CHENG, and M. TOMLINSON. 1998. *Restructuring the Employment Relationship*. Oxford: Oxford University Press.

GERWIN, D. and H. KOLODNY. 1992. *Management of Advanced Manufacturing Technology*. New York: John Wiley & Sons, Inc.

GILLESPIE, R. 1991. *Manufacturing Knowledge: A History of the Hawthorne Experiments*. Cambridge: Cambridge University Press.

GITTLEMAN, M., M. HORRIGAN, and M. JOYCE. 1998. "'Flexible' Workplace Practices: Evidence from a Nationally Representative Survey."*Industrial & Labor Relations Review*, 52, no. 2, pp. 99–115.

GODARD, J. 2004. "A Critical Assessment of the High-Performance Paradigm."*British Journal of Industrial Relations*, 42, no. 2, pp. 349–78.

GRAHAM, L. 1995. *On the Line at Subaru-Isuzu: The Japanese Model and the American Worker*. Ithaca: Cornell University ILR Press.

GRANT, H. M. 1998. "Solving the Labour Problem at Imperial Oil: Welfare Capitalism in the Canadian Petroleum Industry, 1919–1929."*Labour/Le Travail*, 41 (Spring), pp. 69–95.

GUNDERSON, M. and A. SHARPE. 1998. *Forging Business–Labour Partnerships: The Emergence of Sector Councils in Canada*. Toronto: Published in co-operation with the Centre for the Study of Living Standards by University of Toronto Press.

ICHNIOWSKI, C., K. SHAW and G. PRENNUSHI. 1997. "The Effects of Human Resource Management Practices on Productivity: A Study of Steel Finishing Lines." *American Economic Review*, 87, no. 3, pp. 291–313.

JACKSON, E. T. and G. DiGIACOMO. 1997. "Introduction," in Innovative Workplace Practices: Case Studies, *Collective Bargaining Review*. Workplace Information Directorate, Labour Branch, Human Resources Development Canada (January), pp. 85–89.

JACOBY, S. 1997. *Modern Manors: Welfare Capitalism Since the New Deal*. Princeton University Press.

———. 2003. "A Century of Human Resource Management," in *Industrial Relations to Human Resources and Beyond*, edited by B. E. Kaufman, R. A. Beaumont, and R. B. Helfgott. Armonk, NY: ME Sharpe, pp. 147–71.

KANIGEL, R. 1997. *The One Best Way: Frederick Winslow Taylor and the Enigma of Efficiency*. New York, NY: Penguin Books.

KAUFMAN, B. E. and D. G. TARAS. 1999. "Non-union Employee Representation: Introduction."*Journal of Labor Research*, 20, no. 1, pp. 1–8.

KLEIN, J. A. 1988. *The Changing Role of First-Line Supervisors and Middle Managers*. Washington, D.C.: Bureau of Labor–Management Relations and Cooperative Programs, U.S. Department of Labor (BLMR 126).

KLEIN, J. A. and P. A. POSEY. 1986. "A Good Supervisor is a Good Supervisor Anywhere."*Harvard Business Review* (November–December).

KOCHAN, T. A., H. C. KATZ, and N. MOWER. 1984. *Worker Participation and American Unions: Threat or Opportunity?* Kalamazoo, MI: Upjohn.

LAM, H. and Y. RESHEF. 1999. "Are Quality Improvement and Downsizing Compatible?"*Relations industrielles*, 54, no. 4, pp. 727–47.

LAWLER, E. E. and S. A. MOHRMAN. 1985. "Quality Circles After the Fad."*Harvard Business Review*, 63, no. 1 (January–February), pp. 64–71.

LAWLER, E. E., S. A. MOHRMAN, and G. E. LEDFORD. 1992. *Employee Involvement and Total Quality Management*. San Francisco: Jossey Bass.

———. 1995. *Creating High Performance Organizations: Practices and Results of Employee Involvement and Total Quality Management in Fortune 1000 Companies: A Study Commissioned by the Association for Quality Participation*. San Francisco: Jossey Bass.

LEE, C. and R. S. SCHULER. 1982. "A Constructive Replication and Extension of a Role and Expectancy Perception Model of Participation in Decision-Making."*Journal of Occupational Psychology*, 55, pp. 109–18.

LEWCHUK, W. and D. WELLS. 2006. "When Corporations Substitute for Adversarial Unions: Labour Markets and Human Resource Management at Magna."*Relations industrielles*, 61, no. 4, pp. 639–65.

LEWCHUK, W. and D. ROBERTSON. 1996. "Working Conditions under Lean Production: A Worker-Based Benchmarking Study."*Asia Pacific Business Review*, 2, pp. 60–81.

LISCHERON, J. A. and T. D. WALL. 1975. "Employee Participation—An Experimental Field Study."*Human Relations*, 28, pp. 863–84.

LOCKE, E. A. and D. M. SCHWEIGER. 1979. "Participation in Decision-Making: One More Look," in *Research in Organizational Behavior*, Vol. 1, edited by B. M. Staw. Greenwich, CT: JAI Press.

LONG, R. J. 1989. "Patterns of Workplace Innovations in Canada."*Relations industrielles*, 44, no. 4, pp. 805–25.

LOWE, G. S. 2002. "Here in Body, Absent in Productivity: Presenteeism hurts output, quality of work-life and employee health," *Canadian HR Reporter*, 15, pp. 5–6.

MAYO, E. 1933. *The Human Problems of an Industrial Civilization*. Cambridge, MA: Harvard Business School Press.

McCALLUM, M. E. 1990. "Corporate Welfarism in Canada 1919–1939." *Canadian Historical Review*, 71, no. 1, pp. 46–79.

MILLER, K. I. and P. R. MONGE. 1986. "Participation, Satisfaction, and Productivity: A Meta-Analytic Review."*Academy of Management Journal*, 29, no. 4, pp. 727–53.

OSTERMAN, P. 1994. "How Common Is Workplace Transformation and Who Adopts It?"*Industrial and Labor Relations Review*, 47, no. 2, pp. 173–88.

RANKIN, T. 1986. "Integrating QWL and Collective Bargaining."*Worklife Review*, 5, no. 3.

ROBERTSON, D., J. RINEHART, C. HUXLEY, J. WAREHAM, H. ROSENFELD, A. McGOUGH, and S. BENEDICT. 1993. *The CAMI Report: Lean Production in a Unionized Auto Plant*. Willowdale, ON: Canadian Auto Workers.

ROETHLISBERGER, F. J. and W. J. DICKSON. 1939. *Management and the Worker*. Boston: Harvard University Press.

SASHKIN, M. 1976. "Changing Towards Participative Management Approaches: A Model and Methods." *Academy of Management Review*, 1, no. 3, pp. 75–86.

SCHULER, R. S. 1980. "A Role and Expectancy Perception Model of Participation in Decision-Making."*Academy of Management Journal*, 23, pp. 331–40.

TARAS, D. G. 1997. "Why Non-union Representation IS Legal in Canada."*Relations industrielles*, 52, no. 4, pp. 763–86.

———. 2003. "Voice in the North American Workplace: From Employee Representation to Employee Involvement," in *Industrial Relations to Human Resources and Beyond*, edited by B. E. Kaufman, R. A. Beaumont, and R. B. Helfgott. Armonk, NY: ME Sharpe, pp. 293–329.

———. 2006. "Non-union Representation and Employer Intent: How Canadian Courts and Labour Boards Determine the Legal Status of Non-union Plans." *Socio-Economic Review*, 4, no. 2, pp. 321–36.

TARAS, D. G. and A. PONAK. 1999. "Petro-Canada: A Model of the Union Cooperation Strategy within the Canadian Petroleum Industry," in *From Contract to Commitment: Employment Relations at the Firm-level in Canada*, edited by A. Verma and R. P. Chaykowski. Kingston, ON: IRC Press.

TARAS, D. and B. E. KAUFMAN. 2006. "Non-union Employee Representation in North America: Diversity, Controversy and Uncertain Future."*Industrial Relations Journal*, 37, no. 5, pp. 513–42.

TAYLOR, F. W. 1911. *The Principles of Scientific Management*. New York: Harper and Brothers.

———. 1916. "The Principles of Scientific Management."*Bulletin of the Taylor Society* (December), quoted in *Classics of Organization Theory*, 4th Edition, edited by J. M. Shafritz and J. Steven Ott. Fort Worth: Harcourt Brace, 1995.

THACKER, J. W. and M. W. FIELDS. 1987. "Union Involvement in Quality-of-Worklife Efforts: A Longitudinal Investigation."*Personnel Psychology*, 40, pp. 97–111.

TJOSVOLD, D. 1991. *Team Organization: An Enduring Competitive Advantage*. Chichester: John Wiley & Sons.

———. 1998. "Making Employee Involvement Work: Cooperative Goals and Controversy to Reduce Costs."*Human Relations*, 51, no. 2, pp. 201–14.

VERMA, A. 1989. "Joint Participation Programs: Self-help or Suicide for Labor?"*Industrial Relations*, 28, no. 3 (Fall), pp. 401–10.

———. 1990. *The Prospects for Innovation in Canadian Industrial Relations in the 1990s*. Ottawa: Canadian Federation of Labour and World Trade Centres in Canada Joint Committee on Labour Market Adjustment.

VERMA, A. and J. CUTCHER-GERSHENFELD. 1993. "Joint Governance in the Workplace: Beyond Union–Management Cooperation and Worker Participation," in *Employee Representation*, edited by B. E. Kaufman and M. M. Kleiner. Madison, WI: Industrial Relations Research Association.

VERMA, A. and D. IRVINE. 1992. *Investing in People: The Key to Canada's Growth and Prosperity*. Toronto: Information Technology Association of Canada.

VERMA, A. and T. A. KOCHAN. 1985. "The Growth & Nature of the Non-union Sector Within a Firm," in *Challenges and Choices Facing American Labor*, edited by T. A. Kochan. Cambridge, MA: M.I.T. Press, pp. 89–118.

VERMA, A. and R. B. McKERSIE. 1987. "Employee Involvement Programs: The Implications of Non-involvement by Unions."*Industrial and Labor Relations Review*, 40, no. 4, pp. 556–68.

VERMA, A. and N. M. MELTZ. 1994. "Canadian Developments in Industrial Relations and Implications for the U.S." Paper presented to *Conference on Labor Relations Institutions and Economic Performance, Work and Technology Institute*, Washington, D.C. (March 14–15).

VERMA, A. and J. P. WEILER. 1994. *Understanding Change in Canadian Industrial Relations: Firm-level Choices and Responses*. Kingston, ON: IRC Press.

WAGER, T. 1996. *Employee Involvement, Strategic Management and Human Resources: Exploring the Linkages*. Kingston, ON: Queen's University, Industrial Relations Centre.

WAGNER, J. A. 1994. "Participation's Effects on Performance and Satisfaction: A Reconsideration of Research Evidence."*Academy of Management Review*, 19, no. 2, pp. 312–30.

WOOD, S. 1999. "Human Resource Management and Performance." *International Journal of Management Reviews*, 1, no. 4, pp. 367–413.

Chapter 7

ABDURRAHAMAN, A. and M. SKUTERUD. 2005. "Explaining the Deteriorating Entry Earnings of Canada's Immigrant Cohorts, 1996–2000." *Canadian Journal of Economics*, 38, pp. 641–71.

BAKER, M., D. BENJAMIN, and S. STANGER. 1999. "The Highs and Lows of the Minimum Wage Effect: A Time-Series Cross-Section Study of the Canadian Law."*Journal of Labor Economics*, 17, no. 2, pp. 318–50.

BARTEL, A., C. ICHNIOWSKI, and K. SHAW. 2007. "How Does Information Technology Affect Productivity? Plant Level Comparisons of Product Innovation, Process Improvement and Worker Skills."*Quarterly Journal of Economics*, 122, no. 4, pp. 1721–58.

BENJAMIN, D., M. GUNDERSON, T. LEMIEUX, and C. RIDDELL. 2007. *Labour Market Economics; Theory, Evidence and Policy in Canada*, 6th Edition. Toronto: McGraw-Hill Ryerson Press.

BENJAMIN, D., M. GUNDERSON, and W. C. RIDDELL. 2002. *Labour Market Economics: Theory, Evidence and*

Policy in Canada, 5th Edition. Toronto: McGraw-Hill Ryerson.

BLINDER, A. 2006. "Offshoring: The Next Industrial Revolution."*Foreign Affairs*, 85, pp. 113–28.

CAMPOLIETI, M., T. FANG, and M. GUNDERSON. 2005. "Minimum Wage Impacts on Employment Transitions of Youths: 1993–99."*Canadian Journal of Economics*, 38, pp. 81–104.

CAMPOLIETI, M., M. GUNDERSON, and C. RIDDELL. 2006. "Minimum Wage Impacts from a Pre-Specified Research Design: Canada 1981–97."*Industrial Relations*, 45, pp. 195–216.

CARD, D. 1992. "Do Minimum Wages Reduce Employment? A Case Study of California, 1987–89."*Industrial and Labor Relations Review*, 46, no. 1, pp. 38–54.

CARD, D. and A. KRUEGER. 1995. *Myth and Measurement: The New Economics of the Minimum Wage*. Princeton, NJ: Princeton University Press.

CARD, D. and W. C. RIDDELL. 1993. "A Comparative Analysis of Unemployment in Canada and the United States," in *Small Differences That Matter: Labor Markets and Income Maintenance in Canada and the United States*, edited by D. Card and R. B. Freeman. Chicago: University of Chicago Press, pp. 149–89.

DEVORETZ, D. and S. A. LARYEA. 1998. *Canadian Human Capital Transfers: The United States and Beyond*. Commentary no. 115 (October). Toronto: C. D. Howe.

FOOT, D. K. and D. STOFFMAN. 2000. *Boom, Bust and Echo: The Millennium Edition*. Macfarlane, Walter & Ross.

FOOT, D. K. and R. A. VENNE. 1990. "Population, Pyramids and Promotional Prospects."*Canadian Public Policy*, 16, no. 4, pp. 387–98.

FORTIN, P. 1996. "The Great Canadian Slump."*Canadian Journal of Economics*, 29, no. 4, pp. 761–87.

GASTON, N. and D. TREFLER. 1997. "Labour Market Consequences of the Canada–U.S. Free Trade Agreement."*Canadian Journal of Economics*, 30, no. 1, pp. 18–41.

GERA, S. and G. GRENIER. 1994. "Interindustry Wage Differentials and Efficiency Wages: Some Canadian Evidence."*Canadian Journal of Economics*, 27, pp. 81–100.

GOMEZ, R. and M. GUNDERSON. 2005. "Does Economic Integration Lead to Social Policy Convergence? An Analysis of North American Linkages and Social Policy," in *Social and Labour Market Aspects of North American Linkages*, edited by R. Harris and T. Lemieux. Calgary: University of Calgary Press.

GOMEZ, R., M. GUNDERSON, and A. LUCHAK. 2002. "Mandatory Retirement: A Constraint in Transitions to Retirement?"*Employee Relations*, 24, no.4, pp. 403–22.

GUNDERSON, M. 1998. "Harmonization of Labour Policies Under Trade Liberalization." *Industrial Relations/Relations industrielles*, 53, no. 1, pp. 11–40.

HAMERMESH, D. 1993. *Labor Demand*. Princeton, NJ: Princeton University Press.

HEISZ, A. 2007. *Income Inequality and Redistribution in Canada: 1976 to 2004*. Statistics Canada, Analytical Studies Branch Research Paper Series, Catalogue no. 11F0019MIE.

HELLIWELL, J. 1999. "Checking the Brain Drain: Evidence and Implications." Study 99-3. Toronto: University of Toronto Institute for Policy Analysis.

HUMAN RESOURCES DEVELOPMENT CANADA (HRDC), in co-operation with STATISTICS CANADA. 1999. *South of the Border: Graduates from the Class of '95 Who Moved to the United States*. Statistics Canada, Catalogue 81-587-XIE.

IQBAL, M. 1999. *Are We Losing Our Minds? Trends, Determinants, and the Role of Taxes in Brain Drain to the United States*. Conference Board of Canada, pp. 265–99.

JORGENSON, D. W., M. S. HO, and K. STIROH. 2005. "Growth of U.S. Industries and Investments in Information Technology and Higher Education," in *Measuring Capital in the New Economy*, edited by C. Corrado, J. Haltiwanger and D. Sichel.Chicago, IL: University of Chicago Press.

KEYNES, J. M. 1936/1967. *The General Theory of Employment, Interest and Money*. London: Macmillan.

LEE, MARC. 2007. *Eroding Tax Fairness: Tax Incidence in Canada, 1990 to 2005*. Toronto: Canadian Centre for Policy Alternatives.

LEMIEUX, T. 2005. "Trade Liberalization and the Labour Market," in *Social and Labour Market Aspects of North American Linkages*, edited by R. Harris and T. Lemieux. Calgary: University of Calgary Press.

MANNING, A. 2003. *Monopsony in Motion: Imperfect Competition in Labor Markets*. Princeton: Princeton University Press.

McSHANE, S. L. and D. C. McPHILLIPS. 1987. "Predicting Reasonable Notice in Canadian Wrongful Dismissal Cases."*Industrial and Labor Relations Review*, 41, no. 1, pp. 108–17.

METCALF, D. 2007. "Why Has the British National Minimum Wage Had Little or No Impact on Employment?" CEP Discussion Paper No. 781.

PAYETTE, S. 1999. "Contingent Work: Trends, Issues and Challenges for Labour."*Workplace Gazette*, 2, no. 3, pp. 116–19.

PORTER, M. and D. ESTY. 1998. "Industrial Ecology and Competitiveness: Strategic Implications for the Firm." *Journal of Industrial Ecology*, 2, no. 1, pp. 35–43.

RIDDELL, W. C. and A. SHARPE. 1998. "The Canada–U.S. Unemployment Rate Gap: An Introduction and Overview." *Canadian Public Policy*, 24, Special supplement (February), pp. S1–S37.

ROYAL COMMISSION ON THE ECONOMIC UNION. 1985. *Report*. Ottawa: Queen's Printer.

SHARPE, A. 1997. "The Productivity Paradox: An Evaluation of Competing Explanations."*Canadian Business Economics* (Fall), pp. 32–47.

STATISTICS CANADA. 1998. "Brain Drain or Brain Gain? What Do the Data Say?" Presentation, October 1, 1998.

———. 2006. "Canada's Changing Labour Force, 2006 Census: Findings." Available at **www12.statcan.ca/english /census06/analysis/labour/index.cfm**.

———. 2007. CANSIM Table 282-0085, Labour Force Survey Estimates (LFS), Supplementary Unemployment Rates by Sex and Age Group, unadjusted for seasonality, monthly.

WILTON, D. A. and D. M. PRESCOTT. 1992. *Macroeconomics: Theory and Policy in Canada*, 3rd Edition. Don Mills, ON: Addison-Wesley.

YAN, B. 2006. "Demand for Skills in Canada: The Role of Foreign Outsourcing and Information-Communication Technology." *Canadian Journal of Economics*, 39, pp. 53-67.

YUEN, T. 2003. "The Effect of Minimum Wages on Youth Employment in Canada: A Panel Study." *Journal of Human Resources*, 38, pp. 647–72.

Chapter 8

ADAMS, G. W. 1993. *Canadian Labour Law*, 2nd Edition. Aurora: Canada Law Book.

ADELL, B. 2003. "Secondary Picketing After *Pepsi-Cola*: What's Clear, and What Isn't?" *Canadian Labour & Employment Law Journal*, 10, no. 1135–159.

BRUDNEY, J. J. 2005. "Contractual Approaches to Labor Organizing: Supplanting the Election Paradigm?"*Labor and Employment Relations Association Series*, Proceedings of the 57th Annual Meeting.

GUNDERSON, M. 2003. "Age Discrimination in Employment in Canada."*Contemporary Economic Policy*, 21, no. 3, 318–28.

JACKSON, J. 2005. "Collective Bargaining Legislation in Canada," in *Union–Management Relations in Canada*, edited by M. Gunderson, A. Ponak and D. G. Taras. Toronto: Pearson Education Canada.

MIXON, F. G. Jr. and R. W. RESSLER. 1993. "Union Influence and Right-To-Work Law Passage: Evidence from Hazard Model Estimates."*Am. J. Economics & Sociology*, 52, no. 2, pp. 183–92.

"Policy on Discrimination Against Older Persons Because of Age." 2002. Ontario Human Rights Commission. Available at **http://ohrc.on.ca/english/publications/age-policy.shtml**.

SLINN, S. 2005. "An Analysis of the Effects on Parties' Unionization Decisions of the Choice of Union Representation Procedure: The Strategic Dynamic Certification Model."*Osgoode Hall Law Journal*, 43, no. 4,

pp. 407–50.

WEILER, P. C. 1980. *Reconcilable Differences: New Directions in Canadian Labour Law*. Toronto: Carswell.

Chapter 9

ARTHURS, H. W. 2006. *Fairness at Work: Federal Labour Standards for the 21st Century (The Arthurs Report)*. Federal Labour Standards Review. Ottawa: Human Resources and Skills Development Canada. Available at www.hrsdc.gc.ca/en/labour/employment_standards/fls/final/page00.shtml.

CASEY, J., ed. 2003. *Remedies in Labour, Employment, and Human Rights Law*. Toronto: Thomson Carswell.

ENGLAND, G. 2000. *Individual Employment Law*. Toronto: Irwin Law.

ENGLAND, G., R. WOOD, and I. CHRISTIE. 2005. *Employment Law in Canada*, 4th Edition. Toronto: LexisNexis & Butterworths.

LEVITT, H. A. 2003. *The Law of Dismissal in Canada*, 3rd Edition. Aurora: Canada Law Book.

Chapter 10

ANDERSON, J. 1989. "The Structure of Collective Bargaining in Canada," in *Union–Management Relations In Canada*, 2nd Edition, edited by J. Anderson, M. Gunderson, and A. Ponak. Don Mills: Addison-Wesley.

BACHARACH, S. and E. LAWLER. 1981. *Bargaining: Power, Tactics, and Outcomes*. San Francisco: Jossey-Bass.

BAMBER, G., J. H. GITTELL, T. A. KOCHAN, and A. VON NORDENFLYCHT. (forthcoming). *Up in the Air: Can an Industry Compete on Costs Without Destroying Its Workforce? An International Study of the Changing Airline Industry*, manuscript.

BARNETT, V. 2003. "The Use of Information Technology in a Strike." *Journal of Labor Research*, 24, no. 1, pp. 55–72.

CARTER, D. 1993. "The Changing Face of Labour Law." Address to the Annual Spring Industrial Relations Seminar, Queen's University (May 10), mimeo.

CHAMBERLAIN, N. W. and J. W. KUHN. 1986. *Collective Bargaining*, 3rd Edition. New York, NY: McGraw-Hill Book Company.

CHAYKOWSKI, R., J. CUTCHER-GERSHENFELD, T. KOCHAN, and C. SICKLES MERCHANT. 2000. *Facilitating Conflict Resolution in Union–Management Relations: A Guide for Neutrals*. Ithaca, NY: Cornell University.

CHAYKOWSKI, R. P. 1990. "Union and Firm Preferences for Bargaining Outcomes in the Private Sector."*Relations industrielles/Industrial Relations*, 45, no. 2, pp. 326–55.

CHAYKOWSKI, R. P. and M. GRANT. 1995. "From Traditional to Mutual Gains Bargaining."*Collective Bargaining Review*. Ottawa Ont.: Human Resources Development Canada (May), pp. 79–88.

CHAYKOWSKI, R. P. and A. VERMA. 1992. "Adjustment and Restructuring in Canadian Industrial Relations," in *Industrial Relations in Canadian Industry*, edited by R. Chaykowski and A. Verma. Toronto: Holt, Rinehart and Winston.

DELANEY, J. and D. SOCKELL. 1989. "The Mandatory–Permissive Distinction and Collective Bargaining Outcomes." *Industrial and Labor Relations Review*, 42, no. 4, pp. 566–83.

FISHER, R. 1994. "Deter, Compel, or Negotiate?"*Negotiation Journal*, 10, no. 1, pp. 17–32.

FISHER, R. and W. URY. 1983. *Getting to Yes: Negotiating Agreement Without Giving In*. New York, NY: Penguin Books.

FISHER, R., W. URY, and B. PATTON. 1991. *Getting to Yes: Negotiating an Agreement Without Giving In*, 2nd Edition. New York: Houghton Mifflin Company.

FORREST, A. 1989. "The Rise and Fall of National Bargaining in the Canadian Meat-Packing Industry."*Relations industrielles/Industrial Relations*, 44, no. 2, pp. 393–406.

FRIEDMAN, R. 1994. "Missing Ingredients in Mutual Gains Bargaining Theory."*Negotiation Journal* (July), pp. 265–80.

HECKSCHER, C. and L. HALL. 1994. "Mutual Gains and Beyond: Two Levels of Intervention."*Negotiation Journal* (July), pp. 235–48.

HUNTER, L. W. and R. K. McKERSIE. 1992. "Can Mutual Gains Training Change Labour–Management Relationships?"*Negotiation Journal*, 8, no. 4, pp. 319–30.

KATZ, H. 1993. "The Decentralization of Collective Bargaining: A Literature Review and Comparative Analysis."*Industrial and Labor Relations Review*, 47, no. 1 (October), pp. 13–22.

KUMAR, P. and N. MELTZ. 1992. "Industrial Relations in the Canadian Automobile Industry," in *Industrial Relations in Canadian Industry*, edited by R. Chaykowski and A. Verma. Toronto, ON: Holt, Rinehart and Winston.

ROSE, J. 1992. "Industrial Relations in the Construction Industry in the 1980s," in *Industrial Relations in Canadian Industry*, edited by R. Chaykowski and A. Verma. Toronto, ON: Holt, Rinehart and Winston.

ROSS, A. M. 1948. *Trade Union Wage Policy*. Berkeley: University of California Press.

SUSSKIND, L. E. and E. M. LANDRY. 1991. "Implementing a Mutual Gains Approach to Collective Bargaining." *Negotiation Journal*, 7, no. 1 (January), pp. 5–10.

VERMA, A. and R. CHAYKOWSKI. 1999. *Contract and Commitment: Employment Relations in the New Economy*. Kingston, ON: IRC Press.

WALTON, R. E. and R. B. McKERSIE. 1991. *A Behavioral Theory of Labor Negotiations: An Analysis of a Social Interaction System*, 2nd Edition. Ithaca, NY: ILR Press.

Chapter 11

ADAMS, R. J. 1995. "Canadian Industrial Relations in Comparative Perspective," in *Union–Management Relations in Canada*, 3rd Edition, edited by M. Gunderson and A. Ponak. Don Mills: Addison-Wesley, pp. 495–526.

BEAUCAGE, A. and C. LAFLEUR. 1994. "La négociation concessive dans l'industrie manufacturière canadienne pendant les années 1980," in *Proceedings of the XXXth Annual Conference of the Canadian Industrial Relations Association*, edited by E. Déom and A. Smith. Quebec: CIRA.

BETCHERMAN, G., K. McMULLEN, N. LECKIE, and C. CARON. 1994. *The Canadian Workplace in Transition*. Kingston, ON: IRC Press.

CANADIAN CENTRE FOR OCCUPATIONAL HEALTH AND SAFETY. 2007. "National Day of Mourning—April 28." Available at www.ccohs.ca/events/mourning (accessed 22 August 2007).

CELANI, A. and C. L. WEBER. 1998. "Pay-for-Knowledge Systems: Guidelines for Practice." Industrial Relations Centre, Queen's University, Current Issues Series. Kingston, ON: IRC Press.

CHAYKOWSKI, R. P. and G. A. SLOTSVE. 1986. "Union Seniority Rules as a Determinant of Intra-Firm Job Changes."*Relations industrielles/Industrial Relations*, 41, pp. 720–37.

CUPW. 2007. *Agreement Between Canada Post Corporation and the Canadian Union of Postal Workers (Urban Postal Operations)—Expires: January 31, 2011*. Available at www.cupw.ca/index.cfm/ci_id/9661/la_id/1.htm.

FISHER, E. G. and L. M. SHERWOOD. 1984. "Fairness and Managerial Rights in Canadian Arbitral Jurisprudence." *Relations industrielles/Industrial Relations*, 39, pp. 720–37.

FORREST, A. 1993. "Women and Industrial Relations: No Room in the Discourse."*Relations industrielles/Industrial Relations*, 48, pp. 409–40.

GERSUNY, C. 1982. "Origins of Seniority Provisions in Collective Bargaining."*Labor Law Journal*, 33 (August), pp. 518–24.

GILSON, C. H. H. 1985. "Changes in the Nature of Grievance Issues Over the Last Ten Years: Labour Management Relations and the 'Frontier of Control.'"*Relations industrielles/Industrial Relations*, 40, pp. 856–64.

HALL, K. 1999. "Hours Polarization at the End of the 1990s."*Perspectives on Labour and Income*, 11 (Summer), pp. 28–37.

HÉBERT, G., R. BOURQUE, A. GILES, M. GRANT, D. JALETTE, G. TRUDEAU, and G. VALLÉE. 2003. *La Convention collective au Québec*. Boucherville: Gaëtan Morin.

HUMAN RESOURCES AND SOCIAL DEVELOPMENT CANADA. Various dates. *The Workplace Gazette, Collective*

Bargaining Bulletin, and *The Wage Settlement Bulletin*, Government of Canada.

JAMIESON, H. R. and B. R. GREYELL (Commissioners). 1995. *Report of the Industrial Inquiry Commission into Industrial Relations at West Coast Ports* (November 30).

KAPSALIS, C. and P. TOURIGNY. 2004. "Duration of Non-Standard Employment."*Perspectives on Labour and Income*, 12 (December), pp. 5–13.

LAMSON, C. 1986. "On the Line: Women and Fish Plant Jobs in Atlantic Canada."*Relations industrielles/Industrial Relations*, 41, pp. 145–56.

MacDOWELL, L. S. 1978. "The Formation of the Canadian Industrial Relations System During World War Two."*Labour/Le Travailleur*, 3, pp. 175–96.

RICHARD, Justice K. P. (Commissioner). 1997. *The Westray Story: A Predictable Path to Disaster*. Report of the Westray Mine Public Inquiry. Halifax: Province of Nova Scotia.

ROCHON, C. P. 2000. *Work and Family Provisions in Canadian Collective Agreements*. Ottawa: Human Resources and Social Development Canada.

SACK, J. and E. POSKANZER. 1996. *Contract Clauses: Collective Agreement Language in Canada*, 3rd Edition. Toronto: Lancaster House.

SASS, R. 1982. "Safety and Self-Respect."*Policy Options* (July–August), pp. 50–53.

SCOTT, T. 1996. "Human Rights Issues and the Collective Agreement." Industrial Relations Centre, Queen's University, Current Issues Series. Kingston, ON: IRC Press.

VERMA, A. and J. CUTCHER-GERSHENFELD. 1993. "Joint Governance in the Workplace: Beyond Union–Management Cooperation and Worker Participation," in *Employee Representation,* edited by B. E. Kaufman and M. M. Kleiner. Madison, WI: Industrial Relations Research Association.

WARSKETT, R. 1993. "Can a Disappearing Pie Be Shared Equally? Unions, Women, and Wage Fairness," in *Women Challenging Unions: Feminism, Democracy, and Militancy*, edited by L. Briskin and P. McDermott. Toronto: University of Toronto Press.

WELLS, D. 1986. "Autoworkers on the Firing Line," in *On the Job: Confronting the Labour Process in Canada*, edited by C. Heron and R. Storey. Kingston, ON: McGill-Queen's University Press.

WILTON, D. A. 1980. "An Analysis of Canadian Wage Contracts with Cost-of-Living Allowance Clauses." Discussion Paper 165. Ottawa: Economic Council of Canada.

Chapter 12

ABOWD, J. and J. TRACY. 1989. "Market Structure, Strike Activity, and Union Wage Settlements."*Industrial Relations*, 28, pp. 227–50.

AKYEAMPONG, E. 2006. "Increased Work Stoppages." *Perspectives on Labour and Income*, 7, no. 8, pp. 5–9.

ALIGISAKIS, M. 1997. "Labour Disputes in Western Europe: Typology and Tendencies."*International Labour Review*, 136, pp. 73–94.

ALLEN, D. 1994. "How Strikes Influence Work Injury Duration: Evidence from the State of New York." *Proceedings of the Forty-Sixth Annual Meeting*. Madison, WI: Industrial Relations Research Association, pp. 306–14.

ANDERSON, J. C., M. GUNDERSON, and A. PONAK. 1989. "Strikes and Dispute Resolution," in *Union–Management Relations in Canada*, 2nd Edition, edited by J. Anderson, M. Gunderson, and A. Ponak. Don Mills, ON: Addison-Wesley.

ASHENFELTER, O. and G. JOHNSON. 1969. "Bargaining Theory, Trade Unions, and Industrial Activity."*American Economic Review*, 59, pp. 35–49.

BARNETT, V. 2003. "The Use of Information Technology in a Strike."*Research in Labour Economics*, 24, pp. 55–73.

BEATTY, C. and J. GANZ. 1989. "After the Strike: Changing the Teacher Board Relationship."*Relations industrielles/Industrial Relations*, 44, pp. 569–89.

BECKER, B. E. and C. A. OLSON. 1986. "The Impact of Strikes on Shareholder Equity."*Industrial and Labor Relations Review*, 39, pp. 425–38.

BRISKIN, L. 2007. "From Person-Days Lost to Labour Militancy: A New Look at Canadian Work Stoppage Data."*Relations industrielles/Industrial Relations*, 62, pp. 31–61.

BUDD, J. 1994. "The Effect of Multinational Institutions on Strike Activity in Canada."*Industrial and Labor Relations Review*, 47, pp. 401–16.

———. 1996. "Canadian Strike Replacement Legislation and Collective Bargaining: Lessons for the United States."*Industrial Relations*, 35, pp. 245–60.

CAMERON, S. 1983. "An International Comparison of the Volatility of Strike Behaviour."*Relations industrielles/Industrial Relations*, 38, pp. 767–84.

CAMPOLIETI, M., R. HEBDON, and D. HYATT. 2005. "Strike Incidence and Strike Duration: Some New Evidence from Ontario."*Industrial and Labour Relations Review*, 58, pp. 610–30.

CARD, D. 1988. "Longitudinal Analysis of Strike Activity."*Journal of Labor Economics,*6, pp. 147–76.

———. 1990. "Strikes and Wages: A Test of an Asymmetric Information Model."*Quarterly Journal of Economics*, 105, pp. 625–59.

COHEN, I. 1990. "Political Climate and Two Airline Strikes: Century Aviation in 1932 and Continental Airlines in 1983–85."*Industrial and Labor Relations Review*, 43, pp. 308–23.

COHN, S. and A. EATON. 1989. "Historical Limits on Neoclassical Strike Theories: Evidence from French Coal Mining, 1890–1935."*Industrial and Labor Relations Review*, 42, pp. 649–62.

COUSINEAU, J. and R. LACROIX. 1986. "Imperfect Information and Strikes: An Analysis of Canadian Experience, 1967–82."*Industrial and Labor Relations Review*, 39, pp. 377–87.

COUSINEAU, J., R. LACROIX, and D. VACHON. 1991. "Foreign Ownership and Strike Activity in Canada."*Relations industrielles/Industrial Relations*, 46, pp. 616–29.

CRAMTON, P. and J. TRACY. 1992. "Strikes and Holdouts in Wage Bargaining: Theory and Data."*American Economic Review*, 82, pp. 100–21.

———. 1994. "The Determinants of U.S. Labour Disputes. "*Journal of Labour Economics*, 12, pp. 180–209.

———. 1998. "The Use of Replacement Workers in Union Contract Negotiations: The U.S. Experience, 1980–1989." *Journal of Labour Economics*, 16, pp. 667–701.

CRAMTON, P., M. GUNDERSON, and J. TRACY. 1999a. "Impacts of Strike Replacement Bans in Canada."*Labor Law Journal*, 50, pp. 173–79.

———. 1999b. "The Effect of Collective Bargaining Legislation on Strikes and Wages."*Review of Economics and Statistics*, 81, pp. 475–87.

CURRIE, J. and S. McCONNELL. 1991. "Collective Bargaining in the Public Sector: The Effect of Legal Structure on Dispute Costs and Wages."*American Economic Review*, 81, pp. 693–718.

DAVIDSON, W., D. WORRELL, and S. GARRISON. 1988. "Effect of Strike Activity on Firm Value."*Academy of Management Journal*, 31, pp. 387–94.

DeFUSCO, R. and S. FUESS. 1991. "The Effects of Airline Strikes on Struck and Nonstruck Carriers."*Industrial and Labor Relations Review*, 44, pp. 324–33.

DiNARDO, J. and K. HALLOCK. 2002. "When Unions 'Mattered': The Impact of Strikes on Financial Markets."*Industrial and Labor Relations Review*, 55, pp. 219–33.

DUSSAULT, F. and R. LACROIX. 1980. "Activité de Grève: un test des hypothèses explicatives traditionnelles." *Canadian Journal of Economics*, 13, pp. 632–44.

EATON, B. C. 1973. "The Worker and the Profitability of the Strike."*Industrial and Labor Relations Review*, 26, pp. 670–79.

EDWARDS, P. K. 1986. *Conflict at Work: A Materialist Analysis of Workplace Relations.*Oxford: Basil Blackwell.

———. 1992. "Industrial Conflict: Themes and Issues in the Recent Research."*British Journal of Industrial Relations*, 30, pp. 361–404.

ENDERWICK, P. and P. J. BUCKLEY. 1982. "Strike Activity and Foreign Ownership: An Analysis of British Manufacturing 1971–73."*British Journal of Industrial Relations*, 20, pp. 308–21.

FLAHERTY, S. 1987. "Strike Activity, Worker Militancy, and Productivity Change in Manufacturing, 1961–1981." *Industrial and Labor Relations Review*, 4, pp. 585–600.

FORCHHEIMER, K. 1948. "Some International Aspects of the Strike Movement."*Bulletin of the Oxford University Institute of Statistics,*10, pp. 9–24.

FRANKLIN, S. 2001. *Three Strikes: Labor's Heartland Losses and What They Mean for Working Americans*. New York: Guilford Press.

FRANZOSI, R. 1989. "One Hundred Years of Strike Statistics: Methodological and Theoretical Issues in Quantitative Strike Research." *Industrial and Labor Relations Review*, 42, pp. 348–62.

GAREN, J. and J. KRISLOV. 1988. "An Examination of the New American Strike Statistics in Analyzing Aggregate Strike Incidence." *British Journal of Industrial Relations*, 26, pp. 75–84.

GHILARDUCCI, T. 1988. "The Impact of Internal Politics on the 1981 UMWA Strike." *Industrial Relations*, 27, pp. 371–84.

GILSON, C., I. SPENCER, and S. GRANVILLE. 1989. "The Impact of a Strike on the Attitudes and Behaviour of a Rural Community." *Relations industrielles/Industrial Relations*, 44, pp. 785–802.

GODARD, J. 1992. "Strikes as Collective Voice: A Behavioral Analysis of Strike Activity."*Industrial and Labor Relations Review,*46, pp. 161–175.

GRAMM, C. 1986. "The Determinants of Strike Incidence and Severity: A Micro Level Study."*Industrial and Labor Relations Review*, 39, pp. 361–75.

———. 1987. "New Measures of the Propensity to Strike During Contract Negotiations, 1971–1980."*Industrial and Labor Relations Review*, 40, pp. 406–17.

GRAMM, C., W. HENDRICKS, and L. KAHN. 1988. "Inflation Uncertainty and Strike Activity." *Industrial Relations*, 27, pp. 114–29.

GRAMM, C. and J. SCHNELL. 1994. "Difficult Choices: Crossing the Picket Line During the 1987 National Football League Strike."*Journal of Labor Economics,*12, pp. 41–73.

GUNDERSON, M., R. HEBDON, and D. HYATT. 1996. "Collective Bargaining in the Public Sector."*American Economic Review*, 86, pp. 315–26.

GUNDERSON, M., B. HEBDON, D. HYATT, and A. PONAK. 2005. "Strikes and Dispute Resolution," in *Union–Management Relations in Canada*, 5th Edition, edited by M. Gunderson, A. Ponak and D. Taras. Don Mills: Addison-Wesley.

GUNDERSON, M. and D. HYATT. 1996. "Canadian Public Sector Employment Relations in Transition," in *Public Sector Employment in a Time of Transition.*Madison, WI: Industrial Relations Research Association.

GUNDERSON, M., D. HYATT, and A. PONAK. 1995. "Strikes and Dispute Resolution," in *Union–Management Relations in Canada*, 3rd Edition, edited by M. Gunderson and A. Ponak. Don Mills: Addison-Wesley.

GUNDERSON, M., J. KERVIN, and F. REID. 1986. "Logit Estimates of Strike Incidence from Canadian Contract Data."*Journal of Labor Economics*,4, pp. 257–76.

———. 1989. "The Effect of Labour Relations Legislation on Strike Incidence." *Canadian Journal of Economics*, 22, pp. 779–94.

GUNDERSON, M. and A. MELINO. 1987. "Estimating Strike Effects in a General Model of Prices and Quantities." *Journal of Labor Economics*,5, pp. 1–19.

———. 1990. "The Effects of Public Policy on Strike Duration."*Journal of Labor Economics*,8, pp. 295–316.

GUNDERSON, M., A. MELINO, and F. REID. 1990. "The Effects of Canadian Labour Relations Legislation on Strike Incidence and Duration." *Labor Law Journal*, 41, pp. 512–18.

GUNDERSON, M. and F. REID. 1995. "Public Sector Strikes in Canada," in *Public Sector Collective Bargaining in Canada*, edited by G. Swimmer and M. Thompson. Kingston, ON: IRC Press.

HAMEED, S. M. and T. LOMAS. 1975. "Measurement of Production Losses Due to Strikes in Canada: An Input-Output Analysis." *British Journal of Industrial Relations*, 13, pp. 86–93.

HARRISON, A. and M. STEWART. 1989. "Cyclical Fluctuations in Strike Durations."*American Economic Review*,79, pp. 827–41.

HAYES, B. 1984. "Unions and Strikes with Asymmetric Information."*Journal of Labor Economics*,2, pp. 57–83.

HEBDON, R. 1996. "Public Sector Dispute Resolution in Transition," in *Public Sector Employment in a Time of Transition*, edited by D. Belman, M. Gunderson and D. Hyatt. Industrial Relations Research Association, chapter 3.

HEBDON, R., D. HYATT, and M. MAZEROLLE. 1999. "Implications of Small Bargaining Units and Enterprise Unions on Bargaining Disputes." *Relations industrielles/Industrial Relations*, 54, pp. 503–24.

HEBDON, R. and R. STERN. 1998. "Tradeoffs Among Expressions of Industrial Conflict: Public Sector Strike Bans and Grievance Arbitrations."*Industrial and Labour Relations Review*, 51, pp. 204–21.

———. 2003. "Do Public Sector Strike Bans Really Prevent Conflict?"*Industrial Relations*, 42, pp. 493–512.

HEBDON, R. and P. WARRIAN. 1999. "Coercive Bargaining: Public Sector Restructuring Under The Ontario Social Contract 1993–96."*Industrial and Labor Relations Review*, 52, pp.196–212.

HICKS, J. R. 1963. *The Theory of Wages*, 3rd Edition. New York: St. Martin's Press.

HORN, R. N., W. J. McGUIRE, and J. TOMKIEWICZ. 1982. "Work Stoppages by Teachers: An Empirical Analysis."*Journal of Labor Research*,3, pp. 487–96.

HUTCHENS, R., D. LIPSKY, and R. STERN. 1992. "Unemployment Insurance and Strikes."*Journal of Labor Research*,13, pp. 337–54.

ICHNIOWSKI, C. 1988. "Police Recognition Strikes: Illegal and Ill Fated."*Journal of Labor Research*,9, pp. 183–97.

ILO. 1990. *Meeting of Experts on Statistics of Strikes and Lockouts*. Geneva: International Labour Organization.

INGRAM, R., D. METCALF, and J. WADSWORTH. 1993. "Strike Incidence in British Manufacturing in the 1980s." *Industrial and Labor Relations Review*, 46, pp. 704–17.

JONES, J. C. H. and W. D. WALSH. 1984. "Inter-industry Strike Frequencies: Some Pooled Cross-sectional Evidence from Canadian Secondary Manufacturing."*Journal of Labor Research*,5, pp. 419–25.

KAUFMAN, B. 1993. "Research on Strike Models and Outcomes in the 1980s: Accomplishments and Shortcomings," in *Research Frontiers in Industrial Relations and Human Resources*, edited by D. Lewin, O. Mitchell, and P. Sherer. Madison, WI: Industrial Relations Research Association.

KELLY, J. 1988. *Trade Unions and Socialist Politics*. London: Verso.

KENNAN, J. 1980. "Pareto Optimality and the Economics of Strike Duration."*Journal of Labor Research*,1, pp. 77–94.

———. 1986. "The Economics of Strikes," in *The Handbook of Labor Economics*, edited by O. Ashenfelter and R. Layard. Amsterdam: North Holland.

KENNAN, J. and R. WILSON. 1989. "Strategic Bargaining Models and Interpretation of Strike Data."*Journal of Applied Econometrics*, 4, pp. 87–130.

KNIGHT, K. 1989. "Labour Productivity and Strike Activity in British Manufacturing Industries: Some Quantitative Evidence."*British Journal of Industrial Relations*, 27, pp. 365–74.

KRAMER, J. and T. HYCLAK. 2002. "Why Strikes Occur: Evidence from the Capital Markets."*Industrial Relations*, 41, pp. 80–93.

KRAMER, J. and G. VASCONCELLOS. 1996. "The Economic Effects of Strikes on the Shareholders of Nonstruck Competitors."*Industrial and Labor Relations Review*, 49, pp. 213–22.

KRUEGER, A. and A. MAS. 2004. "Strikes, Scabs and Tread Separations: Labor Strife and the Production of Defective Bridgestone/ Firestone Tires."*Journal of Political Economy*, 112, pp. 253–89.

LACROIX, R. 1986a. "A Microeconometric Analysis of the Effects of Strikes on Wages."*Relations industrielles/Industrial Relations*,41, pp. 111–26.

———. 1986b. "Strike Activity in Canada," in *Canadian*

Labour Relations, edited by W. C. Riddell. Toronto: University of Toronto Press.

LACROIX, R. and A. LESPERANCE. 1988. "New Labor Laws and Strike Activity." *Relations industrielles/Industrial Relations*, 43, pp. 812–27.

LANGFORD, T. 1996. "Effects of Strike Participation on the Political Consequences of Canadian Postal Workers." *Relations industrielles/Industrial Relations*, 51, pp. 563–82.

LeROY, M. 1992. "Multivariate Analysis of Unionized Employees' Propensity to Cross Their Own Union's Picket Line." *Journal of Labor Research*, 13, pp. 285–92.

MacDOWELL, L. 1993. "After the Strike: Labour Relations in Oshawa, 1937–1939." *Relations industrielles/Industrial Relations*, 48, pp. 691–710.

MAKI, D. 1983. "A Note on the Output Effects of Canadian Postal Strikes." *Canadian Journal of Economics*, 16, pp. 149–54.

———. 1986. "The Effect of the Cost of Strikes on the Volume of Strike Activity." *Industrial and Labor Relations Review*, 39, pp. 552–63.

MARTIN, J. E. 2001. "A Multiple Motive Perspective on Strike Propensities." *Journal of Organizational Behavior*, 22, pp. 387–407.

MAURO, M. J. 1982. "Strikes as a Result of Imperfect Information." *Industrial and Labor Relations Review*, 35, pp. 522–38.

McCLENDON, J. and B. KLAAS. 1993. "Determinants of Strike-Related Militancy: An Analysis of a University Faculty Strike." *Industrial and Labor Relations Review*, 46, pp. 560–73.

McCONNELL, S. 1989. "Strikes, Wages, and Private Information." *American Economic Review*, 79, pp. 810–15.

———. 1990. "Cyclical Fluctuations in Strike Activity." *Industrial and Labor Relations Review*, 44, pp. 130–43.

McHUGH, R. 1991. "Productivity Effects of Strikes in Struck and Nonstruck Industries." *Industrial and Labor Relations Review*, 44, pp. 722–32.

MILNER, S. and D. METCALF. 1993. "A Century of Strike Activity," in *New Perspectives on Industrial Disputes*, edited by D. Metcalf and S. Milner. London: Routledge.

MONTGOMERY, E. and M. BENEDICT. 1989. "The Impact of Bargainer Experience on Teacher Strikes." *Industrial and Labor Relations Review*, 42, pp. 380–92.

NEUMANN, G. R. 1980. "The Predictability of Strikes: Evidence from the Stock Market." *Industrial and Labor Relations Review*, 33, pp. 525–35.

NEUMANN, G. R. and M. W. REDER. 1984. "Output and Strike Activity in U.S. Manufacturing: How Large Are the Losses?" *Industrial and Labor Relations Review*, 37, pp. 197–211.

NG, I. 1987. "Determinants of Wildcat Strikes in Canadian Manufacturing Industries." *Relations industrielles/Industrial Relations*, 42, pp. 386–96.

———. 1991. "Predictors of Strike Voting Behaviour." *Journal of Labor Research*, 12, pp. 123–34.

———. 1993. "Strike Activity and Post-Strike Perceptions Among University Faculty." *Relations industrielles/Industrial Relations*, 48, pp. 231–47.

NG, I. and D. MAKI. 1988. "Strike Activity of U.S. Institutions in Canada." *British Journal of Industrial Relations*, 26, pp. 63–73.

NOEL, A. and K. GARDNER. 1990. "The Gainers Strike: Capitalist Offensive, Militancy, and the Politics of Industrial Relations in Canada." *Studies in Political Economy*, 31, pp. 31–72.

OLSON, C. A. 1984. "The Role of Rescheduled School Days in Teacher Strikes." *Industrial and Labor Relations Review*, 37, pp. 515–28.

———. 1986. "Strikes, Strike Penalties, and Arbitration in Six States." *Industrial and Labor Relations Review*, 39, pp. 539–51.

———. 1988. "Dispute Resolution in the Public Sector," in *Public Sector Bargaining*, 2nd Edition, edited by B. Aaron et al. Washington, D.C.: Bureau of National Affairs.

ONDRICH, J. and J. SCHNELL. 1993. "Strike Duration and the Degree of Disagreement." *Industrial Relations*, 32, pp. 412–31.

PAARSCH, H. 1990. "Work Stoppages and the Theory of the Offset Factor: Evidence from the British Columbia Logging Industry." *Journal of Labor Economics*, 8, pp. 387–418.

PARTRIDGE, D. 1988. "A Reexamination of the Effectiveness of No-Strike Laws for Public School Teachers." *Journal of Collective Negotiations in the Public Sector*, 17, pp. 257–66.

PERSONS, O. 1995. "The Effects of Automobile Strikes on the Stock Market Value of Steel Suppliers." *Industrial and Labor Relations Review*, 49, pp. 78–87.

PONAK, A. and L. FALKENBERG. 1989. "Resolution of Interest Disputes," in *Collective Bargaining in Canada*, edited by A. Sethi. Toronto: Nelson.

REDER, M. and G. NEUMANN. 1980. "Conflict and Contract: The Case of Strikes." *Journal of Political Economy*, 60, pp. 371–82.

REES, A. 1952. "Industrial Conflict and Business Fluctuations." *Journal of Political Economy*, 60, pp. 371–82.

REID, F. and A. OMAN. 1991. "Do Unions Win Short Strikes and Lose Long Strikes?" *Proceedings of the 28th Conference of the Canadian Industrial Relations Association*. Kingston, ON: CIRA.

ROSE, D. 1991. "Are Strikes Less Effective in Conglomerate Firms?" *Industrial and Labor Relations Review*, 45, pp. 131–44.

SCHNELL, J. F. and C. L. GRAMM. 1987. "Learning by Striking: Estimates of the Teetotaller Effect." *Journal of Labor Economics*, 5, pp. 221–41.

SCHUTT, R. 1982. "Models of Militancy: Support for Strikes and Work Actions Among Public Employees." *Industrial and Labor Relations Review*, 35, pp. 406–22.

SCHWARZ, J. and K. KOZIARA. 1992. "The Effect of Hospital Bargaining Unit Structure on Industrial Relations Outcomes." *Industrial and Labor Relations Review*, 45, pp. 573–90.

SEGELLA, M. 1995. "Industrial Conflict in Developed and Developing Countries: Extending a Western Strike Model." *Relations industrielles/Industrial Relations*, 50, pp. 393–417.

SHALEV, M. 1978. "Problems of Strike Measurement," in *The Resurgence of Class Conflict in Western Europe Since 1968*, edited by C. Crouch and A. Pizzorno. London: MacMillan.

SIEBERT, W. and J. ADDISON. 1981. "Are Strikes Accidental?" *Economic Journal*, 91, pp. 389–404.

SINGH, P. and H. JAIN. 2001. "Striker Replacements in the United States, Canada and Mexico: A Review of Law and Empirical Research." *Industrial Relations*, 40, pp. 22–53.

SKEELS, J., P. McGRATH, and G. ARSHANAPALLI. 1988. "The Importance of Strike Size in Strike Research." *Industrial and Labor Relations Review*, 41, pp. 582–91.

STERN, R. N. 1978. "Methodological Issues in Quantitative Strike Analysis." *Industrial Relations*, 12, pp. 32–42.

STONER, C. and R. ARORA. 1987. "An Investigation of the Relationship Between Selected Variables and the Psychological Health of Strike Participants." *Journal of Occupational Psychology*, 60, pp. 61–71.

SWEENEY, K. and J. DAVIES. 1997. "International Comparisons of Labour Disputes in 1995." *Labour Market Trends*, 105, pp. 121–56.

SWIDINSKY, R. and J. VANDERKAMP. 1982. "A Micro-Economic Analysis of Strike Activity in Canada." *Journal of Labor Research*, 3, pp. 456–71.

TANG, R. Y. W. and A. PONAK. 1986. "Employer Assessment of Strike Costs." *Relations industrielles/Industrial Relations*, 41, pp. 552–70.

TOMKIEWICZ, J., C. TOMKIEWICZ, and O. BRENNER. 1985. "Why Don't Teachers Strike?" *Journal of Collective Negotiations in the Public Sector*, 14, pp. 183–90.

TRACY, J. S. 1986. "An Investigation into the Determinants of U.S. Strike Activity." *American Economic Review*, 76, pp. 423–36.

———. 1987. "An Empirical Test of an Asymmetric Information Model of Strikes." *Journal of Labor Economics*, 5, pp. 149–73.

TURNBULL, P. and D. SAPSFORD. 2001. "Hitting the Bricks: An International Comparative Study of Conflict on the Waterfront," in *Industrial Relations*, 40, pp. 231–57.

VANDERKAMP, J. 1970. "Economic Activity and Strikes in Canada." *Industrial Relations*, 9, pp. 215–320.

VROOMAN, S. 1989. "A Longitudinal Attitude of Strike Activity in U.S. Manufacturing." *American Economic Review*, 79, pp. 816–26.

WHEELER, H. 1985. *Industrial Conflict: An Integrative Theory.* Columbia, SC: University of South Carolina Press.

Chapter 13

AKYEAMPONG, E. B. 2003. "Unionization and the Grievance System." *Perspectives on Labour and Income*, 4, pp. 5–11.

———. 2005. "Collective Bargaining Priorities." *Perspectives*, August, pp. 5–10.

ALLEN, A. D. and D. F. JENNINGS. 1988. "Sounding Out the Nation's Arbitrators: An AAA Survey." *Labor Law Journal*, 39, pp. 423–31.

ALLEN, R. E. and T. J. KEAVENY. 1985. "Factors Differentiating Grievants and Non-Grievants." *Human Relations*, 38, pp. 519–34.

BACHARACH, S. and P. BAMBERGER. 2004. "The Power of Labor to Grieve: The Impact of the Workplace, Labor Market, and Power-Dependence on Employee Grievance Filing." *Industrial and Labor Relations Review*, 57, pp. 518–39.

BAMBERGER, P. and L. DONAHUE. 1999. "Employee Discharge and Reinstatement: Moral Hazards and the Mixed Consequences of Last Chance Agreements." *Industrial and Labor Relations Review*, 53, no. 1, pp. 3–20.

BEMMELS, B. 1988. "The Effect of Grievants' Gender on Arbitration Outcomes." *Industrial and Labor Relations Review*, 41, pp. 251–62.

———. 1990. "Arbitrator Characteristics and Arbitrator Decisions." *Journal of Labor Research*, 11, pp. 181–92.

———. 1991. "Gender Effects in Grievance Arbitration." *Industrial Relations*, 30, pp. 150–62.

———. 1994. "The Determinants of Grievance Initiation." *Industrial and Labor Relations Review*, 47, pp. 285–301.

BEMMELS, B., Y. RESHEF, and K. STRATTON-DEVINE. 1991. "The Roles of Supervisors, Employees, and Stewards in Grievance Initiation." *Industrial and Labor Relations Review*, 45, pp. 15–30.

BLOCK, R. N. and J. STEIBER. 1987. "The Impacts of Attorneys and Arbitrators on Arbitration Awards." *Industrial and Labor Relations Review*, 40, pp. 543–55.

BOROFF, K. E. and D. LEWIN. 1997. "Loyalty, Voice and Intent to Exit a Union Firm: A Conceptual and Empirical Analysis." *Industrial and Labor Relations Review*, 51, pp. 50–63.

BROWN, D. and D. BEATTY. 2006. *Canadian Labour Arbitration*, 4th Edition. Aurora, ON: Canada Law Book.

CAPPELLI, P. and K. CHAUVIN. 1991. "A Test of an Efficiency Model of Grievance Activity." *Industrial and Labor Relations Review*, 45, pp. 3–14.

CHAISSON, G. 1996. *Union Mergers in Hard Times*. Ithaca, New York: Cornell University Press.

COLVIN, J. S. A. 2003. "Institutional Pressures, Human Resource Strategies, and the Rise of Nonunion Dispute Resolution Procedures."*Industrial and Labor Relations Review*, 56, pp. 375–92.

———. 2004. "The Relationship Between Employee Involvement and Workplace Dispute Resolution."*Relations industrielles/Industrial Relations*, 59, pp. 681–704.

DASTMALCHIAN, A. and I. NG. 1990. "Industrial Relations Climate and Grievance Outcomes."*Relations industrielles/Industrial Relations*, 45, pp. 311–25.

DEITSCH, C. R. and D. A. DILTS. 1986. "Factors Affecting Pre-Arbitral Settlement of Rights Disputes: Predicting the Method of Rights Dispute Resolution."*Journal of Labor Research*, 7, pp. 69–78.

EDEN, G. 1994. "Reinstatement in the Nonunion Sector: An Empirical Analysis." *Relations industrielles/Industrial Relations*, 49, pp. 87–103.

EWING, D. W. 1989. *Justice on the Job: Resolving Grievances in the Non-Union Workplace*. Boston: Harvard Business School Press.

FEUILLE, P. 1999. "Grievance Mediation," in *Employment Dispute Resolution and Worker Rights*, edited by A. E. Eaton and J. H. Keefe. Champaign, IL: Industrial Relations Research Association Series.

FEUILLE, P. and G. HILDEBRAND. 1995. "Grievance Procedures and Dispute Resolution," in *Handbook of Human Resource Management*, edited by G. Ferris, S. Rosen and D. Barnum. Cambridge, MA: Blackwell, pp. 340–69.

FOISY, C. 1998. "Is Arbitration Too Slow and Legalistic?" in *Conference Proceedings of the 16th Annual University of Calgary Labour Arbitration Conference*, edited by M. Hughes and A. Ponak. Calgary: Industrial Relations Research Group and University of Calgary.

FRASER, D. and O. B. SHIME. 1989. "The Ontario Grievance Settlement Board," in *Proceedings of the 26th Conference of the Canadian Industrial Relations Association*. Laval, QC: CIRA, pp. 567–78.

FREEMAN, R. B. and J. L. MEDOFF. 1984. *What Do Unions Do?* New York, NY: Basic Books.

GANDZ, J. 1979. "Grievance Initiation and Resolution: A Test of the Behavioural Theory." *Relations industrielles/Industrial Relations*, 34, pp. 778–92.

GANDZ, J. and P. J. WARRIAN. 1977. "Does It Matter Who Arbitrates? A Statistical Analysis of Arbitration Awards in Ontario."*Labour Gazette*, 77, pp. 65–75.

GANDZ, J. and J. D. WHITEHEAD. 1982. "The Relationship Between Industrial Relations Climate and Grievance Initiation and Resolution."*Proceedings of the 34th Annual Meeting*, Industrial Relations Research Association.

Madison, WI: IRRA, pp. 320–28.

GOLDBERG, S. B. 1989. "Grievance Mediation: A Successful Alternative to Labor Arbitration."*Negotiation Journal*, 5, pp. 9–15.

GRAHAM, H. and B. HESHIZER. 1978. "The Effect of Contract Language on Low-Level Settlement of Grievances."*Labor Law Journal*, 30, pp. 427–32.

HARCOURT, M. and S. HARCOURT. 2000. "When Can an Employee Refuse Unsafe Work and Expect to be Protected From Discipline? Evidence From Canada."*Industrial and Labor Relations Review*, 53, pp. 684–703.

HEBDON, R. and R. STERN. 1998. "Tradeoffs Among Expressions of Industrial Conflict: Public Sector Strike Bans and Grievance Arbitrations."*Industrial and Labor Relations Review*, 51, pp. 204–21.

ICHNIOWSKI, C. 1986. "The Effects of Grievance Activity on Productivity."*Industrial and Labor Relations Review*, 40, pp. 75–89.

KATZ, H. C., T. A. KOCHAN, and K. R. GOBEILLE. 1983. "Industrial Relations Performance, Economic Performance, and QWL Programs: An Interplant Analysis."*Industrial and Labor Relations Review*, 37, pp. 3–17.

KATZ, H. C., T. A. KOCHAN, and M. R. WEBER. 1985. "Assessing the Effects of Industrial Relations Systems and Efforts to Improve the Quality of Working Life on Organizational Effectiveness." *Academy of Management Journal*, 28, pp. 509–26.

KLAAS, B. and A. DeNISI. 1989. "Managerial Reactions to Employee Dissent: The Impact of Grievance Activity on Performance Ratings."*Academy of Management Journal*, 32, pp. 705–18.

KNIGHT, T. R. 1986a. "Correlates of Informal Grievance Resolution Among First-Line Supervisors." *Relations industrielles/Industrial Relations*, 41, pp. 281–98.

———. 1986b. "Feedback and Grievance Resolution." *Industrial and Labor Relations Review*, 39, pp. 585–98.

LEWIN, D. 1999. "Theoretical and Empirical Research on the Grievance Procedure and Arbitration: A Critical Review," in *Employment Dispute Resolution and Worker Rights*, edited by A. E. Eaton and J. H. Keefe. Champaign, IL: Industrial Relations Research Association.

LEWIN, D. and R. B. PETERSON. 1988. *The Modern Grievance Procedure in the United States*. Westport, CT: Quorum Books.

———. 1999. "Behavioral Outcomes of Grievance Activity."*Industrial Relations*, 38, pp. 554–76.

McCABE, D. M. 2002. "Administering the Employment Relationship: The Ethics of Conflict Resolution."*Journal of Business Ethics*, 36, pp. 33–48.

MITCHNICK, M. and B. ETHERINGTON. 2002. *Leading Cases on Labour Arbitration*. Toronto: Lancaster House.

———. 2006. *Labour Arbitration in Canada*. Toronto: Lancaster House.

NORSWORTHY, J. R. and C. A. ZABALA. 1985. "Worker Attitudes, Worker Behavior, and Productivity in the U.S. Automobile Industry, 1959–1976."*Industrial and Labor Relations Review*, 38, pp. 544–57.

O'HARE, E. and W. O'DONOHUE. 1998. "Sexual Harassment: Identifying Risk Factors."*Archives of Sexual Behavior*, 27, pp. 561–80.

OLSON-BUCHANAN, J. B. 1996. "Voicing Discontent: What Happens to the Grievance Filer After the Grievance?"*Journal of Applied Psychology*, 81, pp. 52–63.

PALMER, E. and B. PALMER. 1991. *Collective Agreement Arbitration in Canada*, 3rd Edition. Toronto: Butterworths.

PERRY, E. L., C. T. KULIK and J. M. SCHMIDTKE. 1997. "Blowing the Whistle: Determinants of Responses to Sexual Harassment."*Basic and Applied Social Psychology*, 19, pp. 457–82.

PETERSON, R. B. and D. M. McCABE. 1994. "The Nonunion Grievance System in High Performing Firms."*Proceedings of the 1994 IRRA Spring Meeting*. Madison, WI: IRRA, pp. 529–34.

PONAK, A. and J. BENJAMIN. 2007. "Innovation and Problem Solving Under Alberta's Ministerial Appointment System."*Labour Arbitration Yearbook* (Forthcoming).

PONAK, A. and C. OLSON. 1992. "Time Delays in Grievance Arbitration."*Relations industrielles/Industrial Relations*, 47, pp. 690–708.

PONAK, A., B. PAINTER, and D. SHENFIELD. 2005. *Beyond Collision: High Integrity Labour Relations*. National Defence/Canadian Forces—U.N.D.E Case Study.

PONAK, A., W. ZERBE, S. ROSE, and C. OLSON. 1996. "Using Event History Analysis to Model Delay in Grievance Arbitration."*Industrial and Labor Relations Review*, 50, pp. 105–21.

RINGSEIS, E. and A. PONAK. 2007. "Judicial Review of Arbitration Decisions."*Canadian Labour and Employment Law Journal*, 13, no. 2, pp. 301–12.

ROSE, J. B. 1991. "The Emergence of Expedited Arbitration."*Labour Arbitration Yearbook*, 1, pp. 13–22.

THORNICROFT, K. W. 1989. "Arbitrators, Social Values and the Burden of Proof in Substance Abuse Discharge Cases."*Labor Law Journal*, 40, pp. 582–93.

———. 1993. "Accounting for Delay in Grievance Arbitration."*Labor Law Journal*, 44, pp. 543–55.

———. 1994. "Do Lawyers Affect Grievance Arbitration Outcomes?"*Relations industrielles/Industrial Relations*, 49, pp. 357–72.

———. 1995. "Gender Effects in Grievance Arbitration... Revisited."*Labor Studies Journal*, 19, pp. 35–44.

———. 1996. "The Timeliness of Expedited Arbitration in B.C.: The First Two Years."*Labour Arbitration 1996*. Vancouver, BC: Continuing Legal Education Society of BC.

TURNER, J. T. and J. W. ROBINSON. 1972. "A Pilot Study on the Validity of Grievance Settlement Rates as a Predictor of the Union–Management Relationship."*Journal of Industrial Relations*, 14, pp. 314–22.

WAGAR, T. H. 1994. "The Effects of Lawyers on Non-Discipline/Discharge Arbitration Decisions."*Journal of Labor Research*, 15, pp. 283–93.

WHEELER, H. N., B. S. KLASS, and D. M. MAHONEY. 2004. *Workplace Justice Without Unions*. Kalamazoo, MI: W. E. Upjohn Institute for Employment Research.

WHITEHEAD, J. D., E. M. AIM, and L. A. WHITEHEAD. 1988. "Dispute Resolution in Canada: Selected Examples of Recent Innovations," in *Selected SPIDR Proceedings 1987–1988*. New York, NY: SPIDR, pp. 200–18.

ZACK, A. 1999. "Agreement to Arbitrate and Waiver of Rights Under Employment Law," in *Employment Dispute Resolution and Worker Rights*, edited by A. E. Eaton and J. H. Keefe. Champaign, IL: Industrial Relations Research Association.

Chapter 14

ABOWD, J. 1989. "The Effect of Wage Bargains on the Stock Market Value of the Firm."*American Economic Review*, 79, pp. 774–809.

ADDISON, J. and C. R. BELFIELD. 2001. "Updating the Determinants of Firm Performance: Estimation using the 1998 WERS." *British Journal of Industrial Relations*, 39, pp. 341–66.

———. 2004. "Unions and Establishment Performance: Evidence from the British Workplace Industrial/Employee Relations Surveys," in *Changing Role of Unions: New Forms of Representation*, edited by P. Wunnava. New York: M. E. Sharpe, pp. 281–319.

———. 2007. "Union Voice," in *What Do Unions Do?: A Twenty-Year Perspective*, edited by J. Bennett and B. Kaufman. London: Transaction Publishers, pp. 239–74.

ADDISON, J. and A. CASTRO. 1987. "The Importance of Lifetime Jobs: Differences Between Union and Nonunion Workers." *Industrial and Labor Relations Review*, 40, pp. 393–405.

ADDISON, J. and B. HIRSCH. 1989. "Union Effects on Productivity, Profits and Growth." *Journal of Labor Economics*, 7, pp. 72–105.

ADDISON, J. and C. SCHNABEL. 2003. *International Handbook of Trade Unions*. Cheltenham, U.K.: Edward Elgar.

ADDISON, J. and J. WAGNER. 1994. "Unionism and Innovative Activity: Some Cautionary Remarks on the Basis of a Simple Cross-Country Test."*British Journal of Industrial Relations*, 32, pp. 85–98.

ALLEN, S. 1987. "Can Union Labor Ever Cost Less?"*Quarterly Journal of Economics* (May), pp. 347–73.

———. 1988. "Productivity Levels and Productivity Change Under Unionism."*Industrial Relations*,27, pp. 94–113.

ANDREWS, M., M. STEWART, J. SWAFFIELD and R. UPWARD. 1998. "The Estimation of Union Wage Differentials and the Impact of Methodological Choices."*Labor Economics*, 5, pp. 449–74.

BALKIN, D. 1989. "Union Influence on Pay Policy: A Survey."*Journal of Labor Research*, 10, pp. 299–309.

BATT, R., A. COLVIN, and J. KEEFE. 2002. "Employee Voice, Human Resource Practices, and Quit Rates."*Industrial and Labor Relations Review*, 55, pp. 573–94.

BECKER, B. 1995. "Union Rents as a Source of Takeover Gains Among Target Shareholders."*Industrial and Labour Relations Review*, 49, pp. 3–19.

BECKER, B. and C. OLSON. 1989. "Unionism and Shareholder Interests." *Industrial and Labor Relations Review*, 42, pp. 246–62.

———. 1992. "Unions and Firm Profits."*Industrial Relations*,31, pp. 395–415.

BELMAN, D. 1992. "Unions, the Quality of Labour Relations, and Firm Performance," in *Unions and Economic Competitiveness*, edited by L. Mishel and P. Voos. Armonk, NY: M. E. Sharpe, Inc.

BELMAN, D., J. HEYWOOD, and J. LUND. 1997. "Public Sector Earnings and the Extent of Unionization." *Industrial and Labour Relations Review*, 50, pp. 610–28.

BEMMELS, B. 1987. "How Unions Affect Productivity in Manufacturing Plants." *Industrial and Labor Relations Review*,40, pp. 241–53.

BENEDICT, M. and L. WILDER. 1999. "Unionization and Tenure and Rank Outcomes in Ohio Universities."*Journal of Labor Research*, 20, pp. 185–202.

BENJAMIN, D., M. GUNDERSON, T. LEMIEUX, and W. C. RIDDELL. 2007. *Labour Market Economics: Theory, Evidence and Policy in Canada*, 6th Edition. Toronto: McGraw-Hill.

BENNETT, J. and B. KAUFMAN, eds. 2007. *What Do Unions Do?: A Twenty-Year Perspective*. London: Transaction Publishers.

BETCHERMAN, G., K. McMULLEN, N. LECKIE, and C. CARON. 1994. *The Canadian Workplace in Transition*. Kingston, ON: IRC Press.

BETCHERMAN, G., N. LECKIE, and K. McMULLEN. 1997. *Developing Skills in the Canadian Workplace*. Ottawa: Canadian Policy Research Networks.

BETTS, J., C. ODGERS, and M. WILSON. 2001. "The Effects of Unions on Research and Development: An Empirical Analysis Using Multi-Year Data."*Canadian Journal of Economics*, 34, pp. 785–806.

BEYER, J. M., H. M. TRICE, and R. E. HUNT. 1980. "The Impact of Federal Sector Unions on Supervisors' Use of Personnel Policies." *Industrial and Labor Relations Review*, 33, pp. 212–31.

BLACK, S. and L. LYNCH. 2001. "How to Compete: The Impact of Workplace Practices and Information Technology on Productivity."*Review of Economics and Statistics*, 83, pp. 434–45.

BLANCHFLOWER, D. 1999. "Changes Over Time in Union Relative Wage Effects in Great Britain and the United States," in *The History and Practice of Economics, Essays in Honor of Bernard Corry and Maurice Peston*,Vol. 2, edited by S. Daniel, P. Arestis, and J. Grahl. Northhampton, MA: Edward Elgar, pp. 3–32.

BLANCHFLOWER, D. and A. BRYSON. 2007. "What Effect Do Unions Have on Wages Now?" in *What Do Unions Do?: A Twenty-Year Perspective*, edited by J. Bennett and B. Kaufman. London: Transaction Publishers, pp. 79–113.

BLAU, F. D. and L. M. KAHN. 1983. "Unionism, Seniority, and Turnover."*Industrial Relations*,22, pp. 362–73.

BLAU, F. AND L. KAHN. 2004. "Collective Bargaining, Relative Wages and Employment: International Evidence," in *Changing Role of Unions: New Forms of Representation*, edited by P. Wunnava. New York: M. E. Sharpe, pp. 169–228.

BOOTH, A. 1995. *The Economics of the Trade Union*. Cambridge: Cambridge University Press.

BRATSBERG, B. and J. F. RAGAN Jr. 2002. "Changes in the Union Wage Premium by Industry."*Industrial and Labor Relations Review*, 56, pp. 65–82.

BRONARS, S. and G. DEERE. 1990. "Union Representation Elections and Firm Profitability."*Industrial Relations*, 29, pp. 15–37.

———. 1994. "Unionization and Profitability: Evidence of Spillover Effects."*Journal of Political Economy*, 102, pp. 1281–88.

BRONARS, S., G. DEERE, and J. TRACY. 1994. "The Effects of Unions on Firm Behaviour." *Industrial Relations*, 33, pp. 426–51.

BROWN, C., and J. MEDOFF. 1978. "Trade Unions in the Production Process." *Journal of Political Economy*, 86, pp. 355–78.

BROWN, S. and J. SESSIONS. 2004. "Trade Unions and International Competition," in *Changing Role of Unions: New Forms of Representation*, edited by P. Wunnava. New York: M. E. Sharpe.

BRUNELLO, G. 1993. "The Effect of Unions on Firm Performance in Japanese Manufacturing." *Industrial and Labor Relations Review*, 45, pp. 471–87.

BUDD, J. 2007. "The Effect of Unions on Employee Benefits and Non-Wage Compensation," in *What Do Unions Do?: A Twenty-Year Perspective*, edited by J. Bennett and B. Kaufman. London: Transaction Publishers, pp. 160–92.

BUDD, J. and K. MUMFORD. 2004. "Trade Unions and Family-Friendly Policies in Great Britain." *Industrial and Labor Relations Review*, 57, pp. 204–22.

BUDD, J. W. and I. NA. 2000. "The Union Membership Wage Premium for Employees Covered by Collective Bargaining Agreements." *Journal of Labor Economics*, 18, pp. 783–807.

CARD, D. 2001. "The Effect of Unions on Wage Inequality in the U.S. Labor Market." *Industrial and Labor Relations Review*, 54, pp. 296–315.

CARD, D., T. LEMIEUX, and W. C. RIDDELL. 2007. "Unions and Wage Inequality," in *What Do Unions Do?: A Twenty-Year Perspective*, edited by J. Bennett and B. Kaufman. London: Transaction Publishers, pp. 114–59.

CHRISTOFIDES, L. and R. SWIDINSKY. 1994. "Wage Determination by Gender and Visible Minority Status: Evidence from the 1989 LMAS." *Canadian Public Policy*, 20, pp. 34–51.

CHRISTOFIDES, L. and T. STENGOS. 2003. "Wage Rigidity in Canadian Collective Bargaining Agreements."*Industrial Labor Relations Review*, 56, pp. 429–48.

CLARK, K. 1980. "The Impact of Unionization on Productivity: A Case Study."*Industrial and Labor Relations Review*, 33, pp. 451–69.

CLEVELAND, G., M. GUNDERSON, and D. HYATT. 2003. "Union Effects in Low-Wage Services: Evidence from Canadian Childcare." *Industrial and Labor Relations Review*, 56, pp. 295–305.

COHEN, Y. and J. PFEFFER. 1986. "Organizational Hiring Standards."*Administrative Science Quarterly*, 31, pp. 1–24.

CONNOLLY, R., B. HIRSCH, and M. HIRSCHEY. 1986. "Union Rent Seeking, Intangible Capital, and Market Value of the Firm."*Review of Economics and Statistics*, 68, pp. 567–77.

COOKE, W. 1989. "Improving Productivity and Quality Through Collaboration." *Industrial Relations*, 28, pp. 299–319.

———. 1990. "Factors Influencing the Effect of Joint Union–Management Programs on Employee–Supervisor Relations." *Industrial and Labor Relations Review*, 43, pp. 587–603.

———. 1992. "Product Quality Improvement Through Employee Participation: The Effect of Unionization and Joint Union–Management Administration."*Industrial and Labor Relations Review*, 46, pp. 119–34.

———. 1994. "Employee Participation Programs, Group-Based

Incentives, and Company Performance: A Union-Nonunion Comparison." *Industrial and Labor Relations Review*, 47, pp. 594–609.

———. 1997. "The Influence of Industrial Relations Factors on U.S. Foreign Investment."*Industrial and Labour Relations Review*, 51, pp. 3–17.

CORNEO, G. and C. LUCIFORA. 1997. "Wage Formation Under Union Threat Effects." *Labor Economics*, 4, pp. 265–92.

DAVIES, R. J. 1986. "The Structure of Collective Bargaining in Canada," in *Canadian Labour Relations*, edited by W. C. Riddell. Toronto: University of Toronto Press.

DeFINA, R. H. 1983. "Unions, Relative Wages, and Economic Efficiency." *Journal of Labor Economics*, 1, pp. 408–92.

DELERY, J., N. GUPTA, D. SHAW, R. JENKINS, and M. GANSTER. 2000. "Unionization, Compensation, and Voice Effects on Quits and Retention." *Industrial Relations*, 39, pp. 625–45.

DENNY, K. and S. NICKELL. 1991. "Unions and Investment in British Manufacturing Industry." *British Journal of Industrial Relations*, 29, pp. 113–21.

DiNARDO, J., N. M. FORTIN, and T. LEMIEUX. 1996. "Labor Market Institutions and the Distribution of Wages, 1973–1992: A Semiparametric Approach." *Econometrica*, 64, pp. 1001–44.

DOIRON, D. and W. RIDDELL. 1994. "The Impact of Unionization on Male–Female Earnings Differentials in Canada." *Journal of Human Resources*, 29, pp. 504–34.

DOUCOULIAGOS, H. and P. LAROCHE. 2003a. "Unions and Tangible Investments." *Industrial Relations*, 42, pp. 314–37.

———. 2003b. "What Do Unions Do to Productivity: A Meta-Analysis." *Industrial Relations*, 42, pp. 650–91.

DRAGO, R. 1988. "Quality Circle Survival."*Industrial Relations*, 27, pp. 336–51.

DUNCAN, G. and F. STAFFORD. 1980. "Do Union Members Receive Compensating Wage Differentials?" *American Economic Review*, 70, pp. 335–71.

EHRENBERG, R., and J. SCHWARZ. 1986. "Public Sector Labor Markets," in *Handbook of Labor Economics*, edited by O. Ashenfelter and R. Layard. Amsterdam: North-Holland, pp. 1219–68.

FAIRRIS, D. 2003. "Unions and Wage Inequality in Mexico." *Industrial and Labor Relations Review*, 56, pp. 481–97.

FANG, T. and A. VERMA. 2002. "Union Wage Premiums." *Perspectives on Labour and Income*, 14, pp. 17–23.

FERNIE, S. and D. METCALF. 2005. *British Unions: Resurgence or Perdition?* London: Routledge.

FLAHERTY, S. 1987. "Strike Activity, Worker Militancy, and Productivity Change in Manufacturing: 1961–1981." *Industrial and Labor Relations Review*, 40, pp. 585–600.

FORTH, J. and N. MILLWARD. 2002. "Union Effects on Pay Levels in Britain."*Labour Economics*, 9, pp. 547–61.

FREEMAN, R. 1980. "Unionism and the Dispersion of Wages."*Industrial and Labor Relations Review*,34, pp. 3–23.

———. 1981. "The Effect of Unionism on Fringe Benefits." *Industrial and Labor Relations Review*, 34, pp. 489–509.

———. 1986. "Unionism Comes to the Public Sector."*Journal of Economic Literature*, 24, pp. 41–86.

———. 1993. "How Much Has De-unionization Contributed to the Rise of Male Earnings Inequality?" in *Uneven Tides: Rising Inequality in America*, edited by S. Danziger and P. Gottschalk. New York: Russell Sage Foundation.

FREEMAN, R. and L. F. KATZ. 1991. "Industrial Wage and Employment Determination in an Open Economy," in *Immigration, Trade and the Labour Market*, edited by J. M. Abowd and R. Freeman. Chicago: NBER, pp. 235–59.

FREEMAN, R. and M. KLEINER. 1990. "The Impact of New Unionization on Wages and Working Conditions."*Journal of Labor Economics*, 8, pp. 8–25.

———. 1999. "Do Unions Make Enterprises Insolvent?" *Industrial and Labour Relations Review*, 52, pp. 510–27.

FREEMAN, R. and J. MEDOFF. 1979. "The Two Faces of Unionism." *The Public Interest*, 7, pp. 69–93.

———. 1984. *What Do Unions Do?* New York: Basic Books.

GASTON, N. and D. TREFLER. 1995. "Union Wage Sensitivity to Trade and Protection: Theory and Evidence." *Journal of International Economics*, 39, pp. 1–25.

GOLDSCHMIDT, S. M. and L. E. STUART. 1986. "The Extent and Impact of Educational Policy Bargaining." *Industrial and Labor Relations Review*, 39, pp. 350–60.

GRANT, D. 2001. "A Comparison of the Cyclical Behavior of Union and Nonunion Wages in the United States." *The Journal of Human Resources*, 36, pp. 31–57.

GRANT, E. K., R. SWIDINSKY, and J. VANDERKAMP. 1987. "Canadian Union–Non-Union Wage Differentials." *Industrial and Labor Relations Review*, 41, pp. 93–107.

GUNDERSON, M. 2007. "Two Faces of Union Voice in the Public Sector," in *What Do Unions Do?: A Twenty-Year Perspective*, edited by J. Bennett and B. Kaufman. London: Transaction Publishers, pp. 401–22.

GUNDERSON, M., D. HYATT, and W. C. RIDDELL. 1999. *Pay Differences Between the Government and Private Sectors*. Ottawa: Canadian Policy Research Network.

HALL, W. and N. CARROLL. 1973. "The Effects of Teachers' Organizations on Salaries and Class Size." *Industrial and Labor Relations Review*, 26, pp. 834–41.

HAMMER, T. and A. AVGAR. 2007. "The Impact of Unions on Job Satisfaction, Organizational Commitment, and Turnover," in *What Do Unions Do?: A Twenty-Year Perspective*, edited by J. Bennett and B. Kaufman. London: Transaction Publishers, pp. 346–72.

HENDRICKS, W. 1994. "Deregulation and Labor Earnings." *Journal of Labor Research*, 15, pp. 207–34.

HILDRETH, A. 1999. "What Has Happened to the Union Wage Differential in Britain in the 1990s?" *Oxford Bulletin of Economics and Statistics*, 61, pp. 5–31.

HIRSCH, B. 1988. "Trucking Regulation, Unionization, and Labor Earnings, 1973–85." *Journal of Human Resources*, 23, pp. 295–317.

———. 1991a. "Union Coverage and Profitability Among U.S. Firms."*Review of Economics and Statistics*, 73, pp. 69–77.

———. 1991b. *Labor Unions and the Economic Performance of Firms*. Kalamazoo, MI: Upjohn Institute for Employment Research.

———. 1992. "Firm Investment Behavior and Collective Bargaining Strategy." *Industrial Relations*, 31, pp. 95–121.

———. 1993. "Trucking Deregulation and Labor Earnings: Is the Union Premium a Compensating Differential?" *Journal of Labor Economics*, 11, pp. 279–301.

———. 1999. "Unionization and Economic Performance: Evidence on Productivity, Profits, Investment, and Growth." Vancouver: Fraser Institute.

———. 2007. "What Do Unions Do for Economic Performance?" in *What Do Unions Do?: A Twenty-Year Perspective*, edited by J. Bennett and B. Kaufman. London: Transaction Publishers, pp. 193-237.

HIRSCH, B. and D. A. MACPHERSON. 1998. "Earnings and Employment in Trucking: Deregulating a Naturally Competitive Industry," in *Regulatory Reform and Labor Markets*, edited by J. Peoples. Norwell, MA: Kluwer Academic, pp. 61–112.

———. 2000. "Earnings, Rents, and Competition in the Airline Labor Market."*Journal of Labor Economics*, 18, pp. 125–55.

———. 2002. *Union Membership and Earnings Data Book: Compilations from the Current Population Survey (2002 Edition)*. Washington: Bureau of National Affairs.

HIRSCH, B., D. A. MACPHERSON, and E. J. SCHU-MACHER. 2004. "Measuring Union and Non-Union Wage Growth: Puzzles in Search of Solutions," in *Changing Role of Unions: New Forms of Representation*, edited by P. Wunnava. New York: M. E. Sharpe.

HIRSCH, B. and E. J. SCHUMACHER. 1998. "Union, Wages, and Skills."*Journal of Human Resources*, 33, pp. 201–19.

———. 2002. "Private Sector Union Density and the Wage Premium: Past, Present, and Future," in *The Future of Private Sector Unionism in the United States*, edited by J. T. Bennett and B. E. Kaufman. Armonk, NY: M. E. Sharpe, pp. 92–128.

HIRSCHMAN, A. 1970. *Exit, Voice and Loyalty*.Cambridge, MA: Harvard University Press.

HOXBY, C. 1996. "How Teachers' Unions Affect

Production."*Quarterly Journal of Economics*, 111, pp. 671–718.

ICHNIOWSKI, C. 1980. "Economic Effects of the Firefighters' Union." *Industrial and Labor Relations Review*, 33, pp. 198–211.

———. 1986. "The Effects of Grievance Activity on Productivity." *Industrial and Labor Relations Review*, 40, pp. 75–89.

ICHNIOWSKI, C., R. FREEMAN, and H. LAUER. 1989. "Collective Bargaining Laws, Threat Effects, and the Determination of Police Compensation." *Journal of Labor Economics*, 7, pp. 191–209.

JAKUBSON, G. 1991. "Estimation and Testing of the Union Wage Effect Using Panel Data." *Review of Economic Studies*, 58, pp. 971–91.

JARRELL, S. and T. STANLEY. 1990. "A Meta-Analysis of the Union-Nonunion Wage Gap." *Industrial and Labor Relations Review*, 44, pp. 54–67.

JUDGE, T., J. BONO, C. THORENSEN, and G. PATTON. 2001. "The Job Satisfaction–Job Performance Relationship." *Journal of Applied Psychology*, 127, pp. 376–407.

KAHN, L. 1980. "Union Spillover Effects on Unorganized Labor Markets."*Journal of Human Resources*, 15, pp. 87–98.

KALACHEK, E. and F. RAINES. 1980. "Trade Unions and Hiring Standards."*Journal of Labor Research*, 1, pp. 63–76.

KARIER, T. 1995. "U.S. Foreign Production and Unions."*Industrial Relations*, 34, pp. 107–18.

KAUFMAN, B. E. 2002. "Models of Union Wage Determination: What Have We Learned Since Dunlop and Ross?" *Industrial Relations*, 41, pp. 111–58.

KAUFMAN, R. S. and R. T. KAUFMAN. 1987. "Union Effects on Productivity, Personnel Practices, and Survival in the Automotive Parts Industry." *Journal of Labor Research*, 8, pp. 333–50.

KAUFMAN, R. T. 1992. "The Effects of IMPROSHARE on Productivity." *Industrial and Labor Relations Review*, 45, pp. 311–22.

KIM, D. and P. VOOS. 1997. "Unionization, Union Involvement, and the Performance of Gainsharing Programs." *Relations industrielles/Industrial Relations*, 52, pp. 304–29.

KLAFF, D. B. and R. G. EHRENBERG. 2003. "Collective Bargaining and Staff Salaries in American Colleges and Universities."*Industrial and Labor Relations Review*, 57, pp. 92–104.

KOCH, M. and G. HUNDLEY. 1998. "The Effect of Unionism on Recruitment and Selection Methods." *Industrial Relations*, 36, pp. 349–70.

KUHN, P. 1998. "Unions and the Economy: What We Know and What We Should Know." *Canadian Journal of Economics*, 31, pp. 1033–56.

KUMAR, P. and T. STENGOS. 1985. "Measuring the Union Relative Wage Impact: A Methodological Note."*Canadian Journal of Economics*,18, pp. 182–89.

LAPORTA, P. and A. JENKINS. 1996. "Unionization and Profitability in the Canadian Manufacturing Sector." *Relations industrielles/Industrial Relations*, 51, pp. 756–76.

LAWRENCE, C. and R. LAWRENCE. 1985. "Manufacturing Wage Dispersion: An End Game Interpretation."*Brookings Papers on Economic Activity*, 1, pp. 47–106.

LEE, L.-F. 1978. "Unionism and Wage Rates: A Simultaneous Equations Model with Qualitative and Limited Dependent Variables."*International Economic Review*, 19, pp. 415–34.

LEMIEUX, T. 1993. "Unions and Wage Inequality in Canada and the United States," in *Small Differences That Matter: Labor Markets and Income Maintenance in Canada and the United States*, edited by D. Card and R. Freeman. Chicago: University of Chicago Press, pp. 69–107.

———. 1998. "Estimating the Effects of Unions on Wage Inequality in a Panel Data Model with Comparative Advantage and Nonrandom Selection."*Journal of Labor Economics*, 16, pp. 261–91.

LEWIS, H. G. 1963. *Unionism and Relative Wages in the United States*.Chicago: University of Chicago Press.

———. 1983. "Union Relative Wage Effects: A Survey of Macro Estimates."*Journal of Labor Economics*,1, pp. 1–27.

———. 1986a. *Union Relative Wage Effects: A Survey*.Chicago: University of Chicago Press.

———. 1986b. "Union Relative Wage Effects," in *Handbook of Labor Economics*, Vol. 1, edited by O. Ashenfelter and R. Layard. New York: Elsevier Science Publishers.

LONG, R. 1993. "The Effect of Unionization on Employment Growth of Canadian Companies."*Industrial and Labor Relations Review*, 46, pp. 691–703.

LUCHAK, A. 2003. "What Kind of Voice Do Loyal Employees Use?"*British Journal of Industrial Relations*, 41, pp. 115–34.

MACHIN, S. 1991. "Unions and the Capture of Economic Rents: An Investigation Using British Firm Level Data."*International Journal of Industrial Organization*, 9, pp. 261–74.

MACHIN, S. and M. STEWART. 1996. "Trade Unions and Financial Performance."*Oxford Economic Papers*, 48, pp. 213–41.

MACPHERSON, D. A. and J. B. STEWART. 1990. "The Effect of International Competition on Union and Nonunion Wages." *Industrial and Labour Relations Review*, 43, pp. 434–46.

MAKI, D. R. 1983. "Trade Unions and Productivity: Conventional Estimates." *Relations industrielles/Industrial Relations*, 38, pp. 211–25.

MAKI, D. and L. MEREDITH. 1986. "The Effect of Unions on Profitability: Canadian Evidence." *Relations industrielles/Industrial Relations*, 41, pp. 54–68.

MENEZES-FILHO, N. 1997. "Unions and Profitability Over the 1980s: Some Evidence on Union-Firm Bargaining in the United Kingdom."*Economic Journal*,107, pp. 651–70.

MENEZES-FILHO, N., D. ULPH, and J. VAN REENEN. 1998. "R & D and Unionism: Comparative Evidence from British Companies and Establishments." *Industrial and Labor Relations Review*, 52, pp. 45–63.

MENG, R. 1990a. "Union Effects on Wage Dispersion in Canadian Industry." *Economic Letters*, 32, pp. 399–403.

———. 1990b. "The Relationship Between Unions and Job Satisfaction," *Economic Inquiry*, 32, pp.1635–48.

METCALF, D. 2003. "Unions and Productivity, Financial Performance and Investment: International Evidence" in *International Handbook of Trade Unions*, edited by J. Addison and C. Schnabel. Edward Elgar.

MITCHELL, D. 1983. "Unions and Wages in the Public Sector: A Review of Recent Evidence." *Journal of Collective Negotiations in the Public Sector*, 12, pp. 337–53.

MITCHELL, M. and J. STONE. 1992. "Union Effects on Productivity: Evidence From Western U.S. Sawmills." *Industrial and Labor Relations Review*, 46, pp. 135–45.

NEUMARK, D. and M. WACHTER. 1995. "Union Effects on Nonunion Wages: Evidence from Panel Data on Industries and Cities." *Industrial and Labour Relations Review*, 49, pp. 20–38.

NG, I. and D. MAKI. 1994. "Trade Union Influence on Human Resource Management Practices." *Industrial Relations*, 33, pp. 121–35.

ODGERS, C. and J. BETTS. 1997. "Do Unions Reduce Investment? Evidence From Canada." *Industrial and Labor Relations Review*, 51, pp. 518–36.

PEARCE, T., J. GROFF, and J. WINGENDER. 1995. "Union Decertification's Impact on Shareholder Wealth." *Industrial Relations*, 34, pp. 58–72.

PENCAVEL, J. 1991. *Labor Markets Under Trade Unionism: Employment, Wages and Hours.* Cambridge, MA: Basil Blackwell.

———. 2007. "Unionism Viewed Internationally," in *What Do Unions Do?: A Twenty-Year Perspective*, edited by J. Bennett and B. Kaufman. London: Transaction Publishers, pp. 423–58.

REES, A. 1963. "The Effect of Unions on Resource Allocation." *Journal of Law and Economics*, 6, pp. 69–78.

REES, D. 1994. "Does Unionization Increase Faculty Retention?" *Industrial Relations*, 33, pp. 297–321.

RENAUD, S. 1997. "Unions and Wages in Canada." *Selected Papers from the 33rd Annual CIRA Conference.* Quebec: Canadian Industrial Relations Association, pp. 211–26.

———. 1998. "Unions, Wages and Total Compensation in Canada." *Relations industrielles/Industrial Relations*, 53, pp. 710–27.

———. 2002. "Rethinking the Union Membership/Job Satisfaction Relationship: Some Empirical Evidence for Canada." *International Journal of Manpower*, 23, pp. 137–50.

RIDDELL, W. 1993. "Unionization in Canada and the United States: A Tale of Two Countries," in *Small Differences That Matter: Labor Markets and Income Maintenance in Canada and the United States*, edited by D. Card and R. Freeman. Chicago: University of Chicago Press.

ROBINSON, C. 1989. "The Joint Determination of Union Status and Union Wage Effects: Some Tests of Alternative Models." *Journal of Political Economy*, 97, pp. 639–67.

ROBINSON, C. and N. TOMES. 1984. "Union Wage Differentials in the Public and Private Sectors: A Simultaneous Equations Specification."*Journal of Labor Economics*, 2, pp. 106–27.

ROSE, N. L. 1987. "Labor Rent Sharing and Regulation: Evidence from the Trucking Industry."*Journal of Political Economy*, 95, pp. 1146–76.

RUBACK, R. and M. ZIMMERMAN. 1984. "Unionization and Profitability: Evidence from the Capital Market." *Journal of Political Economy*, 92, pp. 1134–57.

SCHEUR, S. 1999. "The Impact of Collective Agreements on Working Time in Denmark." *British Journal of Industrial Relations*, 37, pp. 465–81.

SHIPPEN, B. S. Jr. and A. K. LYNCH. 2002. "How International Trade Affects Union Wages: New Evidence." *Journal of Labor Research*, 23, pp. 131–44.

SIMPSON, W. 1985. "The Impact of Unions on the Structure of Canadian Wages: An Empirical Study with Micro Data." *Canadian Journal of Economics*, 18, pp. 164–81.

SINGH, P. and N. C. AGARWAL. 2002. "Union Presence and Executive Compensation: An Exploratory Study." *Journal of Labor Research*, 23, pp. 631–46.

SLICHTER, S., J. HEALY, and R. LIVERNASH. 1960. *The Impact of Collective Bargaining on Management.*Washington: Brookings Institution.

STEWART, M. 1995. "Union Wage Differentials in an Era of Declining Unionization." *Oxford Bulletin of Economics and Statistics*, 57, pp. 143–66.

SWIDINSKY, R. 1992. "Unionism and the Job Attachment of Canadian Workers." *Relations industrielles/Industrial Relations*, 47, pp. 729–51.

SWIDINSKY, R. and M. KUPFERSCHMIDT. 1991. "Longitudinal Estimates of the Union Effects on Wages, Wage Dispersion and Pension Fringe Benefits." *Relations industrielles/Industrial Relations*, 46, pp. 819–38.

TARAS, D. 2000. "Contemporary Experience with the Rockefeller Plan: Imperial Oil's Joint Industrial Council," in *Non-Union Employee Representation*, edited by B. Kaufman and D. Taras. NY: M. E. Sharpe, pp. 231–58.

TREJO, S. 1993. "Overtime Pay, Overtime Hours and Labor Unions."*Journal of Labor Economics*, 11, pp. 253–78.

VEDDER, R. and L. GALLAWAY. 2002. "The Economic Effects of Labor Unions Revisited." *Journal of Labor Research*, 23, pp. 105–30.

VERMA, A. 2007. "What Do Unions Do at the Workplace: Union Effects on Management and HRM Policies," In *What Do Unions Do?: A Twenty-Year Perspective*, edited by J. Bennett and B. Kaufman. London: Transaction Publisher, pp. 275–312.

VOOS, P. and L. MISHEL. 1986. "The Union Impact on Profits: Evidence from Industry Price-Cost Margin Data."*Journal of Labor Economics*, 4, pp. 105–33.

WAGAR, T. 1997. "Is Labor–Management Climate Important?: Some Canadian Evidence."*Journal of Labor Research*, 18, pp. 163–174.

———. 1998. "The Labour–Management Relationship and Organizational Outcomes." *Relations industrielles/Industrial Relations*, 52, pp. 430–46.

WHITE, F. 1994. "The Union/Non-Union Earnings Differential for Professionals."*Proceedings of the 30th Annual Conference of CIRA*. Quebec: Canadian Industrial Relations Association, pp. 269–79.

WILSON, K. 1995. *The Impact of Unions on United States and Economy-Wide Productivity*. New York: Garland.

WOODBURY, S. 1985. "The Scope of Bargaining Outcomes in Public Schools." *Industrial and Labor Relations Review*, 38, pp. 195–210.

WUNNAVA, P. and B. EWING. 1999. "Union–Nonunion Differentials and Establishment Size." *Journal of Labor Research*, 20, pp. 177–83.

ZWERLING, H. and T. THOMASON. 1995. "Collective Bargaining and the Determinants of Teachers' Salaries." *Journal of Labor Research*, 26, pp. 468–84.

Chapter 15

ADELL, B., M. GRANT, and A. PONAK. 2001. *Strikes in Essential Services*. Kingston, ON: Queen's University, IRC Press.

AKYEAMPONG, E. 2002. "Fact-sheet on Unionization." *Perspectives on Labour and Income* (August, Vol. 3, No. 8), Statistics Canada, Catalogue no. 75-001-XIE.

———. 2004. "The Union Movement in Transition." *Perspectives on Labour and Income* (August, Vol. 5, No. 8), Statistics Canada, Catalogue no. 75-001-XIE.

BEAUMONT, P. 1995. "Canadian Public Sector Industrial Relations in a Wider Setting," in *Public Sector Collective Bargaining*, edited by G. Swimmer and M. Thompson. Kingston, ON: Queen's University, IRC Press.

BORDOGNA, L. 2003. "The Reform of Public Sector

Employment Relations in Industrialized Democracies," in *Going Public: The Role of Labor–Management Relations in Delivering Quality Government Services*, edited by J. Brock and D. Lipsky. Urbana-Champaign: Industrial Relations Research Association.

CHAYKOWSKI, R. 2000. "The National Joint Council of the Public Service of Canada," in *Nonunion Employee Representation*, edited by B. Kaufman and D. Taras. Armonk, NY: M. E. Sharpe.

CYR-RACINE, C.-S. and P. JALETTE. 2007. "What Have Unions Got to Do With Reverse Privatisation?" *Journal of Collective Negotiations*, 31, no.4, 302–17.

EDWARDS, C. 1968. "The Public Service Alliance of Canada." *Relations industrielles/Industrial Relations*, 23, pp. 634–41.

FINKLEMAN, J. and S. GOLDENBERG. 1983. *Collective Bargaining in the Public Service: The Federal Experience in Canada*. 2 vols. Montreal: Institute for Research on Public Policy.

FRYER, J. 1995. "Provincial Public Sector Labour Relations," in *Public Sector Collective Bargaining*, edited by G. Swimmer and M. Thompson. Kingston, ON: Queen's University, IRC Press.

———. 2001. "Working Together in the Public Interest: Advisory Committee on Labour Management Relations in the Federal Public Service." Ottawa: Treasury Board of Canada. Available at www.fryercommittee.com.

GOLDENBERG, S. 1988. "Public Sector Labour Relations in Canada," in *Public Sector Bargaining*, 2nd Edition, edited by B. Aaron, J. Grodin and J. Stern. Madison, WI: Industrial Relations Research Association.

GRANT, M. 2003. "Quebec: Towards a New Social Contract," in *Beyond the National Divide*, edited by M. Thompson, J. Rose, and A. Smith. Montreal & Kingston: McGill-Queen's University Press.

GUNDERSON, M. 1995. "Public Sector Compensation," in *Public Sector Collective Bargaining*, edited by G. Swimmer and M. Thompson. Kingston, ON: Queen's University, IRC Press.

HAIVEN, L. 1995. "Industrial Relations in Health Care: Regulation, Conflict and Transition to the 'Wellness Model," in *Public Sector Collective Bargaining*, edited by G. Swimmer and M. Thompson. Kingston, ON: Queen's University, IRC Press.

HAIVEN, L. and J. HAIVEN. 2002. *The Right to Strike and the Provision of Emergency Services in Canadian Health Care*. Ottawa: Canadian Centre for Policy Alternatives.

HAIVEN, L., S. McBRIDE, and J. SHIELDS. 1991. "The State, Neo-Conservatism, and Industrial Relations," in *Regulating Labour*, edited by L. Haiven, S. McBride, and J. Shields. Toronto: Garamond Press.

HEBDON, R. and P. JALETTE. 2008. "The Restructuring of

Municipal Services: A Canada-United States Comparison." *Environment and Planning C: Government and Policy*, 26, pp. 144–56.

HEBDON, R. and M. MAZEROLLE. 2003. "Regulating Conflict in Public Sector Labour Relations: The Ontario Experience (1984–1993)." *Relations industrielles/Industrial Relations*, 58, no. 4, pp. 667–86.

HÉBERT, G. 1995. "Public Sector Bargaining in Quebec: The Rise and Fall of Centralization," in *Public Sector Collective Bargaining in Canada*, edited by G. Swimmer and M. Thompson. Kingston, ON: Queen's University, IRC Press.

JALETTE, P. 2005. "Réponses syndicales à la sous-traitance." *Just Labour*, 6 & 7, Autumn, pp. 93–103.

JALETTE, P. and P. WARRIAN. 2002. "Contracting-out Provisions in Canadian Collective Agreements: A Moving Target." *Workplace Gazette*, 5, no. 1 (Spring), pp. 64–76.

LOGAN, H. A. 1948. *Trade Unions in Canada*. Toronto: Macmillan.

MUELLER, R. E. 2000. "Public- and Private-Sector Wage Differentials in Canada Revisited." *Industrial Relations*, 39, no. 37, pp. 375–401.

OECD. 2006. *Factbook: Economic, Environmental and Social Statistics*. Paris: Organisation for Economic Co-operation and Development.

PANITCH, L. and D. SWARTZ. 1993. *The Assault on Trade Union Freedoms*. Toronto: Garamond Press.

PONAK, A. 1981. "Unionized Professionals and the Scope of Bargaining." *Industrial and Labor Relations Review*, 34, pp. 396–407.

PONAK, A. and L. FALKENBERG. 1989. "Resolution of Interest Disputes," in *Collective Bargaining in Canada*, edited by A. Sethi. Toronto: Nelson.

PONAK, A., Y. RESHEF, and D. G. TARAS. 2003. "Alberta: Industrial Relations in a Conservative Climate," in *Beyond the National Divide*, edited by M. Thompson, J. Rose, and A. Smith. Montreal & Kingston: McGill-Queen's University Press.

RESHEF, Y. and S. RASTIN. 2003. *Unions in the Time of Revolution: Government Restructuring in Alberta and Ontario*. University of Toronto Press.

ROSE, J. B. 1995. "The Evolution of Public Sector Unionism," in *Public Sector Collective Bargaining*, edited by G. Swimmer and M. Thompson. Kingston, ON: Queen's University, IRC Press.

———. 2004. "Public Sector Bargaining: From Retrenchment to Consolidation." *Relations industrielles/Industrial Relations*, 59, no. 2, pp. 271–94.

STATISTICS CANADA. 2007. "Unionization." *Perspectives on Labour and Income*, Autumn, 19, no. 3, pp. 52–58. Statistics Canada, Catalogue no. 75-001-XIE.

SWIMMER, G. 1995. "Collective Bargaining in the Federal Public Service of Canada—The Last Twenty Years," in *Public Sector Collective Bargaining*, edited by G. Swimmer and M. Thompson. Kingston, ON: Queen's University, IRC Press.

———. 2000. *Public Sector Labour Relations in an Era of Restraint and Restructuring*. Canadian Policy Research Networks.

SWIMMER, G. and T. BARTKIW. 2003. "The Future of Public Sector Collective Bargaining in Canada." *Journal of Labor Research*, XXIV, no. 4, pp. 579–95.

SWIMMER, G. and M. THOMPSON. 1995. *Public Sector Collective Bargaining*. Kingston, ON: Queen's University, IRC Press.

THOMASON, T. 1995. "Labour Relations in Primary and Secondary Education," in *Public Sector Collective Bargaining*, edited by G. Swimmer and M. Thompson. Kingston, ON: Queen's University, IRC Press.

THOMASON, T. and J. BURTON. 2003. "Unionization Trends and Labor–Management Cooperation in the Public Sector," in *Going Public: The Role of Labor–Management Relations in Delivering Quality Government Services*, edited by J. Brock and D. Lipsky. Urbana-Champaign: Industrial Relations Research Association.

THOMPSON, M. 1988. "Public Sector Industrial Relations in Canada: The Impact of Restraint," in *Proceedings of the Annual Spring Meeting, 1988, of the Industrial Relations Research Association*, edited by B. Dennis. Madison, WI: IRRA.

———. 1995. "The Industrial Relations Effects of Privatization: Evidence from Canada," in *Public Sector Collective Bargaining*, edited by G. Swimmer and M. Thompson. Kingston, ON: Queen's University, IRC Press.

———. 2000. "Public Sector Industrial Relations in Canada: Adaptation to Change," in *Strategic Choices in Reforming Public Service Employment: An International Perspective*, edited by C. Dell-Aringa and B. Keller. New York: St. Martin's Press.

THOMPSON, M. and A. PONAK. 1995. "Public Sector Collective Bargaining," in *Union–Management Relations in Canada*, 4th Edition, edited by M. Gunderson and A. Ponak. Don Mills, Ont.: Addison-Wesley.

THOMPSON, M. and G. SWIMMER. 1995. "The Future of Public Sector Industrial Relations," in *Public Sector Collective Bargaining*, edited by G. Swimmer and M. Thompson. Kingston, ON: Queen's University, IRC Press.

WARNER, M. and R. HEBDON. 2001. "Local Government Restructuring: Privatization and Its Alternatives." *Journal of Policy Analysis and Management*, 20, no. 2, pp. 315–36.

WARRIAN, P. 1996. *Hard Bargain: Transforming Public Sector Labour–Management Relations*. Toronto: McGilligan Books.

WEILER, P. C. 1980. *Reconcilable Differences: New Directions in Canadian Labour Law Reform*. Agincourt, ON: Carswell.

Chapter 16

BABCOCK, R. H. 1973. "Samuel Gompers and Quebec Workers." *American Review of Canadian Studies*, 3, pp. 47–66.

BOIVIN, J. 1989. *Les relations patronales-syndicales au Québec*, 2nd Edition. Chicoutimi: Gaétan Morin.

BOIVIN, J. and J. SEXTON. 2007. "Le système québécois de relations du travail en mutation: pour le meilleur ou pour le pire?" in *Nouvelles dynamiques des relations du travail*, 62ème congrès du Département des relations industrielles de l'Université Laval. Québec: Les Presses de l'Université Laval.

COMMISSION DE L'ÉQUITÉ SALARIALE (CÉS). 2006. *La loi sur l'équité salariale, un acquis à maintenir*. Available at **www.ces.gouv.qc.ca/publications/rapp-2006.pdf** (accessed 26 April 2007).

COMMISSION DES DROITS DE LA PERSONNE ET DES DROITS DE LA JEUNESSE. 1998. *Les programmes d'accès à l'égalité au Québec. Bilan et perspectives*. Québec (décembre).

———. 2005. *L'accès à l'égalité en emploi. Rapport triennal 2001–2004. La loi sur l'accès à l'égalité en emploi dans des organismes publics*. Available at **http://142.213.87.17/fr/ publications/docs/Rapport_triennal_PAE_2001-2004.pdf** (accessed 10 May 2007).

CONSEIL DU PATRONAT DU QUEBEC. 2007. *Cap sur la prospérité du Québec, plateforme 2007–2009*. Montréal: Conseil du patronat du Québec.

CONSEIL DU TRÉSOR. 2007. *2007–2008 Expenditure Budget, Volume IV, Additional Information*. Presented by the Chair of the Conseil du trésor. Québec.

CÔTÉ, A. and L. LEMONDE. 1988. *Discrimination et Commission des droits de la personne*. Montréal: Saint-Martin.

CRII (COMPENSATION RESEARCH AND INFORMA-TION INSTITUTE). 1998. *Fourteenth Annual Report*, French version (November), p. 22.

CSF (CONSEIL DU STATUT DE LA FEMME). 1993. *Même poids, même mesure. Avis sur l'équité en emploi*. Québec: Direction des Communications.

CSN. 1992. *Une démarche syndicale pour prendre les devants dans l'organisation du travail*. Available at **www.csn.qc.ca/ Pageshtml2/RechDemarOT1.html**.

DELORME, F., R. FORTIN and L. GOSSELIN. 1994. "L'organisation du monde patronal au Québec: un portrait diversifié," in *Les relations industrielles au Québec. 50 ans d'évolution*. Québec: Presses de l'Université Laval, pp. 167–201.

DELORME, E. and D. VEILLEUX. 1980. *Les syndicats indépendants au Québec: un aperçu de leur situation*. Québec: Ministère du Travail et de la main-d'œuvre.

FOURNIER, L. 1994. *Histoire de la FTQ*. Montréal: Québec-Amérique.

FRASER, M. 1987. *Québec Inc*. Montréal: Éditions de l'Homme.

GÉLINAS, André. 2002. *L'intervention et le retrait de l'État. L'impact sur l'organisation gouvernementale*. Québec: Les Presses de l'Université Laval.

GOUVERNEMENT DU QUÉBEC. 1993a. *La politique en matière de condition féminine. Femmes des années 1990— Portrait statistique*. Québec.

———. 1993b. *Un modèle d'entente de partenariat: le contrat social en entreprise*. Québec: Ministère de l'industrie, du commerce et de la technologie.

———. 1997. *Document de réflexion sur une nouvelle organisation du travail*. Québec: Conseil consultatif du travail et de la main-d'œuvre.

GRANT, M. and B. LÉVESQUE. 1997. "Aperçu des princi-pales transformations des rapports du travail dans les entre-prises: le cas québécois," in *Nouvelles formes d'organisation du travail: études de cas et analyses comparatives*. Montréal: Harmattan.

GRENIER, J.-N. and F.-B. MALO. Forthcoming. "La restruc-turation des services publics et les relations du travail dans l'administration publique québécoise: la stratégie du gou-vernement Libéral."*Management international*, numéro spé-cial sur les restructurations d'entreprises, Patrice Jalette et Linda Rouleau, éditeurs invités.

INSTITUT DE LA STATISTIQUE DU QUÉBEC. 2007. "Portrait des principaux indicateurs du marché du travail 1998–2006."*Annuaire québécois des statistiques du travail*, 3, no 1. Available at **www.stat.gouv.qc.ca/publications/ remuneration/annuaire_travailv3n1_pdf.htm** (accessed 12 September 2007).

LABROSSE, A. 2007. *La présence syndicale au Québec en 2006*. Québec: Direction des études et des politiques, Ministère du travail.

MALO, F.-B. and J.-N. GRENIER. Forthcoming. "La nouvelle gestion publique et la transformation du Réseau québécois de la santé et des services sociaux entre 1987 et 2007. Quels impacts pour les diverses parties prenantes?" in *Sélection des textes du 44ᵉ congrès de l'ACRI*, Université McGill, 4–7 juin 2007.

PORTER, M. E. 1990. *The Competitive Advantage of Nations*. London: Macmillan.

QUARTER, J. and G. MELNYK. 1989. *Partners in Enterprise: The Worker Ownership Phenomenon*. Montréal: Black Rose.

ROUILLARD, J. 1989. *Histoire du syndicalisme québécois*. Montréal: Boréal.

SHAWL, R. 1998. "La présence syndicale au Québec," in *Le marché du travail*, 19, no. 9, pp. 6–10.

STATISTICS CANADA. 1999. *Earnings of Men and Women, 1997.* Catalogue no. 13-217. Ottawa.

———. 2007a. *Average Earnings by Sex and Work Pattern,* CANSIM 202-0102. Ottawa. Available at www40.statcan.ca/l01/cst01/labor01b.htm (accessed 26 April 2007).

———. 2007b. "Population active, occupée et en chômage, et taux d'activité et de chômage, par province." *Enquête sur la population active,* CANSIM 282-0002. Ottawa. Available at www40.statcan.ca/l02/cst01/labor07b_f.htm (accessed 14 September 2007).

TREFF, K. and D. B. PERRY. 1998. *Finances of the Nations.* Toronto: Canadian Tax Foundation.

TRUDEAU, G. 2004. "Les normes minimales du travail: bilan et éléments de prospective," in *Introduction aux Relations industrielles,* edited by Jean Boivin, Gaëtan Morin éditeur, pp. 161–91.

Chapter 17

ACIRRT (Australian Centre for Industrial Relations Research and Training). 1999. *Australia at Work.* Sydney: Prentice-Hall.

BACON, D. 2004. *Children of NAFTA.* Berkeley and London: University of California Press.

BURAWOY, M., J. A. BLUM, S. GEORGE, Z. GILLE, T. GOWAN, L. HANEY, M. KLAWITER, S. H. LOPEZ, S. Ó RIAIN, and M. THAYER. 2000. *Global Ethnography: Forces, Connections, and Imaginations in a Postmodern World.* University of California Press.

CUPE (Canadian Union of Public Employees). 2007. *Healthy, Clean and Green.* Ottawa: CUPE.

CLAWSON, D. 2003. *The Next Upsurge: Labor and the New Social Movements.* Ithaca and London: Cornell University Press.

COHEN, R. and P. KENNEDY. 2000. *Global Sociology.* New York: New York University Press.

DRACHE, D. and H. GLASBEEK. 1992. *The Changing Canadian Workplace.* Toronto: Lorimer.

EDWARDS, P., M. HALL, R. HYMAN, P. MARGINSON, K. SISSON, J. WADDINGTON, and D. WINCHESTER. 1992. "Great Britain: Still Muddling Through," in *Industrial Relations in the New Europe,* edited by A. Ferner and R. Hyman. Oxford: Blackwell.

EVATT FOUNDATION. 1995. *Unions 2001. A Blueprint for Union Activism.* Sydney: Evatt.

FERNER, A. and R. HYMAN. 1992. "Italy," in *Industrial Relations in the New Europe,* edited by A. Ferner and R. Hyman. Oxford: Blackwell.

———, eds. 1998. *Changing Industrial Relations in Europe.* Oxford: Blackwell.

GOETSCHY, J. and P. ROSENBLATT. 1992. "France: The Industrial Relations System at a Turning Point?" in *Industrial Relations in the New Europe,* edited by A. Ferner and R. Hyman. Oxford: Blackwell.

GREENHOUSE, S. 2007. "Labor Union, Redefined, for Freelance Workers." *New York Times,* January 27, 2007.

GUNDERSON, M. and A. VERMA. 2003. "Industrial Relations in the Global Economy," in *From Industrial Relations to Human Relations and Beyond,* edited by B. Kaufman, R. Beaumont and R. Helfott. New York: M. E. Sharpe.

HYMAN, R. 1999. "An Emerging Agenda for Trade Unions?" Institute of International Labour Studies, DP/98/1999.

———. 2001. *Understanding European Unions.* London: Sage.

INOUE, S. 1999. *Japanese Industrial Relations and the Future: Opportunities and Challenges in an Era of Globalisation.* Institute of International Labour Studies, DP/106/99.

INTERGOVERNMENTAL PANEL ON CLIMATE CHANGE. 2007. "Climate Change 2007—Impacts, Adaptation, Vulnerability: Summary for Policy Makers." Working Group II Contribution to the Intergovernmental Panel on Climate Change, 4th Assessment Report, Brussels, April.

ITUC (International Trade Union Confederation). 2006. "Trade Union Climate Change Strategies, The Trade Union Statement to COP12/MOP2." The United Nations Framework Convention on Climate Change, Nairobi, Kenya, 6–17 November.

JACOBI, O., B. KELLER, and W. MULLER-JENTSCH. 1992. "Germany," in *Industrial Relations in the New Europe,* edited by A. Ferner and R. Hyman. Oxford: Blackwell.

JACOBY, S., ed. 1995. *The Workers of Nations: Industrial Relations in a Global Economy.* New York: Oxford University Press.

JENSON, J., E. HAGEN, and C. REDDY. 1988. Feminization of the Labor Force. Oxford UP.

KJELBERG, A. 1992. "Sweden: Can the Model Survive?" in *Industrial Relations in the New Europe,* edited by A. Ferner and R. Hyman. Oxford: Blackwell.

KLEIN, N. 2000. *No Logo.* Toronto: Vintage Canada.

LaBOTZ, D. 1992. *The Mask of Democracy.* Montreal: Black Rose Books.

LICHTENSTEIN, N. 2002. *State of the Union.* Princeton: Princeton University Press.

LIPSIG-MUMMÉ, C. 1997. "The Politics of the New Service Economy," in *Work of the Future: Global Options,* edited by J. Paul, W. Veit and S. Wright. Sydney: Allen and Unwin.

LIPSIG-MUMMÉ, C., J. CURTIN, and I. NIELSEN. 2003. "Making Women Count." April: APOonline.

LIPSIG-MUMMÉ, C. and K. LAXER. 1998. *Organising and Union Membership: A Canadian Profile in 1997*. Canadian Labour Congress and Centre for Research on Work and Society.

LIPSIG-MUMMÉ, C. and S. MCBRIDE. 2007. "Divergent Decline: Trade Unions, Labour Regimes and Globalisation. Australia and Canada Compared."*Just Policy*, #45.

LIPSIG-MUMMÉ, C. and I. NIELSEN. 2003. "Communities of Unionism: The Working Young and the Labour Movement." *AIRAANZ Conference Proceedings*, Melbourne.

LOHR, S. 2006. "Outsourcing Is Climbing Skills Ladder," *New York Times*, February 16, 2006.

MAHON, R. 1999. "Yesterday's Modern Times Are No Longer Modern: Swedish Unions Confront the Second Shift," in *The Brave New World of European Labor*, edited by A. Martin and G. Ross. Oxford: Blackwell.

MARTIN, A. and G. ROSS, et al. 1999. *The Brave New World of European Labor*. Oxford: Blackwell.

MILKMAN, R. and K. VOSS, eds. 2004. *Rebuilding Labor*. Ithaca and London: Cornell University Press.

MONBIOT, G. 2000. *Captive State*. London: Pan Books.

———. 2003. *The Age of Consent*. London: Pan Books.

MUNCK, R. 2002. *Globalisation and Labour*. London: Zed Books.

PEETZ, D. 2006. *The Brave New Workplace*. Crow's Nest (Australia): Allen and Unwin.

RADOSH, R. 1969. *American Labor and United States Foreign Policy*. New York: Vintage Books.

ROSS, A. 1997. "An Appeal to Walt Disney," in *No Sweat*. London: Verso.

ROSS, G. and A. MARTIN. 1998. "Europeanization and the Integration of European Labor." Mimeo.

SILVIA, S. 1999. "Every Which Way But Loose: German Industrial Relations Since 1980," in *The Brave New World of European Labor*, edited by A. Martin and G. Ross. Oxford: Blackwell.

TRUBECK, D. and J. ROTHSTEIN. 1998. "Transnational Regimes and Advocacy in Industrial Relations: A Cure for Globalization?" Labor and Global Economy Research Circle, University of Wisconsin-Madison.

VISSER, J. 2006. "Union Membership Statistics in 24 Countries." *Monthly Labor Review*, 129, pp. 38–49.

VOSKO, L. 2000. *Temporary Work: The Gendered Rise of Precarious Employment*. Toronto: University of Toronto Press.

WINES, M. 2006. "Africa Adds to the Miserable Ranks of Child Workers," *New York Times*, August 24, 2006.

YATES, M. 1998. *Why Unions Matter*. New York: Monthly Review of Books.

Index